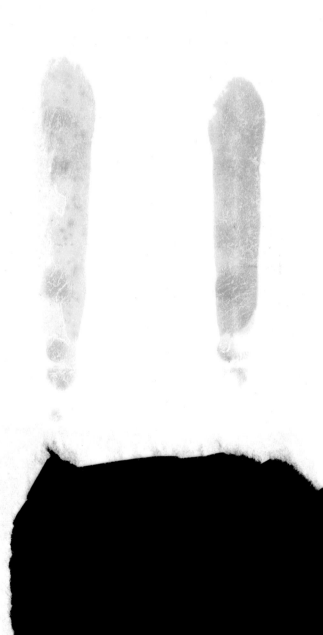

IVC

THE JACOBEAN AND
CAROLINE STAGE

THE JACOBEAN

AND

CAROLINE STAGE

DRAMATIC COMPANIES
AND PLAYERS

BY

GERALD EADES BENTLEY

VOLUME II

OXFORD
AT THE CLARENDON PRESS

Oxford University Press, Ely House, London W. 1

GLASGOW NEW YORK TORONTO MELBOURNE WELLINGTON
CAPE TOWN SALISBURY IBADAN NAIROBI LUSAKA ADDIS ABABA
BOMBAY CALCUTTA MADRAS KARACHI LAHORE DACCA
KUALA LUMPUR HONG KONG

FIRST PUBLISHED 1941
REPRINTED LITHOGRAPHICALLY IN GREAT BRITAIN
AT THE UNIVERSITY PRESS, OXFORD
FROM SHEETS OF THE FIRST EDITION
1949, 1966 (WITH CORRECTIONS)

CONTENTS
VOLUME II

PLAYERS 343

APPENDIX 630
    Wills 631
    The Closing of the Theatres because of Plague . . 652
    The Records of Sir Humphrey Mildmay . . . 673
    Markham's Suit 682
    Heton's Papers 684
    Theatrical Notes from Crosfield's Diary . . . 688
    Miscellaneous 690

INDEX 697

PLAYERS

ACTON, FRANCIS. There is only a suggestion that he may have been an actor because of his appearance among the thirty-nine defendants, mostly actors, in Gervase Markham's suit.

1623, May 21—'ffrancis Acton att the white harte in the ould Balye London,' 10s. (See Appendix, p. 682.)

ADKINSON, WILL. He was probably a minor attendant of the King's company, since his name appears only once in connexion with them. There are numerous mentions of a William Atkinson in the records of St. Mary's Aldermanbury after 1602, but the name is too common to make identification probable.

>1625—'Enter Seruant, Will. Adkinson:' in A King and No King, Act V (K₄ᵛ). (1625 4° B.M.; not in 1619, 1631, or 1639 quartos.)

ADSON, J. (not F., as sometimes given). The stage directions of The Late Lancashire Witches show that Adson was an attendant of the King's company in the summer of 1634, but there is no other record which certainly associates him with the company. It seems to me not improbable that he was one of the musicians of the King's company, and that he may be identified with the flautist and composer. The identification is suggested by the fact that the name is rather an uncommon one and by the consideration that it would have been economical to use a musician as the invisible spirit in The Late Lancashire Witches, for there are over forty roles in the comedy, the musicians were frequently required to play their instruments on the stage, and it would have been easy to have one of them walk on in an invisible cloak.

The allusion to 'Adsons new ayres' in Cavendish's Country Captain might refer to his volume of 1621, or it might refer to newer and unrecorded compositions. Possibly it indicates his popularity with the Blackfriars audience as one of the regular theatre musicians.

I have selected only the most biographically significant of the records of Adson as one of the royal musicians; de Lafontaine prints several others in The King's Musick.

1621—John Adson's Courtly Masquing Ayres, Composed to 5 and 6 Parts, for Violins, Consorts, and Cornets, was published.

1633, Nov. 4—'Warrant to swear John Adson a musician for the flute and cornet in ordinary, in the place of Henry Lanier, deceased.' (King's Musick, p. 86, from L.C., vol. 738, p. 341.)

1634—'Enter an invisible spirit. J. Adson with a brace of greyhounds', in Heywood and Brome's The Late Lancashire Witches, sig. D₄. (1634 4° B.M.).

1640, July 6 and 7—'Warrant to swear William Lanier one of his Majesty's musicians for the wind instruments in ordinary in the room of John Adson, deceased. Also a patent to grant him a fee of 1s. 8d. per diem, and £16 2s. 6d. allowance yearly for a livery.' (*King's Musick*, p. 105, from L.C., vol. 739, p. 408).

c. 1640—Near the beginning of the fourth act of Cavendish's *Country Captain*, Captain Sackbury, who is drunk, calls for a tune from the musicians.

> *Musi.* Doe you meane Master *Adsons* new ayres sir ?
>
> *Cap.* I sir. But they are such phantasticall ayres, as it puts a Poet out of his witts to ryme to them but let me heare——
>
> (1649 ed.)

ALLEN, EDWARD (*see* ALLEYN).

ALLEN, JEREMY. Our only reference to him is as a leader of an unidentified touring company at Coventry.

1640, Aug. 19—'p^d given to Jeremy Allin & leonard Smith togeather wth the rest of theire company being stage-players the 19th of August 1640, . . . xx^s.' (Murray, ii. 254.)

ALLEN, RICHARD. His name appears in the casts for *Epicoene* (1616 folio) and *The Coxcomb* (1679 folio). Chambers thinks that he was absorbed into the Lady Elizabeth's company in 1613 (Chambers, *E.S.* ii. 251). Though there are no references to him after 1616, it is possible that he was a member of the provincial Lady Elizabeth's company (see pp. 177–82). There are several records of Richard Allens in the registers of St. Saviour's and St. Thomas's and in the token books for 1620, 1621, 1623, and 1627, but the name is too common to allow identification.

ALLEN, WILLIAM. His receipt of the livery allowance, and his leading roles in *The Renegado* and *Hannibal and Scipio* indicate that he was an important actor in Queen Henrietta's company throughout its career at the Cockpit; he is named in every list of the company except the short one which Crosfield recorded in his diary in 1634 (see p. 246). Some time before January 1640/1 he had gone to the King's company. Mr. Baldwin (*Organization and Personnel*, p. 64) suggests that he joined the King's men when the Queen's went to pieces in 1636–7, and this suggestion seems not unlikely. His long association with Christopher Beeston at the Cockpit makes it probable that he was the William Allen associated with Mrs. Beeston in recusancy. The 'servante' of the record might mean that he was Beeston's apprentice.

The records from St. Giles in the Fields, in which parish the Cockpit was located, are confusing, since the registers of this parish do not give occupations. The marriage of 1629 seems likely, for one of Allen's fellow members of the Queen's company had been John Blaney. Trueman's assertion of Allen's rank during the wars is somewhat surprising ; perhaps the old theatre-goer had confused the actor with the Allen who was a drum major before the wars (see *C.S.P., Dom.*, 1639–40, p. 550).

Collier's record of the burial at St. Anne's Blackfriars on 18 October 1642 of 'Mr Allen called servant to the Queene' (Bod.) is a misreading of 'M^r. Allin Calcot Servant to the Queene'.

1614, Dec. 20—A true bill for not going to church on this day or in the three months following was entered against a number of people including 'Jane wife of Christofer Beeston yoman, William Allen yoman'; and the like 25 March 1615, 'Jane wife of Christopher Beeston . . . yeoman, and his servante William Allen'; and the like 25 June 1615, 'William Allen yoman, Jane wife of Christopher Beeston yoman'; and the like 1 January 1615/16, 'Jane Beeston wife of Christofer Beeston gentleman, William Allen yoman.' (*Middx. Co. Rec.* ii. 107, 110, 114, 120.)

1625—'Anthonio Grimaldi *the* Renegado. William Allen' in the cast of Massinger's *Renegado* given by Queen Henrietta's men 'at the priuate Play-house in Drurye-Lane'. (1630 4° B.M.)

1625, Oct. 28—'William sonne of William Allen Player' chris. St. G.C.

1626—'Captaine *Landby. William Allin*' in Queen Henrietta's cast for Shirley's *The Wedding.* (1629 4° HN.)

1629, June 29—'William Alleyne and Elizabeth Blane' mar. St. G.F.

c. 1630—'*Mullisheg, K.* of Fesse, *by* M^r. Will. Allen' in the cast of Queen Henrietta's men prefixed to the 1631 4° of Heywood's *The Fair Maid of the West*, Part I; since no actor is listed for the role in Part II, he probably played it there as well. (1631 4° B.M.)

1630, Nov. 20—An order was issued for the delivery of livery 'vnto William Allen for himselfe & thirteene others his ffellowes the Queenes Players'. (*M.S.C.* ii. 352–3.)

>1634—'*Pandolph, M.* Allen' in the cast of Davenport's *King John and Matilda* given by Queen Henrietta's men 'at the Cock-pit in Drury-lane'. (1655 4° B.M.).

1635—'Hannibal. By William Allen' in the cast for Nabbe's *Hannibal and Scipio* given by Queen Henrietta's men 'at their Private house in Drury Lane'. (1637 4° B.M.)

1638, Sept. 30—'Samuell sonne of William & Alice Allen' chris. St. G.F.

1639, Dec. 5—'William Allen & Elisabeth Russell' mar. St. G.F.

1640, Sept. 13—'Robte sonne of William & Alice Allen' chris. St. G.F.

1640/1, Jan. 22—Warrant for swearing him and five others grooms of his Majesty's chamber to attend as players (see p. 64). (*M.S.C.* ii. 397.)

1642, July 10—'Ann Daughter of William and Alice Allen' chris. St. G.F.

1643, Apr. 4—'Mary Daughter of William Allen' bur. St. G.F.

1644, Apr. 28—'Hester Daughter of William and Alice Allen' chris. St. G.F.

1645, Aug. 1—'Hester daughter of William Allen' bur. St. G.F.

1646, July 12—'John sonne of William and Alice Allen' chris. St. G.F.

1647—'William Allen' is ninth in the list of ten King's men who signed the dedication to the Beaumont and Fletcher folio. (1647 folio B.M.)

1647, Sept. 28—'Michaell sonne of William Allen' bur. St. G.F.

1647, Nov. 8—'William Allen' bur. St. Anne's Blackfriars.

1648, May 20—'Elisabeth Daughter of William Allen' bur. St. G.F.

>1649—Wright says that he was one of 'those of principal Note at the *Cockpit'* (Queen Henrietta's), and that in the wars '*Allen* of the *Cockpit*, was a Major, and Quarter Master General at *Oxford*'. (*Hist. Hist.*, pp. 4 and 8; see Appendix, pp. 693 and 694.)

1652, Oct. 7—'William So: of William Allin' bur. St. G.F.

ALLEYN, EDWARD. Alleyn's career as an actor in Worcester's and the Admiral's–Prince Henry's companies was over long before the death of Shakespeare, though his fame was still great. As early as 1605 he had taken the first steps in the purchase of the manor of Dulwich, and by 1616 his interests were centred in Dulwich far more than in London. The deed of foundation of his College of God's Gift at Dulwich was read before a gathering of notables on 13 September 1619, and both before and after this date Alleyn's chief activities were concerned with his foundation, as his diary, 1617–22, and his papers show.

In spite of his new and absorbing interests, Alleyn had not, however, severed all his connexions with the theatre. He still owned the Fortune theatre, and he had a financial interest in the organization of the Palsgrave's company and of Prince Charles's. His diary and the Dulwich papers show that he took charge after the old Fortune burned in 1621 and organized a syndicate to finance a new playhouse, retaining one share for himself.

After the close of the diary in 1622, we have no indication of his activities in connexion with the theatre, and it seems likely that he became more and more absorbed in his foundation.

Since Alleyn's activities in our period were largely philanthropic, and since his career has been so fully set forth elsewhere (*MSS. Dul.*; Collier, *Memoirs of Edward Alleyn; Hens. D.* ii. 1–42), I have thought it best to record here only those events in the last ten years of his life which are definitely connected with theatres, plays, or players.

1615/16, Mar. 20—The Prince's men signed an agreement with Alleyn and Meade in settlement of the company's debt to Henslowe. See pp. 198–9.

1616–17—The Prince's men complained to Alleyn of Meade's treatment of them and said that they had had to leave the Hope. See p. 200, n. 3.

1617—The case of *Alleyne* v. *Edward Travis* shows that he was interested in the Puddle Wharf property after the theatre had been condemned, and that he spent more than £2,000 on the premises before 1623. (Hillebrand, pp. 244–8.)

c. 1617—William Birde wrote Alleyn about a friend of Alleyn's who was a gatherer at the Fortune (*see* John Russell).

1617, Oct. 1—'I came to London in yᵉ coach & went to yᵉ red bull.' (Young, ii. 51.)

1617, Oct. 3—'I went to yᵉ red bull & R for yᵉ younger brother, but 3. 6. 4.' (Ibid.)

1617, Nov. 11—'pd by mortton yᵉ fortune quitt rent—o 1 10.' (Ibid., p. 56.)

1617/18, Mar. 22—'Redman & His wife: Cartwright gannell & parr dind wᵗ vs.' (Ibid., p. 73.)

1618, Apr. 9—'water & ale att yᵉ fortune *as you like itt.*' (Ibid., p. 79. Warner says that the italicized words are an obvious modern forgery.)

1618, May 30—'pd mortone for yᵉ tyeths of yᵉ fortune—o 5 o.' (Ibid., p. 86.)

1618, Aug. 15—Lord Chancellor Bacon wrote to Buckingham, 'I now write to give the King an account of a Patent I have stayed at the Seal. It is of licence to give in mortmain eight hundred pound land, though it be of tenure in chief, to Alleyn that *was* the Player, for an hospital.' (Collier, *H.E.D.P.* iii. 122, n. 1.)

1618, Sept. 13—'I invited to dinner . . . then cam vnlookt for Tho: Allen & His sone mʳ Edmonds mʳ Juby & His wife . . .' (Young, ii. 103.)

1618, Sept. 18—'Dinner att yᵉ marmayd in bred street wᵗ mʳ Edmonds mʳ bromfeeld Tho: Allen & 5 of yᵉ fortune company.' (Ibid., p. 104.)

1618, Sept. 20—'pare & His wife: doc: nott: tuchborne mʳ massie: . . . dind wᵗ vs.' (Ibid., p. 104.)

1618, Oct. 4—'Tho: Allen & His wife sone & daughter Randall wood Jo: Taylore dind wᵗ vs.' (Ibid., p. 109.)

1618, Oct. 13—'I R rent att yᵉ banksid & fortune . . .' (Ibid., p. 110.)

1618, Oct. 22—'pd yᵉ fortune quitt rent by morton—o 1 10.' (Ibid., p. 111.)

1618, Oct. 23—'I dind wᵗ yᵉ company att yᵉ fortune . . .' (Ibid.)

1618, Oct. 30—'I went to London water to yᵉ fortune *saw Romeo.*' (Ibid., p. 112. Warner says that the italicized words are an obvious modern forgery.)

1618, Oct. 31—'. . . after dinner wᵗ yᵉ fortune men att selling the leasse.' (Ibid.)

1618/19, Jan. 8—'ale wᵗ them att yᵉ fortune.' (Ibid., p. 122.)

1618/19, Jan. 12—'I went to yᵉ fortune to R rent . . .' (Ibid.)

1619, Apr. 15—'water from yᵉ fortune—o o 4.' (Ibid., p. 130.)

1619, May 9—'w: pare & His wife Jo: Russel & His wife . . . dind wᵗ vs.' (Ibid., p. 134.)

1619, June 20—'Ther dind wᵗ vs . . . 4 off yᵉ princes men . . .' (Ibid., p. 138.)

1619, July 11—'Ther dind wᵗ vs will borne & His wife . . .' (Ibid., p. 142.)

1619, July 26—'I went to yᵉ fortune wᵗ mʳ Scott . . .' (Ibid., p. 146.)

1619, Aug. 15—'Ther dind wᵗ vs mʳ Taylore mʳ gunell His wife & daughter franc: grace.' (Ibid., p. 147.)

1619, Aug. 22—'Ther dind wᵗ vs mʳ Hobbs mʳ Cartwright & mʳ Jones his man.' (Ibid., p. 148.)

1620, Apr. 5—'I dined wᵗ mʳ Hewitt & ther wase yᵉ princes musitions mʳ ball & mʳ drewe . . .' (Ibid., p. 174.)

1620, Apr. 9—'Ther dind wᵗ vs mʳ gunnell: Cartwright: parr & price yᵉ King of bohemes men.' (Ibid.)

1620, Apr. 12—'pd yᵉ quitt rent for yᵉ fortune dwe att michell Last

—o 1 10. pd ye tyethes for ye fortune bothes theys by morton—
—o 5 o.' (Young, ii. 174.)

1620, May 23—'pd my fyne being ratett . . . ye fortune att 20^l . . .'
(Ibid., p. 177.)

1620, July 23—'ther dind w^t vs will: boarne & His boye . . .' (Ibid.,
p. 185.)

1620, Aug. 13—'John Lowen & His wife dind w^t me.' (Ibid., p. 186.)

1620, Nov. 7—'fortune quitt rent—o 01 10.' (Ibid., p. 193.)

1620/1, Feb. 23—'I went to meet Sr Nic. Stoddard in powles spent
att ye pole Head w^t Hym m^r borne & gunnell—o o 6.' (Ibid.,
p. 202.)

1620/1, Mar. 18—'Charles massy ye Collyar & His sone & canterbury
& His wife dind Here.' (Ibid.)

1620/1, Mar. 24—'pd ye tyeth for ye fortune by morton—o 05 o.'
(Ibid., p. 204.)

1621, Apr. 15—'borne: massey: Cartwright: gunnell: grace: Hunt
dind Here & my Lewsham baly.' (Ibid.)

1621, Aug. 10—'I agreed w^t they princes men for 30^l to quitt all.'
(Ibid., p. 216.)

1621, Aug. 12—'Mr Edmonds: Charles Massey & on other off y^e
compa[n]y dynd Here.' (Ibid.)

1621, Nov. 19—'giuen charles massye att His playe—o 5 o.' (Ibid.,
p. 224.)

1621, Dec. 9—'m̃d this night att 12 of ye clock ye fortune was burnt.'
(Ibid., p. 225.)

1622, Apr. 16—'Dinner att ye Hart in Smithfeeld w^t ye builders off
ye fortune.' (Ibid., p. 234.)

1622, Apr. 26—'water to London 6^d wine w^t ye fortune workmen 12^d.'
(Ibid., p. 235.)

1622, Apr. 28—'I went to westminster to mete ye workmen off ye fortune . . .' (Ibid., p. 236.)

1622, May 1—'I mett ye workmen att Ric gunnells . . .' (Ibid.)

1622, May 3—'I . . . spent att diner w^t Hym & ye fortune builders—
o 07 o.' (Ibid.)

1622, May 6—'I dind w^t ye fortune workmen att angells . . .' (Ibid ,
p. 237.)

1622, May 13—'pd ye first payment for ye fortune building 25^l . . .'
(Ibid.)

1622, May 26—'. . . m^r gunell His cosen brother & wife dind Here.'
(Ibid.)

1622, June 4—'I dind w^t m^r Hemings.' (Ibid., p. 238.)

1622, June 12—'I went to ye Lord off Arundle showed ye fortune plott
. . .' (Ibid.)

1622, June 17—'I dind att ye fortune att Smiths Howse . . .' (Ibid.,
p. 239.)

1622, July 19—' I seald ye Leases off ye fortune dind w^t ye Justices
att angells.' (Ibid., p. 244.)

1622, July 21—'Charls massy & His Cosen ned Collins 2 shagbutts
& a cornett dind Here.' (Ibid., p. 246.)

1622, Aug. 15—'I went to ye fortune to meet w^t m^r thicknis &
others . . .' (Ibid., p. 247.)

1622, Aug. 18—'m^r doughton: m^r gwalter: m^r gunell: m^r garman &
wigpitt w: Cartwright m^r [sic].' (Ibid.)

1622, Sept. 6—'. . . from thenc to yᵉ fortune I dind wᵗ mʳ axell & gaue His wife for ned Laighton 20ˢ I gaue His man 6ᵈ His mayd 6ᵈ . . . I seald att vnderwoods yᵉ fortune Leases & so came Home.' (Ibid., p. 249.)

1622, Sept. 22—'mʳ gunnell & His wife . . . dind Here.' (Ibid.)

1623, June 2—'On Monday, the Lord Duke of Richmond, the lord treasurer, the Earls of Arundel, Pembroke, Montgomery, Carlisle, if not others, all, with Sir Thomas Edmondes, treasurer of the household, Sir John Fearne, Allein, some time a player, now squire of the bears, Inigo Jones, surveyor of the king's works, rode hence on Tuesday, towards Winchester and Southampton, to take order for his majesty's entertainment with the prince and Lady Mary, whither, it is said, the king intends to go and meet them. Which lords are to be here [London] again on Saturday [7 June].' Dr. Meddus to the Rev. Joseph Mead, 5 June 1623. (Birch, *James I*, ii. 402–3.)

1623, June 28—'Joane Alleyn late the wife of the worshipfull Edward Alleyn Esquier Mʳ of his Maᵗˢ Game of Beares Bulls and Masteiue Doggs, and founder of the Colledge of God's guift . . . daughter of the worshipfull Phillipp Henslowe Esquier deceased . . . departed this mortall life without yssue on the 28ᵗʰ daye of June Anno Dñi 1623, and was solemnely interred in the Quier of the Chappell of the aforesaid Colledge on the south side thereof neare to the high alter on the ffirst daye of July following.' (Young, ii. 34.)

1623, Dec. 3—He married Constance, eldest daughter of John Donne, Dean of St. Paul's. (Ibid., p. 35.)

1623, Dec. 20—'But the strangest match in mine opinion is, that Allen the player hath lately married a young daughter of the Dean of Paul's; which, I doubt, will diminish his charity and devotion towards his two hospitals.' John Chamberlain, Esq., to Sir Dudley Carleton, 20 Dec. (Birch, *James I*, ii. 441.)

1626, Nov. 25—He died on this date and was buried the 27th of November. (Young, ii. 40.)

1660—'About this time also *Edward Allen* of *Dulwich* in *Surry*, founded a fair Hospital at *Dulwich*. . . . This man may be an example, who having gotten his wealth by Stage-playing converted it to this pious use, not without a kinde of reputation to the Society of Players.' (Sir Richard Baker, *A Chronicle of the Kings of England* [1660], p. 447.)

ALLINGTON, JOHN. His importance at Blackfriars was probably not great, for he appears only in the ticket of privilege, and even there does not appear in the nine names in the body of the document, but is one of the two added in the marginal list of eleven.

1636/7, Jan. 12—Ticket of privilege as attendant of players granted to 'John Allington' and ten others 'imployed by his Maᵗᵉˢ servantes the Players of the Blackfryers.' (*M.S.C.* ii. 380.)

APPERLEY, JOHN. There is no direct evidence that he was connected with the stage, but many Southwark musicians were.

1612/13, Mar. 18—'John Aperley s of John a musitian' chris. St. S.S.

1615, Oct. 22—'Elizabeth Apperlye d of John a musitian' chris. St. S.S.

1617/18, Mar. 12—'Wm Atterley s of John a Musitian' chris. St. S.S.

1619/20, Mar. 9—'Margaret Apperley d of John a Misitian' chris. St. S.S.

ARCHER (ARZSCHAR, ERTZER), ROBERT. He appears as an English actor in Germany from 1608 until he was dismissed by the Elector of Brandenburg with a payment of 250 thalers as settlement of his claims, 16 May 1616. (See Meissner, *Englischen Comoedianten*, pp. 41 and 52; Herz, *Englische Schauspieler*, pp. 52–3; Cohn, *Sh. in Ger.* lxxxviii.)

ARMESTEAD, EDWARD (*see* ARMIGER, EDWARD).

ARMIGER, EDWARD. Armiger belonged to the obscure Red Bull–King's troupe. In 1629 he was touring with a company from the Red Bull, and in 1634 he is said to belong to the company at the Fortune, which was probably the same troupe. It is probable that the Edmund Armiger whose estate was in question in 1640 is not the same man. Malcolm said that he had found a notice of the burial of Edward Armiger at St. Giles' Cripplegate, 30 September 1635 (*Londinium Redivivum*, iii. 304). There is no such entry as he describes; perhaps only his date is in error, but I failed to find any burial entry for the player before 1653. Unless there was more than one Edward Armiger at St. Giles', the marriage license indicates that the actor was born about 1612.

1629, Nov. 30—William Perry and Richard Weeks, 'his Majestie's sworne servantes,' showed at Reading a license of the Master of the Revels dated 10 November 1629. The clerk at Reading recorded eight names, including 'Edward Armiger', 'all of the Red Bull company'. (Murray, ii. 386.)

1634, July 15—'Edward Armiger, Gent., of St Giles, Cripplegate, Bachelor, 22, & Alse Budsdell, of same, Sp^r, 21, her father's consent; at St Faith's.' (*Marriages, London.*)

1634, July 18—'Edward Armestead' is one of the four who, Kendall told Crosfield, were the chief of the Fortune company. (*Crosfield's Diary*, p. 72.)

1635, Aug. 21—'Edward, sonne of Edward Armiger, Player' chris. St. G.C.

1635, Sept. 2—'Edward sonne of Edward Armiger Player' bur. St. G.C.

1637, May 6—'Henry son: of Edward Armiger Player' bur. St. G.C.

1640 (?)—'John Bradshaw to Mr. Mortimer. I pray Mr. Mortimer to see how a suit in Chancery is proceeded in between Nicholas Bedingfield, of Suffolk, and Petronill Byfield, who pretends to be executor of Edmund Armiger. I hear they were come to examining of witnesses last term. . . .' (*C.S.P., Dom.*, 1640–1, p. 361.)

ASHBORNE, EDWARD. He is known only as an attendant of the King's company, though it is possible that he should be identified with Ashton.

1610, May 9—'A sarvant of Edward Ashborne' bur. St. G.F.

1624, Dec. 27—Herbert exempted 'Edward Ashborne' from arrest as one of twenty attendants of King's. (See pp. 15–16.)

ASHTON, — (*see also* ASHBORNE, EDWARD).

c. 1635—In stage directions for King's revival of *Love's Pilgrimage*, II. i, '*Enter two Servants, Rowl: Ashton*', and IV. i, '*Enter a Servant, Rowl: Ashton*'. (1647 folio B.M. Dated from revival licensed 16 September 1635; *Herbert*, p. 36.)

ASKEN, AARON. A wandering entertainer in Germany, sometimes called Aaron the Dancer. He appears with Robert Reynolds's troupe in 1627 and 1640. (Herz, *Englische Schauspieler*, pp. 31, 55 ff.)

ATKINS, JOHN. There seem to have been at least two John Atkins connected with theatrical affairs. The man who held Globe property and the man who married Alice Heminges may reasonably be assumed to be the same, and perhaps he is the man buried at St. Mary's. The man who sued the players may have been the one who had occupied the Cockpit property, but there is no reason to suppose that he is to be identified with the friend of the Heminges family.

1612/13, Feb. 11—'Jhon Atkyns & Ales Hemming' mar. St. M.A.

c. 1615—The housekeepers of the Globe had granted two small parcels of ground of the Globe property to a John Atkins in trust for John Heminges. (Wallace, *Sh. and Lond. Assoc.*, p. 63, and Baldwin, *Organization and Personnel*, p. 104.)

1616, Aug. 9—The Cockpit properties which Beeston leased were late occupied by John Atkins. (Hotson, p. 89.)

1616, Aug. 25—'Jhon Atkins' bur. St. M.A.

1631, Oct. 18—'A petition of Iohn Atkins against Richard Gunnell William Cartwright Richard Fowler & Mathew Smith Answered of course.' (*M.S.C.* ii. 406.)

1631, Nov. 28—'A petition of Iohn Atkins ag^st Richd Gunnell, Wm Cartwright Richard Fowler & Mathew Smith ye Queene of Bohemias Players Answered (vizt) If Richard Gunnell &c' doe not giue the pet^r satisfaccõn heerin before the expiration of one moneth after the sight heerof, The pet^r may take the ordinary course of Law for his reliefe./' (Ibid.)

1635, Dec. 31—A John Atkins, scrivener, was named as one of the overseers in the will of the King's comedian, John Shank. See Appendix, p. 648.

ATTERLEY, JOHN (*see* APPERLEY, JOHN).

ATTWELL (ATTEWELL, OTTEWELL), HUGH. Early in his career he was an actor for the Queen's Revels company (see Nungezer), but by the beginning of our period he had become a Prince Charles's man. Apparently he remained with this company until his death. It was not Hugh Attwell, but George, possibly his father, who was associated with *Attowell's Jig* (see Baskervill, *Jig*, pp. 238–41). Rowley's elegy tells us that he was a 'little man', and the mention of his six years' fight with Death suggests that he may have been forced to leave the stage some time before his death.

1615/16, Mar. 20—No. 6 to sign debt funding agreement of the players at the Hope, probably Prince's (Charles I) with Alleyn and Meade. (*Hens. Paps.*, pp. 90–1.)

1616–17—No. 6 to sign Prince's (Charles I) letter to Alleyn explaining their disagreement with Jacob Meade and asking for a loan (see p. 200, n. 3). (*Hens. Paps.*, p. 93.)

1618, May 4—'Hugh Atwell, of St Botolph, Aldersgate, London, Gent., & Mary Partridge, of same, widow of John Partridge, late of same, Gardener; at Stepney, co. Middlesex.' (*Marriages, London.*)

1618/19, Jan. 6–Feb. 2—'*New-yeere.* H. Atwell' in Middleton's *Inner Temple Mask or Mask of Heroes.* (1619 4° B.M.)

1621, Sept. 25—Died. Collier (*H.E.D.P.* i. 406–7) quotes from a broadside by William Rowley 'in the Library of the Society of Antiquaries' the following:

For a Funerall Elegie on the Death of Hugh Atwell, Servant to Prince Charles, this fellow-feeling Farewell: who died the 25th of Sept. 1621.

> So, now Hee's downe, the other side may shout:
> But did he not play faire? held he not out
> With courage beyond his bone? full sixe yeares
> To wrastle and tugge with Death! the strong'st feares
> To meet at such a match. They that have seene
> How doubtfull Victorie hath stood betweene,
> Might wonder at it. Sometimes cunningly
> Death gets advantage: by his cheeke and eye
> We thought that ours had beene the weaker part,
> And straight agen the little mans great heart
> Would rouse fresh strength and shake him off awhile:
> Death would retire, but never reconcile.
> They too't agen, agen; they pull, they tugge,
> At last Death gets within, and with a hugge
> The faint soule crushes. This thou maist boast, Death,
> Th'hast throwne him faire, but he was out of breath.
> Refresh thee then (sweet Hugh); on the ground rest:
> The worst is past, and now thou hast the best.
> Rise with fresh breath, and be assur'd before,
> That death shall never wrastle with thee more.
> Oh, hadst thou Death (as warres and battels may
> Present thee so) a field of noble clay
> To entertaine into thy rhewmie cell,
> And thou wouldst have it be presented well,
> Speake thy oration by this man's toung:
> 'Mongst living Princes it hath sweetly sung,
> (While they have sung his praise) but if thy Court
> Be silence-tyde and there dwells no report,
> Lend it to Life to store another flesh:
> We misse it here; wee'l entertain 't afresh.

EPITAPH.

Here lyes the man (and let no lyars tell)
His heart a Saints, his toung a silver bell:
Friend to his friend he stood: by Death he fell:
He chang'd his *Hugh*, yet he remains At-well.

WILL ROWLEY.

AXEN (AXALL, AXELL, AXON), ROBERT. As an actor he appears always with the companies at the Phoenix in Drury Lane, first with Queen Henrietta's men and, after they had moved to the Salisbury Court, with the King and Queen's young company. His known roles do not indicate that he was an important actor. It seems probable to me that the Jackson in the Queen's men's cast for *King John and Matilda* is a slip for Axen, since there is no other known reference to an actor named Jackson in the period, and since the role is about the size of the ones Axen had in three of the company's other plays, the first and second parts of *The Fair Maid of the West* and *Hannibal and Scipio*. The entry from Alleyn's diary may indicate too large an establishment for the actor, but those from St. James's are more likely.

1622, Sept. 6—Alleyn's diary has, 'I went to Doc: backer att ye Charter Howse from thenc to ye fortune I dind wt mr axell & gaue His wife for ned Laighton 20ˢ I gaue His man 6ᵈ His mayd 6ᵈ.' (Young, ii. 249.)

c. 1630—'*An English Merchant; by* Rob. Axell' in cast of Queen Henrietta's men prefixed to the 1631 4° of Heywood's *The Fair Maid of the West*, Part I; '*The Duke of Mantua, By* Rob. Axall' in the cast prefixed to Part II. (1631 4° B.M.)

1630/1, Feb. 6—'Everelda d. of Robert Axon & Mary his wife' chris. St. J.C.

1632/3, Jan. 16—'Symon s. of Robert Axon' chris. St. J.C.

1632/3, Jan. 21—'Simon s. of Robert Axon' bur. St. J.C.

1634, Mar. 28—'Will'm s. of Robert Axon' chris. St. J.C.

1634, Sept. 11—Legacies in the will of Thomas Basse to him, his wife Mary, and his son Thomas. (See Appendix, p. 631.)

>1634—'*Chester*, M. [Mr.] *Iackson*' in cast for Davenport's *King John and Matilda* by Queen Henrietta's men at the Cockpit. (1655 4° B.M.)

1635—Two parts—'*Bomilcar*. By *Robert Axen*.' and '*Gisgon*. By *Robert Axen*.'—in cast for Nabbe's *Hannibal and Scipio* given by Queen Henrietta's company 'at their Private house in *Drury Lane*'. (1637 4° B.M.)

1639, Aug. 10—'Robert Axon' is listed first in the ticket of privilege and certificate for the young company of Cockpit players. (*M.S.C.* ii. 390.)

BABHAM, CHRISTOPHER. His connexion with the stage is obscure. If Blagrave and Beeston are to be trusted, he had at least business relations with the King's men. How Sir Henry Herbert handled the complaint we do not know, but it is certain that Hammerton became an important actor in the King's company. It is not certain that Babham is to be identified with the gentleman jailer.

1632, Nov. 12—William Blagrave and William Beeston petition the Lord Chamberlain for recovery of the boy Stephen Hammerton whom Christopher Babham has stolen from them and employs at Blackfriars; the Lord Chamberlain refers the case to Sir Henry Herbert. (*M.S.C.* ii. 408.)

1635 (?)—A Christopher Babham petitions Secretary Coke to renew his predecessor's orders for £70 to him due upon his fee of gentleman jailer.

    I. Petition of Christopher Babham to Lord Treasurer Portland. Has been employed in the King's service for the better part of his life, to the peril thereof in the time of the great plague, when he attended the Receipt of the Exchequer, after which he served in the office of gentleman-gaoler in the Tower, as also in paying and receiving moneys for victualling the Navy, and in posting day and night to expedite the King's service, by reason whereof the King became indebted to him 70l. upon the fee of gentleman-gaoler, besides 200l. disbursed to Sir Allen Apsley for provisions in the Navy. Prays warrant for payment of the 70l. (*C.S.P., Dom.*, 1635–6, p. 68.)

BACKSTEAD, WILL (see BARKSTED).

BACON, JOHN. A minor attendant of the King's company. The name in the stage directions of the folio has sometimes been read as ' Job. ', but it is clearly ' Joh '. The production in which Bacon performed with the pistol was probably shortly after 16 September 1635, when Sir Henry Herbert relicensed the play. (*Herbert*, p. 36.)

c. 1635—'*Ioh. Bacon ready to shoot off a Pistol*' in stage direction for King's revival of *Love's Pilgrimage*, IV. i. (1647 folio B.M. Dated from renewal license dated 16 September 1635; *Herbert*, p. 36.)

1636/7, Jan. 12—Ticket of privilege as attendant of players granted to him and ten others 'imployed by his Ma^{tes} servantes the Players of the Blackfryers.' (*M.S.C.*, ii. 380.)

BAGSTARE, RICHARD (see BAXTER, RICHARD).

BALLS, FRANCIS. Balls was a minor actor, possibly a hired man, in the King's company. Professor Sisson says in the introduction to his edition of Massinger's *Believe as You List* for the Malone Society (p. xxxiii), 'Francis Balls was probably the son of one Richard Balls, musician to the King, employed also by the King's company at the Blackfriars theatre, who died shortly before 1623. This fact may explain why in one instance (l. 830) he is called "ffan [Fran] Balls" and elsewhere "Mr Balls" (ll. 1362, 2367) . . . my information is derived from Chancery records, as yet unpublished. . . .' It may be observed that Pattrick and Rowland play Demetrius when he is to speak, and Balls when he has a silent part.

1631, May 6 (lic.)—He divided the part of Demetrius ('ffan Balls')
with William Patrick and 'Rowland' in the King's production of
Believe as You List. He was also one of the Attendants of King
Prusias ('m^r Balls:') and one of the Attendants of Marcellus ('m^r
Balls:') in the same production. (Greg, *Dram. Doc.*, pp. 297–9.)

BALLS, RICHARD. A royal musician who was sometimes employed by the King's company (*see* Francis Balls). Viscount
Mandeville's letter shows that he was also a city wait.

1620, Apr. 5—'I dined w^t m^r Hewitt & ther wase ye princes musitions
m^r ball & m^r drewe.' (Alleyn's Diary, Young, ii. 174.)

1622, Oct. 21—'VIII. 48. Letter from H. Mandeville to the Lord
Mayor and Court of Aldermen, soliciting for John Willson the
place of one of the servants of the City for Music and Voice, vacant
by the death of Richard Balls.' (*Remembrancia*, p. 303.)

BAND, THOMAS (*see* BOND, THOMAS).

BANKES, WILLIAM. An actor in Prince Charles's (II) company
who was not sworn groom until 1635, but who had some sort of
protection, or at least convinced his creditors that he had, as early
as 1631. The fact that this is the year of the formation of the
company suggests that he was associated with it from the beginning. The number of petitions against Bankes for debt may
indicate something of his character or they may indicate that he
was a financial agent for the company, though the latter is most
unlikely, since he appears in none of the other lists of the company.
There is no evidence that he was a fraud, as Thomas Barnes (q.v.)
was. It is not at all certain that the William Bankes of Foster
Lane is the same as the actor, though one would surmise that
collecting penalties for oaths might appeal to a man with so many
debts as the player had.

1631, May 6—'A petition of Francis Baber against William Bankes
debt 30^{li}.' (*M.S.C.* ii. 404.)

1631, May 26—'A petition of Francis Baber against William Bankes
debt 30^{li} Answered (vizt) If William Bankes doe not giue the pet^r
satisfaccõn heerin vpon sight heerof The pet^r may take the benefitt
of his Ma^{tes} Lawes for his relief.' (Ibid.)

1631, July 1—'A petition of William Bankes agst Mr Edw: Crofts debt
200^{li}.' (Ibid., p. 405.)

1631, July 8—'A petition of William Bankes against Mr Edward
Crofts debt 200^{li} Answered (vizt) If Mr Edward Crofts doe not giue
ye pet^r satisfaccõn heerin vpon sight heerof The pet^r may take the
ordinary course of law for his reliefe.' (Ibid.)

1631, July 23—'A petition of Edward Hurd against Wm Bankes debt
30^{li} Answered (vizt) Let William Bankes see this petition & satisfie
the pet^r within one moneth after the sight heerof. Or else the pet^r
may take the benefitt of his Ma^{tes} Lawes for his reliefe.' (Ibid.)

1631, July 23—'A petition of William Bankes against Mr William
Askewgh 77^{li}.' (Ibid.)

1632, Oct. 4—'A petition of William Wombwell against Wm Banke;

debt 60^{li} Answered wth leaue graunted vpon sight.' (*M.S.C.* ii. 407.)

1632/3, Feb. 20—'A petition of Wm Bankes & Alexander Bradshaw agst Mr Iohn Wortham.' (Ibid., p. 409.)

1633, Apr. 20—'A peticõn of Raph Bankes against Wm Bankes debt 50^{li} Answered wth leaue graunted [vpon sight] after one weeke after sight.' (Ibid.)

1633, May 10—'A petition of Thomas Bankes agst Wm Bankes.' (Ibid., p. 410.)

1633, May 10—'A petition of Thomas Tennant against Wm Bankes Answered (vizt) I desire my Lord chiefe Iustice to take this pet^{rs} pittifull estate into his fauourable consideration & take such order for the pet^{rs} speedy inlargement as may bee convenient.' (Ibid.)

1634/5, Feb. 24—'A peticõn of Wm Bankes against Mr Iohn Worthã Answered wth leaue graunted after a moneth after sight.' (Ibid., p. 411.)

1635, Dec. 12—'William Bankes' was one of four men named in 'ffower seuerall Warrantes for the swearing of these 4 persones Groomes of the Chamber in ordinary w^{thout} ffee to attend the Prince his Highnes in ye Quality of Players'. (Ibid., p. 377.)

1635/6, Mar. 24—'Appointment by Robert Lesley, one of the gentlemen of the Privy Chamber, of William Banckes of St. Foster's, Foster Lane, London, as his deputy within that parish, for seven years next ensuing, to see that the statute of the 21st James I. for suppressing profane swearing and cursing, be duly put in execution, also to collect penalties for breach of the statute, and to pay the same over to the said Robert Lesly, deducting 2s. 6d. out of every 20s. for his pains. [A printed form with the names and dates filled in in manuscript.]' (*C.S.P., Dom.*, 1635–6, p. 320.)

1636, June 28—'A peticõn of Wm Vanham against Wm Bankes debt 130^{li} Answered (vizt) Let the pet^r discharge Bankes of the Arrest made vpon Bankes w^{thout} leaue. And after that, if Bankes shall refuse to giue him satisfaccõn for his iust debt the pet^r may take the ordinary couse of Law for his reliefe.' (*M.S.C.* ii. 411.)

BARBOR, EDMOND. Probably not an actor, but he is among the thirty-nine sued by Markham, at least twenty-nine of whom were actors.

1623, May 21—In Markham's suit as 'Edmond Barbor on Charkenwell hill', 22s. (See Appendix, p. 682.)

BARFIELD (BAREFIELD, BARFFEILDE, BARRFOOTE, BURFEILD); ROGER. Barfield was one of three leaders of a travelling Queen Anne's company in 1606 (Murray, ii. 400). His absence from later dramatic records, as well as his designation as 'Gentleman' at St. Giles', suggests that he had left the stage before the death of Shakespeare. The Roger Barfield, trumpeter, is not improbably the player, for it is noteworthy that his first appearance as a royal musician comes between his designation as a player at St. Giles' and his designation as a gentleman. One would think trumpeting a not uncongenial employment for a former provincial actor.

BARKSTED PLAYERS

1609/10, Feb. 28—'Lease from Edward Alleyn, of St. Saviour's, Southwark, esq., to Edmond Williams, of the parish of St. Giles without Cripplegate, "packthredmaker", of two messuages in Whitecrosse Street, in the par. of St. Giles, in the tenure of the said Edmond Williams and Roger Barffeilde, for 14 years, at a rent of 3*l.*' (*MSS. Dul.*, p. 237.)

1610/11, Jan. 2—'Isabell daughter of Roger Barfield Player' chris. St. G.C.

1610–11—'Roger Burfeild' is last in a list of six trumpeters named in an allowance for wages and liveries granted to Prince Henry's servants. He is in the lowest of the wage groups, receiving £13. 6s. 8d. yearly wages and £13. 2s. 10d. for livery. (*King's Musick*, p. 49, from L.C., vol. 592, p. 14.)

1612—'Roger Barfeild' received mourning allowance as one of the 'trumpeters of the late Prince Henry of Wales'. (Ibid., from L.C., vol. 555.)

1614, July 3—'Susan dau. of Roger Barfield, Gentleman' bur. St. G.C.

1616, July 12—'Anthony sonne of Roger Barfield gentleman' chris. St. G.C.

1618—'Roger Barfeild' is listed as one of the twenty-eight trumpeters of Queen Anne in the accounts for her funeral. (*King's Musick*, p. 52, from L.C., vol. 556.)

1625—In the list headed 'The Chamber of King Charles', the fifth and last of the trumpeters listed is 'Roger Barrfeild'. (Ibid., p. 59, from L.C., vol. 557.)

1625, May 28—In a warrant for liveries and banners to be delivered to seventeen trumpeters, the name of 'Roger Barfoote' appears fifth. (Ibid., pp. 55–6, from L.C., vol. 813, p. 10.)

1625, July 4—'Warrant to the Treasurer of the Chamber, to pay to Josias Broome, Nicholas Transome, William Arnold, Roger Barefield, and Robert Broome, his Majesty's Trumpeters, 16d. each per day for wages.' (*C.S.P., Dom.*, 1625–6, p. 543.)

1626, May 28—A warrant for twenty-three King's Trumpeters contains the name of 'Roger Barrfoote' and all the others of the above warrant. (P.R.O. L.C. 5/51, p. 10.)

BARKSTED (BACKSTEAD, BARKSTEAD, BAXTED, BUCKSTEAD), WILLIAM. Before 1616 he belonged to the Queen's Revels, then to the Lady Elizabeth's, and then to Prince Charles's men, and in that time he published *Myrrha* and *Hiren* (see Nungezer and *D.N.B.*). After March 1615/16 there is no direct evidence to connect him with the stage or even to prove that he was alive, though Taylor's anecdotes suggest that he had some popularity, and the use of 'late' in 1638 but not in 1629 might imply that he had died between the two dates. Hazlitt's identification of Barkstead as the 'Mr. Wm. Buckstead Comedian' whose name is signed to 'A Prologue to a playe to the cuntry people' (MS. Ashmole, 38, art. 198) is probable (Hazlitt, *Handbook*, p. 26). It is generally thought that his name on the title-pages of certain copies of the 1631 edition of *The Insatiate Countess*, the omission of the play from the Marston collection of 1633, and the character of much of the verse of the play indicate that Barkstead finished Marston's play.

1615/16, Mar. 20—No. 7 to sign the debt-funding agreement of the players of the Hope, probably Prince's men, with Alleyn and Meade. (*Hens. Paps.*, pp. 90–1 ; see above, p. 199.)

1629—Anecdote No. 11 in John Taylor's *Wit and Mirth* begins, 'Will Barkstead the Plaier cast his Chamber-lye out of his window in the night'. (*All the Workes of Iohn Taylor The Water-Poet*, 1630, B.M.)

1631—The third edition of *The Insatiate Countess* has alternate title-pages, one of which says, 'Written, By William Barksteed', and the other, 'Written by Iohn Marston'.

1638—The fourth anecdote in *Taylor's Feast* concérns 'Will Baxted, a late well knowne fine Comedian'. (1638 4° HN, pp. 10–15.)

BARNES, THOMAS. Barnes was not a player at all, but a carpenter who perpetrated a fraud by posing as one of the Lady Elizabeth's men, apparently with the connivance of Joseph Moore, the leading member of the company. The Lord Chamberlain's records set forth the events clearly enough. Other players no doubt presumed on the protection of their livery, but I know of no other case so fully set forth as this one.

1629, July 2—The L.C. Books record a warrant to swear 'Thomas Barnes A groome of ye Chamber in ordinary'; in the margin is, 'Queene of Bohemia's Players'. (*M.S.C.* ii. 350.)

1631, June 20—Two women petition the Lord Chamberlain for redress against Thomas Barnes, who has ejected them from their house without reason. (Ibid., p. 405.)

1631/2, Jan. 11—'A petition of Drue Heydon against Thomas Barnes debt 52^li Answered of course.' (Ibid., p. 406.)

1631/2, Jan. 23—'A petition of Edward Gerrard ag^st Thomas Barnes debt 600^li ingagem^t. . . .' (Ibid.)

1631/2, Jan. 23—To a petition of Drue Heydon against Thomas Barnes, the Lord Chamberlain answers that he has questioned Barnes, who can say in his defence only that he is a Queen of Bohemia's player. Upon further questioning, the Lord Chamberlain discovers that Barnes is a carpenter who never had any knowledge of stage playing, and discharges him from his Majesty's service. (Ibid., pp. 406–7.)

1631/2, Jan. 23—'Tho Barnes discharged his seruice' is the marginal notation to the following: 'Wheras by virtue of a Warraunt vnder my hand of the second of Iuly 1629 one Thomas Barnes was sworne his Ma^tes servant in the place of a Groome of the Chamber in ordinary vpon p^rtence that Hee was one of the Company of Players, which by his Ma^tes fauour had a lycence to practice vnder the name of the Queene of Bohemias [Players] servantes wheras in truth the sayd Barnes is by profession a Carpenter & neuer did nor doth professe the quality of a stageplayer but was dishonestly & sinisterly obtruded vpon mee by the false & fraudulent suggestion of one Ioseph Moore that followed the busines in the name of the company

out of a corrupt end to deriue vnto him selfe a benefitt by intituling
the sayd Barnes vnto ye previledge & proteccõn of his Ma^{tes} service
as now appeareth vnto mee vpon the seuerall petitions of diuerse
persons of good credit from some of whome the sayd Barnes doth
most iniuriously and scandalously detayne their iust & due debtes
& others of them Hee hath drawne to bee bound for him in great
sommes of money, which since, hee hath suffered to bee forfeited &
therby hath exposed those which were ingaged for him vnto the
danger of imprisonm^t & apparent ruine of their estates. ffor reformation heerof & to the end that his Ma^{tes} service may bee purged
from the stayne of soe dishonest foule proceedinges. Theis are to
will & require you to call the sayd Barnes before you & him to
dismisse & discharge out of his Ma^{tes} service & all relation therunto
& to cause his name to bee blotted and razed out of the list of his
Ma^{tes} servantes Heerof you may not fayle & this shall bee yor warr^t.
Whitehall the 23th of Ian. 1631.' Addressed 'To ye gent' vshers
dayly Wayters & to euery of them./' (Ibid., pp. 356–7.)

1631/2, Jan. 26—'A petition of Edward Gerrard & Edward Bankes
against Thomas Barnes debt 50^{li} . . .' (Ibid., p. 407.)

BARRETT, JOHN. The records connect him with only one company, the King's Revels. The fact that he had a son in 1637 is
good evidence that the production of *Messalina* in which he played
the empress must have taken place long before 1640, the year
which is usually suggested for the production.

c. 1634?—'*Messallina* Empresse—*Iohn Barret*' in King's Revels cast
for Richards's *Messalina, the Roman Empress.* (1640 ed. B.M.)

1634/5, Mar. 10—In full list of players at Norwich. Some of them
seem to be King's Revels men, though the records do not give the
name of the company; probably two companies. (See pp. 286 and
288–9.)

1637, Nov. 12—'William, son of John Barrett, Player' chris. St. G.C.
1638, Nov. 11—'Gustavous, sonne of John Barratt, Player' chris.
St. G.C.
1639/40, Jan. 31—'William sonne of John Barrett Player' bur. St.
G.C.
1640, Mar. 31—'John Barratt player' bur. St. G.C.
1640, May 8—'Gustavous sonne of John Barratt Playe^r' bur. St. G.C.

BARRETT, WALTER. When a Lady Elizabeth's company got
into trouble at Coventry, in March 1615, the names of the actors
were copied from the patent of 31 May 1613. One of these actors
was Walter Barrett. Eleven years later he was still a provincial
actor.

1613, May 31—Named in patent to Lady Elizabeth's of this date
which was copied at Coventry 28 March 1615. (See *R.E.S.* i. 183.)
1624, Apr. 9—'Walter Barrett' named as an associate of William
Perry in a confirmation of licence of 31 October 1617 to 'Children
of the Revels to the late Queene Anna' shown at Exeter. (*Hist.
MSS. Com.*, Records of the City of Exeter, p. 171, and Murray, ii.
273.) *See* James Jones.

BASSE, THOMAS. He was a Lady Elizabeth's man in 1611 and 1613, but before June 1617 he had become a fellow and sharer of Queen Anne's company, according to the Baskerviles. Evidently he had become a member between June 1616 and June 1617, since he is not mentioned by the Baskerviles in connexion with the agreement of the former date. After the break-up of Queen Anne's company he joined with several of his fellows to start the Children of the Revels, a company which appears never to have begun performing. From 1622 until 1634 we have no record of him. It is noteworthy that all the legatees in his will, outside his own family, are members of Queen Henrietta's company or their families—Axon, Robbins, Perkins, Bowyer, and the two Beestons. He may have cherished ex-Queen Anne's men exclusively, but it is possible that he had an unknown position at the Phoenix in the reign of Charles I.

1617, June 3—The Baskerviles say that he refused to sign the new agreement of Queen Anne's men on this date, though he was a fellow and sharer of the company. (Fleay, *Stage*, pp. 285–8.)

1619, >May 13—As a member of Queen Anne's company, he was eleventh of sixteen men named to receive black cloth for her funeral procession. (*M.S.C.* ii. 325.)

1622, July 8—He is the fourth of seven late Queen Anne's men named in a warrant for a Privy Seal and another for a Signet Bill for licensing the Children of the Revels. (Murray, ii. 193–4; see above, pp. 167–8.)

1622—Herbert listed him in his office book as fourth of the seven 'chiefe players at the Red Bull, called the players of the Revells'. (*Herbert*, p. 63; see above, p. 167.)

1634, Sept. 11—Made his nuncupative will, giving his residence as St. James's Clerkenwell, and mentioning several actors. (See Appendix, p. 631.)

1634, Oct. 3—His will was proved by his wife Dorcas. (See ibid.)

BATTY. Since *Ned Gibs* (Edward Gibbs) is known to have been an actor as well as a fencer, it is possible that Batty was too.

1664—One of several gentlemen who have been talking of the days before the wars says, 'You talk of your Players, I am for the Fencers, there are none living now like old *Bradshaw*, old *Batty*, *Chatterton* and *Ned Gibs*'. ([Tatham] *Knavery in All Trades*, E$_1$, 1664 4° HN.)

BAXTED, WILL (see BARKSTED, WILL).

BAXTER, RICHARD. Essential facts about his career have been discovered by Professor C. J. Sisson, who says (*B.A.Y.L.*, p. xxxiii), 'I may note here that Richard Baxter was born in 1593, was a hired man in Queen Anne's company at the Red Bull from about the time of the opening of that theatre in 1605–6, until he left them, probably in 1623, to join the King's company. . . . My information is derived from Chancery records, as yet unpublished.' Professor Sisson's date for the beginning of Baxter's career with Queen Anne's seems a bit early, since he would have been only twelve or thirteen in 1606, rather young for a hired man. His importance with the King's company cannot have been great.

He is sometimes said to have played Stremon's boy in *The Mad Lover*, but he was far too old for a boy's role in 1630. It is more likely that he played the servant. The compositor no doubt thought the bookholder's note of the actor's name an insertion and added the 'and'.

The entries from Clerkenwell cannot be too certainly connected with the actor because of the commonness of the name, but most of them seem to belong to the same man, and St. James's Clerkenwell is a most likely place of residence for a man who spent fifteen or twenty years acting at the Red Bull. If he is the Richard Baxter who was acting at the Restoration, as Downes implies (pp. 1–2; see Hotson, pp. 242–3), his stage career must be one of the longest of the seventeenth century.

1593—He was born. See Sisson, *B.A.Y.L.*, p. xxxiii.

1605-6—Hired man in Queen Anne's company at Red Bull from about the time of the opening until about 1623. (Ibid.)

1614, Oct. 2—'Richarde Baxter & Joane Elitt' mar. St. J.C.

1616, Dec. 25—'Constance d. of Richard Baxter' chris. St. J.C.

1617, Oct. 21—'Constance d. of Richard Baxter' bur. St. J.C.

1618, Sept. 2—'Richard s. of Richard Baxter' chris. St. J.C.

1620, Aug. 23—'Robart s. of Richard Baxter [& Joane his wife]' chris. St. J.C.

1621/2, Jan. 27—'Mychaell s. of Richard Baxter & Jone his wife' chris. St. J.C.

1622, Mar.-Apr.—A sword in his hands injured a feltmaker's apprentice named Gill on the stage of the Red Bull. Gill wrote, threatening him and the company with the revenge of the apprentices unless he was given satisfaction.' Gill was taken before the Justice of the Peace, and the apprentices were warned. Baxter appears innocent. (*Middx. Co. Rec.* ii. 165-6; 175-6.)

1622, Dec. 2—'Susan d. of Richard Baxter' bur. St. J.C.

1624, Apr. 9—'Richard Backster' was named in the confirmation of the licence of 31 October 1617 to the Children of the Revels to the late Queen Anne which was shown at Exeter. (*Hist. MSS. Com.*, Records of the City of Exeter, p. 171, and Murray, ii. 273.) *See* James Jones.

1624, June 30—'John s. of Richard Baxter & Jone his wife' chris. St. J.C.

1624/5, Jan. 26—'Jane d. of Richard Baxter' bur. St. J.C.

1625, Sept. 10—'John s. of Richard Baxter' bur. St. J.C.

1628, July 10—'A petition of Iohn Hamond agst Mr Baxter debt 200^{li}.' (*M.S.C.* ii. 402.)

1628—'Richard Baxter' was twelfth in the King's cast for *The Lover's Melancholy*, lic. 24 November; roles not given. (1629 4° B.M.; *Herbert*, p. 32.)

1629, Dec. 23—'John s. of Richard Baxter & Jane his wife' chris. St. J.C.

c. 1630—A stage direction in *The Mad Lover*, IV. i, says, '*Enter a Servant and R. Bax, and Stremon at the doore*'. Apparently he sings Charon's lines in a two-part song with Stremon. (First folio B.M.)

1631, Apr. 20—'Eliz. d. of Richard Baxter & Jone his wife' chris. St. J.C.

1631, May 6 (lic.)—He divided the part of Calistus with Thomas Hobbes, and played Titus and an attendant on Marcellus in the King's production of *Believe As You List* (*R: Bax, R: Baxt:, R: Baxter:*). (Sisson, *B.A.Y.L.*, pp. xxxi ff.)

1636, May 17—He was fifth in a partial list of minor King's men named in a pass for players. (*M.S.C.* ii. 378–9.)

1636/7, Jan. 12—'Richd Bagstare' with ten others was granted a ticket of privilege as an attendant of the players 'imployed by his Ma^tes servantes the Players of the Blackfryers'. (Ibid., p. 380.)

1648—In January 1663/4 he gave evidence in a Chancery suit, apparently as one of a company of actors who in 1648 'did by stealth and in secret places Act together here in England some Playes and Interludes'. (Boswell, 'Cartwright', p. 130.)

BAYLY, EDWARD. He appears only as a provincial player.

1628, June 7—'Edward Bayly' is one of thirteen players named in a licence of this date granted by Sir Henry Herbert to Ellis Guest's company and shown at Norwich 2 July 1628. (Murray, ii. 353.)

BEDOWE, ELLIS. Bedowe is a very shadowy figure. The appearance of his name in the list which George Stutville gave to the clerk at Norwich may indicate that he belonged to the King's Revels company, but it is not certain (see pp. 286 and 288–9). It is possible also that he may be the Ellis of the stage directions of *The Poor Man's Comfort* and of *The Wasp*, but Ellis Worth (q.v.), a much better known actor, seems a more likely candidate in each case.

1634/5, Mar. 10—In complete list of players at Norwich. (Part of them are King's Revels men, though the records do not give the name of the company; perhaps it was only a temporary amalgamation.) (Murray, ii. 356.)

BEE, WILLIAM. He appears only as a companion of Francis Wambus in his defiance of the Norwich authorities in 1624. Is it possible that the Norwich clerk meant William Beeston, whose father was a member of the Lady Elizabeth's company at this time?

1624, May 26—Discharged from Norwich gaol with Francis Wambus, with whom he had apparently been imprisoned, 26 April 1624, though his name is not mentioned at the time of imprisonment. (*See* Wambus.)

1624, Sept. 28—Townsend agreed to pay the jailer the charges for Bee and Wambus. (*See* Wambus.)

BEELAND (BECKLAND, BELAND, BILAND, BYLAND), AMBROSE. He was evidently one of the musicians who served the King's company at the Globe and Blackfriars, perhaps one of those whose skill led Whitelocke to say 'the Blackefryar's Musicke . . . were then esteemed the best of common musitians in London' (Burney, *Music*, ii. 299). His long career as a royal violinist indicates that he must have been quite a young man when Sir Henry Herbert exempted him from arrest. Numerous other records of his musical career are to be found in *King's Musick*.

1624, Dec. 27—He is the fourth of twenty-one attendants of the King's company exempted from arrest by Sir Henry Herbert. (See above, pp. 15–16.)

1628, Dec. 14—The Lord Chamberlain issued a warrant for the apprehension of 'Ambrose Beeland and Henry Wilson Fidlers at yᵉ complaint of Mʳ Hemmings'. (*M.S.C.* ii. 348.)

c. 1630?—In the prompt notes of the MS. play, *The Wasp*, at Alnwick Castle, appears the name 'Ambros'. The company to whom the play belonged is unknown, but conceivably Beeland is indicated. (Greg, *Dram. Doc.*, p. 360.)

1639/40, Feb. 11 and 13—'Warrant to swear Ambrose Beeland a musician to his Majesty for the violins in ordinary, in the place of James Johnson, deceased. Also for the payment of 1s. 8d. per diem as wages and £16 2s. 6d. yearly for a livery allowance.' (*King's Musick*, p. 104, from L.C., vol. 739, p. 373.)

1641, Apr. 17—'Ambrose Byland' is one of the violinists among the King's musicians exempted from payment of subsidies. (*H.E.D.P.* ii. 35 n.)

1641, Nov. 8—'Ambrose Biland' was one of seven King's violinists who approved a petition of Margaret Dorney that her son Richard be admitted to the musician's place formerly occupied by his father. (*King's Musick*, p. 108, from L.C., vol. 740, p. 3.)

1661, Aug. 3—'Certificate that Davies Mell and Ambrose Beeland, who were sworn musicians for the violins to his late Majesty, are to continue in their said places to his present Majesty, as they have done since his Majesty's happy restoration.' (Ibid., p. 135, from L.C., vol. 741, p. 317.)

1671/2, Mar. 19—'Warrant to admit Edmund Flower one of his Majesty's musicians in ordinary for the violin, in place of Ambrose Beeland, surrendered.' (Ibid., p. 242, from L.C., vol. 744, p. 14.)

BEESTON (*alias* HUTCHINSON), CHRISTOPHER. From his erection of the Phoenix in 1617 to his death in 1638, Christopher Beeston was probably the most important theatrical figure in London, but he had had at least twenty years' experience on the stage before he built his theatre. Probably his career began under the auspices of Augustine Phillips, who left thirty shillings (the same sum he left to Shakespeare and to Condell) 'To my s[er]uante Xpofer Besone' He appeared with Phillips in the cast of *Every Man in His Humour* and perhaps in *2 Seven Deadly Sins*, and in 1604 he named his son Augustine. By 1602 Beeston was in the Earl of Worcester's company; at the accession of James he became a Queen Anne's man, and he remained in her service until her death in 1619. He seems to have become the dominant member in this company and to have succeeded Thomas Greene as business manager in 1612, for in the Baskervile suits both Beeston's fellows and the Baskerviles say that he was the business manager, and the actors say that he was the member of greatest substance. Beeston says that he entered the service of Prince Charles at the Queen's death, and the records of that company indicate that he brought them to his theatre, the Phoenix, where they appear to have played for about three years.

From at least 1604 to 1610 Beeston lived in the parish of St. Leonard's Shoreditch, where his children Augustine, Christopher, Jane, and Robert were baptised and buried, but in 1611, 1614, and 1615 he appears in St. James's Clerkenwell, nearer to the Red Bull in which the Queen's men performed. He certainly owned a house in that parish in 1616. After he moved to Clerkenwell, his wife Jane and his servant William Allen, probably the actor (q.v.), are reported several times for staying away from church. One gets the impression that Beeston was probably one of the players who led Prynne to make his sweeping generalization, 'the most of our present English *Actors* (as I am credibly informed) being professed Papists'. Evidently Beeston moved to the parish of St. Giles in the Field when his new theatre in that parish was completed; the investigation of the riot of 1617 suggests that he was living in the house attached to the theatre (see above, pp. 161–3, and Hotson, p. 90).

As a member and manager of Queen Anne's company, Beeston was an associate of Thomas Heywood, and the friendship between the dramatist and the manager seems to have been lifelong (see Clark, *Heywood*, passim). Beeston wrote verses for Heywood's *Apology for Actors* in 1612, and in 1634 he paid for a plate in Heywood's *Hierarchie of the Blessed Angels*.

There are repeated suggestions that Beeston was more shrewd than honest in his business dealings with the actors. Perkins, Worth, and Cumber said so in 1619, and John King said the same thing in 1620. While there are no direct charges about his conduct when Prince Charles's men left the Cockpit or when the Lady Elizabeth's and then Queen Henrietta's men did later, it is rather suspicious that the old company should always have left in reduced circumstances, that the new company should apparently prosper, and that so many plays should have remained at the Cockpit when the various companies left. A Beeston's Diary would probably offer many parallels to Henslowe's Diary and might well be equally valuable. The hints we get of Beeston's relations with the Master of the Revels and his adroit petition to the Privy Council suggest that he was a very clever manager.

After Beeston built the Cockpit in 1616 and 1617, he was always a member of the company occupying his theatre—Queen Anne's,

Prince Charles's, Lady Elizabeth's, Queen Henrietta's, Beeston's Boys, the latter two of which he probably organized himself. It is probable, however, that he ceased to act, for he does not appear in any of the six casts of Queen's men. In 1634 Kendall told Crosfield in his account of the Queen's men that Beeston was 'Their master', and when the new company was formed to succeed the Queen's men, Beeston was officially sworn their governor. His will shows that he owned two-thirds of the shares in the company and furnished the theatre and the costumes. His activities as Master of the Queen's men and Governor of the King and Queen's young company are detailed below and are self-explanatory. It is probably a tribute to Beeston's management that his company got into trouble soon after his death and was frequently in difficulties before the closing of the theatres.

1616, Mar. 30—Swinnerton and Lee showed the 1609 licence of Queen Anne's men with Beeston's name at Norwich, but Beeston probably was not there. (Murray, ii. 340–1.)

1616, Easter—'True Bill, for not going to church, chapel or any usual place of Common Prayer on the said 1st of January [1615/16], nor at any time during the three months then next ensuing—against . . . Jane Beeston wife of Christofer Beeston gentleman, William Allen yoman, . . . late of St. James's-in-Clerkenwell co. Midd.' (*Middx. Co. Rec.* ii. 119–20.) The fuller version of this record in *Middx. Sessions*, iii. 216, reads, 'Jane, wife of Christopher Beeston *alias* Hutchenson, gentleman, William Allen, Katherine Cashe *alias* Nurse *alias* Hutchenson, spinster'.

1616, June—With nine other members of the Queen's company, Beeston signed a new debt-funding agreement with the Baskeriles. (Fleay, *Stage*, p. 275.)

1616, Aug. 9—Beeston leased from John Best and six trustees 'All that edifices or building called the Cockpits, and the Cockhouses and sheds thereunto adjoining'. The rent was £45 a year, and the lease was to run thirty-one years from 29 September 1616. (Hotson, p. 89.)

1616, Sept. 5 or 6—In the records of the Sessions of the Peace and Gaol Delivery of these dates occur the following items: 'John Shepp'erd of "Lillypott Lane," London, bricklayer, committed for working upon a new foundation in Drury Lane, and handed in bail to Richard Smith of Holborn upon condition that he shall appear before the Lords of the Council at their first sitting at Whitehall, and in the meantime not to go on in the building and withall to do his best endeavour to bring forth Mr. Beeston to-morrow in court, then his appearance to be spared and Beeston to be bound. On 10 September, A.D. 1616, discharged by order of the Justices.' 'Whereas the Court is informed that there is a new building to hand to be set and erected "in Drury Lane nere Lincolnes Inne feilds att and adioyninge to the Cockepitt", contrary to the law and his Majesty's proclamations; it is therefore ordered that the said new building shall presently be stayed, and the workmen committed to prison that shall hereafter presume to go forward in the said new building, and also such as shall set them on-work having had warning already to forbear; and further it is ordered that all other new buildings whatsoever be likewise stayed.' (*Middx. Sessions*, iii. 310 and 310–11.)

1616, Sept. 18—A letter from the Council to the High Sheriff of Middlesex about persons erecting new buildings contrary to the law, contains 'A note of such persons as are greate offendors in building contrary to his Majesty's proclamacions, etc., and such as are fittest to be made an example . . . Clarkenwell. Christopher Beeston hath erected a base tenement, not of bricke, and, having been formerly prohibited, did promise to make it only an addition to his owne dwelling howse, but since hath made a tenement of it, distant from his howse, and neere to his Majesty's passage. To be pulled downe.' (*Acts P.C.*, 1616, 1617, pp. 14–15.)

1616, Oct. 4—Process was begun against 'Christofer Beeston and the rest of the players of the Redd. Bull' for highway repair arrears. (*Middx. Co. Rec.* ii. 235.)

1616, Oct. 7—Attached to a letter to the High Sheriff of Middlesex, ordering the demolition of illegal new buildings, is a report of William and John Gore, late Sheriffs, telling what they have done; 'For Christopher Bastones house, it is for the most parte puld downe, not to be inhabited'. (*Acts P.C.*, 1616, 1617, p. 36.)

1616/17, Mar. 20—In the Middlesex Sessions of this date, 'on the chief movers of a notable riot' fifty persons were charged, most of them with 'riotous assalte and spoyle done upon the dwellinge house of . . .' or with 'breaking the dwellinge house of . . .' or with riotous destruction of one sort or another. The first four charged were Henry Baldwin, who pleaded not guilty when charged 'for breaking the dwellinge house of Christopher Beeston and diverse goods', and John Grymes, Christopher Longe, and Christopher Lewes, who pleaded guilty when charged 'for a riotous assalte and spoyle done upon the dwellinge house of Christopher Beeston' and were sent back in irons for various terms, fined, and charged to find sureties for their good conduct. (*Middx. Co. Rec.* ii. 219–23.) Probably the four men were among the rioting apprentices who had wrecked the new Cockpit theatre on Shrove Tuesday, two weeks before, and Beeston's house was the one adjoining the theatre. (See above, pp. 161–3.)

1617, May 31—Beeston's name was copied by the clerk from the licence shown by a travelling Queen Anne's company at Norwich, but it is not likely that he was with them. (Murray, ii. 343.)

1617, June 3—Beeston and seven other 'ffellowes and Sharers' of Queen Anne's company signed a new debt funding agreement with the Baskerviles. Beeston and Cumber signed a bond for £63 and another for £10. They agreed to continue to pay as long as they or any four of them should play together. (Fleay, *Stage*, pp. 285–8.)

1617, July 16—'True Bill, for not going to church, chapel or any usual place of Common Prayer on the said day [25 March 1617], nor at any time during the three months then next ensuing,—against . . . Jane wife of Christopher Hutchenson *alias* Beeston gentleman . . . late of St. James's Clerkenwell co. Midd.' (*Middx. Co. Rec.* ii. 128.)

1617, Sept. 29—The Privy Council wrote the High Sheriff of Middle-

sex, 'Whereas about a twelvemoneth since an expresse comaunde-
ment was given unto the then sherife of Middlesex, your predecessor, for pulling downe certeyne howses within the county of
Middlesex neere adjoyninge unto the citty of London, suche as
had been newly erected contrary to his Majestie's proclamacions
and in highe contempt thereof, amongst which nomber there was
a base tenement erected by one Christopher Beeston in Clarkenwell, neere unto his Majestie's passage, pulled downe and demolished by vertue of the sayd order, which since is buylt up agayne,
and his Majesty of late passing that way hath taken speciall notice
thereof, being highly offended with the presumption. Yow shall
therefore by vertue of this our letter make your present repaire
unto the place, and to cause the sayd buylding, ymmediatly and
without delay, before to morrow at night at the furthest, being the
last of this moneth, to be pulled downe to the grownde and utterly
demolished. And to take sufficient bondes of the owner to his
Majestie's use that neyther in that place nor in any other he shall
erect any buylding hereafter contrary to his Majestie's proclamacions on that behalfe, or ells, in case of refusall, to committ him to
prison till he submitt himselfe. All which wee require yow at your
perill to see performed punctually and precisely as you will answer
your neglect unto his Majestie. And soe, etc.' (*Acts P.C.*, 1616,
1617, p. 334.)

1617, Oct. 2—Beeston, with five other Queen Anne's men, petitioned
the Sessions of the Peace for relief from charges for highway repairs
about the Red Bull theatre. (*Middx. Co. Rec.* ii. 170.)

c. 1617—In his deposition in *Smith* v. *Beeston*, 5 May 1620, John King
says that the company of Queen Anne began to break up about
three years before (i.e. 1617) and that Beeston took their apparel
and converted it to his own use and sold some to other companies.
(Wallace, *Three Theatres*, p. 48.)

1619, >May 13—As a member of Queen Anne's company he was
allowed black cloth to wear in her funeral procession on this date.
'3. The Q: Plaiers . . . Christopher Beeston—iiij yards'. (*M.S.C.*
ii. 325.)

1619, Nov. 18—When sued by John Smith, Worth, Cumber, and
Perkins say that Beeston had kept the company accounts fraudulently for the past seven or eight years, that he 'hath of late given
over his coate & condicion & separated & Devided himself from
these Defend^{tes} carriing awaie nott onely all the furniture &
apparell . . .' and that '. . . there was greate variance & striffe
betweene the said Defend^{tes} & the said Beeston vpon there
separacion . . .' (Wallace, *Three Theatres*, pp. 36, 38.)

1619, Nov. 23—In his reply to John Smith, Beeston describes himself as '. . . havinge had a long tyme of sicknes, and at this tyme
being very sickely and vnfitt to followe suytes'. He also declared
that the members of Queen Anne's company were now dispersed
and broken up and that 'after her Ma^{tes} Decease, he entred into
the service of the most noble Prince Charles'. (Ibid., pp. 39, 40.)

1622—In Sir Henry Herbert's lists of the various companies, the
list of the Lady Elizabeth's men begins, 'The chiefe of them at the
Phoenix. Christopher Beeston, . . .' (*Herbert*, p. 63.)

1622, Oct. 3—Beeston is one of the six actors of the Red Bull named in an order for repair of the highways about the theatre. (See above, p. 169, n. 2.)

1623—Worth, Cumber, and Blaney were the only original members of the 1617 Queen Anne's left, and in petitioning to be relieved of payments they accuse Mrs. Baskervile of bribing Beeston to her interest. They say, '. . . your oratours and the rest of thier fellowes at that tyme and long before and since did put the managing of thier whole businesses and affaires belonging vnto them ioyntly as they were players in trust vnto Christopher Hutchinson alias Beeston', and later, 'your oratours and the rest of thier said fellowes condiscended to seale the same, they being altogether ruled by the said Christopher Hutchinson alias Beeston who had the sole managing of all thier affayres'. Mrs. Baskervile in her reply denies bribing Beeston and says 'That shee beleiueth it to bee true that the Compl^tes and the rest of their said companie, before and since the decease of her said late husband Thomas Greene, did putt much affiance in the said Huttchinson alias Beeston concerninge the managing of their affaires, Butt knoweth not that the said Huttchinson had anie such power ouer the said Companie of Players as in the said Bill is alleaged'. (Fleay, *Stage*, pp. 274, 276, and 289.)

1623—'Receaved from Mr. Biston, as from ye Cockpitt, for and towards ye building of ye church . . . £10. 7s.' (Parton, *St. Giles*, Assessment Book, p. 235.)

1629, June 19—The Lord Chamberlain signed a warrant for liveries for 'ye Queenes Comoedians' to 'Christopher Biston for himselfe & thirteene others his fellowes'. (*M.S.C.* ii. 350.)

1630/1, Feb. 2—In the L.C. Warrant Books is a copy of a letter sent to the Sheriff of Middlesex: 'S^r. I vnderstand that Sr Iohn Wentworth is arrested vpon an execution at the suite of one Beeston & now remayning in your Custody . . .' (See ibid., pp. 353–4.)

1631, May 25—'A warrant for payment of 170^li. vnto Mr Christopher Beeston for himselfe & the rest of the Queenes Players for sixteene Playes by them Acted betweene the 10th of October & the 20th of Februarie. 1631.' (Ibid. i. 355.)

1632, Nov. 18—Beeston promised Sir Henry Herbert that Shirley's play *The Ball* would be reformed, and that 'he would not suffer it to be done by the poett any more'. (*Herbert*, p. 19.)

1632, Dec. 5—'Christopher Beeston' was paid £100 for nine plays at Court 'in October &c. 1631'. (*M.S.C.* ii. 359.)

1633, May 4—Beeston secured an additional term to his lease of the Cockpit and adjacent property from John Best's widow, to run until 28 September 1656. (Hotson, p. 91.)

1633, Aug. 15—'Received of Biston, for an ould play called *Hymen's Holliday*, newly revived at their house, being a play given unto him for my use, this 15 Aug. 1633, 3l. o. o. Received of him for some alterations in it 1l. o. o.' (*Herbert*, p. 35.) 'Meetinge with him at the ould exchange, he gave my wife a payre of gloves, that cost him at least twenty shillings.' (This item directly follows the preceding one in *Variorum*, iii. 233, and apparently refers to Christopher Beeston. The date is very doubtful. Ibid., p. 67.)

1634, July 18—Kendall told Crosfield he was 'master' of the Queen's company at the Phoenix. See p. 688. (*Crosfield's Diary*, p. 72.)

1634, >Nov. 7—He paid for the engraving of the plate of 'The Powers' in Heywood's *Hierarchie of the Blessed Angels*, and his kindness is acknowledged by the legend under the plate, '*Ex sumptib*: CHRISTOPH: BEESTON *Generos*'. Perhaps it is only chance and not an actor's design that his name and William Beeston's are printed in larger type than that used for any of the other seven donors. (1635 folio B.M.)

1634, Dec. 11—Thomas Basse left rings to him, his wife Elizabeth, and his son William. (See p. 631.)

1634, Dec. 16—Warrant to 'Christopher Beeston one of the Queenes Ma^tes Players' for liveries for himself and thirteen fellows. (*M.S.C.* ii. 374.)

1634, Dec. 31—He was paid for productions by Queen Henrietta's company at court in 1633. (Ibid.)

1634/5, Feb. 20—Beeston agreed to allow the French players to use the Cockpit for performances during Lent. (See pp. 233–4.)

1635/6, Mar. 24—He was paid for eight plays given by the Queen's men at court. (*M.S.C.* ii. 378.)

1636, July 10—'Xpofer son of John Beeston Carpento^r' chris. St. G.C.

1636/7, Feb. 21—'A Warrant to sweare Mr Christopher Bieston his Ma^tes servant in ye place of Gouuernor of the new Company of the Kinges & Queenes boyes.' (*M.S.C.* ii. 382.)

1636/7, Feb. 24 (?)—'Mr. Beeston was commanded to make a company of boyes, and began to play at the Cockpit with them the same day.' (*Herbert*, p. 66). See above, pp. 324–6, on the date.

1622–38—'Meetinge with him [Beeston, the manager of the Cockpit Playhouse] at the ould exchange, he gave my wife a payre of gloves, that cost him at least twenty shillings.' (*Herbert*, p. 67.)

1637, May 10—He was paid for nine plays given by the Queen's company at court and two by the new company (Beeston's Boys). (*M.S.C.* ii. 383.)

1637, May 12—Called before the Privy Council with William Beeston, Ezekial Fenn, Theophilus Bird, and Michael Moone; plays at the Cockpit stopped until further orders (see p. 327). (*M.S.C.* i. 392.)

1637, May ?—'Petition of Christopher Beeston to the Council. Petitioner being commanded to erect and prepare a company of young actors for their Majesties' service, and being desirous to know how they profited by his instructions, invited some noblemen and gentlemen to see them act at his house, the Cockpit. For which, since he perceives that it is imputed as a fault, he is very sorry, and craves pardon.' (*C.S.P., Dom.*, 1636–7, p. 254.)

1637, June 10—The Lord Chamberlain wrote the Stationers' Company that no plays must be published without the permission of Beeston as manager of the King and Queen's young company, or his successors in management. (*M.S.C.* ii. 384–5.)

1637, Sept. 17—He petitioned the Board for permission for his company to practice; the petition was granted for September 29 if there were no increase in the plague. (*C.S.P., Dom.*, 1637, p. 420.)

1638, Oct. 4—Made his will, which was proved 30 October. (See pp. 631–3.) 'By his will . . . he bequeathed to his son William some freehold land and houses in St. Leonard's, Shoreditch, and a plot of ground in Lincoln's Inn Fields (parish of St. Giles-in-the-

Field), enclosed with a brick wall. From a later suit in Chancery I have extracted some new information concerning Christopher Beeston's holdings in Shoreditch. Besides some property in Hog Lane, Shoreditch, he owned several houses in King's Head Yard, between Hog Lane and a ten-acre plot known as "the Curtain". Katherine Crosse, who owned this large property, let a piece of it to Christopher Beeston. The Curtain estate included the site of the Curtain Playhouse. . . . Beeston, as we know, acted with Queen Anne's Company at this theatre in and after 1604. The last mention of the Curtain hitherto discovered is from the year 1627. . . . I have uncovered another record which testifies that the building was still standing in 1660.' (Hotson, p. 92.)

1638, Oct. 15—'Christopher Hutchinson alias Beeston' bur. St. G.F.

1660, Dec.—In his brief, prepared in 1660 for re-establishing his old prerogatives as Master of the Revels, Sir Henry Herbert wrote, 'To proue that Mister Beeston payd me 60li. per annum besids usuall Fees & allowances for Court plaies'. (*Herbert*, p. 101.)

BEESTON, ELIZABETH. She was the second wife (at least) of Christopher. The terms of his will indicate that she must have been active in the affairs of the King and Queen's young company after her husband's death, and, by implication, probably before.

1638, Oct. 4—She received theatrical legacies in the will of her husband (see p. 632).

1640, July 7—Borrowed £150 from the actor William Wilbraham and gave a mortgage on the Cockpit property as security. (Hotson, p. 94.)

BEESTON, ROBERT. His name appears in several lists of Queen Anne's men before 1616, but there is no certain record of him as an actor after that year.

1617, July 16—'Andrea wife of Robert Beeston yoman . . . late of St. James's Clerkenwell' is listed in the True Bill for recusancy. (*Middx. Co. Rec.* ii. 128.)

1630, June 29—'Robte Beetson and Elisabeth Craven' mar. St. G.F.

BEESTON, WILLIAM. William was the son of Christopher Beeston and probably acted in his father's companies from his boyhood, for in a lawsuit in 1666 he described himself as 'being bred up in the art of stage playing, and being skilled in that science' (Hotson, p. 107). There are, however, no records of his early connexion with the stage unless he was the William Bee at Norwich (q.v.). The first certain theatrical record of William Beeston is the petition for the recovery of Stephen Hammerton, a petition which suggests that Beeston was associated with Blagrave in the management of the Salisbury Court. He was back at the Cockpit by 1637, and his father seems to have thought of William as his successor, since he left him most of his real estate and a one-twelfth interest in the King and Queen's young company. He was sworn as governor, but soon after was imprisoned for his indiscretions and succeeded by Davenant. He

must, however, have returned eventually to his old post, for
Davenant was involved in the Army Plot and fled with the others
in May 1641, and Beeston reappears in his old post in the L.C.
books for 1641 (see above; p. 335). His activities during the Interregnum are most interesting, but not of fundamental importance
here. Some of the more conspicuous of them are noted below.

It is most interesting to note the tributes to Beeston's ability
as a director or dramatic coach in training the boy players. Most
of the leading actors of the time must have been engaged in training apprentices, but, so far as I can recall, Beeston is the first
whose ability is mentioned. Thus it is not only as a Restoration
manager that he is an important link between the Caroline and
the Restoration stage, but as the master whose acting technique
must have been apparent in the work of several of the most
conspicuous Restoration actors.

There were at least two William Beestons living in the parish of
St. Giles in the Field in the reign of Charles I. I have found seventeen entries concerning their families in the parish registers before
1651 (*R.E.S.* vi. 152–3). The Chancery Complaint of 1658 which
Leslie Hotson found (Hotson, pp. 100–6) enables us to distinguish fairly well between these Beestons, for the stage manager
says that he had married the widow of Thomas Bowen Mercer.
Therefore he is the man who married Alice Bowen in 1642. It
must have been the other Beeston who married Margaret Howson
in 1633, for children are born to Margaret and William Beeston
both before and after the actor's marriage in 1642. I take it,
therefore, that all references to William and Margaret Beeston
are to the other William, and I have eliminated all entries which
mention Margaret or which, while not naming Margaret, record
the burial of children christened as hers. Thus there can be no
doubt that the entries of 1642 and 1644 refer to the Cockpit
manager, but it is possible that the children buried in 1637 and
1639 belonged to the other William Beeston, probably the man
buried 15 February 1650/1.

1624, May 26—*See* William Bee.
1624, June 29—'Grant to Wm. Beeston of the outlawry of Sir Edw.
  Raleigh, and of the extent of certain of his lands in Farnborough,
  co. Warwick, till he is satisfied of his just debt, with costs.' (*C.S.P.,
  Dom.*, 1623–5, p. 287.)
1624, Sept. 28—*See* William Bee.
1626/7, Feb. 14—A William Beeston petitions the Lord Chamberlain
  against Sir John Wentworth and is given permission to sue after
  three months. (*M.S.C.* ii. 401.)
1632, Nov. 12—With William Blagrave, he petitions the Lord Chamberlain for the recovery of a boy named Stephen Hammerton,
  whom Christopher Babham has stolen from them and uses at
  Blackfriars. The Lord Chamberlain refers the case to Sir Henry
  Herbert. (Ibid., p. 408.)

1633, Oct. 28—'William Beeston & Margrett Howson' mar. St. G.F. 'P: L' in margin.

1634, Sept. 11—He was left a ring in the will of Thomas Basse. (See p. 631.)

1634, >Nov. 7—Beeston paid for the engraving of the plate of 'The Virtues' for Heywood's *Hierarchie of the Blessed Angels*, and his munificence is acknowledged by the legend under the plate, '*Ex sumptib*: GULIELMI: BEESTON: *Generos*.' Perhaps it is only chance that his name and that of Christopher Beeston appear in larger type than those of the other seven donors. (1635 folio B.M.)

1637, May 12—He was called before the Privy Council with Christopher Beeston, Theophilus Birde, Ezechiel Fenn, and Michael Moone; playing at the Cockpit was stopped until further order. (*M.S.C.* i. 392.)

1637, June 27—'Mary Daughter of William Beeston' bur. St. G.F.

1638, Oct. 4 and 7—His father's will (see pp. 631–3) gave him a half share in the King and Queen's young company; thus the company had four shares, Christopher's wife Elizabeth one and a half, and William one half. By the will he also received certain properties.

1638—At the end of Brome's *Antipodes* (acted by the Queen's company at Salisbury Court in 1638, printed in 1640) is a note signed by the author· '. . . it was, at first, intended for the Cock-pit Stage, in the right of my most deserving Friend Mr. William Beeston, unto whom it properly appertained. . . .' (1640 ed. B.M.)

1639, Apr. 5—'A warrt to sweare Mr Wm Bieston his Mates servant in Ordinary in ye Quality and vnder the Title of Gouuernor & Instructer of the Kings & Queens young Company of Actors.' (*M.S.C.* ii. 389.)

1639, July 27—'A stilborn Child of William Beeston' bur. St. G.F.

1639, Aug. 10—Upon complaint of 'William Bieston Gent' Gouuernor &c' of the kinges and Queenes young Company of Players at the Cockpitt in Drury Lane', 'all other Companyes of Actors heerby concernable' were forbidden 'to intermedle wth or Act' any of a list of plays. (*M.S.C.* ii. 389–90.)

1640, May 3—For acting an unlicensed play, 'William Bieston and the Company of Players of the Cockpitt in Drury Lane' were forbidden 'to Act any Playes whatsoeuer vntill they shall bee restored . . . vnto their former Liberty'. (Ibid., pp. 393–4.) Herbert says that the offensive play 'had relation to the passages of the King's journey into the north, and was complained of by His Majesty to me, with command to punish the offenders'. (Adams, p. 359.)

1640, May 4—Herbert wrote in his Office Book, 'On Monday the 4 May, 1640, William Beeston was taken by a messenger and committed to the Marshalsea by my Lord Chamberlain's warrant, for playing a play without license. The same day the company at the Cockpit was commanded by my Lord Chamberlain's warrant to forbear playing, for playing when they were forbidden by me, and for other disobedience, and lay still Monday, Tuesday, and Wednesday. On Thursday, at my Lord Chamberlain's entreaty, I gave them their liberty, and upon their petition of submission subscribed by the players, I restored them to their liberty on Thursday.' (Adams, p. 360.)

c. 1640—The Epilogue of Brome's *The Court Beggar* (printed 1653;

the title-page says that it was acted at the Cockpit by the King's
men in 1632, but this statement is certainly wrong; see pp. 337–8)
obviously refers to him and was perhaps added to the play about
this time. 'There's wit in that now. But this small Poet vents
none but his own, and his by whose care and directions this Stage
is govern'd, who has for many yeares both in his fathers dayes, and
since directed Poets to write & Players to speak till he traind up
these youths here to what they are now. I some of 'em from before
they were able to say a grace of two lines long to have more parts
in their pates then would fill so many Dry-fats. And to be serious
with you, if after all this, by the venemous practise of some, who
study nothing more then his destruction, he should faile us, both
Poets and Players would be at losse in Reputation.' (1653 ed.)

1640/1, Feb. 25—Beeston made a bond of £400 penalty to Michael
Bowyer. (See p. 387.)

1641—In an 'Establishment list of Servants of the Chamber in 1641'
is 'Gouernor of ye Cockpitt Players—William Bieston'. (M.S.C. ii.
326.)

1642, July 15—'LC William Hutchinson alias Beeston and Alice
Bowen' mar. St. G.F.

> 1642—Wright says, '*Burt* was a Boy first under *Shank* at the *Black-
friers*, then under *Beeston* at the *Cockpit*'. (*Hist. Hist.*, p. 3.)

1644, Apr. 1—'Jane Daughter of William and Alice Hutchinson als
Beeston' chris. St. G.F.

1649—John Herne, son of the original lessor, made a deed of sale of
the Salisbury Court to Beeston for £600; the deed was never signed,
probably because of damage done to the theatre by apprentices.
(Adams, p. 380.)

1650–1—'In the winter of 1650–1651 Beeston had repaired the Drury
Lane house for plays and had begun to train a company of boys.'
(Hotson, p. 50.)

1652, May 25—Beeston, through Theophilus Bird as agent, got the
Salisbury Court from Herne for £408. (Adams, p. 381.)

1652—Kirkman dedicated his translation, *The Loves and Adventures
of Clerico and Logis*, to Beeston with the following eulogy 'To His
much honored Friend Will. Beeston, Esq;'.

'Divers times (in my hearing) to the admiration of the whol
Company, you have most judiciously discoursed of Poësie: which
is the cause J presume to chuse you for my Patron and Pro-
tector; who are the happiest interpreter and judg of our English
Stage-Playes this Nation ever produced; which the Poets and
Actors of these times, cannot (without ingratitude) deny; for I
have heard the chief, and most ingenious of them acknowledg
their Fames & Profits essentially sprung from your instructions,
judgment and fancy. . . . I doubt not though they fail to receive
incouragement from you, your son, Mr George Beeston (whom
knowing men conclude, a hopeful inheritor of his Fathers rare
ingenuity) may receive them with a gracious allowance.' (1652
ed. B.M.)

1652/3, Mar. 2–9—Mr. Hotson thinks he was the 'ill *Beest*' who be-
trayed the players at Gibbon's Tennis Court to the soldiers. (See
Hotson, pp. 49–50.)

1654—Flecknoe's *Love's Dominion*, 'A Dramatique Piece, Full of

Excellent Moralitie; Written as a Pattern for the REFORMED STAGE' and published in 1654, has a Postscript at the end: 'That this Piece may receive no disadvantage (as I hope it will no prejudice) by the publishing it, I let thee understand (Gentle Reader) if ever it be acted, I intitle to my right in it, (not departing in the mean time with my right of altering my mind) Mr. Will. Beeston, who by Reason of his long Practice and Experience in this way, as also for having brought up most of the Actors extant, I think the fittest Man for this Charge and Imployment.' (1654 ed. HN.)

1682—Aubrey says he 'died at his house in Bishopsgate street without, about Bartholomew-tyde, 1682.' (Aubrey, *Brief Lives*, i. 97.)

BEHEL, JACOB (*see* PEDEL, JACOB).

BENFIELD, RICHARD. Not a player, but evidently a friend of players. (See Appendix, pp. 633-5.)

BENFIELD, ROBERT. Benfield did not begin his acting career in the King's company, as the Burbages point out in their reply to the suit about shares in the company in 1635 (*M.S.C.* ii. 371), but came to the company, as the cast of *The Duchess of Malfi* would suggest, to replace William Ostler. Baldwin (*Organization and Personnel*, p. 51) thinks that he came to the company in 1615. He had formerly been a member of the Lady Elizabeth's company, and probably of the Queen's Revels before that. We know some half-dozen of his roles from the casts of the company, and, as Professor Baldwin has pointed out, he 'takes dignified parts, such as kings, senators, and old men, regularly ranking third or fourth in number of lines' (ibid., p. 183). On the basis of these known parts, Baldwin has worked out a series of roles for him in all the plays of the Beaumont and Fletcher folios produced after his admission to the company. He seems to have been a steady and reliable rather than a conspicuous member of the King's company.

It seems to me likely that all the entries in the St. Giles' registers refer to the King's man, though he is not always called player. The burial record in 1649 probably refers to the actor because it falls between his last known act as a member of the company and the Morrisons' reference to him as dead in 1655.

1616—No. 2 in King's cast for *The Mad Lover*. (1679 folio B.M.)

1616–18—No. 6 in King's cast of *The Knight of Malta*. (Ibid.)

1617, Oct. 15—'Robert s of Robert Benfield' bur. St. Bartholomew the Great. (Bod.)

1619, Mar. 27—No. 8 in patent to King's company. (*M.S.C.* i. 280-2.)

1619, May 19—No. 8 in livery allowance for King's. (*Hist. MSS. Com.*, Report IV, Part I, p. 299.)

1619 ?—No. 4 in King's cast of *The Humorous Lieutenant*. (1679 folio B.M.)

c. 1619–20—No. 5 in King's cast of *The Custom of the Country*. (Ibid.)

1619–21—No. 6 in King's cast of *The Island Princess*. (Ibid.)

1619–21—No. 3 in King's cast of *Women Pleased*. (1679 folio B.M.)

1619–22—No. 4 in King's cast of *The Little French Lawyer*. (Ibid.)

1619–23—'Antonio, 1 W Ostler. 2 R. Benfeild' in the cast of King's
  men prefixed to the 1623 edition of *The Duchess of Malfi*. Apparently Benfield took the part in the revival 1619–23. (1623 4° B.M.)
c. 1620—No. 3 in King's cast of *The False One*. (1679 folio B.M.)
c. 1621—No. 2 in King's cast of *The Double Marriage*. (Ibid.)
1621—No. 3 in King's cast of *The Pilgrim*. (Ibid.)
1621, Apr. 7—In livery allowance list for King's men. (*Hist. MSS.
  Com.*, Report IV, Part I, p. 299.)
1622, May 14—No. 2 in King's cast of *The Prophetess*. (1679 folio
  B.M.)
1622, Oct. 24—No. 6 in King's cast of *The Spanish Curate*. (Ibid.)
1623, Aug. 29—No. 6 in King's cast of *The Maid in the Mill*. (Ibid.)
1623, Dec. 6—No. 2 in King's cast of *The Lover's Progress*. (Ibid.)
1623—No. 22 in the list of actors in the Shakespeare folio.
1624, May 27—No. 4 in King's cast of *A Wife for a Month*. (1679 folio
  B.M.)
1624, Dec. 20—No. 5 in submission of King's men for playing *The
  Spanish Viceroy* (see pp. 14–15). (*Herbert*, p. 21.)
1625, >May 5—As a member of the King's company, he received black
  cloth for James's funeral procession; his name—'Robert Benn-
  feild—iiij yards'—was eleventh in the list. (*M.S.C.* ii. 325–6.)
1625, June 24—No. 6 in King's patent. (Ibid., i. 282.)
1626—'*Iunius Rusticus*—Robert Benfield' in King's cast of Massinger's *The Roman Actor*, licensed 11 October 1626. (1629 4° B.M.)
1627/8, Jan. 1—' James sonn of Robert Benfield gent' chris. St. G.C.
1628—No. 3 in King's cast for *The Lover's Melancholy*, licensed 24
  November. (1629 4° B.M.)
1628/9, Jan. 21—' Mary wife of Robert Bennyfield player' bur. St. G.C.
1629, May 6—' Robert Benfield' was sixth in the cloak allowance for
  the King's men. (See pp. 82–3.) (*M.S.C.* ii. 350.)
1629—'*Ladislaus* King of Hungarie—*Robert Benfield*' in King's cast
  of Massinger's *The Picture*, licensed 8 June. (1630 4° B.M.)
1629?—'M^r. *Benfield, the King*' in King's cast for Carlell's *The Deserving Favorite*. (1629 4° Chi.)
c. 1630—' Makewell—A Doc: of Phisicke—Robert Benfield' in King's
  cast given in the MS. of Clavell's (?) *The Soddered Citizen*. (*Soddered Citizen*, p. 3.)
1631, May 6 (lic.)—'Mr Benfeild' was Marcellus in King's production
  of *Believe as You List*. (Sisson, *B.A.Y.L.*, pp. xxxi and 99.)
1631—The MS. of Arthur Wilson's *The Swisser* (B.M. Add. MS.
  36759) gives his name in the cast for the 1631 Blackfriars production:

| Antharis } | Two old noble men | { Benfeild. |
| Clephis } | Mortall Enemies | { Penn. |

(Feuillerat, *The Swisser*.)
1631, June 10—' Received of Mr. Benfielde, in the name of the kings
  company, for a gratuity for ther liberty gaind unto them of playinge, upon the cessation of the plague, this 10 of June, 1631,—
  3*l.* 10*s. od.*'—' This (Sir Henry Herbert adds) was taken upon
  Pericles at the Globe.' (*Herbert*, p. 64.)
1631, July 21—' Bartholomew sonne of Robert Benfeild Gentleman'
  bur. St. G.C.
1631, Aug. 1—' Eliz Dau of Robert Benfield Player' bur. St. G.C.

1632—'DE-GARD, A Noble stayd Gentleman . . . Acted by Mr. *Robert Benfield*' in the cast for the King's 1632 revival of *The Wild Goose Chase* printed in the 1652 edition. (B.M. copy.)

1633, Oct. 24—'Lowins and Swanston were sorry for their ill manners, and craved my pardon, which I gave them in presence of Mr. Taylor and Mr. Benfeilde.' (*Herbert*, p. 21; see above, p. 37.)

1634-5—Both the Burbages and John Shank assert in their petitions to the Lord Chamberlain in 1635 that for the year Whitsun Monday 1634–Whitsun Monday 1635 Benfield gained from the King's company 'as hee was a Player and noe Howskeeper 180^{li}' (*M.S.C.* ii. 368, 372.)

1635, >July 12—Benfield, Pollard, and Swanston petitioned the Lord Chamberlain that Shank, Cuthbert Burbage, and Mrs. Robinson be forced to sell them each one share in the Globe. They further petitioned that Shank be forced to sell one of his shares in the Blackfriars to be divided among the three of them. (Ibid., pp. 362-4.)

1635, July 12—The Lord Chamberlain complied with the request of Benfield, Pollard, and Swanston. (Ibid., p. 365.)

1635, Aug. 1—Since the actors were unable to agree on the price of the shares, Sir Henry Herbert, Sir John Finett, and Daniell Bedingfield were appointed to arbitrate. (Ibid., p. 373.) (Shank's will of 31 December 1635 indicates that he still claimed all his shares. See pp. 646-8.)

1636, Apr. 7—Witness of will of John Honyman. (See p. 645.)

1639, Aug. 26—The will of Richard Benfield of Gray's Inn makes Robert Benfield (apparently) his executor and leaves legacies to him and his daughter Anne and 40s. to his maidservant Katherine Sadler. (See pp. 633-5.)

1647—His name—'Robert Benfeild'—stands seventh in the list of King's men who signed the dedication of the Beaumont and Fletcher folio.

1647/8, Jan. 28—One of seven King's men who signed a bond for an old King's company debt. (*See* Theophilus Bird, p. 379.)

1649, July 28—'Rob: Bennifeild gentleman' bur. St. G.C.

1655, Easter term—Thomas Morrison and his wife, formerly wife of Michael Bowyer, in their suit against Theophilus Bird 'deny that Benfield also died worth more than £1500 and that a London apothecary named Warburton and his wife Ann (Benfield's only daughter) are his heirs'. (Hotson, p. 33.)

1664—In a coffee-house scene in the third act of Tatham's (?) *Knavery in All Trades*, a gentleman has mentioned a current play.

> *third* . . . Bur (*sic*) sir, they say 'tis done rarely well.
> *fourth.* I cannot believe it, 'tis impossible they should do any thing so well as I have seen things done.
> *fifth.* When *Taylor Lowen*, and *Pollard* were alive.
> *fourth.* Did you not know *Benfield*, and Swautted?
> *fifth.* Did I not know 'em? yes, and hum'd them off a hundred times.

(1664 4° HN.)

BIEL, JACOB (*see* PEDEL, JACOB).

BIRCHE, George. Birche is first heard of when he marries the daughter of Richard Cowley two months before her father's death, but only two weeks after she had been named as executrix in his will. This circumstance sounds a little as if the father had arranged or at least hastened the marriage, and it is probably connected with Birche's appearance a few months later as an actor in the King's company. It is not unlikely, however, that he was connected with the company in some minor capacity before his marriage. Professor Baldwin (*Organization and Personnel*, pp. 55–8 and 209) thinks that he succeeded to the 'line' and to the membership of Condall in 1623, and this surmise seems possible. His disappearance in 1625 may be due, as has been suggested, to his death in the plague of that year. It seems to me most unlikely that he was the 'George Birch, a poor man' buried at St. James's Clerkenwell, 3 April 1635.

1618/19, Jan. 28—'George Birch & Elizabeth Cowley wth licence' mar. St. S.S. (See will of Richard Cowley, p. 642.)

1619, Aug.—Probably the '[ ]r Bir' who brings on a chair according to the prompter's notes for the King's production of *Barnavelt*. (Greg, *Dram. Doc.*, p. 273.)

1619–21—No. 7 in King's cast for *The Island Princess*. (1679 folio B.M.)

1619?—No. 7 in King's cast for *The Laws of Candy*. (Ibid.)

c. 1620—No. 8 in King's cast for *The False One*. (Ibid.)

c. 1621—No. 4 in King's cast for *The Double Marriage*. (Ibid.)

1621—No. 7 in King's cast for *The Pilgrim*. (Ibid.)

1622, May 14—No. 7 in King's cast for *The Prophetess*. (Ibid.)

1623, May 21—'George Burgh att the vpper end of Shoreditch,' 5s., in Markham's suit. (See p. 682.)

1623, Nov. 18—'Bridgett Birche d of George a Player' chris. St. S.S.

1623, Dec. 6—No. 4 in King's cast for *The Lover's Progress*. (1679 folio B.M.)

1624, May 27—No. 6 in King's cast for *A Wife for a Month*. (Ibid.)

1624, Dec. 20—'Burght' was No. 6 in submission of King's men for playing *The Spanish Viceroy*. (See above, pp. 14–15.)

1625, >May 5—As a member of the King's company, he received black cloth for James's funeral procession: 'The King Players . . . George Birche—iiij yards.' He was fourth in the list. (*M.S.C.* ii. 325; see above, pp. 80–1.)

1625, June 24—No. 11 in patent for King's men. (Ibid. i. 282–3.)

1635, Apr. 3—'George Birch, a poor man' bur. St. J.C.

BIRD (*alias* bourne), Theophilus. He was probably the son of the Admiral's–Prince Henry's–Palsgrave's actor, William Bird (q.v.), and may have appeared as a child with that company, but he first appears in female roles for Queen Henrietta's men, graduating to male roles by 1635, when he had a fairly prominent part as Massanissa in *Hannibal and Scipio*. When the Queen's company was forced out of the Cockpit, Bird stayed on, perhaps because he had already become Christopher Beeston's son-in-law

Some time between 1638 and 1641, probably in 1640, he went over to the King's company; he remained with them until the closing of the theatres, and had a part in their ventures during the Interregnum. For his Restoration career, see Hotson.

It is odd that we find Bird's name affixed to the prologues of two plays (an unusual occurrence) and to the dedication of one, all of which were written in whole or in part by John Ford. This may be only a coincidence, but it seems to suggest a friendship between the dramatist and the player.

Because of Bird's signature to the two Ford prologues, one is tempted to guess that he was the T. B. whose initials appear after the epilogue in the 1661 edition of *Love Will Find out the Way* (i.e. Shirley's *Constant Maid*), an occurrence which led the printer to attribute the play to T. B. The play, like *The Lady's Trial* and *The Witch of Edmonton*, was performed by a company of which Bird was a member.

A facsimile of Bird's signature may be seen in the *Shakespeare Society Papers*, iv. 101.

1608, Dec. 7—'Theophilus Borne s of William Borne baptized; Hoxton' St. Leonard's Shoreditch. (Bod.)

1625—'Pavlina, *Sister to* Vitelli. Theo. Bourne' in Massinger's *The Renegado* by Queen Henrietta's men at the private playhouse in Drury Lane. (1630 4° B.M.)

c. 1630—'Toota, *Queen of* Fesse, *and wife of* Mullisheg. *By* Theophilus Bourne' in the cast of Queen Henrietta's men prefixed to the 1631 4° of Heywood's *The Fair Maid of the West*, Part II; he does not appear in the cast for Part I. (1631 4° B.M.)

c. 1635 ?—'*Mr.* Bird' is found at the end of the prologue to the 1658 edition of *The Witch of Edmonton*, by Rowley, Dekker, Ford, &c. This signature must belong to a revival at the Cockpit, for the prologue says,

> But as the year doth with his plenty bring
> As well a latter as a former Spring;
> So has this Witch enjoy'd the first, and reason
> Presumes she may partake the other season:
> In Acts deserving name, the Proverb says,
> Once good, and ever; Why not so in Plays?
> Why not in this?

1635—'Massanissa. By Theophilus Bird' in Nabbe's *Hannibal and Scipio* given by Queen Henrietta's men 'at their Private house in Drury Lane'. (1637 4° B.M.)

1637, May 12—He was called before the Privy Council with William and Christopher Beeston, Ezekiel Fenn, and Michael Moone; playing was stopped at the Cockpit until further orders. (*M.S.C.* i. 392.)

1638, Oct. 4—Christopher Beeston's will of this date names Bird as the husband of Beeston's eldest daughter, Anne, and mentions their son Christopher. (See p. 632.)

1638, Oct. 27—'Christopher son of Theophilus Bird' bur. St. G.F.

1638—His name, 'Mr. Bird', is found at the end of the prologue of Ford's *The Lady's Trial*. (1639 4° B.M.)

1640/1, Jan. 19—A ticket of privilege was issued for 'Theophilus Bird' as 'a sworne servant to the Kinges Ma^{tye} and of the Company of his Ma^{tes} Players at the Blackfryers'. He was the only one of the six players sworn 22 January to be granted a ticket of privilege. (*M.S.C.* ii. 397.)

1640/1, Jan. 22—He is named with five others in a warrant swearing them grooms of his Majesty's chambers 'to attend his Ma^{tye} in the Quality of Players and to bee of the Company of his Ma^{tes} servantes at ye Blackfryers'. (Ibid., 397.)

1642, Mar. 27—'Elizabeth Daughter of Theophilus Bird' bur. St. G.F.

>1642—Trueman says '*Bird*' was one of 'those of principal Note at the *Cockpit*'. (*Hist. Hist.*, p. 4.)

1647—His name—'Theophilus Byrd'—stands tenth in the list of ten King's men who signed the dedication of the Beaumont and Fletcher folio. (1647 folio B.M.)

1647/8, Jan. 28—'John Lowen, Richard Robinson, Robert Benfield, Thomas Pollard, Hugh Clarke, Stephen Hamerton, and Theophilus Bird entered on a new bond of £360 conditioned on the payment to Morrison of £147 12s. on or before 30 July, 1648.' (Hotson, p. 32, from a Chancery suit of 1655.)

1652, Mar. 25—As agent for William Beeston, Bird signed the deed of sale of the Salisbury Court theatre to Beeston from John Herne (II). (Hotson, p. 103.)

1656—The dedication of Ford and Dekker's *The Sun's Darling* to Thomas Wriothesley, Earl of Southampton, is signed 'Theophilus Bird. Andrew Penneycuicke.' (1656 4° HN.)

BIRD (*alias* BORNE), WILLIAM. He had been an actor for at least twenty years before the death of Shakespeare, first as a Pembroke's man, then in the Admiral's–Prince Henry's–Palsgrave's company. He appears frequently in Henslowe's Diary as an agent for the company. (See Chambers, *E.S.*, Nungezer, and *Hens. D.* for his career before 1616.) The references to him from 1616 to 1621 indicate that he was one of the leaders of the Palsgrave's men in this time. He appears in none of the lists after 1621. If he is the man who was buried in Shoreditch in January 1623/4, he must have retired from the company some two years before his death.

c. 1617—He wrote Alleyn for the company about a dishonest gatherer whom Alleyn had appointed. (*MSS. Dul.*, p. 49.) *See* John Russell.

1618, Apr. 19—'ther dind w^t vs Jo. Mathew & His wife m^r beamond & another w: borne & His sone . . . ' (Alleyn's Diary, Young, ii. 81.)

1618, Oct. 31—He was the second of the Palsgrave's men who signed the lease of the Fortune from Edward Alleyn. (See pp. 138–9.)

1619, July 11—'Ther dind w^t vs will borne & His wife m^r borne a surgian:' (Alleyn's Diary, Young, ii. 142.)

1620, July 23—'ther dind w^t vs will: boarne & His boye m^r Skragg . . . ' (Ibid., p. 185.)

1620/1, Feb. 23—'I went to meet Sr Nic. Stoddard in powles spent att ye pole Head w^t Hym m^r borne & gunell.' (Ibid., p. 202.)

1621, Apr. 15—'borne: massey: Cartwright: gunnell: grace: Hunt dind Here.' (Ibid., p. 204.)

1622, May 20—He occupied a tenement adjoining the Fortune play-house. (*MSS. Dul.*, p. 243.)

1623/4, Jan. 22—'Willm Bird *alias* Borne, was buried the 22 of Januarie, Hollywell Street', St. Leonard's Shoreditch. (Bod.)

BLACKSON, —. He is known only from his appearance in the MSS. of Middleton's play. Though the play became the property of the King's men, Mr. Bald says, with reason, that the actors' names probably date from earlier productions. (Bald, *Hengist, King of Kent*, pp. xx–xxi.)

<1616—'Blackson' and 'Black[son]' appear in the stage directions of the MSS. of Middleton's *Hengist, King of Kent*. Apparently he took part in the dumb shows. (Bald, *Hengist, King of Kent*, pp. xvii and xxviii.)

BLAGRAVE (BLAGROVE), WILLIAM. One would guess that William Blagrave, deputy to Sir Henry Herbert, belonged to the family of Thomas Blagrave who had served as Master of the Revels under Elizabeth (see Feuillerat), but he is not mentioned in the Blagrave genealogy (*Harl. Soc. Pub.* lxv. 83). Other Blagraves were court musicians in the reign of Charles I (*King's Musick, passim*). William appeared as deputy to Sir Henry Herbert in 1624 and continued to act in this capacity until 1635, when he disappears. Besides his official duties he had a private theatrical enterprise of his own at this time in the Salisbury Court playhouse.

1624, Mar. 30—'From Mr. Blagrave, in the name of the Cockpit com-pany, for this Lent, this 30th March, 1624. £2. o. o.' (*Herbert*, p. 48.)

1624, >Sept.—Benjamin Garfield testified that before *Keep the Widow Waking* was acted he gave twenty shillings to Blagrave to forbid it, which Blagrave promised to do but did not. (Sisson, *Keep the Widow Waking*, pp. 248–9.)

1629, July 6—He and Richard Gunnell leased ground at Salisbury Court from the Earl of Dorset for a playhouse, for a term of forty-one and a half years, at £25 the first half-year and £100 annually each year thereafter. They paid this rent of £100 to Herne each year until 1642, and on the ground they built a dwelling-house and a playhouse which cost them £1,000. (Hotson, pp. 100–1.)

1629, July 21—Herbert received the 'benefitt of the summers day from the kinges company, being brought mee by Blagrave . . .' (*Herbert*, p. 43.)

1629, Nov. 22—Herbert received the 'benefitt of the winters day from the kinges company being brought mee by Blagrave . . .' (Ibid., p. 44.)

1631, Dec. 1—Herbert records, 'Received of Mr. Blagrave, in the name of the kings company, for the benefitt of my winter day . . . 13*l*. 0s. 0*d*.' (Ibid.)

1632, Nov. 12—With William Beeston, Blagrave petitioned the Lord Chamberlain for the recovery of the boy Stephen Hammerton, whom Christopher Babham had inveigled from them and was using at Blackfriars; the case was referred to Sir Henry Herbert. (*M.S.C.* ii. 408.)

1633, June 6—Herbert received his benefit 'of yᵉ kings company, for my summers day, by Blagrave'. (*Herbert*, p. 44.)

1634, July 20—'A peticõn of the Kings Players complayning of intermingleing some passages of witches in old playes to yᵉ pʳiudice of their designed Comedy of the Lancashire witches' was referred to Blagrave, in the absence of Sir Henry Herbert. (*M.S.C.* ii. 410.)

1634/5, Jan. 24—'A Warrᵗ for paymᵗ of xxxˡⁱ vnto Wᵐ Blagraue for himselfe & the rest of his Company for three playes Acted by the Children of the Reuells at Whitehall in Anno 1631. Mᵈ their Bill was signed by Sʳ Henry Herbert Mʳ of the Reuells & passed Ian 24. 1634.' (Ibid., p. 375.)

1634/5, Jan. 30—Another warrant covering payment for these same three plays was entered this date. (Ibid.)

1635—The visiting French company 'gave Blagrave three pounds for his paines'. (*Herbert*, p. 62.)

1635, Aug. 1—Laud and the High Commissioners wrote requesting 'articles and additionals exhibited on behalf of William Blagrave against John Pregion, notary public'. Witnesses were to be called in Lincoln Cathedral in September on behalf of Blagrave. (*C.S.P., Dom.*, 1635, p. 311.)

1635, Sept. 16—'Received of Blagrove from the King's Company, for the renewing of *Love's Pilgrimage*, the 16th of September, 1635,— £1. 0. 0.' (*Herbert*, p. 36.)

1635, Oct. 15—As Deputy to the Master of the Revels, he licensed Glapthorne's *Lady Mother*. (Ibid., p. 37.)

1635, Dec. 31—He witnessed the will of John Shank. (See p. 648.)

BLAKE, JOHN. His only connexion with theatrical affairs, so far as we know, was as an investor.

1623/4, Feb. 20—Alleyn granted John Blake, glazier, of High Holborn, in St. Giles in the Fields, a lease of a half-share of the new Fortune. (*Hens. Paps.*, pp. 30, 112.)

BLANEY, JOHN. Blaney first appears as an actor in the old Queen's Revels company, but he seems to have been a Queen Anne's man by the time of the first agreement with the Baskerviles, and he is mentioned as a fellow and sharer in the later agreements. He remained with Queen Anne's or with derivative companies until he went to Queen Henrietta's.

1616, June—He was named in the Baskervile suit as a member of Queen Anne's at the time of the second settlement in favour of Francis Browne. (Fleay, *Stage*, p. 275.)

1617, June 3—He signed the new agreement of Queen Anne's with Susan Baskervile; she says he was a fellow and sharer at the time. (Ibid., pp. 285–8.)

1619, >May 13—As a member of Queen Anne's company, he was the twelfth listed to receive black cloth for her funeral procession. 'The Q: Plaiers . . . Iohn Blany—iiij yards.' (*M.S.C.* ii. 325.)

1622, July 8—He was fifth in a list of seven late Queen Anne's in a warrant for the Privy Seal for licensing the Children of the Revels. (Murray, ii. 193–4; see above, pp. 167–8.)

1622—'John Blany' was listed in Herbert's office book as among the 'chiefe players at the Red Bull, called the players of the Revells'. (*Herbert*, p. 63.)

1623, May 21—He was referred to as 'Iohn Blanye neare the Red Bull in Sᵗ Iohns Streete' in Markham's suit. (See pp. 682–3.)

1623, May 23—With Worth and Cumber, he pleaded to be excused from payments to the Baskeriles, since most of their fellows were 'dead, or departed'. Worth, Cumber, and Blaney were the only original members of the 1617 Queen Anne's company left. (Fleay, *Stage*, pp. 270–9.)

1625—'Asambeg, *Viceroy of* Tunis. Iohn Blanye,' appears in the cast for Massinger's *The Renegado*, given by Queen Henrietta's men 'at the priuate Play-house in Drurye-Lane', licensed by Herbert 17 April 1624, and printed in 1630. (1630 4° B.M.; *Herbert*, p. 28.)

BOND (BAND), THOMAS. Mr. W. J. Lawrence says that Bond was a 'country player from 1623 to 1627' (*M.L.R.* xxv. 209), but I know of no evidence for this statement save his appearance at Norwich in 1624. We know of his membership in only two companies, the Red Bull Revels company and Prince Charles's (II). The extant records of his activities do not point to any great prominence, and it is somewhat surprising to find his portrait at Dulwich with actors like Field and Burbage, Cartwright, Perkins, and Alleyn. It is even more surprising to find Kemble's assertion that he was the third man to play Bussy D'Ambois. This identification is almost certainly wrong, since there is no record of Bond in the King's company, whose membership is so well known. Though Thomas Bond was a common name in the time (one was an Oxford student in 1629, another a property holder in Wiltshire in the same year, and one was receiver general of fines in 1640), it seems likely that the man buried at St. James's was the actor, because the actor was associated for years with the theatre in that parish and with other actors there. The date fits with his disappearance from other records.

1622–3 ?—His name appears in the prompter's notes in the MS. of *The Two Noble Ladies* (B.M. MS. Egerton 1994), whose title-page says it was acted at the Red Bull by the Company of the Revels: 'Tritons in: Bond Stutf.'[1] Probably Bond's name belonged to the Revels performance indicated, though it may have been inserted by some prompter for a later performance. (Greg, *Dram. Doc.*, pp. 216, 277.)

1624, Apr. 9—'Thomas Band' was named in the confirmation of a licence of 31 October 1617 to the Children of the Revels to the late Queen Anne shown at Exeter and Norwich. (*Hist. MSS. Com.*,

---

[1] Miss Rhoads (who transcribed the MS. for the Malone Society) reads 'm: Bond', though she is not certain. Dr. Greg (*Dram. Doc.*, p. 277) reads 'in: Bond'. It looks to me like 'm' rather than 'in', though 'in' seems to make better sense.

Records of the City of Exeter, p. 171, and Murray, ii. 273.) *See* James Jones.

1627, July 16—'Thomas Bonde & Susan Hunter' mar. St. J.C. (Note that the will of William Browne [p. 636] mentions a legacy to Thomas Bond and his wife Susan, Browne's sister. If this is the Susan, she must have been married before.)

1629, May 25—'Eliz. d. of Thomas Bond & Susan vx.' chris. St.J.C.

1631, Dec.—'*Miscellanio, his Tutor.* Thomas Bond' in the cast of *Holland's Leaguer,* acted by Prince Charles's (II) men at Salisbury Court this month. (*Herbert,* p. 45; 1632 4° B.M.)

1632, *c.* 10–15 May—'Thomas Bond' was the eighth name listed in a warrant for swearing 'groomes of the Chamber in ordinary wthout ffee to attend the Prince his Highnes in ye quality of players'. (*M.S.C.* ii. 358; see above, p. 303.)

1632, Dec. 10—William Crome (q.v.) petitioned the Lord Chamberlain against Bond and five others of 'ye princes Players'. A petition of 21 December was 'Answered wth leaue graunted vpon sight'. (*M.S.C.* ii. 408.)

1632/3, Feb. 18—'A petition of Thomas Osberne agst Thomas Bond debt 15^{li}.' (Ibid., p. 409.)

1634, Apr. 7—Kemble told F. G. Waldron that he thought he had seen in some old tract that Tom Bond was the third man referred to in the prologue to *Bussy D'Ambois* (1641 ed.) as playing Bussy at the revival. (Waldron, *Sh. Miscellany,* pp. 25–6.)

1634, Oct. 23—William Browne in his will left a legacy to Thomas Bond, his brother-in-law, and to Bond's wife Susan. (See p. 636.)

1635, Apr. 25—'Thomas Bond, householder' bur. St. J.C.

BORNE, Theophilus (*see* BIRD, THEOPHILUS).

BORNE, William (*see* BIRD, WILLIAM).

BORROSE, —. The possibility that he was a player is fairly remote.

1643, Dec. 5—'M^r. Borrose from the Playhouse' bur. St. Anne's Blackfriars.

BOSGRAVE, George. He first appears as a boy in a 1613 Lady Elizabeth's patent shown at Coventry in 1615, and his only other record with an acting troupe shows him again in a provincial company. His participation in the illegal plague funeral in 1636 suggests his association with trumpeters, as does an unpublished entry in the L.C. papers at the Public Record Office noting his apprehension with Edward Hodgeson and three others for usurping the bills of the king's trumpeter.

1613, May 31—He was listed as a boy in a patent for Lady Elizabeth's of this date which was copied at Coventry 28 March 1615. (*R.E.S.* i. 183.)

1623/4, Feb. 20—Alleyn granted to George Bosgrave, 'of the parish of St. Giles without Cripplegate, gent.', a lease of a half-share of the new Fortune. (*Hens. Paps.,* pp. 30, 112.)

1624, Apr. 9—He was named in the confirmation of a licence of 31 October 1617 to the Children of the Revels to the late Queen Anne which was shown at Exeter. (*Hist. MSS. Com.*, Records of the City of Exeter, p. 171; Murray, ii. 272–3.) *See* James Jones.

1633/4 (?)—James Hodgson, Edward Hodgson, Gregory Saunders, George Bosgrave, and Francis Newton were apprehended for usurping the bills of the King's trumpeter. (P.R.O., L.C. 5/132, p. 357.)

1636, Oct. 3—'Record of the committal of eleven persons to Newgate, "untill his Majesties pleasure bee knowne, for goeing with one Samuell Underhill a trumpeter who died of the plague, to his grave with trumpettes sounded and swords drawne in the night time in Shorditch"; the eleven persons so committed being—Thomas Creswell of Barbican, Thomas Woodford of Hosierlane, Edward Bosseley of Criplegate, John Pett of Whitecrosstreete, Edward Hodgson of Cowcrosse, Abraham Rogers of Whitecrostreete, John Carre of St. Johnstreet, George Rickner of Whitecrostreete, George Bosgrave of Golding Lane, Adam Rose of Grubstreete, and William Johnson of Whitecrostreete.' (*Middx. Co. Rec.* iii. 62.)

1636, Dec. 1—'True Bill that, at twelve o'clock in the night of the said day at St. Leonard's-in-Shorditch co. Midd., Thomas Cresswell, Thomas Wadd (? Woodford), Edward Bosseley, John Pett, Edward Hodgson, Abraham Rogers, John Carre, George Rickner, George Bosgrave, Adam Rose, William Johnson, Philip Knight, Launcelot Giles, Edward Jupe, Henry Griffin, Francis Langley and John Wilkinson, all seventeen late of the said parish yomen, riotously and unlawfully as rioters and disturbers of the King's peace, assembled and came together, with swordes, linckes, and torches lighted and with trumpettes sounded, to the great terror and dread of the King's lieges and subjects there living. Ten of the rioters confessed the indictment and were fined three shillings and four pence each. The other seven were at large.' (Ibid., pp. 63–4.)

BOURNE, THEOPHILUS (*see* BIRD, THEOPHILUS).

BOURNE, WILLIAM (*see* BIRD, WILLIAM).

BOURNE (BOARNE, BOORNE, BOWRNE), THOMAS. We have only one record of this actor's dramatic activity, and that in the obscure group at Norwich in 1634/5 which was probably a combined provincial company and the London King's Revels company (see above, pp. 286 and 288–9). There is, however, abundant evidence that for fifteen years or more he was known as a player. The name is not sufficiently uncommon to make it at all certain that the two petitions refer to the player; a London bookseller of the same name who took up his freedom 15 January 1622/3 and who was still in business in 1628 is just as likely to be the petitioner. (*Dictionary of Printers.*) The copious St. Giles' records indicate that W. J. Lawrence is almost certainly wrong in his identification of the Thomas Borne of the Norwich record with Theophilus Bourne *alias* Bird. (*M.L.R.* xxv. 209.)

1625, Sept. 1—'Eliz dau: of Thomas Bourne, gent' bur. St. G.C.

1627, Apr. 19—'Susan Dau: of Thomas Boorne Player' bur. St. G.C.

1628, Dec. 14—'Eliz: Dau of Thomas Boarne Player' chris. St. G.C.

1628/9, Feb. 13—'Eliz: Dau: of Tho: Boarne, yoeman' bur. St. G.C.

1629/30, Jan. 17—'ffrancis sonne of Thomas Boarne, Player' chris. St. G.C.

1630, May 7—'ffrancis sonne of Thomas Bourne Player' bur. St. G.C.

1631, June 5—'Richard sonne of Thomas Bowrne Player' chris. St. G.C.

1634, July 27—'Mary daughter of Tho: Bourne Player' chris. St. G.C.

1634—John Murray and Thomas Boorne had received a grant concerning frauds practised in foreign 'baltrie' and brasswork imported into England. Petitioners now interested and pray Council to give order for passing of the grant. (C.S.P., Dom., 1634–5, p. 389.)

1634/5, Mar. 10—His name appears in the complete list of players entered in the Norwich records. (Some of the players seem to belong to the King's Revels, though the records do not give the name of the company; probably they were an amalgamated group. See above, pp. 286 and 288–9.) (Murray, ii. 356.)

1636, Dec. 14—'Temperance daugr: of Tho: Bourne Player' chris. St. G.C.

1636/7, Mar. 20—'Richard son: of Tho: Bourne Player' bur. St. G.C.

1637, Apr. 7—'Temperance daugr: of Tho Bourne Player' bur. St. G.C.

1637, Apr. 8—'Mary daugr of Thomas Bourne Player' bur. St. G.C.

1638, Aug. 29—'Constance daugr of Thomas Bourne Player' chris. St. G.C. (Collier in his Bodleian MS. records a burial item of Constance 12 June 1640, but I did not find it.)

1640, June 25—Thomas Bourne, William Morgan, and other recusants petition to compound at one-third of their goods before conviction. (C.S.P., Dom., 1640, pp. 343–4.)

1642, May 16—'Edmund sonne of Thomas Bourne player' chris. St. G.C.

BOWERS, RICHARD. Another inconspicuous assistant of the King's company. One would prefer to think him the man buried in 1645/6, but he may have been the father of the children.

1636/7, Jan. 12—Ticket of privilege granted to 'Richd Bowers' and ten others 'imployed by his Mates servantes the Players of the Blackfryers'. (M.S.C. ii. 380.)

1645/6, Feb. 2—'Richard Bowers from the Play-house' bur. St. Anne's Blackfriars.

1647, Aug. 5—'John sonne to Richard and Mary Bowers' bur. St. Anne's Blackfriars.

1648, July 9—'Mary daughter to Richard and Mary Bowers' bur. St. Anne's Blackfriars.

1650/1, Feb. 26—'Jeremiah son to Richard and Mary Bowers' chris. St. Anne's Blackfriars.

BOWYER, MICHAEL. Though Bowyer was known as an actor at least as early as 1621, we know nothing of his dramatic activities until he appears with Queen Henrietta's company, organized in

1625. His important romantic roles in the plays of this company offer strong evidence that he was both an experienced and a successful actor when he came to the troupe. Kendall told Crosfield in 1634 that Bowyer was one of the leaders of the company, apparently ranking him after Beeston. Both Turner and Perkins, however, appear in more of the business transactions of the organization than Bowyer does.

Some time between 1635 and 1641, Bowyer left Queen Henrietta's company and became a King's man. Theophilus Bird's statements in 1655 make it apparent that Bowyer must have made the transfer before Bird did, but Bird's date of 1635 cannot be accepted, because we know that Bird was still with Beeston at the Cockpit in 1637. It is probable, as Mr. Baldwin has pointed out (*Organization and Personnel*, pp. 64–5), that Bowyer left the Queen's company when it was threatened with extinction in the plague of 1636–7, for he is not mentioned among the leaders of the company whom Sir Henry Herbert transferred to the Salisbury Court in 1637, nor was he among those who appeared as leaders of Beeston's Boys in the same year.

The loan which Bird says Bowyer made the King's company when he joined them, William Beeston's bond to him, and the legacies in his will indicate that he was a man of some substance. The large bequest to Richard Perkins suggests that there may have been friendships among the Queen's men of as long standing as those among the King's men which have so frequently occasioned remark.

1621, Aug. 16—'William Bowyer, sonne to Michael Bowyer, a Stage Player and Isabell his wife' chris. St. Bodolph, Aldgate. (Denkinger p. 98.)

1621, Aug. 16—'William Bowyer, sonne to Michael Bowyer a Stage-player' bur. St. Bodolph, Aldgate. (Ibid.)

1622. Sept. 1—'William Bowyer sonne to Michael Bowyer Stage-player and Elizabeth his wife' chris. St. Bodolph, Aldgate. (Ibid., p. 98.)

1622, Sept. 11—'William Bowyer, sonne to Michael Bowyer, a stage-player' bur. St. Bodolph, Aldgate. (Ibid.)

1625—'Vitelli, *A Gentelman of* Venice *disguis'd* Michael Bowier' in the cast for Massinger's *The Renegado* presented by Queen Henrietta's men at the 'priuate Play-house in Drurye-Lane', licensed 17 April 1624 and printed in 1630. (1630 4° B.M.)

1626—'*Beauford*, a passionate louer of *Gratiana*. *Michael Bowyer*' in the Queen Henrietta's cast given in Shirley's *The Wedding*. (1629 4° HN.)

c. 1630—His name is in the cast of Queen Henrietta's men prefixed to the first part of Heywood's *The Fair Maid of the West* in the 1631 4°: 'Mr. Spencer. *By* Mr. Michael Bowyer.' Since no actor for the part of Spencer is given in the cast prefixed to the second part of the play, he probably had the role in the second part as well. (1631 ed. B.M.)

>1634—'King *John*, M. [Mr.] *Bowyer.*' in the Queen Henrietta's cast of Davenport's *King John and Matilda.* (1655 4° B.M.)

1634, July 18—Kendall told Crosfield that 'Mr Boyer' was one of the 'Queen's servants at yᵉ Phoenix in Drury Lane'. (*Crosfield's Diary*, p. 72.)

1634, Sept. 11—Bowyer was left a ring in the will of Thomas Basse. (See p. 631.)

1635—'Scipio. By Michael Bowyer' appears in the cast for Nabbes's *Hannibal and Scipio* given by Queen Henrietta's men 'at their Private house in Drury Lane'. (1637 4° B.M.)

c. 1636 or 1637—In 1655 Theophilus Bird said that he was admitted to the King's company about 1635 (must have been at least May 1637; see above, pp. 56–7) and 'was persuaded to join with eleven other members in a bond of £400 to Richard Perkins, in trust for Bowyer, for the payment of the £200' which Bowyer had loaned to the company on joining them, evidently some time before Bird did. (Hotson, pp. 31–2.)

1639—Robert Davenport dedicated *A Crowne for a Conquerour, and Too Late to Call Backe Yesterday. Two Poems, the one Divine, the other Morall* 'To my noble friends, Mʳ Richard Robinson, And Mʳ Michael Bowyer' (1639 4° HN). Mr. Baldwin thinks this linking of the names indicates that Bowyer was a King's man in 1639 (*Organization and Personnel*, p. 64).

1640/1, Jan. 22—He is named with five others in a warrant for swearing them grooms of his Majesty's Chamber to attend as players. (*M.S.C.* ii. 397.)

1640/1, Feb. 25—'I find that, five weeks before Davenant's flight [6 May 1641], William Beeston entered into a bond of £400 penalty to Michael Bowyer, . . . (L. C. 4/66. 25 Feb., 1640/1). While we know nothing of the purpose of this bond, it may possibly have had something to do with Beeston's reinstatement in 1641 as governor of the Cockpit players.' (Hotson, p. 129, note 36.)

>1642—Trueman says that he was one of 'Those of principal Note at the *Cockpit*' (Queen Henrietta's). (*Hist. Hist.*, p. 4.)

<1642—In 1655 Theophilus Bird said that after the closing of the theatres, Bowyer, Pollard, and others seized the apparel, hangings, and books of the company and sold them for their own use. (Hotson, p. 32.)

1645, Sept. 26—He made his will, giving his address as Hounslow in Middlesex. He left a legacy to Richard Perkins of St. Giles in the Fields of £50 or 5s. a week for life and made his wife Elizabeth executrix and chief legatee. (See pp. 635–6.)

1645, Nov. 7—His will was probated.

1646, Apr. 1—His wife Elizabeth married Thomas Morrison. (Hotson, p. 32.)

BRADSHAW, Richard. A Richard Bradshaw appeared as a provincial player in the last seven or eight years of the reign of Elizabeth, and he appears several times in Henslowe's diary and in the Alleyn papers between 1598 and 1605 (see Nungezer). The Richard Bradshaw of 1630 and 1633 must have been a different actor, for it is unlikely that a man could have been acting for twenty-five years in the provinces without leaving another record. Yet it is curious that a second actor of the name should also have performed in the provinces only. The Lord Dudley's player of 1595 was probably at least thirty, since he was a leader of the troupe; surely he would not have been still dashing about the country at the age of sixty-eight. On the whole it seems to me more probable that there were two Richard Bradshaws, provincial actors.

The very interesting examination of the players at Banbury tells more of the methods of provincial companies than it does of Bradshaw. All the actors agree, however, that Bradshaw was the master of the company.

It is not certain that the player and the fencer are to be identified, but Gibbs (q.v.) was a player, and some of the others may have been too.

1630 ?—'Richard Bradshawe hath licens and company' at Reading. (Murray, ii. 386.)

1633, May 2 and 3—Six suspicious strolling actors, examined by the mayor and justices of Banbury, assert that the company was under the direction of Richard Bradshaw, who had gone to London to renew the commission and recruit players. (*See* Bartholomew Jones, Richard Whiting, and Edward Damport.)

1664—One of a group of gentlemen who are talking about the theatre of the old days says, 'You talk of your Players, I am for the Fencers, there are none living now like old *Bradshaw*, old *Batty*, *Chatterton* and *Ned Gibs*.' ([Tatham,] *Knavery in All Trades*, E_1, 1664 4° HN.)

BRADSTREET, JOHN. An English actor who first appeared in Germany in 1591/2 and continued to act there for a number of years. Since he did not die until 1618, he may have acted after 1616. (Chambers, ii. 304.)

BRAY, ANTONY. Unknown except for the one list. He might possibly be the same as Anthony Brew.

1634/5, Mar. 10—He is named in the list of twenty-eight players, part of them King's Revels men, which was entered in the Norwich records. (There were probably two companies; see pp. 286 and 288-9.) (Murray, ii. 356.)

BREW, ANTHONY. Brew's roles in *The Two Noble Ladies* suggest that he was a hired man in the Revels company, but it is possible that the prompter's notes were not made for the performance mentioned on the title-page. It has been suggested that this actor might be the Anthony Brewer who wrote *The Lovesick King*. On this subject Miss Hope Dodds has a very interesting theory (*M.L.R.* xix [1924], 158) that *The Lovesick King* was written at the expense of the corporation of Newcastle for presentation before James when he visited that city in May 1617. She thinks that Brewer took much of his material for the play from *Edmond*

Ironside, another play in the repertory of his company. This is a very tempting speculation, but unfortunately, though there is evidence of indebtedness to *Edmond Ironside*, of a Newcastle origin for the play, and of possible allusions to James, there is no evidence at all of the company which presented it, of a date as late as 1617, or of the identity of Anthony Brewer dramatist and Anth. Brew. player. This is regrettable, for one would like to be able to accept Miss Dodds's neatly constructed account of the play.

1622–3 ?—His name appears in the prompter's notes in the MS. of *The Two Noble Ladies* (B.M. MS. Egerton 1994), whose title-page says it was acted at the Red Bull by the Company of the Revels: 'Ent. Anth Brew:' (fol. 232[9]ᵃ). Here he was a Lord of Babylon. Apparently he is also the 'Anth' who is twice noted in the part of a soldier (fols. 227[4]ᵃ and 235[12]ᵇ). (Greg, *Dram. Doc.*, pp. 274, 276, 277.)

BRIDGE, EDWARD. Probably not an actor, but his inclusion with such a large number of actors in Markham's suit suggests that he may have been. (See below, p. 683.)

BRIGGES, JOHN (*see* BUGGE, JOHN).

BRIGGS, ROBERT. Briggs is known only from his appearance in the MSS. of Middleton's *Hengist, King of Kent*. Though this play became the property of the King's men, Mr. Bald says, with reason, that the actors' names probably date from earlier productions. (Bald, *Hengist, King of Kent*, pp. xx–xxi.)

<1616—'Brigs', 'Rob: Briggs', and 'Bri' appear in the two MSS. of Middleton's *Hengist, King of Kent*. He seems to have taken part in the dumb shows and to have played a gentleman. (Bald, *Hengist, King of Kent*, pp. xvii and xxviii.)

BROME, RICHARD. The only significant evidence that Brome was an actor is to be found in the Lord Chamberlain's record of 1628, though a number of Jonson's allusions to his servant have been strained to indicate that Brome was a player. (Thaler, *Modern Language Notes*, xxxvi. 88–90.) The uncertainty of the identity and status of the 'Richard Broome' of the record is increased by the fact that the Lady Elizabeth's company of 1628 is a most obscure group, in the swearing of at least one of whose members there was certainly fraud. (See above, pp. 188–90.) In the light of Brome's later association with the Salisbury Court theatre, it seems not impossible that he was sworn in order to be protected as dramatist and reviser for the company rather than as a player. I have listed below the facts which have a bearing on his association with the companies, as well as one or two occurrences of the name which have not been published before.

1616, July 8—'Richard Broome & francis Lott wedow' mar. St. Michael Bassishaw. (Challen, *Marriages*.)

1627, Dec. 4—'Richard Broome & Joane Dylke, L. vg.' mar. St. Gregory by St. Paul. (Ibid.)

1628, June 30—'Richard Broome' was fourth in a list of the 'Queene of Bohemia's Players' made grooms of his Majesty's chamber. (*M.S.C.* ii. 347; see above, pp. 188–9.)

1631, Dec. 12—'A petion (*sic*) of Iohn Bonus &c against Richd Broome Answered of course eod [12 December 1631].' (L.C. 5/183, p. 116; not in *M.S.C.* ii.)

1635, July 20—He signed a contract with the Salisbury Court theatre to write three plays a year, as well as prologues, epilogues, songs, and revised scenes for old plays, for three years at a salary of 15*s.* a week plus the first day's profits for each new play as a benefit. In spite of the contract he wrote one or two plays for the Cockpit in this period. (Andrews, *Brome*, pp. 13–15.)

1638, Aug.—'In 1638 it was agreed that the contract [with the Salisbury Court] should be continued seven years longer, at [a salary of] 20 shillings a week for Brome's exclusive services.' He delivered one play sometime after Christmas in the winter of 1638–9 and another play just before Easter 1639 on this contract. The company refused to accept the latter and (whether for this reason or not we do not know) Brome left the Salisbury Court to write for William Beeston at the Cockpit. (Ibid., pp. 14–15.)

1638—The epilogue to *The Antipodes*, acted in 1638 by Queen Henrietta's men at Salisbury Court, says, '. . . it was, at first, intended for the Cock-pit Stage, in the right of my most deserving Friend Mr. William Beeston, unto whom it properly appertained . . . it was generally applauded, and well acted at Salisbury Court'. (1640 ed. B.M.)

1642, Sept. 16—'Lucia Daughter of Richard Brome esq^r and Sara vxor' chris. St. G.F.

BROMEFIELD, RICHARD. A provincial actor in 1628. How many of the other records reveal the player I cannot be sure; certainly the last two refer to different men.

1618, Sept. 18—Perhaps he is the 'm^r Bromfeeld' mentioned in Alleyn's diary; see the entry under John Edmonds. (Alleyn's Diary, Young, ii. 104.)

1618, Sept. 28—'Dined att ye bull Head w^t m^r bromefeeld & tuchborne.' (Ibid., p. 105.)

1628, June 7—'Richard Bromefild' and twelve others were named in the new licence of this date granted to Ellis Guest's company by Sir Henry Herbert. (Murray, ii. 353.)

1628, July 2—With Ellis Guest's company of thirteen players, he was at Norwich with the licence of 7 June. (Ibid.)

1632/3, Jan. 21—'Richard Bromefeild, drowned' bur. St. J.C.

1636, June 3—'Particular of sundry sums underwritten to be adventured in the fishings of Great Britain and Ireland, but not yet paid.' £100 and £50 adventured; Richard Bromfield in the latter group. (*C.S.P., Dom.*, 1635–6, pp. 532–3.)

BROUGHTON, AMBROSE. Probably not an actor, but his inclusion with such a large number of actors in Markham's suit suggests that he may have been. (See p. 682.)

BROWNE (*alias* BASKERVILE), FRANCIS. He is connected with the theatre by virtue of his membership in the Baskervile family which is so closely associated with Queen Anne's men in its last years.

1616, June—His life was substituted for that of Susan Baskervile's husband as the term of the pension to be paid daily by Queen Anne's men. (Fleay, *Stage*, p. 283.)

1617, June 3—He was dead by this time, as William Brown's life is substituted in the agreement. (Ibid., p. 275.)

BROWNE, JOSEPH. Only the parish registers give evidence of his connexion with the stage.

1636, Dec. 4—'Lucretia daug^r of Joseph Browne, Play^r' chris; buried 10 June 1637, St. G.C.

1639/40, Feb. 9—'William, sonne of Joseph Browne, Playe^r' chris. St. G.C.

BROWNE, RICHARD. Probably not an actor, but his inclusion with such a large number of actors in Markham's suit suggests that he might have been. (See p. 683.)

BROWNE, ROBERT. A Robert Browne appears as a member of the Earl of Worcester's troupe as early as 1582/3, and there are a few other records of him as a player in England, but most of his acting career was spent in Germany, where he appears to have been one of the best known of the popular English actors from 1590 to 1607. From 1608 to 1612 there are records of a Robert Browne, player, in England, the chief of which informs us that he was one of the patentees of the Queen's Revels company. After a break of six years in which there are no records of a Robert Browne, player, the name appears again among the actors in Germany where Robert Browne was leader of a company from 1618 to 1620. (See Nungezer; Herz, *Englische Schauspieler*, pp. 21–3; and Meissner, *Englischen Comoedianten*, pp. 43, 65–6.)

BROWNE, ROBERT. The puppet showman is probably not the Robert Browne of German fame, who would have been about eighty at the time of the Norwich visit. He might have been the Robert son of Robert Browne, stage player, who was baptized at St. Saviour's 19 October 1595. (See *T.L.S.*, 15 November 1928, p. 856.)

1637/8, Jan. 12—'To Robert Browne, Georg Hall, & Richard Jones players by warant, who had a motion to shew expressing the worlds abuses' at Coventry. (Murray, ii. 253.)

1639, Oct. 9—'Robert Browne and George Hall did this day exhibit a lycense . . . to shewe an Italian Motion but . . . he sayth his motion is noe Italian motion but made in London,' at Norwich. (Ibid., p. 359.)

BROWNE, WILLIAM. William Browne was not improbably introduced to the stage by his stepfather, Thomas Greene, the famous comedian, for he was a minor when Greene died, and four years after his stepfather's death he was a hired man in Greene's former company. From 1617, when he was a hired man of Queen Anne's company, until the formation of Prince Charles's company, about 1631, nothing is known of Browne's dramatic activity. His part in *Holland's Leaguer* and his position in the warrant of May 1632 indicate that he was fairly prominent in the Prince's company, though not one of the leaders.

1609/10, Feb. 17—'William Browne & Alice Longe' mar. St. J.C.

1612, July 25—His stepfather, Thomas Greene, left him £40 to be paid 'when he shall come to the age of twenty and one yeares', and an annuity of £4 until then. (Fleay, *Stage*, p. 193.)

c. 1616—The Baskervile suit says that before the settlement of 3 June 1617, Queen Anne's had fallen in arrears with Browne's wages as hired man. (Ibid., p. 284.)

1617, June 3—His life was substituted for that of Francis Browne as the term of the daily Baskervile pension from Queen Anne's. (Ibid., pp. 275, 285.)

1621/2, Feb. 14—'William Browne & Bridget Mason' mar. St. J.C. (His will, p. 637, mentions his son-in-law 'Phillipp Mássam'.)

1623, June 16—Browne and his mother, Susan Baskervile, answered the complaint of the players, Worth, Cumber, and Blaney, concerning the pension which the Queen's company had granted them in payment of Thomas Greene's share in the company and of various loans which the Baskerviles had made to the company. (Fleay, *Stage*, pp. 279–92.)

1626, Apr. 28—'William Browne & Ann Baylie' mar. St. J.C. (His will, p. 637, mentions his wife Anne.)

1631, Dec.—'Philautus, a Lord inamored of himselfe. William Browne' in the cast of *Holland's Leaguer*, acted by Prince Charles's (II) men at Salisbury Court. (1632 4° B.M.; *Herbert*, p. 33.)

1632, May 10–15—'William Browne' was fifth in a warrant to swear eleven men as grooms of the Chamber in ordinary to attend the Prince 'in ye quality of players'. (*M.S.C.* ii. 358; see above, p. 303.)

1632, Dec. 10—William Crome (q.v.) petitioned the Lord Chamberlain against Browne and five others of 'ye princes Players'. A petition of 21 December was 'Answered wth leaue graunted vpon sight'. (*M.S.C.* ii. 408.)

1634, Oct. 23—'William Browne of the parish of St James Clarkenwell . . . gent' made his will. He left legacies to Thomas Bond and his wife Susan and others; said he was a member and sharer of the Red Bull company and that they owed him money. His chief beneficiary was his wife Anne; his mother, Susan Baskervile, was made executrix. (See below, pp. 636–7.)

1634, Nov. 6—'Will'm Browne, householder' bur. St. J.C.

1634, Nov. 10—His will was probated.

BRYAN (BRYANT), MARY. An investor in the shares of the Fortune theatre.

1623/4, Mar. 24—Alleyn granted 'Marie Brian, of Clerkenwell, widow' one share in the new Fortune. (*Hens. Paps.*, pp. 30, 112.)

1625, Dec. 22—She made her will, but there is no mention of theatres or actors. It was probated 27 January 1625/6. (P.C.C. 7 Hele.)

1625/6, Jan. 7—'Mrs Mary Bryan' bur. St. J.C.

1639, July 15—Her share went to Tobias Lisley. (*MSS. Dul.*, pp. 54–5.)

BUCKLE, JOHN. Though Kendall told Crosfield that Buckle was one of the leaders of a company (apparently the Red Bull–King's), little else is known of him. Both the parish register items seem likely to represent this player, since no Buckley is otherwise known, and since one parish contained the Fortune and the other contained the Red Bull and was adjacent to the Fortune parish.

1634, July 18—In the list of London players which Kendall gave Crosfield is '4. The Fortune in Golden Lane, ye cheife Mr Wm Cartwright, Edward Armestead, John Buckle, John Kirke.' (This was probably the Red Bull company; *see* William Cartwright and pp. 274–5.) (*Crosfield's Diary*, p. 72.)

1638, July 12—'Eliz. d. of John Buckle' bur. St. J.C.

1652/3, Jan. 4—'Mary Wife of John Buckley player' bur. St. G.C.

BUCKSTEAD, WILLIAM (*see* BARKSTEAD, WILLIAM).

BUGGE, JOHN.[1] Bugge appears as a player only in the obscure Queen of Bohemia's company of 1628, and the charges made against him by the College of Physicians emphasize the dubious character of that company, though the dishonesty of Bugge is not demonstrated, as is that of his fellow in the company, Thomas Barnes. It seems a good guess that Andrew Bugge had something to do with John's practice of physic. The John Bugge in Benfield's will is probably the player, as Benfield seems to have had a rather large acquaintance among actors.

1628/9, Jan. 10—'A Warraunt to sweare Iohn Bugge one of the Queene of Bohemia's Players A Groome of ye chamber in ordinary wthout ffee.' (*M.S.C.* ii. 348.)

1628/9, Mar. 4—'Andrew son of the reputed wife of Andrew Bugge Chirurgeon in bitted (?) and bagg yard in old street bonds taken' chris. St. G.C.

1630/1, Feb. 7—'A petition of the President & Censors of the Colledge of Phisitions against diuerse Emperickes (vizt) Butler A glouer, Trigg A last maker, Bugges one of the Queene of Bohemias Players sometimes an Apothecary & . . . others for practising of Phisique agst ye Charter of the Colledge . . .' (*M.S.C.* ii. 403.)

1632, May 18—'A petition of Francis Heath against John Bugge debt 50li Answered of course eod [18 May 1632].' (Lord Chamberlain's Papers 5/183, p. 123.)

1633, Apr. 27—'A petition of Richard Elton agst Iohn Bugge debt xxli Answered wth leaue graunted after one weeke after sight.' (*M.S.C.* ii. 409.)

[1] According to the *Hist. MSS. Com.* report on the MSS. of the College of Physicians (Report VIII, p. 229), the name is given as Brigges in the documents of the college. Bugge occurs often enough, however, to leave no doubt that the name should be so spelled.

1635, June 24—'Mary daughter of John Buggs Gentlem' bur. St. G.C.
1639, Aug. 26—Richard Benfield of Gray's Inn in his will left £15
'to my lovinge freind John Bugges Doctor in Phisicke'. (See
p. 634.)

BUKLANK, ALEXANDER. A ghost name created by Halliwell-
Phillipps's misreading of the name of Alexander Bullard in B.M.
Add. MS. 19256.

BULLARD, ALEXANDER. A minor attendant of the King's company. The name is usually given as Buklank, since Sir Henry
Herbert's document has usually been printed from Halliwell-
Phillipps's transcript, but this transcript is not accurate. (See
above, pp. 15–16.)

1624, Dec. 27—Herbert exempted him from arrest as an attendant
of the King's company. (*Herbert*, p. 74; see above, pp. 15–16.)

BURBAGE, CUTHBERT. Though he was never, so far as is known,
an actor himself, Cuthbert Burbage was the son of an actor, the
builder of the first theatre, and the brother of the most famous
actor of his time. He seems to have been interested in theatres
all his life ; certainly he was acting for his father in connexion with
the Theatre by 1589, and he still held shares in the Globe and
Blackfriars at his death in 1636.

There are numerous indications of Cuthbert's friendship with
the players of his brother's company, and one of them, Nicholas
Tooley, seems to have lived with him in St. Leonard's Shoreditch,
where he is found all his life. Cuthbert Burbage is found in the
Visitations of London in 1634, where his arms are given and where
he records that he has adopted his grandson, James Moxie, who
is called (obviously in memory of his great-grandfather, 'the first
builder of playhowses') James Burbage. (See Stopes, *Burbage*,
for a fuller account of his life.)

1617/18, Jan. 13—With John Heminges, John Shank, and Thomas
Ravenscroft, Burbage witnessed the will of Richard Cowley. (See
p. 642.)
1618/19, Mar. 12—Witnessed his brother Richard's will. (See p. 638.)
1623, June 3—The will of Nicholas Tooley, who was buried from
Burbage's house, left legacies to Mrs. Burbage, 'in whose howse I
doe now lodge', and to Mrs. Condell. Burbage and Condell were
made executors and chief legatees. (See pp. 649–51.)
1635—In the players' petition, Benfield, Pollard, and Swanston say
that the Burbages had owned half the Globe, but that now Cuthbert
owned three and one-half of the sixteen shares in the Globe and one
of the eight in the Blackfriars. (*M.S.C.* ii. 362–4.)
1635—The reply of Cuthbert Burbage and his sister-in-law Winifred
to Benfield, Pollard, and Swanston gives the history of the Burbages' theatrical undertakings. (Ibid., pp. 370–2.)
1635, Sept. 1—He was made executor in the will of Elizabeth Condell.
(See p. 638.)

1636, Sept. 17—'Cuthbert Burbardge was buryed ye 17th day of September 1636.' (Stopes, *Burbage*, p. 133, from the Registers of St. Leonard's Shoreditch.)

BURBAGE, RICHARD. The most famous actor of the Elizabethan stage was the son of James Burbage, the builder of the first theatre, and the younger brother of Cuthbert (q.v.). He was probably born about the summer of 1573 (Baldwin, *Organization and Personnel*, pp. 238–9), and he became active in theatrical affairs at least as early as 1590, or several years earlier, if his brother's statement that he acted for thirty-five years is to be trusted. With his brother Cuthbert he inherited and developed his father's interest in the Theatre and Blackfriars. Like his brother, he spent his life in the parish of St. Leonard's Shoreditch, where his seven children were baptized, and where five of them and both their parents were buried. It was probably at St. Leonard's that his wife, Winifred, married his fellow, Richard Robinson (q.v.), not long after Burbage's death.

Richard Burbage was for about a quarter of a century the leading actor and one of the chief assets of Shakespeare's company. Mr. Baldwin thinks that he had become their leading actor by 1592 (ibid., p. 237), and there is no doubt that he continued in this position until his death in 1619, though in the last three years of his life the company's plays seem often to have had two leading roles, taken by Burbage and Field.

A number of his roles are known from contemporary reference: Ferdinand in *The Duchess of Malfi*, Malvole in *The Malcontent*, Richard in *Richard III*, Hamlet, Lear, and Othello. After a careful, though not always convincing, analysis of Burbage's known roles and a study of the company's plays, Mr. Baldwin concludes that Burbage played the following parts in the other plays of Shakespeare: Henry V, Romeo, Talbot, Richard in *2* and *3 Henry VI*, Lucius in *Titus Andronicus*, Demetrius, Lucentio, King John, Richard II, Prince Hal, Bassanio, Berowne, Claudio, Brutus, Orlando, Orsino, Ford, Angelo, Timon, Macbeth, Antony, Bertram, Pericles, Coriolanus, Posthumus, Leontes, Prospero, Wolsey, and Arcite. In the plays of the Beaumont and Fletcher folio Mr. Baldwin thinks that he probably acted Philaster, Amintor, Arbaces, Jacomo, Antonio, Aecius, Caratach, Don John, Philippo, Memnon, Crates, Theodoret, Mountferrat, and Archas. In many of these parts the personal appearance and the talents of Richard Burbage undoubtedly influenced the dramatist as he wrote, though it is impossible to determine just how extensive this influence was.

Burbage's talent as a painter is referred to in several places, and one of the pictures at Dulwich College is attributed to him in the early catalogue (*MSS. Dul.*, p. 205). At Dulwich there is also a small and not very satisfactory picture of Burbage himself, which is reproduced in Sir Edmund Chambers's *William Shake-speare* (i. 76).

There are many references to Burbage at the time of his death, one pointing out that there was more mourning for him than for Queen Anne, who died about ten days before him. The allusions to Richard Burbage, which continue for many years after his death, have been frequently published (Stopes, *Burbage*; Nungezer), and I have reprinted only one or two which have not appeared before.

1616, Mar. 25—He was a legatee in Shakespeare's will. (Chambers, *Shakespeare*, ii. 172.)

1616, Oct. 14—'Wynefryd Burbadge, daughter of Richard Burbadge, 14th Oct., 1616, Holywell Street,' bur. St. Leonard's, Shoreditch. (Stopes, *Burbage*, p. 140.)

1616, Nov. 6—'William Burbadge, son of Richard Burbadge' chris. St. Leonard's Shoreditch. (Ibid., p. 141.)

1616—He was mentioned in Jonson's *Masque of Christmas*. See Hemminges.

1616—No. 1 in King's cast of *The Mad Lover*. (1679 folio B.M.)

1616–17—No. 1 in King's cast of *The Queen of Corinth*. (Ibid.)

1616–18—No. 1 in King's cast of *The Knight of Malta*. (Ibid.)

1617, July 17—John Chamberlain writing to Sir Dudley Carleton of Lady Coke's charges against her husband says that she 'declaimed bitterly against him, and so carries herself, that divers said Burbage could not have acted better'. (Birch, *James I*, ii. 20.)

1617/18, Jan. 13—With Cuthbert Burbage, Hemminges, and Ravenscroft, he witnessed the nuncupative will of Richard Cowley. (See p. 642.)

1618, Nov. 16—No. 1 in King's cast of *The Loyal Subject*. (1679 folio B.M.)

1618/19, Mar. 16—'Richard Burbadge, Player, was buried the 16th March, 1618–9, Halywell Street,' St. Leonard's Shoreditch. (Stopes, *Burbage*, p. 140.) According to a MS. funeral elegy in the Huth collection, he had died on the 13th. (Ibid., p. 120.) Part of an elegy on Burbage in *H.E.D.P.* i. 412–13, probably the same as the Huth MS., gives his parts.

1618/19, Mar. 19—In a letter to Carleton, Chamberlain says, 'Burbage, the great actor, dead, worth 300l. in land'. (*C.S.P., Dom.*, 1619–23, p. 26.)

1619, Mar. 27—His name is second in a patent for the King's men. (*M.S.C.* i. 280–2.)

1619, Aug. 5—'Sara Burbedge, daughter of Winifred Burbadge, widow, 5th Aug., 1619, Halliwell Street,' chris. St. Leonard's Shoreditch. (Stopes, *Burbage*, p. 141.) 'Sara Burbadge, 29 April, 1625, Hallywell Street,' bur. St. Leonard's. (Ibid., p. 140.)

1623—'Richard Burbadge' is second in the actor list in the Shakespeare folio.

1623, June 3—In his will Nicholas Tooley speaks with affection of 'my late Master, Richard Burbadge, deceased'. (See p. 649.)

1624—In comparing Jesuit tricks to plays, John Gee says in his *New Shreds of the Old Snare*, 'Would any man thinke that *Burbege* should be cõtent with a single share, who was the flower and life of his company, the *Loadstone* of the Auditory, and the *Roscius* of the Stage?' (1624 ed. B.M., p. 21.)

BURROUGHS, — (*see* BORROSE, —).

BURT, NICHOLAS. Burt was a very well-known Restoration actor and is said to have been active on the Caroline stage, but there is no certain contemporary evidence for his early connexion with the theatre. Mr. Baldwin assumes that he was really Nicholas Birche, son of George Birche (q.v.), born in 1619 or 1620, and apprenticed to the Shakespearean company about 1632. (*Organization and Personnel*, pp. 58 n., 194, 195.) Since there are several extant signatures of Nicholas Burt and numerous references to him, all of which spell his name Burt or Burtt, and since there is no evidence whatever that George Birche ever had a son Nicholas, or any other son for that matter, Mr. Baldwin's assumptions appear somewhat arbitrary.

While there is no contemporary corroboration of Wright's statements about the early career of Burt, there is no reason to doubt them. The transfer to Beeston would probably have occurred at the time of Shank's death in 1635/6, when Beeston may have been collecting boys for the proposed young company.

1631, May 6—'Nick' played a Carthaginian officer, an attendant of the King of Prusias, and an attendant of Marcellus in the King's production of *Believe as You List*. Professor Sisson conjectures that Nick was Nicholas Burt, but this seems unlikely, since the roles are those of a hired man and not of a boy, and Wright says that Burt was a boy at this time. Nicholas Underhill (q.v.) seems a more likely candidate. (Sisson, *B.A.Y.L.*, pp. xxxi ff. and xxxiv.)

>1636—Wright says '*Burt* was a Boy first under *Shank* at the *Blackfriers* . . .' (See p. 692.)

1637?—Wright says that Burt was a boy 'then under *Beeston* at the *Cockpit*; and *Mohun* and *Shatterel* were in the same Condition with him, at the last Place. There *Burt* used to Play the principal Women's Parts, in particular *Clariana* in *Love's Cruelty*'. (See p. 692.)

<1642—Wright says that after the closing of the theatres, '*Hart* was a Lieutenant of Horse under Sir *Thomas Dallison*, in *Prince Rupert's* Regiment, *Burt* was a Cornet in the same Troop, and *Shatterel* Quartermaster.' (See p. 694.)

1648—Wright says that after the wars the actors made up one company from the remnants of several and acted for a time at the Cockpit. They were raided by the soldiers when they were performing 'the *Bloudy Brother*, (in which *Lowin* Acted Aubrey, *Tayler* Rollo, *Pollard* the Cook, *Burt* Latorch, and I think *Hart* Otto) . . .' (See p. 695.)

BURTON, ANTONY. Known only as a provincial actor.

1628, June 7—He was named in the new licence granted to Ellis Guest's company by Sir Henry Herbert and shown at Norwich 2 July. (Murray, ii. 353.)

BYLAND, AMBROSE (*see* BEELAND, AMBROSE).

CAMBY, —. In his account of the last stand of Newcastle's Whitecoats at Marston Moor, William Lilly quotes a remark of 'Captain *Camby*, then a Trooper under *Cromwell*, and an Actor, who was the third or fourth Man that entred amongst them'. (*Mr. William Lilly's History of His Life and Times, From the Year 1602, to 1681* [2nd ed.; London, 1715], p. 79.) Nothing is known of such an actor, or of such an officer, but Lilly may have known whereof he spoke. There is no apparent reason for dishonesty.

CANE (CAIN, CAUE, DE CAINE, KANE, KAYNE, KEIN, KEYNE, KEYNES, RAYNE), ANDREW. Before he became a player Cane was probably a goldsmith, for Kendall referred to him as a goldsmith in 1634, and he appears several times as a goldsmith after the closing of the theatres. The 'stall' mentioned in the christening entry of 1623 may have been connected with his first profession.

Cane's first appearance as a player in 1622 is confusing, for Sir Henry Herbert seems to indicate that he was both a Palsgrave's man and a Lady Elizabeth's man. Professor Murray is probably right (Murray, i. 215–16) in suggesting that he was a Lady Elizabeth's man recently transferred to the Palsgrave's. I can take no stock in Fleay's notion (*Biog. Chron.* i. 295) that 'Andrew our elder journeyman' in v. 2 of the first part of Heywood's *Fair Maid of the West* is an allusion to Andrew Cane. Cane must have been of some importance in the last days of the Palsgrave's company, for he was one of the six whom Gunnell thought it advisable to attach to the theatre by a bond. This bond suggests that Cane was probably a member of the obscure King and Queen of Bohemia's company in the first five or six years of Charles's reign, but there is no reliable evidence.

He appears in the first lists of Prince Charles's (II) company, though the precise date of his joining is unknown because of the obscurity of the origins of that organization. There are numerous evidences of his importance as a Prince's man—his role in *Holland's Leaguer*, Kendall's statement, his prominent place in licences of the company, and his payment for court performances. Cane evidently continued a Prince's man until the closing of the theatres, no doubt to the profit of the company, as is suggested by the references to him as the popular clown of the Fortune or the Red Bull, the two theatres in which the last eight or ten years of the company seem to have been spent. It is not surprising to find Cane acting surreptitiously at the Red Bull after the war had begun, but it is somewhat startling to find that he was coining for the King at Oxford.

The Stage-Players Complaint has woodcuts of two men on the title-page, one of which is probably intended for Andrew Cane and the other for Timothy Reed. The dialogue of the pamphlet suggests, but not too clearly, that Cane was known for his rapid speech and Reed for his nimble heels.

1619/20, Jan. 24—'Thomas Cane s of Andrew Cane and Mary his wife,' Holywell Street, chris. St. Leonard's Shoreditch. (Bod.)

1622, >July 8—Sir Henry Herbert lists '— Kane' among the six 'Palsgrave's servants'. (*Herbert*, p. 63.)

1622, >July 8—'Andrew Cane' was listed in Herbert's office-book as one of 'the chiefe of them at the Phoenix'. (Ibid.)

1623, Apr. 18—'Hester a fowndlyne the parents unknowne taken up at Andrew Keines stall' chris. St. G.C.

1624, Apr. 30—In a suit of 1654 it is revealed that on this date Andrew Cane, Charles Massey, William Cartwright, William Stratford, Richard Price, and Richard Fowler signed a bond to Richard Gunnell to continue to play together at the Fortune and not break the company. Cane said in 1654 that none of the six broke the bond. (Hotson, pp. 51–4.)

1631, Dec.—'A lycence vnto Andrew Kayne And others by the name of Seruants to the Prince to exercise and practise all manner of plaies in their new playhowse in Salisbury Court (and not else where wthin the Citties of London or Westm^{er} or the Suburbs thereof or wthin 5 miles Compasse of the same) and also in any other Cittie or borough wthin his Ma:^{ts} dominions or in any place heretofore vsed for that purpose Signified and p[ro]cur by the Lo: Visc: Dorchest^{er}.' (P.R.O. 2/90, C 82/2077.)

1631—A document in private hands reads, 'Grant of permission to Andrew Rayne [obviously a misreading of Andrew Kayne] and others, the qualities of Playing as well in their present Theatre, Salisbury Court, as elsewhere, 1631.' (*N. & Q.*, Series II, ii. 145.)

1631, Dec. 7—In the Norwich accounts under date of 9 March 1635/6 the following statement was entered: 'A licence signed by his Matie & vnder his privie signet was this day shewed in Court whereby lycence is given to Andrew Kayne to play Comedyes Test 7° Decembris Anno Septimo Caroli Regis.' (Murray, ii. 358.)

1631, Dec.—'*Trimalchio, a humorous gallant.* Andrew Keyne.' in the cast of *Holland's Leaguer*, which was acted by Prince Charles's (II) at the Salisbury Court. (*Herbert*, p. 45; 1632 4° B.M.)

1632, May 10–15—'Andrew Kayne' was second in a warrant to swear eleven men as grooms of the Chamber 'to attend the Prince his Highnes in ye quality of players'. (*M.S.C.* ii. 358.)

1634, July 18—Kendall told Crosfield that among the London players were '3. The Princes Servants at ye Red-bull in St Johns street, ye cheife Mr Cane a goldsmith, Mr Worth Mr Smith'. (*Crosfield's Diary*, p. 72.)

1635, Nov. 3—Joseph Moore presented at Norwich a licence authorizing 'Andrew Kayne Elis Worth & others' to play at the Salisbury Court theatre and elsewhere. (Murray, ii. 358.)

1635, Dec. 10—'Andrew Kayne' was named with Moore and Worth in a warrant for seven plays presented at Whitehall and Hampton Court by Prince Charles's men. (*M.S.C.* ii. 377.)

1637—Cane's reputation seems to be compared with Timothy Reade's (they are later associated in *The Stage-Players Complaint*) in the poem by 'D. E.' prefixed to Thomas Heywood's *Pleasant Dialogues and Drammas*, published in 1637.

> Who can deny but Poets take their birth
> From some thing that's more excellent than earth ?.
> Since those harmonious strains that fill our eares,
> Proclaime their neere allyance with the Spheares,
> And shewes their Art all Arts as farre exceed
> As doth the fiery-Cane, the weakest Reed.

1639, Sept. 29—Objections were raised concerning the libellous words spoken by 'Cain' in *The Whore New Vamped*, produced by the Prince's men at the Red Bull. The King ordered actor, poet, and licensor punished. (See pp. 314–15; *M.S.C.* i. 394–5; *C.S.P.*, *Dom.*, 1639, pp. 529–30.)

1639, Oct. 21—'Ezechiell Heath, a boy from Andrew Keynes' bur. St. J.C.

1639, Nov. 9—'Henrye Dutton, servant to Andrew Keyne' bur. St. J.C.

1639, Nov. 29—'Andrew Streete, servant to Andrew Keyne' bur. St. J.C.

1639, Dec. 3—'Thomas Johnson, servant to Andrew Keyne' bur. St. J.C.

1639/40, Jan. 4—'Marye d of Andrew Keyne' bur. St. J.C.

1640, May 4—'Andrew Kayne' and Joseph Moore were payees for Prince Charles's for three plays presented at Richmond. (*M.S.C.* ii. 394.)

1640/1, Jan. 21—'Richard Swallow, servt to Andrew Kayne, Player' bur. St. G.C.

1641, autumn—The *Stage-Players Complaint* was published, with the sub-title, *In A Pleasant Dialogue between Cane of the Fortune and Reed of the Friers*. The dialogue between the two famous comedians concerns theatrical and political affairs.

1642, Dec. 12—'While the Lord Mayor and the Court of Common Council were sitting at Guildhall on 12 December, 1642, the populace, intent on obtaining a hearing for their petitions, surged in and made a riot: "some Proctors, some Tapsters, some Players, witnesse Cain the Clown at the Bull, and others came in great multitude, and filled the Hall and Yard."' (Hotson, p. 7, from *An Exact and True Relation*, B.M., E. 130.15.)

1644, June 17–24—'*Mercurius Britanicus* . . . gives us a further trace of him two years after this riot, in a curious reference to him as engraver, at Oxford, of the dies for the debased coinage of the Royalist Army:

> I could wish that the Coine for his Majesties souldiers might not come too fast that way to this City, which is graved in the West, by the *quondam* foole of the Red Bull, now stampt for a knave in brasse, I mean farthing tokens, made now in the West. . . . The losse the Subject sustaines by Farthings is so great that it deserves a redresse.

That Cane is here meant is clear from the fact that he was a goldsmith by trade.' (Ibid.)

c. 1644—In the suit of 'And. deCaine v. Wm. Wintershall and wife Margaret' the Wintershalls say that they have had to delay their action against Cane 'by reason of the death and insolvency of the said obligors and the absence of the said complainant, who being at Oxford in the late king's army could not be proceeded against'. (Ibid., p. 53.)

1648—'Indeed we need not any more *Stage-plays*, we thanke them for suppressing them, they save us money; for Ile undertake we can laugh as heartily at *Foxley*, *Peters*, and others of their godly Ministers as ever we did at *Cane* at the *Red Bull*, *Tom: Pollard* in the humorous Lieutenant, *Robins* the Changeling, or any humorist of them all.' (Ibid., p. 37, from *A Key to the Cabinet of the Parliament*.)

1649/50, Jan. 22–9—'But your own Play-houses at *Westminster*, *Whitehall*, *Darby-house*, *Somerset-house*, &c. are the only Stages where Players must come, and who those players must be, I'le tell you; all in Parliament Robes K——s F——s and Rebels; those are the men now in request: *Andr. Cane* is out of date & all other his complices: alas poor players they are acting their parts in prison, for their presumptions to break a Parliament Crack. On Tuesday *Janu.* 21 1649. bee it known unto all men, the State *Janizaries* rob'd the Play-house in *St Johns streete*, imprisoned the Players, and listed all the Lords, Ladies and Gentlewomen, who are either to serve the States or pay money, if their mightynesse please to command it for so great a contempt as breaking an Act made upon the Stage at *Westminster*.' (Ibid., p. 46, from *Mercurius Pragmaticus [for King Charls II]*.)

1652, Dec. 9—He signed the petition of goldsmiths to Parliament as 'Andrew Decayne'. (Ibid., p. 7.)

1654—*Pleasant Notes upon Don Quixot* refers to him as a stage favourite. (See p. 691.)

1673—In Henry Chapman's *The City of Bath Described* is 'THE APPENDIX, Without which a Pamphlet now a dayes, finds as as (*sic*) small acceptance as a Comedy did formerly, at the *Fortune* Play-house, without a Jig of *Andrew Kein's* into the bargain'. (1673 4° B.M.)

CAPON, JOHN. A well-known comedian during the Commonwealth (see Rollins, 'Commonwealth Drama', pp. 306–7). Though I have found no records of him before the wars, he may well have got his training before the theatres were closed.

CARPENTER, WILLIAM. Carpenter first appears as a Lady Elizabeth's man in 1611, but in our period he is known only as a Prince Charles's (I) man. The St. Giles' entries in 1617 and 1618 indicate that the player was called gentleman in those registers, but they do not necessarily prove that *all* the William Carpenter entries refer to the player. Probably the Marshalsea porter was another man.

1617, Sept. 30—'Robert, sonne of William Carpenter, Player' chris. St. G.C.

1618. Apr. 14—'Robert Sonne of William Carpenter gent' bur. St. G.C.

1618/19, Jan. or Feb.—'*Time*. W. Carpenter' in Middleton's *Inner*

Temple Mask or Mask of Heroes, in which five Prince Charles's men had parts. (1619 4° B.M.)

1619, Sept. 8—'William sonne of William Carpenter gent.' chris. St. G.C.

1620/1, Feb. 25—'Elizabeth daughter of William Carpenter gent' chris. St. G.C.

1621, Nov. 8—'Elizabeth daghter of William Carpenter, gentle' bur. St. G.C.

1623, May 21—'William Carpenter porter at the Marshallsey', 5s., in Markham's suit. (See p. 682.)

1624/5—He was named, apparently as a Red Bull actor, in information laid before the Star Chamber in the *Keep the Widow Waking* suit, but he is not referred to again in the suit. Mr. Sisson says, 'It is evident that these two [Carpenter and Worth] were selected to answer for the company.' (See above, pp. 208–9, and Sisson, *Keep the Widow Waking*, pp. 235–6.)

1625, >May 5—He was fourth in the list of eight Prince's men who received livery for James's funeral: 'William Carpenter—iiij yards.' (See above, p. 209, and M.S.C. ii. 326.)

1625, Sept. 9—'William Carpenter' bur. St. J.C.

1637, July 26—Buried 'Anne wife of Wm: Carpenter, gent' St. G.C.

1644, Nov. 29—'ffrancesse dau: of Wm Carpenter Gent' chris. St. G.C.

CARR, JOHN. Known only as a provincial player. The name is not sufficiently distinctive for identification with the man committed in 1636, though the offence might well be that of a player.

1631, Sept. 23—He was payee with Robert Knipton for the 'players of the Revells' at Coventry. (Murray, ii. 251.)

1636, Oct. 3—A John Carre of St. John's street was committed for helping to bury Samuel Underhill, trumpeter, a plague victim, with illegal splendour. (*See* George Bosgrave.)

CARTWRIGHT, WILLIAM, Senior. There were two William Cartwrights who were actors, father and son, and it is often impossible to distinguish between them with certainty. The father had been on the stage for at least eighteen years before the death of Shakespeare, appearing as an Admiral's–Prince Henry's–Palsgrave's man. The frequency with which he appears in Alleyn's Diary in 1618–22 indicates that he was of some importance in the negotiations between Edward Alleyn and the men of the Palsgrave's company in those years, and his signature of the bond of six members of the company to Richard Gunnell in 1624 shows that Gunnell also thought him of importance in the organization. His activities in the next few years are obscure, but he appears to have been a member of the King and Queen of Bohemia's company (see above, pp. 260–9) and later of the Red Bull–King's company and the King's Revels troupe. The group of players with which he appears at Norwich is obscure. Part of them are surely Revels men, but whether Cartwright belonged to the Revels group or the other, one cannot tell. When *Messalina* was performed, he was undoubtedly a Revels player, and this is his last appearance in a dramatic record.

Some of the petitions to the Lord Chamberlain may well refer to William Cartwright Junior, and some to still a third William Cartwright. I have simply noted them all.

The William Cartwrights in the parish registers are almost as confusing as those in the L.C. papers. Since Markham's suit seems to indicate that the elder actor lived in the parish of St. Giles' Cripplegate in 1623, when his son was about sixteen, and since Miss Boswell (Boswell, 'Cartwright', pp. 123–42) seems confident that the Cartwright at St. Giles in the Fields is the Restoration actor, I have given all the Cripplegate entries to the father, though it does not seem quite right that he should have married four wives after he was at least fifty-five. The registers of St. Giles' Cripplegate are said (*Londinium Redivivum*, iii. 304) to contain the record of the burial of William Cartwright the Fortune player in the year 1650, but I failed to find it, though I made a second search covering the period from December 1649 to March 1651.

There are three portraits of William Cartwright, actor, in the gallery at Dulwich which have caused some confusion, but Miss Boswell (op. cit.) says that two portray the Restoration actor, donor of the pictures, and that the one entitled 'Oul Mr. Cartwright' is the Palsgrave's man.

1617/18, Mar. 22—Dined with Alleyn (*see* Gunnell).

1618, Oct. 31—He is seventh in the list of Palsgrave's men who signed the lease of the Fortune from Edward Alleyn. (See pp. 138–9.)

1619, Aug. 22—'Ther dind w^t vs . . . m^r Cartwright'. (Alleyn's Diary, Young, ii. 148.)

1620, Apr. 9—Dined with Edward Alleyn with three other Palsgrave's men. (See p. 140.)

1621, Apr. 15—With four other Palsgrave's men, dined with Alleyn. (See p. 140.)

1621, June 19—'Jane wife of William Cartwright, yeoman' bur. St. G.C.

1622, Aug. 18—With five others, dined with Alleyn. (See p. 142.)

1623, May 21—'William Cartwrighte att the vpper end of white Crosse Streete', 6s. in Markham's suit. (See p. 682.)

1624, Apr. 30—He and Cane, Massey, Stratford, Price, and Fowler signed a bond with Richard Gunnell to continue to play together at the Fortune. (See pp. 148–9.)

1627, May 23—A Thomas Saul petitioned the Lord Chamberlain for a £50 debt against William Cartwright, Gunnell, Price, and Fowler. (*M.S.C.* ii. 401.)

1629—Professor Adams thinks that he was one of the original organization of the King's Revels for the new Salisbury Court. (Adams, p. 374.)

1629/30, Feb. 16—'A petition of Roger Dowdeswell, William Cartwright and Alice Rayer vid against Thomas Cole. . . .' The petition was repeated 9 February 1630/1. (*M.S.C.* ii. 402, 404.)

1631, Oct. 18—'A petition of Iohn Atkins against Richard Gunnell William Cartwright Richard Fowler & Mathew Smith.' The petition was repeated 28 November 1631 and 'Answered (vizt) If Richard Gunnell &c doe not giue the pet^r satisfaccõn heerin before the expiration of one moneth after the sight heerof, The pet^r may take the ordinary course of Law for his reliefe'. (*M.S.C.* ii. 406.)

1632/3, Jan. 22—'A petition of Isaak Harsenett against Wm Cartwright.' (Ibid., p. 409.)

1633, Apr. 11—'A petition of Iohn Ayloffe against Wm Cartwright.' (Ibid., p. 409.)

1633, May 10—'A petition of Isaak Hasnett agst Wm Cartwright Answered wth leaue graunted vpon sight.' (Ibid., p. 410.)

1633, Oct. 11—'A petition of William Stoner against Wm Cartwright debt xx^{li} Answered wth leaue graunted after one weeke after sight.' (Ibid.)

1634, July 18—Kendall told Crosfield that among the London players were '4. The Fortune in Golden Lane, ye cheife Mr Wm Cartwright, Edward Armestead, John Buckle, John Kirke'. (*Crosfield's Diary,* p. 72; see 688.)

c. 1634?—'*Claudius* Emperour—*Will. Cartwright* Sen.' in the King's Revels cast given in Richards's *Messalina.* (1640 ed. B.M.)

1634/5, Feb. 21—'A peticõn of Thomas Style agst Wm Cartwright debt 13^{li} Answered wth leaue after one weeke after sight.' (*M.S.C.* ii. 411.)

1634/5, Mar. 10—His name is in the full list of players recorded at Norwich. Some of them seem to be King's Revels men, though the records do not give the name of the company, which was probably an amalgamation. (Murray, ii. 356.)

1636, May 12—'Received of ould Cartwright for allowing the [Fortune] company to add scenes to an ould play, and to give it out for a new one, . . . £1. o. o.' (*Herbert,* p. 37.) The word Fortune was added by Malone, probably because he thought Cartwright was of that company.

1636, June 10—'A peticõn of William Cartwright agst Edward Houghton for Assaultes. Answered wth leaue granted after one weeke after sight.' (*M.S.C.* ii. 411.)

1636/7, Jan. 31—'William Cartwright and Tomazine Kendall' mar. St. G.C.

1637, Apr. 17—'A peticõn of William Cartwright against Ewin Birch; Answered wth leaue graunted after one weeke after sight.' (*M.S.C.* ii. 412.)

1637, July 6—'Tomazine, wife of William Cartwright, Playe^r' bur. St. G.C.

1637, July 25—'Wm: Cartwright and Ellen Collins' mar. St. G.C. 'Licent' in margin.

1642, May 12—'Katherine wife of Wm Cartwright Player' buried St. G.C.

1650/1, Mar. 14—'Ann Wife of Willi Cartwright player' bur. St. G.C.

CARTWRIGHT, WILLIAM, Junior. Young Cartwright's career has been most fully studied by Miss Eleanore Boswell (*M.L.R.* xxiv: 125–42). If, as she has pointed out, he was born in 1606 or 1607, he must have had theatrical experience before his first recorded appearance as an actor, in 1634/5. It is not unlikely that he had been a boy actor with his father at the Fortune. Like his father, he cannot certainly be assigned to the Revels company from the Norwich record. Since Wright associates him with the Salisbury Court, he must have belonged to Queen Henrietta's company in the last years before the closing of the theatres.

In addition to his surreptitious acting during the Commonwealth, Cartwright must have been a bookseller, for Aubrey says (*Surrey*, v. 356) that the donor of the collection of plays at Dulwich was 'Mr. *Cartwright*, a Bookseller, who lived at the End of *Turn-Stile Alley*. . . . This *Cartwright* was an Excellent Player, and besides his Plays gave many Pictures'. His only known book is *The Actor's Vindication*, in the dedication of which W. C. speaks of 'our Qualitie'.

Miss Boswell says that two pictures at Dulwich, 'Young Mr Cartwright Actour' and the young man 'in a black dress with a great doge', portray the Restoration actor.

It is not unlikely that some of the petitions to the Lord Chamberlain listed under William Cartwright, senior, refer to his son.

1606–7—He was born about this time, for he was in his eightieth year 17 December 1686. (Boswell, 'Cartwright', p. 133.)

1633, May 1—He married Elisabeth Cooke at St. Giles in the Fields (Ibid., p. 127.)

1634/5, Mar. 10—His name is in the full list of players at Norwich; some of them seem to be King's Revels men, though the records do not give the name of the company, which was probably an amalgamation. (Murray, ii. 356; see above, pp. 286 and 288–9.)

1636, Apr. 28—He married Andria Robins. (Boswell, 'Cartwright', p. 127.)

>1642—Wright says that before the wars Cartwright and Wintershall 'belong'd to the private House in *Salisbury-Court*'. (See p. 692.)

1648—He was one of a group of actors who performed by stealth at the Cockpit. (Boswell, 'Cartwright', p. 130.)

1652, May 12—His wife Andria was buried St. G.F. (Ibid., p. 127.)

1654, Nov. 19—'William Cartwright, of St. Giles in the Fields, and Jane Hodgson, of our parish' mar. St. J.C. (Ibid., p. 128.)

CARVER, WILLIAM.

1624, Dec. 27—Sir Henry Herbert exempted him from arrest as an attendant of King's. (*Herbert*, p. 74; see above, pp. 15–16.)

CASTLE, THOMAS. His name is included here because he has not appeared in an actor list before, though he may not have been an actor after the death of Shakespeare. His parish would suggest that he was a hired man at the Fortune.

1608, Oct. 9—'Nicholas sonne of Thomas Castle, Player' chris. St. G.C.

1610, Apr. 15—'Hester daughter of Thomas Castle, Player' chris. St. G.C.

CASSE, ROBERT.

1650, Nov. 10—'Robert Casse' is one of four members mentioned in a letter from Emperor Ferdinand III requesting safe conduct for a company of English comedians in Germany. (Cohn, *Sh. in Ger.*, p. *c.*)

CAUE, ANDREW (*see* CANE, ANDREW).

CHAMBERS, WILLIAM. A minor attendant of King's. The 1629 death item seems the more likely.

1624, Dec. 27—Sir Henry Herbert exempted him from arrest as an attendant of King's. (*Herbert*, p. 74; see pp. 15–16.)
1629, Nov. 30—'William Chambers' bur. St. Anne's Blackfriars.
1642/3, Mar. 2—'William Chambers' bur. St. G.F.

CHATTERTON, —. Probably he was only a fencer, but he may have been, like Ned Gibbs (q.v.), a player as well.

1664—One of several gentlemen talking of old times before the war says, 'You talk of your Players, I am for the Fencers, there are none living now like old *Bradshaw*, old *Batty*, *Chatterton* and *Ned Gibs.*' ([Tatham,] *Knavery in All Trades*, E₁, 1664 4° HN.)

CHERRINGTON, WILL. He appears only in the mysterious cast for Jordan's *Money is an Asse*, which Jordan said in 1668 was written and acted when he was not yet full fifteen years old (*R.E.S.* i. 219). The prologue says, 'We never had more Tutor, then the Poet,' implies that the actors are all children, says they have had no setters-on but their own resolution, and that there are only eight of them. Five of the eight actors appeared in the long list of actors given at Norwich in 1634/5, suggesting that they may have been boys of the King's Revels company.

c. 1635?—'Feminia *Wil. Cherrington*' is in the cast for Thomas Jordan's *Money is an Asse* printed in the 1668 4°. (1668 4° B.M.)

CLARK (CLARKE, CLEARKE, CLERKE), HUGH. Clark must have had dramatic training before his first appearance in *The Wedding*, for he had the female lead in that play, as he did in *The Fair Maid of the West*. Before 1634 he was taking adult roles and had become, according to Kendall, one of the leaders of Queen Henrietta's company. The date of his transfer to the King's company was probably, as Baldwin suggests (*Organization and Personnel*, p. 64), late in 1636 or early in 1637, for the Queen's old company broke at this time. The marriage date seems a little early for the Gratiana of *The Wedding*, but it is not impossible.

1626—'*Gratiana*, Sir *Iohns* Daughter. *Hugh Clarke*' in the Queen Henrietta's cast for Shirley's *The Wedding*. (1629 4° HN.)
1627, May 6—'Hugh Clark and Judith Brown alias Robins' mar. St. G.F.
c. 1630—'Besse Bridges, *The fair Maid of the west*; by Hugh Clark' in the cast of Queen Henrietta's men printed in the 1631 quarto of Heywood's *The Fair Maid of the West*, Part I. Since the role is

assigned to no one in the cast prefixed to the second part, Clark probably played it there as well. (1631 4° B.M.)

> 1634—'*Hubert*, M. [Mr.] *Clarke*' in cast for Davenport's *King John and Matilda*, presented by Queen Henrietta's men at the Cockpit. (1655 4° B.M.)

1634, July 18—He was probably the 'Clarke' who Kendall told Crosfield was one of the chief of Queen Henrietta's company. (*Crosfield's Diary*, p. 72.)

1635—'Nuntius. By Hugh Clerke.' and 'Syphax. By Hugh Clerke.' in Nabbes's *Hannibal and Scipio*, given by Queen Henrietta's men 'at their Private house in Drury Lane'. (1637 4° B.M.)

1638, Nov. 27 ?—The second prologue printed after *The Custom of the Country* in the 1647 folio is prefixed by the words '*For my Sonne Clarke*'. (1647 folio B.M.)

1640/1, Jan. 22—'Hugh Clarke' is fourth in the list of six men named in the warrant for swearing 'each of them A Groome of his Ma^tes Chamber in Ordinary without ffee to attend his Ma^tye in the Quality of Players and to bee of the Company of his Ma^ts servants at ye Blackfryers'. (*M.S.C.* ii. 397.)

1647—'Hugh Clearke' stands fourth in the list of ten King's men who signed the dedication of the Beaumont and Fletcher folio. (1647 folio B.M.)

1647/8, Jan. 28—He was one of seven King's men who entered into a bond for the payment of an old company debt. (*See* Theophilus Bird.)

1653, Oct. 7—'Hugh Clarke' bur. St. J.C.

CLARK, SILL. The 'Princes Servants' who are referred to on the title-page of Day's play might be Prince Henry's, Prince Charles's (I), or Prince Charles's (II). It is, consequently, difficult to date the stage direction which mentions Sill Clark. The date of publication of the play makes a little more likely the conjecture that Prince Charles's (II) is the company referred to, rather than the others.

1659—The 1659 4° of Day's *The Blind Beggar of Bednall-Green* contains at Act IV (H₄ᵛ) the following stage direction: '*Enter old* Playnsey, *old* Strowd, *and Captain* Westford, Sill. *Clark.*'

CLARKE, ROBERT. Probably a hired man of the King's company. St. Anne's Blackfriars is a likely residence for him.

1617, Nov. 7—'Ezekiell sonne of Robert Clarke, Player' bur. St. G.C.
1624, Dec. 27—Herbert exempted him from arrest as an attendant of the King's company. (*Herbert*, p. 74; see above, pp. 15–16.)
1629, July 30—'Eliz. wife to Robert Cleark' bur. St. Anne's Blackfriars.

CLAY (CLEY), HENRY. Another functionary of the extensive King's company.

1620, Nov. 8—'John sonne of Henry Cley gentleman' chris. St. G.C.
1624, Dec. 27—Herbert exempted 'Henry Clay' from arrest as an attendant of the King's company. (*Herbert*, p. 74; see above, pp. 15–16.)

1626, Aug. 27—'Susanna Da: of Henry Cley Player' chris. St. G.C. (Collier [Bod.] has misread this name as Oley.)

CLAY, NATHANIEL. A provincial player.

1618, Apr.—'Nath. Clay' is named in a 'Letter of Assistance' as one of the leaders of the 'Children of Her Majesty's Royal Chamber of Bristol'. (*C.S.P., Dom.*, 1611–18, p. 549.)

1630, Nov 12—'Nathaniell Clay' is one of the names in a licence from the Master of the Revels dated 30 December 1629 which was shown at Reading the following November. The group was probably a provincial King's Revels company; see Kempston. (Murray, ii. 386.)

CLAYTON, RICHARD. If Clayton was an actor at the Fortune in 1623, as the court messenger reported, he must have been connected with the Palsgrave's company, who then occupied the theatre. Probably he was a hired man, since he is mentioned in none of the records of the troupe.

1623, May 21—In Gervase Markham's suit among the 'Thirty-nine Defendants, chiefly Actors' is 'Richard Claytone in Goulding Lane'. (See p. 682.)

1623/4, Jan. 29—In the course of Markham's suit the court messenger reported that he had warned Clayton and three others, 'all Actors at the fortune'. (See p. 683.)

1634, Apr. 7—'Richard Clayton, Player' bur. St. G.C.

CLUN, WALTER. If Wright is to be trusted, Clun must have been apprenticed to one of the King's men before the closing of the theatres. His absence from contemporary records is no evidence against Wright, since boys were not often named. For his career after the Restoration, see Hotson and Nungezer.

> 1642—Wright says that '*Hart* and *Clun*, were bred up Boys at the *Blackfriers*; and Acted Womens Parts'. (*Hist. Hist.*, p. 3; see p. 692.)

COBORNE, EDWARD (*see* COLBORNE, EDWARD).

COLBORNE, EDWARD.[1] The player of the St. Giles' registers is probably the same as the Edward Colbrand who appeared as a Prince Henry's man in 1610 and 1612 and in the new patent of the company granted to them as the Palsgrave's servants in January 1612/13. The names of the children indicate that the player, yeoman, and gentleman were probably, but not certainly, the same man.

1610/11, Mar. 24—'Margaret dau of Edward Colburne, Player' chris. St. G.C.

1613, June 3—'Elizabeth daughter of Edward Cobern player' chris. St. G.C.

---

[1] Of the thirteen entries at St. Giles, nine are spelled Coborn and four Colborne. I think the name was probably Colborne, pronounced like Holborn.

1614, June 19—' Edward sonne of Edward Coborn yoeman ' chris. St. G.C.

1616, Nov. 23—' John sonne of Edward Coborne, Player' chris. St. G.C.

1621, Dec. 17—' Elizabeth daughter of Edward Coborne yoeman' chris. St. G.C.

1624, Aug. 30—' Bartholomew, sonne of Edward Coborne, gentlema[n]' chris. St. G.C.

1625, July 6—' Martha dau of Edward Coleborne, gent' bur. St. G.C.

1625, July 11—' Edward sonne of Edward Coborne, gent' bur. St. G.C.

1625, July 17—' Eliz wyfe of Edward Colborne, gent' bur. St. G.C.

1625, July 19—' Alice s^r to Edward Coborne, gent' bur. St. G.C.

1625, July 20—' Margaret dau of Edward Coborne gent' bur. St. G.C.

1625, July 21—' John sonne of Edw Coborne, gent' bur. St. G.C.

COLLEWELL, RICHARD. A provincial player who would probably never have been known had his company not got into difficulties with the local authorities at Banbury and eventually been sent on to London to be examined upon suspicion of forgery.

1633, May 2—' Examination of Richard Collewell. Has been of this company two years past, and is servant to Edward Whiting. They lay at Leicester five weeks and played there, and from thence went to the next town and played there. At Coventry they had a reward, but played not. Played at Solihull, Monday, Tuesday, and Wednesday this last week. Were at Keinton and played stage plays Monday, Tuesday, and Wednesday last. His master went from Keinton on Saturday last towards London.' (C.S.P., Dom., 1633-4, p. 49.)

1633, May 3—' Further examination of the same. The commission under the privy seal was bought by his master, Bradshaw, of Edward Whiting of Nottingham.' (Ibid.)

1633, May 22—He was fetched with others of the company of Richard Bradshaw to London at the Order of the Privy Council from the jail at Banbury where he had been imprisoned for playing with a forged licence. The players were accused of giving false names, so Collewell may be merely an alias. (M.S.C. i. 384–5.)

1633, June 3—The company appeared in London before the Privy Council. (Ibid., p. 385.)

1633, June 8—Discharged upon bond. (Ibid.)

COLLINS, EDWARD.

1636/7, Jan. 12—His name was ninth in a list of eleven attendants ' imployed by his Ma^{tes} servantes the Players of the Blackfryers' who were granted tickets of privilege. (M.S.C. ii. 380.)

COLLINS, JEFFREY.

1624, Dec. 27—His name was sixth in a list of twenty-one attendants of the King's players who were exempted from arrest. (Herbert, p. 74; see above, pp. 15–16.)

CONDELL, ELIZABETH. As the wife of one of the managers of the King's company, she inherited some of his theatrical property.

1627, Dec. 13—She was made executrix and chief beneficiary in the will of her husband, Henry. (See p. 641.)

1635, Sept. 1—She made her will bequeathing theatrical property. (See pp. 638–40.)

1635, Oct. 3—'Mrs Cundell''bur. St. M.A.

1635/6, Feb. 8—Her will was probated. (See p. 640.)

CONDELL, HENRY. Condell first appears as 'Harry' in the cast for *2 Seven Deadly Sins* about 1592, but Mr. Baldwin (*Organization and Personnel*, p. 273) thinks that he had been Heminges's apprentice before 1589, taking the regal feminine roles in Shakespeare's early plays. Interesting as this may be, there is very slight evidence for it.

He appears regularly in the business and dramatic records of the company before the death of Shakespeare. According to Baldwin (ibid., pp. 260 ff., 208 ff.), he played the parts of the dignified young man, Benvolio, Don Pedro, Oliver, Horatio, from 1598 to 1603, and later 'honest' old soldiers, but the only role which we have definitely assigned to him is that of the Cardinal in *The Duchess of Malfi*. After 1619 he appears less frequently in the records of the company, and Mr. Baldwin (ibid., pp. 56 ff.) thinks that he was superannuated in that year and only an honorary member of the company until his death. The evidence for this conclusion is the infrequency of Condell's appearance in the company records of these later years and the rise of George Birche, who appears to have succeeded to his roles; the evidence does not make the conclusion inevitable, but it does suggest it.

Condell and Heminges had been associated for years in the affairs of the parish of St. Mary's Aldermanbury, as well as in the affairs of the company, before they began their more famous collaboration in the editorship of the first folio. Both of them were buried from the parish church, though they were living in other parishes at the time of their deaths. It is most fitting that in 1896 a monument should have been erected to their memory just outside the parish church.

Condell's friendship with his fellows is seen in his legacies in the wills of Phillips, Cooke, Shakespeare, Tooley, and Underwood; and his honesty and business acumen are shown by the fact that he appears as trustee or executor in three of these wills. There is another testimonial to his friendly relations with his fellow actors in the plague pamphlet, *The Runaways Answer to a Rod for Runaways*, 1625, in which a group of unknown actors thanks Condell for his generous entertainment of them at Fulham.

Though never famous as an actor, Condell must have been one of the most familiar and respected members of his profession in Jacobean London.

1615—He was appointed a member of the Wardmote Inquest at St. Mary's Aldermanbury and reappointed in 1616. (Barnard, *New Links*, p. 14.)

1616, Mar. 25—Shakespeare in his will left 26s. 8d. a piece 'to my ffellowes' Heminges, Burbage, and Condell. (Chambers, *Shake-speare*, ii. 170–4.)

1616—He was fourth in the King's cast for *The Mad Lover*. (1679 folio B.M.)

1616–17—No. 2 in the King's cast for *The Queen of Corinth*. (Ibid.)

1616–18—No. 5 in King's cast for *The Knight of Malta*. (1679 folio B.M.) Baldwin thinks he played Gomera (*Organization and Personnel*, p. 208.)

1617, May 23—With William Washbourne, Condell, whose residence is given as St. Mary's Aldermanbury, London, purchased John Savage's moiety of a 300-acre estate in Gloucestershire. (Barnard, *New Links*, pp. 1–2.)

1617—'Harry Condell' is signed to the Marriage and Baptismal Registers of St. Mary's Aldermanbury, both times as Harry. (Probably not his autograph; see Barnard, *New Links*, pp. 14–15.)

1618—He was appointed Constable in St. Mary's Aldermanbury. (Ibid., p. 15.)

1618, Nov. 16—No. 2 in King's cast for *The Loyal Subject*. (1679 folio B.M.) Baldwin thinks he played Boroskie (*Organization and Personnel*, p. 208.)

1619, Mar. 27—No. 3 in patent for King's. (*M.S.C.* i. 280–2.)

1619, May 19—No. 2 in King's list for livery allowance. (*Hist. MSS. Com.*, Report IV, Part I, p. 299.)

1619, Aug. 18—Washbourne and Condell conveyed their Gloucestershire property to Edward Sheldon, of Beoley, Worcester, and Samuel Burton, Archdeacon of Gloucester. (Barnard, *New Links*, pp. 3–4.)

1619—The Parish Minute Book of St. Mary's Aldermanbury says, ' John Hemynges and Henry Condall were appointed feoffees for our parish land.' (Ibid., pp. 15–16.)

1619 ?—No. 1 in King's cast for *The Humorous Lieutenant*. (1679 folio B.M.) Baldwin thinks he played Antigonus (*Organization and Personnel*, p. 208.)

1620, Apr. 20—Heminges and Condell, described as 'of greate lyveinge wealth and power', were sued by John Witter for a one-sixth share of the actors' moiety of the Globe which he alleges had belonged to Augustine Phillips, the first husband of Witter's wife. (Wallace, *Sh. and Lond. Assoc.*, pp. 47–76.)

1620, Nov. 29—The suit of Witter against Heminges and Condell was finally dismissed. (Ibid., p. 76.)

1621, Apr. 7—'Henry Cundale' is in the livery allowance for King's. (*Hist. MSS. Com.*, Report IV, Part I, p. 299.)

1621, June 15, July 3, and Nov. 15—He is among the thirty-one parishioners named in the three deeds made when St. Mary's Aldermanbury purchased a parsonage and advowson. (Barnard, *New Links*, pp. 19–20.)

1621/2, Feb. 7—'A warrant for apprehension of William Thomas sen and Will: Thomas jun at the suite of Henry Condall.' (Murray, ii. 192.)

1623, June 3—He was made executor and joint residuary legatee in the will of Nicholas Tooley, who also left a special legacy for Mrs. Condall. (See pp. 649–51.)

1623—With Heminges he edited the Shakespeare Folio.

1623—No. 8 in the list of King's men in the Shakespeare Folio.

1624—Mr. Barnard says that he appears in parish papers as owner of two houses in St. Mary's Aldermanbury in this year. (Barnard, *New Links*, p. 13, from Pierson C. Carter, *The History of the Church and Parish of St. Mary the Virgin, Aldermanbury*, p. 88.)

1624, Oct. 4—He was made an executor in the will of John Underwood. (See p. 651.)

1623–5—The following lines in recognition of the work of Condell and Heminges are quoted by Sir Israel Gollancz from an early-seventeenth-century commonplace book of the Salusbury family now in the National Library of Wales (*T.L.S.*, 26 January 1922, p. 56):

To my good freandes Mr. John Hemings & Henry Condell.

To

Yow *tha*t joyntly wi*t*h vndaunted paynes
vowtsafed to chawnte to us thease noble straynes
how mutch yo*w* merrytt by it is not sedd
butt yo*w* have pleased *the* lyving loved *the* deadd.
Raysede from *the* woambe of earth a Richer myne
then Curteys Cowlde wi*t*h all his Castelyne
Assotiatts they dydd butt digg for Gowlde
Butt Yow for Treasure mutch moare manifollde.

1625, >May 5—He was second in the list of King's men to receive black cloth for James's funeral procession: 'Henrie Condoll—iiij yards.' (*M.S.C.* ii. 325.)

1625, June 9—He made an indenture of apprenticeship for eight years for his son William to Edward Pate, haberdasher. (Barnard, *New Links*, pp. 37–8.)

1625, June 24—No. 2 in patent for King's. (*M.S.C.* i. 282; see above, pp. 17–18.)

1625, Sept. 10—A group of players addressed *The Runaways Answer to a Rod for Runaways* to him, thanking him for his farewell entertainment at his 'Countrey-house at Fulham'. The dedication is signed B.V., S.O., T.O., A.L., and V.S. I cannot identify the players. (1625 4° B.M.)

1626, Apr. 1—A deed of St. Mary's Aldermanbury names Heminges and Condell, among others, as 'now or late parishioners'. (Barnard, *New Links*, p. 20.)

1627, May 2—Condell replied to a complaint in Chancery brought by Mathew Baldron and his wife, formerly the wife of Thomas Massam. The suit concerns a messuage in the Strand called the Helmet which Condell had inherited at least twenty years before. A few years later Mrs. Condell sold the property for £1,450. (Ibid., pp. 21–3; see below, pp. 638–40.)

1627, Dec. 13—He made his will at Fulham. (See pp. 640–2.)

1627, Dec. 29—'Mr Condall [A pencil X against this entry.—Ed.]' bur. St. M.A.

1629/30, Mar. 4—'Henry Condall [Against this entry is placed a X in pencil.—Ed.]' bur. St. M.A. Evidently the actor's son, baptized 6 May 1610.

1635, Sept. 1—His wife Elizabeth made her will, with references to theatres and players; it was probated 8 February 1635/6. (See pp. 638–40.)

1635, Oct. 3—'Mrs Cundell' bur. St. M.A.

CONDELL, William. William was the errant son of the King's actor. For the wild courses of the apprentice William after his father's death, see the summaries of the suit brought by Mrs. Condell and William against the latter's former master. (Barnard, *New Links*, pp. 37–47.)

1611, May 26—'William s. of Henry Condell' chris. St. M.A.

1625, June 9—In a Chancery suit of May, 1633, Edward Pate and William Bagnall say that in an indenture of 9 June 1625 Henry Condell apprenticed his younger son William, aged fourteen, to Edward Pate, haberdasher, in order that he might learn the trade of a hosier. (Barnard, *New Links*, pp. 37–8.)

1635, Sept. 1—The will of his mother, Elizabeth, speaks of his wild courses and makes her legacies to him conditional. She left a silver porringer to his wife Elizabeth. (See below, pp. 638–40.)

1647/8, Mar. 5—'Judith daughter of William and Elisabeth Condall' chris. St. G.F.

COOCK, William (*see* COOKE, WILLIAM).

COOKE, William. A minor player who was for a time a member of Prince Charles's (II) company. It is doubtful whether the puppeteer and the cozener are the same man as the player, but it may be. A William Cooke was one of the lessees of the White-friars theatre in March 1607/8, but he is not likely to have been an actor in Prince Charles's company twenty-five years later.

1632, Dec. 10—William Crome petitioned against Cooke and five others of 'ye princes Players'. On 21 December the Lord Chamberlain granted permission to sue. (*M.S.C.* ii. 408.)

1633, May 3—William Cooke and Fluellen Morgan leased a licence from Edward Whiting, 'and they two went with it with a puppet play until they had spent all, then they pawned the commission for four shillings'. (*C.S.P., Dom.*, 1633–4, p. 49.)

1635, Dec. 12—He is one of the men named in the 'ffower seuerall Warrantes for the swearing of these 4 persones Groomes of the Chamber in ordinary wthout ffee to attend the Prince his Highnes in ye Quality of Players'. (*M.S.C.* ii. 377.)

1640—'Complaint of Robert Fitzmorris, esquire, that William Cooke with one "Wabes and Dillon", tailors, had by "covine" (?) and practice between them cheated, cosened and made away with a suit of clothes belonging to Fitzmorris, worth £8, which Cooke had sold to a player. Order for Cooke to remain in prison till he gives satisfaction for the same.' (Middlesex Session Books Calendar, 1638–44, p. 89.)

1644, Nov.–1645—He was probably the 'William Coock' in the company of English players at the Hague. (*See* Jeremiah Kite.)

COOLING, John. Known only from his epitaph.

1626—One of the epitaphs in H[enry] P[arrott's] *Cures for the Itch*, 1626, is,   *On* Iohn Cooling, *a Player.*

      Death hath too soon remou'ed from vs *Io. Cooling*
      That was so well belou'd, and liu'd by fooling.   G₃ᵛ.

The epitaph is reprinted as the forty-third in *Wits Recreation*, 1641.

CORDEN, GEORG. Probably only a provincial player.

1639/40, Jan. 9—'p^d given to Georg Corden servaunt to the Earle of Leic, Willm Johnson servaunt to the lord Clifford Georg Sanderson servant to the Lord Goring & 13 more assistants players who had the Kings patent to play' at Coventry. (Murray, ii. 254.)

COSTINE, JOHN. Another provincial player. He may possibly be the same as the William Costine who was paid with two others for showing an Italian motion at Coventry in 1632–3 (Murray, ii. 252).

1636, July 3—'to Jon Costine a player wth 10 in his compeny to avide the Towne & not to playe, these Dangeuse tymes' at Manchester. (Murray, ii. 331.)

COTTON, JOHN. A theatrical speculator whose project failed.

1620—With John Williams (q.v.) and Thomas Dixon, he received permission to build an amphitheatre for shows and sports, but the permission was withdrawn 29 September 1620. (C. S. P., Dom., 1619–23, p. 181; Adams, pp. 412–14.)

COWLEY, RICHARD. Cowley's career was nearly over by the time of the death of Shakespeare, but he had been associated with the company for more than twenty years, perhaps first as an apprentice to the comedian William Kemp, to whose Dogberry he is known to have played Verges. Mr. Baldwin assigns him secondary comic parts—Gobbo, Silence, Aguecheek, William—and thinks that he succeeded to Bryan's membership in the company about 1597 (Organization and Personnel, pp. 254–5, 257, 399, 430).

1616, Sept. 28—'Elizabeth Cowley, wife of Richard Cowley, 28th September, 1616, Holywell Street', bur. St. Leonard's Shoreditch. (Stopes, Burbage, p. 140.)
1617/18, Jan. 13—Made his will; Cuthbert Burbage, Heminges, Shank, and Ravenscroft witnessed it. (See below, p. 642.)
1618/19, Jan. 28—His daughter Elizabeth married George Birche. (See Birche and p. 642.)
1618/19, Mar. 12—'Richard Cowley, Player, 12th March, 1618, Halliwell Street', bur. St. Leonard's Shoreditch. (Stopes, Burbage, p. 140.)
1623—'Richard Cowly' was tenth in the list of actors in the Shakespeare Folio.

COX, ROBERT. The fame of this actor did not develop until after the closing of the theatres, but he appeared on the stage before that time. Professor Rollins thinks that he was the Robert Cox admitted to the Merchant Taylors' School in 1618 and born in 1604 (Stud. Phil. xx. 60). The man living in St. Giles' Cripplegate in the thirties may have been the player, but the name is too common to make identification certain. He must have had some experience on the stage before he was granted a ticket of privilege as one of the Cockpit company in 1639. For a full discussion of his

Commonwealth career, see Hyder E. Rollins in *Stud. Phil.* xviii. 307 ff., and Elson, *Wits*, passim.

1632, Dec. 9—'Robert sonne of Robert Cox gentle' chris. St. G.C.; bur. 19 December.

1633, Dec. 13—'Andrew son: of Robert Cox, gent' chris. St. G.C.

1636, Sept. 23—'Beatrice daugr of Robert Cox yeoman' chris. St. G.C.; bur. 25 November.

1639, Aug. 10—'Robert Coxe' was sixth in the list of 'ye young Company' of Cockpit players. (*M.S.C.* ii. 390–1.)

1653, June 9—In reporting the arrest of players who were performing at the Red Bull on this date, *Mercurius Democritus* (June 22–9) says that one of them was 'one Mr. *Cox* an *Actor* (a very honest though impoverished man, who is not only as well as others, put by the practice of his Calling, but charged with a poor Wife, and 5 helplesse Infants)'. (Hyder E. Rollins, *T.L.S.*, 3 August 1922.)

1654, Sept. 30—'Katherine d. of Robert Coxe' bur. St. J.C.

1655, Dec. 12—'Robert Coxe, a Player' bur. St. J.C.

1672—Kirkman, in the preface to *The Wits, or Sport upon Sport*, a collection of drolls, says, 'and as meanly as you may think of these Drols, they were then Acted by the best Comedians then and now in being; and I may say, by some that then exceeded all now living, by Name, the incomparable *Robert Cox*, who was not only the principal Actor, but also the Contriver and Author of most of these Farces'. (Hotson, p. 48.)

1698—Langbaine says of him: 'This Author was a celebrated Comedian in King *Charles* the First's time: on the Suppression of the Stage he made several Drolls, and, with his Companions, Acted them by stealth, both in *London* and the Country Towns: He Acted the chief parts himself, and so very naturally, that at *Oxon* he gain'd great Applause.' (Langbaine, p. 28.)

CRANE, RALPH. Crane was a scrivener who made part of his living by transcribing plays for their authors or for gentlemen of literary taste or for the players themselves; in at least one instance for the use of the players in the theatre. Mr. F. P. Wilson, who has investigated Crane's career most thoroughly, says that he was born in London, probably between 1550 and 1560, since he was an old man in 1621. Crane says that his father was a freeman of the Merchant Taylors' company, and Thomas Lodge, who dedicated *Scillaes Metamorphosis* to Crane in 1589, says that he had travelled abroad. Crane was early employed as a household servant to Mrs. Dorothy Osborne, a clerk to Sir Anthony Ashley, and an underwriter in the Privy Seal Office. He says that he had worked chiefly for lawyers. His employment in the playhouse was probably occasional, as is implied in his verses in *The Workes of Mercy*. His hand has been identified in six non-dramatic MSS. and in five dramatic MSS. For a full account of Ralph Crane and the character of his work, see Wilson, 'Crane'.

1619, July–Aug.—He transcribed *Sir John van Olden Barnavelt* for the King's players, and the transcript was used as a prompt copy in the theatre. (Wilson, 'Crane', pp. 203–5, and Frijlinck, *Barna-velt*.)

1621—He published *The Workes of Mercy*, a volume of religious verse with dedications to at least three different patrons: Dorothy Osborne, John, Earl of Bridgewater, and Lewin Munck. He wrote (1621 ed. HN.),

> And some imployment hath my vsefull *Pen*
> Had 'mongst those ciuill, well-deseruing *men*,
> That grace the *Stage* with *honour* and *delight*,
> Of whose true honesties I much could write,
> But will comprise't (as in a Caske of Gold)
> Vnder the *Kingly Seruice* they doe hold.

1622 (?)—Transcribed 'A Song in seuerall parts' by Thomas Middle-ton, which was performed at the feast of the Lord Mayor, Edward Barkham, for aldermen and other guests in the Easter holidays of this year. (Wilson, 'Crane', pp. 197–8.)

1624 (?)—He made two transcripts of *A Game at Chess* (MSS. Malone 25, Bodleian, and Lansdown 690, B.M.). The Malone MS. was evidently prepared for Middleton himself and is dedicated by him to William Hammond. (Wilson, 'Crane', pp. 208–10.)

<1625—*The Workes of Mercy* was republished as *The Pilgrime's New-yeares-Gift*.

1625, Nov. 27—He transcribed Fletcher's *Demetrius and Enanthe* (*The Humorous Lieutenant*) and dedicated the dated MS. to Sir Kenelm Digby. (Greg, *Dram. Doc.*, pp. 359–60.)

1626, Oct. 23—The Bodleian MS. Rawl. poet. 61 is a 186 page tran-script by Crane of five sets of poems and treatises, one of which is dated 23 October 1626. Another is by Crane himself, and a third is 'Londons Lamentable Estate', on the plague of 1625, by 'Ph. M.' Harl. 6930 is partially the same, but has no dedication and no date. (Wilson, 'Crane', pp. 199–200.)

1620–7 (?)—Crane transcribed *The Witch* (MS. Malone 12, Bodleian) for Middleton, who dedicated it to Thomas Holmes. In his dedica-tion Middleton says that the play was long since acted and that he has dragged it from obscurity. (Ibid., p. 208.)

1632, Dec.—He prepared Harl. 3357, which is the same as MS. Rawl. poet. 61, omitting Crane's work and Ph. M.'s and including an Eclogue of Thomas Randolph's. The dedication, to Sir Francis Ashley, brother of Sir Anthony, asks him to consider it ' (for Age, Affliction, Greif and Want tell Me, it will be so) the Vltimum Vale, of Him that hono[rs] your Name'. (Ibid., p. 200.)

CRATE, CHRISTOPHER. It is possible that his acting career did not begin until after the closing of the theatres, but it seems un-likely that any man should have chosen to begin such a profitless profession after 1642. He lived in the Fortune parish.

1649, May 13—'Kathe wife of Christo: Crate player' bur. St. G.C.

CRAWFORD, JAMES. The form of this entry is not the usual one for the payment of provincial players at Coventry. Perhaps Crawford was an amateur.

1617, Dec. 21—'Paid vnto Mr James Crauford for acting a Comedye' at Coventry. (Murray, ii. 247–8.)

CROME, WILLIAM. Sir Henry Herbert's accusation suggests that Crome made a business oi supplying the players with costumes. It is possible, as Miss Boswell suggests (M.S.C. ii. 408), that the William Crome who was suing the Prince's players in 1632 was the same Crome who was involved with their successors at the Salisbury Court in February 1634/5.

1632, Dec. 10—'A petition of William Crome against William Browne Henry Graddell, Iames Sneller, Thomas Bond William Cooke & William Hall ye princes Players answered of course.' (M.S.C. ii. 408.)

1632, Dec. 21—'A petition of William Crome against the Princes Players Answered wth leaue graunted vpon sight.' (Ibid.)

1634/5, Feb. 17—'I committed Cromes, a broker in Longe Lane, the 16 of Februi. 1634, to the Marshalsey, for lending a church-robe with the name of JESUS upon it, to the players in Salisbury Court, to present a Flamen, a priest of the heathens. Upon his petition of submission, and acknowledgment of his faulte, I releasd him, the 17 Februi. 1634.' (Herbert, p. 64.)

CUMBER, JOHN. Cumber's dramatic career was spent in Queen Anne's or derivative companies. John Smith said in his complaint that Beeston, Worth, Perkins, and Cumber were the responsible members of Queen Anne's company from 1612 to 1616 (Wallace, Three Theatres, pp. 32 ff.), and Cumber appears regularly as a defendant in the Baskerviles' attempts to collect their money from the company. He is probably the man who was buried at St. Mary's Aldermanbury, in spite of the spelling of the name, for Markham's suit records that he did live in Aldermanbury in 1623, and the bill written on the day of his burial speaks of him as 'newly deceased'.

Mr. W. J. Lawrence says categorically (T.L.S., 23 March 1922) that The Two Merry Milk Maids, published in 1620 as acted 'by the Companie of the Reuels', was written by John Cumber. The title-page says that the play was written by I. C., but the only other reason I know for suggesting Cumber's authorship is its production by a company of which he was probably a member. This evidence alone seems scarcely adequate to lift Cumber to the status of a dramatist.

1616, June—The Baskervile suit said that he was a member of Queen Anne's at the time of the second settlement in favour of Francis Browne. (Fleay, Stage, pp. 270–97.)

1617, June 3—As a fellow and sharer of Queen Anne's company, he signed the new agreement with the Baskerviles. (Ibid., pp. 285–8.)

1619, >May 13—As a member of Queen Anne's company, he was allowed black cloth to wear in her funeral procession: 'Iohn Cumber —iiij yards.' (M.S.C. ii. 325.)

1619—Worth, Perkins, and Cumber, when sued by John Smith,

declared that the responsibility for the company debt was Beeston's and not theirs, for he had kept the company accounts fraudulently for the last seven or eight years. (Chambers, *E.S.* ii. 238–40; Wallace, *Three Theatres*, p. 36.)

1620, May 22—Mr. W. J. Lawrence thinks that *The Two Merry Milk-maids*, entered in the Stationers' Register this date and published this year as by I. C. and presented before the King by the Company of the Revels, was written by the actor. (*T.L.S.*, 23 March 1922.)

1622, July 8—He was the sixth of seven members of the late Queen Anne's company named in a warrant for licensing the Children of the Revels. (Murray, ii. 193–4; see above, pp. 167–9.)

1622—He was listed in Herbert's office book as among the 'chiefe players at the Red Bull, called the players of the Revells'. (*Herbert*, p. 63.)

1623, May 21—In Markham's suit as 'Iohn Cumber in Alderman-burye', 5s. (See p. 682.)

1623, May 23—With Worth and Blaney he pleaded to be excused from payments to Susan Baskervile, since most of their fellows were 'dead, or departed'. Worth, Cumber, and Blaney were the only original members of the 1617 Queen Anne's company left. (Fleay, *Stage*, 270–9.)

1623, June 16—'John Combe' bur. St. M.A.

1623, June 16—He is referred to in the Answer to the players' Bill as 'John Comber newly deceased'. (Fleay, *Stage*, p. 279.)

CURT or CURTIS (*see also* CURTIS, GREVILLE). The man whose Christian name and nickname appear in the first edition and the MS. of two of the King's men's plays is pretty surely Curtis Greville, but the inadequacy of our knowledge of the hired men of the companies of the time will not allow certainty.

c. 1625–6—The name 'Curtis' occurs in the stage directions of *The Two Noble Kinsmen*, iv. 1, and v. 3. (1634 4° B.M., pp. 64 and 80.)

1631, May 6 (lic.)—According to the stage directions of Massinger's *Believe as You List*, 'Curt:' and 'Curtis' acted the Third Merchant. (Sisson, *B.A.Y.L.*, pp. xxxi ff.)

DABORNE, ROBERT. Before 1616 Daborne was very active as a dramatist and in 1610 was one of the patentees for the Queen's Revels company. So far as is known, he had no connexion with the stage in 1616, and by 1618 he had taken orders, for he published *An Assize Sermon* in that year. In the token books of St. Saviour's Southwark, 'Robert Daborne & ux' are listed in 'Clincke libtye' in 1616, and in 1617 Daborne alone occurs 'By the Clinke'.

DAMPORT, EDWARD (*see* DAVENPORT, EDWARD). He was a member of Richard Bradshaw's provincial company which was arrested at Banbury in May 1633, and eventually sent to the Privy Council because the Banbury authorities had reason to suspect Bradshaw's licence. Damport's depositions give his version of the company's affairs. It is possible that he is the same as the Edward

Davenport (q.v.) who was one of the King and Queen's young company in 1639. See Bartholomew Jones for a fuller version of the Banbury affair. (There is no reason whatever for identifying the Banbury company with the King's Revels, as Fleay does, *Stage*, pp. 330–1.)

1633, May 2—'Examination of Edward Damport. Has gone with this company up and down the country playing stage plays these two years last past. His father promised his master, Edward Whiting, that he should serve him seven years. His old master had the commission under the privy seal which is now in question, before it came to him. His old master, Edward Whiting, liveth in Coventry, and is now in London. They played under this commission lately at Meriden, Solihull, and other places. At Keinton they played twice or thrice, and came from thence this Thursday morning.

'Further examination of the same. His master's name is Richard Bradshaw. Heard that Edward Whiting let the commission to some man that pawned it. He was at Nottingham when his master gave 20s. in earnest for this commission, and was to pay either 10l. or 20l., and gave bond for the money. Whiting made assignment thereof, and the money was to be paid at the year's end. His master had the commission before he bought it, and delivered it up to Whiting, who gave it back to Bradshaw.' (*C.S.P., Dom.*, 1633–4, p. 48.)

1633, May 22—Summoned with Richard Bradshaw's company before the Privy Council because the authorities suspected their licence. They are accused of giving false names. (Murray, ii. 163–7; *M.S.C.* i. 384–5.)

1633, June 3—Appeared before the Privy Council. (*M.S.C.* i. 385.)

1633, June 8—Discharged upon bond. (Ibid.)

DANIEL, JOHN. John Daniel was originally one of Prince Charles's musicians, but in 1615 he became manager of the provincial company, the Youths of her Majesty's Royal Chamber of Bristol, in the place of his brother Samuel (*M.S.C.* i. 279). The history of the provincial companies is so tangled that it is impossible to tell whether Daniel's company was the same in all three of his provincial appearances or not. (For Murray's reading of the evidence, see Murray, ii. 14–15.) There is no assurance that the receiver of stolen plate was the provincial actor.

1615, July 17—At the instigation of the Queen, he was given permission to make up a company of the Youths of her Majesty's Royal Chamber of Bristol, in place of his brother Samuel Daniel. (*M.S.C.* i. 279; *C.S.P., Dom.*, 1611–18, p. 549.)

1616–17—'John Danyell one of the Company of the Quenes Maties Players' was paid at Norwich for forbearing to play. (Murray, ii. 370.)

1619, Sept. 4—He was made executor of the will of his brother Samuel. (*Sh. Soc. Paps.* iv. 156–7.)

1623/4, Mar. 18—'Geven to John Daniell who had a Pattent for the Children of Bristoll' at Leicester. (Murray, ii. 316.)

1625, May 28—Notes of third audience at Whitehall: '... the pardons of Birch and Daniel the buyers of the Duchess of Richmond's stolen plate, but the parties refuse to accept the pardon in hope of the parliament.' (*Hist. MSS. Com.*, Report XII, App. I, 199.)

DANIEL, WILLIAM. A provincial player who led itinerant troupes up and down the country for at least fifteen years. In spite of the Canterbury entry of 1621–2, Daniel probably was never connected with the King's company. Such slips as this are common in provincial records. The protest of 1623 implies that Daniel had been travelling with a fraudulent exemplification of the patent of the Palsgrave's company. In July 1616 the Lord Chamberlain had sent out an order for the confiscation of exemplifications, naming several players and the companies in whose names they travelled, and requiring them to appear before him in London (Murray, ii. 343–4). Again in November 1622 he had ordered the confiscation of fraudulent commissions and licences, and the order had been carried by Gilbert Reason, who delivered the protest against Daniel in 1623 (ibid., pp. 351–2). It was probably in connexion with the Lord Chamberlain's campaign of the previous year that Reason brought the protest in 1623.

The patent of 28 November 1634, which Daniel showed at Norwich, seems regular enough and was apparently issued to him as leader of a provincial King's Revels company. In this capacity he seems to have continued to travel as late as 1636.

1621–2—'To William Daniell the cheife of the Kings Players to ridd them out of the Cittie w^thout actinge xx^s allowed by Burgmoth' at Canterbury. (Murray, ii. 231.)

1623, May 31—'The Company of the players of the ffortune howse in London doe vnder their hands ptest against Willm Danyell who hath iniuriously gotten their Letters Patents.' Appended to a record of the visit of Gilbert Reason and the Prince's players to Norwich. (Ibid., p. 347.)

1634, Nov. 28—'A Patent vnder the hand & seale of Sr Henry Herbert Master of the Revells bearinge date the 28th of November 1634 made to Willm Danyell Willm Hart John Townesend Samuell Minion Hugh Haughton Thomas Doughton and the rest of their Company not exceedinge the number of ffiftene psons to play Comedies &c was this day brought & shewed by the said Willm Daniell', shown at Norwich 3 September 1635. (Ibid., p. 357.)

1634–5—He was payee for an unnamed company at Norwich. (Ibid., p. 372.)

1635, June—'Paid given to William Daniell who brought a comission for the Revels vizt, for himself & 16 more' at Coventry. (Ibid., p. 252.)

1635, Sept. 1—A William Danyell was made a trustee for Sir William Acton in the will of Elizabeth Condell. (See p. 640.)

1635, Sept. 3—He was at Norwich with the license of 28 November 1634. (Murray, ii. 357.)

1636, Apr. 22—'Paid given to Richard Drington [Errington] & William Daniel players of the Revels', at Coventry. (Ibid., p. 252.)

1636–7—'Item payd vnto William Daniell one of the Kings Revells because he should not playe', because of the plague, at Gloucester. (Ibid., p. 285.)

1636, Dec. 5—He was payee for 'the Revells' at Coventry. (Ibid., p. 253.)

DANNER, JOHN. A ghost name raised by Mrs. Stopes's misreading of a Lord Chamberlain's warrant. See John Daunce.

D'AUNAY, JOSIAS (see FLORIDOR, JOSIAS).

DAUNCE, JOHN. As an actor he is known only as a member of the peculiar Lady Elizabeth's company of 1628 (see pp. 188–90). He may, or may not, be the King's messenger and the parishioner of St. Giles.

1629, July 2—In the L.C. Warrant Books is recorded a warrant to 'sweare Iohn Daunce a groome in ordinary'; in the margin is written 'Queene of Bohemia's Players'. (M.S.C. ii. 350.)

1631, Apr. 11—'John Dance & Sara Rositer, L. F.', mar. St. Gregory by St. Paul. (Challen, Marriages.)

1635, June 7—'John Dance & Mary Skooleing', mar. St. G.F.

1640, June 25—'A warrt for the swearing of Iohn Dance one of the Eight Messengers of his Mats Chamber in Ordinary in ye roome of Edward Gomond deceased. Iune 25. 1640.' (Unpublished L.C. Warrant Books, L.C. 5/134, p. 406, P.R.O.)

1640, June 18—'Ann Daughter of John Dance', bur. St. G.F.

1640, Nov. 4—'John Dance' bur. St. G.F.

DAUSSE, ROBERT (see DAWES, ROBERT).

DAVENANT, WILLIAM. Though his first play had been licensed as early as January 1626/7, Davenant is not known to have had a closer connexion with the theatre before 1639, when his project for a large, new theatre is revealed by the patent for its erection. His agreement to forgo the privileges of his patent was probably due to the protests of the housekeepers of other London theatres. He did not, however, give up his interest in theatre management, for after Beeston's removal as Governor of the King and Queen's young company, Davenant was appointed to serve in his place. He did not, however, continue in this capacity until the theatres closed, contrary to the usual statement. In May 1641, less than a year after his appointment, his complicity in the Army plot was discovered, and he fled for France, though he was captured in Kent. Evidently Beeston returned to his old post, for in a Lord Chamberlain's list of 1641 he appears as Governor of the Cockpit players (see p. 335).

1639, Mar. 26—Davenant secured from King Charles a royal patent to erect a large theatre in Fleet Street near the Three Kings Ordinary, 'in the parishes of Saint Dunstan's in the West, London, or in Saint Bride's, London'. (Adams, pp. 424–7.)

1639, Oct. 2—He renounced all the rights of his patent and promised not to build a theatre any place in London or Westminster. (Ibid., pp. 428–30.)

1640, June 27—He was appointed manager of Beeston's Boys (the King and Queen's young company) by the Lord Chamberlain after William Beeston's removal for abuse of privilege. (See pp. 332–5.)

1641, May 6—Davenant fled for France with Jermyn and others involved in the Army plot. (Gardiner, ix. 360.)

DAVENPORT, EDWARD (*see* DAMPORT, EDWARD). One cannot be certain that the Cockpit player, the messenger, and the husband of Rebecca were all the same man. It is possible that the Cockpit player is the same as Edward Damport (q.v.), who was a provincial actor in 1633.

1638/9, Jan. 9—'Edward sonne of Edmond & Rebecca Davenport' chris. St. G.F.

1639, Aug. 10—'Edward Dauenport' was seventh in the list of the young company of Cockpit players. (*M.S.C.* ii. 390–1.)

1640, Oct. 5—'A warr^t to sweare Tho. Dixon A Messenger of the Chamber in ordinary in ye roome of Edmund Dauenport deceased. Octob. 5. 1640.' (Unpublished L.C. Warrant Books, L.C. 5/134, p. 418, P.R.O.)

DAWES, ROBERT. There is only a vague suggestion that Dawes was an actor after the death of Shakespeare. He was a patented member of the Duke of York's company in 1610, and a Lady Elizabeth's man contracted to Henslowe and Mead in 1614. The Revels Office scrap on which his name, if it is his name, appears is most uncertain in date and cannot be associated with any company, though Lady Elizabeth's is a plausible guess.

1614–18 ?—Sir George Buc made a correction in the MS. of his 'A COMMENTARY Vpon the New Roulle of Winchester . . .' (now in the possession of Major G. Halswell, of Wylmington Hayes, Honiton, Devon) upon the back of a scrap from the Revels Office. The Revels Office entry, which has been deleted, reads as follows:

> Cupid's festivall comed
> Intrat in off. Rev
> 18 Deceb p Histr. Dausse Rob

R. C. Bald dates the MS. 1614–18 from references to living members of the families treated, but the discarded Revels Office scrap might have been written before the book was begun, or, if Buc continued to revise his MS., after 1618. (*T.L.S.*, 17 March 1927, p. 193.)

DAY, THOMAS. An actor during the Commonwealth was pretty sure to have had experience before the closing of the theatres, as Cartwright and Baxter, who are coupled with Day in this record, had had.

The player 'by stealth' is not likely to have been the same as the Thomas Day, one of the Children of the Chapel who performed in *Cynthia's Revels* and *The Poetaster* at the beginning of the century, and whose musical development seems to have continued as Musician to Prince Henry, Organist of Westminster Abbey, Master of the Choristers, and Master of the Children of the Chapel Royal. The musician is said to have died in 1654 (Rimbault, *Chapel Royal*, p. 205).

1648—In January 1663/4 a Thomas Day gave evidence in a Chancery suit, apparently as one of a company of actors which in 1648 'did by stealth and in secret places Act together here in England some Playes and Interludes'. (Boswell, 'Cartwright', p. 130.)

DE CAINE, ANDREW (*see* CANE, ANDREW).

DE LAU, HURFRIES (*see* LAW, HURFRIES DE).

DISTLE (DISTLEY, DISHLEY), —. The leader of a troupe of provincial players who first appears in March 1609/10 and then again in October 1612 and March 1612/13. In the 1612 record his company is called 'my Lo: Dudleye his plaeres', and Murray (ii. 42) assumes that his company was always Lord Dudley's, though it is never so called again. Distle's troupe was not improbably a local organization, since four of its six appearances are recorded at Gawthorpe Hall, and it is never recorded farther afield than Leicester.

1616, Nov. 7—'to Distle and his companie' 6s. 8d. was paid at Gawthorpe Hall, Lancs. (Murray, ii. 395.)
1629—'Dishley and his ffellowes' were at Leicester. (Ibid., p. 317.)
1635/6, Feb. 19—'Dishley and his companie' were at Doncaster. (Ibid., p. 257.)

DIXON, THOMAS. A theatrical speculator all of whose known projects failed. There is a reference to the second one in Act II, scene 3, of Marmion's *Holland's Leaguer*.

1620, Sept. 29—The King wrote to the Privy Council to revoke a licence previously granted to John Cotton, John Williams, and Thomas Dixon, to build an amphitheatre 'intended principally for martiall exercises, and extraordinary shewes and solemnyties', with the privilege to close other shows and sports one day a month on fourteen days warning. (*H.E.D.P.* i. 405–8 and 444–5.)
>1626, Aug. 12—Cotton and Williams again applied for permission to build an amphitheatre in Lincoln's Inn Fields, and, according to the Lord Keeper, their intention was to present 'common plaies, or ordinary sports, now used or shewed at the Beare-garden or the common Playhouses about London, for all sorts of beholders, with a restraint to all other plaies and shewes, for one day in the weeke upon two daies warning'. On 28 September 1626 the Lord Keeper recommended that the grant should not be passed. (*H.E.D.P.* i. 442–5.)

DOBSON, JOHN. Known only from the minor comic role which he had in *The Wedding*.

1626—'*Cameleon*, *Rawbones* man. *Iohn Dobson*' in the cast for Shirley's *The Wedding*, given by Queen Henrietta's men. (1629 4º HN.)

DORSET, EDWARD SACKVILLE, EARL OF. There are indications that Dorset's interest in theatres and actors was greater than one would have expected from a noble lord. He probably pushed the warrant for liveries as Lord Chamberlain to the Queen (see below, p. 661, n. 1), and his leasing of his grounds and buildings for the Salisbury Court theatre was evidently part of his attempt to clear his estate, which his brother had left heavily involved, but the activities which Heton mentions do not seem to be those of an official for the Queen or of an embarrassed land-owner. He seems to have taken an unusual interest in the Queen's men and in any occupants of the Salisbury Court theatre. I have listed the facts which might have a bearing on his actions in connexion with the players.

1628, July 16—He was appointed Lord Chamberlain to Queen Henrietta Maria. (*D.N.B.*)

1629, June 19—To the L.C. warrant for liveries for the Queen's company is appended, 'M^d his Ma^{tes} pleasure was signifyed by my Lord of Dorsett'. (*M.S.C.* ii. 350.)

1629, July 6—According to a complaint in Chancery in 1658, Sir Henry Compton, Sir John Sackville, and others in trust for Edward, Earl of Dorset, let to William Blagrave and Richard Gunnell a plot of ground in Salisbury Court for a term of forty-one and one-half years from 24 June 1629. (Hotson, p. 100.)

1629, Oct. 24—Sir George Gresley wrote to Sir Thomas Puckering: 'My Lord of Dorset is become a great husband; for he hath let his house in Salisbury Court unto the queen for the Ambassador Leiger of France, which is daily expected to come over, to lie in, and giveth for it £350 by the year, and for the rest of his stables and outhouses towards the water side, he hath let for £1000 fine and £100 by the year rent, unto the master of the revels, to make a playhouse for the children of the revels.' (Birch, *Charles I*, ii. 35.)

1630—Mary, Countess of Dorset, was appointed governess to Charles, Prince of Wales, and later to James, Duke of York. (*D.N.B.*)

1636, May 10—'His ma^{tie}: being this day p^{r}sent in Councell, & takeing into consideraċon how dangerous it mought be in theise tymes of Infecċon to suffer the vsuall Assemblies and confluence of people at Play houses; Hath thought fitt and ordered that the Lo: Chamblaine of the Queens ma^{ts}: Household, should be hereby prayed & required to cause the Players, that are her ma^{ts}: Servants to forbeare all Stage Playes & other Enterludes whatsoeuer vntill further order./' (*M.S.C.* i. 391.)

c. 1636—Heton wrote in his 'Instructions', 'When her M^{ts} servants were at the Cockpitt, beinge all at liberty, they disperst themselves to severall Companies, soe that had not my lo: of Dorsett taken care to make up a new Company for the Queene, she had not had any at all.' (See Appendix, p. 684.)

>1639—'How much I haue done for the vphoulding of this Company, I gaue you some p'ticulers of in a peticon to my lo: of Dorsett.

'And wheras my lo: of Dorsett had gotten for a former Company at Salisberry Co't the Princes service, they being left at liberty, took their opportunity of another house, and left the house in Salisberry Co^{r}t destitute both of a service and Company.' (Ibid.)

DOUGHTON, THOMAS (see DOWNTON, THOMAS).

DOVER, ANTHONY. As wardrobe keeper he was probably associated with whatever company occupied the Salisbury Court theatre.

1634, July 18—Kendall told Crosfield in regard to the Salisbury Court players, 'other servants there are as 2 Close keepers Richard Kendall Anthony Dover &c.' (Crosfield's Diary, p. 72; see p. 688.)

1634/5, Mar. 10—'Antony Dover' is seventeenth in the list of twenty-seven players at Norwich. Probably two companies, though one is evidently the Revels company (see pp. 286 and 288–9). (Murray, ii. 356.)

DOWLE, ROWLAND. His full name appears only once, in the ticket of privilege for the minor functionaries of the King's company in 1636/7, but he is pretty surely the Rowland or Rowl: referred to so frequently in the stage directions of plays acted by the King's company. No other man to whom the name would apply is to be found in the long lists of King's men of this time, and the roles which he had are just those which would be assigned to a hired man.

Professor Baldwin (Organization and Personnel, p. 88), Professor Murray (Murray, i. 236 n.) and others have thought a speech in The Witch of Edmonton, II. 1, where one of several countrymen is addressed as 'Fellow Rowland', an indication that he acted in the 1621 production and was therefore connected with the Prince's company. I can see no reason why this name should be taken as a book-keeper's insertion and therefore the name of an actor. Prompters did not insert actors' names in the dialogue but in the stage directions (vide the instances below). The omission of the name from the dramatis personae is of no significance; several others are omitted, and Rowland is a good name for a country fellow. In The Coxcomb, on the other hand, the name occurs only in the stage directions, though the editors of the 1679 folio and most subsequent ones have mistaken it for a character's name.

1631, May 6—He was probably the Rowland who had several parts in the King's production of Believe as You List, licensed on this date. He divided the part of Demetrius ('Rowland:') with William Patrick and Francis Balls; he was one of the Carthaginian officers ('Rowland:'); he was one of the attendants on King Prusias ('Rowl:'); he was the Jailor's assistant ('Rowl:'); and he was one of the attendants on Marcellus ('Rowland:' 'Rowl:'). (Sisson, B.A.Y.L., pp. xxxi ff.)

c. 1635—He appears twice in the stage directions of Love's Pilgrimage, probably for the revival which Herbert licensed 16 September 1635 (Herbert, 36): II. 1, 'Enter two Servants, Rowl: Ashton'; and IV. 1, 'Enter a Servant, Rowl: Ashton'. (1647 folio HN.)

1636—It was probably for a revival of 1636 (Herbert, p. 75) that his name was inserted in the stage directions of The Coxcomb, V. 3: 'Enter . . . Andrugio, and his man Rowland.' (Ibid.)

1636/7, Jan. 12—'Rowland Dowle' is seventh in the ticket of privilege granted eleven men 'imployed by his Ma^tes servantes the Players of the Blackfryers'. (*M.S.C.* ii. 380.)

1638—It was probably for the revival of 1638 that his name was inserted in the stage directions of *The Chances*: 'Ent. Rowl. with wine', Act III, scene 2. (1647 folio HN.)

DOWNTON (DOWTONNE, DOUTONE, DOWTEN, DOWGHTON, DOWTON, DENYGTEN, DOUGHTEN, DOUNTON), THOMAS. Downton first appears in the registers of St. Saviour's in 1592, where he is called a musician. Thereafter there are many references to him in the Henslowe and Alleyn papers, the records of the Admiral's men, the registers of St. Saviour's, the records of Prince Henry's company, the registers of St. Giles' Cripplegate, and in the early records of the Palsgrave's company (see Chambers, *E.S.* ii. 313, and Nungezer).

After the death of Shakespeare he probably remained a Palsgrave's man until his marriage to Jane Easton and the vintner's business, for Wilson's letter to Alleyn implies that Downton was a leader of the company in 1617. Following his rise in the world he seems to have remained friendly with Edward Alleyn and the Palsgrave's men, but there is no indication of any further connexion with an acting company. His will, which contains an interesting reference to his library, has no reference to theatrical affairs. The set of acrostic verses on Thomas Dowton, printed from a MS. in the possession of J. F. Herbert (*Sh. Soc. Paps.* i. 19), gives no indication whether they refer to the actor or not.

1617, Oct. 8—'John Daye svant to Thomas Doughten Playe^r' bur. St. G.C.

>1617, Nov. 2—William Wilson refers to Downton and Juby as leaders of the Palsgrave's men. *See* William Wilson.

1617, Nov. 14—'Anne wife of Thomas Doughton Player' bur. St. G.C.

1617/18, Feb. 15—'Thomas Downton of St Giles without Cripplegate, London, gent, and Jane Easton, late wife of Oliver Easton, vintner, were married by licence' at St. Bartholomew the Great. (Bod.)

1618, Oct. 31—He witnessed Alleyn's lease of the Fortune to the Palsgrave's company. (See above, pp. 138–9.)

1619, June 11—'Jane daughter of Thomas Downton Vintener' bur. St. G.C.

1622, Aug. 18—'m^r doughton: m^r gwalter: m^r gunell: m^r garman & wigpitt w. Cartwright m^r (*sic*) [dined here].' (Alleyn's Diary, Young, ii. 247.)

1625, July 28—'Jeffrey Langworthy sh^r to Thomas Downton' bur. St. G.C.

1625, Aug. 5—Thomas Downton, Vintner, of St. Giles' Cripplegate, made his will, making his wife Jane his executrix. He speaks of her estate before marriage. (See below, pp. 642–3.)

DOWNTON (DOUGHTON), THOMAS. The provincial actor, Thomas Doughton, may well have been the son of the Palsgrave's man of the same name whose christening is registered at St. Saviour's 12 July 1601, 'Thomas Dowton s of Thomas a player', and whose father says of him in his will, 'because my sonne hath bine a desperate sonne to me I giue a desperat Legacye'. The career of a provincial player would probably not be an incompatible one for a desperate son.

Professor Murray (Murray, ii. 8–9 and 102–5) thinks that the first company mentioned was a provincial Queen Henrietta's company and the second a provincial King's Revels. He may be right, but the evidence is so slight and so contradictory that nearly all conclusions about the provincial companies are hazardous.

1628, June 7—'Tho: dougton' was named in the new licence of this date granted to Ellis Guest's company by Sir Henry Herbert and presented at Norwich 2 July 1628. (Murray, ii. 353.)

1635, Sept. 3—'Thomas Doughton' is the last of six players named in a licence of 28 November 1634 shown at Norwich on this date. (Ibid., p. 357.)

DREWE, BARTHOLOMEW. Since Bartholomew is completely unknown except for the St. Saviour's entry, there is only a possibility that he may have been the Prince's musician who dined with Alleyn.

1614, Nov. 12—'George Drewe s of Bartholomewe a player' chris. St. S.S.

1620, Apr. 5—'I dined w^t m^r Hewitt & ther wase ye princes musitions m^r ball & m^r drewe.' (Alleyn's Diary, Young, ii. 174.)

DREWE, THOMAS. Drewe was an actor in Queen Anne's company from about 1613 to the break-up of the company in 1619, and he probably stayed on at the Red Bull, if the highway repair order of 1622 is to be taken at its face value. Probably the Prince's musician who dined with Alleyn in 1620 was another Drewe, but not certainly. There is no evidence for or against the identification of the gentleman waiter and the actor.

Mr. W. J. Lawrence has announced that the actor was also a dramatist ('Found: A Missing Jacobean Dramatist', *T.L.S.*, 23 March 1922). This is an interesting possibility, but the evidence for it is very slight. There *was* a dramatist named Thomas Drew or Drue who wrote *The History of the Duchess of Suffolk*, published anonymously in 1631, but licensed to the Palsgrave's company for acting in 1623/4 as by Mr. Drew and by the Stationers' company in 1629 as by Thomas Drue. He probably also wrote the lost *Woman's Mistake* which was entered in the S.R. 9 September 1653 as by T. Drue, and he may be the T. D. who appears as author on the 1639 title-page of *The Bloody Banquet*. Unfortunately, however, there is nothing to connect the actor and the dramatist except the name and the probability that *The Bloody Banquet* was a Red Bull play. The chief evidence against the identification of actor and dramatist is the appearance in 1621 of

Daniel Ben Alexander, the Converted Jew, first written in Syriacke and High Dutch by Himself. Translated . . . into French by S. Lecherpiere. And out of French into English, by Thomas Drewe. This does not sound like the work of an actor, but the translator might have written *The History of the Duchess of Suffolk* and *The Woman's Mistake.* Until more facts about the actor or the dramatist are found we can only say that there is a possibility that they may be the same.

1612/13, Mar. 21—'Elizabeth d. of Tho. Drewe' chris. St. J.C.

1613, Mar. 29—'Elizabeth d. of Thomas Drewe' bur. St. J.C.

c. 1613–14—The Baskervile suit in 1623 names him as a member of Queen Anne's at the time of the original agreement with Susan Baskervile. (*See* Ellis Worth.)

1614, July 10—'Francis s. of Thomas Drew' chris. St. J.C.

1616, June—He was named in the Baskervile suit as a member of Queen Anne's at the time of the second settlement in favour of Francis Browne. (Fleay, *Stage,* 270–97.)

1617, May 18—'Elizabeth d. of Thomas Drewe' chris. St. J.C.

1617, June 3—He signed the new agreement of Queen Anne's with Susan Baskervile. She says he was a fellow and sharer at the time. (Fleay, *Stage,* pp. 285–8.)

1617, June 19—'Francis s. of Thomas Drewe' bur. St. J.C.

1617, Oct. 2—He and five others petitioned the Sessions of the Peace for the Red Bull (Queen Anne's) company. (See *Middx. Co. Rec.* ii. 170.)

1618, Sept. 20—'Robart s. of Thomas Drew' chris. St. J.C.

1619, > May 13—He was the sixteenth member of Queen Anne's company listed to receive black cloth for her funeral procession—'Thomas Drewe—iiij yards'. (*M.S.C.* ii. 325.)

1620, Apr. 5—'I dined wt mr Hewitt & ther wase ye princes musitions mr ball & mr drewe.' (Alleyn's Diary, Young, ii. 174.)

1622, May 5—'Thomas Drewe of this parish and Mary Todd of Endfield in the Countie of Middlesex were married by banes' at St. Bartholomew the Great. (Bod.)

1622, Oct. 3—He was one of six Red Bull actors named in an order for repairing the highway. (See p. 169, n. 2.)

1623/4, Jan. 2—'For the Palsgrave's Company; *The History of the Dutchess of Suffolk*; which being full of dangerous matter was much reformed by me; I had two pounds for my pains: Written by Mr. Drew.' It was entered S.R. 13 November 1629 as by Thomas Drue, but printed anonymously in 1631. (*Herbert,* p. 18.)

1635, Dec. 8—'A warrt to sweare Mr Thomas Drue A Gentleman Wayter to his Maty extraordinary. Dec. 8. 1635.' (*M.S.C.* ii. 376.)

1638, Mar. 26—'Thomas Drewe & Katherine Baldwine' mar. St. J.C.

1653, Sept. 9—Possibly he was the Drew who collaborated with Davenport on *The Woman's Mistake,* entered S.R. on this date.

DRINGTON, RICHARD (*see* ERRINGTON, RICHARD).

DUKE, JOHN. A member of Queen Anne's company who is sometimes said to have acted after the death of Shakespeare because he is named in Norwich accounts of 1616 and 1617

(Murray, ii. 340, 343). Most of the names in both these accounts have simply been copied from licences of 1609 and 1612; they are not evidence of the presence of the actors named. Thomas Greene, who appears in both records, died in 1612. Duke's death is probably recorded in the burial registers of St. James's Clerkenwell, the parish of his company's theatre, 31 May 1613, 'John Duke, householder' (St. J.C.).

DULANDT (DOWLAND?), ROBERT.

1623, Aug. 30—As one of the musicians of the Duke of Wolgast, he petitioned with Richard Jones and Johan Kostressen for permission to return to England. (Meyer, *Shakespeare Jahrbuch*, xxxviii. 209.)

EARLE, JOHN.

1640, Apr. 25—'Iohn Earle' is last in a list of four 'Ticketts of Preueledge for the Princes Players hired men'. (*M.S.C.* ii. 394–5.)

EATON, WILLIAM. Gilbert Reason appeared with a provincial Prince Charles's company from 1612 to 1625, but only once is Eaton found in the records with him, though he may have been one of the unknown members of the troupe for years   Reason disappears in 1625, and it is probable that Eaton transferred to Ellis Guest's company and is the William Eyton whose name was copied from that company's licence at Norwich in 1628.

1622, Dec. 23—'Paid which was given to Gilbert Reason and Mr William Eaton players to the Prince his high' at Coventry. (Murray, ii. 249.)

1628, June 7—'Wm Eyton' was fourth in a list of thirteen in a licence of this date under the hand of Sir Henry Herbert, shown at Norwich 2 July 1628. Ellis Guest was leader of the company, which is not named. (Ibid., p. 353.)

ECCLESTON (EGLESTONE), WILLIAM. Eccleston was in the King's company in 1610 and 1611 when he had parts in Jonson's *Alchemist* and *Catiline*, but several documents of 1611 and 1613 show that he transferred to Lady Elizabeth's company. He was back in the King's company in time to have a part in *Bonduca*, and Mr. Baldwin thinks that he succeeded to the share of Alexander Cooke between March 1613 and March 1614 (*Organization and Personnel*, p. 50). Thereafter he appeared in numerous lists of the company, including the cast for *The Spanish Curate*, which was licensed for performance 24 October 1622. After this date he appears only in the list in the Shakespeare folio and in Nicholas Tooley's will, neither of which is any evidence that he was acting when the record was made. Mr. Baldwin concludes, with reason, that he must have left the company in the spring of 1623, probably on quarter day (ibid., p. 58).

From his analysis of the plays and actors of the King's company, Mr. Baldwin concludes that Eccleston's 'line' was that of 'the sprightly, sometimes petulant, young man, given to the foibles of youth, such as singing and seeking excitement in sword play or in love. A typical manifestation of this sprightly youth is the singing, roistering, usually young soldier, who is an expert swordsman', and he assigns him such roles as Junius in *Bonduca*, Peter in *The Chances*, Duarte in *The Custom of the Country*, Ptolemy in *The False One*, and Raymond in *The Sea Voyage*. Eccleston also played, according to Mr. Baldwin, a number of female roles in Shakespeare's plays when he was an apprentice, but since there is no evidence that he was an apprentice with the King's company, these are scarcely worth noting.

Mr. Baldwin also argues ingeniously, though not plausibly, that 'as a merry old gentleman of some seventy-five years, and in touch with his old fellows' Eccleston made out the actor lists for the second folio of 1679 (*Organization and Personnel*, pp. 391–3). The picture delights the imagination, but there is little to recommend it to the reason.

1616—'William Eglestone' was sixth in King's cast for *The Mad Lover*. (1679 folio B.M.)

1618, Nov. 16—'William Eglestone' was eighth in King's cast for *The Loyal Subject*. (Ibid.)

1619, Mar. 27—'William Ecclestone' was tenth in a licence for the King's company. (*M.S.C.* i. 280–2.)

1619, May 19—'William Eccleston' was ninth in a livery allowance for the King's men. (*Hist. MSS. Com.*, Report IV, Part I, p. 299.)

1619 ?—'William Eglestone' was sixth in King's cast for *The Humorous Lieutenant*. (1679 folio B.M.)

1619 ?—'William Eglestone' was second in King's cast for *The Laws of Candy*. (Ibid.)

c. 1619–20—'William Eglestone' was sixth in King's cast for *The Custom of the Country*. (Ibid.)

1619–21—'Will. Egleston' was sixth in King's cast for *Women Pleased*. (Ibid.)

1619–21—'William Eglestone' was third in King's cast for *The Island Princess*. (Ibid.)

1619–22—'William Egleston' was sixth in King's cast for *The Little French Lawyer*. (Ibid.)

1621, Apr. 7—His name was ninth in the livery allowance list for the King's men. (*Hist. MSS. Com.*, Report IV, Part I, p. 299.)

1622, June 22—'William Eglestone' was second in King's cast for *The Sea Voyage*. (1679 folio B.M.)

1622—'William Eglestone' was fourth in King's cast for *The Spanish Curate*. (Ibid.)

1623—'William Ecclestone' was twentieth in the list of King's men in the Shakespeare Folio.

1623, June 3—Nicholas Tooley in his will said, 'I doe release and forgiue vnto John Vnderwood and William Ecclestone all such sommes of monie as they doe severallie owe vnto mee'. (See Appendix, p. 650.)

1652—Conceivably he was the W. E. who wrote verses to *The Wild*

Goose Chase, published for the benefit of Lowin and Taylor. (*See* John Lowin.)

EDMONDS (EDMANS), JOHN. 'John Edmans' and Robert Gough were left the wearing apparel and arms of Thomas Pope by his will of 1603, a bequest which suggests that they were his apprentices in the Shakespearian company. Upon this slender suggestion, Mr. Baldwin has built up for Edmonds a career in the company from 1598 to 1609 and even assigned him the creation of the role of Cleopatra, among others; there is, however, no direct evidence that he ever acted in the Shakespearian company at all. He lived in the parish of St. Saviour's, as is indicated by the christening of his children, and he acquired a half-share in the Globe through marriage with Mary Clarke, a fellow legatee in the will of Thomas Pope, but the only company in whose records he is found is Queen Anne's. There is only a possibility that he is the Edmonds who dined several times with Alleyn and the actors.

Though a John Edmonds was buried at St. Saviour's 20 September 1634, he is not called player in that record, and the fact that there was a labourer, a sailor, a basket-maker, and a brewer's servant of the same name in the parish makes identification impossible.

1618, Apr.—A 'Letter of Assistance from the Council for Martin Slatier, John Edmondes, and Nath. Clay, to act interludes and stage plays in Bristol or any city, &c., under the power of the patent to John Daniel' was shown at Exeter in June 1618. (*C.S.P., Dom.*, 1611–18, p. 549.)

1618, June 30—'Mr Edmonds dind w^t me.' (Alleyn's Diary, Young, ii. 93.)

1618, Sept. 18—'Dinner att ye marmayd in bred street w^t m^r Edmonds m^r bromfeeld Tho: Allen & 5 of ye fortune company'. (Ibid., p. 104.)

1619, >May 13—'Iohn Edmondes' was fourteenth in the list of Queen Anne's men who received 'iiij yards' of black cloth for Queen Anne's funeral procession. (*M.S.C.* ii. 325.)

1621, Aug. 12—'Mr Edmonds: Charles Massey & on other off ye compa[n]y dynd Here.' (Alleyn's Diary, Young, ii. 216.)

EGLESTONE, WILLIAM (*see* ECCLESTON, WILLIAM).

ELLIS (*see* GUEST, ELLIS; BEDOWE, ELLIS; WORTH, ELLIS).

ERRINGTON, RICHARD. Errington was an ex-pewterer who became a leader of provincial acting companies. He first appears as a leader of a provincial King's company, but before 1631 (Murray, i. 272–3, suggests that it was in November 1629) he had joined the company of Ellis Guest, a company which is called Queen Henrietta's a year or so later (Murray, ii. 104, 354). By 1636 Errington had joined Daniel's King's Revels company. It is significant that Errington always appears as a leader in the companies with which he is found.

1622–3—Payment was made at Norwich to 'Mr Irington & other of his Ma^ts Company of Players'. (Murray, ii. 371.)

1627, Nov. 22—He made a deposition at Ludlow in connexion with a drunken riot outside the house in which his company was acting: 'Richard Errington, of the Citty of London, pewterer, aged l^tie yeares or thereaboute . . . beinge one of the Company of his Majesties players who then were actinge in the said howse, & this deponent takeinge money att the doore . . .' (Murray, ii. 326.)

1631, July 18—At Reading 'Ellys Guest, Richard Errington and their company' showed their licence of 15 July 1631 from the Master of the Revels for six months. (Ibid., pp. 386–7.)

1636, Apr. 22—'Richard Drington & William Daniel players of the Revels' were given a fee at Coventry. (Ibid., p. 252.)

ESTOTVILLE, George (see STUTVILLE, GEORGE).

EVANS, Gouldwais. He may have had nothing to do with the theatre, but so many of the musicians who lived in theatrical districts like Clerkenwell and Southwark did that it seems worth while to record such facts about them as appear.

1625, Oct. 23—'Gouldwaies Evans & Eliz. Richardson' mar. St. J.C.

1626/7, Feb. 4—'Joseph s. of Gouldwaies Evans & Eliz. vx' chris. St. J.C.

1629, Aug. 13—'William s of Gouldwais Evans a musitoan' chris. St. S.S.

1631, Dec. 25—'Judith d. of Gouldwaies Evans' chris. St. J.C.

1635, Aug. 2—'Andrewe s. of Gouldwayes Evans' chris. St. J.C.

EYDWARTT, Johann. He may have been a German rather than an English actor.

1627, Apr. 1–May 6—In the list of 'English Comedians' (Robert Reynolds's company) who were lodged at private houses in Torgan during the marriage celebrations of Princess Sophia and the Landgrave of Hesse-Darmstadt was 'Johann Eydtwartt'. (Cohn, *Sh. in Ger.*, p. xcvii.)

EYTON, William (see EATON, WILLIAM).

FARNABY, Richard. Probably the son of the composer Giles Farnaby, Richard himself was a composer, several of whose compositions are to be found in the 'Fitzwilliam Virginal Book' (Fellowes, *English Madrigal Composers*, p. 233). He was in Germany in 1624 (Meyer, *Shakespeare Jahrbuch*, xxxviii. 209).

FAULKNER, Thomas. I cannot tell what was meant by 'an inhabitant at the Fortune Playehouse'. The phrase suggests a caretaker at the theatre, but it might mean an actor, or, conceivably, a spectator.

1626, May 16—Recognizances were taken for the appearance of James Carver and Thomas Alderson, charged with rioting at the Fortune and '. . . beatinge and assaultinge of Thomas Faulkener an inhabitant at the Fortune Playehouse'. (*Middx. Co. Rec.* iii. 161–2.)

1646, May 12—Recognizances were taken 'For the appearance of Thomas Faulkner . . . to answer for "assaulting and pumping of Margarett Emmerson uppon the" same "false report"'. (Ibid., p. 181.)

FENN, EZEKIEL. It seems highly probable that Fenn was the boy born in the parish of St. Martin's in the Fields in 1620, for the name is unusual, and the date fits well with his career. Thus he was eleven when he played Sophonisba, the leading female role in *Hannibal and Scipio,* and not more than nineteen when he took his first man's part. He must have been a fairly experienced boy actor by 1635, since in that year he was cast for the important role of Sophonisba and the even more important one of Winifred. When Queen Henrietta's company was broken, Fenn stayed on with Beeston at the Cockpit and was probably a person of some authority, since he was one of those called by the Privy Council in May 1637. If the prologue which Glapthorne wrote was really delivered in the theatre, it indicates that Fenn must have had quite a following to make it profitable for the company so to call him to the attention of the audience.

1620, Apr. 9—'Ezekiell Fenne fs. Mauritii et Lucie' chris. St. M.F.

1635—'*Sophonisba.* By *Ezekiel Fenn*' in Nabbe's *Hannibal and Scipio* presented by Queen Henrietta's company 'at their Private house in *Drury Lane*'. (1637 4° B.M.)

c. 1635 ?—The quarto of *The Witch of Edmonton* has an Epilogue, spoken by Winifred, the heroine, and signed 'Phen.', which evidently belongs to a revival of the play by Queen Henrietta's men about 1635. (See above, pp. 251–2.)

1637, May 12—'Ezech: Fenn' was called before the Privy Council with William and Christopher Beeston, Theophilus Bird, and Michael Moone, and plays at the Cockpit were ordered stopped until further orders. (*M.S.C.* i. 392.)

1639—The 1639 quarto of Henry Glapthorne's *Poems* contains the following:

For *Ezekial Fen* at his first Acting
a Mans Part

PROLOGVE.

Suppose a Merchant when he lanches forth
An untry'd Vessell, doubtfull of its worth,
Dare not adventure on that infant Peece
The glorious fetching of a golden Fleece
From the remot'st Indies. 'Tis so with mee,
Whose Innocence and timerous Modestie
Does blush at my own shadow, prone to feare
Each Wave a Billow that arises here;
The Company's my Merchant, nor dare they
Expose my weak frame on so rough a Sea,

'Lesse you (their skilful Pilots) please to stear
By mild direction of your Eye and Ear
Their new rigg'd Bark. This is their hopes and mine
Promise my selfe; if you like North-stars shine,
I like a daring, and adventrous Man,
Seeking new paths i'th' angry Ocean,
In threatning Tempests, when the surges rise, ·
And give salt kisses to the neighb'ring Skies,
When blustring *Boreas* with impetuous breath
Gives the spread Sailes a wound to let in Death,
Cracks the tall Mast, forcing the Ship (though loth)
On its carv'd Prow to wear a Crown of froth;
Will face all perils boldly, to attain
Harbour in safety; then set forth againe. ·

1639, Aug. 10—'Ezechiell Fenne' was eighth in the list of the young company of Cockpit Players for tickets of privilege. (*M.S.C.*, ii. 390–1.)

FERRET, JAMES.

1634/5, Mar. 10—His name is in the long list of players recorded at Norwich. (Some of the players belonged to the King's Revels, though the records do not give the name of the company; probably two companies are listed together here. See above, pp. 286 and 288–9.)

FERRIS, DEAVID (?).

1629, Nov. 10—'Deavid[?] Ferris' was fourth in the list of players named in the licence granted to William Perry and Richard Weeks, 'all of the Red Bull company', which was shown at Reading 30 November 1629. (Murray, ii. 386.)

FIELD, HENRY.

1634/5, Mar. 10—His name is in the long list of players copied at Norwich. Some of the players belonged to the King's Revels, though the records do not give the name of the company; probably two companies are concerned. (Ibid., p. 356; and see above, pp. 286 and 288–9.)

FIELD, NATHAN. Nathan Field was the son of the Puritan preacher and writer John Field and the brother of Theophilus, Bishop of Llandaff, and of Nathaniel, the printer, with whom he has been often confused, even some of his contemporaries giving him his brother's name. Nathan's career has been most fully discussed by Miss Roberta Brinkley in her book *Nathan Field, the Actor-Playwright*, 1928.

The actor, whose picture in the gallery at Dulwich College displays a dark and dashing young man (reproduced in Chambers, *Shakespeare*, i. 82), was born in 1587. He was introduced to the stage at the age of about twelve or thirteen, when he was seized by James Robinson and impressed as one of the Children of the Chapel. He appeared several times as an actor in the Queen's

Revels, and probably became a protégé of Ben Jonson in this time. When the Lady Elizabeth's company was formed, Field became the leader and thereafter appeared several times in negotiations with Henslowe for the company and in casts of the company's plays. He had become a very well-known actor before he left the Lady Elizabeth's company, probably in 1616, Mr. Baldwin thinks to succeed to Shakespeare's share as a patented member of the King's company (*Organization and Personnel*, p. 51).

Field was evidently prominent in the King's company until his death, which occurred before August 1620, when his sister was granted letters of administration, and probably, though not certainly, after May 1619, when his name appeared in the livery list for the company.

Mr. Baldwin (ibid., pp. 204–5) thinks that Field regularly played the young lover roles in dual leads with Burbage—such parts as Euphanes in *The Queen of Corinth*, Miranda in *The Knight of Malta*, Polydore in *The Mad Lover*, Thierry in *Thierry and Theodoret*, and Young Archas in *The Loyal Subject*. He is known to have played Bussy, probably in a King's revival of the play. Such roles are quite compatible with his contemporary reputation as a ladies' man.

Field's unaided work as a dramatist was done before he came to the King's company, *A Woman Is a Weathercock* for the Queen's Revels and *Amends for Ladies* for Lady Elizabeth's. His acknowledged collaborations, *The Fatal Dowry* and *The Jeweller of Amsterdam*, were written after he transferred to King James's company and were probably both written for that company. There has been much disagreement about his attributed collaborations, but Miss Brinkley, who has studied his work most fully, limits them to *Four Plays in One*, *The Queen of Corinth*, *The Knight of Malta*, and *The Honest Man's Fortune*, the first and last probably written for Lady Elizabeth's and *The Queen of Corinth* and *The Knight of Malta* for the King's men.

1616—No. 3 in King's cast for *The Mad Lover*. (1679 folio B.M.)

1616—'Field, the Player, to —— Sutton, Preacher at St. Mary Overy's. Remonstrates against his condemnations from the pulpit of all players. Though, like other trades, that of actors has many corruptions, it is not condemned in Scripture, and, being patronized by the King, it is disloyal to preach against it.' (*C.S.P., Dom.*, 1611–18, p. 419; reprinted Halliwell–Phillipps, *Illustrations*, pp. 115–17.)

1616–17—No. 5 in King's cast for *The Queen of Corinth*. (1679 folio B.M.)

1616–18—No. 2 in King's cast for *The Knight of Malta*. (Ibid.)

1618, Nov. 16—No. 5 in King's cast for *The Loyal Subject*. (Ibid.)

1617–19—He became the owner of one-eighth of the actor's moiety of the Globe, or one-sixteenth of the entire property. (Wallace, *Sh. and Lond. Assoc.*, p. 63, and Adams, 'Housekeepers of the Globe', *Mod. Phil.* xvii. 6.)

1618—He published *Amends for Ladies*, which had been acted before 1611.

1619—Ben Jonson told Drummond that ' Nid field was his Schollar, & he had read to him the Satyres of Horace & some Epigrames of Martiall'. (*Ben Jonson*, i. 137.)

1619, Mar. 27—He was seventh in the patent list of the King's company. (*M.S.C.* i. 280–2.)

1619, May 24—'.The Bishop of Llandaff shall be advanced higher, to be Bishop of Chichester; Chichester to Norwich; and Dr. Field (Field, the player's brother), shall succeed Llandaff.' (Rev. Thomas Lorkin to Sir Thomas Puckering, London, 24 May 1619. Birch, *James I*, ii. 167.)

1619, May 19—He was fourth in the livery allowance list for the King's men. (*Hist. MSS. Com.*, Report IV, Part I, p. 299.)

1619, June 5—Sir William Trumbull wrote from Brussels to Lord Hay that he was told that the Earl of Argyll was privy to the payment of £15 or £16 for the nursing of a child 'which the world sayes is daughter to my lady (Argyll) and N(at) Feild the Player'. (*Athenaeum* (1882), i. 103.) Sir Edmund Chambers says that more than one MS. commonplace book contains an epigram with some such heading as *On Nathaniell Feild suspected for too much familiarity with his Mᵣⁱˢ Lady May*. (Chambers, *E.S.* ii. 317.)

1620, Aug. 2—Letters of administration, in which he was called a bachelor, of St. Giles in the Fields, were granted his sister. (*See* Brinkley, p. 153.)

1620–7—The children of Nathaniel Field which Collier, *Mem. Act.* and Bod., shows at St. Anne's Blackfriars in these years seem to be those of the actor's brother Nathaniel, the printer. (*See* Brinkley.)

1623—'Nathan Field' was No. 17 in the actor list in the Shakespeare Folio.

1629—There is an unimportant jest (No. 30) on him in John Taylor's *Wit and Mirth*, reprinted in Hazlitt, *Old English Jest Books*, vol. iii.

1632—*The Fatal Dowry*, by P. M. and N. F., was published.

1634, Apr. 7—The prologue to the King's revival of *Bussy D'Ambois* of this date refers to him as Bussy: 'Field is gone, Whose Action first did give it name.' (1641 4° B.M.) He may have been the first Bussy for the King's company; he can scarcely have created the role.

>1642—Wright says, 'Some of these Chappel Boys, when they grew Men, became Actors at the Black-friers; such were *Nathan Feild*, and *John Underwood*.' (*Hist. Hist.*, p. 16.)

1664—Flecknoe in his 'Short Discourse of the English Stage' (published in *Love's Kingdom*) says, 'In this time were Poets and Actors in their greatest flourish, Johnson, Shakespear, with Beaumont and Fletcher, their Poets, and Field and Burbidge their Actors.' (Hazlitt, *Drama and Stage*, p. 277; reiterated p. 279.)

1670—In his *Epigrams of All Sorts* (1670) Richard Flecknoe includes a complaint on the mutilation of one of his plays, which concludes:

> May, never *Poet* write for them agen:
> But they be forc'd to Act *old Plays* like those
> For want of new, are forc'd to wear *old Cloathes*;
> And come o' th' *Stage* all tattered and poor,
> In old cast sutes, which *Field* and *Burbadge* woar.

FINTRYE, ROBERT. Though there are no records of his activity after Shakespeare's death, Fintrye is listed here because he may well have acted in the later period and because no information about him is to be found in any of the modern books on actors.

1613, May 31—'Robert Fintrye' is listed as a boy in a patent for Lady Elizabeth's of this date copied at Coventry 28 March 1615. ('Stage Gleanings', p. 183.)

FISHER, JOHN.

1622, May 20—Alleyn granted 'John ffisher of London Barber Chirurgion' a lease of a half-share of the new Fortune. (*Hens. Paps.*, pp. 29, 112.)

FLORIDOR, JOSIAS. Floridor was the stage name of Josias de Soulas, the leader of the company of French players who came to London in February 1634/5 and acted at court, in the Cockpit in Drury Lane, and in M. Le Febure's riding academy (*see* Adams, pp. 420-4). For his French career, see Frederick Hawkins, *Annals of the French Stage* (1884), i. 148 ff.

1635, May 5—'Josias D'Aunay, Hurfries de Lau, and others' were granted a warrant to act at a new house in Drury Lane. (*Herbert*, p. 61. Mr. Adams says that this Josias D'Aunay is either the real name of or an error for Josias Floridor, whose 'real name is supposed to have been Josias de Soulas. Perhaps we should insert a comma after " Josias".')
1635, May 10—The Lord Chamberlain issued a warrant for £30 'vnto Mons' Iosias Floridor for him selfe & the rest of the ffrench Players for three playes Acted by them at ye Cockpitt'. (*M.S.C.* ii. 376.)
1635/6, Jan. 8—The Lord Chamberlain issued a warrant for £10 'vnto Iosias Floridor for him selfe & the rest of the ffrench Players for A Tragedy by them Acted before his Matye in December last'. (Ibid., p. 378.)

FOSTER, ALEXANDER. Foster appears as a Lady Elizabeth's man in 1611 and 1612; the payment to him in 1616 was probably for plays presented when the Lady Elizabeth's men and Prince Charles's were acting together (see p. 198), for he never appears as a member of Prince Charles's company. There is no indication that Foster was anything but a provincial actor from 1616, when the Lady Elizabeth's company was reduced to a provincial status, until 1628, when the new licence was issued. It should be noted that Foster's name appears a number of times in provincial records when it has simply been copied from the licence which the leader of the company brought; there is no evidence to show that he was present.

It is probable that the items from the State Papers and *Hist.*

MSS. Com. refer to another Alexander Foster who was page of the bedchamber; the petitions from the L.C. warrant books perhaps refer to the same man. One cannot, however, be certain about this.

1616, Apr. 29—Foster was paid for four plays at Court as 'one of the Princes highnes Players'. (Chambers, *E.S.* iv. 183.)

1617/18, Mar. 20—On 23 May 1618 John Townsend presented at Norwich a licence of this date permitting 'Alexander ffoster John Townsend Joseph Moore & ffr Wamus servants to the Lady Elizabeth' to play. (Murray, ii. 344–5.)

1619, July 18—Alexander Foster, page of the bedchamber, was granted the office of Bailiff in Wales. (*C.S.P., Dom.,* 1619–23, p. 64.)

1619, Dec. 13—The same man was given the reversion of the Clerk of the Bills. (Ibid., p. 103.)

1620/1, Jan. 28—Another reference to Foster's grant of the office of Bailiff. (Ibid., p. 216.)

1621/2, Mar. 13—The L.C. Warrant Books contain a bill for 'John Townsend Alexander Foster & Joseph Moore the Lady Elizabeths graces her player^s'. (Murray, ii. 193.)

1621/2, Mar. 20—A later stage of the above bill was copied into the Mayor's Court Book at Norwich on 10 May 1623. (Murray, ii. 346–7.)

1624, June 2—Alexander Foster was made lessee of the profits of the Court of Soham in Cambridgeshire. (*Hist. MSS. Com.,* Report XII, App. 1, p. 164.)

1628, June 30—'Alexander Foster' was second in a list of 'Queene of Bohemia's Players' named in a warrant for swearing them Grooms of the Chamber. (See pp. 188–9.)

1628, July 17—'Alexander Foster' is the third of three men named in a warrant for a new licence for the 'Queene of Bohemias Players' and mentioned as a leader of the old Lady Elizabeth's company. (*M.S.C.* ii. 347–8.)

1628, Dec. 9—One of four leaders named in a docquet for a new licence for Lady Elizabeth's. (*C.S.P., Dom.,* 1628–9, p. 406.)

1629, Dec. 20—'A petition of Captaine Alexander Moore against Robert Moore Alexander Foster & William Rogers.' (L.C. Warrant Book 5/183, p. 64, P.R.O.)

1629, Dec. 24—'At this daye Joseph Moore, Alexander Foster, Robert Guilman and John Towensend, sworne servantes to his Majestie, with the rest of their Company', were paid 20s. to 'forbeare their playeing' at Reading. (Murray, ii. 386.)

1629/30, Feb. 6—'A petition of William Steuens against Iohn Lilly & Alexander Foster, debt 18^li.' The Lord Chamberlain gave Lilly and Foster one month of grace. (L.C. Warrant Book 5/183, p. 69, P.R.O.)

1630, Nov. 30—'A petition of Peter Hayward against Alexander Foster.' (Ibid., p. 91.)

1643, Sept. 9—'To Alex: foster &c: 3: more his Ma: good & Loyall Souldyers for this reliefe.' (MS. Diary of Sir Humphrey Mildmay, B.M. MS. Harl. 454, fo. 146.)

FOUCH, RICHARD.

1631, Dec.—'*Margery her maid*. Richard Fouch' in the cast of *Holland's Leaguer*, acted by Prince Charles's men at the Salisbury Court theatre this month. (*Herbert*, p. 45; 1632 4° B.M.)

FOWLER, RICHARD. Fowler seems to have been a rather important player at the Fortune from the time of the reorganization of the Palsgrave's men in 1618 until the closing of the theatres. He was apparently a member of the little known King and Queen of Bohemia's company at that theatre and later of Prince Charles's (II). The obscurity of these companies at the Fortune in the reign of Charles I is reflected in the paucity of our information about their chief players.

The definite statement in *Knavery in All Trades* about Fowler's roles is in complete accord with Gayton's allusion. The Fortune had a reputation for noisy plays, and Fowler must have been instrumental in maintaining it. The *Rebellion* allusion suggests the same type of part as the other two; indeed, it is not impossible that the tailor means to remind the audience of Fowler in the role of old Jeronimo.

Fowler's part in *Holland's Leaguer* is not that of a conqueror, but then not even the Fortune could produce heroic plays exclusively.

1618, Sept. 16—'Jane daughter of Richard ffowler gentleman' chris. St. G.C.

1618, Oct. 31—He was tenth of the Palsgrave's men to sign the lease of the Fortune from Edward Alleyn. (See above, pp. 138–9.)

1620/1, Feb. 17—'Richard sonne of Richard ffowler Player' chris. St. G.C. He was buried 8 August 1625.

1622—Herbert names him as one of the nine leading members of the Palsgrave's company. (*Herbert*, p. 63.)

1622/3, Feb. 26—'Addam sonne of Richard ffowler Player' chris. St. G.C. 'Adam sonne of Richard ffowler' bur. 2 July 1623.

1623, May 21—'Richard ffowler in Redcrosse Streete', 5s., in Markham's suit. (See Appendix, p. 682.)

1624, Apr. 30—With five other players he signed a bond with Richard Gunnell to continue to play together as the Palsgrave's company at the Fortune. (See pp. 148–9.)

1624, Dec. 15—'Thomas sonne of Richard ffowler Player' chris. St. G.C.; bur. 20 June 1634.

1627, Apr. 4—'Richard Fowler and Elizabeth Freeman, *by banes*' mar. St. B.B.

1627, May 23—Thomas Saul petitioned the Lord Chamberlain against Fowler, Gunnell, Price, and Cartwright for a £50 debt. (*M.S.C.* ii. 401.)

1631, Dec.—'*Snarle, friend to Philautus*. Richard Fowler' in the cast of *Holland's Leaguer*, acted by Prince Charles's (II) at Salisbury Court this month. (*Herbert*, p. 45; 1632 4° B.M.)

1631, Oct. 18—John Atkins petitioned the Lord Chamberlain against Gunnell, Cartwright, Matthew Smith, and Fowler. (*M.S.C.* ii. 406.)

1631, Nov. 28—Atkins's petition was repeated; this time the four men were called 'yᵉ Queene of Bohemias Players'. Atkins was given permission to sue after one month. (*M.S.C.* ii. 406.)

1632, May 10–15—'Richard Fowler' was fourth in a list of eleven men named in a 'warraunt to sweare these seuerall persons following groomes of the Chamber in ordinary wᵗʰout ffee to attend the Prince his Highnes in yᵉ quality of players'. (Ibid., p. 358.)

1639/40, Feb. 13—In the Acts of the Court of High Commission, vol. ccccxxxiv, fol. 105, listed in *C.S.P., Dom.*, 1640, p. 396, is 'Richard Fowler . . . a commission decreed'.

1639—In Act v, scene 2, of Rawlins's play, *The Rebellion* (S.R. 20 November 1639), acted by the King's Revels, four tailors prepare to perform a play. After several punning allusions to the players, they decide to act *The Spanish Tragedy*.

> 2 *Tay.* Who shall act *Ieronimo*?
> 3 *Tay.* That will I:
> Marke if I doe not gape wider than the widest
> Mouth'd Fowler of them all, hang me:
> 'Who calls *Jeronimo* from his naked bed: haugh!
> Now for the passionate part—
> 'Alas it is my sonne *Horatio*. (1640 4° HN.)

1643, Sept. 11—'Richard ffowler Stage Player' bur. St. G.C.

1654—Gayton tells of a Shrove Tuesday riot in the theatre when the players performed several pieces at the demand of the audience, but the spectators threw apples, stones, nuts, tiles, and oranges none the less: 'It was not then the most mimicall nor fighting man, *Fowler*, nor *Andrew Cane* could pacifie; Prologues nor Epilogues would prevaile.' (See Appendix, p. 691.)

1664—In the third act of *Knavery in All Trades* (1664 4° HN), several gentlemen are in a coffee-house talking of the theatre before the wars:

> *fourth.* But did you know *Mat Smith, Elis Worth,* and *Fowler* at the Fortune?
> *fifth.* Yes, and I will tell you by a good token; *Fowler* you know was appointed for the Conquering parts, and it being given out he was to play the Part of a great Captain and mighty Warriour, drew much Company; the Play began, and ended with his Valour; but at the end of the Fourth Act he laid so heavily about him, that some Mutes who stood for Souldiers, fell down as they were dead e're he had toucht their trembling Targets; so he branisht his Sword and made his *Exit*; ne're minding to bring off his dead men; which they perceiving, crauld into the Tyreing house, at which, *Fowler* grew angry and told 'em, Dogs you should have laine there till you had been fetcht off; and so they crauld out again, which gave the People such an occasion of Laughter, they cry'd that again, that again, that again.

GARRET, JOHN (*see above*, p. 171, n. b).

GASCOIGNE [GASCOINE, GASCOYNE], WILLIAM. One of the many minor functionaries at the Globe and Blackfriars.

1624, Dec. 27—'William Gascoyne' was the last named in a list of twenty-one men exempted from arrest by Herbert in their capacity as 'Musitions and other necessary attendantes' of the King's company. (*Herbert*, p. 74.)

1631, May 6 (lic.)—'Gascoine: & Hubert' open the trap door for Antiochus in King's production of *Believe as You List*, IV. I. (Sisson, *B.A.Y.L.*, p. 60.)

1640, June 29—'Jane Gascoigne' bur. St. G.F.

1641, July 16—'Alice Daughter of William & Alice Gascoigne' chris. St. G.F. 'Alice Daughter of William Gascoigne' bur. 23 July 1642.

GELLIUS, GEDEON. It seems probable that an actor of this date would have had experience before the closing of the theatres.

1650, Nov. 10—'Gedeon Gellius [Giles?]' is one of four men mentioned in a letter from the Emperor Fredinand III requesting safe conduct for a company of English comedians in Germany. (Cohn, *Sh. in Ger.*, p. c.)

GEORGE. Though the play in which his name appears was probably written late in the sixteenth century, the prompter's notes may well be for a revival. Because of the uncertainty as to date and company it is impossible to identify George.

In the MS. of *Thomas of Woodstock, or Richard II* (B.M. Egerton 1994, fol. 172b) is the stage direction, 'Enter a seruant'. Above it is written, 'George'. (Greg, *Dram. Doc.*, p. 254.)

GERDLER, ADAM. Perhaps he was a popular amateur rather than a professional actor.

1635—'To Adam Gerdler, whom my Lord sent for from York to act a part in "The Knight of the Burning Pestell"' at Craven District. (Account Books of the Clifford Family.) (Murray, ii. 255.)

GIBBES, GEORGE. A ghost name from Mrs. Stopes's misreading, followed by Nungezer, of George Giles in the licence for the Queen of Bohemia's men, 30 June 1628.

GIBBORNE, THOMAS (*see* GILBORNE, THOMAS).

GIBBS (GIBES, GIBS), ANTHONY. His appearance in the prompter's notes in the MS. of *Two Noble Ladies* probably indicates that he was a hired man in the Revels company, though it is possible that his name was not entered for the performance designated on the title-page of the MS. Ellis Guest's company is a motley group, most of whose actors cannot be traced elsewhere.

1622–3 ?—In the prompter's notes in the MS. of *The Two Noble Ladies* (B.M. MS. Egerton 1994), whose title-page says it was acted at the Red Bull by the company of the Revels, Gibbs appears four times as a soldier: 'Anth: Gibs:' (fol. 227[4]ª), 'Tay. Gib: Stage k:' (fol. 233 [10]ª), 'Anth: Gibs:' (fol. 235[12]b), and 'Tay: Gibs:' (fol. 236[13]b). (Greg, *Dram. Doc.*, pp. 276–7.)

1628, June 7—'Antony Gibes' is the last of thirteen men named in a new licence of this date granted to Ellis Guest's unnamed company by Sir Henry Herbert and presented at Norwich 2 July 1628. (Murray, ii. 353.)

GIBBS, EDWARD. Crosfield's designation implies that he was of more value to the Revels company for his fencing exhibitions than for his histrionic ability, and the reminiscences of the gentleman in *Knavery in All Trades* suggest the same thing. By 1639 he belonged to Their Majesties' Young Company, and he may have been with them as early as 1636–7 when the company was formed. There is no assurance that the later entries refer to the actor-fencer, but he may have been involved in the Dreydon divorce.

1634, July 18—Kendall told Crosfield that among those at Salisbury Court was '3. Edward Gibbs a fencer'. (*Crosfield's Diary*, p. 72; see Appendix, p. 688.)

1639, Aug. 10—'Edward Gibbes' was tenth in the list of the young company of Cockpit players for a ticket of privilege. (*M.S.C.* ii. 390–1.)

1639/40, Jan. 30—In the Acts of the Court of High Commission, vol. ccccxxxiv, fol. 68b, is the following: 'Sir John Dreydon, Edward Gibbs, and Lady Bridget Kingsmill, widow. . . . Commission was introduced upon the articles. Publication decreed.' (*C.S.P., Dom.*, 1640, p. 385.)

1639/40, Feb. 6—For the same three, a 'defence decreed by the first session of next term'. (Ibid., p. 392.)

1641, Dec. 7—'Edward sonne of Edward and Jone Gibbes' chris. St. G.F.

1641, Dec. 22—'Susan wife of Edward Gibbs' bur. St. J.C.

1641/2, Feb. 3—'Edward Gibbes and Jone ffletcher' mar. St. G.F.

1642/3, Jan. 19—'Mary Daughter of Edward Gibbs' bur. St. G.F.

1664—In the third act of Tatham's (?) *Knavery in All Trades*, several gentlemen have been discussing the theatre in the days before the wars, when one says, 'You talk of your Players, I am for the Fencers, there are none living now like old *Bradshaw*, old *Batty*, *Chatterton*, and *Ned Gibs*'. (1664 4° HN.)

GIBBS, ROBERT. The parish and the mention of Gunnell, manager of the Fortune, make it likely that both items concern one individual, possibly a hired man at the Fortune. The Robert Gibbs of St. Dionis Backchurch in 1638 (see *London, 1638*) seems too wealthy for an actor.

1622/3, Jan. 30.—'Thomas Willington seruant to Richard Gunnell from the house of Robert Gibbes' bur. St. G.C.

1648, Nov. 16—'Ailce: [*sic*] wife of Rob: Gibbs player' bur. St. G.C.

GIBSON. Probably a hired man in Lady Elizabeth's company. It is possible that the direction on fol. 54ᵃ of *The Captives* indicates that his name was Jack Gibson, but it is more likely that two men are intended, Jack and Gibson. Gibson may be the same as the H. Gibson of *Edmond Ironside*.

1624, Sept. 3—In the stage directions of the MS. of *The Captives* (acted at the Cockpit, probably by Lady Elizabeth's company) appears: 'Iack: Gibsen', apparently to set a chair (fol. 54ᵃ); 'Gib:'

as one of several country fellows and '[Gi]bs: Cont: fellowes' (fol. 61ᵇ) ; and 'fact: Gibson' as a factor (fol. 69ᵃ). (Greg, *Dram. Doc.*, pp. 285–7.)

GIBSON, H. Of the four actors whose names appear in the stage directions of *Edmond Ironside*, Gibson is the only one not known to have been a Prince Charles's man about 1632. He was probably a hired man in that company; his role is of the type which would usually be assigned to a hired man.

c. 1632—His name appears in the stage directions of the MS. of *Edmond Ironside* (Egerton 1994), evidently revived *c.* 1632. Gibson appears fol. 105ᵃ, 'Ent Mess[e]nger H Gibson'; fol. 105ᵇ, 'H. Gibs:'; fol. 107ᵃ, 'Enter H: Gibs:', anticipating the entrance of a messenger. (See Greg, *Dram. Doc.*, p. 259, and *Edmond Ironside*.)

GILBOURNE (GIBBORNE ?), THOMAS.

1624, Apr. 21—Alleyn granted 'Thomas Gilbourne, citizen and cloth-worker of London', a lease of one share of the new Fortune. Dr. Greg says the name is 'Thomas Gibborne (or Gilbourne)'. (*Hens. Paps.*, pp. 30 n. and 112.)

1642—He made his will as citizen and clothworker of London, but there is no mention of theatres or players. (P.C.C. 102 Campbell.)

GILBURNE, SAMUEL. In his will Augustine Phillips calls Gilburne his apprentice, but his name in the folio list is the only other evidence of a stage career. Sir Edmund Chambers suggests that Gilburne was apprenticed to Phillips as a musician and not as an actor (Chambers, *Shakespeare*, ii. 85–6). His ownership of a folio demonstrates his continued dramatic interest, but not his professional activity. It seems likely that he acted only as an apprentice and left the profession before he became old enough to get his name into records.

1623—'Samuel Gilburne' was fourteenth in the actor list in the Shakespeare Folio.

< 1623—In his notes on the first folios in the Folger Library, Mr. Shane Leslie says, '12, Gilburne copy with signature of Samuel Gilburne, the Elizabethan actor'. (*T.L.S.*, 20 September 1934.) Professor J. Q. Adams writes me that the name 'Samuel Gilburne' is found on the page of the folio carrying the actors' list, that the volume carries no other name or scribbling, that Mr. Folger, Dr. Rosenbach, and various booksellers have presumed that the name was the actor's signature, but that no other evidence for identification is known.

GILES, GEORGE. This player's name has not been included in actor lists before because of Mrs. Stopes's misreading of his name as Gibbes. (*Sh. Jahr.* xlvi. 94.)

1628, June 30—'George Giles' was eighth in a list of the 'Queene of Bohemias Players' sworn 'Groomes of his Matᵉˢ Chamber'. (*M.S.C.* ii. 347; see above, pp. 188–9.)

1629, Nov. 10—'A petition of Edmund Turney agst. George Giles debt 19^{li} od money.' (*M.S.C.* ii. 402.)

1634, Nov. 7—'A peticõn of Peter Ireland agst George Gyles debt 10^{li} od money.' (Ibid., p. 411.)

GILES, GIDEON (*see* GELLIUS, GEDEON).

GILMAN (GUILMAN, GYLMAN), ROBERT. One of the leaders of the new Lady Elizabeth's company of 1628 (see above, pp. 188–91). It is rather odd that he appears neither before nor after this time.

1628, June 30—'Robert Gylman' is third in a list of 'Queene of Bohemias Players' sworn 'Groomes of his Ma^{tes} Chamber'. (*M.S.C.* ii. 347; see above, pp. 188–9.)

1628, July 17—'Robert Gilman' is named second as a leader of the 'Queene of Bohemias Players' in a warrant for a new licence, but he is not mentioned as one of the old Lady Elizabeth's company. (Ibid., and see above, p. 189.)

1628, Dec. 9—'Robert Guilman' is mentioned with Moore, Foster, and Townsend as leaders of Lady Elizabeth's in the docquet for a licence. (*C.S.P., Dom.*, 1628–9, p. 406.)

1629, Dec. 24—'Robert Guilman' and three others, 'sworne servantes to his Majestie', appeared at Reading with their company and a licence of 15 December 1628. (Murray, ii. 386.)

GOAD (GOADE, GODE, GOOD), CHRISTOPHER. Goad was evidently known as an actor to his contemporaries for several years before he first appears as a Queen Henrietta's man in the cast of *The Fair Maid of the West*. All his roles in the casts of Queen Henrietta's plays are small, but he was probably of more importance in the King's Revels company, for his role in *Messalina* is a prominent one.

Mr. Adams (Adams, p. 374) and others have said that Goad was one of the original members of the King's Revels company in 1629, but we have no information whatever about the original membership of this company and good reason to think that Goad was still a Queen Henrietta's man in 1630.

The actor has been confused with the '*Christ. Goade Bac. Art. & Coll. Regal Soc.*' who signed verses in *Lacrymae Cantabrigiensis* (1619). This Christopher Goad was the son of Roger Goad, Provost of King's, Cambridge, and himself a popular lecturer when he was 'deposed from above' in 1638 (Smith, *Sir Henry Wotton*, ii. 394). Goad the player has also been suggested as the author of the verses signed C. G. which are prefixed to the 1640 quarto of Rawlins's *Rebellion*, acted by the King's Revels. Because of Goad's association with the company, this suggestion is not absurd, but the initials are too common to allow any certainty. A C. G. also wrote verses for Tatham's *Fancies' Theatre*, Brome's *Sparagus Garden*, and Nabbes's *Unfortunate Mother*, all published in the same year; in the last he consoled Nabbes for the failure of his play with a reminder of the failure of a play of Jonson's.

Since the player was surely the man recorded in the registers of St. Giles' Cripplegate, I think the Christopher Goad of Clerkenwell was another man, though it is possible that they are the same.

?—Possibly his name is intended in the 'G[ ]ad' of the prompter's note, probably made for a revival, in the MS. of *Thomas of Woodstock, or Richard II* (B.M. Egerton 1994, fol. 162ᵃ). The actor had the part of the 'Mayre'. *See* Richard and Henry Gradwell. (Greg, *Dram. Doc.*, p. 253.)

1623, May 13—'Daughter of Christopher Good Player' bur. St. G.C.

1626, Aug. 20—'Michael son of Xpofer Goade Player' chris. St. G.C.

1628, July 31—'Eliz: Dau: of Christopher Goad, gent' bur. St. G.C.

1629, July 23—'Constance d. of Xpofer Gode & Ruth vx.' chris. St. J.C.

c. 1630—'Mʳ Forset, *a Gentleman*; by Christoph. Goad' and '*A Spanish Cap. by* C. Goad' in the cast of Queen Henrietta's men prefixed to the 1631 4⁰ of Heywood's *Fair Maid of the West*, Part I; in the cast for Part II he appears as '*The D. of Farara. By* Christoph. Goad'. (1631 4⁰ B.M.)

1631, Oct. 19—'Xpofer s. of Xpofer Goade' chris. St. J.C.; bur. 2 January 1631/2.

1632, Nov. 28—'John s. of Xpofer Goade' chris. St. J.C.; bur. 18 January 1632/3.

>1634—'*Oxford*, M. [Mr.] *Goat*' in the cast for Davenport's *King John and Matilda*, given by Queen Henrietta's men at the Cockpit. (1655 4⁰ B.M.)

1634, July 18—Kendall told Crosfield that among the players at Salisbury Court was '5. Christofer Goad'. (*Crosfield's Diary*, p. 72; see Appendix, p. 688.)

c. 1634 ?—'*Silius*, chiefe Favorite to the Empresse—*Christopher Goad*' in the King's Revels cast for Richards's *Messalina*. (1640 ed. B.M.)

1634/5, Mar. 10—'XXofer Goade' is in the long list of players recorded at Norwich. Some of them seem to be King's Revels men, though the records do not give the name of the company, which probably was an amalgamation. (Murray, ii. 356; see above, pp. 286 and 288–9.)

1636, Oct. 3—'Ruth dau. of Xpofer Goade Playeʳ' chris. St. G.C.

1639, Apr. 28—'Timothy sonne of Christopher Goad Player' chris. St. G.C.

1640, Sept. 16—'Symon sonne of Xpofer Goad Player' bur. St. G.C.

1640, Sept. 23—'Eliza daugʳ of Xpofer Goad Player' chris. St. G.C.

1641/2, Jan. 16—'Marye d. of Christopher Gode' bur. St. J.C.

GODWIN, Richard.

1631, Dec.—'*Faustina, sister to Philautus*. Richard Godwin', in the cast of *Holland's Leaguer*, acted by Prince Charles's (II) at Salisbury Court. (*Herbert*, p. 45, and 1632 quarto B.M.)

1639, Nov. 10—'Richard Godwyn' bur. St. G.F.

GOFFE (*see* GOUGH).

GOLDING. Evidently the passage refers to an actor at the

Fortune as 'forty pound golding'. It may be that 'golding' is a punning allusion to his name; if so, I cannot tell who he was.

1639—In Act v, Sc. 2 of Rawlins's *Rebellion* (S.R. 20 Nov. 1639), four tailors preparing to act a play indulge in the following punning dialogue:

> *Old.* Now for the credit of the Taylers.
>
> 3 *Tay.* Nay, Master and we doe not act as they say,
> With any Players in the Globe of the World,
> Let us be baited like a Bull for a company of
> Strutting Coxecombes: nay we can act I can tell you.
>
> .   .   .   .
>
> 1 *Tay.* Well play; we are to play a play.
>
> 3 *Tay.* Play a play a play, ha, ha, ha; O egredious nonsensensicall wigeon, thou shame to our crosse-legg'd corporation; thou fellow of a sound, play a play; why forty pound golding of the beggers *Theater* speakes better, yet has a marke for the sage audience to exercise their dexterity, in throwing of rotten apples whilst my stout Actor pockets, and then eates up the injury: play a play, it makes my worship laugh yfaith'. (1640 4° HN.)

GOSSON, HENRY. Perhaps not an actor, but his inclusion with such a large number of actors in Markham's suit suggests that he might have been.

1623, May 21—'Henry Gosson over the gate att London bridge', 5s., in Markham's suit. (See Appendix, p. 682.)

GOUGH (GOFFE), ALEXANDER. The son of a player in the King's company, Alexander Gough was probably an apprentice in the company at an early age; at any rate he was entrusted with an important role by the time he was twelve. Though he must have been too old for female parts by 1636, when he received a player's pass at the age of twenty-two, he is known only as a 'Woman Actor', as Wright calls him. Since he was associated with the players during the interregnum, it appears that he performed with the company for six or seven years before the closing of the theatres without getting into any of the extant official records or leaving any impression in his adult roles. He never became a sharer in the company.

The dedication of *The Passionate Lovers* and the title-page of *The Queen* confirm Wright's assertion about Gough's acquaintance with persons of quality.

From his analysis of roles Mr. Baldwin says that Gough's 'line' was that of the modest lady (*Organization and Personnel*, p. 191). There is evidence for this conclusion in *The Wild Goose Chase* and in *The Swisser*, which Baldwin did not consider, but there is a sharp contradiction in Gough's role of Fewtricks, the impudent and mischievous page of *The Soddered Citizen*. In this play Gough and William Trigg have just the reverse of the modest and madcap lines which Mr. Baldwin assigns to them. For this reason Baldwin's attribution to Gough of Clara in *Rule a Wife and Have a Wife* and Juliana in *The Fair Maid of the Inn* must be doubted.

1614, Aug. 7—'Alexander Goffe, s of Robert; a player' chris. St. S.S.

1626—'*Caenis, Vespatians* Concubine. Alexander Govgh' in the King's cast for *The Roman Actor*, lic. 11 Oct. (1629 4° B.M.)

1628—'Alexander Govgh' was No. 17 in the King's cast for *The Lovers' Melancholy*, lic. 24 November. The roles are not given, but the position of his name indicates a woman's part. (1629 4° B.M.)

1629—'*Acanthe* a maid of honor. *Alexander Goffe*' in King's cast for *The Picture*, lic. 8 June. (1630 4° B.M.)

c. 1630—'ffewtricks—his Boye—Allex: Goffe' in King's cast in the MS. of Clavell's (?) *Soddered Citizen*. (*Soddered Citizen*, p. 3.)

1631—In the MS. of Arthur Wilson's *The Swisser* (B.M. Add. MS. 36759) his name appears in the cast for the Blackfriars production, 'Eurinia, A Captiue . . . *Goffe*'. (Feuillerat, *The Swisser*.)

1632—'*Sander Gough*' took the part of Lillia-Bianca in the King's 1632 revival of *The Wild Goose Chase*. (1652 ed. B.M.)

1636, May 17—His name was sixth in a partial list of minor King's men for players' pass. (*M.S.C.* ii. 378–9.)

1649–58—Wright says that when the players acted secretly in Cromwell's time, '*Alexander Goffe*, the Woman Actor at *Blackfriers*, (who had made himself known to Persons of Quality) used to be the Jackal and give notice of Time and Place'. (*Hist. Hist.*, p. 9. Mr. Hotson suggests 1647 as the date of these activities [Hotson, pp. 23–4].)

1652—The quarto of Jonson, Fletcher, and Middleton's *The Widow* printed by Moseley has an epistle to the reader signed '*Alexander Gough*'. The sentence, 'I believed it of more value to present you this lively piece . . .', indicates his responsibility for publication. (1652 4° HN.)

1653—The anonymous play *The Queen, or The Excellency of Her Sex* was printed as 'Found out by a Person of Honour, and given to the Publisher Alexander Goughe'. Gough signed the dedicatory epistle to Lady Catherine Mohun. There are two sets of complimentary verses to Gough on his publication of the play. (1653 4° HN.)

1655—The 8° of Carlell's *Passionate Lovers*, I and II, printed for Moseley, has a dedicatory epistle to Mary, Duchess of Richmond and Lennox, beginning 'I Humbly offer Your Grace the last sacrifice of this nature that is in my power', and signed 'Alex. Goughe'. Did he publish it? (1655 8° HN.)

GOUGH (GOFFE), ROBERT. Robert Gough, the brother-in-law of Augustine Phillips, first appears in the plot of *Seven Deadly Sins*, about 1592. Apparently he had been the apprentice of Thomas Pope, and Mr. Baldwin thinks that he had played the tender sentimental lady, that William Eccleston was his 'running mate', and that Gough played Juliet, Portia, Luciana, Katherine in *Love's Labour's Lost*, and Lady Mortimer in *1 Henry IV* (*Organization and Personnel*, pp. 274–5, 416, 418). The evidence for all these assignments is not very convincing, but Mr. Baldwin is on somewhat firmer ground when he contends that Gough succeeded to the membership of his brother-in-law, Phillips (*Organization and Personnel*, pp. 51–2. 282). He is called 'Mr.' in the prompter's notes in the MS. of *The Second Maiden's Tragedy* (1611), usually an indication of membership.

Gough's adult roles are not very important ones, and the evidence suggests that he withdrew from the company when he was made messenger, for he does not appear in the list of eleven members who signed the submission to Herbert in *The Spanish Viceroy* affair in 1624 (see *Herbert*, p. 21).

There is much evidence of his residence in Southwark, and there can be little doubt that he was the man buried in 1624/5, though Collier was wrong in saying that he is called player in the registers. He is found in the token books of St. Saviour's from 1604 to 1623, in Austen's Rents, 1612–21, and 'Palmers Rents the Musitian' in 1623 (Bentley, *T.L.S.*, 15 November 1928).

1619, Mar. 27—'Robert Gough' is ninth in the list of twelve King's men in the Signet Bill for the licence of 1619. (*M.S.C.* i. 280–2.)

1619, May 19—'Robert Goffe' was seventh in Pembroke's livery allowance list for King's. (*Hist. MSS. Com.*, Report IV, p. 299.)

1619, Aug.—In the prompter's notes in the MS. of *Sir John van Olden Barnavelt* is the stage direction, 'Enter Leidenberge & m^r Gough' (B.M. MS. Add. 18653, fol. 10 [9]^a), indicating that he played the part of an attendant. (Greg, *Dram. Doc.*, p. 273.)

1621, Apr. 7—'Robert Gough' was in Pembroke's livery allowance list of King's men. (*Hist. MSS. Com.*, Report IV, p. 299.)

1621, Oct.—A Robert Gough is sworn in as 'one of the 40 messengers in the place of Thomas Roberts'. (Bald, p. 22 n., from Petyt MS. No. 515.7 in the Library of the Inner Temple.)

1623—'Robert Goughe' was No. 23 in the actor list in the Shakespeare Folio.

1623, May 21—'Roberte Gough on the Banckesyde', 5s., in Markham's suit. (See Appendix, p. 682.)

1623/4, Jan. 29—He is mentioned in a further notice of Markham's suit.

1624, Aug. 30—A warrant directed 'Robert Goffe one of the Messengers of his Ma^{ts}: Chamber to bring one Midleton sonne to Midleton the Poet before theire Llo:p^s to answer &c.' (*M.S.C.* i. 381.)

1624/5, Feb. 19—'Robert Gough a man' bur. St. S.S.

GRACE, FRANCIS. Grace appeared as a member of Prince Henry's company in 1610 and again when the company became the Palsgrave's men in January 1612/13. He was a prominent member of the Palsgrave's company from that date until his death in 1623/4. He was a friend of Edward Alleyn, as the diary suggests, and was probably Alleyn's tenant, though the tenant may have been Richard Grace.

1617/18, Jan. 30—Alleyn noted in his diary, 'pd for repairing graces Howse in gowlding Lane—0–12–8'. (Young, ii. 69.)

1617/18, Mar. 24—'pd baxster more for graces Howse Reparing . . . 0.10.3.' (Ibid., 74.)

1618, Oct. 31—He was the third of the Palsgrave's men to sign the lease of the Fortune from Alleyn. (See pp. 138–9.)

1619, Aug. 15—'Ther dind w^t vs m^r Taylore m^r gunell His wife & daughter franc: grace.' (Young, ii. 147.)

1621, Apr. 15—'borne: massey: Cartwright: gunnell: grace: Hunt dind Here.' (Ibid., p. 204.)

1622—He was first in Herbert's list of the members of Palsgrave's. (*Herbert*, p. 63.)

1623, May 21—'ffrancke Grace att the George Alley in Gouldinge lane', 10s., in Markham's suit. (See Appendix, p. 682.)

1623/4, Feb. 2—'ffranck Grace, Player' bur. St. G.C.

GRACE, RICHARD. That Richard Grace was the younger brother of Francis is an easy guess, but there is no evidence as to what their relationship was. Markham's suit shows that Richard was an actor by January 1623/4, and the change of his designation in the parish registers from 'yoman' to 'player' about the same time suggests that he may have become a hired man in the Palsgrave's company shortly before Francis's death. He was probably of little importance in the company, since his name does not appear in a single official record of the theatres.

Malcolm says (*Londinium Redivivum*, iii. 304) that Richard Grace was buried at St. Giles' in 1627. A comparison with the extracts from the parish registers given below provides a fair sample of the gross inaccuracies of this book.

1617/18, Jan. 30—It may have been his house which Alleyn repaired; *see* Francis Grace.

1619, May 26—'Sara daughter of Richard Grace yeoman' bur. St. G.C.

1619, Aug. 30—'Margaret daughter of Richard Grace yeoman' chris. St. G.C.

1621/2, Jan. 16—'John sonne of Richard Grace yeoman' chris. St. G.C.

1623, May 21—'Richard Grace in Gouldinge Lane', 5s., in Markham's suit. (See Appendix, p. 683.)

1623/4, Jan. 29—Markham's suit says he was an actor at the Fortune. (See ibid.)

1625, Aug. 12—'Eliz dau of Richard Grace yoman' bur. St. G.C.

1627, May 4—'Charles son of Ric: Grace Player' chris. St. G.C.

1628/9, Jan. 16—'Elizabeth Dau. of Richard Grace Player' chris. St. G.C.; bur. 19 May 1630.

1630, May 18—'Phillip & James sonnes of the reputed ffather James Bolland Seifringman in the house of Richard Grace Player' chris. St. G.C.; bur. 21 May 1630.

1630, Aug. 4—'Increase dau of Richard Grace Player' chris. St. G.C.; bur. 26 Oct. 1630.

1631, June 1—'Richard Grace & Katherine Denshfield, L. vg.' mar. St. Gregory by St. Paul. (Challen, *Marriages*.)

1631/2, Mar. 5—'Richard sonne of Richard Grace Player' chris. St.
 G.C.; bur. 26 May 1632.
1634, Apr. 22—'Richard Grace Plaier' bur. St. G.C.

GRADWELL (GRADELL), **HENRY**. He is known only as a Prince
Charles's man, but the appearance of 'G[ ]ad' in *Thomas of Woodstock* may possibly point to his earlier association with some other
company. Unfortunately, both the date of the performance and
the identity of 'G[ ]ad' is extremely uncertain. Though nothing
is known of Gradwell as an actor after 1632, it seems likely that
he was the man who lived in Clerkenwell until 1651.

?—Conceivably Gradwell was indicated in 'G[ ]ad' in the prompter's
 notes in *Thomas of Woodstock or Richard II*, Egerton 1994, fol.
 162ª. The date of the performance is very uncertain; probably the
 notes were made for a revival. 'G[ ]ad' might refer to Richard
 Gradwell or to Christopher Goad. (Greg, *Dram. Doc.*, p. 253.)
1628, Dec. 14—'Francys s. of Henry Graddell & Alice his wife' chris.
 St. J.C.
1630, July 10—'Jane d. of Henry Craddell & Alice vx' chris. St. J.C.
1631, Nov. 27—'Alice d. of Henry Graddell' chris. St. J.C.
1631, Dec.—'*Capritio, a young Novice*. Henry Gradwell', in cast of
 Holland's Leaguer, acted by Prince Charles's (II) men at Salisbury
 Court this month. (*Herbert*, p. 45; 1632 4º B.M.)
1632, May 10–15—'Henry Gradwell' was ninth in a list of eleven
 men sworn 'groomes of the Chamber in ordinary wᵗʰout ffee to
 attend the Prince his Highnes in yᵉ quality of players'. (*M.S.C.* ii.
 358; see above, p. 303.)
c. 1632—Probably he is the 'mʳ gradell' who appears twice in the
 prompter's notes in the MS. of *Edmond Ironside* (B.M. Egerton
 MS. 1994), which was apparently written about 1590–1600, but
 revived about 1632, probably by Prince Charles's men (see above,
 p. 323). He appears fol. 104ᵇ 'm: Grad:' and 107ª 'mʳ gradell'.
 The second entry indicates that he had the part of a Herald. It is
 possible that these stage directions refer to Richard Gradwell.
 (Greg, *Dram. Doc.*, p. 259.)
1632, Sept. 17—'Jane d. of Henry Grudwell [Gradwell?]' bur. St.
 J.C.
1632, Dec. 10—'Henry Graddell' was one of six 'princes Players'
 petitioned against by William Crome (q.v.). At Crome's second
 petition, 21 December 1632, the Lord Chamberlain 'Answered wᵗʰ
 leaue graunted vpon sight'. (*M.S.C.* ii. 408.)
1651, Oct. 9—'Hen. Graddell' bur. St. J.C.
1658, May 3—'Alice Gradwell, widdow' bur. St. J.C.

GRADWELL (GRADELL), **RICHARD**. Though Richard Gradwell
is known only from parish registers, he may be the actor in
Thomas of Woodstock. It is unlikely that he was the actor in
Edmond Ironside, since 'mʳ' probably indicates that that man
wàs a sharer, and sharers are usually found in company records.

?—Possibly he was the 'G[ ]ad' of *Thomas of Woodstock or Richard II*.
 See Henry Gradwell.

1630/1, Jan. 19—'Eliz Dau of Richard Gradell Gentleman' chris. St. G.C.

c. 1632—*See* Henry Gradwell.

1632, Aug. 5—'Anne dau. of Richard Gradwell Player' chris. St. G.C.

1633/4, Mar. 16—'Richard son: of Richard Gradwell Play^r' chris. St. G.C.

GRAY, MARGARET (*see* GREY, MARGARET).

GREENE, JOHN. Greene was one of the most important English actors in Germany from 1606 to 1627 (Chambers, *E.S.* ii. 280–7). He had a company at Prague in 1617 and one at Cologne and Utrecht in 1620, at Frankfort and Dresden in 1626, and at Frankfort, Nuremberg, Dresden, and Torgau in 1627. (See Meissner, *Englischen Comoedianten*, pp. 43, 50, 51, 58; Herz, *Englische Schauspieler*, pp. 24–32; Meissner, *Jahrbuch*, xix. 139.)

GREENE, THOMAS. An important actor in Queen Anne's company who appears in provincial records and miscellaneous references after 1616, though he died in August 1612. Greene left most of his estate, including his share in Queen Anne's and a debt they owed him, to his wife Susan, who married James Baskervile in 1613. The attempts of the Baskerviles to collect provide most of our knowledge of the later days of the company.

GREVILLE (GREVILL, GRIVELL, GRIVILL), CURTIS. Greville's first appearance as a player in Herbert's list of 1622 is confusing, because Herbert lists him both as a Palsgrave's man and as a Lady Elizabeth's man. Professor Murray's suggestion (Murray, i. 215–16) that Cane and Greville, both of whom appear in the two lists, had just transferred to the Palsgrave's at this time for the opening of the new Fortune and that Herbert had neglected to remove their names from the Lady Elizabeth's list, is the best that has been made. It should be noted, however, that the suggestion is better for Cane, who does appear later as a Palsgrave's man, than for Greville, who never appears again as a member of either company.

By 1626 he was a hired man in the King's company, probably having come at the time of the reorganization of the companies in 1625. In none of the six King's plays in which he is known to have acted did he have a very important role; perhaps Mountayne is the largest. Most of them are mildly comic. In *The Swisser* Andrucho (Lowin) calls Asprandus (Smith) and Iseas (Greville) 'you two little Pigmies', but the speech is probably intended to call attention to the bulk of Lowen rather than the smallness of Smith and Greville.

By 1634 Greville had joined the Revels company, probably as a hired man again, since Crosfield's list implies that only the *first* seven were sharers.

1615, Dec. 23—'Curtis Grovell & Catherine Fawne mar. St. Andrew's in the Wardrobe. (Bod.)

1621/2, Jan. 16—'Elizabeth daughter of Bridget the reputed wife of Robert Birredge, from Curtyse Grevills howse' chris. St. G.C.; bur. 21 Feb. 1621/2.

1622—Sir Henry Herbert mentions him as a member of Palsgrave's and, in the same entry, as one of 'the chiefe of them at the Phoenix'. (*Herbert*, p. 63; see pp. 183-4.)

c. 1625-6—'Curtis' in the stage directions for King's revival of *The Two Noble Kinsmen*, IV. 2, and v. 3. (1634 4° B.M.; on the date see Chambers, *Shakespeare*, i. 530). He played a messenger and an attendant.

1626—'*Latinus* a Player—Cvrtise Grevill' in King's cast for Massinger's *The Roman Actor*, lic. 11 October. (1629 4° B.M.)

1628—'Cvrteise Grivill' was tenth in King's cast for *The Lover's Melancholy*, lic. 24 November. (1629 4° B.M.)

c. 1630—'*Mountayne—A Goldsmith*—Curtoys Grivell' in King's cast given in the MS. of Clavell's (?) *Soddered Citizen*. (*Soddered Citizen*, p. 3.)

1631, May 6 (lic.)—'Curt:' and 'Curtis:' in the King's cast for *Believe as You List*, IV. 3; his part was that of third merchant. (Sisson, *B.A.Y.L.*, pp. xxxi ff.)

1631—In the MS. of Arthur Wilson's *The Swisser* (B.M. Add. MS. 36759) his name is given in the cast for the Blackfriars production:

Asprandus			Smith
Iseas	}	Two Gentlemen {	Greuill

(Feuillerat, *The Swisser*, p. 3.)

1634, July 18—Kendall told Crosfield that among the players at Salisbury Court was '9. Courteous Grevill'. (*Crosfield's Diary*, p. 72.)

GREY, MARGARET.

1623, Aug. 1—Alleyn granted 'Margaret Grey, of London, widow', a lease of a half share in the Fortune. (*Hens. Paps.*, pp. 30, 112.)

1623/4, Jan. 29—Alleyn granted her a lease of one share of the new Fortune and the taphouse belonging to the theatre and five other tenements in Whitecross Street and Goulding Lane for forty-nine and a half years at a rent of £10. 13*s.* 10*d.* (Ibid.)

GRIMES, ARTHURET (*see* GRYMES, ANTHONY).

GRYMES, ANTHONY. 'Anthony Grymes' and 'Arthuret Grimes' probably shelter the same provincial player; to me Arthuret looks a little more like a mistake than Anthony. It is likely that 'Grynes' is the Coventry reading of the same name.

1625/6, Mar. 6—'Item geuen to Ellis Geste, Thomas Swinerton, Arthuret Grimes, and others, going about with a Pattent from the M^r of the Revells' at Leicester. (Murray, ii. 316.)

1628, June 7—'Anthony Grymes' is third in the list of thirteen players named in the new licence granted to Ellis Guest's company and presented at Norwich 2 July 1628. (Ibid., p. 353.)

1633, Dec.—'Paid given to Grynes & other players who came by warrant' at Coventry. (Ibid., p. 252.)

GRYMES, Thomas. It is possible that the theatrical costumer, who surely must have been serving the players before the closing of the theatres, may have been the same as the child actor at the Chapel who is recorded in Clifton's suit in 1601. (See Chambers, *E.S.* ii. 43–4.)

1647—When Dulwich College sued Tobias Lisle and Thomas Grymes in Chancery for arrears in rent for the Fortune playhouse, Grymes replied that he had no lease, but 'that he, having a very great stock of Apparrell both for men and women, did furnishe the actors of the playhowse, and therefore they allowed him a part or share out of the playhowse and paid him other somes of money out of the proffittes of the howse and still [are] indetted to him'. (*MSS. Dul.*, pp. 245–6.)

GUEST (GARST, GEST, GESTE, GEYST, GOST), ELLIS (ELIAS, ELLICE, ELLYS). Guest was a rather prominent provincial player, but there are no records of his performance in London. Generally his company is unnamed in the records, but in 1629 he appeared as a Lady Elizabeth's man, probably fraudulently, and in 1633 as the leader of a provincial Queen Henrietta's company. It is possible that he was the 'Ellis' who appears in the stage directions of *The Wasp* and *The Poor Man's Comfort*, but Ellis Worth (q.v.) is a more likely candidate.

1612/13, Jan. 9—'Ellice Geyst the sonne of Elice Geyst supposed: She was brought a bedd in her fathers howse whose name is Robert Steward surgion, dwellinge at the Bull ouer against leaden hall,' chris. St. Peter Cornhill. (*Harl. Soc. Pub.*)

1612/13, Feb. 2—'Ellice the supposed sonne of Ellice Gest: the mother of the saide childe dwelleth wth her ffather Robt Steward wthin the bull y',' bur. St. Peter Cornhill. (Ibid.)

1624/5, Mar. 16—'Ellis Gest' was one of the leaders of the company to whom Sir Henry Herbert granted a licence of this date; it was presented at Norwich 28 May 1625. (Murray, ii. 352–3, 371.)

1625/6, Mar. 6—'Ellis Geste, Thomas Swinerton, Arthuret Grimes' with their company at Leicester. (Ibid., p. 316.)

1628, June 7—Ellis Guest is named first in the new licence granted to an unnamed company by Sir Henry Herbert and presented at Norwich 2 July 1628. (Ibid., p. 353.)

1629, June 27—At Norwich he presented a warrant dated 8 June 1629 and called himself one of the company of Joseph Moore, Alexander Foster, Robert Guilman, and John Townsend, saying that the rest of the company was still at Thetford. Elizabeth's men were elsewhere at this time, and this is the only instance that connects Guest with them; Murray thinks the licence a forgery or the entry a mistake of the Norwich clerk. (Ibid. i. 259–60; ii. 353.)

1629—'Item geven to Mr Guest, a player, & his Companie' at Leicester. (Ibid. ii. 317.)

1630—'Ellys Garst hath licens and company' at Reading. (Ibid., p. 386.)

c. 1630 ?—He was possibly the 'Ellis' who is named as an actor in the

MS. of *The Wasp*; see Ellis Bedowe and Ellis Worth. (Greg, *Dram. Doc.*, p. 360.)

1631, July 18—'Ellys Guest, Richard Errington and their company' showed their licence of 15 July at Reading. (Murray, ii. 386–7.)

1633, June 22—'Elias Gost and his Company of the Quenes players' were at Norwich. (Ibid., p. 354.)

1634, Sept. 13—A licence of the Revels office of 25 June 1634 was presented at Norwich by 'Elias Guest one of the players in the said lycence'. He was paid 40s., but did not play. (Ibid., pp. 355, 372.)

GUILMAN, ROBERT (*see* GILMAN, ROBERT).

GUNNELL, RICHARD. Gunnell was an important figure in the Jacobean and Caroline theatre as actor, theatre manager, and dramatist. He is first heard of when Prince Henry's men become the Palsgrave's in January 1612/13. Alleyn's diary indicates his importance in the company and, apparently, the friendship existing between Alleyn and Gunnell. He was one of four Palsgrave's men to hold shares in the new Fortune, only Massey and Gunnell holding full shares. It seems that he became manager of the theatre and a dramatist for the company at about the same time, for Herbert licensed two of his plays in 1623 and 1624, and in 1624 Gunnell bound the other chief members of the company to him to continue at the Fortune. He appears in Herbert's office-book as manager in 1624 and 1625.

After 1625 Gunnell's Fortune enterprise seems to have been in difficulties, for there are repeated petitions against him and his associates for debt. (See the King and Queen of Bohemia's company, pp. 260–9.) Probably he had given up acting and turned wholly to management about 1625, for the Lord Chamberlain says in 1631/2 that he is not one of his Majesty's servants.

In 1629 he joined with Blagrave in building the Salisbury Court theatre, and he probably continued to manage companies there until his death, for Kendall told Crosfield in July 1634 that Gunnell was the chief man of the King's Revels, and Andrew Cane said that he died in that year. He was probably succeeded at Salisbury Court by Richard Heton, who was paid for the company's plays in 1636/7 and who drew up his plans for the company a year or so later.

The suit of *deCaine* v. *Wintershall*, together with records of Gunnell's activities in 1633/4 and 1634, makes it clear that he must have died in 1634. Malcolm's record of his death in January 1629/30 (*Londinium Redivivum*, iii. 304) is no more reliable than most of the other extracts from the St. Giles' Cripplegate registers in this volume.

Kendall confirms Prynne's charge of Catholicism against Gunnell.

1613/14, Jan. 15—'Martyne dau of Richard Gunnell, Player' chris. St. G.C.

1615, Sept. 9—'Margaret daughter of Richard Gunnell Play^r' chris.
St. G.C.

1616—*A Description of New England*, by Captain John Smith, has
eight sets of commendatory verses. One is:

> To that worthy and generous Gentleman, my verie
> good friend, Captaine Smith.
>
> May Fate thy Proiect prosper, that thy name
> May be eternised with liuing fame:
> Though foule Detraction Honour would peruert,
> And Enuie euer waits vpon desert:
> In spight of Pelias, when his hate lies colde,
> Returne as Iason with a fleece of Golde.
> Then after-ages shall record thy praise,
> That a New-England to this Ile didst raise:
> And when thou dy'st (as all that liue must die)
> Thy fame liue heere; thou, with Eternitie.
>
> R: Gunnell.

1617/18, Mar. 22—'Redman & His wife: Cartwright gannell & parr
dind w^t vs.' (Alleyn's Diary, Young, ii. 73.)

1618, Oct. 31—'Richard Gumnell' is named in the lease of the Fortune from Edward Alleyn, and 'R Gunll' was fourth of Palsgrave's
to sign it. (*Hens. Paps.*, pp. 27–8; see above, pp. 138–9.)

1619, Aug. 15—He and his wife and daughter dined with Alleyn. *See*
Francis Grace.

1620, Apr. 9—'Ther dind w^t vs m^r gunnell: Cartwright: parr & price
ye King of bohemes men.' (Alleyn's Diary, Young, ii. 174.)

1620, Apr. 20—'Edward sonne of Richard Gunnell, gentle' chris. St.
G.C.

1620/1, Feb. 23—'I went to meet Sr Nic. Stoddard in powles spent att
ye pole Head w^t Hym m^r borne & gunell.' (Young, ii. 202.)

1621, Apr. 15—He and others of the Palsgrave's men dined with
Alleyn. *See* William Bird.

1621/2, Jan. 17—'Anne daughter of Richard Gunnell gentleman'
chris. St. G.C.

1622, May 1—'I mett ye workmen att Ric gunnells.' (Alleyn's Diary,
Young, ii. 236.)

1622, May 20—Alleyn granted 'Richard Gunnell, of London, gent', a
lease of a whole share of the new Fortune. (*Hens. Paps.*, pp. 29, 112.)

1622, May 26—'Tho Allen His wife sone & daughter m^r gunell His
cosen brother & wife dind Here.' (Alleyn's Diary, Young, ii. 237.)

1622, Aug. 18—Dined with Alleyn; see Thomas Downton.

1622, Sept. 22—'m^r gunnell & His wife Starkey & His wife w^t a pigg
goodman walker dind Here.' (Alleyn's Diary, Young, ii. 249.)

1622, Dec. 30—'Recognizances, taken before Richard Lowther esq.
J.P., of Ronald Maddox of Salsbery Court in Fleete Street in the
city of London taylor and John Thompsone of Bowlane in St.
Aldermary in London taylor, in the sum of twenty pounds each;
For the appearance of Richard Peagott bodymaker at the next
Session of the Peace, "to aunswer the complaint of Mr. Gunnell the
Player".' (*Middx. Co. Rec.* ii. 173.)

1622/3, Jan. 30—'Thomas Willington seruant to Richard Gunnell
from the house of Robert Gibbes' bur. St. G.C.

1623, June 21—'Daughter of Richard Gunnell, Player' bur. St. G.C.

1623, Dec. 4—'For the Palsgrave's Players; *The Hungarian Lion*: Written by Gunnel.' Not extant. (*Herbert*, p. 26.)

1624, Apr. 17—'For the Fortune; *The way to content all Women, or how a Man may please his Wife*: Written by Mr. Gunnel.' Not extant. (Ibid., p. 28.)

1624, Apr. 30—Cane, Massey, Cartwright, Stratford, Price, and Fowler signed a bond with Gunnell to continue to play together as Palsgrave's at the Fortune. (Hotson, pp. 52-3.)

1624, July 10—'Ellenor daughter of Richard Gunnell player' chris. St. G.C.

1624, Nov. 3—'For the Palsgrave's Company; A new Play, called, *The Masque*. The masque book was allowed of for the press; and was brought me by Mr. Jon[son] the 29th December 1624.' (*Herbert*, p. 30.) Mr. Adams says in a note, 'This entry seems to be confused. I should like to identify the "new play called *The Masque*" with the play entered in Warburton's list as "A Mask" by R. Govell. Since "R. Govell" is not otherwise heard of, I suspect that this is Warburton's reading of "R. Gunell". . . . "Mr. Jon" may be either Ben Jonson, or Inigo Jones; but Herbert seems to have used the spelling "Johnson".'

1624/5, Feb. 1—'Hellen daughter of Richard Gunnell gentleman' bur. St. G.C.

1624/5, Mar. 15—'From Mr. Gunnel, in the name of the dancers of the ropes, for Lent, this 15 March, 1624. £1. 0. 0.' (*Herbert*, p. 48.)

1624/5, Mar. 19—'From Mr. Gunnel, to allowe of a Masque for the dancers of the ropes, this 19 March, 1624. £2. 0. 0.' (*Variorum*, iii. 66; omitted from *Herbert*.)

1627, May 23—Thomas Saul petitioned the Lord Chamberlain against Gunnell, Cartwright, Price, and Fowler for a £50 debt. (*M.S.C.* ii. 401.)

1629, July 6—He and William Blagrave leased ground for a playhouse at the lower end of Salisbury Court from the Earl of Dorset, for forty-one and a half years. The rental, which was £25 for the first half year and £100 a year thereafter, was paid to Herne each year until the closing of the theatres. On this ground Gunnell and Blagrave built a dwelling and a playhouse at a cost of £1,000. (Hotson, pp. 100-1.)

1630, Apr. 14—'Penelope Dau of Richard Gunnell, Player' bur. St. G.C.

1630, Dec. 2—'Edward sonne of Richard Gunnell Player' bur. St. G.C.

<1630 ?—His daughter Margaret married William Wintershall, the actor, at some unspecified date. (Hotson, pp. 52-3.)

1630/1, Feb. 7—'John sonne of Barbara the reputed wife Dermiere gentleman from Richard Gunnell Player in Redcrostreete' chris. St. G.C.

1631, Oct. 18—John Atkins petitioned the Lord Chamberlain against Gunnell, Cartwright, Matthew Smith, and Fowler. (*M.S.C.* ii. 406.)

1631, Nov. 28—Atkins's second petition called them 'ye Queene of Bohemias Players'. Permission was given to sue after one month. (Ibid.)

1631/2, Jan. 26—William Whitbee petitioned against Gunnell for a debt of £16. The Lord Chamberlain gave permission to sue, stating that 'I vnderstand not Richard Gunnell to bee any of his Ma^{tes} servantes either in ye quality of a stage player or otherwise'. (Ibid., p. 407.)

1633—It was evidently Gunnell to whom Prynne referred in his remark, 'the most of our present English *Actors* (as I am credibly informed) being professed *Papists*, as is the Founder of the late erected new *Play-house*:' (*Histriomastix*, p. 142).

1633/4, Mar. 22—Michaell Grigg petitioned against Gunnell for a debt of £19. 17*s.* 8*d.* Leave granted to sue after one week. (*M.S.C.* ii. 410.)

1633/4, Mar. 23—'John the son of Richard Gunnell in the Well Yard, was buried' at St. Bartholomew the Less. (Bod.)

1634, July 13—Kendall told Crosfield that 'Mr. Gunnell a Papist' was among the chief men at Salisbury Court and that he was 'akin to ye Nappers'. (*Crosfield's Diary*, p. 72.)

1634—In the suit *And. deCaine v. Wm. Wintershall and wife Margaret* in 1654, Cane said that Gunnell died in 1634, and Wintershall said he died intestate in 1633 or 1634, leaving a widow, Elizabeth, and two daughters, Anne and Margaret. (Hotson, p. 52.)

<1634—In this suit Wintershall said that Gunnell's widow Elizabeth administered his estate and afterwards married John Robinson, who was possibly the player. (Ibid.)

1637—Among the 'Elegiack Poems' of Thomas Jordan's *Poeticall Varieties or Varietie of Fancies*, 1637, is:

An Elegie on his Inestimable friend, M^r. Richard Gunnell, Gent.

Goe sell your *smiles* for *weeping,* change your *mirth*
For *mourning dirges,* lave the pretious *earth*
Of my inestimable friend with teares
(Fertill as them the cheeke of *Aprill* weares,
When *Flora* propagates her blessing on
Th' approaching *Daffadills*) *under this stone*
Lyes his neglected ashes, Oh that they
Who knew his *vertues* best should let his *Clay*
Lye unregarded so, and not appeare
With a full *sorrow,* in each eye a teare
Once, daily ore his *urne,* how can they thinke
A pleasing thought, sit and securely drinke
Insatiate carrowses; these are they
Can lose both friends and sorrowes in one day
(Not worth my observation) let me turne
Againe to my sad duty, where ile mourne
Till my corporeall essence doe become
A glyding rivulet; and pay the *summe*
To thy deare memory; my streame shall lend
A drop to none les he hath lost a friend:
The melancholly mad-man that will prove
His *passion* for his *Mistresse* is but *love,*
Were best be thrifty in his teares, for I
Will not supply him though his *mistresse* dye;
My ford is thine deare *Gunnell* and for thee

My *Christall Channell* flowes so currently,
Tagus and great *Pactolus* may be proud
Of their *red sands*, let me my Rivers shrowd
Incourse *Meanders*, where the waters shall
In a griev'd murmure, *Gunnell, Gunnell*, call,
It is for thee I *flow*, for thee I *glide*,
I had retain'd my *floods* hadst thou not *dyed*.
And little water birds shall chaunt this *theame*,
Thy *Iordan* mourner is a Iordan *streame*.

1637, Nov.—In reply to a suit for non-payment of rent on the Fortune
theatre, it was explained that 'Marrant and Roods [Rhodes] were
assignees of leases . . . originally granted by Edw. Alleyn to Charles
Masseye, the actor, John Fisher, Thomas Wiggett, and Richard
Gannill'. (*MSS. Dul.*, p. 54.)

c. 1641—Elizabeth Robinson, formerly wife of Richard Gunnell,
made her will. (Hotson, p. 52.)

GWALTER, WILLIAM.

1622, May 20—Alleyn granted 'William Gwalter Cittizen and
Jnholder of London' a lease of two shares in the Fortune. (*Hens.
Paps.*, pp. 29, 112.)

1622, Aug. 18—He dined with Alleyn; *see* Thomas Downton.

1623, June 19 and 20—He parted with one of his shares to Robert
Leigh. (*Hens. Paps.*, pp. 30, 112.)

1631, Oct. 6—A William Gwalter was one of the high constables of
the hundred of Ossulston, co. Middx. (*Middx. Co. Rec.* iii. 40)

GYLMAN, ROBERT (*see* GILMAN, ROBERT).

HALEY, RICHARD (*see* HAWLEY, RICHARD).

HALL, GEORGE. Certainly Hall was an entertainer, but whether
the Norwich record means that he was also an actor is impossible
to determine.

1637/8, Jan. 12—'paid given to Robert Browne, Georg Hall, &
Richard Jones players by warant, who had a motion to shew
expressing the worlds abuses' at Coventry. (Murray, ii. 253.)

1639, Oct. 9—He was with Browne at Norwich; *see* Robert Browne.

HALL, WILLIAM. The fact that Hall appears in the list of grooms
sworn as Prince Charles's players, but not in the company's cast
of *Holland's Leaguer*, indicates either that he was an obscure
member of the company or that he did not join until after the
production of *Holland's Leaguer*. The latter conclusion seems more
probable because of the importance of his place in the company
suggested by his inclusion in the list of six whom Crome wished
to sue.

His role for the King's Revels is an average one, neither leading
not obscure. The parish register entries show that he was a player
for some time, but tell us nothing of his company.

1632, May 10–15—'William Hall' was tenth in a list of eleven men
named in a warrant for swearing them 'groomes of the Chamber in

ordinary wthout ffee to attend the Prince his Highnes in ye quality of players'. (*M.S.C.* ii. 358.)

1632, Dec. 10—William Crome petitioned against William Browne, Graddell, Sneller, Bond, Cooke, and Hall, 'ye princes Players'. On 21 December 1632 leave to sue was granted. (Ibid., p. 408.)

c. 1634 ?—'*Mela Seneca's* Brother—*Will. Hall*' in the King's Revels cast for *Messalina.* (1640 ed. B.M.)

1637/8, Mar. 19—' A warr^t of app^rhension against Richard Bullocke vpon ye complaint of Wm Hall for an Arrest 19 March 1637.' (*M.S.C.* ii. 387.)

1640, Oct. 19—'William Hall and Jone Harredye' mar. St. G.C.

1641, Sept. 25—'William sonne of Wm. Hall, Player' chris. St. G.C.

1644, June 12—'Ann dau: Willm Hall player' chris. St. G.C.

1645, Aug. 20—'ffrances dau: of Willi Hall Player' chris. St. G.C.

1648, Sept. 1—'Afrika Dau of Willi Hall player' chris. St. G.C.

1651/2, Feb. 25—'ffran Dau of Willi Hall player' bur. St. G.C.

1651/2, Mar. 20—'Sarah Dau of Willi Hall plaier' bur. St. G.C.

HALLEY, Richard (*see* HAWLEY, RICHARD).

HALSEY, Bernard.

1622/3, Feb. 3—'Daughter of Bernard Halsey, Tumbler' bur. St. G.C.

HAMERTON, Henry. Possibly Henry Hamerton and Henry Hammersley were not the same player, but the similarity of the names and the association of the Prince's men with the theatre in St. Giles's parish suggest that they were.

1626, Apr. 16—'Affryca, Da of Henry Hammersley, Player' chris. St. G.C.

1635, Dec. 12—'Henry Hamerton' was named with three others in a warrant to swear them grooms to attend the Prince in the quality of players. (*M.S.C.* ii. 377.)

HAMLEN (HAMLETT), Robert. Hamlen had signed the Lady Elizabeth's (?) bond to Henslowe in 1611 and the debt-funding agreement of the players at the Hope, apparently Prince Charles's, in March 1615/16. He seems to have remained with Prince Charles's until the general reorganization of the companies in 1625, when he disappears.

1616–17 ?—' Robt hamlen' was fifth to sign Prince's (Charles I) letter to Alleyn explaining their disagreement with Jacob Meade and asking for a loan. (*Hens. Paps.*, p. 93; see above, p. 200, n. 3.)

1625, > May 5—As a member of the Prince's company, 'Robert Hamlett' received 'iiij yards' of black cloth for the King's funeral procession. (*M.S.C.* ii. 326.)

HAMLUC, W. Hamluc is generally said to be an actor's name slipped into the text of *The Witch of Edmonton*, though it is quite possible that the dramatists may have selected the name and that no actor is indicated at all. If Hamluc and Mago were actors, it is probable that they took part in the Prince's production of about

1621, rather than the Queen Henrietta's performance of about 1635 or 1636 (see above, p. 251).

c. 1621—The list of the dramatis personae of *The Witch of Edmonton* gives 'W. Hamluc' and 'W. Mago' as two country men. 'Haml.' has two speeches; the name also occurs in a stage direction, '*Enter* W. Hamlac, *with Thatch and a Link*' (IV. 1). (1658 4° B.M.)

HAMMERTON, NICHOLAS. One would guess that Nicholas belonged to the playing family of Stephen and Henry Hammerton, but there is no evidence.

1634/5, Jan. 3—'Richard sonne of Nicholas Hammerton, Play^r' bur. St. G.C.

HAMMERTON, STEPHEN. The petition of Beeston and Blagrave to recover the boy Stephen implies that Hammerton had been performing at the Salisbury Court, for Blagrave was one of the owners of that theatre. It is generally said that Hammerton was not taken from Blackfriars, but one cannot be certain, for there is nothing in the records to prove that he did not return to the Salisbury Court for two or three years after 1632. The prestige of the King's men, however, makes such an action unlikely.

The records of Hammerton's popularity and the evidence of his roles completely verify Wright's statement about him published in 1699. The character and number of the epilogue references to Hammerton make it clear that he was the matinee idol of Blackfriars in the forties.

Mr. Baldwin (*Organization and Personnel*, p. 194) notes that Hammerton became a full member of the company in 1640/1 and deduces that he must have begun his apprenticeship before January 1630/1. This conclusion is not impossible, but the Beeston-Blagrave petition does not prove it, nor does it prove that Hammerton was one of the original King's Revels actors in 1629.

The Stephen Hammerton of York obviously was not the actor, but he at least suggests the origin of the King's man.

1632—'ORIANA, the faire betroth'd of *Mirabell*, . . . Acted by Mr. *Steph. Hammerton*' in the King's cast for the 1632 revival of *The Wild Goose Chase*, printed in 1652. (1652 ed. B.M.)

1632, Nov. 1 and Dec. 3—'Mary Hammerton wife of Stephen Hammerton of Hellifeild co. York esq.' was indicted with others for not attending church for the past month. All are designated as late of St. Margaret's, Westminster. Jeaffreson says that they were probably visiting country gentry, for there was a family of the name which included several Stephens at Hellifield in Yorkshire. (*Middx. Co. Rec.* iii. 46, 132.)

1632, Nov. 12—William Blagrave and William Beeston petitioned the Lord Chamberlain to recover 'a boy named Stephen Hamerton' from Christopher Babham, who had inveigled him from them and used him at Blackfriars. The Lord Chamberlain referred the case to Herbert. (*M.S.C.* ii. 408.)

1640—The epilogue to Shirley's *The Doubtful Heir* has the lines:

> *How did the action please ye, was it well ?*
> *How did King* Stephen *do, and tother Prince ?*

Since the king in the play is named not Stephen but Ferdinand, it is probable that Stephen Hammerton had this role. (1652 ed. B.M.)

c. 1640—The epilogue to Suckling's *The Goblins* (acted by King's at Blackfriars) in telling of the reaction of various groups in the audience to plays says,

> *The women—Oh if* Stephen *should be kil'd,*
> *Or misse the Lady, how the plot is spil'd ?*

Evidently Hammerton played Orsabrin. (1648 ed. Chi.)

1641—In Killigrew's *The Parson's Wedding*, the Captain, whose recital of the epilogue is interrupted by the Lady Love-all, tries to put her off with, 'Think on't, *Stephen* is as handsome, when the Play is done, as Mr. *Wild* was in the Scene.' He concludes the play with, 'What say you, Gentlemen, will you lend your hands to joyn them ; the Match you see is made ; if you refuse, *Stephen* misses the Wench, and then you cannot justly blame the Poet. For you know, they say, that alone is enough to spoil the Play.' (1664 ed. B.M.)

1640/1, Jan. 22—A warrant was issued for swearing him and five others as Grooms of His Majesty's Chamber to attend as players. (*M.S.C.* ii. 397.)

>1642—Wright says, '*Amyntor* was Play'd by *Stephen Hammerton*, (who was at first a most noted and beautiful Woman Actor, but afterwards he acted with equal Grace and Applause, a Young Lover's Part).' (*Hist. Hist.*, p. 4.)

1647—His name—'Stephen Hammerton'—stands fifth in the list of ten King's men who signed the dedication of the Beaumont and Fletcher folio.

1647—Henry Harington's verses in the Beaumont and Fletcher folio evidently allude to him:

> *Ladies can't say*
> *Though* Stephen *miscarri'd that so did the play:*
> *Judgement could ne're to this opinion leane*
> *That* Lowen, *Tailor, ere could grace thy Scene:*

1647/8, Jan. 28—He was one of seven King's men to enter into a bond for payment of a King's company debt. (*See* Theophilus Bird.)

HANLY, RICHARD (*see* HAWLEY, RICHARD).

HANSON, NICHOLAS. It is improbable that the provincial player is the legatee in the will of Michael Bowyer, but he might be.

1623, June 14—'Nicholas Hanson' brought to Norwich a licence of 28 May 1622. The name of the company was not given, but Mr. Murray (ii. 11) thinks it was the Children of the King's Revels. (Murray, ii. 347–8.)

1628, Apr.—'Paid & given to the Kings Revells, to Nicholas Hanson one of that company' at Coventry. (Ibid., p. 250.)

1645, Sept. 20—A Nicholas Awnsham of Hounslow was a legatee and witness in the will of Michael Bowyer. (See Appendix, pp. 635–6.)

HARRIS, JOHN. Though there is only one record of the appearance of Harris as a player, there is ample evidence, after 1642, that he was thought of as a former player's boy. Muddman (Williams, *English Journalism*, pp. 106–7) says that after the closing of the theatres he became a printer at Oxford, issued a newsbook, *Mercurius Militaris*, for the army, and clamoured for the death of Charles. In 1654 he was convicted of obtaining £900 by forging Cromwell's signature. In 1660 he was hanged for theft and burglary.

1634/5, Mar. 10—His name was sixteenth in the list of twenty-eight players at Norwich. Some of them belong to the King's Revels, though the records do not give the name of the organization. Probably the list includes two companies. (Murray, ii. 356; see above, pp. 286 and 288–9.)

1648, Dec. 12—In *Mercurius Impartialis* (B.M. E476.3) he is described as 'sometimes a Players Boy'. (Hotson, p. 15.)

1649/50, Feb. 25—*Royall Diurnall* (B.M. E594.6) says he was 'once a Strowlers boy, or a Players boy of the Company of the Revells'. (Ibid.)

1649/50, Mar. 13–20—In *The Man in the Moon* (B.M. E596.3) he is called 'a Players Boy, knowne by the name of *Jack of Oxford*'. (Ibid.)

HARRISON, RICHARD. It is odd that Harrison appears only in these two documents about the repair of highways near the Red Bull and not in any of the longer lists of Queen Anne's or Revels men. If he was an obscure hired man, why should he appear in such documents, presumably concerned with company leaders? Possibly he was a resident caretaker of some sort at the Red Bull.

1617, Oct. 2—He was one of six players who petitioned the Sessions of the Peace for the Red Bull (Queen Anne's) company. (*Middx. Co. Rec.* ii. 170.)

1622, Oct. 3—The same six Red Bull actors were named in an order for repairing the highways. (See p. 169, n. 2.)

HART, CHARLES. The only evidence we have for Hart's career before 1642 is the statement of Wright, who is generally trustworthy.

In spite of frequent assertions to the contrary, there is no evidence that Charles Hart was in any way connected with the Shakespeare family. Shakespeare's nephew, William Hart (q.v.), who is often said to have been Charles's father, died a bachelor (*Shakspeareana Genealogica*, p. 398).

Most of Mr. Baldwin's discussion is based on the assumption that Charles was the son of William, and is therefore of little value, except his observation that if Hart had the important role of the Duchess when *The Cardinal* was licensed in 1641, he must have been apprenticed several years earlier.

Charles Hart was a very famous actor on the Restoration stage. He died in 1683.

> 1642—Wright says, '*Hart* and *Clun*, were bred up Boys at the *Blackfriers*; and Acted Womens Parts, *Hart* was *Robinson's* Boy or Apprentice: He Acted the Dutchess in the Tragedy of *the Cardinal*, which was the first Part that gave him Reputation.' He also says that '*Hart* was a lieutenant of Horse under Sir *Thomas Dallison*, in *Prince Rupert's*, Regiment'. (*Hist. Hist.*, pp. 3, 8.)

HART, WILLIAM. William Hart is generally said to have been the son of Shakespeare's sister Joan. I know, however, of no evidence to support this identification except the facts that Shakespeare did have a nephew William Hart, and that the actor was connected with Shakespeare's company. The St. Giles' entries about William Hart, player, disturb the old assumption. Either the actor was *not* Joan Hart's son, or the William Hart buried at Stratford in 1639 was not Shakespeare's nephew; perhaps there were two actors named William Hart. The first possibility seems to me the more likely, since no real evidence has ever been adduced to show that the Stratford man was an actor (see *Shakspeareana Genealogica*, pp. 397–8).

The actor William Hart was receiving money from the King's company, presumably as a hired man, in January 1630/1, touring with a Revels company in 1634 and 1635, and back as a King's man in 1636.

The odd 'Weaver als Player' designation in the parish registers in 1638 and 1639 suggests that he had abandoned his occupation of weaver to go on the stage.

Because of the confusion of the Harts, I have included all items about Shakespeare's nephew, the King's actor, and possibly a third William Hart who planned to go abroad in 1639.

1600, Aug. 28—'Wilhelmus filius Wilhelmi Hart' chris. Trinity Church, Stratford-on-Avon. (*Shakspeareana Genealogica*, p. 397.)

1616, Mar. 25—He was left a legacy of £5 in the will of his uncle, William Shakespeare. (Chambers, *Shakespeare*, ii. 172.)

1630/1, Jan. 10—'A petition of William Measure agst Wm Hart debt 7^{li} Answered (vizt) I desire Sr Henry Herbert Kn^t to make stay of soe much money as shall appeare to bee iustly due vnto the pet^r [out of the *del.*] from his Ma^{tye} out of the first moneys payable vnto Wm Hart & to make payment therof vnto the pet^r or his Assigne Accordingly And This shall bee his warr^t. Jan. 10. 1630.' (P.R.O., L.C. 5/183.)

1634, Nov. 28—One of six leaders mentioned in a licence of this date for a new unnamed company; the licence was shown at Norwich 3 September 1635. Mr. Murray thinks it was a King's Revels company. (Murray, ii. 8, 357.)

1635/6, Mar. 16—'Anne daughter of William hart Gentlem[an]' chris. St. G.C.

1636, May 17—His name was seventh in a list of minor King's men in players' pass. (*M.S.C.* ii. 378–9.)

1636/7, Jan. 12—His name was third in a list of eleven 'Dependantes on the Players' of Blackfriars who were granted tickets of privilege. (*M.S.C.* ii. 380.)

1638, July 29—'Winifred dau. of William Harte, Weaver als Player' chris. St. G.C.

1639, Mar. 29—'Will'mus Hart' bur. Trinity Church, Stratford-on-Avon. (*Shakspeareana Genealogica*, p. 398.)

1639, May 26—'Minute of a pass for Searles Proude and William Hart to go into the Low Countries with two servants.' (*C.S.P., Dom.*, 1639, p. 232.)

1639, July 19—'Winifred daug^r of William Harte weaver' bur. St. G.C. In the margin is 'als Player'.

1639, Nov. 23—'Mary daug^r: of William Harte Player' bur. St. G.C.

1650, Nov. 9—'Willi Hart Player from the hospitall' bur. St. G.C.

HARVEY, WILLIAM.

1628, June 7—'W^m harvye' is seventh in a list of thirteen named in the new licence of this date granted to Ellis Guest's unnamed company by Sir Henry Herbert and presented at Norwich 2 July 1628. (Murray, ii. 353.)

HATFIELD, GEORGE. A ghost name from Fleay's misreading of George Stutfield (q.v.).

HAUGHTON, HUGH. It seems likely that the Lady Elizabeth's boy and the leader of the provincial company are the same. The actor in the masque seems more likely to have been a stage-struck domestic servant, but he might have been our provincial ex-actor.

1613, May 31—'Hughe Haughton' was named as a boy in a patent to Lady Elizabeth's of this date copied at Coventry 28 March 1615. (See *R.E.S.* i. 183.)

1634, Nov. 28—He was named as one of the six leaders in a licence of this date for an unnamed company presented at Norwich 3 September 1635. Mr. Murray thinks the company was the King's Revels. (Murray, ii. 8, 357.)

1640/1—In Sir Thomas Salusbury's *Masque at Knowsley*, Dr. Almanacke discusses Christmas's will with him. Almanacke reminds Christmas of various persons to whom he should leave legacies.

> *Alm.*: Honest Hugh Haughton S^r
> *Ch.*: O my privie servant: I have a purpose to settle an annuity upon him, Provided allwayes, That if hee act not once at the least, euery Christmas, or talks of anything else, till Shrouetyde followinge, this legacie shalbee voyde, and of none effect.

'Hu. Haughton' in the part of December speaks the eight-line epilogue. (R. J. Broadbent, ed., *A Masque at Knowsley*, reprinted from the *Transactions of the Historic Society of Lancashire and Cheshire*, 1926, p. 11.) The masque, which is strongly reminiscent of Middleton's *Inner Temple Masque*, was performed at Knowsley Hall on Twelfth Night 1640/1.

HAUGHTON, ROBERT (*see* HOUGHTON, ROBERT).

HAWLEY (HALEY, HALLEY, HANLEY, HANLY, HAWLE), RICHARD.
At first glance it seems doubtful if all these spellings should be
taken to conceal the same man, but a little analysis of the records
seems to me to make it highly probable. The records of Roger and
Joan show that Hawley, Halley, and Haley are the same man.
The ticket of privilege and the players' pass for the King's men
(in which four names are duplicated) show that Halley and Hanley
are the same, a confusion which seems odd until one remembers
that the name was probably Hawley, sometimes spelled Hauley,
and that clerks often mistook a 'u' for an 'n', especially when
either spelling made a common name.

Hawley was probably a hired man in the King's company who,
if he is to be identified with the Hanly at Norwich, as I think he
should be, had begun his career as a provincial actor.

1628, June 7—'Richard Hanly' is tenth in a list of thirteen men
named in a new licence of this date granted to Ellis Guest's unnamed company and shown at Norwich 2 July 1628. (Murray, ii.
353.)

1630, Apr. 8—'Richard Hawle and Margrett Gibbens' mar. St. G.F.

1632, Dec. 16—'Roger, sonne of Richard Halley player' chris. St.
G.C. 'Roger son: of Richard Hawley, Player' bur. 4 Oct. 1636.

1633/4, Jan. 5—'Joanna Da: of Richard Haley Player' chris. St. G.C.
'Jone daug^r of Richard Hawley Player' bur. 22 Aug. 1634.

1635, Apr. 8—'ffrancis sonn of Richard Hawley Player' chris. St.
G.C.

1636, May 17—'Richd Hanley' was eighth in a list of minor King's
men in players' pass. (M.S.C. ii. 378.)

1636, July 27—'Thomazine daug^r: of Richard Hawley Player' chris.
St. G.C. 'Thomazine daug^r: of Rich: Hawley Player' bur. 1 Sept.
1636.

1636, Aug. 2—'Frances dau: of Richard Hawley Player' bur. St.
G.C.

1636/7, Jan. 12—A ticket of privilege as attendant of the players was
granted to 'Richd Halley' and ten others 'imployed by his Ma^{tes} servantes the Players of Blackfryers'. (M.S.C. ii. 380.)

1638, Apr. 1—'Joyce daug^r: of Richard Hawley, Player' chris. St.
G.C.

1639, July 21—'Sara wife of Richard Hawley, Player' bur. St. G.C.

1640, Nov. 20—'Richard Haley' bur. St. G.F.

HEARNE, JOHN (see HERNE, JOHN).

HEMINGES (HEMINGE, HEMMINGE, HEMMINGES), JOHN. John
Heminges's career as an actor was over by the time of the death
of his fellow, William Shakespeare. Though his name appears in
the casts for *The Alchemist* and *Catiline*, it is not found in any
casts after 1611—e.g., *Bonduca*, *Valentinian*, or *The Duchess of
Malfi*—and Mr. Baldwin deduces, apparently with reason, that he
had retired from the stage and devoted himself to managerial
activities by 1612 or 1613 (*Organization and Personnel*, p. 250)..

Heminges first appears as a Strange's man in 1593, though his confirmation of arms in 1628/9 says that he had been a servant of Queen Elizabeth, and Sir Edmund Chambers thinks that he was probably the 'John Hemminge gent' who married Rebecca, widow of the player William Knell, on 10 March 1587/8 (Chambers, *E.S.* ii. 320). He seems to have been one of the original Lord Chamberlain's men, and he remained an important member of the company until his death in 1630, having more to do with their financial transactions than any other man. From 1596 to 1630 Heminges almost invariably received the company's payments for performances at court, though in his last two years Lowin and Taylor generally received the money with him.

As an actor, Heminges's roles, according to Mr. Baldwin (op. cit., pp. 218, 249 ff.), were mostly those of 'the more or less comic, peppery old man', the 'father, counsellor, servant, with all the privileges of oddity or whimsicality attaching to age'. Mr. Baldwin thinks he played such parts as Capulet, Brabantio, Polonius, Leonato, Kent, Gonzalo, Cleremont, Calianax. In these years of his prime, Heminges lived in the parish of St. Mary's Aldermanbury, where he was married, where fourteen of his children were baptized, where he was a churchwarden and sidesman, and where he and his wife were buried.

Heminges was an original shareholder in both the Globe and Blackfriars. In the former his interest increased from one-tenth in 1598 to one-fourth at the time of his death, and in the latter from one-seventh in 1608 to, apparently, one-fourth at the time of his death. John Shank summarizes this financial interest of John Heminges in 1635:

And wheras Iohn Heminges the father of William Hemings of whome yor suppłt made purchase of the sayd partes inioyed the same 30 yeeres wthout any molestacõn beeing the most of the most of [*sic*] the sayd yeeres both Player & Houskeeper, and after Hee gaue ouer playing diuerse yeeres, & his sonne Wm Hemings fower yeers after . . . (*M.S.C.* ii. 369).

At the death of Shakespeare, then, John Heminges was no longer an actor but one of the chief stockholders in the company and a sort of general manager. He has left most records as the man who collected the court fees,[1] but there are hints that he was more important to the company in other capacities. Herbert's office-book suggests that Heminges was the man who dealt with all government officials for the company, and in a time of such centralized control this function was extremely important. Heminges on occasion, possibly as a regular thing, represented all the London companies; witness Herbert's record of January 1618/19. He was able to gain special favours for the company, as

---

[1] Not all court payments to Heminges are listed below. See above, p. 94, n. a.

is indicated in Herbert's record of 11 April 1627; he even served in November 1628 as a sort of special assistant for the Lord Chamberlain. (It is interesting to note that after Heminges's death the Lord Chamberlain asked Sir Henry Herbert to perform this function [see William Hart].) The passage from Jonson's *Masque of Christmas* suggests that Heminges was even active in recruiting the company.

The activities of Heminges and his fellow Condell in the preparation of the First Folio are their greatest claims to fame, but such activities lie outside the scope of this study. For such a task no two men in the company, and possibly no two men in London, were so well qualified by their long personal and professional acquaintance with the author and by their knowledge of his services to the company.

Though Heminges spent most of his adult life in the parish of St. Mary's Aldermanbury and evidently considered that parish his home, there is some evidence that he spent the last years of his life near the Globe. Witter said in 1619 that Heminges owned a house on the Globe property. Heminges's will seems to indicate that he no longer resided in St. Mary's Aldermanbury, and his name is found in the token books of St. Saviour's in 1623 near Globe Alley and in 1624 and 1628 at Blackboy Alley. These facts suggest that in his last years he occupied his house near the Globe.

1616, Mar. 25—He was a legatee in the will of Shakespeare. (Chambers, *Shakespeare*, ii. 172.)

1616, Christmas—In *The Masque of Christmas*, Jonson introduces Venus as a deaf tirewoman seeking her son Cupid.

> *Venus*: I forsooth, he'le say his part I warrant him, as well as ere a Play boy of 'em all: I could ha' had money enough for him, an I would ha beene tempted, an ha' let him out by the weeke, to the Kings Players: Master *Burbadge* has beene about and about with me; and so has old Mr. *Hemings* too, they ha' need of him. (1640 folio B.M.)

1616/17, Jan. 22—He was paid for a play given by King's at court. (Chambers, *E.S.* iv. 183.)

1617, Apr. 24—He was paid for a play given by King's at court. (Ibid.)

1617?, Christmas—A messenger was sent from St. James's 'to wodstrete to heminges the player', apparently in connexion with a court masque. (Mary Sullivan, *Court Masques of James I*, p. 181, n. 2, from *Exchequer of Receipt Miscellaneous*.)

1617/18, Jan. 13—He witnessed the will of Richard Cowley. (See Appendix, p. 642.)

1618, Apr. 20—Payment for two plays given before the King at Easter by the King's company was made 'To John Heminges &c.' (Cunningham, *Revels*, p. xlv.)

1618, May 15—Payment was made 'To the said John Heminges' for another play before the King. (Ibid.)

1618/19, Jan. 29—'Of John Hemminges, in the name of the four companys, for toleration in the holy-dayes, 44s. January 29, 1618.' (*Herbert*, p. 48.)

1619, Mar. 27—His name was the first one listed in a patent for the King's company. (*M.S.C.* i. 280–2.)

1619, Apr. 20—Heminges and Condell, described as 'of greate lyve-inge wealth and power', were sued by John Witter for a one-sixth share of the actors' moiety of the Globe which he alleged had belonged to Augustine Phillips, the first husband of Witter's wife. (Wallace, *Sh. and Lond. Assoc.*, pp. 47–51.)

1619, May 10—Witter, in his replication in *Witter v. Heminges and Condell*, says that on the Globe grounds Heminges had 'a faire howse newe builded to his owne vse for wᶜʰ he payeth but twentie shillinges yearely in all at the most'. (Ibid., p 72.)

1619, May 19—His name was first in a livery allowance list for the King's men. (*Hist. MSS. Com.*, Report IV, Part I, p. 299.)

1619, Sept. 2—'Rebecca wyfe of Mʳ John Hemmings' bur. St. M.A.

1619—'John Hemynges and Henry Condall were appointed feoffees for our parish land.' (Barnard, *New Links*, pp. 15–16, quoted from St. Mary's Aldermanbury Parish Minute Book.)

<1619—The Burley MS. containing a number of poems by John Donne has also the following epitaph on Burbage by Ben Jonson: (H. J. C. Grierson, ed., *The Poems of John Donne* (1912), i. 443):

Epi: B: Jo:

Tell me who can when a player dies
In wᶜʰ of his shapes againe hee shall rise?
What need hee stand at the iudgment throne
Who hath a heaven and a hell of his owne.
 Then feare not Burbage heavens angry rodd,
 When thy fellows are angells & old Hemmĩgs is God.

1620, Nov. 29—The suit of Witter against Heminges and Condell was finally dismissed. (Wallace, *Sh. & Lond. Assoc.*, p. 76.)

1621, Apr. 7—Heminges's name was first in the livery allowance list for King's. (*Hist. MSS. Com.*, Report IV, Part I, p. 299.)

1622, Mar. 27—He was paid for six plays given by King's at court. (Murray, ii. 193.)

1622, June 4—'I dind wᵗ mʳ Hemings.' (Alleyn's Diary, Young, ii. 238.)

>1623—With Henry Condell he edited the Shakespeare Folio.

1623—'John Hemmings' was third in the list of King's men in the Folio.

1623–5—See Condell for verses commemorative of Heminges and Condell's work as editors of the First Folio.

1623, Aug. 19—Herbert reallowed *The Winter's Tale* 'on Mr. Hemmings his worde that there was nothing profane added or re-formed, thogh the allowed booke was missinge'. (*Herbert*, p. 25.)

1623–28?—Malone says that after Heminges's retirement he 'took some concern in the management of the theatre, and used to present Sir Henry, as Master of the Revels, with his New-Year's gift for three or four years afterwards'. (Ibid., p. 67.)

1624, Oct. 4—As Underwood's 'fellow', Heminges was made legatee and overseer in his will. (See Appendix, p. 651.)

1625, > May 5—His name—' Iohn Hemmings—iiij yards '—stood first in the list of 'The King Players' who received black cloth for James's funeral procession. (*M.S.C.* ii. 325.)

1625, June 24—His name stood first in a patent for the King's men. (Ibid. i. 282–3.)

1626, Apr. 1—A deed of St. Mary's Aldermanbury refers to Heminges and Condell, among others, as 'now or late parishioners'. (Barnard, *New Links*, p. 20.)

1626, July 17—' [Received] from Mr. Hemmings for a courtesie done him about their Blackfriers hous,—3*l.* o. o.' (*Herbert*, p. 64.)

1626/7, Mar. 20—'From Mr. Hemminges, for this Lent allowanse, £2. o. o.' (Ibid., p. 48.)

1627, Apr. 11—' [Received] from Mr. Hemming, in their company's name, to forbid the playing of Shakespeare's plays, to the Red Bull Company, this 11 of April, 1627,—5*l.* o. o.' (Ibid., p. 64.)

1627, Dec. 13—He was made a legatee and an overseer in the will of Henry Condell. (See Appendix, p. 641.)

1628, Apr. 10—With Lowin and Taylor he was paid £100 for King's plays in 1627. (*See* Taylor.)

1628, May 9—' Iohn Hemings ' was paid for *The Dumb Bawd of Venice*, performed by King's at court 15 April 1628. (*M.S.C.* ii. 347.)

1628, Nov. 24—' A petition of Henry Ienkins against Richard Sharp debt 50^s answered (vizt) I desire Mr Hemings to satisfye the pet^r out of ye first moneys acrueing to Richard Sharpe either for his share or diuedent &c And this shall bee his warraunt. Nouember 24th 1628.' (L.C. Petition Book, 5/183, p. 43. P.R.O.)

1628, Dec. 14—The Lord Chamberlain issued a warrant for the apprehension of 'Ambrose Beeland and Henry Wilson Fidlers at ye complaint of Mr Hemmings'. (*M.S.C.* ii. 348.)

1628/9, Feb. 27—' Iohn Hemings ' was paid £160 for sixteen plays given before the King at Christmas 1628; the company is not mentioned. (Ibid., p. 349.)

1628/9, Mar. 2—The Garter King of Arms issued a confirmation of his family's arms to ' John Hemings of London Gent. of long tyme Servant to Queen Elizabeth of happie Memory, also to King James hir Royal Successor and to King Charles his Sonne now raigning which John was Sonne and Heire of George Hemings of Draytwiche in the Countye of Worcester Gent'. (*Variorum*, iii. 188.)

1629, May 5—' A Certifficate for Mr Iohn Hemmings.' (*M.S.C.* ii. 349.)

1629, May 6—' Iohn Hemmings ' was the first name listed in a cloak allowance for King's. (Ibid., p. 350.)

1629, May 6—' Iohn Hemings ' was paid £10 for the production of *The Love-Sick Maid* at court Easter Monday; the company was not named. (Ibid., p. 349.)

1630, Apr. 3—' A warr^t for payment of 120^{li} vnto Iohn Hemings for 12 Playes Acted before his Mat^{ie}: at Christmas 1629 signed ye 3^d of Aprill. 1630.' (Ibid., p. 352.)

1630, Sept. 20—The King's order for a payment of £100 for the relief of the players begins, 'Whereas we have given order, that our servant John Heming, and the rest of our Players . . .' (*H.E.D.P.* i. 459.)

1630, Oct. 9—Heminges made his will, as citizen and grocer, of London; it was proved 11 October. See Appendix, pp. 643–5.

1630, Oct. 12—' John Hemmings, player' bur. St. M.A.

HEMINGES, William. Though William Heminges appears never to have been an actor and, according to John Shank in 1635, 'never had any thing to doe wth the sayd [Globe and Black-friars] Stage' (*M.S.C.* ii. 369), he did inherit his father's shares in both theatres, though he soon sold them to John Shank. He was familiar with poets and dramatists of the time, .as his *Elegy on Randolph's Finger* shows, and was the author of at least three plays. Anthony à Wood said (Wood, *Athenae*) that Heminges had 'left behind him greater monuments of his work and ability' than his published plays. What they were no one knows—perhaps Anthony à Wood didn't.

1602, Oct. 3—'William s. of Jhon Hemming' chris. St. M.A.

1621—He was elected King's scholar at Christ Church, Oxford, from Westminster school. (Wood, *Athenae*, iii. 277.)

1628—Received his M.A. from Oxford. (Ibid.)

1628, Dec. 13—'Note of two caveats entered by command of his Majesty, that no grant of a prebend in Christ Church, Oxon, be passed before John Morris, B.D., and Hebrew Professor in that University, be placed there; and that William Hemming, son of John Hemming, his Majesty's servant, have the next Canon's place that becomes void in the said cathedral.' (*C.S.P., Dom.*, 1628–9, p. 408.)

c. 1632—Wrote his *Elegy on Randolph's Finger*, which contains the famous lines 'On the Time Poets'. See *Hemminges' Elegy*, passim.

c. 1632—Wrote lines from Ludgate prison; apparently he was imprisoned as a debtor. (Ibid., p. 20.)

1632/3, Mar.—'Soon after his father's death he [William Heminges] commenced a dramatick poet, having produced in March, 1632–3, a comedy entitled *The Coursinge of a Hare, or the Madcapp*, which was performed at the Fortune theatre, but is now lost. MS. Herbert.' (*Herbert*, p. 34.)

c. 1633—In his answer to the Lord Chamberlain (18 May–12 July 1635), John Shank said that about two years before he had bought one share in the Globe and one in the Blackfriars from William Heminges. (*See* Shank.)

c. 1634—In the same answer Shank says that about eleven months before he had bought one more share in the Blackfriars and two more in the Globe from Heminges for which he had paid £350,' & your suppℓt hath besides disbursed to the said Wm Hemings diuerse other small sumes of money, since Hee was in prison'. (*M.S.C.*, ii. 367.)

1638/9, Feb. 6—'Ruth supposed Daughter of William Hanings & [blank]' chris. St. G.F.

1644, Oct. 13—'Edward s. of William Heam'ings & Rebecka vx' chris. St. J.C. 'Edward sonne of William Hemings' bur. 22 Jan. 1648/9, St. G.F.

1646/7, Jan. 24—'William s. of William Hemings & Rebecca vx' chris. St. J.C. 'William sonne of William Hemings' bur. 9 Feb. 1648/9, St. G.F.

1653—His *Fatal Contract* was published by A.T. and A.P. (probably Anthony Turner and Andrew Pennycuicke), who speak of his death, apparently some time before 1653. (1653 4° HN.)

1662—His *Jewes Tragedy* was published.

HERBERT, HENRY. Henry Herbert bought the office of Master of the Revels from Sir John Astley on 20 July 1623. He continued in this office until the closing of the theatres, and he succeeded to a certain extent in reasserting his powers after the Restoration. As Master of the Revels he was the most important official having regular and direct dealings with the players. His office-book for the period 1622–42 is the most important single document for the study of the Jacobean and Caroline theatre. Though the MS. has disappeared, many extracts from it were taken by Malone and Chalmers, and these, with the exception of a few published by Mr. W. J. Lawrence in the *T.L.S.* for 29 November 1923, have been conveniently gathered together by Professor J. Q. Adams in *The Dramatic Records of Sir Henry Herbert.* Sir Henry and his activities are discussed in pp. 3–18 of this book.

HERNE, JOHN.

1627/8, Jan. 2—'Susanna Dau: of Mr John Hearne gent' bur. St. G.C.
1628/9, Jan. 28—'Beniamyne Son of Mr John Hearne, gent' chris. St. G.C.
1629, July 15—John Herne, of Lincoln's Inn, Esquire, bought from the Earl of Dorset for £950 for a term of sixty-one years the rent and reversion of the property which had been leased to Gunnell and Blagrave for the Salisbury Court theatre. Herne received his rent of £100 per annum until 1642. (*Sh. Soc. Paps.* iv. 91–5; Hotson, pp. 100–2.)

HETON, RICHARD. Heton was manager of the Salisbury Court theatre in February 1636/7. A late lawsuit says that Gunnell, the former manager, had died about 1634, and it is possible that Heton had succeeded him. His only known official act is his collection of money for plays given at court, but his intentions are well known from the documents which Cunningham published (see Appendix, pp. 684–7). A great deal can be learned about Heton by reading these documents of 1639. He was ambitious to become a second Henslowe, breaking companies and dismissing actors as he pleased. Unfortunately it is not known whether he ever succeeded in carrying through his proposals.

There is no assurance that the Richard Heaton of St. Giles or the Richard Heaton of St. Clement Danes may be identified with the manager.

1630, Nov. 16—'William Ellis, Thomas Tyldesley, and Richard Dyot, Commissioners for compounding with Recusants in co. York, to Attorney General Heath. They have compounded with Richard Heaton, of St. Clement Danes, co. Middlesex, for his Majesty's two-third parts of the lands of Dame Grace Babthorpe, widow of Sir Ralph Babthorpe, under the yearly rent of 66*l.* 13*s.* 4*d.*, and desire that a lease may be made to Heaton accordingly.' (*C.S.P., Dom.*, 1629–31, p. 383.)
1631, July 24—'Lease to Richard Heaton, of two-third parts of the lands of Thomas Worsley and Dame Grace Babthorpe, in co. York,

due to the King by reason of their recusancy, resuming to the Crown a yearly rent of 106*l*. 13*s*. 4*d*.' (*C.S.P.*, *Dom*., 1631–3, p. 120.)

1636/7, Feb. 18—He was paid for three plays by the Salisbury Court players (King's Revels) given before the King in October 1635 and February 1635/6 at Hampton Court and St. James. (*M.S.C.* ii. 381–2.)

1639—His notes of his plans for a new agreement and patent for Queen Henrietta's at Salisbury Court were designed to keep them completely under his control. He calls himself 'one of the Sewers of the Chamber to . . . the Queene'. (See below, pp. 684–6.)

1639, Apr. 28—'A Crisom Child of Richard Heaton' bur. St. G.F.

1639, Sept. 14—He made further notes concerning a new agreement with the Queen's men. (See below, pp. 686–7.)

1640, Nov. 17—'Hellen daughter of Richard Heaton' bur. St. G.F.

1641, Apr. 26—'Hellen Daughter of Richard & Elizabeth Heaton' chris. St. G.F.

HEYWOOD, Thomas. Not Heywood's career as a dramatist but his acting career is our concern here. In the nineties he appeared as an Admiral's man, but his long career was with the Worcester–Queen Anne's company. His name occurs in most of the documents of Queen Anne's throughout the history of the company, and he seems to have been a sharer in the company until its final break-up. The number of plays which he wrote for Lady Elizabeth's and Queen Henrietta's companies and his association with Christopher Beeston (q.v.) suggest that he had some close connexion with the Cockpit, but there is no direct evidence that he acted after the break-up of Queen Anne's. The lines in *Musarum Deliciae* (1640), which have sometimes been taken as an indication that Heywood was still acting, clearly refer to writing plays as 'groveling on the stage', compared to another type of composition, 'thy pleasingest flight was somewhat high, When thou didst touch the angels Hyerarchie'. His familiarity with affairs at the Cockpit, however, is clearly shown in the prologues and prefaces for *The Jew of Malta* (1633) and *Love's Mistress* (1636).

Heywood's residence in the last twenty-odd years of his life was in St. James's Clerkenwell, but it has not always been noticed that several of his children are recorded in the registers of St. Saviour's Southwark in the first decade of the seventeenth century (see Bentley, *T.L.S.*).

1616, Mar. 30—'Thomas hayward' was named in a licence for Queen Anne's presented at Norwich; all but Swinnerton and Lee were absent. (Murray, ii. 340.)

1616, June—He was named in the Baskervile suit as a member of Queen Anne's at the time of the second settlement in favour of Francis Browne. (Fleay, *Stage*, pp. 270–97.)

1617, May 31—'Thomas Hayward' played with Queen Anne's at Norwich. (Murray, ii. 343.)

1617, June 3—He signed the new agreement with the Baskerviles as a fellow and sharer of Queen Anne's and signed two extra bonds as well (Fleay, *Stage*, pp. 285–8.)

1617, Oct. 2—He petitioned the Sessions of the Peace on behalf of the Red Bull (Queen Anne's). (*Middx. Co. Rec.* ii. 170.)

1619, >May 13—'Thomas Heywood' was fifth in the list of Queen Anne's men allowed black cloth to wear in her funeral procession. (*M.S.C.* ii. 325.)

1622, Oct. 3—He was one of six Red Bull actors named in an order for the repairing of the highways. (See above, p. 169, n. 2.)

1623, May 21—Markham's suit lists 'Thomas Haywarde neare Clarkenwell Hill', 5s. (See Appendix, p. 682.)

1641, Aug. 16—'Tho Heywood, Poet b^d in ye Church,' St. J.C.

1671—Francis Kirkman, the bookseller, in a note at the end of his catalogue of all the plays ever published, appended to the 1671 edition of John Dancer's *Nicomede*, says of Heywood, '. . . he was very laborious; for he not only Acted almost every day, but also obliged himself to write a sheet every day, for several years together; but many of his Playes being composed and written loosely in Taverns, occasions them to be so mean . . .' (Greg, *Handlist*, pp. xlv–xlvi.)

HILL, JOHN. Collier (Bod.) misread Alice's name as Nill, and he was followed by Chambers and Nungezer. The residence which Errington's servant gave in 1627 makes it doubtful that Alice was his daughter. It is possible that she was the daughter of John Hull, an English actor in Germany in 1600 and 1601. (Herz, *Englische Schauspieler*, p. 38.)

1601, Aug. 13—'Alyce hill d of John a player' chris. St. S.S.

1627, Nov. 22—'John Hill of Pocklington, in the countie of Yorke,' a servant of Richard Errington, 'one of the Company of his Majesties players', made a deposition about a brawl which occurred at Ludlow when the company was acting there. (Murray, ii. 326.)

HINT, ROBERT.

1629, Nov. 10—'Robert Hint' is seventh in a list of eight players named in a licence of this date granted to William Perry and Richard Weekes, 'his Majestie's sworne servantes', which was shown at Reading 30 November. (Murray, ii. 386.)

HITCHENS, FRANCIS. Hitchens's parish suggests that he was connected with the Fortune, but there is no evidence. The identification of the player and the gunner is only a possibility.

1624, Nov. 17—'Katherine dau of Frances Hitchens Playo^r' bur. St. G.C.

1627/8, Feb. 3—'ffrancis Hitchens, Drummer' bui. St. G.C.

1630/1, Mar. 21—'Kenrick Edisbury to [Sir Edward] Nicholas [Secretary to the Admiralty]. Recommends Francis Kitchin as gunner for the Fortune, pink.' Further references to the same man 22 March 1630/1, November 1633, and October 1634. (*C.S.P., Dom.*)

HOBBES, THOMAS. Hobbes first appears when his fellow actor in the Duke of York's company, William Rowley, dedicated his *Search for Money* (1609) to 'his entire and deare-esteemed friend, Maister *Thomas Hobbs*'. With others of the company Hobbes became a Prince Charles's man after the death of Prince Henry, and, though the records of this company are not very full, apparently continued a member until the company went to pieces when their patron became King.

Hobbes and one or two of his fellows were fortunate enough to become King's men at the reorganization of the companies in 1625, but though the entry of 23 May 1625 and that of 6 May 1629 indicate that he was a member, there is no evidence of his ever having important roles in the company's plays.

Professor Sisson points out (*B.A.Y.L.*, p. xxv) that the unusual form of the prompter's anticipatory stage direction at line 661 of Massinger's manuscript of *Believe as You List* ('*Mr Hobs: calld vp*') implies that Hobbes had duties at the front of the house from which he had to be called.

1615, Aug. 23—'Thomas Hobbs & Mary Taylor' mar. St. J.C.

1616, Aug. 4—'Alice d. of Thomas Hobbes' chris. St. J.C.

1618, Aug. 25—'Anne d. of Thomas Hobbes' bur. St. J.C.

1618, Aug. 30—'Jo: boger & marie mr Hobbs & His frend dind wt vs & good man Haynes.' (Alleyn's Diary, Young, ii. 100.)

1619, Aug. 22—'Ther dind wt vs mr Hobbs mr Cartwright & mr Jones his man.' (Alleyn's Diary, Young, ii. 148.)

1623, May 21—Markham's suit lists 'Thomas Hobbes att the vpper end of Shoreditch', 6s. (See Appendix, p. 683.)

1625, >May 5—'Thomas Hobbs' was eighth in the list of players of the Prince's company who received black cloth for James's funeral procession. (*M.S.C.* ii. 326.)

1625, May 23—In Coke's notes of business for his second audience at Whitehall and under the head of 'King Charles his servants' is 'Thomas Hobbs, comedian, now left out of the number new sworn, being engaged for the stock debt of their company in 500*l*. desireth to be sworn as the rest are or to be disengaged'. (*Hist. MSS. Com.*, Report XII, App. 1, p. 198.) Apparently Hobbes was a King's man on this date, though not a patented member. He does not appear in the patent of 24 June 1625; probably this omission had something to do with his objections.

1626/7, Jan. 3–9—A Richard Holden petitioned the Lord Chamberlain against Joseph Taylor, Anthony Smith, and Thomas Hobbes. (*M.S.C.* ii. 400.)

1628, Nov. 24—Fleay (*B.C.E.D.* i. 233), followed by Murray (Murray, i. opp. 172) and Baldwin (*Organization and Personnel*, p. 176), erroneously includes his name in *The Lover's Melancholy* cast and omits that of John Honyman.

1629, May 6—'Thomas Hobbes' was eleventh in a list of King's men for cloak allowance. (*M.S.C.* ii. 350.)

1629, Dec. 3—'A petition of ye widow Pinder against Thomas Hobbes debt 21li.' (Ibid., p. 402.)

1631, May 6 (lic.)—He divided the part of Calistus ('Mr Hobs:, mr Hobs:') with Richard Baxter in the King's production of *Believe As You List*. (Sisson, *B.A.Y.L.*, pp. xxxi ff.)

1636, May 17—He was second in a list of minor King's men for a Player's pass. (*M.S.C.* ii. 378–9.)

HOLCOMB (HOLCOME), THOMAS. In his petition to the Lord Chamberlain in 1635, John Shank seems to imply that Holcomb had been his apprentice, for he says that he had 'payd his part of 200ˡⁱ for other boyes since his coming to yᵉ Company, Iohn Honiman, Thomas Holcome and diuerse others & at this time maintaines 3 more for the sayd service'. (*M.S.C.* ii. 369.) Holcomb's inclusion in several casts of the Beaumont and Fletcher folio, where only one or two boys are mentioned, indicates the importance of his roles, though his only known part is the insignificant one of the Provost's wife in *Barnavelt*. On the basis of such slight evidence Mr. Baldwin argues rather impetuously that Holcomb had the parts of 'the longing woman and the watery-mouthed maid' (*Organization and Personnel*, pp. 223–4), and assigns him such roles as Leocadia in *Love's Pilgrimage*, Honora in *The Loyal Subject*, Rosellia in *The Sea Voyage*, and Leucippe in *The Humorous Lieutenant*.

1616–17—No. 8 in King's cast for *The Queen of Corinth*. (1679 folio B.M.)
1616–18—No. 8 in King's cast for *The Knight of Malta*. (Ibid.)
1619, Aug.—The prompter's notes show that he was the Provost's wife ('T: Holc') in King's production of *Barnavelt*. (Greg, *Dram. Doc.*, p. 273.)
c. 1619–20—No. 8 in King's cast for *The Custom of the Country*. (1679 folio B.M.)
1619–21—No. 8 in King's cast for *Women Pleased*. (Ibid.)
1619–22—No. 8 in King's cast for *The Little French Lawyer*. (Ibid.)
1622, May 14—No. 8 in King's cast for *The Prophetess*. (Ibid.)
1624, July 24—'George sonne of Thomas Holcome Plaier' chris. St. G.C.
1625, Sept. 1—'Thomas Holcome, Player' bur. St. G.C.
1625/6, Jan. 13—His widow married Ellis Worth, the actor (q.v.).

HOLLAND, AARON. Holland was the builder and owner of the ground rents of the Red Bull theatre. His activities in connexion with the theatre, mostly before 1616, are known from suits in the Court of Requests unearthed by C. W. Wallace and published in the *Nebraska University Studies*, ix. 291–315. Professor Sisson has discovered another suit, as yet unpublished, from which he learned that Holland had sold his lease and his share in the profits of the Red Bull before 6 November 1623, retaining only a small annuity for life. (Sisson, *Keep the Widow Waking*, pp. 235–6.)

HOLMAN, THOMAS.
1630, Nov. 12—'Memorandum, Robert Kimpton, Nathaniell Clay, Thomas Holman, and others named in the licence from the Master of Revells, dated the 30ᵗʰ of December 1629, tendred themselves to play in Towne, but did not, and were here in Lent last.' At Reading. (Murray, ii. 386.)

HOLT (HOULT), JAMES. A Queen Anne's man who appears in the patents of 1604 and 1609 and several times in the provinces. Though a patent bearing his name was shown several times in the provinces after 1616, there is no evidence that he was present; in fact, men who were dead at the time the patent was shown appear in these patents with him. He is unknown after the funeral of Queen Anne.

1616, Mar. 30—Named in a licence for Queen Anne's presented at Norwich. (Murray, ii. 340.)

1617, May 31—Named in a licence for Queen Anne's presented at Norwich. (Ibid,, p. 343.)

1619, >May 13—As a member of Queen Anne's company, 'Iames Hoult' was the sixth member of the Queen's company listed to receive black cloth to wear in her funeral procession. (*M.S.C.* ii. 325.)

HONYMAN (HONEYMAN, HONIMAN, HONNYMAN, HUNNIEMAN, HUNNYMAN), JOHN. Honyman's roles indicate that he was one of the most important boy actors in the company from about 1626 to about 1630, and though he died before attaining (so far as we know) to any very important adult roles, his contemporaries seem to have thought him of great promise. Of his literary work, which impressed Sir Aston Cokayne, nothing whatever is known; Cokayne implies that he had written plays.

Mr. Baldwin (*Organization and Personnel*, p. 198) thinks that in addition to his assigned roles Honyman played Olinda in *The Lover's Progress*, Maria in *A Wife for a Month*, Ismenia in *The Maid in the Mill*, and Bianca in *The Fair Maid of the Inn*. Mr. Baldwin's reconstruction of Honyman's career in the company is badly askew because he assumes that Honyman succeeded to Thompson's place at the latter's death in 1630, whereas Thompson did not die until 1634, three or four years after Honyman had had his first adult role in *The Soddered Citizen*.

John Honyman's family is easily traced in the records of St. Botolph's Bishopsgate. His father married Ellen Chancellor 12 August 1611, and John is the first of their children recorded at St. Botolph's. A brother Anthony and a sister Alice both died young. His brother Richard (q.v.), whom he mentions in his will, survived him. Sometime before 1627 his father died and his mother married John Thomas, Glover, possibly the occasion for John's apprenticeship to the King's company. On 8 July 1635 his mother married John Sweetman, to whom she was married when John Honyman made his will and to whom he left a bequest.

1612/13, Feb. 7—'John, son of Richard Honyman' chris. St. B.B.

1617< >1635—In his answer to the players' petition to the Lord Chamberlain (18 May–12 July 1635), John Shank, describing his efforts on behalf of the company, said that he had 'payd his part of 200^{li} for other boyes since his coming to ye Company, Iohn Honiman, Thomas Holcome and diuerse others & at this time maintaines 3 more for the sayd service'. (*M.S.C.* ii. 369.)

1626—'*Domitilla* cousin germane to *Caesar*—Iohn Hvnnieman' in King's cast for Massinger's *The Roman Actor*, lic. 11 October. (1629 4° B.M.)

1628—'Iohn Honyman' was fourteenth (apparently a boy) in King's
cast of *The Lover's Melancholy*, lic. 24 November. (1629 4° B.M.)
Fleay, followed by Murray and Baldwin, has omitted Honyman
and inserted Hobbes.

1629—'*Sophia* wife to *Mathias*. *Iohn Hunnieman*', in King's cast for
Massinger's *The Picture*, lic. 8 June. (1630 4° B.M.)

1629?—'*Iohn Honiman, Clarinda*,' in King's cast for Carlell's *The
Deserving Favorite*. (1629 4° B.M.)

c. 1630—'*Sly—his Servant*—John Honyman' in King's cast in the
MS. of Clavell's (?) *The Soddered Citizen*. (*Sod. Cit.*, p. 3.)

1631, May 6 (lic.)—'I: Hony:' was First Merchant in the stage directions (iv. 3) for King's production of Massinger's *Believe as You
List*. (Sisson, *B.A.Y.L.*, pp. xxxi ff.)

1632—'A young FACTOR by Mr. *John Hony-man*' in cast for King's
1632 revival of *The Wild Goose Chase*, printed in 1652. (B.M. copy.)
Mr. W. J. Lawrence says (*R.E.S.* iii. 222) that Honyman also took
the part of Mariana. In the dramatis personae in the first edition
of the play eleven roles are given, each with the name of the actor who
took the part, then comes Mariana, with no actor assigned, and
then A Young Factor, assigned to Honyman. Apparently Mr.
Lawrence assumes that the printer meant to indicate that Honyman took both roles, though there is nothing in the punctuation or
format of the page to indicate this. The part of Mariana is quite a
small one, with only one speech and that of five lines. It would have
been quite possible for Honyman to double the parts, but I see no
reason to assume that he did. The Young Factor is much the
larger part of the two.

1633, Apr. 15—'A Warraunt to sweare Iohn Honyman A Groome
of ye Chamber in ordinary wthout ffee to attend in ye quality of a
Player.' (*M.S.C.* ii. 360.)

1636, Apr. 7—'Johm Honyman one of his Maties Servants the Players'
made his will. Most of his property went to his mother, Ellen
Sweetman, part for herself and part in trust for his brother Richard.
He left twenty shillings for a ring for his stepfather, John Sweetman, and a ten-shilling ring to each of his fellows. His mother was
made executrix. Will Browne, Robert Benfield, and William Burbage witnessed the will. (See Appendix, p. 645.)

1636, Apr. 13—'John Honnyman, Player' bur. St. G.C.

1637—In the section of 'Elegiac Poems' in Thomas Jordan's *Poeticall
Varieties or Varieties of Fancie*, 1637, dedicated to John Ford of
Gray's Inn, is the following:

*An Epitaph on his kind friend M*r*. Iohn
Honiman, Gent.*

Thou that couldst never weepe, and know'st not why
Teares should be spent but in *mans infancy*,
Come and repent thy *error* for here lyes
A *Theame* for *Angels* to write Elegies,
Had they the losse as we have; such a one
As *nature* kild for his perfection,
And when she sends those vertues backe agen
His stocke shall serve for twenty vertuous men.

In *Aprill* dyed this *Aprill* to finde *May*
In Paradise, or celebrate a day
With some celestiall creature, had he beene
Design'd for other then a *Cherubin*;
Earth would have gave him choice; he was a man
So sweetly good, that he who wisely can
Describe at large, must such another be,
Or court no *Muses* but *Divinitie*.

    Here will I rest, for feare the *Readers* eyes
    Vpon his *urne* become a *Sacrifice*.

1658—*Small Poems of Divers Sorts* (1658 ed. B.M.) by Sir Aston Cokayne contains the following (pp. 140–1).

To Mr. John Honyman

On hopefull youth, and let thy happy strain
Redeem the Glory of the Stage again:
Lessen the Loss of *Shakespeares* death by thy
Successful Pen, and fortunate phantasie.
He did not onely write but act; And so
Thou dost not onely act, but writest too:
Between you there no difference appears
But what may be made up with equal years.
This is my Suffrage, and I scorn my Pen
Should crown the heads of undeserving men.

1784—Davies (*Dramatic Miscellanies*, i. 328), in discussing the downfall of the theatres at the Civil War, says, 'The two most celebrated of these performers, were John Thomson and John Hunnieman. The last was the author of a play, with the name of which I should be glad to enrich the dramatic catalogue, but I cannot learn whether it was a tragedy, a comedy, or a mixture of both.'

HONYMAN (HONEYMAN, HONIMAN, HONNYMAN, HUNNYMAN), RICHARD. Richard Honyman was five years younger than his brother John, the King's man. The relationship between the two is clearly established by John's will, which mentions his minor brother Richard and his mother Ellen Sweetman, and by the records of the various members of the family at St. Botolph's. (*See* John Honyman.) Richard's marriage two months after his brother's death suggests that he may have been encouraged by his legacy. Richard was dead by 1657, when his wife remarried.

His position as a hired man of the Prince's company cannot have been a very prominent one.

1618, May 10—'Richard, son of Richard Hunnyman and Hellin' chris. St. B.B.

1636, Apr. 7—His brother John (q.v.) left a legacy to him, apparently as a minor. (See Appendix, p. 645.)

1636, June 15—'Richard Honiman and Rachell Wharton. *l*' mar. St. B.B.

1640, Apr. 25—'Richd Honiman' is second in a list of the 'Princes Players hired men' who are not to be 'hindred or diverted . . . or otherwise molested', (*M.S.C.* ii. 394–5.)

1657, Nov. 12—'Hugh Day, *cooper*, and Rachell Honeyman, *wid*, both of this parish, married *by* Mr. Stephens. Banns.' mar. St. B.B.

HORNE, JAMES. Horne is somewhat difficult to place, for though he received livery on two occasions, there is no evidence that he was ever of much importance in the company. Mr. Baldwin shows reason to believe that he came into the organization between Easter and Christmas 1621 (*Organization and Personnel*, p. 54), but his argument that Horne was a comedian and sometimes played female roles is weak. (Ibid., pp. 192, 368.)

1615, Dec. 19—'James Horne, of St Botolph, Bishopsgate, London, Chandler, & Dorothy Hamond, of St Swithin's, London, Spinster; at St Botolph, Bishopsgate', mar. (*Marriages, London.*) They were married 31 Dec. 1615 St. B.B.

1621—His name was eighth in King's cast for *The Pilgrim*. (1679 folio B.M.)

1625, > May 5—'Iames Horne' was thirteenth in the list of King's men who received black cloth for James's funeral procession. (*M.S.C.* ii. 326.)

1626—'2. Lictors. George Vernon. Iames Horne.' in King's cast for Massinger's *The Roman Actor*, lic. 11 October. (1629 4° B.M.)

1628—'Iames Horne' was fifteenth in King's cast for *The Lover's Melancholy*, lic. 24 November. The roles are not given, but the position of his name indicates that he took a woman's part. (1629 4° B.M.)

1629, May 6—'Iames Horne' was fourteenth in a list of King's men for cloak allowance. (*M.S.C.* ii. 350.)

HORTON, EDWARD. Horton's one known role of any size, that of Mariana in *The Deserving Favorite*, is too nondescript to tell us anything about him, but his appearance in the stage directions of *The Mad Lover* indicates that he was a singing boy and small at the time of the revival from which the stage prompter's directions seem to date. The lines following the entrance in which his name occurs indicate that Stremon and his boy are well known as musicians, and the boy is addressed, 'And how does small Tim Treble here, the heart on't?' Apparently the boy Horton sang the part of Charon to Stremon's Orpheus in the entertainment in IV. I, as Weber pointed out in his edition of the play. According to the stage directions of the folio, Stremon enters alone as Orpheus, but his two-part song requires a singer for Charon's part, and the introduction of the boy as a singer earlier in the play makes it fairly obvious that he has simply been omitted from the stage direction in Act IV.

1629?—'*Edward Horton, Mariana*' in King's cast for Carlell's *The Deserving Favorite*. (1629 4° B.M.)

c. 1630—His name occurs in the stage directions in King's revival of *The Mad Lover*, ii. 2: '*Enter Stremon and his Boy Ed. Hor.*' (1647 folio B.M.)

4595.2 K

HOUGHTON, ROBERT. Since Houghton appears only in the records of this one affair, it may be that the Banbury Puritans cured him of the histrionic urge.

1633, May 2—He was examined at Banbury concerning the fraudulent use of a licence, and the following evidence was sent to the Privy Council: 'Examination of Robert Houghton. Came to this company the Thursday before Easter last, and played his part in stage plays at Sir William Spencer's, [and] at Keinton two or three days this week. Received nothing but meat and drink from them.' (C.S.P., Dom., 1633–4, p. 49.)

1633, May 3—'Further examination of the same. Edward Whiting let the commission in question to William Cooke and Fluellen Morgan, and they two went with it with a puppet play until they had spent all, then they pawned the commission for four shillings. Mr. Bradshaw, hearing of it, redeemed, and afterwards bought it.' (Ibid.)

1633, May 22—He was fetched with others of the company of Richard Bradshaw at the order of the Privy Council from the jail at Banbury, where he had been imprisoned for playing with a forged licence. Since he was accused of giving a false name, the name given here may be assumed. (M.S.C. i. 384–5; Murray, ii. 166.)

1633, June 3—He appeared before the Privy Council in London. (M.S.C. i. 385.)

1633, June 8—Discharged upon bond. (Ibid. See Bartholomew Jones.)

HOWES, OLIVER. A ghost name from Mrs. Stopes's misreading, followed by Nungezer, of Oliver Jones in the licence for the Queen of Bohemia's men of 30 June 1628.

HOYT, ROBERT (see HUYT, ROBERT).

HUBERT. Probably the Christian name of a hired man or musician.

1631, May 6 (lic.)—'Gascoine: & Hubert' open the trap door for Antiochus in King's production of Believe as You List, iv. 1. (Sisson, B.A.Y.L., p. 60.)

HUNNYMAN, JOHN (see HONYMAN, JOHN).

HUNNYMAN, RICHARD (see HONYMAN, RICHARD).

HUNT, JOHN. Possibly a son of the Thomas Hunt who had been an Admiral's man in the late nineties and a Lady Elizabeth's man in 1611.

1613, May 31—Named as a boy in a patent to Lady Elizabeth's of this date which was copied at Coventry 28 March 1615. (See R.E.S. i. 183.)

HUNT, Robert. A ghost name from the misreading of 'Robert Huyt' in the Maidment and Logan edition of Shakerley Marmion, followed by Nungezer.

HUNT, Thomas. A Thomas Hunt appears at the end of the sixteenth century in the Admiral's plots for *Frederick and Basilea, Troilus and Cressida,* and *The Battle of Alcazar.* There is no other record of him until he is found among the signatories to the Lady Elizabeth's men's bond to Henslowe in 1611. It is just possible that he was the Hunt who dined with Alleyn, an identification suggested by his presence in the company of other Palsgrave's men.

1621, Apr. 15—'borne: massey: Cartwright: gunnell: grace: Hunt dind Here & my Lewsham baly.' (Alleyn's Diary, Young, ii. 204.)

HUTCHINSON, Christopher⎫
HUTCHINSON, Elizabeth ⎬ *see* BEESTON.
HUTCHINSON, William ⎭

HUYT, Robert. It has been suggested that this name was Hunt, Hoyt, or White. Since no actor of any of these names is known, I think we can only accept the spelling in the first quarto. Hoyt seems to me the most likely pronunciation.

1631, Dec. '*Ieffry, tenant to Philautus.* Robert Huyt,' in the cast of *Holland's Leaguer,* acted by Prince Charles's (II) men at Salisbury Court this month. (*Herbert,* p. 45; 1632 4° B.M.)

IRINGTON, — (*see* ERRINGTON, RICHARD).

ISLIPP, Adam.

1622, May 20—Alleyn granted 'Adam Jslipp of London Stationer.' a lease of one share in the new Fortune. (*Hens. Paps.,* pp. 29 and 112.)

1639, Sept. 4—He made his will as citizen and stationer of London, but made no mention of theatres or players. The will was probated 25 September 1639. (Somerset House, P.C.C. Harvey 151.)

IVORY, Abraham. Mr. W. J. Lawrence suggests (*T.L.S.,* 26 April 1928) that the Abraham Ivory of Buckingham's *Rehearsal* who 'had formerly been a considerable actor of women's parts' was the same as the Abraham in the following account of a raid on the players at the Cockpit in *The Kingdom's Weekly Intelligencer,* 2–9 January 1648/9 (Hotson, p. 40).

. . . Abraham had a black Satten gown on, and before he came into the durt, he was very neat in his white laced pumps. The people not expecting such a pageant looked and laughed at all the rest, and not knowing who he was, they asked, what had that Lady done?

JACK. It is possible that Jack is simply the Christian name of the Gibson who appeared in this play, but more likely that two separate actors are indicated. Jack was probably a hired man in the Lady Elizabeth's company.

1624, Sept. 3—His name occurs in the stage directions of the MS. of

Heywood's *The Captives*, licensed by Herbert this date. (*See* Gibson. Greg, *Dram. Doc.*, p. 285.)

JACKSON. I think that Jackson is a printer's slip for Axen (q.v.), a well-known actor of Queen Henrietta's company at this time.

> 1634—'*Chester*, M. [Mr.] *Iackson*' is in the cast for Davenport's *King John and Matilda*, given by Queen Henrietta's men at the Cockpit. (1655 4° B.M.)

JACKSON, EDWARD.

1622, May 20—Alleyn granted 'Edward Jackson of London gent' a lease of one share of the new Fortune. (*Hens. Paps.*, pp. 29 and 112.)

JARMAN, ANTHONY.

1622, May 20—Alleyn granted 'Anthony Jarman Cittizen and Carpinter of London' a lease of one share of the new Fortune. (*Hens. Paps.*, pp. 29 and 112.)

1622, Aug. 18—He dined with Alleyn (*see* Thomas Downton).

JARVICE. If, as seems possible, Jarvice was the name of a man, and not a character, he was a musician, probably for the King's Revels at Salisbury Court (see p. 300).

1635, Oct. 15—In Glapthorne's *Lady Mother*, licensed on this date, Sucket says to a musician, called simply Musician, 'Ever, ever whil'st you live, *Jarvice*; the dauncers alwayes payes the musike.' (Bullen, *Old Plays*, ii. 132.)

JAY, TOM. On 14 September 1655 there was a raid by the soldiers on the players at the Red Bull (*see* Hotson, pp. 56–8). A ballad on the affair seems to refer to an actor Tom Jay. (*See* John Wright.) If Jay acted during the Commonwealth, he is almost sure to have been an actor before 1642, for surely no one took up this luckless profession after the closing of the theatres.

JEFFES, ANTHONY. He was an actor for at least fifteen years in the Admiral's–Prince Henry's company, but about 1612 he retired from the company and became a brewer. He appears in the St. Giles' Cripplegate registers four times as a player, 1605–9, and seven times as a brewer, 1610–21.

1616, Oct. 30—'Richard sonne of Anthony Jeffes, Brewer' chris. St. G.C.

1619, May 23—'William sonne of Anthony Jeffs Brewer' chris. St. G.C.

1620, May 20—'William Andrewes servant to Anthony Jeffs brewer' bur. St. G.C.

1620, Oct. 22—Warner suggests that he was the 'm^r Jeffe' of the party who dined with Edward Alleyn at Dulwich on his wedding day. (Alleyn's Diary, Young, ii. 192 and n. 3.)

1620/1, Mar. 23—'Sara daughter of Anthony Jeffes Brewer' chris. St. G.C.

JEFFES, HUMPHREY. Jeffes appeared regularly as an Admiral's–Prince Henry's–Palsgrave's player from 1598 to 1616. Probably he was a member until his death, for there is no list of the company between the short one of 1616 and the list of ten who signed the Fortune lease two months after Jeffes's burial. Both his associates in the Lord Chamberlain's list of provincial Palsgrave's men signed the lease.

1616, July 16—Pembroke sent out an order asking provincial officials to seize the duplicate patents of several named players and take bonds of them to appear at Whitehall for contempt. Among the players named are 'Charles Marshall, Homfry Jeffes and Willm Parr:' of the Palsgrave's company. (Murray, ii. 343–4. See above, p. 178, for full letter.)
1617, June 4—The above order was copied at Norwich. (Ibid.)
1618, Aug. 21—'Humphrie Jeffes, Plaier' bur. St. G.C.

JEWELL, JOHN. It is impossible to tell why his name was removed from the list of Grooms; perhaps he had not been a player at all.

1628, June 30—'Iohn Iewell' was tenth in the list of the 'Queene of Bohemia's Players' sworn grooms of His Majesty's Chamber, but his name has been deleted and that of 'Oliuer Iones' substituted. (See pp. 188–9.)

JOHNSON, RICHARD. The Revels man may be the same as the provincial player at Banbury who once gave his name as Richard Johnson and once as Richard Whiting (q.v.); otherwise he is unknown except for his role in *Messalina*.

c. 1634 ?—'*Montanus* a Knight in *Rome* defence vertuously inclined. *Rich. Iohnson*.' in the King's Revels cast for Richards' *Messalina, the Roman Empress*. (1640 ed. B.M.)

JOHNSON, WILLIAM. There is only a possibility that the Johnson who was one of the leaders of the odd provincial troupe and the friend of the King's trumpeter were the same man.

1636, Oct. 3—'William Johnson of Whitecrostreete' was committed for burying Samuel Underhill, a trumpeter, with illegal splendour. (*See* George Bosgrave.)
1639/40, Jan. 9—'Given to Georg Corden Servaunt to the Earle of Leic, Willm Johnson servaunt to the lord Clifford Georg Sander-son servant to the Lord Goring & 13 more assistants players who had the Kings patent to play' at Coventry. (Murray, ii. 254.)

JOLLY, GEORGE. Jolly was a very well-known actor in Germany from at least 1648 until 1660 and an important manager in England after the Restoration (Hotson, pp. 167–94), but the records printed below offer the first evidence that he was an actor before the closing of the theatres. Though there is no direct indication of his company, it is likely that he was connected with Prince Charles's men at the Fortune, for Mathew Smith (q.v.) was a prominent member of that company, and Jolly seems to have lived with him, possibly as an apprentice. The Fortune, at which the Prince's men were then performing, was located in the parish of St. Giles.

I doubt if the barber chirurgion who had a daughter in 1630 can be identified with the actor who was still active in 1673. Possibly the barber was the father of the actor.

1629/30, Jan. 8—'Mary daughter of George Jolley Barber Chirurgion of St Martins Aldersgate in the house of William Perkins in Morelane' chris. St G.C.

1640, July 9—'John sonne of George Jolly Player in ye house of Mathew Smith Playe^r in Whitcrostrt' chris. St. G.C.

1640, July 13—'John sonne of George Jolly Player' bur. St. G.C.

JONES, BARTHOLOMEW. This minor provincial actor would probably have remained entirely unknown if his company had not made the mistake of visiting Puritan Banbury. There must have been many dubious touring companies of this sort in the time.

1633, May 2—'Examination of Bartholomew Jones [at Banbury]. Has gone with this company up and down the country these two years, and has acted his part in divers places. They played by virtue of this commission at Leicester, Market Bosworth, Stanton, Solihull, Meriden, and Stratford, at Sir Thomas Lucy's, and divers other places. At Coventry and other places where they played not they received rewards. The commission under the privy seal was one Edward Whiting's, and he and Richard Bradshaw were partners, and were both gone to London.' (*C.S.P., Dom.*, 1633–4, p. 47.)

1633, May 3—'Further examination of the same. Bradshaw bought the commission of Edward Whiting at Nottingham some two years since. They made use of this commission because the other was out of date. He saw Bradshaw pay Whiting three pieces for this commission. Bradshaw went from Keinton, co. Warwick, on Saturday last towards London. Appointed to meet them on Monday next at Thame, co. Oxford. The commission from the Master of the Revels was rased by one of their company that is gone from them. The Master of the Revels will give allowance to the rasing if he be paid.' (Ibid.)

1633, May 6—The above examinations were enclosed in a letter from the Lord Mayor and Justices of Banbury to the Privy Council. With the examinations the Mayor and Justices say they 'Send a patent of licence pretended by the bearers to be granted by his Majesty, and a commission from the Master of the Revels. The patent they suspect, the commission they find rased. The parties are wandering rogues, if not more dangerous persons, as appears by their examinations, in which it is apparent they have changed their names. Have committed them to prison until their Lordships' pleasure be signified.' (Ibid.)

1633, May 22—The Privy Council entirely approves the actions and suspicions of the Lord Mayor and Justices and orders Jones and Richard Whiting, Edward Damport, Drew Turnor, Robert Haughton, and Richard Collwell fetched from the jail at Banbury. Since the men are accused of giving false names, these may be assumed. (*M.S.C.* i. 384–5.)

1633, June 3—The players appeared in London before the Privy Council. (Ibid., p. 385.)

1633, June 8—'This day the Players form'ly sent for from Banbury were discharged out of the Messeng^{rs} custody vpon Bond giuen to be forthcoming whensoeu' they should be called for.' (Ibid.)

JONES, EDWARD. Jones may have been some sort of a caretaker at the theatre, which was not demolished until August 1655 (Adams, p. 233); it is possible, however, that there was some adjacent tenement which was distinguished in this way in the parish.

1646/7, Feb. 2—'Edward Jones at ye Play-house' bur. St. Anne's Blackfriars.

JONES, JAMES. There were too many Joneses in seventeenth-century London to make it very likely that Elizabeth was the daughter of the provincial actor, though the parish of St. Giles in the Fields was a theatrical neighbourhood.

1613, May 31—He was named as a boy in a patent to Lady Elizabeth's of this date which was copied at Coventry 28 March 1615. (See *R.E.S.* i. 183.)

1624, Apr. 9—The Exeter records show that James Jones was named in a confirmation of this date attached to a patent of 31 October 1617 and brought to Exeter and Norwich by William Perry in 1624. The Norwich record supplements the Exeter one, which is confused. The reference in the Exeter record to the company as 'Children of the Revells of the late Queene Anna' must have been copied from the confirmation, as the licence was issued more than a year before the death of Queen Anne. (*Hist. MSS. Com.*, Records of the City of Exeter, p. 171, and Murray, ii. 273, 347.)

1639, Aug. 18—'Elizabeth Daughter of James and Ann Jones' chris. St. G.F.

JONES, JOHN. A Jack Jones appears in the Admiral's plot for *Tamar Cam* in 1602, and three children of John Jones were baptized at St. Bodolph's Aldgate in 1609, 1610, and 1615; in the last baptismal entry the father is called a player. Neither the parish clerks nor, apparently, anyone else drew a very sharp line between actors and miscellaneous entertainers in the seventeenth century (*see* Edward Gibbs).

1625, May 7—'John Jones and Boxer Tumblers' were at Norwich (Murray, ii. 371.)

1630—'Indictment of John Jones of St. Michaels in Bedwardine Labourer for performing at Upton on Severn under a so called license from Sir Henry Harbert Knight Master of the Revels in these words "... I have by these presents lycensed and authorized

John Jones Anne his wife Richard Payne Richard Jones and their assistants to set forth and shew . . . motion with divers stories in it as also tumbling vaulting sleight of hand and other such like feats of activity . . .'' Such license being false and counterfeit.' (Murray, ii. 410–11, from *Worcestershire County Records*, 1900, i. 470.)

JONES, OLIVER. Oliver Jones is known only as a member of the curious Queen of Bohemia's company of 1628 (see pp. 188–90). He cannot be certainly identified with the man married at St. James's, but the combination of names is not common.

1626, Nov. 14—'Oliuer Jones & Eliz Price lic.' mar. St. J.C.
1628, June 30—'Oliuer Iones' is tenth in a list of 'Queen of Bohemia's Players' sworn Grooms of the Chamber to His Majesty. His name has been substituted for that of 'Iohn Iewell' deleted. (*M.S.C.* ii. 347.)

JONES, RICHARD. Jones is frequently mentioned in the Dulwich manuscripts. As early as 1583 he was a Worcester's man, and he went to Germany with that company in 1593. From 1594 to 1602 he appears as an Admiral's man, in 1610 as a Revels patentee. For the next fifteen years he is heard of only in Germany. An undated letter—apparently written before the death of Philip Henslowe—on the same subject as that of 1620 shows that Harris Jones was the wife of Richard and that she had inherited the Leopard's Head from her father.

I think it probable that the provincial entertainer of 1630 and 1638 was another Richard Jones; fifty-five years seems too long for a man to continue to act.

It has been said (Nungezer; Chambers, *E.S.*) that a Richard Jones is traceable in the token books of St. Saviour's. This is a bit misleading, for while the token books do carry the name Richard Jones frequently, the registers show numerous Richard Joneses living in the parish—a baker, a tailor, a merchant, a waterman, a carrier, a basketmaker, a gentleman, and a poor man—but no player.

1620, Apr. 1—'Haris Joones to Mr Edward Allinn
'Ladro (?) from Dansicke the firste of Apriell, 1620. My aproved good ffrinde Mr Allin, your helleth wished in the lord wriith your good wife, trvsting in God you ar both in good hellth, as I was at the wryting her of. Thes few lines is to intreate your worshype to stand owr good frinde as you hath bin before. I sente you a leeter of atorny by Mr Babties [Baptist ?] abowte the lebickes hed [Leopard's Head]; I cnowe not whither you hath reseafed it or no. I woulld intreate your worship to sende me word how Mr Rowly hath delte with me for my rente by this baer [bearer] her of. My husband is with the prince, and as yt I am here in Dansicke lockinge evry daye [to] gooe to him. Thvs desierin God to bles you with your good wife, I commyt you to the almyty God. Your pore frinde to command, Haris Joones. H. I.' (*MSS. Dul.*, pp. 52–3.)

1623, Aug. 30—Richard Jones, Johan Kostressen, and Robert Dulandt, musicians, petitioned the Duke of Wolgast for permission to return to England. (Meyer, *Sh. Jahr.* xxxviii. 209.)

1624, July 10—Having failed in his English project, Jones petitioned the Duke of Wolgast to be re-employed. (Ibid., p. 210.)

1630—Richard Jones and two others were indicted at Worcester for forging a licence from the Master of the Revels. (*See* John Jones.)

1637/8, Jan. 12—'Robert Browne, Georg Hall, & Richard Jones players by warant, who had a motion to shew expressing the worlds abuses', were at Coventry this date. (Murray, ii. 253.)

JORDAN, THOMAS. Jordan is an interesting, if somewhat obscure, figure, whose literary compositions and swindles after the Restoration show him to have been a man of no small impudence. His membership in the company of the King's Revels before the closing of the theatres is demonstrated by the *Messalina* cast and perhaps by the Norwich list. He may well have remained with this company through their transformation into Queen Henrietta's men in 1637 and on to the closing of the theatres, but there is no evidence of his company affiliations after the *Messalina* cast.

One of the most puzzling of Jordan's works is *Money Is an Ass*, which he says was written and acted when he was fifteen. The prologue implies that the actors were all boys, says that there were only eight of them, that the play had never been acted before, and that Jordan had been their only director. Of the cast of eight whose names appear in the first quarto, five are named in the long list of players copied at Norwich in March 1634/5. The most I can make of this is that Jordan wrote the play for himself and the other boys of the Revels company and that their masters allowed them to act it, probably on tour. Jordan's well-known mendacity forces one to accept any of his statements with reservations.

The prologue to *Tricks of Youth* implies—though it by no means proves—that Jordan was connected with the surreptitious acting at the Red Bull before the Restoration, as do the last six lines in his prologue for *The Tamer Tamed*, acted June 24, 1660 (quoted here from *A Nursery of Novelties* [1665?], p. 20).

> Pray keep your seats, you do not sit in fear
> As in the dangerous dayes of *Oliver*;
> It is not now (in good time be it spoke)
> *Enter* the Red-Coats, *Exit* Hat and Cloak.
> But such a prosp'rous change doth now attend ye,
> That those who did affront ye, shall defend ye.

The prologue to *The Tricks of Youth* I have taken from the HN copy which lacks the first four lines, evidently because someone has cut out Jordan's stamped dedication from the recto of the leaf. These lines are supplied from the B.M. copy of the book, very kindly transcribed for me by Mr. Arundel Esdaile. The prologue

is not dated in *The Tricks of Youth*, but the reprint of it in
A Nursery of Novelties, p. 15, is dated 16 August 1660. *The Nursery of Novelties* version of the poem shows numerous alterations
in capitalization and punctuation, and line 20 has been changed
to read, 'And are secur'd, but our magnifick Ladies', and line 24
to read, 'Nullifies them, and gives us a new Essence'.

I cannot feel very confident about any of the parish register
entries concerning Thomas Jordans. The marriage of 1632 is
surely too early to be that of the Revels boy; the burials of 1638
might possibly be those of his wife and son.

1632, June 14—'Thomas Jordan & Anne Baggont' mar. St. Andrew's
    by the Wardrobe. (Bod.)
c. 1634 ?—'*Lepida* mother to *Messalina—Tho. Iordan*' is in the cast
    for the King's Revels production of Nathaniel Richards's *Messalina*.
    (1640 ed. B.M.)
1634/5, Mar. 10—His name is in the full list of players at Norwich;
    some seem to be King's Revels men, though the records do not
    give the name of the company, which was probably an amalgama-
    tion. (Murray, ii. 356; see above, pp. 286 and 288–9.)
c. 1635—'Captain Penniless—*Tho. Jordain*' stands first in the cast for
    his play, *Money Is an Ass*, in the 1668 quarto. He says in the
    verses to certain copies of the play,

> The Play was writ by Me, & pleas'd the Stage
> When I was not full fifteen Years of Age.
>   (1668 4° B.M. and *R.E.S.* i. 219.)

1637—Jordan's *Poetical Varieties*, published this year, is dedicated
    to 'The Mecoenas of Candid Industry, M^r. Iohn Ford of *Grayes-
    Inne*, Gent', and contains elegies on John Honyman and Richard
    Gunnell and a number of commendatory verses, of which the
    following are extracts (1637 4° B.M.):

> Of my friend M^r. *Thomas Jordan, Tetrastichon.*
>   Tho. Heywood.
>
> To my Friend M^r. *Tho. Jordan* on his Poems,
>   Which I title, His *Vnder-wood.*
>
> . . . That one so young should hold
> The club up gainst the Giant ignorance.
>   Rich. Brome.
>
> To M^r. *Thomas Jordan* on his Fancies.
>
> We that are old in th'art must leake,
> And worne with often usage breake;
> Thy yonger pot the Muses will
> With their best waters alwayes fill;
>   When we are gone, the World shall see,
>   A full-brim'd Helicon in thee.
>   Tho. Nabbes.
>
> To his Friend the Author M^r. *Thomas Jordan,*
>   on his Varieties.
>   Ed. May.

On my Friend and adopted sonne M^r. *Thomas
Jordan* the Infant-Poet of our Age.

J. B.

1638, July 21—'Elisabeth wife to Thomas Jordan' bur. St. Anne's
Blackfriars.

1638—In Jordan's *Wit in a Wildernesse of Promiscuous Poetry*
(N.D.) is '*A Poem composed, and spoken by the Author to the late
King at the Dedication of* Mr. Tho. Bushel's *Rock at Euston in Oxon,
1638, in the person of* Caliope'. The quarto is not dated, but it contains an epitaph on a man who died in 1653.

1638, Sept. 19—'Richard sonne of Thomas Jordan' bur. St. G.F.

> 1640—He contributed complimentary verses to the 1640 edition of
Nathaniel Richards's *Messalina*. (1640 ed. B.M.)

1640—'T. Iourdan' contributed commendatory verses to Rawlins's
Rebellion, acted 'by his Majesties Company of Revells'. (1640 4°
HN.)

1641, Aug. 2—Sir Henry Herbert licensed Jordan's *Walks of Islington
and Hogsdon*. The licence is printed after the epilogue in the 1657
edition of the play. (1657 4° HN.)

1642—Jordan printed his Royalist tract, *Rules to Know a Loyal King
from a disloyal Subject.*

1660, Aug. 16—In the second issue of *The Walks of Islington and
Hogsdon*, called *Tricks of Youth* (some copies dated 1663), is the set
of verses quoted below. When Jordan reprinted them in his
Nursery of Novelties, he entitled them, '*A Prologue to the King,
August 16, 1660.*'

> Sure such a Glory, so Serene, so Bright,
> Started from Chaos when God cal'd for Light;
> For like that glittering Birth of Beams, you do
> Transluminate this Western world, from you.
> Our Saint, our Soul, our Soveraign, our King,
> We live and grow, as the Sun broods the Spring.
> Then (as in Loyalty oblig'd) 'tis fit
> We render part of our small Stock, our Wit,
> Which hath so long been crampt under their rage,
> Who durst not see their actions on the Stage;
> That numb'd with a stupidity, we fear
> We shall assault the softnesse of your ear.
> We have been so perplext with Gun and Drum,
> *Look to your Hats and Clokes, the Red-coats come.*
> *D'amboys* is routed, *Hotspur* quits the field,
> *Falstaff's* out-filch'd, all in Confusion yeild,
> Even Auditor and Actor, what before
> Did make the *Red Bull* laugh, now makes him roar.
> We curse the Misery in which our Trade is,
> And are imprison'd, but our large siz'd Ladies
> (Thinking to 'scape them) are torn by the throats
> And like Wine Porters put in Petty-coats) [*sic*]
> Dragg'd to the *Muse* for Plotters; But *Your Presence*
> Hath nullified their power, and given us Essence.
> Till YOU came hither all was so forlorn,
> We wisht we had been buried, or unborn;

All things were *Retrograde*, the Night and Day
Were shrinking to *Prima Materia*.
We liv'd in such a strange distorted Age,
Men durst not see their Figures on the Stage;
But furious as the deform'd Lady was,
Who for revenge broke her owne *Looking-glasse*,
They crackt our *Mirror*, and now none but YOU
Dread Majesty, can mend, or make us new.

T. J.

1685—He is said to have died in this year, since a successor was appointed for him as city poet. (*D.N.B.*)

JUBY (JEUBE, JEWBE, JEWBEY, JEWBY, JEWEBEY, JUBE, JUBEY, JUBIE, JUBYE), EDWARD. Juby was a prominent member of the Admiral's–Prince Henry's–Palsgrave's company from 1594 to his death in 1618. He appears frequently in Henslowe's Diary as a member of the company, and a letter of Charles Massey to Edward Alleyn in 1613, as well as William Wilson's letter in 1617, implies that Juby was business manager of the Palsgrave's men; his position in the list of signatories to the Fortune lease in 1618 indicates his seniority if not his management of the company.

He lived in the parish of St. Saviour's Southwark, where his children appear in the registers from 1599 to 1617. (See Bentley, *T.L.S.*) In most of these years the token books of the parish show him to have lived in Oares Rents, and the accounts in Henslowe's Diary show that he was a tenant of Henslowe at that place in March 1602/3.

Richard Juby and William Juby, who were also Admiral's men, disappear after 1602.

1617, Aug. 11—'Tabitha Jubey a childe' bur. St. S.S. (She was baptized as the daughter of Edward Juby 'a player' 15 September 1614.)

>1617, Nov. 2—William Wilson refers to Juby and Downton as leaders of the Palsgrave's men. (*See* William Wilson.)

1618, Sept. 13—'m^r Juby & His wife' dined with Alleyn unexpectedly. (Young, ii. 103.)

1618, Oct. 31—He was the first member of Palsgrave's who signed the lease of the Fortune from Edward Alleyn. (*Hens. Paps.*, pp. 27–8.)

1618, Nov. 20—'Edward Jubye a man buried in the church' St. S.S.

1622—His widow Frances held his share of the Fortune lease. *See* Frances Juby.

JUBY, FRANCES.

1622, Apr. 28—'m^rs Jobye, wido Hudsone: Jo: goodman: & mighell: & dawly din Here.' (Alleyn's Diary, Young, ii. 236.)

1622, May 20—Alleyn granted 'ffrauncis Juby of Southwark in the County of Surrey widowe' a lease of one-half share of the new Fortune. (*Hens. Paps.*, pp. 29 and 112.)

KANE ⎫
KAYNE ⎬ *see* CANE, ANDREW.
KEIN ⎭

KELLOCK, JOHN. He probably served the Prince in some capacity other than that of a player.

1618, Oct. 4—'Philladelpha Kellock d of John the Princes servant' chris. St. S.S.
1627, June 25—He made his will, which contains nothing of interest; it was probated 15 August. (P.C.C. 82 Skynner.)

KEMPSTON (KIMPTON, KNIPTON), ROBERT. He was evidently a leader of the provincial King's Revels company.

1629, Dec. 30—'Robert Kimpton', Nathanial Clay, and Thomas Holman were named in the licence from the Master of the Revels which was shown at Reading 12 November 1630. (Murray, ii. 386.)
1631, Sept. 23—'Paid given to Robert Knipton & John Carr players of the Revells the 23th of September last as appeareth by a bill', 5s., at Coventry. (Ibid., p. 251.)
1632, Sept. 8—'This day Robt Kempston and other of his Company of the Revells . . . are lycenced to play' at Norwich. (Ibid., p. 354.)

KENDALL, RICHARD. It seems likely that Kendall's position as wardrobe keeper at Salisbury Court was related to his apprenticeship to a tailor. The information which he gave Crosfield suggests that the acting companies may have had more to do with the creation of their own costumes than has been suspected. The fact that the wardrobe keeper accompanied the troupe on tour is interesting; no doubt Kendall was drafted for minor roles in King's Revels plays.

I know of no evidence either for or against Kendall's identification with the man who married Joan Nabbes in 1635.

1634, July 18—Crosfield's diary has under this date, 'One Richard Kendall about ye age of 50 or upwards, belonging to ye Company of players of Salsbury Court that came to Oxford this yeare came to see me & related unto me diverse particular stories vizt.
1. of his particular state & education in his youth at Kirkby Lonsdall where he served his Apprenticeship to a Talor, & afterward went to Cambridge where he stayd but litle, & then went to London where he became servant to Sir Wm Slingsby—and nowe he is one of ye 2. Keepers of the Wardrobe of the said Company.' (Crosfield's Diary, pp. 71–2.)
1634/5, Mar. 10—His name is in the full list of players at Norwich. Some of them seem to be King's Revels men, though the records do not give the name of the company, which was probably an amalgamation (see pp. 286 and 288–9). (Murray, ii. 356.)
1635, Oct. 25—'Richard Kendall & Joane Nabes of this p. by banes, p. Mr Morse' mar. St. Martin Orgar. (Challen, Marriages.)

KEYES, RALPH.

1623, May 21—Markham's suit mentions 'Raphe Keyes att the Crosse Keyes in Knighte Ryder streete London'. He was possibly an actor, as most of the others sued were. (See Appendix, p. 682.)

KEYES, Robert.

1623, May 21—Markham's suit mentions 'Roberte Keyes of S^t: Brydes Lane'. He was possibly an actor, as most of the others sued were. (See Appendix, p. 683.)

KEYNE, KEYNES, Andrew (*see* cane, andrew).

KIMPTON, Robert (*see* kempston, robert).

KING, John. He testified in *Smith* v. *Beeston*, 5 May 1620, as 'John Kinge of London gent of thage of fortie six yeares or thereabout*es*'. (Wallace, *Three Theatres*, p. 47.) Though he is not called a player, the information which he shows in his testimony would not be easily obtained by any except one fairly closely connected with the Red Bull while Queen Anne's men or the Revels company were there.

KIRKE (kerke, kirk, kyrke), John. It is by no means certain that all these notices of Kirke refer to the same man, but there is enough evidence to make them worth consideration.

Mr. W. J. Lawrence has no hesitation in identifying the actor and the dramatist (*Stud. Phil.* xxi. 586 ff.), and though the evidence is slight, the fact that both actor and dramatist are associated with the Red Bull theatre is significant.

Kirke's career as an actor seems to have been mostly at the Red Bull, first as a member of the Red Bull company and then as a Prince Charles's man (see above, pp. 271–5). In 1640, however, the Princes' men went to the Fortune and apparently remained there until the closing of the theatres.

The Kirke who brought the two plays to Herbert in June 1642 was probably a manager or bookkeeper, for it was generally these officials and not the dramatists who brought plays to be licensed. It is not impossible that the Prince's player should have become a responsible manager in the company, for Crosfield said that in 1634 he was one of the leaders of the Red Bull company, and he may have become equally valuable after he transferred to Prince Charles's men.

Finally, there is some reason to identify the actor and the John Kirke in St. James's Clerkenwell, for this is the parish of the Red Bull with which the actor was so long associated, and the rather unusual Christian name, Parry, given to John Kirke's son in 1641 suggests a tribute to William Perry, the veteran leader of the provincial troupe to which John Kirke had belonged.

If Thomas Jordan's poem commemorates the player, as it may, since Jordan wrote elegiac verses to Gunnell and Honyman without reference to their theatrical careers, then we have evidence that Kirke became a merchant after the close of the theatres. One cannot be sure even of this, however, for Jordan was quite capable of making his old poem of 1643 serve for another John Kirke in 1665.

1629, Nov. 10—'John Kerke' is named just after the leaders of the troupe in a licence of this date granted to William Perry and Richard Weekes, 'his Majestie's sworne servantes . . . all of the Red Bull company'; it was shown at Reading 30 November 1629. Eight men were named. (Murray, ii. 386.)

1633, Nov. 6—'Marie d. of John Kirke' chris. St. J.C.

1634, July 18—Kendall told Crosfield, 'The Fortune in Golden Lane, yᵉ cheife Mr Wᵐ Cartwright, Edward Armestead, John Buckle, John Kirke.' (Crosfield's Diary, p. 72 ; see Appendix, p. 688.)

1634, Sept. 19—'Marie d of John Kirke' bur. St. J.C.

1635, Dec. 12—'Iohn Kirke' and three others were named in a warrant to swear them Grooms of the Chamber in ordinary without fee to attend the Prince in the quality of players. (M.S.C. ii. 377.)

1638—The rent of a 'John Kerke' in St. Michael le Querne was assessed at £20. (London, 1638, p. 152.)

1638—The 1638 quarto of Henry Shirley's The Martyr'd Soldier, acted by Queen Henrietta's men, has a dedication to Sir Kenelm Digby; it is signed 'I. K.' in the HN copy, but Bullen says (Old Plays, i. 172) that in some copies 'John Kirke' is given in full.

1638, July 13—His Seven Champions of Christendome was entered S.R. and published the same year. The title-page says it was 'Acted at the Cocke-pit, and at the Red-Bull in St. Johns Streete, with a generall liking'. (1638 4° B.M.)

1641, May 1—'Parrye s. of John Kyrke & Eliz. vx' chris. St. J.C. 'Parrye s. of John Kyrke' bur. 2 Dec. 1642.

1642, June 8—'Received of Mr. Kirke, for a new play which I burnte for the ribaldry and offense that was in it' £2. (Herbert, p. 39.)

1642, June 8—'Received of Mr. Kirke for another new play called The Irishe Rebellion, the 8 June, 1642' £2. (Ibid.)

1642/3, Mar. 22—'John s. of John Kyrke & Eliz. vx' chris. St. J.C. 'John s. of John Kyrke' bur. 12 Oct. 1647.

1643—The following poem is in Thomas Jordan's Piety and Poesy (1643 ed. B.M.) :

> An Epitaph on my worthy Friend, Mr. John Kirk.
>
> Reader, Within this Dormitory, lies
> The wet Memento of a Widdows Eys;
> A Kirk, though not of Scotland, One in whom
> Loyalty liv'd, and Faction found no room:
> No Conventicle Christian, but he Died
> A Kirk of England by the Mothers side.
> In brief, to let you know what you have lost,
> Kirk was a Temple of the Holy Ghost.

The same poem was printed in Jordan's Nursery of Novelties, 1665 (?), where it is entitled, 'An Epitaph on Mr John Kirke, Merchant.'

KITE, JEREMY (JEREMIAS). The St. Giles' registers and the list of English actors at The Hague leave no doubt that there was an actor named Kite, but the easy confusion of the name with Knight makes it uncertain whether we have any English references to him outside the parish registers.

1627, Apr. 4—'Wm son of Jerymie Kite Player' chris. St. G.C.

1628—'Mr Kite, a playe' & his Companie' at Leicester. The name is probably a mistake for Knight (see Knight, —). (Murray, ii. 317.)

1632/3, Feb. 20—'ffrancis da: of Jeremy Kite Player' chris. St. G.C.

1644, Nov.–1645—The names of an English company of actors residing at The Hague at least from November 1644 to 1645, as recorded in an act passed by notary, were 'Jeremias Kite, William Coock, Thomas Loffday, Edward Schottnel [sic], Nathan Peet and his son'. The entry is quoted by J. H. van Lennep in *N. & Q.*, Second Series, ix. 48–9, from L. Ph. C. van den Bergh, *'s Graven-haagsche Bijzonderheden* (1857), pp. 20–3.

KNELLER, JAMES. Kneller is known only from these two provincial records. It is possible that James Kneller is a misreading of James Sneller (q.v.).

1613, May 31—Named as a boy in a patent for Lady Elizabeth's company of this date which was copied at Coventry 28 March 1615. (See *R.E.S.* i. 183.)

1624, Apr. 9—The Exeter records show that James Kneller was named in a confirmation of this date attached to a patent of 31 October 1617 and brought to Exeter and Norwich by William Perry in 1624. The Norwich record supplements the Exeter one, which is confused. The reference in the Exeter record to the company as 'Children of the Revells of the late Queene Anna' must have been copied from the confirmation, as the licence was issued more than a year before the death of Queen Anne. (*Hist. MSS. Com.*, Records of the City of Exeter, p. 171, and Murray, ii. 273, 347.)

KNIGHT, —. The extant records leave us confused among at least two men named Knight and one named Kite. The Knight who was bookkeeper for the King's company in 1632 and 1633 was probably either Anthony or Edward, since the King's men would surely need an exemption for their bookkeeper, and since it is a little improbable that three Knights should be connected with the company. I should think Edward the more likely, since he is placed first in the list, and the bookkeeper would be more important than musicians and hired men.

I know of no evidence either for or against the identification of Anthony Knight and the provincial player.

It seems to me safest to assume that neither 'Knight' nor 'Kite' in the Leicester records of 1628 is a mistake, but that the two entries refer to distinct companies, for it was not usual for a company to appear at the same town twice in one year. It is curious that the only known references to Knight's company and to Kite's company occur at Leicester in the same year.

1628—'Knight and his Companie, beinge Players' were at Leicester (Chamberlain's Accounts). (Murray, ii. 317.)

1628—'Mr Kite, a playe' & his Companie' were at Leicester. This item immediately follows the preceding one in Murray's extracts, but none of the five 1628 items is dated, so that the man mentioned might be either Knight as above, or Jeremy Kite.

1632, Oct. 12—'Received of Knight, for allowing of Ben Johnsons play called *Humours Reconcil'd, or the Magnetick Lady*, to bee acted, this 12th of Octob. 1632, 2*l*. o. o.' (*Herbert*, p. 34.)

1633, Oct. 21—On October 18th Sir Henry Herbert had sent to the King's men to stop a performance of *The Tamer Tamed*. After he had got hold of the MS. and expurgated it, he wrote the following note which he copied in his office book:

'Mr. Knight,

In many things you have saved mee labour; yet wher your judgment or penn fayled you, I have made boulde to use mine. Purge ther parts, as I have the booke. And I hope every hearer and player will thinke that I have done God good servise, and the quality no wronge; who hath no greater enemies than oaths, prophaness, and publique ribaldry, wh^{ch} for the future I doe absolutely forbid to bee presented unto mee in any playbooke; as you will answer it at your perill.'

'This was subscribed to their play of *The Tamer Tamd*, and directed to Knight, their book-keeper.' (*Herbert*, p. 21.)

1636, Oct. 3 and Dec. 1—A Philip Knight, with sixteen others, several of them actors and all of St. Leonard's Shoreditch, buried Thomas Undrill with illegal splendour. (*See* George Bosgrave.)

KNIGHT, ANTHONY (*see also* KNIGHT, —).

1624, Dec. 27—'Anthony Knight' stands sixteenth in the list of twenty-one men, 'Musitions and other necessary attendantes', whom Herbert exempted from arrest as being necessary to the King's company (see above, pp. 15–16). (*Herbert*, p. 74.)

KNIGHT, EDWARD (*see also* KNIGHT, —).

1615/16, Mar. 20—'Edw: Knight:' witnessed an agreement between Alleyn and Meade of the one part and the Prince's men of the other. (*Hens. Paps.*, p. 91.)

1623, May 21—Markham's suit names 'Edwarde Knighte att the George Alley in Goulding Lane'. (See Appendix, p. 682.)

1624, Dec. 27—'Edward Knight' stands first in the list of twenty-one attendants of the King's company whom Herbert exempted from arrest. (*Herbert*, p. 74.)

KNIPTON, ROBERT (*see* KEMPSTON, ROBERT).

KOSTRESSEN, JOHAN. With Richard Jones and Robert Dulandt, two other musicians in the service of the Duke of Wolgast, Kostressen petitioned on 30 August 1623 to leave Wolgast and return to England. (Meyer, *Sh. Jahr.* xxxviii. 209.)

LACY, JOHN. That the famous Restoration actor and dramatist had become a player before the closing of the theatres we know from Aubrey and from the record of his ticket of privilege as one of Beeston's Boys. Aubrey says that Lacy was born in Yorkshire,

near Doncaster, and that Ben Jonson took a note of his Yorkshire words and proverbs for his *Tale of a Tub*. (Aubrey, *Brief Lives*, ii. 28.) Since he was famous as a dancer in the Restoration, one would guess that he had danced at the Cockpit.

The apprenticeship to Ogilby (q.v.) arouses one's curiosity. Aubrey seems to say that Lacy was apprenticed to Ogilby and at 'the . . . playhouse' at the same time. The fact that Ogilby built the first Dublin theatre a few years later and attracted to it James Shirley, a playwright of the Cockpit, suggests that Ogilby may have had some familiarity with the Cockpit, which was not too far from his dancing school in Gray's Inn Lane.

For Lacy's career as a Restoration actor, see Nungezer, Hotson, and the *D.N.B.*

1631—'Came to London to the . . . playhouse, 1631. His master was . . . Apprentice (as were also . . . and Isaac) to Mr. John Ogilby.' (Aubrey, *Brief Lives*, ii. 28.)

1639, Aug. 10—'Iohn Lacie:' was third in a list 'of ye young Company of at ye Cockpitt Players' for a ticket of privilege. (*M.S.C.* ii. 390–1.)

1642—Lacy was 'lievetenant and quartermaster to the lord Gerard'. (Aubrey, *Brief Lives*, ii. 28.)

1681, Sept. 17—'He made his *exit* on Saturday September 17th 1681, and was buryed in the farther churchyard of St Martyn's in the fields on the Monday following, aged . . .' (Ibid., pp. 28–9.)

LANCASTER, SILVESTER.

1640, Apr. 25—'Siluester Lancaster' was first in a list of the 'Princes Players hired men' who were not to be 'hindred or diverted . . . or otherwise molested'. (*M.S.C.* ii. 394–5.)

LAU, HURFRIES DE. De Lau was a member of the French company which visited England in 1635 and, after acting at the Cockpit during Lent, received permission to remodel Le Febure's riding academy for their theatre. (*M.S.C.* ii. 375.)

1635, May 5—'A warrant granted to Josias D'Aunay, Hurfries de Lau, and others, for to act playes at a new house in Drury-lane, during pleasure, ye 5 may, 1635.' (*Herbert*, p. 61.)

LEE (LEIGH), ROBERT. Lee's earliest appearance was *c.* 1590 as a Strange's man, but he is first known as an important actor in Queen Anne's company in March 1603/4. All his later appearances are as a Queen Anne's man, chiefly in the provinces, where he was long a leader of the road company. His name is to be found in the registers of St. Bodolph's Aldgate from February 1594/5 to 1608, and he is probably the Robert Lee who appears thereafter in St. James's Clerkenwell, which would be a convenient residence for an actor always in Red Bull companies.

1616, Mar. 30—'Robert Lee' was eighth in a licence for Queen's presented at Norwich; all but Swinnerton and Lee were absent. (Murray, ii. 340–1.)

1616, May 20—'Roberte Lee' was paid for four plays given by the Queen's company at court. (Chambers, *E.S.* iv. 183.)

1617, May 31—Robert Lee brought to Norwich a 1611 exemplification of Queen Anne's 1609 licence and got leave to perform for three days. (Murray, ii. 343.)

1617, Oct. 31—One of four leaders named in a patent of this date which was shown at Norwich 29 August 1618 (*see* Rossiter). (Ibid., p. 345.)

1619, >May 13—As a member of Queen Anne's company, 'Robert Leighe' was first in the list of players allowed black cloth to wear in her funeral procession. (*M.S.C.* ii. 325.)

1619/20, Feb. 24—Lee and Long, with the rest of their company (not named, but probably Anne's) were granted a licence. (Ibid. i. 284.)

1622, July 8—'Robert Lee' was named first in the warrant for the licence for seven late Queen Anne's men to bring up children as the Children of the Revels. (Murray, ii. 193–4.)

1622, Nov.—Lee, Perkins, and other comedians to the late Queen Anne were named in a warrant for a licence. (*M.S.C.* i. 284.)

1622—'Robert Lee' was first in Herbert's office book list of the 'chiefe players at the Red Bull, called the players of the Revells'. (*Herbert*, p. 63.)

1623, May 21—Markham's suit names 'Roberte Leigh in Clarkenwell Close', 5s. (See Appendix, p 682.)

1623, May 24—His name appears in a licence for Queen Anne's shown at Norwich by William Perry. (Murray, ii. 347.)

1623, June 20—'Robert Leigh' received from Alleyn and with Gwalter's consent one of the latter's two shares in the Fortune. (*MSS. Dul.*, p. 244.)

1640/1, Jan. 31—'Robert s. of Robert Lee' bur. St. J.C.

LILLIE, GEORGE. It does not seem very likely that the player ought to be identified with the Barking taverner, but the Queen of Bohemia's company of 1628 was a curious organization, and it would be no more surprising to find that Lillie was a taverner than to find that Barnes (q.v.) was a carpenter.

1628, June 30—'George Lillie' was seventh in a list of 'Queene of Bohemia's Players' made grooms of His Majesty's chamber (see above, pp. 188–9). (*M.S.C.* ii. 347.)

1633, Oct. 11—'A peticon of Wm Garrett against George Lillie debt 20^{li}.' (Ibid., p. 410.)

1634, July 18—A George Lilly was a taverner at Barking, Essex. (*C.S.P., Dom.*, 1634–5, p. 158.)

LILLIE, JOHN. The coupling of the names of John Lillie and Alexander Foster, both of whom were Lady Elizabeth's men, suggests that the debtors were players and may have been sued for a company debt.

1628, June 30—'Iohn Lillie' was fifth in a list of 'Queene of Bohemia's Players' sworn grooms of his Majesty's chamber (see above, pp. 188–9). (*M.S.C.* ii. 347.)

1629/30, Feb. 6—'A petition of William Steuens against Iohn Lilly & Alexander Foster, debt 18^{li}. Answered (vizt) If Lilly & Foster doe

·not giue yᵉ petʳ satisfacčon heerin before yᵉ expiration of one moneth after yᵉ sight heerof, the petʳ may take yᵉ ordinary course of Law for his releife. Febr. 6ᵗʰ 1629[/30].' (P.R.O., L.C. 5/183, p. 69.)

LOFFDAY, Thomas (see LOVEDAY, THOMAS).

LONG, Nicholas.

Long, who appears only as a provincial player, was leading a company of Queen's Revels boys in 1612 and a Lady Elizabeth's troupe in March 1613/14. He was an associate of Philip Rosseter (q.v.).

1617, Oct. 31—'Robt Lee Philip Rossiter Willm Perry & Nicholas Longe' showed a licence of this date at Norwich on 29 August 1618. (Murray, ii. 345.)

1619/20, Feb. 24—'Robert Lee and Nicholas Longe wᵗʰ the rest of their Companie' (unnamed, but probably a new organization of the late Queene Anne's company) received a licence. (M.S.C. i. 284.)

1620, May 20—'Mʳ Longe brought his Maᵗⁱᵉˢ Patent to play &c dated in ffebruary last' at Norwich; company not named. (Murray, ii. 345.)

1621/2, Jan. 21—'Nicholas Longe, Player' bur. St. G.C.

LOVEDAY (LOFFDAY), Thomas.

Loveday, who was a boy when he appeared in *Money Is an Ass*, was acting when the companies began after the Restoration. (See Hotson.)

1634/5, Mar. 10—His name is in the full list of players at Norwich; many of them seem to be King's Revels men, though the records do not give the name of the company, which was probably an amalgamation. (Murray, i. 279, and ii. 356; see above, pp. 286 and 288–9.)

c. 1635—'Clutch, *Tho. Loveday*' appears in the cast for Thomas Jordan's *Money Is an Ass* which is printed in the 1668 quarto. (B.M. 4°.)

1644, Nov.–1645—'Thomas Loffday' was one of the English company residing at The Hague. (*See* Jeremiah Kite.)

LOVELL, Thomas.

Lovell's only appearances before the closing of the theatres show him to have been a boy actor. It is probable that he belonged to acting companies during the Interregnum, since he appears as a member of Davenant's company in November 1660. (See Hotson, p. 206.)

1634/5, Mar. 10—His name is in the full list of players at Norwich; many of them seem to be King's Revels men, though the records do not give the name of the company, which was probably an amalgamation. (Murray, i. 279, and ii. 356; see above, pp. 286 and 288–9.)

c. 1635—'Money. *Tho. Lovel*' appears in the cast for Thomas Jordan's *Money Is an Ass* which was printed in the 1668 quarto. (B.M. 4°.)

LOWE, Nicholas.

1628, June 7—'Nicolas Lowe' is eighth in a list of thirteen actors named in a new licence granted to Ellis Guest's unnamed company on this date and shown at Norwich 2 July 1628. (Murray, ii. 353.)

c. 1635—'Credit. *Nich. Lowe*' appears in the cast for Thomas Jordan's *Money Is an Ass* which was printed in the 1668 quarto. (B.M. 4°.)

LOWEN, G. Upon the basis of the solitary known allusion to G. Lowen, Mr. Baldwin (*Organization and Personnel*, pp. 198, 223, 377–8) builds up a career for him in the King's company from 1615 to 1623, assigns him a 'line', fits him to roles in sixteen plays, and discovers a number of his physical characteristics. This superstructure of conjecture seems a trifle top-heavy for its basis in fact.

1619, Aug.—The prompter's notes show that 'G: Lowen' played Barnavelt's daughter in King's production of *Barnavelt*. (Frijlinck, *Barnavelt*, pp. 53, 55; Greg, *Dram. Doc.*, p. 272.)[1]

LOWIN (LOWEN, LOWENS, LEWIN, LOWINE, LOWING, LOWINS, LOWYN), JOHN. John Lowin, who ranks with Hemings and Condell as the best known of Shakespeare's fellows and with Taylor as the most famous members of the Caroline company, was baptized at St. Giles' Cripplegate, 9 December 1576, the son of Richard Lowin, a carpenter. He was apprenticed in 1593 to Nicholas Rudyard, goldsmith, for eight years, and first appears as a player shortly after the termination of his apprenticeship, in 1602. No doubt it was his apprenticeship in the company which lead to his taking part in the pageant for the inauguration of a Goldsmith Lord Mayor in 1611.

Though he first appeared as a Worcester's man in 1602, he had entered the King's company by the time of the performance of *Sejanus* in 1603, probably about June. (Baldwin, *Organization and Personnel*, pp. 48–9.) He is probably the I. L. *Roscio* who published *Conclusions upon Dances* in 1607, and possibly the John Lowin who married Joan Hall, widow, at St. Botolph's Bishopsgate, on 29 October in the same year, though there was another John Lowin in that parish, baptized in 1582 and married to Elizabeth Clement in 1642.

It is not difficult to determine the type of role generally assigned to Lowin, for more than a dozen of his characterizations are known from extant casts and from the discussions in *Historia Histrionica*. He is the bluff and outspoken character, sometimes the honest friend, sometimes villain. As Mr. Baldwin phrases it, 'the fundamental characteristic of Lowin is a certain bluff gruffness, which may be of the "honest" soldier type, or that of the rather domineering villain. Hence he is both comedian and villain'. (*Organization*

[1] Dr. Greg (p. 273) says that he played Barnavelt's wife, but this must be an error, since the directions seem to indicate fairly clearly that Lowen was the daughter. Furthermore, Dr. Greg assigns the part of the wife to 'nich' on the same page and does not assign the daughter.

and Personnel, p. 186 n.) He probably played Valentinian in *Valentinian,* Petilius in *Bonduca,* Leontius in *The Humorous Lieutenant,* Antonio in *The Maid in the Mill,* Piniero in *The Island Princess,* and Alberto in *The Fair Maid of the Inn.* (Ibid., pp. 200–2.) In many of his lines Lowin's great size is referred to, a characteristic which probably played its part in securing for him the post of King's Porter.

Lowin was not only a leading actor in the company but, after the death of John Heminges, one of its managers. Evidently Lowin and Taylor were selected as Heminges's successors before his death, for in 1628 they were joined with him in the receipt of payment for plays performed at court. Thereafter Lowin and Taylor, with the assistance of Swanston in the later days, regularly received grants and payments for the company; apparently they were generally thought of as the responsible members of the organization, for in 1634 Kendall told Crosfield that Lowin and Taylor were the masters of the King's company.

It was probably about the time that they succeeded Heminges as managers of the company that Lowin and Taylor became housekeepers in the Globe and Blackfriars; the shares in the Globe which they held between them were the same in number as those which had been held by Heminges.

Lowin seems to have spent most of his adult life in the parish of St. Saviour's Southwark, for he is listed in the token books 'At the further end of Mayden Lane' in 1601 and 1602, and 'Nere the Playhouse' from 1609 to 1623; he appears in the registers of the parish in 1638/9 and perhaps in 1619/20.

At the outbreak of the wars Lowin was too old to serve—indeed, one wonders if his services to the company had not been limited largely to managerial functions, as Heminges's had been, in the last few years of acting—and Wright says that he kept an inn at Brentford, where he died very old. Two burial entries have been noted as the actor's, one at St. Martin's-in-the-Fields in 1659, and another at St. Paul's, Covent Garden, in 1669 (*Mem. Act.,* p. 179), and both have been given by most writers on the actors since Collier. These two records must be rejected in favour of the St. Clement Danes entry given below, for it is the only one of the three which calls Lowin a player.

Lowin's portrait in the Ashmolean bears on the canvas the inscription, 'Aetat 64 A1640', which verifies the baptismal entry at St. Giles' Cripplegate as that of the actor. The frame of the Ashmolean portrait has 'b1575 D1659'. This is a much later addition than the inscription on the canvas, the birth date is demonstrably wrong, and I think that the St. Clement Danes entry shows that the death date is wrong. The acceptance of the player at St. Clement Danes as the King's man does not contradict Wright's statement about Lowin's great age (seventy-seven) or his death at Brentford, for it is no more impossible for Lowin to have died at Brentford and been buried at St. Clement Danes than for Condell to have died at Fulham and been buried at St. Mary's Aldermanbury.

1616—No. 5 in King's cast for *The Mad Lover*. (1679 folio B.M.)

1616–17—No. 6 in King's cast for *The Queen of Corinth*. (Ibid.)

1616–18—No. 7 in King's cast for *The Knight of Malta*. (Ibid.)

1617–18—He was overseer of Paris Garden. (Chambers, *E.S.* ii. 329.)

1618, Nov. 16—No. 3 in King's cast for *The Loyal Subject*. (1679 folio B.M.)

1619, Mar. 27—His name was fourth in a patent for the King's company. (*M.S.C.* i. 280–2.)

1619, May 19—'John Lowen' was third in the list of King's men for livery allowance. (*Hist. MSS. Com.*, Report IV, p. 299.)

1619?—No. 2 in King's cast for *The Humorous Lieutenant*. (1679 folio B.M.)

1619?—No. 5 in King's cast for *The Laws of Candy*. (Ibid.)

c. 1619–20—No. 2 in King's cast for *The Custom of the Country*. (Ibid.)

1619–21—No. 5 in King's cast for *Women Pleased*. (Ibid.)

1619–21—No. 1 in King's cast for *The Island Princess*. (Ibid.)

1619–22—No. 2 in King's cast for *The Little French Lawyer*. (Ibid.)

1619–23—'Bosola, I. Lowin' is in the cast of King's men prefixed to the 1623 quarto of *The Duchess of Malfi*. Since only one name is given, he apparently had the part in both the original production >1614 and the revival of 1619–23. (1623 4° B.M.)

1619/20, Feb. 1—'John Lewin & Katherine Wooden with licence' mar. St. S.S.

1620, Aug. 13—'John Lowen & His wife dind w^t me.' (Alleyn's Diary, Young, ii. 186.)

c. 1620—No. 1 in King's cast for *The False One*. (1679 folio B.M.)

1621—No. 5 in King's cast for *The Pilgrim*. (Ibid.)

1621, Apr. 7—His name was third in a livery allowance list of King's men. (*Hist. MSS. Com.*, Report IV, p. 299.)

c. 1621—No. 5 in King's cast for *The Double Marriage*. (1679 folio B.M.)

1622, May 14—No. 1 in King's cast for *The Prophetess*. (Ibid.)

1622, June 22—No. 4 in King's cast for *The Sea Voyage*. (Ibid.)

1622, Oct. 24—No. 2 in King's cast for *The Spanish Curate*. (Ibid.)

1623—'John Lowine' was eleventh in the actor list in the Shakespeare folio.

1623, May 21—Markham's suit names 'Iohn Lowen of Lambeth'. (See Appendix, p. 683.)

1623, Aug. 29—No. 2 in King's cast for *The Maid in the Mill*. (1679 folio B.M.)

1623, Dec. 6—No. 5 in King's cast for *The Lover's Progress*. (Ibid.)

1624, Oct. 4—Underwood in his will made 'John Lowyn' a legatee and overseer. (See Appendix, p. 651.)

1624, Dec. 20—His name was seventh in the submission of the King's men for playing *The Spanish Viceroy*. (*Herbert*, p. 21; see above, pp. 14–15.)

1625, >May 5—As a member of King's, 'Iohn Lowen' received 4

yards of black cloth for James's funeral procession; his name was fifteenth in the list. (*M.S.C.* ii. 326.)

1625, May 12—'A note by Sir John Coke, one of the Masters of Requests, for his first audience with Charles I. on May 12, 1625 (*H.M.C. Cowper MSS.* i. 194), contains the following: "King James' servants . . . John Lowen, porter, who bought his place, being a player, for 200*l.*, to be confirmed in it. . . . His majesty's comedians to be sworn again in ordinary."' (*R.E.S.* i. [1925], 184.)

1625, June 24—His name was third in the list for a patent for King's. (*M.S.C.* i. 282–3.)

1626—'*Domitianus Caesar*—Iohn Lowin' is in King's cast for Massinger's *The Roman Actor*, lic. 11 October. (1629 4º B.M.)

1626, Nov. 3—'A peticõn of Iohn Nicols agst: Iohn Lowen and Rich: Robinson. debt. 20^{li}. Answ: of Course.' (*M.S.C.* ii. 400.) The same petition appears again dated 13 or 14 November. (Ibid.)

1628, Apr. 10—With Heminges and Taylor he was paid £100 for plays given by King's in 1627. (Ibid., p. 346.)

1628—No. 1 in King's cast for *The Lover's Melancholy*, lic. 24 November. (1629 4º B.M.)

1629, May 6—No. 2 in list of King's for cloak allowance. (*M.S.C.* ii. 350.)

1629—'*Eubulus* an old Counsaylor—*Iohn Lewin*' in King's cast for Massinger's *The Picture*, lic. 8 June. (1630 4º B.M.)

1629, June 29—The L.C. Books record a warrant for 'ye app^{r}hension of Richard Ewer at ye complaint of Iohn Lowen'. (*M.S.C.* ii. 350.)

1629?—'M^r. *Lewin, Iacomo*' in King's cast of Carlell's *The Deserving Favorite*. (1629 4º B.M.)

c. 1630—'*Vndermyne*—*A wealthy Cittizen*—John Lowen' in King's cast in the MS. of Clavell's (?) *The Soddered Citizen*. (*Sod. Cit.*, p. 3.)

1630/1, Feb. 18—'Received of Mr. Taylor and Lowins, in the name of their company, for the benefitt of my winter day, upon the second day of Ben Jonson's play of *Every Man in his Humour*, this 18 day of February, 1630—12*l.* 4*s.* 0*d.*' (*Herbert*, p. 44.)

1630/1, Feb. 18—'A license to Mr. Lowins, on the 18th of February 1630, for allowing of *a Dutch vaulter*, at their Houses, [the Globe, and Blackfriars.]' (Ibid., p. 47.)

1630/1, Mar. 17—A warrant for 'Iohn Lowing in the behalfe of himselfe and the rest of his Company his Ma^{tes} Players' to be paid £260 for plays given by King's at Hampton Court and Whitehall. (*M.S.C.* ii. 354–5.)

1631, May 6 (lic.)—'Mr Lowin:' played Titus Flaminius in King's production of *Believe as You List*. (Sisson, *B.A.Y.L.*, pp. xxxi ff.)

1631—The MS. of Arthur Wilson's *The Swisser* (B.M. Add. MS. 36759) gives his name in the cast for the Blackfriars' production: 'Andrucho, A Swisser otherwise Count Aribert banisht . . . Lowin.' (Feuillerat, *The Swisser*.) In this play (iii. 2, ll. 112–13) Asprandus says to Andrucho,

> Then thy great Beard and Bulke
> Will grace the Gallowes well.

c. 1631—Lowin and Taylor acquired shares as housekeepers in the Globe and Blackfriars, as is evidenced by the statement in the petition of Benfield, Swanston, and Pollard, 'Mr Tailor and Mr Lowen were long since admitted to purchase 4 partes betwixt them from the rest', and by the list at the end of their petition, showing that Lowin and Taylor each owned two housekeeper's shares in the Globe and one in the Blackfriars. (*M.S.C.* ii. 363–4.)

1631/2, Feb. 22—'A Warraunt for payment of 120^{li} vnto Iohn Lowing Ioseph Taylor & Elliard Swanson for themselues & the rest of their fellowes his Ma^{tes} Comædians' for plays given at Christmas. (Ibid., p. 358.)

1632—'BELLEUR, . . . of a stout blunt humor. . . . Most naturally Acted by Mr. *John Lowin*' in King's cast for the 1632 revival of *The Wild Goose Chase*, printed 1652. (B.M. copy.)

1632—Alexander Gill's slanderous verses on Jonson's *Magnetic Lady* conclude with a reference to 'Lowine' and Taylor as lights of the stage. (*See* Joseph Taylor.)

1632/3, Mar. 16—'A Warraunt for payment of 270^{li} vnto Iohn Lowen Ioseph Taylor & Ellyard Swanston his Ma^{tes} Comædians' for one rehearsal and twenty-three plays at court between 3 May 1632 and 3 March 1632/3. (*M.S.C.* ii. 360.)

1633, Apr. 15— A warraunt for Liueryes for 14 of his Ma^{tes} Players . . . to bee đđ to Iohn Lowen.' (Ibid.)

1633, May 6—A warrant to recruit actors for the King's company was directed 'To Iohn Lowen and Ioseph Taylor'. (Ibid., p. 361.)

1633, Oct. 24—Lowin and Swanston apologized for their 'ill manners' in the matter of Fletcher's *The Tamer Tamed*. (*Herbert*, p. 21.)

1634, Apr. 26—'A Warrant to sweare William Smith A Groome of the Chamber extraordinary. Apr. 26. 1634. Io. Lowen.' (*M.S.C.* ii. 373.)

1634, Apr. 27—'A Warraunt for payment of 220^{li} vnto Iohn Lowen Ioseph Taylor & Elliard Swanston for themselues & the rest of their fellowes the kings Players' for plays acted during the past year. (Ibid.)

1634, July 18—Kendall told Crosfield, 'The Kings Company at ye private house of Blackfriars: The masters or cheife whereof are
⎰Mr Talor
⎱Mr Lowen.' (*Crosfield's Diary*, p. 72.)

1635, Apr. 3—'A warr^t . . . for Liueryes for 14 of his Ma^{tes} Players to bee đđ to Iohn Lowen.' (*M.S.C.* ii. 376.)

1635, May 24—'A warr^t for payment of 250^{li} vnto Iohn Lowen for himselfe & the rest of ye kings Players for 20 playes.' (Ibid.)

1635, Sept. 1—'Mr Lowen' was made an overseer of the will of Elizabeth Condell. (See Appendix, p. 639.)

1635, Nov. 16—It was probably Lowin who delivered the prologue to *The Platonic Lovers*, containing the lines:

> Well, I (your Servant) who have labour'd heere
> In Buskins, and in Socks, this thirty yeare,
> I'th truth of my experience . .

Lowin was the only King's man who had been a member of the company for over thirty years in 1635, though Richard Robinson had probably begun performing boy's parts for the company twenty-eight or nine years before.

1635, Dec. 31—He was mentioned in the will of John Shank.

apparently as a sort of treasurer of the company. (See Appendix, p. 647.)

1636, Aug. 5—' : . . Sir Henry, upon conference with the Earl of Essex, the Lord Chamberlain, concerning the plague, which had increased to a hundred deaths a week, sent warrants, by Mr. Louens, on the 5th of August, to the several playhouses, for the purpose of preventing their representations.' (*Herbert*, p. 65.)

1636, Sept. 4—'Joane Lowin in the Church' bur. St. S.S.

1636, Dec. 13—A warrant was issued for the payment 'to John Lowen and Joseph Taylor, on behalf of their company', of a weekly allowance of £20 for the Christmas season at Hampton Court. (*C.S.P., Dom.*, 1636–7, p. 228, and see above, p. 53.)

1636/7, Mar. 12—A warrant was issued for £240 'to bee payd unto John Lowen and Joseph Taylor or either of them' for twenty-two plays given by the King's company at court, but Swanston signed all the receipts. (Law, *Forgeries*, App.)

1637, Apr. 22—A warrant was issued for the delivery of sixteen liveries 'vnto Iohn Lowen, Ioseph Taylor & Eilardt Swanston'. (*M.S.C.* ii. 383.)

1637, June 10—The Lord Chamberlain wrote the Stationers' Company that no plays were to be published without 'some Certificate in writeing vnder the handes of Iohn Lowen & Ioseph Taylor for the Kings servantes & of Christopher Bieston for ye Kings & Queenes young Company', or their successors in management. (Ibid., pp. 384–5.)

1637/8, Mar. 15—A warrant was issued 'for the payment of 150li vnto Iohn Lowen, Ioseph Taylor & Eillart Swanston or any of them' for fourteen plays given by the King's company at court. (Ibid., p. 387.)

1638, May 4—John Lowen, clerk, and others petitioned concerning one Symes and a tenement in Birchen Lane, London, called the Bull; case again referred to trial at law. (*C.S.P., Dom.*, 1637–8, p. 404.)

1638, June 2—'Received of Mr. Lowens for my paines about Messinger's play called *The King and the Subject*, 2 June, 1638, 1l. o. o.' (*Herbert*, p. 22 ; see above, pp. 60–1, for more about this play.)

1638/9, Jan. 29—'John s. of John Lowin one of ye kings players' chris. St. S.S.

1638/9, Mar. 12—A warrant was issued for the payment of £300 'vnto Iohn Lowen, Ioseph Taylor & Eillardt Swanston or any one of them' for twenty-four plays given by the King's company at court. (*M.S.C.* ii. 388–9.)

1638/9, Mar. 14—'A warrt for Liueryes for 16 of ye Kinges Players ... to bee dd to Iohn Lowen, Ioseph Taylor & Eillardt Swanston.' (Ibid., p. 389.)

1640, Apr. 4—'A warrt for payment of 230li vnto Iohn Lowen, Ioseph Taylor & Eillardt Swanston for himselfe & the rest of the Company of ye Players for one & Twenty Playes Acted before their Mats.' (Ibid., p. 392.)

1640/1, Mar. 20—'A warrt for payment of 160li vnto the Kinges Players for Playes Acted before his Matye the Queene & Prince ... to bee payd to Iohn Lowen. Ioseph Taylor & Eillardt Swanston or any of them.' (Ibid., p. 397.)

1640/1, Mar. 20—'A warr^t to the great Wardrobe for Liueryes . . . for Iohn Lowen, Ioseph Taylor & Eillardt Swanston and fifteene others their fellowes.' (Ibid., pp. 397-8.)

1647—'John Lowin' stands first in the list of ten King's men who signed the dedication of the Beaumont and Fletcher folio.

1647—Harrington, in his verses for the first Beaumont and Fletcher folio, mentions Lowin and Taylor as famous actors of the King's company. (*See* Stephen Hammerton.)

1647/8, Jan.—One of seven members of the King's company to enter into a bond for the payment of old company debt. (*See* Theophilus Bird.)

1648—'Lowin Acted Aubrey' in the production of *Rollo or the Bloody Brother* when troops raided the Cockpit. (*Hist. Hist.*, p. 9.)

1652—The title-page of the 1652 edition of *The Wild Goose Chase* says, 'Retriv'd for the publick delight of all the Ingenious; And private Benefit Of John Lowin, And Joseph Taylor, Servants to His late Majestie. By a Person of Honour.' The dedication, which ends, 'But be the *Comoedie* at your *Mercy* as *We* are. Onely we wish, that you may have the same *kind Joy* in *Perusing* of it, as we had in the *Acting. So Exeunt'*, is signed by Lowin and Taylor. One of the prefatory verses is entitled, 'An Epigram upon the long lost and fortunately recovered WILD-GOOSE CHASE, and as seasonably bestowed on Mr. JOHN LOWEN and Mr. JOSEPH TAYLOR, for their best advantage', and reads,

> In this late dearth of wit, when *Jose* and *Jack*
> Were hunger-bit for want of fowl and Sack,
> His nobleness found out this happy meanes
> To mend their dyet with these WILD-GOOSE scenes,
> By which he hath revived in a day
> Two Poets, and two Actors, with one Play.

The verse is signed W. E., whom Collier and others have conjectured to be the old King's player, William Eccleston.

1653, Aug. 24—'John Lowin the player buried' St. Clement Danes.

1664—In a coffee house scene in the third act of Tatham's (?) *Knavery in All Trades* (1664 4° HN), a gentleman has mentioned a current play.

> *third.* . . . Bur (*sic*) sir, they say 'tis done rarely well.
> *fourth.* I cannot believe it, 'tis impossible they should do any thing so well as I have seen things done.
> *fifth.* When *Taylor Lowen*, and *Pollard* were alive.
> *fourth.* Did you not know *Benfield*, and Swautted?
> *fifth.* Did I not know 'em? Yes, and hum'd them off a hundred times.

1676—He is praised by Snarl in Shadwell's *Virtuoso*. (*See* Swanston.)

1699—Wright says, '*Lowin* used to Act, with mighty Applause, *Falstaffe, Morose, Vulpone*, and *Mammon* in the *Alchymist*; *Melancius* in the *Maid's* Tragedy' (*Hist. Hist.*, p. 4); that he was superannuated when the wars began (ibid., p. 7); and that '*Lowin* in his latter Days kept an Inn (the three Pidgions) at *Brentford*, where he Dyed very Old, (for he was an Actor of eminent Note in the Reign of K. *James* the first) and his Poverty was as great as his Age' (ibid., p. 10).

1708—In telling of the Restoration performance of *Henry VIII*, Downes says, 'The part of the King was so right and justly done by Mr. *Betterton*, he being Instructed in it by Sir *William*, who had it from Old Mr. *Lowen*, that had his Instructions from Mr. *Shakespear* himself . . .' (Downes, p. 24.)

LYLY, GEORGE (*see* LILLIE, GEORGE).

LYLY, JOHN (*see* LILLIE, JOHN).

MAGO, WILLIAM. Mago was perhaps a Prince's hired man in 1621 and an employee of the King's company, probably a hired man, at least from 1624 to 1631.

c. 1621—The list of the dramatis personae of *The Witch of Edmonton* gives 'W. Hamluc' and 'W. Mago' as two countrymen. (1658 4° B.M.) (*See* W. Hamluc.)

1624, Dec. 27—Herbert exempted him from arrest as a member of the King's company. (*Herbert*, p. 74, and see above, pp. 15–16.)

1631, May 6 (lic.)—He was a Carthaginian Officer ('wᵐ Mago:') and an attendant on King Prusias ('Wᵐ Mag⟨o⟩') in King's production of Massinger's *Believe As You List*. (Sisson, *B.A.Y.L.*, pp. xxxi-ff.)

MAIVRIN or MAROVIN. The first reading is Murray's, the second Bolingbroke's. Both are rather odd names and suggest misreadings.

1634/5, Mar. 10—His name is twenty-second of twenty-eight in a full list of players at Norwich; some of them seem to be King's Revels men, though the records do not give the name of the company, which was probably an amalgamation. (Murray, ii. 356, and see above, pp. 286 and 288–9.)

MANNERY (MANNEROY, MANURAY), SAMUEL. The actor, first a boy with the Prince's company and later, probably, a hired man with Beeston's Boys, is probably the man found in the parish registers of St. Giles in the Fields, for the name is unusual, and the parish is that of the theatre in which he was employed.

1631, Dec.—'Bawd. Samuell Mannery' in cast of *Holland's Leaguer* acted by Prince Charles's men at Salisbury Court. (*Herbert*, p. 45; 1632 4° B.M.)

1638, Oct. 28—'LC. Samuell Mannery & Mary ffinch' mar. St. G.F.

1639, Aug. 10—'Samuell Manuray' was twelfth in a ticket of privilege for the young company at the Cockpit. (*M.S.C.* ii. 390–1.)

1639, Sept. 1—'A Crisom Child of Samuell Manneroy' bur. St. G.F.

1642/3, Mar. 17—'Samuell sonne of Samuell & Mary Manneroy' chris. St. G.F.

1648, Sept. 25—'A stilborn Child of Samuell Manneroy' bur. St. G.F.

1648, Nov. 1—'Samuell Manneroy' bur. St. G.F.

1649, Apr. 18—'Ann Daughter of Samuell Manneroy' bur. St. G.F.

MAROVIN (*see* MAIVRIN).

MARRANT, EDWARD. One of the tenants of the Fortune Theatre in 1637 when, with Margaret Gray and John Rhodes, he was sued in Chancery by Dulwich College for arrears in rent. (Young, ii. 262.)

MARSHALL, CHARLES. In June 1616 the Lord Chamberlain sent out an order condemning the use of duplicate patents and naming, among others, Charles Marshall as a leader of a touring Palsgrave's company. Since Charles Massey was a well-known leader of that company, and since the other leaders were also well-known Palsgrave's men, it seems probable that Charles Marshall is a mistake for Charles Massey. (*See* Charles Massey and William Parr.)

MARTYN, CHARLES.

1615, Mar. 28—He was named as a boy in a patent to Lady Eliza-beth's of 31 May 1613 which was copied at Coventry on this date. (See *R.E.S.* i. 183.)

MASKELL, THOMAS. Maskell was probably a showman, in spite of the fact that he was called a player at Manchester, but it is possible that six men may have formed a touring company, as they had in Elizabeth's days.

1635, Dec. 23—He was at Norwich with a licence of 20 June 1635 to 'sett forth an Italian motion'. (Murray, ii. 358.)

1635/6, Feb. 18—At Manchester 'Tho Maskall a player & 5 more [were paid] to voyd the Town'. (Ibid., p. 331.)

MASSEY (MARCY, MASSIE, MASSY, MERCY), CHARLES. Massey first appears in a plot of the Admiral's men in 1597 and is regularly found in the Admiral's–Prince Henry's–Palsgrave's company from that time until his death in 1625. Dr. Greg points out (*Hens. D.* ii. 297) that throughout his career he was intimately associated with Samuel Rowley. His friendship with Edward Alleyn is indicated in Alleyn's diary. He seems to have been one of the most substantial members of the company from the time of the building of the new theatre until his death.

Like several other members of this troupe, Massey was an occasional playwright. In April 1602 the Admiral's company paid him £5 for a play called *Malcolm King of Scots*, and in March 1602/3 £2 in earnest of *The Siege of Dunkirk with Alleyn the Pirate*. Both these plays have disappeared, but one was still in the repertory of the company in 1621, or else Massey had written another, when Alleyn gave him five shillings 'att His playe'. It is possible that Alleyn may have meant an actor's benefit performance of the type popular in the Restoration, but I know of no evidence that this custom existed before the Civil War.

That the marriage in St. Gregory by St. Paul was that of the actor is proved by the mention of his widow Elianor in 1635.

1605, Apr. 4—'Charles Massey & Elinor Colman lic fac' mar. St. Gregory by St. Paul. (Challen, *Marriages*.)

1616, June 16—The Lord Chamberlain wrote to local officials condemning several players and their exemplifications of patents. He mentions 'Charles Marshall, Homfry Jeffes and Willm Parr: three of Prince Palatynes Company'. Probably Massey was intended, not Marshall. (*See* William Parr.)

1618, Sept. 20—'m^r massie' dined with Alleyn. (Young, ii. 104.)

1618, Oct. 31—He was the fifth member of Palsgrave's to sign the lease of the Fortune from Edward Alleyn. (See above, pp. 138–9.)

1620/1, Jan. 21—' John sonne of Charles Mercy, gentleman' bur. St. G.C.

1620/1, Mar. 18—'Charles massy ye Collyar & His sone & canterbury & His wife dind Here.' (Young, ii. 202.)

1621, Apr. 15—'borne: massey: Cartwright: Gunnell: grace: Hunt dind Here.' (Ibid., p. 204.)

1621, Apr. 24—'Margaret daughter of Charles Mercy yeoman' chris. St. G.C. 'Margaret daughter of Charles Mercy Playe^r' bur. 24 December 1621.

1621, Aug. 12—'Mr Edmonds: Charles Massey & on other off ye compa[n]y dynd Here.' (Young, ii. 216.)

1621, Nov. 19—'giuen charles massye att His playe—o–5–o.' (Ibid., p. 224.)

1622, May 20—Alleyn granted him a lease of a half share (one twenty-fourth part) of the new Fortune for £41. 13. 4. (*Hens. Paps.*, pp. 28–30, 112.)

1622, May 20—He was granted a whole share—in addition to the half share which he already held—of the new Fortune. (Ibid., p. 112.)

1622—He was second in Herbert's list of the members of Palsgrave's. (*Herbert*, p. 63.)

1622, July 21—'Charls massy & His Cosen ned Collins 2 shagbutts & a cornett dind Here.' (Alleyn's Diary, Young, ii. 246.)

1622/3, Mar. 14—He surrendered one share in the Fortune to Alleyn, leaving him with a half share. (*Hens. Paps.*, p. 112.)

1624, Apr. 30—He and five others signed a bond with Richard Gunnell to continue to play together as the Palsgrave's company at the Fortune. (Hotson, p. 52; see above, pp. 148–9.)

1625, July 20—' John sonne of Charles Mercy, gent' bur. St. G.C.

1625, Aug. 3—'Charles Mercy gēt' bur. St. G.C.

1635, Dec. 6—In the answer of the Fortune lessees, November, 1637, to a bill in Chancery against them for non-payment of rent, they say that Massey had died before 6 December 1635 and had left a widow Elianor. (*MSS. Dul.*, p. 54.)

MASSEY, GEORGE. It is not known whether George Massey was related to Charles or not, but one would suspect it because of their connexion with the same enterprise and their residence in the same parish.

1622, May 20—Alleyn granted 'George Massye, citizen and merchant tailor of London', a lease of a half share in the new Fortune. (*Hens. Paps.*, p. 112.)

1624, Sept. 14—'George Massey gentleman bur. St. G.C.

1635—A memorandum of the non-payment of rent on George Massey's share in the Fortune is found among Henslowe's papers. (*Hens. Paps.*, p. 112.)

MATCHIT, AMB.

c. 1635 ?—'Felixina *Amb. Matchit*' appears in the cast for Thomas Jordan's *Money Is an Ass* which is printed in the 1668 quarto. (1668 4° B.M.) *See* Thomas Jordan.

MAY, EDWARD. The name May was rather common in Caroline London, and one cannot be sure just how many records refer to a single individual.[1] The player Edward was undoubtedly with Prince Charles's company in 1631; in 1634/5 he was at Norwich, probably with the King's Revels. There is some reason to believe that the player was the poet of *Poetical Varieties*, since he and Thomas Jordan had been associated in the Norwich list three years before. The May in the stage directions of *Edmond Ironside* was probably the Prince Charles's player, because the names in *Edmond Ironside* all seem to be from that company. (See above, p. 323.)

The identity of the May in *Wit without Money* and the E. M. of *The Poor Man's Comfort* is less certain, for we have no reliable evidence that Edward was ever a Queen Henrietta's man. Indeed, we have only Mr. Lawrence's categorical statement to assure us that E. M. stands for Edward May at all. That Edward May joined Queen Henrietta's company about 1635 and got his name in the first quartos of *Wit without Money* and *The Poor Man's Comfort* as an actor in that company is not an unreasonable hypothesis, but his membership cannot be definitely accepted on the basis of such evidence.

Obviously there were at least two Edward Mays in St. Giles in the Fields; if it is ever established that Edward was the May of *Wit without Money*, then he might reasonably be identified as one of the men in St. Giles, the parish of the Queen's theatre.

1631, Dec.—'*Fidelio, friend to Philautus*. Edward May' in the cast of *Holland's Leaguer* acted by Prince Charles's men at Salisbury Court this month. (*Herbert*, p. 45; 1632 4° B.M.)

c. 1632—Probably he is the 'may' who appears (fol. 107ª) in the prompter's notes in the MS. of *Edmond Ironside* (B.M. Egerton 1994), apparently written 1590–1600, but revived about 1632, probably by Prince Charles's men (see above, p. 323). The stage directions indicate that he played the part of '1 Balife'. (Greg, *Dram. Doc.*, p. 259.)

[1] There was an Edward May, physician, who published a medical pamphlet in 1639, and an Edward May 'Gent' (possibly the same man) who published *Epigrams Divine and Moral* in 1633. Certainly the former was not the actor, and I cannot believe that the latter was.

I am less certain about the 'Ed. May' whose commendatory verses are the first of twelve sets published before Thomas Beedome's *Poems, Divine and Humane*, 1641. This man was a friend of Beedome and of Henry Glapthorne, the editor of the volume, for he speaks of Beedome's ghost as addressing Glapthorne, 'Thanks my deare Wilbore [according to J. H. Walter in *T.L.S.*, 19 September 1936, "bore" is a common appendage to nicknames in Glapthorne's native East Anglia] for thy love and care', and he concludes his praise of Glapthorne's editorship by saying,

I by that friend am sent
To bring this first stone to his Monument.

The association with Glapthorne and Nabbes, the only other writers of commendatory verses in this volume whose names are signed, suggests the actor, but the verse seems too fluent for a minor theatrical functionary.

1634/5, Mar. 10—His name is in the full list of players at Norwich. Some of them seem to be King's Revels men, though the records do not give the name of the company, which was probably an amalgamation. (Murray, ii. 356; see above, pp. 286 and 288–9.)

1635?—Daborne's *Poor Man's Comfort* (whose 1655 title-page says, 'divers times Acted at the Cock-pit in Drury lane') has a prologue signed 'Per E. M.'. Mr. W. J. Lawrence (*M.L.R.* xxv. 211) identifies E. M. with Edward May and thinks the prologue was written for a Queen Henrietta's revival of 1635.

c. 1636—The 1639 4° of *Wit without Money* (presented by the Queen's company at the Phoenix, according to the title-page) has the stage direction, Act V, H₃v, '*Enter Vncle and Merchant: May with a torch*'. (B.M. 4°, pointed out by Mr. Lawrence, *M.L.R.* xxv. 211.)

1637—Prefixed to Thomas Jordan's *Poetical Varieties*, published in this year, are some commendatory verses, 'To his friend the Author Mᵣ Thomas Jordan on his Varieties', signed 'Ed. May'. (1637 ed. HN.)

1641, Sept. 24—'Edward May' bur. St. G.C.

1641, Oct. 7—'Clare Daughter of Edward May' bur. St. G.C.

1641/2, Feb. 11—'ffrancis daughter of Edward May' bur. St. G.C.

1647, July 1—'Edward May and Mary Maynwaring' mar. St. G.C.

MAY, NATHAN. Nathan May appears once in the provinces as a leader of a provincial troupe, in 1615. Though his name never occurs again, he is included here because of the possibility that he might be the May of *Edmond Ironside* or *Wit without Money*. (*See* Edward May.)

1614/15, Feb. 27—'Willm Hovell, Willm Perry & Nathan May' showed a licence of this date at Norwich 17 June 1615. (Murray, ii. 340.) The company is unnamed, but Mr. Murray says (ibid., p. 10) with little evidence that it was the King's Revels.

MEADE, JACOB. Jacob Meade touches theatrical affairs at two points: as part owner of the Hope theatre, used for plays for eight or ten months after the death of Shakespeare, and as the great impresario of bull-baiting and bear-baiting, a form of entertainment in close competition with the drama. He is mentioned in numerous documents at Dulwich, chiefly in connexion with the Bear Garden.

Meade was a resident of St. Saviour's Southwark, where he is found in the parish registers and in the token books at various times from 1598 to 1623. The Jacob Meade, waterman, who appears in the registers and token books in 1630 was probably his son.

1615/16, Mar. 20—The Prince's men signed an agreement with Alleyn and Meade in settlement of the company's debt to Henslowe. (See above, p. 199, n. 2.)

1619, Sept. 22—'I dind wᵗ Jacob [Meade] mᵣ adye & mᵣ foster & wee concluded our matters both wᵗ Hym & Tho: Angell blessed be yᵉ god off peac.' (Young, ii. 154.)

1624, July 9—'Jacob Meade a man the kinges shvant' bur. St. S.S.

MEGUS, William.

1622, May 19—'Katherine Megus, d. of William Megus player up ground' bur. St. S.S. (Bod.)

MICHAEL. I cannot identify this King's man.

1619, Aug.—The prompter's notes in the MS. of *Sir John van Olden Barnavelt* show that an actor named Michael ('migh', 'mighell') played a captain, a soldier, and a huntsman in the King's production. (Greg, *Dram. Doc.*, p. 273.)

MINION, Samuel.

1634, Nov. 28—'Samuell Minion' is the fourth of six leaders mentioned in a licence for an unnamed company, probably the new King's Revels, which was shown at Norwich 3 September 1635. (Murray, ii. 8–9, 357.)

MINSHAW (MINSHALL?), Edward. The St. Giles registers suggest that Minshaw had come down in the world to reach the state of player; perhaps he had not been an actor before the closing of the theatres. There is only a bare possibility that Minshall and Minshaw are the same.

1635, Oct. 16—'Edward Minshall, Gent., of Sᵗ Andrew's, Holborn, Bachelor, 21, son of Huon Minshall, Gent., of Middlewich, co. Chester, who consents, & Joane Merrell, of Sᵗ Andrew's, Holborn, Spinster, 20, dau. of John Merrell, of Sᵗ Dunstan's West, Scrivener, decᵈ; consent of mother Anne Merrell, of Sᵗ Andrew's, Holborn, Widow; at Sᵗ Clement Danes.' (*Marriages, London*.)

1640/1, Jan. 5—'Mary daughter of Edward & Joyce Minshall' chris. St. G.F.

1643, May 28—'Edward sonne of Edward and Joyce Minshall' chris. St. G.F.

1643, Sept. 13—'Julyan sonne of Edward Minshall' bur. St. G.F.

1647, June 30—'Jane Daughtʳ of Edw Minshaw gentl' chris. St. G.C.

1649, Aug. 5—'John sonne of Edw. Minshaw gentleman' chris. St. G.C. 'John sonne of Edw. Minshaw player' bur. 14 September 1650.

1651, Apr. 6—'Willi sonne of Edw: Minshaw gentle' chris. St. G.C.

1652, Aug. 26—'Edw. sonne of Edw Minshaw musitian' bur. St. G.C.

MISTALE or MISDALE. One of the readings of the name is Murray's, and the other is Bolingbroke's.

1634/5, Mar. 10—His name is in the full list of players at Norwich. Some of them seem to be King's Revels men, though the records do not give the name of the company, which was probably an amalgamation. (Murray, i. 279, ii. 356; see above, pp. 286 and 288–9.)

MOHUN (MOONE), Michael. Wright's notes on the actor leave no doubt that Moone and Mohun were the same man, though all the Moone records are before the closing of the theatres and all the Mohun records after. He was evidently a man of some importance at the Cockpit or he would not have been mentioned in the two

restraining orders, and to be of importance he must have been an adult by 1637. If, therefore, he was a boy under Beeston at the Cockpit, he must have been there before the formation of Beeston's Boys in 1636, in other words in Queen Henrietta's company.

Mohun was an important figure in the formation of the companies when the theatres reopened after the restoration of Charles II. For his Restoration career, see Hotson.

1637, May 12—Christopher and William Beeston, Theophilus Bird, Ezekiel Fenn, and 'Michaell Moone' were ordered brought before the Privy Council, and playing was ordered stopped at the Cockpit until further notice. (*M.S.C.* i. 392.)

1639, Aug. 10—'Michaell Moone' is fifth in the list of twelve members of the young company at the Cockpit granted tickets of privilege. (Ibid. ii. 390–1.)

1640, May 3—William Beeston, George Stutville, and '[*blank*] Moone' were ordered to be apprehended and committed to the Marshalsea for acting an unlicensed play at the Cockpit and then refusing to close the theatre on Herbert's order. (Ibid., p. 394.)

> 1642—'*Burt* was a Boy first under *Shank* at the *Black-friers*, then under *Beeston* at the *Cockpit*; and *Mohun*, and *Shatterel* were in the same Condition with him, at the last Place. There *Burt* used to Play the principal Women's Parts, in particular *Clariana* in *Love's Cruelty*; and at the same time *Mohun* Acted *Bellamente* [in *Love's Cruelty*], which Part he retain'd after the Restauration.' (*Hist. Hist.*, p. 3; see Appendix, p. 692.)

1642 <–> 1660—Wright says that during the wars most of the actors went into the King's armies. '*Mohun* was a Captain, (and after the Wars were ended here, served in *Flanders*, where he received Pay as a Major).' (Ibid., p. 8; see Appendix, p. 694.)

1657/8, February. Sir Charles Cotterell wrote to Secretary Nicholas of an entertainment given by Newcastle for several members of the royal family at Antwerp at which 'The King was brought in with music, and all being placed, Major Mohun, the player, in a black satin robe and garland of bays, made a speech in verse of his lordship's own poetry, complimenting the King in his highest hyperbole. . . . Then they danced again 2 hours more, and Major Mohun ended all with another speech, prophesying his Majesty's reestablishment'. (*C.S.P., Dom.*, 1657–8, p. 311.)

MONKE, WILLIAM. Many, though by no means all, of the musicians in Southwark were connected with the theatres.

1619, June 10—'Samuell Monke s of Willm a Musitian' chris. St. S.S.

MOONE, MICHAEL (*see* MOHUN, MICHAEL).

MOORE, JOSEPH. Joseph Moore first appears as one of the two leaders of the Lady Elizabeth's company in 1611, and from that time until 1631 he is one of the most conspicuous of the leaders of provincial troupes; he is always found with the Lady Elizabeth's men. According to his fellow, Francis Wambus (q.v.), Moore left the stage for a year or two around 1620 to keep an inn at Chichester, but by 1622 he was acting again, for in this year Herbert said that he was one of the chief men at the Phoenix—Lady Elizabeth's. He is not conspicuous again in the provinces until the formation of the Lady Elizabeth's of 1628, a company which he led in the provinces until he became a Prince Charles's man in 1631. The Lord Chamberlain's charge that Moore acted fraudulently in the case of Barnes cannot be taken too seriously since Moore was allowed to continue as a company leader. His status with Prince Charles's is rather puzzling. He is named first in their licence shown at Norwich, and he is always mentioned in the payments which the company received for performances at court—the usual indications of company leaders—yet he is not mentioned in the one extant cast of the company, and he is in neither of the two lists of Prince Charles's men sworn Grooms of the Chamber. There can be no doubt that he *was* a leader of the company. It is possible that, like Heminges in his later years, he was a financial agent rather than an actor. Probably he would not need to be sworn Groom as a Prince Charles's man since he had been sworn in 1628 as a Lady Elizabeth's servant.

The actor cannot, of course, have been the Joseph Moore at Winchester, who may have been his son. He is probably the man in the Barbican in 1623, and he may have been the resident of St. Andrew's in the Wardrobe, conveniently close to Salisbury Court, in 1638.

1617, June 4—'Joseph More' as the Lord Chamberlain's messenger brought Pembroke's restraining order against four touring companies to Norwich. (Murray, ii. 343–4. See above, pp. 178–9.)

1617, June 5—Townsend and Moore brought the Lady Elizabeth's company and the licence of 27 April 1611 to Norwich. (Ibid., p. 341.)

1617, July 11—Moore and Townsend were payees for three plays given before James on his journey to Scotland. (Cunningham, *Revels*, p. xliv.)

1617/18, Mar. 20—Foster, Townsend, Moore, and Waymus were granted a new licence of this date to play as the Lady Elizabeth's company in London and the provinces; it was shown by Townsend at Norwich 23 May 1618. (Murray, ii. 344–5.)

1619/20, Feb. 8—'Joseph Moore & others' presented a 1611 licence when the company visited Norwich. Professor Murray thinks this visit is misdated and should be dated 1618/19. (Ibid., p. 345.)

1620, Apr. 22—When the company visited Norwich on this date, Waymus declared that Moore, though still a member of the company, had not been with them for a year but 'nowe kepeth an Inn in Chichester'. (Ibid.)

1621, May 2—He was named in the licence for Lady Elizabeth's of 20 March 1617/18 shown at Norwich, but only Townsend was there. (Ibid., p. 346.)

1621/2, Mar. 13—He was named with Townsend, Foster, and Waymus in a Lord Chamberlain's warrant for the Lady Elizabeth's men. (Ibid., p. 193.)

1621/2, Mar. 20—He was named in a licence for Lady Elizabeth's of this date which was shown at Norwich 10 May 1623. (Murray, ii. 346–7.)

1622—He is second of the seven named in Herbert's office book as among 'the chiefe of them at the Phoenix' (Lady Elizabeth's company). (*Herbert*, p. 63.)

1623, May 21—In Markham's suit as 'Joseph More att the Harowe in Barbican', 5s. (See Appendix, p. 682.)

1623, July 26—'Letter to the Master and Fellows of New College, Winchester, recommending Joseph Moore to a scholar's place there.' (*C.S.P., Dom.*, 1623–5, p. 30.)

1624, Apr.—He was summoned before the Mayor of Norwich for trying to play in defiance of the Mayor's orders, but he did not appear, and the summons was probably issued only because his name was in the licence. (Murray, ii. 348–50.)

1628, June 30—'Ioseph Moore' was first of the 'Queene of Bonemia's Players' listed in a warrant for swearing them Grooms of the Chamber. (See above, pp. 188–9.)

1628, July 17—'Ioseph Moore' is one of four mentioned as belonging to the old Lady Elizabeth's company and the first of three mentioned as belonging to the new 'Queene of Bohemia's Players'. (See above, p. 189.)

1628, Dec. 9—Mentioned as one of four leaders in a docquet for a new licence for Lady Elizabeth's. (*C.S.P., Dom.*, 1628–9, p. 406.)

1629—'Mr Moore & his Companie, beinge the Ladie Elizabeth her Players', were paid £1 at Leicester. (Murray, ii. 317.)

1629, June 8—He was named in the warrant of this date presented by Ellis Guest at Norwich 27 June; Guest was alone. (*See* Guest.)

1629, Dec. 24—Moore is the first of the four 'sworne servantes to his Majestie' named in the licence of 15 December 1628 which was shown at Reading on this date. (Ibid., p. 386.)

1629/30, Mar. 3—As the leader of an unnamed company (evidently the Lady Elizabeth's), he presented a warrant of 15 December 1628 at Norwich. (Ibid., p. 353.)

1630, June—'Paid to Joseph More & others that was sworne Servants to the King' for not playing at Coventry. (Ibid., p. 251.)

1631, Mar. 30—With Townsend he was payee for Lady Elizabeth's at Coventry. (Ibid.)

1631, Aug. 13—He was the leader of Lady Elizabeth's company at Reading. (Ibid., p. 387.)

1631, Dec. 7—His name was in a warrant of this date for Prince Charles's company, which was shown at Norwich 21 February 1637/8. (Ibid., p. 358; see above, p. 302.)

1631/2, Jan. 23—The Lord Chamberlain declared that in 1629 Thomas Barnes, a carpenter, had been sworn a player 'by the false & fraudulent suggestion of one Ioseph Moore that followed the busines in the name of the company [Queen of Bohemia's] out of a corrupt end to deriue vnto him selfe a benefitt'. (*M.S.C.* ii. 356–7.)

1633, Apr. 27—'A petition of Thomas Dauenport against Ioseph Moore debt 27li Answered of course.' (Ibid., p. 409.)

1635, Nov. 3—At Norwich presented a licence authorizing a company (apparently Prince Charles's) to play at Salisbury Court and elsewhere. (Murray, ii. 358.)

1635, Dec. 10—'Ioseph Moore Andre Kayne & Ellis Worth. mentioned only' in a warrant for the payment of £100 for seven plays presented by Prince Charles's company in 1634–5. (*M.S.C.* ii. 377.)

1637/8, Mar. 21—'Ioseph Moore for himselfe & the rest of yᵉ Princes Players' was paid for three plays at court in 1636. (Ibid., p. 387.)

1638—He was possibly the 'Joseph More' whose moderated rent (i.e. three-fourths of the whole) in St. Andrews in the Wardrobe was assessed at £2. (*London, 1638*, p. 27.)

1640, May 4—Moore and Cane were named in a warrant for the payment of £60 to the Prince's company for three plays acted at Richmond. (*M.S.C.* ii. 394.)

MORE, ROGER (*see* NORE, ROGER).

MORGAN, FLUELLEN.

1633, May 3—Fluellen Morgan and William Cooke hired a commission from Edward Whiting and travelled with a puppet show until they went bankrupt, according to the testimony of Robert Houghton (q.v.) on this date.

MORRIS, MATHIAS.

c. 1634 ?—'*Sylana* wife to *Silius*—*Mathias Morris*' in the King's Revels cast for Richards's *Messalina*. (1640 ed. B.M.)

MOSSOCK, ANN. This record indicates that the provincial clerks were inclined to dub entertainers of all sorts players.

1638, July 12—'Paid given to Robert Tayler and Ann Mossock, players who came by warrant to shew the worlds creation', at Coventry. (Murray, ii. 253.)

MOUNTSETT (MOUNTFORD ?), JOHN. It is possible that Mountsett was the dancer referred to in *Mercurius Fumigosus* and that he travelled with a company of dancers and acrobats like the Peadles (q.v.).

1638, Aug. 22—John Mountsett came to Norwich with 'eleaven in his Company' and presented a signet bill of 8 June 1635. (Murray, ii. 359.)

1654, Aug. 23–30—*Mercurius Fumigosus* of this date, in speaking of dancers, praises 'the lately desceased *Mountford*, *Peadle*, and now *Christ. Whitehead*'. (Quoted in Rollins, 'Commonwealth Drama', p. 315.)

NAVARRO, JOHN.

1635, Dec. 23—'A Warrant for the payment of xˡⁱ vnto Iohn Nauarro for himselfe and the rest of the Company of Spanish Players for A play presented before his Maᵗʸ.' (*M.S.C.* ii. 377.)

NEWTON, JOHN. Throughout his career, so far as is known, Newton was connected with the Duke of York–Prince Charles's company. He first appears in the patent of 1610. By 1615 he was important in the management of the company, for he and William Rowley represented Prince Charles's men before the Privy Council, as Heminges and Burbage represented the King's men.

Newton's role in *The Inner Temple Masque* suggests that he played the lean clown to Rowley's fat clown in the Prince's company, for Doctor Almanac speaks of 'his gauntnes, his thin chitterlings' (A₃), and Plumporridge (Rowley) calls him 'A leane spinie Rascall with a Dogge in's belly' (A₃ᵛ).

It seems to me not unlikely that the parish clerk of St. Giles' Cripplegate made a mistake in the Christian name in the burial entry of 1625 and that John Newton was the player buried. No other record of a William Newton, player, is known, and John disappears at just the time of William's burial.

1616–17—Newton was the fourth to sign the Prince's company's letter to Alleyn explaining their disagreement with Jacob Meade and asking for a loan. (*Hens. Paps.*, p. 93; see above, p. 200, n. 3.)

1618/19, Jan. or Feb.—'*A Fasting-day* I. Newton' in Middleton's *Inner Temple Masque or Masque of Heroes.* (1619 4° B.M.)

1625, >May 5—'Iohn Newton' was sixth in the list of Prince's men who received black cloth for James's funeral procession. (*M.S.C.* ii. 326; see above, p. 209.)

1625, Aug. 3—'William Newton Player' bur. St. G.C.

NEWTON, WILLIAM (*see* NEWTON, JOHN).

1625, Aug. 3—'William Newton Player' bur. St. G.C.

NICK (*see* BURT, NICHOLAS, and UNDERHILL, NICHOLAS).

Both these records of Nick probably indicate an actor's Christian name, but there is no general agreement as to what actor; Nicholas Burt and Nicholas Underhill, both of whom are known to have been actors in the King's company, are the generally suggested candidates. Professor Sisson thinks that the Nick of *Believe as You List* was Nicholas Burt, but this identification is improbable, for Wright says that Burt was still a boy when he left the King's company to act for Beeston, and Nick's roles in *Believe as You List* are all adult parts. Moreover, they are much the same as the part which Nicholas Underhill had in *The Soddered Citizen*.

Professor Baldwin suggests (*Organization and Personnel*, p. 370) that the 'nick' of *Barnavelt* is a misreading of rich, but both Dr. Greg and Miss Frijlinck read 'nick'. I have consulted the manuscript with Professor Baldwin's suggested emendation in mind, but there seems to me no doubt that the reading of Dr. Greg and Miss Frijlinck is correct. The date of *Barnavelt*, 1619, must be too early for Nicholas Burt, for I cannot believe that an actor as well known after the Restoration as he could have acted for twenty-three years before the closing of the theatres without leaving records.

I am inclined to think, therefore, that both Nicks are Nicholas Underhill.

1619, Aug.—The prompter's notes in the MS. of *Sir John van Olden Barnavelt* show that a boy of this name ('nick') played Barnavelt's wife in the King's production of this play. (Greg, *Dram. Doc.*, p. 272.)

1631, May 6 (lic.)—A player called Nick played a Carthaginian officer, an attendant of King Prusias, and an attendant of Marcellus in the King's production of *Believe as You List*. His name is always given 'Nick' in the MS. (Sisson, *B.A.Y.L.*, pp. xxxi ff.)

NICOLINI, FRANCIS. The following entry was copied from Sir Henry Herbert's office book and published by George Chalmers without date:

> 'A warrant was given to Francis Nicolini, an Italian, and his Company, "to dance on the ropes, to use *Interludes*, and *masques*, and to *sell his powders, and balsams*:."' (*Herbert*, p. 47.)

NILL, JOHN. A ghost name from Collier's misreading, followed by Chambers and Nungezer, of the St. Saviour registers. *See* John Hill.

NORE (NOAR, NOARE, NOER), ROGER. The recurrences and various spellings of the name in the St. Giles records leave no doubt that Roger's name was Nore and not More. Though Mrs. Stopes (*Sh. Jahr.*, 1910) and Miss Boswell (*M.S.C.* ii. 394) read the Lord Chamberlain's warrant as More, I cannot agree with them. I have examined the manuscript at the Record Office twice, and it seems to me that the initial letter is quite like other capital N's on the page and quite distinct from the other capital M's. I think they were both misled by the commonness of the name More and the strangeness of Nore. The latter, however, is found in other London parishes; St. Botolph's Bishopsgate, for example.

St. Giles' Cripplegate would have been a convenient residence for a hired man of the Prince's company, for in 1640 and after, the company was acting at the Fortune in that parish.

1640, Apr. 25—'Roger Nore' is third of four 'Princes Players hired men' who were granted a ticket of privilege. (*M.S.C.* ii. 394-5 [but Miss Boswell has transcribed the name 'More'; see above].)

1640, Oct. 18—'Roger sonne of Roger Nore Player' chris. St. G.C. He was buried 7 November 1640.

1642, Oct. 10—'Eliz: dau of Roger Noer player' bur. St. G.C.

1648, Oct. 18—'John: sonne of Roger Noare player' bur. St. G.C.

1648, Oct. 31—'Amellicoe: [Ancellicoe?] Dau: of Roger Noare play' bur. St. G.C.

1648/9, Mar. 19—'Roger Noare player' bur. St. G.C.

1649, Sept. 27—'John: sonne: of: Roger Noar gentleman Deceased' chris. St. G.C.

OGILBY, JOHN. There is no direct evidence of John Ogilby's connexion with the theatre in London before the Civil Wars, but one or two facts lead me to suspect that some sort of connexion with the Phoenix in Drury Lane may one day be discovered.

Aubrey says that John Lacy, the well-known Restoration actor, came to London 'to the . . . playhouse, 1631' and that he was apprenticed to John Ogilby, the dancing master in Gray's Inn Lane (*see* John Lacy). Aubrey seems to say that Lacy was apprenticed to Ogilby and was a boy actor at the same time.

In the second place, Ogilby's dancing seems to have been of the spectacular sort which was popular in the theatres; witness Aubrey's account of Ogilby's injury when cutting high capers in the Duke of Buckingham's masque (Aubrey, *Brief Lives*, ii. 100).

In the third place, Ogilby built the first Irish theatre in Dublin in 1635, managed it himself until it was closed in 1641, and wrote at least one play for his actors (Adams, pp. 417–19). This enterprise suggests that Ogilby had had some sort of experience with theatres before.

Finally, when Ogilby built his theatre he persuaded James Shirley to come over to Ireland to write for it. At this time, Shirley had been for ten years the chief poet for the Phoenix in Drury Lane.

These facts by no means prove Ogilby's connexion with the Phoenix, or any other London theatre, but they do seem to suggest an interesting possibility.

OLEY, HENRY. A ghost name from Collier's misreading of the St. Giles' Cripplegate registers. *See* Henry Clay.

ORTON, THOMAS.

1641/2, Mar. 17—'Mary dau: of Tho: Orton Player' chris. St. G.C.

OTTEWELL, HUGH (*see* ATTWELL, HUGH).

PAGE, JOHN. John Page was one of Queen Henrietta's boys who stayed on with Beeston at the Cockpit to act with Beeston's Boys. He had the role of a rather merry wench in the secondary plot of Shirley's *Wedding*; in *Hannibal and Scipio* he was an adult with an average number of lines, but was on the stage much and had one long speech.

There are twenty-three entries concerning at least four different John Pages in the registers of St. James's Clerkenwell, 1615 to 1670. I have given only the two which seem most likely to concern the actor.

1615, Aug. 6—'John s. of Will'm Page' chris. St. J.C.

1626—'*Iane*, Iustice *Landbys* daughter, *Iohn Page*' in the Queen Henrietta's cast of Shirley's *The Wedding*. (1629 4° HN.)

1635—'Lelius. By Iohn Page' in the cast for Nabbes's *Hannibal and Scipio*, presented by Queen Henrietta's at the Cockpit. (1637 4° B.M.)

1639, Aug. 10—'Iohn Page' was fourth in the list of twelve members of 'yᵉ young Company of [*sic*] at yᵉ Cockpitt Players' named in a ticket of privilege. (*M.S.C.* ii. 390–1.)

1641, Aug. 16—'John s. of Will. Page' bur. St. J.C.

PALLANT, ROBERT sr. Pallant was connected with several dramatic companies, but he does not seem to have been of much importance in any of them. In 1592 he was a Strange's man, in 1602 Worcester's, in 1603–13 ? Queen Anne's, in 1614 Lady Elizabeth's, 1616 Prince Charles's, 1619 Queen Anne's. It is possible that he belonged to Queen Anne's provincial company throughout his Jacobean career and that his connexion with the other companies was recognized as only temporary. He appears in none of the official lists of Queen Anne's after 1616 except the livery allowance for the Queen's funeral.

Pallant was a friend of Thomas Heywood, the dramatist and Queen's player, for he wrote commendatory verses for Heywood's *Apology for Actors.*

Robert Pallant was long a resident of St. Saviour's Southwark. His children were baptized there 1605–14; he appears in the token books in 'Langlies Rents now Soares' 1614–20; and he was buried in this parish in 1619.

1615/16, Jan. 6—'After the will [of Philip Henslowe] was signed Robert Pallant came to see the invalid and asked him "how he did and whether he did know him the said Pallant or not", and to that the said Philip answered, saying, "Thou art Robin Pallant, I know thee well enough." Then after some further conversation Pallant took his leave, whereupon Henslowe grasped his hand and shaking it, "did bid him hartely farewell."' (*Hens. D.* ii. 19–20.)

1615/16, Mar. 20—He was second to sign the debt-funding agreement of the players at the Hope, probably the Prince's company, with Alleyn and Meade. (*Hens. Paps.*, pp. 90–1.)

1616–17—He was first to sign the Prince's company letter to Alleyn asking his help in finding money and a theatre. (Ibid., p. 93; see above, p. 200, n. 3.)

1616, Mar. 30—He was named in a licence for Queen's of 15 Apr. 1609 which was presented at Norwich; all but Swinnerton and Lee were absent. (Murray, ii. 340–1.)

1617, May 31—Lee presented the same licence at Norwich. (Ibid., p. 343.)

1619, >May 13—'Robert Pallant' was fourth in the list of Queen's players allowed black cloth to wear in her funeral procession. (*M.S.C.* ii. 325.)

1619, Sept. 4—'Robert Pallant a man in the church' bur. St. S.S.

PALLANT, ROBERT, jr. The boy of the King's company was probably the son of the Queen's man. His roles in *The Duchess of Malfi* have generally been accepted as indicating his various parts in one performance, but this assumption is absurd, for no individual could have played the four officers, all of whom appear in the same scene, and the actor who played Cariola could have taken none of these roles, for Cariola appears in the same scene with them. Obviously the officers should not be included in the brackets at all. One actor might have played Cariola and the Doctor, but surely the King's company could have spared hired men better fitted for the Doctor's part than the boy who played Cariola. Is it possible that the bracket indicates that Pallant played Cariola in the first performance when he was about nine and the Doctor in the second, when he was about eighteen, the year before he was certified as a hired man of the King's company?

Mr. Baldwin (*Organization and Personnel*, pp. 222, 380) attributes several roles to Pallant, but they are assigned on the assumption that Pallant had the 'line' of the witty waiting-maid from 1623 to 1625. These attributions are most dubious, for the characters in this line are referred to as 'a child', 'little', 'of low stature', 'a little piece of mischief', and Pallant was eighteen to twenty in the years in question.

1605, Sept. 28—'Robert Pallant s. of Robert a player' chris. St. S.S.
c. 1614 and 1619–23—The cast of King's men prefixed to the 1623 4°
of *The Duchess of Malfi* contains the following (1623 4° B.M.):

> The Doctor,
> Cariola,   ⎱ R. Pallant
> Court Officers. ⎰

1624, Dec. 27—'Roberte Pallant' was eleventh in a list of twenty-one men, 'all imployed by the Kinges Maiesties servantes in theire quallity of Playinge as Musitions and other necessary attendantes', who were granted a protection from arrest by Herbert. (*Herbert*, p. 74.)

PARR, WILLIAM. Parr, who is first found as an Admiral's man in 1602, is not known to have been associated with any company except this one and its derivatives, Prince Henry's and the Palsgrave's.

He was evidently a friend of Edward Alleyn, and he may have been the son of William Parr christened in 1581, though the name is a common one.

1581, Nov. 4—'William sonne to Richard Parr' chris. St. Anne's Blackfriars. (Bod.)
1616, July 16—Pembroke sent out an order asking provincial officials to seize the duplicate patents of several named players and to take bonds of them to appear at Whitehall for contempt. Among the players named are 'one Charles Marshall, Homfry Jeffes and Willm Parr: three of Prince Palatynes Company of Playors'. (Murray, ii. 343–4; see above, pp. 178–9.)
1617, Nov. 16—'Mr E. Staughton: pare Steuans & ther wyfes dind wt vs.' (Alleyn's Diary, Young, ii. 57.)
1617/18, Mar. 22—He dined with Alleyn; *see* Gunnell.
1618, May 31—'pare & His wife' dined with Alleyn with others. (Ibid., p. 174.)
1618, Oct. 31—He was ninth of the ten Palsgrave's men to sign the lease of the Fortune from Edward Alleyn. (See above, pp. 138–9.)
1620, Apr. 9—'Ther dind wt vs mr gunnell: Cartwright: parr & price ye King of bohemes men.' (Alleyn's Diary, Young, ii. 174.)

PATRICK, WILLIAM. Patrick was a hired man in the King's company probably as early as 1622. His known roles are all quite minor ones.

1622, June 20—'Margarett Patrick d of Willm a player' chris. St. S.S.
1623, May 21—In Markham's suit as 'William Pattricke on the Banckesyde neare the Bargehouse', 5s. See Appendix, p. 682.

1624, Dec. 27—He is second in the list of twenty-one whom Herbert exempted from arrest as attendants of King's. (*Herbert*, p. 74.)

1626—'*Palphurius Sura*, a Senator. William Pattricke' in King's cast for Massinger's *Roman Actor*, lic. 11 October. (1629 4° B.M.)

1631, May 6 (lic.)—He divided the part of Demetrius ('Wᵐ Pattrick') with Francis Balls and 'Rowland' in the King's production of *Believe as You List*. He also played a Roman Captain ('wᵐ patt:') in the same production. (Sisson, *B.A.Y.L.*, pp. xxxi ff.)

1636, May 17—He was fourth in a list of eighteen minor King's men named in a players' pass. (*M.S.C.* ii. 378–9.)

1636/7, Jan. 12—His name was fourth in a list of eleven men 'imployed by his Maᵗᵉˢ servantes the Players of the Blackfryers' granted a ticket of privilege. (Ibid., p. 380.)

1638—He was perhaps the 'William Patricke' whose moderated rental was estimated at £7. 10. 0 in the parish of St. Helen's within Bishopsgate. (*London, 1638*, p. 69.)

PEADLE (PEDLE), ABRAHAM. The Peadle family, rope dancers, are first heard of in Germany in 1614 and 1615, but their troupe is found most frequently in the provinces in England. The fact that Peadle is called an actor at the Fortune probably does not indicate that he was a Palsgrave's man, as has sometimes been said; it is more likely that his troupe of rope dancers was the one which occasionally performed at the Fortune and for which Gunnell, the Fortune manager, twice paid fees to Herbert in March 1624/5 (*see* Gunnell).

Jacob Peadle's petition probably refers to the rope dancer, for Jacob and Abraham Peadle were performing together in Germany in 1614 and 1615.

1616, June 17—He was at Norwich with William Peadle, sr., and William Peadle, jr., and a company of rope dancers; they had a licence dated 14 May 1616. (Murray, ii. 342.)

1620, June 14—The same company was again at Norwich. (Ibid., p. 346.)

1623, May 21—In Markham's suit as 'Abraham Pedle at George Alley in Gouldinge lane'. (See Appendix, pp. 682–3.)

1623/4, Jan. 29—Markham's suit calls Clayton, Grace, Stratford, and Peadle actors at the Fortune. (Ibid.)

1631 [Feb. 8?]—'Petition of Jacob Peadle, administrator of his brother, Abraham Peadle, to the Committee of the Council of War for poor Soldiers. Abraham Peadle was drum-major to General Morgan's company for 13½ months at seven rix dollars per month. There is due the sum mentioned in the annexed account. Prays order for receipt. (Annexed, Account above mentioned, which shows 14l. 10s. to be due.)' (*C.S.P., Dom.*, 1629–31, p. 501.)

PEADLE, JACOB. Probably the Jacob Peadle who was administering the estate of his brother Abraham Peadle (q.v.) in 1631 was the same as the Jacob Pedel or Behel who was with the English actors in Germany in 1597 and 1614–15 (Cohn, *Sh. in Ger.*, p. lxxxviii; Herz, *Englische Schauspieler*, pp. 34 ff.; Meissner, *Englischen Comoedianten*, p. 41).

PEADLE, Thomas. Probably Thomas Peadle had been appearing with his father's troupe for some time before his name got into the Coventry records.

1639, Dec. 24—'Willm peadle & Thomas Peadle his sonn & fower children & Charles Sale', who had a 'comission for dauncing & vaulting & other feats of activity', were paid at Coventry. (Murray, ii. 253–4.)

PEADLE (PEDEL), WILLIAM, sr. William Peadle, like Abraham, was a dancer and acrobat. In 1608 he was much admired in Holland as a pantomimist; in 1614 and 1615 he was in Germany. It is impossible to distinguish William senior and William junior with certainty; I should guess that William junior was the man at Coventry in 1639, and the man at St. Giles' Cripplegate. Probably his father was the man whom Collier found mentioned as tumbler and gentleman in the St. Saviour's parish registers in 1610, 1617, and 1629 (Bod.). I ignored the tumblers and rope dancers at St. Saviour's.

1616, June 17—William Peadle, sr., and William Peadle, jr., were at Norwich with Abraham Peadle and a company of rope dancers; they had a licence dated 14 May 1616. (Murray, ii. 342.)

1617, Aug. 8—'Cornelius sonne of William Peadle gentle' chris. St. G.C.

1618, May 9—John Castleton was convicted of stealing a brown gelding belonging to William Peadle of St. Giles in the Fields. (*Middx. Co. Rec.*, ii. 136.)

1619, Dec. 14—'Anne daughter of William Peadle gentleman' chris. St. G.C.; buried 15 December 1619.

1620, June 14—He was at Norwich with William Peadle, jr., and Abraham Peadle and a licensed company of rope dancers. (Murray, ii. 346.)

1620, Nov. 29—'William Peadle & other players, Dauncers vpon Ropes', were paid at Coventry. (Murray, ii. 248.)

1620/1, Jan. 31—'Anne daughter of William Peadle, gentleman' chris. St. G.C.

1639, Dec. 24—'Willm peadle & Thomas Peadle his sonn & fower children & Charles Sale', who had a 'comission for dauncing & vaulting & other feats of activity', were paid at Coventry. (Murray, ii. 253.)

PEADLE (PEDLE), WILLIAM, jr. Probably William, jr., was the son of William, sr. They cannot be clearly distinguished.

1616, June 17—He was at Norwich with William Peadle, sr., and Abraham Peadle and a licensed company of rope dancers. (Murray, ii. 342.)

1617, Aug. 8—'Cornelius sonne of William Peadle gentle' chris. St. G.C.

1619, Dec. 14—'Anne daughter of William Peadle gentleman' chris. St. G.C.; buried 15 December 1619.

1620, June 14—At Norwich with William Peadle, sr., and Abraham Peadle and a licensed company of rope dancers. (Murray, ii. 346.)

1620/1, Jan. 31—'Anne daughter of William Peadle, gentleman' chris. St. G.C.

1639, Dec. 24—'Willm peadle & Thomas Peadle his sonn & fower children & Charles Sale', who had a 'comission for dauncing & vaulting & other feats of activity', were at Coventry. (Murray, ii. 253.)

1654—He is probably the Peadle whose dancing at the Red Bull is praised in *Mercurius Fumigosus*. (See Rollins, 'Commonwealth Drama', p. 315.)

PEET, NATHAN.

1644, Nov.–1644/5, Feb.—'Nathan Peet and his son' were in the English company residing at the Hague. (*See* Jeremiah Kite.)

PENN (PEN, PENNE), WILLIAM.

Penn began his stage career as a boy at least as early as 1609, for in that year he appeared in the Queen's Revels' production of *Epicoene*. By 1616 he was a Prince's man, and he retained his membership in this company until 1625. It was probably in this year, when the King's company was being overhauled at the beginning of the new reign, that Penn went to that company with his fellows Thomas Hobbes and Anthony Smith. (See Baldwin, *Organization and Personnel*, p. 55.)

The cloak allowance of 1629 indicates that Penn had become a sharer in the company by that date. We have no indication that he was ever a very important member; his roles are usually small; he several times played the part of a dignified old man. He fails to appear in a number of the casts of plays produced during his years with the company.

It is fortunate that William Penn is so well identified in the parish registers, for the name is very common. His occupation and the name of his wife identify him at St. Bodolph's; his wife's name identifies him at St. James's; and his occupation identifies him again at St. Giles.

1615/16, Mar. 20—He was tenth to sign the debt-funding agreement of the players at the Hope, probably Prince's, with Alleyn and Meade. (*Hens. Paps.*, pp. 90–1.)

1616, June 30—'William Penne of S⁺ Leonarde parish in Shordich and Sibilla West of our parish' mar. St. Bodolph's Aldgate. (Denkinger, p. 104.)

1617, Nov. 21—'Marie Penne, daughter to William Penne, a Stage-player and Sibbill his wife of Houndsditch' chris. St. Bodolph's Aldgate. (Ibid.)

1619, Mar. 31—'William Penne, sonne to William Penne, a Stage-player, and Sibill his wife' chris. St. Bodolph's Aldgate. (Ibid.)

1623, May 21—He lived 'at the George Alley in Gouldinge lane', according to Markham's suit. (See Appendix, p. 682.)

1625, >May 5—'William Penn' was fifth in the list of Prince's men who received black cloth for King James's funeral. (*M.S.C.* ii. 326; see above, p. 209.)

1625, Aug. 18—'William s. of William Penn' bur. St. J.C.

1625, Nov. 30—'Robert s. of William Penn & Sibbell vx' chris. St. J.C.

1628—'William Penn' was ninth in the King's company's cast for *The Lover's Melancholy*, lic. 24 November (roles not given). (1629 4° B.M.)

1629, May 6—'Wᵐ Pen' was twelfth in the list of King's men granted liveries. (*M.S.C.* ii. 350; see above, p. 24.)

1629—'*Iulio Baptista* a great scholler. *William Pen.*' in the King's cast for Massinger's *The Picture*, lic. 8 June. (1630 4° B.M.)

1631, May 6 (lic.)—According to the stage directions, he played the Second Merchant and the Jailer ('wᵐ Pen:' 'wᵐ penn') in the King's production of *Believe as You List*. (Sisson, *B.A.Y.L.*, pp. xxxi ff.)

1631—In the MS. of Arthur Wilson's *The Swisser* (B.M. Add. MS. 36759), his name is given in the cast for the Blackfriars' production (Feuillerat, *The Swisser*):

> Antharis ⎫ Two old noble men .   .   . Benfeild.
> Clephis ⎭ Mortall Enemies .   .   .   . Penn.

1632—'NANTOLET, Father to *Rosalura* and *Lillia-Bianca* . . . Acted by Mr. *William Penn*' in the King's cast for the 1632 King's revival of *The Wild Goose Chase*, printed 1652. (1652 ed. B.M.)

1635/6, Jan. 6—'John, sonne of William Penn, Player' chris. St. G.C.

1636, May 17—'Wᵐ Pen' is the first of the King's men listed for a players' pass. (*M.S.C.* ii. 378–9.)

1636, Oct. 18—'Wm: son: of Wm: Penn Playerʳ' bur. St. G.C.

1636, Nov. 2—'Anne daugʳ: of William Pen Playerʳ' bur. St. G.C.

PENNYCUICKE (PENNEYCUICK, PENNICOOKE, PENNYCOOKE), ANDREW. We have only Pennycuicke's statement as proof that he ever was an actor, and Pennycuicke's deceptions in the dedications of the books he published do not encourage one to believe him implicitly. (See Rudolph Kirk, *The City Madam*, pp. 9–15.) Still, it is a little difficult to imagine why anyone would want to make false pretentions to the actor's profession at a time when it was no more esteemed than it was in the years 1655–8.

Of the plays which Pennycuicke brought out, three had originally been produced by Queen Henrietta's men and one by the King's men in 1632. Mr. Baldwin (*Organization and Personnel*, pp. 195–6) interprets these facts to mean that Pennycuicke had become an apprentice (perhaps to Shank) in the King's company by 1632, and that he later transferred to the Cockpit, probably on Shank's death, and acted with Beeston's Boys. To me, it seems that such a history of Pennycuicke takes far too much for granted. It is not likely that an actor performed for ten years at the Blackfriars and the Cockpit—especially if one of his roles was as important as Matilda—without leaving any records. The title-page of *The City Madam* does not necessarily mean that Pennycuicke acted for the King's company, or even, certainly, that he acted in that particular play. Neither of his statements about his histrionic experience is sufficiently specific to attach him very surely to a company. His publication of three Queen's plays does suggest a connexion with Queen Henrietta's or Beeston's Boys, or at least a close friendship with some former member of those companies. The record of his birth in 1620—it seems unlikely that there could have been two men with such a name—shows that he would have been too old for Matilda after the closing of the theatres and suggests that he performed the part as one of Beeston's Boys, or even as a Queen Henrietta's apprentice.

Pennycuicke's residence in 1647 and 1652 in St. Giles in the Fields is a slight confirmation of the notion that he was performing with Beeston's Boys when they were acting in the theatre in that parish at the time that Parliament stopped all acting.

1620, Oct. 1—'Andreas Pennicooke fs. Jacobi et Margarete' chris. St. M.F.

1647, Oct. 19—'Andrew Penneycuick and Dorothy kinde' mar. St. G.F.

1652, Dec. 4—'A stilborne Childe of Andrew Pennicooke' bur. St. G.F.

1653—Heminges's *Fatal Contract*, 'Acted with great Applause by her *Majesties* Servants' has a dedication to James Compton, Earl of Northampton, which is signed 'A. T.' and 'A. P.' Perhaps the initials stand for Andrew Pennycuicke (for whom the play was printed) and Anthony Turner; certainly Turner and possibly Pennycuicke had acted with the company which performed the play. (1653 4° HN.)

1655—In the dedication to his edition of Davenport's *King John and Matilda*, printed in this year, Pennycuicke says, 'my selfe being the last that that [*sic*] Acted Matilda in it'. His name is not given in the cast, and it is not likely that he meant that he had played in the production for which the cast is given, i.e. >1634. (1655 4° B.M.)

1656—The dedication of Ford and Dekker's *The Sun's Darling* to Thomas Wriothesley, Earl of Southampton, is signed, 'Theophilus Bird. Andrew Penneycuicke'. (1657 4° B.M.)

1658—The title-page of *The City Madam*, lic. 25 May 1632 and acted at Blackfriars, says that the play was printed for Andrew Pennycuicke, 'one of the Actors'. The second edition of 1659 contains a dedication to Lady Ann, Countess of Oxford, which is signed by him. (1658 and 1659 4°'s B.M.)

PERKINS (PARKINS, PERCKENS, PIRKYNS, PYRKYNS), RICHARD. Perkins was probably the best known actor in Queen Henrietta's company, and, so far as we can tell now, the actor of longest experience. (Beeston seems not to have acted in the company's plays.) In 1602 he was receiving money from Henslowe to make purchases for Worcester's men for a performance of Heywood's play. He appears regularly as a Worcester's–Queen Anne's man until the disintegration of that company, and his friendship for Heywood lasted even longer, for he wrote verses for Heywood's *Apology* in 1609, and Heywood went out of his way to call attention to Perkins's acting in 1633. The actor made an impression on John Webster, too, for Webster singled him out for praise in a note appended to the 1612 quarto of *The White Devil*.

The suits marking the break-up of Queen Anne's company in the two or three years following the death of Shakespeare all point to Perkins as one of the three or four chief members of the company. With the other leaders of the old organization, he was concerned in the formation of the Revels company, but in 1623 or 1624 he became a King's man, as we know from his livery allowance. This addition of Perkins to the King's company in 1623 or 1624 and his desertion of the leading company of the day for the new Queen Henrietta's group two or three years later are puzzling. Mr. Baldwin (*Organization and Personnel*, p. 118) thinks that Perkins was not a member of King's at all, but a special type of hired man entitled to livery. This solution is not very convincing, but it is odd that Perkins should have deserted a company like the King's men. His old fellow, Christopher Beeston, must have been very persuasive.

As a member of Queen Henrietta's men, Perkins is found in all known lists of the company except the *Renegado* cast and Crosfield's odd list, and he replaces Christopher Beeston as recipient of the company's livery allowances after the reorganization at Salisbury Court. There is reason to think that Perkins and a few of his fellows were rather shabbily treated by Beeston during the plague of 1636–7, and that the reorganized Queen's men at Salisbury Court had little of the prestige of the old company at the Cockpit (see pp. 237–45).

Perkins's known roles, as well as the testimony of Webster and Heywood and Pennycuicke, establish his importance as an actor in rather a variety of parts: romantic villain, dignified father, honest, plain-spoken old man.

We have Wright's evidence that Perkins lived in Clerkenwell, at least towards the end of his life. Probably he had lived there in his early years as well, for it would have been a more convenient residence in the fifteen years he performed at the Red Bull than later when he was acting at the Phoenix and Salisbury Court, and Markham's messenger found him in Clerkenwell in 1623. Wright's statement about his death pretty well identifies the actor and the man buried in 1650, and the testimony of Perkins's wife in 1620 identifies the actor and the husband of the woman buried at St. James's Clerkenwell in 1621. The Richard Perkins buried in 1625 may have been the actor's son. Unfortunately the name is too common to make other identifications, though one is tempted to guess that the Richard son of John Perkins christened at St. James's Clerkenwell in October 1585 was the actor, and that he is also to be seen in at least a few of the records of Richard Perkins at St. Giles in the Fields. (See Bentley, *R.E.S.*, p. 162.)

There is a portrait of him, No. 423, in the gallery at Dulwich College.

1616, Mar. 30—He was named in a Queen Anne's licence of 15 April 1609 which was presented at Norwich on this date; all but Swinnerton and Lee were absent. (Murray, ii. 340–1.)

1617, May 31—The same patent was shown again at Norwich. (Ibid., p. 343.)

1617, June 3—He refused to sign the new agreement of Queen Anne's with Susan Baskervile, though the Baskerviles say that he was a fellow and sharer at the time. (Fleay, *Stage*, pp. 285–8.)

1617, Oct. 2—He petitioned the Sessions of the Peace for the Red Bull company (Queen Anne's). (See above, p. 163.)

1619, >May 13—'Richard Parkins' was second in the list of Queen Anne's men allowed black cloth to wear in her funeral procession. (*M.S.C.* ii. 325.)

1619—When John Smith sued Beeston, Perkins, Worth, and Cumber as the most substantial members of the old Queen Anne's company, the latter three declared that Beeston had kept the company accounts fraudulently for the last seven or eight years. (Wallace, *Three Theatres*, pp. 321–5.)

1620, June 27—'Elizabeth Perkins (wief of Richard Perkins of the parish of Clarkinwell gent)' testified to the whereabouts of Emanuel Read in *John Smith* v. *Christopher Beeston*. (Ibid., pp. 335–6.)

1621, Mar. 31—'Elizabeth wife of Richard Perkins' bur. St. J.C.

1621, Nov. 5—'Richard Perkins & Philadelphia Kelly of this p' mar. All Hallows, Lombard Street. (Challen, *Marriages*.)

1622, July 8—He was the second of six 'late Commedians to Queene Anne deceased' named in a warrant for the licensing of the Children of the Revels. (Murray, ii. 193–4.)

1622, Oct. 3—He was one of six Red Bull actors named in an order for repairing the highways. (See above, p. 169, n. 2.)

1622, Nov.—'A Warr^t: vnder the Signet to licence Robert Lee Richard Perkins and others Comedians to the late Queene Anne to exercise the quality & Arte of Stage players as they haue bin heretofore accoustomed.' (*M.S.C.* i. 284.)

1622—'Richard Perkings' was second in Herbert's office book list of 'the chiefe players at the Red Bull, called the players of the Revells'. (*Herbert*, p. 63.)

1623, May 21—He lived 'att the vpper end of St Iohns Streete', according to Markham's suit. (See Appendix, p. 682.)

1623/4—'a liuerie for a Player,/ By warrant/

To George Johnson draper for 3 yardes of
Bastard Scarlett for a livery for Richard Perkins } 004:00:00
one of his Mat^s Players at 26^s 8^d p yard.

To Richard Miller for $\frac{1}{4}$ of a yard of Crimson } 000:26:00'
Veluett for a cape at 26^s 8^d

(*M.S.C.* ii. 328.) Perkins evidently came to the company after the general warrant had been issued at Easter, 1623.

1625, >May 5—As a member of the King's company, 'Richard Perkins' was third in the list to receive black cloth for James's funeral procession. (Ibid., p. 325.)

1625, Sept. 10—'Richard Perkins' bur. St. J.C.

1626—'Sir *Iohn Belfare, Richard Perkins*', in the cast of Queen Henrietta's men prefixed to Shirley's *The Wedding*. (1629 4° HN.)

c. 1630—'*Captain* Goodlack, Spencers *friend*; *by* M^r. Rich. Perkins', in the cast for Part I of Heywood's *The Fair Maid of the West*. Since no actor is named for this character in the cast for Part II, he probably had the role there as well. (1631 4° B.M.)

1633—The prologue and epilogue which Heywood wrote for the Queen's revival of Marlowe's *Jew of Malta* and which were published in the 1633 quarto point out that Perkins played the Jew, though he did not hope to equal Alleyn in the part. The prologue says:

.... *nor is't hate*
* Perkins.   *To merit*: *in* him who doth personate*
                Our Jew *this day, nor is it his ambition*
                To exceed, or equall, being of condition
                More modest; ...

and the epilogue:

                In Graving, with Pigmalion *to contend*;
                Or Painting with Apelles; *doubtlesse the end*
                Must be disgrace: *our Actor did not so,*
                He onely aym'd to goe, but not out-goe.

>1634—'*Fitzwater*, M. [Mr.] *Perkins*, Whose action gave Grace to the Play', in the Queen's cast for Davenport's *King John and Matilda*. (1655 4° B.M.)

1634, Sept. 11—He was left a ring in the will of Thomas Basse. (See Appendix, p. 631.)

1635—'Hanno. By Richard Perkins' in the cast for Nabbes's *Hannibal and Scipio*, presented by Queen Henrietta's at the Cockpit. (1637 4° B.M.)

c. 1635—In 1635 Theophilus Bird said that he had joined the King's men about 1635 (but he must have meant about 1640, for he was still an important player at the Cockpit in 1637) and signed a bond of £400 to Richard Perkins in trust for Michael Bowyer. Apparently Perkins was acting just as a friend of Bowyer's. (See Hotson, pp. 31–4.)

1637, c. Oct. 2—'I disposed of Perkins, Sumner, Sherlock and Turner, to Salisbury Court, and joynd them with the best of that company.' (*Herbert*, p. 66.)

1638, Dec. 20—'A warr^t for Liueryes for the Queenes Players ... to bee đđ to Richard Perkins for him self & 13 others his fellowes.' (*M.S.C.* ii. 388.)

1640/1, Jan. 8—Liveries were ordered to be delivered 'vnto Richard Perkins & Anthony Turner for them selues & twelue others their fellowes in all fowerteene & of the Queenes Ma^tes Company of Players'. (Ibid., p. 396.)

1645, Sept. 26—Legacy in Michael Bowyer's will. (Appendix, p. 635.)

1650, Apr. 20—'Richard Perkins' bur. St. J.C.

>1660—Trueman says that 'Perkins' was one of 'those of principal Note at the *Cockpit* [Queen Henrietta's company]', and that after the closing of the theatres '*Perkins* and *Sumner* of the *Cockpit*, kept House together at *Clerkenwel*, and were there Buried ... some Years before the Restauration'. (*Hist. Hist.*, pp. 4 and 10.)

PERRY (PERRIE, PIERRY, TERRY), WILLIAM. William Perry is probably the most conspicuous of the provincial players. He is first heard of as a boy in a 1613 licence for Lady Elizabeth's company which was shown at Norwich in 1615 (*R.E.S.* i. 183), but by 1617 he was leading a provincial company, and as a company leader he is known for twenty-five years.

The company with which he appeared at Norwich in 1617 was probably some sort of amalgamation of a provincial Queen Anne's company, a Queen's Revels troupe, and a King's Revels company, as the names of the leaders would suggest. Perry seems to have toured as the leader of this group, later called the Children of the Revels to the late Queen Anne, for six or seven years.

William Perry is the most frequently named of the obscure Red Bull–King's troupe which played in the provinces and usually at the Red Bull in London through most of the reign of Charles I (see pp. 270–80). He regularly led the company in the provinces, and presumably he appeared with them in London, but of this there is no record. The title 'His Majesty's servants for the city of York' implies that Perry's troupe had some special association with that city, but evidence is lacking.

There is no assurance that he was the poor man buried at St. James's in 1648, though poverty might well be the lot of a provincial player after the prohibition of acting.

1616, July 16—A letter of this date which was copied in the Norwich records 4 June 1617 ordered four different exemplifications returned to London, their bearers to give bond for their appearance in Whitehall on a fixed day; among others the letter names 'William Perrie haueinge gotten a warrant whereby he and a certaine Company of idle psons wth him doe travel and play under the name and title of the Children of his Ma^{ts} Revels, to the great abuse of his Ma^{ts} srvice'. (Murray, ii. 343–4; see above, pp. 178–9, for the letter in full.)

1617, Oct. 31—The names of Robert Lee, Philip Rossiter, William Perry, and Nicholas Long were copied from a commission of this date at Norwich 29 August 1618. (Ibid., p. 345.)

1619—'Given to Terry and his Companye of Playors, haveinge Large Aucthoritie' at Leicester. (Ibid., p. 313.)

1623, May 24—'William Perry & other of ye late Queene Ann her Company of players' were paid 40s. for not playing at Norwich. (Ibid., pp. 347, 371.)

1624, Apr.—He was named in a confirmation of a licence to the Children of the Revels to the late Queen Anne which was shown at Exeter and at Norwich in May, 1624. (*Hist. MSS. Com.*, Records of the City of Exeter, p. 171; Murray, ii. 272–3 and 347.)

1628, Sept. 7—'William s. of William Perrye & Jone vx' chris. St. J.C.

1629, Sept. 5—'A Warraunt to sweare William Perry A Groome of ye Chamber in ordinary wthout ffee.' (*M.S.C.* ii. 351.)

1629, Sept. 18—'Commission to Wm. Perrey for making up and

keeping a company of players, to present all usual stage plays, by the name of His Majesty's servants for the city of York.' (*C.S.P., Dom.*, 1629–31, p. 59.)

1629, Nov. 10—Eight men were named in a licence of this date which was granted to William Perry and Richard Weeks, 'his Majestie's sworn servantes . . . of the Red Bull company', and shown at Reading 30 November 1629. (Murray, ii. 386.)

1630, Nov. 2—Perry, Weeks, and their company were at Reading. (Ibid., p. 386.)

1632, July 15—'Mr Perry & his company of players' were at Doncaster. (Ibid., p. 257.)

1632, Nov. 28—'A petition of Richard Mapes against William Perry, a player Answered of course.' The petition was repeated 5 December, 'wth leaue graunted after one weeke expired after sight'. (*M.S.C.* ii. 408.)

1632–3—'Mr Perry one of the Kings players that came with a comission' was at Coventry. (Murray, ii. 252.)

1632/3, Feb. 19—'Mr Perry, a Player, and his Companie' were paid at Leicester. (Ibid., p. 318.)

1632/3, Feb. 27—'A warrt to ye signet to draw vp a Bill for the Kinges hand for A lycence vnto William Perry and his Associates to practize the quality of stage playes in ye Citty of Yorke & else where wthin his Maties dominions.' (*M.S.C.* ii. 360.)

1633, July 3—Perry appeared at Norwich with a licence of 30 Apr. 1633. On 6 July 1633 he was paid a gratuity of £3 for forbearing to play in the city. (Murray, ii. 354, 372.)

1633/4, Mar. 1—At Norwich 'Willm Perry brought into this Court his Maties warrant.' The records for 15, 19, and 22 Mar. show that the company continued to play 'beyond the tyme agreed vpon', insisting that their patent allowed them to play forty days. The Norwich fathers finally decided to petition for the prohibition of all stage plays in the town, 'by reason that the maintenance of the Inhabitants here doth consist of worke & makinge of manufactures'. (Ibid., pp. 354–5; see above, p. 274.)

1633/4, Mar. 13—'A peticōn of Alexander Charley against Wm Perry a player debt 40li Answered wth leaue graunted vpon sight. March 13. 1633.' (L.C. Warrant Books, 5/183, p. 142, P.R.O.)

1634–5—The Bristol authorities paid 'one Perry a plaier' for not playing. (Murray, ii. 219.)

1635, >Nov. 22—'Item geven to Mr Perrie, a Player, and his Companie to passe by the Towne and not play', £1, at Leicester. (Ibid., p. 318.)

1635/6, Mar.—Perry with his company played at Canterbury during Lent. The Mayor wrote to the Archbishop complaining of the consequent disorders; in his letter of 5 Apr. thanking the Archbishop for forbidding players in Canterbury during Lent, he said, 'the players complained of are of the company of the Fortune playhouse, and the principal of them were Weekes and Perry. The latter was the man that most affronted the writer, saying that he would play whether the mayor would or not, and when on complaints of citizens who could not restrain their servants from being at the plays till near midnight, the writer desired Perry to keep better hours or he would acquaint the Lords with their disorder,

Perry replied he cared not.' (Murray, i. 274–6; *C.S.P., Dom.*, 1635–6, pp. 321, 334–5, and 354–5.)

1636, Apr. 24—'Mr Perrie, one of the King's players' was paid 20s. at Doncaster. (Murray, ii. 257.)

1636, May 11—'This day Richard Wicks & other servants to his Matie beinge his Maties players granted to Wm Perry & others did bringe in a warrant dated' 30 Apr. 1633, at Norwich. (Ibid., p. 358.)

1642—'given to Mr Pierry & his company who came by comission to play x^s', at Coventry. (Ibid., p. 254.)

1648, June 29—'Wm Perry, a poor man' bur. St. J.C.

PETERS, HUGH. In spite of the charges of his enemies, there is little likelihood that Hugh Peters was ever an actor, but the assertion is so frequently made that it ought to be mentioned. A writer in *Mercurius Pragmaticus* said in 1647 that '*Sam Rowley* and he were a *Pylades*, and *Orestes*, when he played a womans part at the Curtaine Play-house, which is the reason his garbe is so emphaticall in the Pulpit' (quoted from Hotson, p. 15). The *Man in the Moon* says that Peters was '*Book-holder* at the Bull-play-house' (ibid.), and Dr. Young said that Hugh Peters had been jester or fool in Shakespeare's company (ibid., p. 73, n. 56). Even Genest says that he has heard that Peters was a player for a time after he left Cambridge. (Genest, i. 16.)

Most of these tales indicate nothing more than the spite of the Royalists, which prompted them to make whatever charges they thought would be most damaging to the reverend Hugh. It is possible, however, that some confused account may have its origin in the fact that Peters's English church in Rotterdam was a building which had originally been intended for a playhouse. (See *Chetham Society Publications*, i. 6.)

PETTINGHAM, HENRY.

1636/7, Jan. 12—Pettingham's name was fifth in a list of eleven 'persons Dependantes on the Players' who were granted tickets of privilege; the list was headed by Baxter, '[who] is imployed by his Ma^tes servantes the Players of the Blackfryers'. (*M.S.C.* ii. 380.)

PETTINGTON, HENRY. A ghost name from Mrs. Stopes's misreading, followed by Mr. Baldwin and Mr. Nungezer, of Henry Pettingham.

PICKLEHERRING (*see* REYNOLDS, ROBERT).

PLUMFIELD, THOMAS.

1632, May 10–15—'Thomas Plumfield' was seventh in a list of eleven men sworn 'groomes of the Chamber in ordinary w^thout ffee to attend the Prince his Highnes in ye quality of players'. (*M.S.C.* ii. 358.)

1632, Dec. 5—'A petition of Thomas Greene against Thomas Plumfield a player debt 5^li Answered wth leaue graunted w^thin a weeke after sight.' (L.C. Warrant Books, 5/183, p. 129, P.R.O.)

POLLARD, THOMAS. Thomas Pollard was a comedian with the King's company for a quarter of a century and was, in his later years at any rate, a very well-known figure. There is some contradiction about the beginning of his career. In the Sharers' Papers of 1635, John Shank said that he had 'still of his owne purse supplyed the company for the service of his Ma^{ty} wth boyes as Thomas Pollard, Iohn Thompson. . . .' But in these same papers the Burbages say, 'these new men [i.e. Swanston, Benfield, and Pollard] that were neuer bred from Children in the kings service.' (*M.S.C.* ii. 369, 371.) The contradiction could be reconciled if we supposed that Pollard had been Shank's apprentice in the Palsgrave's company at the Fortune and had come with his master to the King's company shortly before or after finishing his apprenticeship. If this were true, the Burbages would be right in saying that Pollard had not been bred up in the King's service, and Shank would be right, with a quibble, in saying that he had cared for Pollard as a boy out of his own purse and supplied him to the company. Moreover, it is not incompatible with what we know of Pollard's age to suppose that he was somewhere around twenty when Shank came to the company within a year or two of 1615. I suggest, therefore, that Pollard may have begun his career as Shank's apprentice in the Palsgrave's company; unfortunately this suggestion can be no more than a conjecture at present.

By 1623, and probably earlier, Pollard had been cast in the comic roles in which he was to make a reputation. Eight or nine of his parts are known, quite enough to show the sort of character the audience could expect him to portray—Pinac in *The Wild Goose Chase*, Brainsick in *The Soddered Citizen*, the Lieutenant in *The Humorous Lieutenant*, Timentes in *The Swisser*.

Mr. Baldwin thinks (*Organization and Personnel*, pp. 57–8) that Pollard succeeded to membership in the company about the spring of 1623, and this conjecture seems probable. Certainly he was a member by 1624 when he signed the submission of the company to Sir Henry Herbert in *The Spanish Viceroy* matter.

With Benfield and Swanston, Pollard petitioned the Lord Chamberlain in 1635 to force the housekeepers of the Blackfriars and the Globe to sell them shares in order that they might participate more fully in the earnings of the company. Probably they got their shares, for the Lord Chamberlain ordered the housekeepers to satisfy them, but Shank's will indicates that at the end of 1635 the matter was not yet fully settled.

The will of Richard Benfield in 1639 suggests that Pollard was a companion of Swanston off the stage as well as on, and perhaps something of a boon companion. The assertion of Bird in 1655 that Pollard and Bowyer had seized the assets of the company when the theatre closed can mean little to us without further details. Bird makes it sound as if Pollard and Bowyer were embezzlers, but he must have been distorting the facts, for Pollard was still associated with his old fellows in the company bond of January 1647/8 and in the dedication of the Beaumont and Fletcher folio in 1647.

Wright's statement that Pollard lived single obviously applies to his life after the wars began and does not necessarily indicate that he was not the Thomas Pollard who married in 1629 and 1635. On the other hand, there is nothing to support the identification, and the name was a fairly common one; there were at least two Thomas Pollards, neither of whom can have been the player, in the parish of St. Botolph's Bishopsgate, 1605–25. Bird's statement that Pollard died worth £500 and that his estate was administered by Perryn of Buckingham tends to corroborate Wright's report.

1616–17—No. 4 in King's cast for *The Queen of Corinth*. (1679 folio B.M.)

1619, Aug.—The prompter's notes show that he played Holderus and a servant ('T. p.' 'Tho. po.') in the King's production of *Sir John van Olden Barnavelt*. (Greg, *Dram. Doc.*, p. 273.)

1619?—No. 8 in King's cast for *The Humorous Lieutenant*. (1679 folio B.M.)

1619?—No. 8 in King's cast for *The Laws of Candy*. (Ibid.)

1619–23—'Siluio, T. Pollard,' in the cast of King's men prefixed to 1623 quarto of *The Duchess of Malfi*. Apparently he had the part in the revival of 1619–23. (1623 4° B.M.)

1619–21—No. 8 in King's cast for *The Island Princess*. (Ibid.)

1622, Aug. 23—'Grant to Thos. Pollard and Joan Woodruff of pardon for incest.' (*C.S.P., Dom.*, 1619–23, p. 442.)

1622, Oct. 24—No. 5 in King's cast for *The Spanish Curate*. (1679 folio B.M.)

1623, Aug. 29—No. 7 in King's cast for *The Maid in the Mill*. (Ibid.)

1623, Dec. 6—No. 3 in King's cast for *The Lover's Progress*. (Ibid.)

1624, Dec. 20—No. 4 in submission of King's for playing *The Spanish Viceroy*. (Herbert, p. 21; see above, pp. 14–15.)

1625, >May 5—'Tho: Pollarde' was fourteenth in the list of King's men who received black cloth for James's funeral procession. (*M.S.C.* ii. 326.)

1625, June 24—No. 13 in a patent for King's. (Ibid. i. 282–3.)

1626, Oct. 11—'*Aelius, Lamia*, and *Stephanos* . . . Thomas Pollard', in King's cast for Massinger's *The Roman Actor*, lic. this date. (1629 4° B.M.)

1628, Nov. 24—No. 8 in King's cast for *The Lover's Melancholy*, lic. this date. (1629 4° B.M.)

1629, May 6—No. 9 in cloak allowance for King's. (*M.S.C.* ii. 350.)

1629, July 1—'Thomas Pollard & ffrancis Gord L. vg.', mar. St. Gregory by St. Paul. (Challen, *Marriages*.)

1629, June 8—'*Vbaldo*', one of '2. wild courtiers. *Thomas Pollard*', in King's cast for Massinger's *The Picture*, lic. this date. (1630 4° B.M.)

c. 1630—'*Brainsicke—A deboyst young gent & a Prisoner*—Tho: Pollard', also '*Birdlyme—A Scrivener—Brain: disguis'd*', in King's cast given in the MS. of Clavell's (?) *Soddered Citizen*. (*Sod. Cit.*, p. 3.)

1631, May 6 (lic.)—The prompter's notes for the King's play, *Believe as You List*, show that 'M^r pollard:' played Berecinthius. (Sisson, *B.A.Y.L.*, pp. xxxi ff.)

1631—The MS. of Arthur Wilson's *The Swisser* (B.M. Add. MS. 36759) gives his name in the cast for the Blackfriars production: 'Timentes, A fearefull Generall... Pollard.' (Feuillerat, *The Swisser*.)

1632—'PINAC ... of a lively spirit ... Admirably well Acted by Mr. *Thomas Pollard*', in the cast for the King's 1632 revival of *The Wild Goose Chase* printed in the 1652 edition. (1652 ed. B.M.)

1635, May 18—Both the Burbages and John Shank assert in their petition to the Lord Chamberlain in 1635 that for the year Whitsun Monday 1634 to Whitsun Monday 1635 Pollard gained from the King's company 'as hee was a Player and noe Howskeeper 180^li' (*M.S.C.* ii. 368, 372.)

1635, May 18—July 12—Benfield, Pollard, and Swanston petitioned the Lord Chamberlain that John Shank, Cuthbert Burbage, and Mrs. Robinson be forced to sell them each one share in the Globe theatre. They further petitioned that Shank be forced to sell one of his shares in Blackfriars to be divided among the three of them. (*M.S.C.* ii. 362-4.)

1635, May 21—'Thomas Pollard & Elizabeth Winden, L. vg.' mar. St. Gregory by St. Paul. (Challen, *Marriages*.)

1635, July 12—The Lord Chamberlain complied with the request of the petitioners. (*M.S.C.* ii. 365.)

1635, Aug. 1—Since the actors were unable to agree on the price of the shares, Sir Henry Herbert, Sir John Finett, and Daniel Bedingfield were appointed to arbitrate. (Ibid., p. 373.) Shank's will of 30 December 1635 indicates that he still claimed all his shares. (See Appendix, p. 647.)

1639, Aug. 26—Richard Benfield of Gray's Inn bequeathed 40s. for a ring 'to my Gossipp Eliardt Swanston and Thomas Pollard'. (See Appendix, p. 634.)

1641, Nov. 25—The epilogue to Shirley's *The Cardinal*, lic. this date, begins: '*Within*. Mr. *Pollard*, wher's Mr. *Pollard* for the Epilogue? He is thrust upon the Stage, and falls.' (1652 ed. B.M.)

1642—In a Chancery Suit of 1655, Theophilus Bird said that at the closing of the theatres in 1642 Pollard and Bowyer seized the apparel, hangings, and playbooks of the company and converted them to their own use. (Hotson, p. 32.)

1647—His name stands eighth in the list of ten King's men who signed the dedication of the Beaumont and Fletcher Folio. (1647 folio B.M.)

1647/8, Jan. 28—One of seven members of King's to sign a bond for an old company debt; see Theophilus Bird. (Hotson, p. 32.)

1648—Pollard played the Cook in *Rollo or The Bloody Brother* acted by combined players when soldiers raided the Cockpit. (*Hist. Hist.*, p. 9.)

1648—*A Key to the Cabinet of Parliament* refers to his clowning in *The Humorous Lieutenant*. (*See* Andrew Cane.)

1655—In Theophilus Bird's suit at Easter term, the defendants say,
'They do not know whether it is true (as Bird alleges) that Pollard
died worth £500 and that "one Richard Perryn of the town of
Buckingham, saddler," is administrator of his estate.' (Hotson,
p. 33.)

1664—In a coffee-house scene in the third act of Tatham's (?) *Knavery
in All Trades*, a gentleman has mentioned a current play.

    third . . . Bur [*sic*] sir, they say 'tis done rarely well.

    fourth. I cannot believe it, 'tis impossible they should do any
thing so well as I have seen things done.

    fifth. When *Taylor Lowen*, and *Pollard* were alive.

    fourth. Did you not know *Benfield* and Swautted ?

    fifth. Did I not know 'em ? yes, and hum'd them off a hundred
times. (1664 4° HN.)

1699—Wright says that '*Pollard*, and *Robinson* were Comedians' at
Blackfriars, and that Lowin, Taylor, and Pollard were superannuated when the wars began. '*Pollard* who Lived Single, and
had a Competent Estate; Retired to some Relations he had in the
Country, and there ended his Life . . . some Years before the Restauration.' (*Hist. Hist.*, pp. 4, 7, 10.)

POWELL, EDWARD. Dyce conjectured that the Edward
Powell who wrote complimentary verses for the 1646 edition of
Shirley's poems and for the 1647 Beaumont and Fletcher folio
was the 'Mr. *Powell*, an ancient Player, lately dead', who Langbaine said was the father of the actor and playwright, George
Powell. If Dyce is right, Edward Powell probably performed
before the closing of the theatres. It seems to me much more
likely, however, that Martin Powell, the Restoration actor, was
the father of George, that Edward was quite a different person,
and that there is no evidence of an actor named Powell before the
closing of the theatres. (See Dyce, *Shirley*, i, p. xcvi, and Langbaine, p. 113.)

PRAT, SAMUELL. The entry may refer to a household rather than
a theatrical servant.

1615, Nov. 7—'Samuell Prat seruant to one of the players,' bur. St.
Anne's Blackfriars.

PRICE (PRYORE ?), RICHARD. Throughout his known career
Richard Price was an actor at the Fortune, belonging certainly to
the Prince Henry–Palsgrave's company, and probably to the King
and Queen of Bohemia's company. It is possible that he had been
an Admiral's man before 1603, for 'Price' was assigned the part of
Scott in the MS. cast for *The Shoemakers' Holiday*. This cast,
however, is probably a forgery. (See *Sh. Soc. Papers*, iv. 114;
Chambers, *E.S.* ii. 159; and *Hens. D.* ii. 203.) Price must be the
'Pryore' of the list of Prince Henry's men in his Book of the
Household in 1610, and he is in the list of the company granted
cloth for Prince Henry's funeral procession and in the list of the

company when it was licensed as the Palsgrave's men two months later. In all important subsequent lists of the company Price appears. His presence in the bond to Gunnell probably indicates that Gunnell thought him of some importance to the company.

Richard Price, the Palsgrave's man, certainly lived in the parish of St. Giles' Cripplegate, where the Fortune was located, but it is possible that there was another Richard Price in the same parish. If the man accused of counterfeiting was the actor, he had moved from Golding Lane to White Cross Street late in 1622 or early in 1623. It seems to me equally possible, however, that the alleged counterfeiter was the man called yeoman in the parish registers. while the actor was the man called player and gentleman, the designation used in his Fortune lease.

The name is too common to place much reliance on the marriage of March 1605/6.

1605/6, Mar. 2—'Richard Price of St Giles in the ffielde & Joane Dudlowe per baynes' mar. St. Clement Eastcheap. (Challen, *Marriages.*)

1618, Oct. 31—He was eighth of the Palsgrave's men to sign the lease of the Fortune from Edward Alleyn. (See above, pp. 138–9.)

1620, Apr. 9—'Ther dind w^t vs m^r gunnell: Cartwright: parr & price ye King of bohemes men.' (Alleyn's Diary, Young, ii. 174.)

1620, Apr. 24—'Richard sonne of Richard Price Gentleman' chris. St. G.C. Buried 29 Apr.

1621, Nov. 23—'Richard sonne of Richard Price gentleman' chris. St. G.C.

1622—He was third in the list of Palsgrave's men in Sir Henry Herbert's office book. (See above, p. 147.)

1622, May 20—Alleyn granted him a lease of a half-share in the new Fortune; he was described as 'Richard Price of London gent.' (*Hens. Paps.*, pp. 30, 112.)

1622, Dec. 4—'A True Bill for making and coining on the same aforesaid 26th of October at Goldinglane, co. Midd., eight pieces of false and counterfeit money made in the likeness of Queene Elizabethes shillinges, against Richard Price, late of Golding lane aforesaid and his wife Mary. Putting themselves "Not Guilty," Richard and Mary were acquitted; Richard however being required to find sureties for his good behaviour.' (*Middx. Co. Rec.* ii. 170.)

1623, May 21—According to Markham's suit, he lived 'in White Crosse Streete'. (See Appendix, p. 683.)

1624, Apr. 30—He and five others signed a bond with Richard Gunnell to continue to play together as Palsgrave's at the Fortune. (See above, pp. 148–9.)

1624, May 15—'Mary daughter of Richard Price yeomã' bur. St. G.C.

1625, Apr. 19—'Henry son of Richard Price gentleman' bur. St. G.C.

1625, July 12—'Morgan sonne of Richard Price Player' chris. St. G.C. Buried 16 July.

1625, Aug. 23—'Martin Swayne s^r to Richard Price, gent' bur. St. G.C.

1627, Apr. 25—'Mary dau of Richard Price Player' chris. St. G.C.

1627, May 23—Thomas Saul petitioned the Lord Chamberlain against Gunnell, Cartwright, Price, and Fowler for a debt of £50. (*M.S.C.* ii. 401.)

1627, July 23—'Richard Price Player' bur. St. G.C.

1628, Apr. 16—'Richard and Mary son and Dau: of Rich: Price Player deceased' bur. St. G.C.

PUDSEY, EDWARD. An English actor in Germany in 1628 and 1640 (Herz, *Englische Schauspieler*, pp. 32 and 55.) He may be, as Chambers suggests (*E.S.* ii. 335), the Edward Pudsey whose commonplace book contains many Shakespearian quotations, but the identification rests on the name only.

PUNCTEUS, JOHN. At an unknown date Sir Henry Herbert issued a licence to 'John Puncteus, a Frenchman, professing *Physick*, with ten in his Company, to exercise *the quality of playing*, for a year, and to *sell his drugs*' (*Herbert*, p. 47). The number in the company is large, and, though Puncteus was obviously conducting a medicine show, it is possible that his group really performed plays.

RAINESCROFTE, THOMAS (*see* RAVENSCROFT, THOMAS).

RANDOLPH, THOMAS. Fleay noticed certain allusions in Randolph's verse which seemed to indicate that he had been connected with a London dramatic company. He noticed further that the first scene of *The Muses' Looking Glass* contained speeches which showed that the play had been performed in a new theatre and that later on in this scene the Salisbury Court theatre was conspicuously omitted from a list of London playhouses. Putting these facts together, Fleay decided that the company alluded to in the verses was Prince Charles's (II) men and that Randolph was the assistant manager of the company in 1632 and 1633 (*Biog. Chron.* ii. 166–7). This conclusion has been generally rejected because there is no indication that Randolph was in London 1632–3, and it seems unlikely that a Cambridge don would have managed an ordinary acting company. (See Thorn-Drury, *Poems*, pp. xv–xvii).

Since Fleay's time, however, other evidence suggesting Randolph's theatrical associations has come to light. In 1923 Professor G. C. Moore Smith published the entire poem, *William Heminges' Elegy on Randolph's Finger*, from which the extract, 'On the Time Poets', had been often quoted. In one passage Heminges describes the indignation of certain Puritans against Randolph (lines 195–206):

> And wᶜʰ was worse that lately he did pen
> vyle thinges for pigmeyes gaynst the Sonns of men,
> The Righteous man and the regenerate
> being laught to scorne thare by the reprobate.
> 'brother, sayd on, you spurr youʳ Zeale to slow
> to checke att thes thinges when the learned knowe

Thes arre but scarrs: the woundes dothe deeper lye:
Who knowes but hee wrightes to a Monastarye
and those whome wee call players may In tyme
Luther abuse and fence for Bellermyne?
The Pope has Iuglinge trickes and can vse slightes
to Conuerte Players Into Iesuittes.'

In this passage the association of Randolph and players is not only fairly clear, but the players are called 'pigmeyes'. Another addition to our information since Fleay wrote is Mr. W. J. Lawrence's discovery that both Randolph's *Amyntas* and his *Muses' Looking Glass* (in which a Puritan calls the theatre audience which is to laugh at him 'the lew'd Reprobate') were licensed for the Children of the King's Revels in 1630 (see above, p. 291). Thus the 'vyle thinges for pigmeyes' is *The Muses' Looking Glass* for the boys of the King's Revels. Note further that Mr. Lawrence found that both these plays were licensed in 1630, the year in which Cambridge was closed from April to November because of the plague. This fact fits the allusion of two lines—the last two quoted below—of Randolph's *Eclogue to Master Jonson*. In this poem, after speaking of his love of Aristotle at Cambridge, Randolph goes on (Thorn-Drury, *Poems*, pp. 108–9):

And yet I let this true delight alone,
Call'd thence to keep the flock of *Corydon*.
Ah woe is me, anothers flock to keep;
The care is mine, the master shears the sheep!
A flock it was that would not keep together;
A flock that had no fleece, when it came hither.
Nor would it learn to listen to my layes,
For 'twas a flock made up of severall strayes:
And now I would return to *Cham*, I hear
A desolation frights the *Muses* there!

I suggest, therefore, that though Fleay was undoubtedly wrong about the years of Randolph's theatrical activity, wrong about the company, and probably wrong about the position he held, it is quite probable that Randolph *was* associated with the King's Revels in, and probably a few months before, 1630. It is somewhat more probable that he served as a theatre poet under contract—a position which Brome held at this theatre a few years later—than as a manager. It seems likely that he wrote or revised *Amyntas* and *The Muses' Looking Glass* for this company, and perhaps *The Drinking Academy* as well, for that play was written for boys, possibly at this time, its allusions indicate a London audience, and its prologue suggests a public and not a private performance.

If this suggestion of Randolph's employment at the Salisbury Court is accepted, the 'flock' of the *Eclogue* refers to the King's Revels boys, the master who sheared the sheep was probably

Blagrave or Gunnell, and 'A flock that had no fleece, when it came hither' (a line which puzzled Thorn-Drury) refers to the fact that the King's Revels, probably a new company in 1629, owned no repertory of plays when it came to the Salisbury Court, and therefore Randolph's work was doubly strenuous. The next couplet, presumably, refers to unknown difficulties which Randolph had with the company and to the fact that the company was rather a scratch team—a fact known from the personnel of the organization (see pp. 289–91). The final couplet refers to his desire to return to Cambridge and his prevention by the plague of 1630. This interpretation seems to me to fit better the allusions in Randolph's work and Sir Henry Herbert's licences than any other which has been offered.

RAVENSCROFT, THOMAS. Mr. W. J. Lawrence thinks that the fact that Ravenscroft witnessed Richard Cowley's will with Burbage, Heminges, and Shank, taken in connexion with his earlier association with boys' companies, implies that he was connected with Blackfriars theatre. While not impossible, this conjecture seems a bit far fetched. (See Appendix, p. 642, and *M.L.R.* xix. 423.)

RAYNE, ANDREW (*see* CANE, ANDREW).

READE, EMANUEL. Reade first appears in the casts of *The Coxcomb* and *The Honest Man's Fortune*; therefore he was a Lady Elizabeth's man before he joined Queen Anne's company. The testimony of Elizabeth Perkins indicates that he was a friend of Christopher Beeston and that he had left the company some time before its break-up.

1616, June—He was named in the Baskervile suit as a member of Queen Anne's at the time of the second settlement in favour of Francis Browne. (Fleay, *Stage*, p. 275.)

1617, June 3—He refused to sign the new agreement of Queen Anne's with Susan Baskervile, though the Baskerviles say that he was a fellow and sharer of the company at the time. (Ibid., pp. 285–8.)

1620, June 16—Beeston declared in *Smith* v. *Beeston* that 'Emanuell Reade gent . . . about three weekes past went into Ireland, whose returne is not expected till some tyme in Michaelmas terme next' (Wallace, *Three Theatres*, p. 49), but on the 27th of June Elizabeth Perkins, wife of Richard Perkins, testified that 'Emanuell Reade hath made his abode in Jreland by the space of two or three yeares last past or theareaboutes with his wief & familie and about Easter last did come into England and did lye often tymes in the howse of the said xpofer Beeston & was much in his company whilest he was in England And about Whitsontyde last the saide Emanuell Reade went againe into Jreland & at his departure he sayde that he thought he should never returne agayne into England'. (Ibid., pp. 49–50.)

READE (REED, RHEADE), TIMOTHY. Though not many facts about the stage career of Timothy Reade are known, the allusions to him immediately before and after the closing of the theatres make it clear that he was a popular comedian. Sometime between 1626 and 1634 he evidently transferred from Queen Henrietta's men to the King's Revels; later, however, he seems to have gone back to the Queen's men, probably in 1637, when Sir Henry Herbert says that he joined Perkins, Sumner, Sherlock, and Turner to the best of the company at Salisbury Court—the King's Revels (see p. 236 ff.).

The evidence for his later career in the Queen's company is the reference to Reade as a Salisbury Court player in 1641 ('Friers' of the title evidently means Whitefriars or Salisbury Court, not Blackfriars) when Queen Henrietta's men were occupying that theatre. This change is also indicated, indirectly, in the dialogue of Goffe's *Careless Shepherdess*. Landlord and Thrift are evidently talking about their joy in watching the same comedian, Reade. Landlord says that he saw the comedian on this stage, i.e. the Salisbury Court where *The Careless Shepherdess* was acted, and would like to see him act *The Changeling* again. Now *The Changeling* was the property of Queen Henrietta's men (see pp. 254–5). Before Queen Henrietta's had left the Phoenix, William Robbins (q.v.) had been famous in this role, but Robbins had apparently gone to the King's men when the Queen's men came to Salisbury Court. Thus Landlord had seen Reade, Robbins's successor as comedian of Queen Henrietta's company, play the part of the Changeling for the Queen's company on the stage of the Salisbury Court some time in 1637 or later.

The dialogue of *The Stage-Players' Complaint* implies that Reade was famous for his nimble feet and Cane for his facile tongue, but one could wish for a more definite statement.

1626—'*Cardona. Tymothy Read*' in the cast of Queen Henrietta's men prefixed to Shirley's *The Wedding*. (1629 4° HN.)

1634, July 18—Kendall told Crosfield that '4. Tim*othy* Reed' was one of the chief of the company at Salisbury Court. (See Appendix, p. 688.)

1634/5, Mar. 10—His name is in the full list of players recorded at Norwich; several of the players were King's Revels men, though the records do not give the name of the company, which was probably an amalgamation. (Murray, ii. 356; see above, pp. 286 and 288–9.)

1637—His reputation seems to be compared with that of Andrew Cane (with whom he is also associated in *The Stage-Players' Complaint*) in the poem by 'D. E.' prefixed to Thomas Heywood's *Pleasant Dialogues and Drammas*, 1637.

> Who can deny but Poets take their birth
> From some thing that's more excellent than earth?
> Since those harmonious strains that fill our eares,
> Proclaime their neere allyance with the Spheares,

> And shewes their Art all Arts as farre exceed
> As doth the fiery-Cane, the weakest Reed.

1641—*The Stage-Players' Complaint* was issued in the autumn of this year, with the sub-title, *In A Pleasant Dialogue between Cane of the Fortune and Reed of the Friers*. The dialogue between the two famous comedians concerns theatrical and political affairs. One of the two dancers in the woodcut on the title-page was probably intended for Reade.

1644/5, Mar. 7—'Edward sonne of Timothy Read' bur. St. G.C.

1646, July 28—'Pennella da: of Tymothy Read player.' bur. St. G.C.

1647, Oct. 6—'A Stage-Play was to have been acted in Salisbury Court this day (and bills stuck up about it) called *A King and no King*, formerly acted at the Black-Fryers, by his Majesties servants, about 8. yeares since, written by *Francis Beaumont* and *Iohn Fletcher*.

'The Sheriffes of the City of *London* with their Officers went thither, and found a great number of people; some young Lords, and other eminent persons; and the men and women with the Boxes, (that took monies) fled. The Sheriffes brought away *Tim Reade* the Foole, and the people cryed out for their monies, but slunke away like a company of drowned Mice without it.' (Hotson, p. 26, from *Perfect Occurrences*.)

1654—'. . . when as at a Bartholmewtide, the Fights and Travels of this great *Knight-Errant* [Don Quixote] are to be seen, and himselfe represented (for these honours came after his death) to the life, by *Timotheo Reado* of *Tiveri-æ*, who was the most incomparable mimicke upon the face of the Earth.' (Edmond Gayton, *Pleasant Notes upon Don Quixot*, 1654, pp. 85–6.)

1656—A country gentleman and a citizen, in the Praeludium to Goffe's *The Careless Shepherdess* (1656 4° B.M., pp. 4–5), discuss their taste in plays while sitting on the stage of the Salisbury Court:

Landl.   Why I would have the Fool in every Act,
        Be't Comedy, or Tragedy, I'ave laugh'd
        Untill I cry'd again, to see what Faces
        The Rogue will make: O it does me good
        To see him hold out 's Chin hang down his hands,
        And twirle his Bawble. There is nere a part
        About him but breaks jests. I heard a fellow
        Once on this Stage cry, *Doodle, Doodle, Dooe*,
        Beyond compare; I'de give the other shilling
        To see him act the Changling once again.

Thri.   And so would I, his part has all the wit,
        For none speaks Craps and Quibbles besides him:
        I'd rather see him leap, laugh, or cry,
        Then hear the gravest Speech in all the *Play*.
        I never saw *Rheade* peeping through the Curtain,
        But ravishing joy enter'd into my heart.

REASON (RAISON), GILBERT. The earliest known occurrence of Reason's name is in the 1610 patent for Prince Charles's men. By 1617 he was touring with an exemplification of the company's patent, and the evidence indicates that he was the leader of the provincial Prince's company until 1625, when both the provincial and the London companies disappear. Evidently the Lord Chamberlain's order of 1617 did not destroy Reason's company or even compromise him very seriously at the Revels Office, for Reason himself carried a similar order a few years later. These orders of the Lord Chamberlain are rather curious; there is a suggestion that they were intended more to clear the way for a favoured provincial organization than to regulate licensing. It is odd that one order carried by a Lady Elizabeth's man appears when Lady Elizabeth's are forced on the road after a partial amalgamation with the Prince's men and that a second order carried by a Prince's man appears when Lady Elizabeth's begins a London career again (see pp. 177–9, 182–3, and 205) forcing the Prince's men out of the Phoenix. Reason's appearance in the cloak allowance does not necessarily indicate that he was active in the London company; provincial players were sometimes used to swell the lists in these funeral allowances.

It is unfortunate that the MS. notes in the Chicago copy of *A Looking Glass for London and England* cannot be dated. The designation 'Mr.' would indicate that Reason was of some importance in the company which presented the play, and this status is not incompatible with his known position in the provincial Prince's company.

1617, June 4—Pembroke sent an order of 16 July 1616 to Norwich stating that 'also Gilberte Reason one of the prince his highnes Playoᵣˢ hauing likewise sepated himselfe from his Company hath also taken forth another exemplification or duplicate of the patent granted to that Company', and asking that he be sent back to London, with six others of other companies. (See above, pp. 178–9, for full letter, and Murray, ii. 343–4.)

1621, Aug. 24—'Gilbert Reason one of the Prinns Players' (Charles I) and his company played at Coventry. (Murray, ii. 249.)

1622, Nov. 20—A Lord Chamberlain's letter of this date ordering the seizure of irregular patents in the provinces was brought to Norwich by Reason in January, 1624/5. (Ibid., pp. 351–2.)

1622, Dec. 23—'Gilbert Reason and Mʳ William Eaton players to the Prince his high' were paid twenty shillings at Coventry. (Ibid., p. 249.)

1623, May 31—Gilbert Reason brought a company of Prince's men to Norwich with an exemplification dated 31 May 1613 for their patent of 30 March 1610. (Ibid., p. 347.)

1624–5—'Gilbert Reason & the rest of the Company of the Princes players as a gratuity to them' were given 43s. at Norwich. (Ibid., p. 371.)

1624/5, Jan. 29—The Mayors' Court Books for this date refer to the above item, which is taken from the Chamberlains' Accounts: 'This day Gilbert Reason brought in & shewed to this Court an Exemplificaĉon of a patent as servants to the Prince to play &c.

And there was made a warrant for xliii^s to be gyven them as a gratuity.' Reason also showed at this time the Lord Chamberlain's warrant for the seizure of irregular patents. (Ibid., pp. 351–2.)

1625, >May 7—As a member of the Prince's company, 'Gilbert Raison' was seventh to receive black cloth for James's funeral procession. (*M.S.C.* ii. 326.)

N.D.—Line 1540 of Greene and Lodge's *Looking Glass for London and England* has the stage direction 'Enter the Priests of the sun with Miters on their heads carrying fire in their hands'. The University of Chicago quarto of this play, which has many contemporary manuscript notes, corrections, and stage directions, has an addition to this stage direction. After 'sun' a caret is inserted, and interlined above is 'Mr Reason'. Evidently Reason played the Priest of the Sun in the production for which the prompter's notes were made. (See C. R. Baskervill, 'A Prompt Copy of *A Looking Glass for London and England*', *Mod. Phil.*, xxx [August 1932], 37, Plate VII.)

REIGNOLDS, WILLIAM. Since William Reignolds appears only once as an actor and is found in none of the later casts of Queen Henrietta's men, it is possible that he was really a musician.

1625—'Francisco, *A Jesuite.* William Reignalds' in the Queen Henrietta's cast for Massinger's *Renegado.* (1630 4° B.M.)

1636, Aug. 18—'Wm Reignolds, musitian' bur. St. G.C.

1642/3, Jan. 10—'Will'm Reignolds & Amye Smith' mar. St. J.C.

REYNOLDS, ROBERT. Robert Reynolds was a Queen Anne's man, but he seems to have foreseen the difficulties in which the company would be involved; at any rate, by 1616 he had begun an acting career in Germany, where he made no small reputation, often appearing under the clown-name of Pickleherring. There are records of his activities in Germany in 1616, 1618, 1626, 1627, 1628, 1631, and 1640. In the earlier years he performed in the companies of Robert Browne and John Greene, but in 1627 he seems to have succeeded to the leadership of Greene's company. (Herz, *Englische Schauspieler*, pp. 30–2, 54–8, 114.)

He may be the Robert Reignouldes who was married in St. James's Clerkenwell in 1626, for he had lived in this parish ten years before.

1615/16, Jan. 1 and 1616/17, Mar. 1—'Robert Reynoldes yoman, his wife Jane Reynoldes,' of St. J.C., and 'Jane wife of . . . Reynoldes stageplayer' of St. John's, indicted for non-attendance at church. (*Middx. Co. Rec.* ii. 120, 127.)

1616, June—Named in the Baskervile suit as a member of Queen Anne's at the time of the second settlement in favour of Francis Browne. (Fleay, *Stage*, p. 275.)

1617, June 3—He refused to sign the new agreement of Queen Anne's with Susan Baskervile, though the Baskerviles said he was a fellow and sharer of the company at the time. (Ibid., pp. 285–8.)

1626, May 1—'Robert Reignouldes & Margery Powell' mar. St. J.C.

REYNOLDS, WILLIAM (*see* REIGNOLDS, WILLIAM).

RHODES (ROADS, ROADES, RODES, ROODS), JOHN. I suspect that there was more than one John Rhodes connected with the theatre in London in the seventeenth century. One was a bookseller in 1628 and in 1641, probably the bookseller who formed the company at the Cockpit in 1659. This same man, since he is found at the Cockpit in 1659, was probably the John Rhodes who Mr. Hotson found had become keeper of the Cockpit by 1644 (Hotson, p. 90). If he lived at the Cockpit in 1644, he was probably the John Rhodes whose wife Ann was buried in that parish in 1644, and perhaps the John Rhodes, draper—the bookseller was a member of the Drapers' Company in 1641—who lived in the adjoining parish of St. Martin's in 1656.

The other records do not fit together quite so well. The King's man of 1624 was probably the 'I: Rho:' who acted in the King's play in February 1624/5. Mr. Baldwin (*Organization and Personnel*, pp. 127–8) has identified this man with the 'Jhon' (q.v.) whose hand appears in several of the MSS. of the King's company and with the Cockpit manager of 1659. His evidence is quite inadequate. It is equally probable that this John Rhodes was the musician buried at St. Giles' Cripplegate in February 1635/6.

Finally, there is the John Rhodes who owned part of the Fortune playhouse in 1637 and 1648. It seems reasonable to identify this man with the John Rhodes of the Fortune Playhouse against whom the King's company complained in 1639. The statement about the assignment of the leases in 1637 suggests that he may have succeeded Richard Gunnell [Gannill] as manager of the Fortune.

It is possible that all these records except that of the burial of the musician really do outline the career of one versatile man, but it seems to me a bit improbable that a bookseller who had kept seven apprentices before 1641 could also have had a career as a King's man and have run the Fortune. Downes and Gildon indicate that the King's man and the bookseller were one, though Downes's parenthetical phrase suggests that he was not sure of his information, and in any case he was writing too late to be a very reliable authority about theatrical affairs before 1642. The best interpretation of the evidence that I can make at present is that the Fortune manager was a second John Rhodes and the musician a third.

1624, Dec. 27—'Theise are to Certefie you That . . . John Rhodes, . . . are all imployed by the Kinges Maiesties servantes in theire quallity of Playinge as Musitions and other necessary attendantes. . . .' (*Herbert*, p. 74; see above, pp. 15–16.)

1624/5, Feb. 8—He is probably the 'I: Rho:' who appears (fol. 5a) with 'G: Ver:' (George Vernon) as a creditor in the prompter's notes in the MS. of *The Honest Man's Fortune* (Dyce MS. 9). The play was first performed in 1613, but it was probably in the later performance by the King's men for which Herbert issued a licence 8 Feb. 1624/5 that Rhodes and Vernon appeared. (Greg, *Dram. Doc.*, p. 291.)

1628, Sept. 13—A John Rhodes was one of ten second-hand book-sellers in Little Britain who were ordered to bring a catalogue of their books to the Archbishop of Canterbury. (*Dictionary of Printers*, p. 255, from *C.S.P., Dom.*, Charles I, vol. 117 [9].)

1632—Upon the complaint of George Stutvile, a warrant was issued for the apprehension of 'Iohn Ierom gent. [*blank*] Roades a Sta-tioner & [*blank*] Booker A serjeant at mace in London'. (*M.S.C.* ii. 359.)

1635/6, Feb. 22—'John Roads, Musitian' bur. St. G.C.

1637, Nov.—Among the Dulwich MSS. is a 'Bill in Chancery pre-ferred by Dulwich College against Margaret Gray, Edward Mar-rant, and John Roods for the non-payment of rent upon leases of the Fortune Theatre'. The answers of the defendants explain that 'Marrant and Roods were assignees of leases . . . originally granted by Edw. Alleyn to Charles Masseye, the actor, John Fisher, Thomas Wiggett and Richard Gannill'. (*MSS. Dul.*, p. 54.)

1639, Oct. 28—'Another [warrant] for Iohn Rodes of ye fortune Playhouse vpon ye complaint of the blackfryers Company for selling their Playes. eod [28 October 1639] Ios: Butler messengr.' (*M.S.C.* ii. 391.)

1641—In the records of the Drapers' Company under the heading, 'List of Members of the Company assessed for the Poll Tax, 1641,' and the sub-heading, 'Those of the generality or Yoemandry of the said Company wch wee conceive not able to pay iiili,' occurs the following entry, 'John Rhodes in little brittaine Bookeseller 7'. The '7' refers to the number of apprentices he had taken during his lifetime. (A. H. Johnson, *The History of the Worshipful Company of Drapers*, iv. 155. Mr. Baldwin, *Organization and Personnel*, p. 128 n., notes that among these apprentices must have been Betterton and Kynaston.)

1644, Oct. 21—'Ann Wife of John Rodes' bur. St. G.F.

1647–9—A court order was issued in the suit about arrears in the Fortune rent between 'Dulwich College and Tobias Lisle, Thomas Grimes, John Rhodes, and others'. (*MSS. Dul.*, p. 56.)

1648—'Answers of John Roades [or Rhodes] and Susan Baskerville to a bill of Dulwich College, that they have paid all arrears of rent on their leases of the Fortune up to 1640, but that since then "stage playes and playhowses have bene suppressed", and they are therefore not answerable for rent, being forbidden by the terms of their leases to put the premises to any other use; 1648. With a demurrer on the part of the College; 1649. ff. 150, 158.' (Ibid., p. 341.)

1656, Apr. 23—John Rhodes was sworn as a witness as 'of St. Martin's-in-the-Fields, Citizen and Draper of London, aged 50 years and upwards'. (Hotson, p. 99.)

1659—In *Roscius Anglicanus* John Downes writes: 'In the Year 1659, General *Monk*, Marching then his Army out of *Scotland* to *London*. Mr. *Rhodes* a Bookseller being Wardrobe-Keeper formerly (as I am inform'd) to King *Charles* the First's, Company of Comedians in *Black-Friars*; getting a License from the then Governing State, fitted up a House then for Acting call'd the *Cock-Pit* in *Drury-Lane*, and in a short time Compleated his Company.' (1708 ed. B.M. Mr. Hotson [Hotson, p. 197] doubts the story of Rhodes's licence from Monk, though he agrees that Rhodes was in charge of a company at the Cockpit.)

1708—'Mr. *Thomas Betterton* was born in *Tuttle-street, Westminster*; his Father being Under-Cook to King *Charles the First*: And when he was now come to Years sufficient, his Father bound him Apprentice to one Mr. *Rhodes* a Bookseller, at the Bible at *Charing-Cross*, and he had for his Under-Prentice Mr. *Kynaston*.

'But that which prepar'd Mr. *Betterton* and his Fellow-Prentice for the Stage, was that his Master *Rhodes* having formerly been *Wardrobe* Keeper to the King's Company of *Comedians* in the *Black-Fryars*, on General *Monck's* March to *London*, in 1659. with his Army, got a Licence from the Powers then in being, to set up a Company of Players in the *Cockpit* in *Drury-lane*, and soon made his Company compleat, his Apprentices, Mr. *Betterton* for Mens Parts, and Mr. *Kynaston* for Womens Parts, being at the Head of them.' (Gildon, *Life of Betterton*, p. 5.)

RICE, JOHN. John Rice was an apprentice in the King's company in 1607 when Heminges lent him, 'a very proper Child, well spoken', to the Merchant Tailors' company to deliver a speech before King James. He appeared with Burbage in another pageant in 1610 as a nymph, but by 1611 he was a Lady Elizabeth's man. How long he remained with Lady Elizabeth's company is not known, but he was a King's man by 1619 and a member by 1621, when he appeared in a livery allowance list. Mr. Baldwin shows good reason for believing that Rice succeeded to Nathan Field's place as a member of the company (*Organization and Personnel*, p. 52). He had left the company by 1629, for he does not appear in the livery list of that year, and his absence from the cast of *The Roman Actor* in 1626 and *The Lover's Melancholy* in 1628 suggests but does not prove that he had left by 1626; Mr. Baldwin thinks that he was one of the three members who dropped out at the time of the reorganization in 1625 (ibid., p. 56).

Heminges's mention of John Rice in his will indicates that the actor's withdrawal from the company was not occasioned by his death—the usual explanation of the disappearance of a member of the King's company.

Markham's suit and Heminges's will show that Rice lived in St. Saviour's, but it is impossible to identify him certainly in the records because there was another man of the name in the parish, a joiner. The actor was probably the John Rice who is found in the token books 'Nere the Playhouse' in 1617 and 1619–23.

1616, May 1—'John Rice & Mabell Hayward' mar. St. S.S. (*The Genealogist*, N.S., vii. 168.)

1619, Aug.—The prompter's notes in the MS. of *Sir John van Olden Barnavelt* show that he played a captain and a servant ('Io: R.', 'Io: Ri.', 'Io: Ric', 'Io: Rice', 'm^r Rice') in the King's production. (Greg, *Dram. Doc.*, pp. 271–3.)

1619–23—'The Marquesse of Pescara, I. Rice' in the King's cast prefixed to the 1623 4° of *The Duchess of Malfi*. Since only one name is given for this role, he apparently had the part in both the original production >1614 and the revival of 1619–23. (1623 4° B.M.)

c. 1620—No. 7 in King's cast of *The False One*. (1679 folio B.M.)

1621, Apr. 7—He was named in the livery allowance for the King's men. (*Hist. MSS. Com.*, Report IV, p. 299.)

1623—'Iohn Rice' was twenty-sixth in the actor list in the Shakespeare folio.

1623, May 21—He is named in Markham's suit as 'Iohn Rice of the Bancksyde'. (See Appendix, p. 683.)

1624, Dec. 20—No. 9 in King's submission for playing *The Spanish Viceroy*. (*Herbert*, p. 21.)

1625, >May 5—'Iohn Rice' was twelfth in the list of King's men who received black cloth for James's funeral procession. (*M.S.C.* ii. 326.)

1625, June 24—No. 9 in patent for King's. (Ibid. i. 282–3.)

1630, Oct. 9—Heminges left 20s. to 'John Rice Clerke of St Saviours in Southwarke', and made 'my loving freinds Mr Burbage and Mr Rice' overseers. (See Appendix, pp. 644–5.)

RICK, G. (*see* RICKNER, GEORGE).

RICKNER, GEORGE. It is impossible to tell why Rickner's name was deleted from the list of King's attendants exempted from arrest, but the 'G: Rick:' of *The Honest Man's Fortune* suggests that the name is not a scribe's error, but that a man of the name had been connected with the company.

1624, Dec. 17—His name has been deleted from Sir Henry Herbert's exemption from arrest of the attendants of the King's men. (See above, pp. 15–16.)

1624/5, Feb. 8—In the prompter's notes in the MS. of *The Honest Man's Fortune* (Dyce MS. 9) 'G: Rick:' appears as a servant (fols. 6^b and 7^b). (Greg, *Dram. Doc.*, p. 291.)

1636, Oct. 3 and Dec. 1—See George Bosgrave.

ROBBINS (ROBINS, ROBINSON, ROBSON), WILLIAM. The actor William Robbins was sometimes called William Robinson, as is shown by his appearance as William Robinson in the Queen's cast for Heywood's *The Fair Maid of the West* in the 1631 quarto and as William Robbins in the same company's cast for Massinger's *Renegado* in the 1630 quarto. The roles in the two plays are quite similar comic parts and would obviously have been taken by the same actor. Much confusion has been caused by the use of these two names in referring to the Queen's comedian and by the consequent confusion of William Robbins and Richard Robinson (q.v.).

Robbins was one of the Queen Anne's men who held together after the Queen's death and formed the Revels company at the Red Bull. He was one of the earliest members of Queen Henrietta's company, for he appears in the first list of that troupe (see above, pp. 220–2), and he is in most of the other lists before the break-up in 1637. His known roles and the contemporary references to him both show that Robbins was a comedian and that the Changeling, which he performed in the play of this name inherited by the Queen's men from Lady Elizabeth's, was one of his famous characterizations.

Though it is not known when Robbins joined the King's company, it was probably at the time of the changes in the companies during the long plague closing in 1636–7; there is no record that he ever appeared with Queen Henrietta's men after that company was reorganized at Salisbury Court.

Robbins's death at Basing House made something of a stir at the time; Peters and the author of *Perfect Occurrences* imply that his comedian's mockery was in part responsible for his death.

1609, Apr. 14—'Alice d of William Robbins' chris. St. J.C.

1616, June—He was named in the Baskervile suit as a member of Queen Anne's at the time of the second settlement in favour of Francis Browne. (Fleay, *Stage*, p. 275.)

1617, June 3—He signed the new agreement of Queen's with Susan Baskervile; she says he was a fellow and sharer at the time. (Ibid., pp. 285–8.)

1619, >May 13—'William Robinson' was thirteenth in the list of Queen Anne's men to receive black cloth for her funeral procession. (*M.S.C.* ii. 325.)

1622, July 8—'Will: Robins' was seventh in a list of seven Queen Anne's men named in a warrant for the Privy Seal for licensing the Children of the Revels; the bill was signed 25 July. (Murray, ii. 193–4.)

1622, July 30—'William Robins & Cisley Browne; lic' mar. St. J.C.

1622—'William Robbins' was seventh in Herbert's list of the seven 'chiefe players at the Red Bull, called the players of the Revells'. (*Herbert*, p. 63; see above, pp. 165–9.)

1623, May 21—In Markham's suit as 'William Robins on Clarkenwell hill', 5s. (See Appendix, p. 683.)

1625, Oct. 16—At Coventry five shillings was 'paid to Martyn Slatier, Robson, & Silvester late servants to the late queene Anne'. (Murray, ii. 250.)

1625—'Carazie *an Eunuch*. William Robins' in the Queen Henrietta's cast for Massinger's *Renegado*. (1630 4° B.M.)

1626—'Rawbone, a thin Citizen, *William Robins*' in the Queen Henrietta's cast for Shirley's *Wedding*. (1629 4° HN.)

c. 1630—'Clem, *a drawer of wine under* Besse Bridges; *by* Mr. William Robinson', in the cast of Queen Henrietta's men prefixed to the 1631 4° of Heywood's *Fair Maid of the West*, Part I; since 'Clem, *the Clown*' is assigned to no actor in the cast for Part II, Robinson probably played the part there as well. (1631 4° B.M.)

1634, July 18—He is probably the 'Robinson' whom Kendall referred to as a Queen's man in conversation with Crosfield. (*Crosfield's Diary*, p. 72; see Appendix, p. 688.)

1634, Sept. 11—William Robins and his wife Cecily were left rings in the will of Thomas Basse. (See Appendix, p. 631.)

1640/1, Jan. 22—'William Robins' is named second in a 'warrt for the swearing of the six persons heerafter mentioned each of them A Groome of his Ma^{tes} Chamber in Ordinary without ffee to attend his Ma^{tye} in the Quality of Players and to bee of the Company of his Ma^{ts} servants at ye Blackfryers'. (*M.S.C.* ii. 397.)

1645, Oct. 14—Wright says that ' *Robins* a Comedian' was one of 'Those of principal Note at the *Cockpit*' (*Hist. Hist.*, pp. 4–5), and that ' *Robinson* was Kill'd at the Taking of a Place (I think *Basing House*) by *Harrison*, he that was after Hang'd at *Charing-cross*, who refused him Quarter, and Shot him in the Head when he had laid down his Arms; abusing Scripture at the same time, in saying, *Cursed is he that doth the Work of the Lord negligently*'. (Ibid., pp. 7–8.) Wright may have got his information from the report of Hugh Peters to Parliament on his view of Basing House immediately after it was taken. 'There lay dead upon the ground, Major *Cuffle* (a man of great account amongst them, and a notorious Papist) slain by the hands of Major *Harrison*; (that godly and gallant Gentleman) and *Robinson* the Player, who a little before the Storm, was known to be mocking and scorning the Parliament, & our Army. . . .' (Sprigg, *Anglia Rediviva*, pp. 139–40, 1647 ed. HN.)

That Wright and Peters meant William Robbins and not Richard Robinson is shown by a reference in *A Diary or an Exact Journall* for 9–16 Oct. 1645: 'Robinson the Player . . . he was in Drury Lane a Comodian, but now hee acted his own Tragedy.' Other contemporary references to his death are, ' Robinson the Fool slain, as he was turning and acting like a Player' (*Perfect Occurrences*, 10–17 Oct.); ' *Slaine*. Major *Robinson* ' (*Perfect Diurnal*, 13–20 Oct.); and ' Slain . . . *Robinson* the Players son' (*The Kingdomes Weekly Intelligencer*, 14–21 Oct.). (Hotson, p. 72.)

1648—*See* Andrew Cane for a reference to ' Robins the Changeling' in *A Key to the Cabinet of Parliament*.

ROBINSON, JOHN. John Robinson is found with no company except the King's Revels. Mr. Hotson's conjecture that the John Robinson whom Elizabeth Gunnell married was the player receives some support from the fact that Gunnell had been connected with both the Salisbury Court and the Fortune, the two theatres in which the King's Revels performed. Moreover, Robinson was buried in Gunnell's parish, and the fact that his wife made her will in 1641 in favour of her daughters suggests that the Robinson she had married was dead in that year.

1634, July 18—Kendall told Crosfield that among the players of Salisbury Court was ' 8. John Robinson'. (*Crosfield's Diary*, p. 72; see Appendix, p. 688.)

c. 1634 ?—'*Saufellus* chiefe of Counsell to *Silius* and *Messallina*— *Iohn Robinson*', in the King's Revels cast for Richards's *Messalina*. (1640 8° B.M.)

<1634—A Chancery suit of 1654 says that after the death of her husband, Richard Gunnell, Elizabeth Gunnell married a John Robinson. Mr. Hotson thinks that perhaps this was the actor. (Hotson, p. 52.)

1634/5, Mar. 10—John Robinson is found in the long list of players at Norwich; many of them were King's Revels men, though probably two companies are listed together. (Murray, ii. 356; see above, pp. 286 and 288–9.)

1640—'Jo. Robinson' contributed the following verses to *Messalina* (1640 ed. B.M.):

> To his Friend M^r. *Nathanael Richards,* upon
> his Tragedy of *Messallina.*
>
> If it be good to write the *truth* of ill
> And *Vertues* excellence, 'tis in thy skill
> (Respected Friend) thy nimble *Scenes* discover
> *Romes lust-burnt Emp'resse* and her vertuous *Mother*
> So truly to the life; judgement may see,
> (Praysing this *Peece*) I doe not flatter thee.
> Men here may reade Heaven's Art to chastise Lust;
> Rich *Vertue* in a *Play,* so cleare; no rust,
> Bred by the *squint* ey'd *critickes* conquering breath
> Can e're deface it; *Mesallina's* death
>> Adds life unto the *Stage*; where though she die
>> Defam'd; true *justice* crownes this Tragedy.

1641, Apr. 27—'John Robinson, Player' bur. St. G.C.

ROBINSON, RICHARD. As a boy actor in the King's company, Richard Robinson appears before 1616 in the casts of *Bonduca* and *Catiline* and in the stage directions of *The Second Maid's Tragedy.* Jonson's praise of Robinson as a female impersonator is no small tribute. Sir Edmund Chambers suggests that he may have been the son of James Robinson, one of the managers of the Children of the Chapel Royal, and one of the boys of that company before he came to King's (*E.S.* ii. 336). Since he witnessed Richard Burbage's will and seems to have married Burbage's widow, it is not improbable that he was Burbage's apprentice.

Robinson had evidently become a sharer in the King's company by 1619, for he appears in the patent and the livery allowance of that year, and he is called 'Mr.' by the prompter in the stage directions of *Barnavelt.* Mr. Baldwin thinks, with some show of reason, that Robinson succeeded to the place of Cowley some time in March 1618/19 (*Organization and Personnel,* p. 51).

The assigned roles of Robinson in the plays after 1619 indicate that he was not one of the most prominent of the actors in the company, and Cowley's reference in 1638 to his popularity is somewhat surprising; perhaps he had a special vogue with the Westminster boys, or perhaps Cowley, like some of his contemporaries, referred to William Robbins (q.v.) as Robinson. Even more surprising is Wright's statement that Pollard and Robinson were comedians, for though Pollard had many comic roles, Robinson is not known to have had any. Wright was surely confusing Robinson with Robbins, the former comedian of Queen Henrietta's company who was a King's man in the last years of the Caroline stage. Though most of his information was accurate,

Wright undoubtedly confused Robbins and Robinson in his account of the latter's death in 1645, for the King's man is known to have been alive in 1647 and January 1647/8 (*see* William Robbins), and it is not, therefore, unthinkable that he should have got the roles of the two men confused.

The letter of Sir Henry Wotton in 1631 indicates that Robinson was a collector and, presumably, a man of some means. It is a pity that Sir Henry could not have been more specific about the qualities of *The Italian Night Masque* which made it so rare in Robinson's opinion.

Evidently Robinson was still maintaining his connexion with his former fellows up to the time of his death in March, 1647/8.

1616, Sept. 5 or 6—At the Sessions of the Peace and Gaol Delivery held on these dates, recognizances were taken of 'Thomas Weston of East Smithfield, scrivener, for Richard Robson of St. Anne's, Blackfriars, charged with incontinency'. Robson was 'Respited to the next and then came and discharged'. (*Middx. Sessions*, iii. 298.)

1616—*The Devil Is an Ass*, given by King's this year, has the following lines (ii. 8) between Ingine and Merecraft (1631 ed. B.M.):

> MER. . . . But, where's this *Lady*?
> If we could get a witty boy, now, *Ingine*;
> That were an excellent cracke: I could instruct him,
> To the true height. For any thing takes this *dottrel*.
> ING. Why, Sir your best will be one o'the players!
> MER. No, there's no trusting them. They'll talke on't,
> And tell their *Poets*. ING. What if they doe? the iest
> will brooke the Stage. But, there be some of 'hem
> Are very honest Lads. There's *Dicke Robinson*
> A very pretty fellow, and comes often
> To a Gentlemans chamber, a friends of mine. We had
> The merriest supper of it there, one night,
> The Gentlemans Land-lady invited him
> To'a Gossips feast. Now, he Sir brought *Dick Robinson*,
> Drest like a Lawyers wife, amongst 'hem all;
> (I lent him cloathes) but, to see him behaue it;
> And lay the law; and carue; and drinke vnto 'hem;
> And then talke baudy: and send frolicks! o!
> It would haue burst your buttons, or not left you
> A seame. MER. They say hee's an ingenious youth!
> ING. O Sir! and dresses himselfe, the best! beyond
> Forty o' your very *Ladies*! did you ne'r see him?
> MER. No, I do seldome see those toyes. But thinke you,
> That we may haue him? ING. Sir, the young Gentleman
> I tell you of, can command him. Shall I attempt it?
> MER. Yes, doe it.

'1618/19, Mar. 12—He witnessed Richard Burbage's will. (See Appendix, p. 638.)

1619, Mar. 27—No. 11 in King's patent. (*M.S.C.* i. 280–2.)

1619, May 19—No. 11 in list of King's for livery allowance. (*Hist. MSS. Com.*, Report IV, p. 299.)

1619, Aug.—The prompter's notes in the MS. of *Sir John van Olden Barnavelt* show that he had the parts of a captain and an ambassador ('m^r Rob.') in the King's production. (Greg, *Dram. Doc.*, p. 273.)

<1619—He was probably the Richard Robinson who married Richard Burbage's widow. (See the item of 2 May 1642 and above, pp. 43–6.)

c. 1621—No. 6 in King's cast for *The Double Marriage.* (1679 folio B.M.)

1621, Apr. 7—No. 11 in list of King's men for livery allowance. (*Hist. MSS. Com.*, Report IV, p. 299.)

1619–23—'Cardinall, 1 H. Cundaile. 2 R Robinson' in King's cast prefixed to the 1623 4° of *The Duchess of Malfi.* Apparently he took the part in the revival 1619–23. (1623 4° B.M.)

1623—No. 24 in actor list in the Shakespeare folio.

1623, June 3—When Nicholas Tooley made his will, Robinson owed him £29. 13*s.* which Tooley bequeathed to Sara Burbage. (See Appendix, pp. 649–50.)

1623, May 21—According to Markham's suit, he lived 'att the vpper end of Shoreditch'. (See Appendix, p. 682.)

1624, May 27—No. 2 in King's cast for *A Wife for a Month.* (1679 folio B.M.)

1624, Dec. 20—No. 2 in submission of King's for *The Spanish Viceroy.* (*Herbert*, p. 21; see above, pp. 14–15.)

1625, >May 5—He was sixth in the list of King's men who received black cloth for James's funeral. (*M.S.C.* ii. 325.)

1625, June 24—No. 5 in patent for King's. (Ibid. i. 282–3.)

1626—'*Aesopus* a Player. Richard Robinson' in King's cast for Massinger's *The Roman Actor*, lic. 11 October. (1629 4° B.M.)

1626, Nov. 3—'A peticõn of Iohn Nicols agst: Iohn Lowen and Rich: Robinson. debt. 20^{li} Answ: of Course.' The petition was repeated 13 or 14 November. (*M.S.C.* ii. 400.)

1626, Nov. 3<>7—'A peticõn of Tho: Mallory agst: Rich: Robinson. 8^{li} debt. Answ: of Course.' (Ibid.)

1629, May 6—'Richard Robinson' was fourth in a list of King's men for cloak allowances. (Ibid., p. 350.)

1629?—'M^r. Robinson, Count Orsinio, and Hermite' in King's cast for Carlell's *The Deserving Favorite.* (1629 4° B.M.)

1631, May 6 (lic.)—He played Lentulus ('Mr Robinson', 'm^r Rob:') in King's production of *Believe as You List.* (Sisson, *B.A.Y.L.*, pp. xxxi ff.)

1631?—In an undated letter Sir Henry Wotton wrote to Sir Gervase Clifton, 'I should have seen some pictures and other rarities in the house of Robinson, one of the King's players, as to-morrow, who an hour since sent me word that he cannot be at home to receive me, by reason of a new play which they are to repeat to-morrow in the afternoon, and which they are publicly to act on Wednesday— the rarest thing, as he conceiveth, that hath ever been seen on a stage, called *The Italian Night Masque.*' (Smith, *Sir Henry Wotton*, ii. 333. Dated 1631 from the suggested identification with *The Italian Night-Piece, or, The Unfortunate Piety*, entered S.R. 9 Sept. 1653. Massinger's play, *The Unfortunate Piety*, was licensed by Herbert for the King's company 13 June 1631 [*Herbert*, p. 33].)

1632—'LA-CASTRE, the Indulgent Father . . . Acted by Mr. *Richard Robinson*', in the cast for the King's 1632 revival of *The Wild Goose Chase* which was printed in the 1652 edition. (1652 ed. B.M.)

1638—The 'Epistle Dedicatorie' to the 1638 edition of Cowley's *Love's Riddle* (1638 ed. B.M.) says of the play,

> Nor has't a part for Robinson, whom they
> At schoole, account essentiall to a Play.

1639—Robert Davenport dedicated *A Crowne for a Conquerour*; and *Too Late to Call Backe Yesterday* 'To my noble friends, Mr Richard Robinson, And Mr Michael Bowyer'. (1639 4° HN.)

1641—The pamphlet, 'An Answer To a printed paper Entitled Articles Exhibited in Parliament, Against Mr. John Sqvier, *Viccar* of Saint *Leonard Shoreditch*. *August* 7. 1641', concludes with a testimonial to Squire signed by some two hundred men, presumably his parishioners. The names of 'Richard Robinson' and 'William Burbage' are given consecutively in the list. (1641 4° B.M.)

1642, May 2—'Winifred, the wyfe of Mr. Richard Robinson, 2nd May, 1642', bur. St. Leonard's Shoreditch. (Stopes, *Burbage*, p. 140.)

>1642—Wright says, '*Hart* and *Clun*, were bred up Boys at the *Blackfriers*. . . . *Hart* was *Robinson's* Boy or Apprentice'. '*Pollard*, and *Robinson* were Comedians' at Blackfriars. (*Hist. Hist.*, pp. 3, 4.)

1645, Oct. 14—*See* William Robbins.

1647—His name—'Richard Robinson'—stands second in the list of ten King's men who signed the dedication of the Beaumont and Fletcher folio.

1647/8, Jan. 28—One of seven King's men who signed a bond for the payment of an old King's debt. (*See* Theophilus Bird.)

1647/8, Mar. 23—'Richard Robinson a Player' bur. St. Anne's Blackfriars.

ROBINSON, THOMAS. An English actor in Germany in 1627 and 1628 and probably later. (See Herz, *Englische Schauspieler*, pp. 31, 32, and 54 ff.)

ROBINSON, WILLIAMS (*see* ROBBINS, WILLIAM).

ROE, WILLIAM. An English actor in Germany in 1640 and 1650. (See Herz, *Englische Schauspieler*, pp. 55 ff., and Cohn, *Sh. in Ger.*, p. c.)

ROGERS, EDWARD. A boy who appears in the first two known casts of Queen Henrietta's men but never later.

1625—'Donvsa, *neece to* Amvrath. Edward Rogers', in Massinger's *Renegado*, presented by Queen Henrietta's company at Drury Lane. (1630 4° B.M.)

1626—'*Milliscent, Cardonaes* daughter. *Edward Rogers*', in the Queen Henrietta's cast for Shirley's *Wedding*. (1629 4° HN.)

ROGERS, WILLIAM. William Rogers is known as a player only from the 1628 list of the peculiar Queen of Bohemia's company.

The identification of the player and the jeweller seems dubious, but it would be no more remarkable than the identification of Thomas Barnes, carpenter, and Thomas Barnes, player, in this same Queen of Bohemia's company.

1628, June 30—'Wm Rogers' is sixth in a list of 'Queene of Bohemia's Players' made Grooms of His Majesty's chamber. (See above, pp. 188–9.)

1635 (?)—Hester Rogers, widow of William Rogers, jeweller, petitioned the King for money long owed for jewels. (*C.S.P., Dom.*, 1635–6, pp. 7–8.)

ROODS, JOHN (*see* RHODES, JOHN).

ROSSETER (ROSSITER), PHILIP. Rosseter was a musician who became involved, through boy actors and theatrical property, in dramatic affairs in London. From 1609 to 1617 he was prominent as a patentee of the Queen's Revels, a lessee of Whitefriars, a manager with Philip Henslowe, and the builder of Rosseter's Blackfriars or the Puddle Wharf theatre. (See the *D.N.B.* account of Rosseter, and Adams, pp. 342–7.)

After the death of Shakespeare, Rosseter was no longer important in theatrical affairs, though he was one of the patentees of the provincial company which seems to have been an amalgamation of Rosseter's Queen's Revels and Perry's King's Revels and Lee's provincial Queen Anne's men. He continued to appear as a royal lutanist until 1623.

1617, Oct. 31—Named with Lee, Perry, and Long in a licence. (Murray, ii. 345.)

1618, Aug. 29—At Norwich, 'Robt Lee Philip Rossiter Willm Perry & Nicholas Longe brought into the Court a comission' of 31 October 1617. (Ibid.)

1619/20, Mar. 1—In his will Thomas Campion bequeathed 'all that he had unto Mr. Philip Rosseter, and wished that his estate had bin farr more'. (*D.N.B.*)

1621, Dec. 28—'A warrant for allowance of strings for the base lute of v^{li} to Phillipp Rossiter for a whole yere ended at Chrissmas 1621.' (Murray, ii. 192.)

1623, May 5—He died on this day, according to his nuncupative will. (Hillebrand, p. 250.)

1623, May 21—His nuncupative will (P.C.C. 41 Swan) was proved. 'There is no information provided in the will. . . . Present were Hugh and Dudley Rossiter and Elizabeth, wife of Wm. Simpson.' (Ibid., p. 250, n. 47.)

ROWL (*see* DOWLE, ROWLAND).

ROWLAND. In the first scene of the second act of *The Witch of Edmonton* a countryman is addressed as 'Fellow Rowland'. Since the man addressed is one of the three countrymen who are not individually designated in the dramatis personae, Professor

Murray (Murray, i. 236 n.) and others have assumed that Rowland was the name of an actor. Actors' names, however often they may slip into the stage directions, are not likely to slip into the dialogue ; I see no reason that one of the playwrights might not have thought Rowland a suitable name for a country fellow and used it only in a speech.

The Rowland who is found in the stage directions of several King's plays was pretty surely Rowland Dowle, q.v.

ROWLEY, SAMUEL. Samuel Rowley, the dramatist, had an active career on the stage from 1597 to January 1612/13 as an Admiral's–Prince Henry's–Palsgrave's man, but there is no evidence that he was an actor after 1613. The fact that he wrote two plays and revised a third for the Palsgrave's company in less than nine months suggests that he had become a dramatist under contract for that theatre.

The dramatist may be the Samuel Rowley whose marriage Mark Eccles found recorded in the registers of St. Michael, Crooked Lane, in 1594: 'Samewell Rowley was married to Alice Coley the vij of Aprill.' The theatrical name of the bride is suggestive, but Rowley's name is not sufficiently uncommon to allow of certainty. A merchant-tailor named Samuel Rowley was buried at St. Giles' Cripplegate in 1620 (see *P.M.L.A.* xliv. 817), but he surely cannot have been the actor-dramatist ; Clode has no records of a merchant-tailor of the name.

Mercurius Pragmaticus was almost certainly lying about Hugh Peters (q.v.), and he cannot carry much weight as an authority on the acting career of Rowley. Except for the brief occupancy of Prince Charles's men in 1622 (see pp. 204–7), no dramatic company is known to have been attached to the Curtain between 1616 and 1642.

1623, July 27—'For the Palsgrave's Players, a Tragedy of *Richard the Third, or the English Profit*, with the Reformation, written by Samuel Rowley.' (*Herbert*, p. 24.)

1623, Oct. 29—'For the Palsgrave's Players ; a new Comedy, called, *Hardshifte for Husbands, or Bilboes the best blade*, Written by Samuel Rowley.' (Ibid., p. 26.)

1624, Apr. 6—'For the Fortune ; a new Comedy, called, *A Match or no Match*: Written by Mr. Rowleye.' (Ibid., p. 27.)

1647—'*Mercurius Pragmaticus* in 1647 said of Hugh Peters, the famous Independent divine: "he has a fine wit I can tell you, *Sam Rowley* and he were a *Pylades*, and *Orestes*, when he played a womans part at the Curtaine Play-house. . . ."' (Hotson, p. 15.)

ROWLEY, WILLIAM. The dramatist was an important member of the Duke of York–Prince Charles's (I) company for ten or twelve years and a member of the King's company for the last two or three years of his life. He first appears as an actor in 1609 in a purchase of costumes by five leading Duke of York's men from

John Heminges. By 1612 he was receiving payment for the company's performances at court, and he and John Newton represented them before the Privy Council in 1615.

Rowley was still a Prince Charles's man in January 1618/19, when several members of the company took part in the *Inner Temple Masque*. The title of Rowley's elegy on the death of Hugh Attewell in 1621 implies that Attewell was Rowley's fellow in 1621 and therefore that Rowley was still a Prince's man in that year.

By 1623 Rowley had become a King's man, and he appears four times in lists of the company before his death in 1626. Mr. Baldwin (*Organization and Personnel*, pp. 57–8) presents evidence that he succeeded to the place of Tooley in 1623. This transfer to the King's men seems clear enough until one comes to the disconcerting fact that Rowley was granted livery for King James's funeral as a Prince Charles's man. I can account for his appearance in this list only by the assumption that Rowley had not yet been sworn as a King's man, and that since he still appeared in the Lord Chamberlain's records as a Prince's player it was thought better to grant him livery as a member of that organization than to omit him altogether. There seems to have been a somewhat similar difficulty about the official status of Rowley's fellow Thomas Hobbes (q.v.) at this time.

The evidence of the *Keep the Widow Waking* suit shows that Rowley died between 1624 and 24 March 1625/6. (Sisson, *Keep the Widow Waking*, p. 237.) There can be little doubt that he was the householder buried at Clerkenwell in February 1625/6. The William Rowley who married Isabell Tooley at St. Giles' Cripplegate 27 November 1637 must have been another man, tempting as the association of the names is.

The rape-seed story, common as it is, suggests some knowledge of William Rowley, for he was performing at the Curtain in 1622 and 1623 (see above, pp. 204–7).

There is ample evidence that Rowley's typical acting role was that of a fat clown. In *The Inner Temple Masque* Plumporridge is said to move 'like one of the great porridge-tubs Going to the counter'. He was a clown in his own *All's Lost by Lust*; he seems to have been the fat bishop in *A Game at Chess*; and the fat clown role appears in several of the plays written for the King's company while he was a member. Mr. Baldwin has good reason for assigning him the parts of Bustopha in *The Maid in the Mill*, Tony in *A Wife for a Month*, the Cook in the original cast of *Rollo or The Bloody Brother*, Cacafogo in *Rule a Wife and Have a Wife*, and the Clown in *The Fair Maid of the Inn* (*Organization and Personnel*, pp. 214, 382).

1615/16, Mar. 20—He was the first to sign the debt-funding agreement of Prince's with Alleyn and Meade. (*Hens. Paps.*, pp. 90–1.)

1616–17—He was second to sign the letter of the Prince's men to Alleyn asking for his help in finding a theatre and a loan. (Ibid., p. 93 ; see above, p. 200, n. 3.)

1618/19, Jan. or Feb.—'Plumporridge. W. Rowley' in the cast of Middleton's *Inner Temple Masque or Masque of Heroes*. (1619 4° B.M.)

1620—John Taylor's *Praise of Hempseed* mentions him in the following lines (Stork, *Rowley*, pp. 11–12):

> And many there are living at this day
> Which do in paper their true worth display,
> As Davis, Drayton and the learned Dun (Donne),
> Johnson and Chapman, Master Middleton,
> With Rowley, Fletcher, Withers, Massinger,
> Heywood, and all the rest where'er they are.

>1620—The 1633 title-page of Rowley's *All's Lost by Lust*, acted not later than 1620, says, '*Divers times Acted by the Lady* Elizabeths Servants. And now lately by her Maiesties Servants, with great applause, at the *Phoenix* in *Drury Lane*'. The dramatis personae of this edition has '*Iaques*, a simple clownish Gentleman, his sonne, personated by the Poet'. (1633 4° HN.; see above, p. 215.)

1621—He wrote an elegy on the death of his fellow, Hugh Attwell (q.v.).

1623, Aug. 29—No. 4 in King's cast for *The Maid in the Mill*. (1679 folio B.M.)

1624, Aug.—Apparently he played the fat bishop in Middleton's *A Game at Chess*. His known roles and the date of his death fit the allusion in Jonson's *Staple of News*, iii. 2:

> Tho. O! yes.
> There is a *Legacy* left to the *Kings Players*,
> Both for their various shifting of their *Scene*,
> And dext'rous change o' their persons to all shapes,
> And all disguises: by the right reuerend
> *Archbishop* of *Spalato*. Lic. He is dead,
> That plai'd him! Tho. Then, h'has lost his share o' the Legacy.

(De Winter, *Staple of News*, pp. 66–7.) The play was acted in Feb. 1625/6 (ibid., p. xviii), and first published in 1631. Though no separate copies of the 1631 edition are extant, a number of them were bound into the folio of 1640. See also R. C. Bald, *T.L.S.*, 6 Feb. 1930, p. 102. The scene in question is iii. 2, not iii. 1, as stated in the letter.

1624, >Sept.—Dekker testified 24 March 1625/6 that Rowley was one of the authors of *Keep the Widow Waking*. (Sisson, *Keep the Widow Waking*, p. 258.)

1624, Dec. 20—No. 10 in submission of King's for playing *The Spanish Viceroy*. (*Herbert*, p. 21, and see above, pp. 14–15.)

1625, >May 5—'William Rowley' was the third member of Prince's listed in a warrant for black cloth for King James's funeral procession. (*M.S.C.* ii. 326.)

1625, June 24—No. 8 in patent for King's. (Ibid. i. 282–3.)

1625/6, Feb. 11—'William Rowley, householder', bur. St. J.C.

1625/6, Feb. 16—'Grace relict of William Rowley' appeared before Henry Durham, notary public, and renounced the administration of his estate. (Miss M. J. Dickson, *T.L.S.*, 28 Mar. 1929.)

1632—The title-page of *A New Wonder, A Woman Never Vext* says that it was '*Written by* William Rowley, *one of his Maiesties Servants*'. (1632 4° B.M.)

1639—The old joke about rape seed is told about William Rowley in *A Banquet of Jests*. The anecdote begins, 'A Handsome young fellow having seene a Play at the *Curtaine*, comes to *William Rowley* after the Play was done, and entreated him if his leisure served, that he might give him a Pottle of Wine, to be better acquainted with him. Hee thankt him, and told him, if hee pleased to goe as farre as the Kings head at the Spittle gate, hee would as soone as hee had made himselfe ready follow him, and accept of his kindnesse.' (1639 ed. HN, pp. 50–1.)

RUSSELL, JOHN. The extant records indicate that John Russell's chief asset was the friendship of Edward Alleyn. Bird's letter implies that Russell was a hired man in the Palsgrave's company who was tolerated only because of Alleyn and who was something of a problem for the company. His continued residence in one of the Fortune tenements after the new theatre was built in 1622 suggests that his connexion with the Palsgrave's men may have continued too.

c. 1617?—The following letter, inscribed 'To his loving frend, Mr. Allin, giue these', is undated. (J. P. Collier, *Alleyn Papers* [Shakespeare Society], 1843, pp. 32–3.)

Sir, There is one Jhon Russell, that by youre apoyntment was made a gatherer with vs, but my fellowes finding [him often] falce to vs, haue many tymes warned him from taking the box; and he as often, with moste damnable othes, hath vowde neuer to touch: yet, notwithstanding his execrable othes, he hath taken the box, and many tymes moste vnconsionablye gatherd, for which we haue resolud he shall neuer more come to the doore. Yet, for your sake, he shall haue his wages, to be a nessessary attendaunt on the stage, and if he will pleasure himself and vs to mend our garments, when he hath leysure, weele pay him for that to. I pray send vs word if this motion will satisfye you; for him, his dishonestye is such we knowe it will not. Thus yealding ourselues in that and a farr greater matter to be comaunded by you, I committ you to God. Your loving frend to comaund, W. Birde.

1618, July 8—'botell ale att Jo: Russells'. (Alleyn's Diary, Young, ii. 94.)

1618, Oct. 31—In the Palsgrave's lease of the Fortune from Alleyn, Russell is mentioned as occupying a tenement of two rooms adjoining the playhouse, for which he paid 24s. per year rent by a ninety-nine year lease dated 20 June 1617. (*Hens. Paps.*, pp. 27–8.)

1619, May 9—'w: pare & His wife Jo: Russel & His wife toby Harison & ye carver & garrell dind wt vs.' (Alleyn's Diary, Young, ii. 134.)

1619, Aug. 8—'pd: Jo: Russell His Legacie giuen by my mother Henslowe.' (Ibid., p. 146.)

1619, Aug. 10—'pd Jo: Rusell when He Receiued His 10^l . . . o 10 6.'
(Ibid., p. 147.)

1619, Sept.—In his list of household expenses for the quarter ending
at Michaelmas, Alleyn records, 'to Jo: Russell for orace . . . o 10 6'.
(Ibid., p. 155.)

1622, May 20—In a lease to Charles Massey of part of the new Fortune, Russell is mentioned as occupying a tenement in the new
building. (*MSS. Dul.*, p. 243; *Hens. Paps.*, pp. 28–9.)

SACKVILLE, EDWARD (*see* DORSET, EARL OF).

SACKVILLE, THOMAS. Sackville was an English player in
Germany from 1592 to at least 1602. Though he remained in
Germany until his death in 1628, he was a merchant and appar-
ently never a player in the last twenty or twenty-five years of his
life. (See Herz, *Englische Schauspieler*, pp. 10, 11, 17, 32–6, and
Cohn, *Sh. in Ger.*, pp. xxix, xxxiii–xxxv.)

SANDERS, WILLIAM. There is only a possibility that the attendant of the King's company may have been the father of Elizabeth
or the husband of Thomasin Pascal.

1610, Sept. 5—'Elizabeth Sanders the Daster of William' bur. St.
G.F.

1624, Dec. 27—Herbert exempted him from arrest as an attendant of
King's. (*Herbert*, p. 74; see above, pp. 15–16.)

1633/4, Mar. 6—'Willm. Sanders & Thomasin Pascal. l[icence]' mar.
St. Anne's Blackfriars.

1643, Dec. 12—'William Sanders from Captaine Hammonds' bur. St.
Anne's Blackfriars.

SANDERSON, GEORG. A strolling player who may have been
the same as Gregory Sanderson (q.v.).

1639/40, Jan. 9—'given to Georg Corden Servaunt to the Earle of
Leic, Willm Johnson servaunt to the lord Clifford Georg Sanderson
servant to the Lord Goring & 13 more assistants players who had
the Kings patent to play xlviii^s ii^d . . .' at Coventry. (Murray, ii.
254.)

SANDERSON, GREGORY. Sanderson is probably the most likely
candidate for the Sands of Daborne's *Poor Man's Comfort*, since
he is the only one known to have been attached to the Cockpit,
where the play was presented.

c. 1617—Perhaps the 'Sands' in the stage directions of Daborne's
Poor Man's Comfort. (*See* James Sands.)

1619, >May 13—'Gregorie Saunderson' was fifteenth in the list of
Queen Anne's men who received black cloth for her funeral procession. (*M.S.C.* ii. 325.)

SANDS, JAMES. The only certain records of James Sands are in
the wills of Augustine Phillips (1605) and William Sly (1608); in
the former he is called Phillips's apprentice. Sir Edmund Chambers suggests (Chambers, *Shakespeare*, ii. 85–6) that Sands was

probably apprenticed to Phillips as a musician. On the basis of Phillips's will, Mr. Baldwin outlines a career for Sands in Shakespeare's company from 1601 to 1613. (Baldwin, *Organization*, pp. 278–9, 382, 410, 423–5.) The name in the stage directions of *The Poor Man's Comfort* is the only reason for thinking that he was ever connected with Queen Anne's (or any later) company—a rather flimsy reason when the better claim of Gregory Sanderson and the equally good one of Thomas Sands are considered.

It has been several times noted that a James Sands appears in the token books of St. Saviour's Southwark in various years from 1593 to 1632. It has not been pointed out, however, that several children of James Sands, waterman, are baptized in the parish from 1594/5 to 1612. The waterman is certainly the man in the token books—in the earlier entries, at any rate, when the player was too young to have been mentioned in the token-book lists.

c. 1617—In the 1655 quarto of Daborne's *Poor Man's Comfort*, Act II, is the stage direction, '*Enter 2. Lords, Sands, Ellis*'.

SANDS, THOMAS. If one could be sure that the stage directions of *The Poor Man's Comfort* belonged to a 1617 performance and those of *Money Is an Ass* to a 1635 performance, Thomas Sands would be out of the question as one of the Lords in the former play. The stage directions of *The Poor Man's Comfort* may, however, belong to a late revival, and the date of Jordan's play is most uncertain.

c. 1617—Conceivably the 'Sands' in the stage directions of Daborne's *Poor Man's Comfort*. (*See* James Sands.)

1634/5, Mar. 10—His name is in the long list of players at Norwich; some of them are King's Revels men, though the records do not give the name of the company, which was probably an amalgamation. (Murray, ii. 356; see above, pp. 286 and 288–9.)

c. 1635?—'Callumney. *Tho. Sandes*', appears in the cast for Thomas Jordan's *Money Is an Ass* which is printed in the 1668 quarto. (1668 4° B.M.) (*See* Thomas Jordan.)

SAVAGE, RAPHE. A Raphe Savage was one of the defendants in the *Keep the Widow Waking* suit in 1624. Professor Sisson thinks that he had succeeded to Aaron Holland's interests in the Red Bull theatre. (Sisson, *Keep the Widow Waking*, pp. 236–7.) Thomas Dekker said in his deposition that the four dramatists wrote the play 'vpp on the instrucc̃ons giuen them by one Raph Savage' (ibid., p. 258), a statement which implies that Savage was concerned in the management of the company at the Red Bull.

SAVILL, ARTHUR.

1631, Dec.—'*Quartilla, Gentlewoman to Triphœna*. Arthur Savill', appears in the cast of *Holland's Leaguer*, acted by Prince Charles's (II) men at Salisbury Court this month. (*Herbert*, p. 45, and 1632 4° B.M.)

SCHADLEUTNER, Sebastian. A man of this name was at Nuremberg in 1623 with the company of John Spencer, the English actor. (Herz, *Englische Schauspieler*, p. 52.)

SCHOTTNELL, Edward (*see* SHATTERELL, EDWARD).

SEABROOK, Thomas. He is known only as a member of the strange Lady Elizabeth's of 1628 (see above, pp. 188–90). There is no evidence either to identify him with or distinguish him from the Thomas Seabrooke of Bagshot Park or the Thomas Seabrook of the Court of High Commission.

1629, July 2—The L.C. Books record a warrant 'to sweare Thomas Seabrooke A Groome of the Chamber in ordinary'. In the margin is written, 'Queene of Bohemia's Players'. (*M.S.C.* ii. 350.)

1630/1, Mar. 5—'Grant to George Dawbridgecourt of the office of keeper of Bagshot Park, in the Forest of Windsor and co. Surrey, with the fee of 5*l.* 6*s.* 8*d.* per annum, on surrender of Thos. Seabrooke.' (*C.S.P., Dom.*, 1629–31, p. 527.)

1639, Nov. 14 and 21—The case of a Thomas Seabrook is mentioned in the Acts of the Court of High Commission, but no charges are referred to. (Ibid., 1639–40, pp. 273, 278.)

SEBECK, Henry. The fact that though a Lady Elizabeth's company appears frequently in the provinces between 1616 and 1622, Sebeck is mentioned only once in provincial records, and then as a leader, makes one suspicious. Possibly he had obtained the company's licence illegitimately.

1617, June 7—Henry Sebeck brought the Lady Elizabeth's patent of 27 April 1611 to Norwich and was given permission to play in time taken from Robert Lee and his company. (Murray, ii. 344.)

SHAKERLEY, Edward. It is curious that Shakerley is known as a player over a period of only two years, for he had a rather large role as the comic servant in *The Renegado*. He may have died in 1625 or 1626, but he must have had acting experience before 1624. It is conceivable that he was the 'Edward Shacklock' who appears in the registers of St. Bodolph's Aldgate in 1617 and 1620, who lived in 'Red Lion alley' in that parish, and who is once called 'Musition' in the registers (*M.L.N.* xlvi [1931], 398).

1623, May 21—In Markham's suit as 'Edwarde Shakerley in Clarken-well Close', 5*s*. (See Appendix, p. 682.)

1624, Nov. 29—'A certificate graunted to Edward Shackerly not to bee arested or imprisoned dureing the tyme of the Revells, the 29th of Nouember 1624.' (Halliwell-Phillipps, *Collections*, p. 17.)

1625—'Gazet *seruant to* Vitelli. Edward Shakerley', in Massinger's *Renegado*, presented by Queen Henrietta's company in Drury Lane. (1630 4° B.M.)

SHANBROOKE, John. Shanbrooke's occupation is known only from parish registers; his theatrical connexions are wholly un-known. One would guess from his residence that he was a hired man in the Palsgrave's company. I suspected that the Sara Dambroake buried from John Shank's house in 1624 was his widow, but her name is given again as Dambrooke in her will, which was witnessed by John and Winifred Shank.

1610, June 10—'William, sonne of John Shanbrooke, Player' chris. St. G.C.

1612, July 26—'Rachell, Dau. of John Shanbrooke, Plaier' chris. St. G.C.

1618, June 4—'Elizabeth daughter to John Shambrooke gent.' bur. St. G.C.

1618, Sept. 17—'John Shambrooke Player' bur. St. G.C.

SHANK (SCHANKS, SHANCK, SHANCKE, SHANCKES, SHANCKS, SHANKE, SHANKES, SHANKS, SHANUCKE), JOHN, sr. There were two John Shanks, players, apparently father and son, besides men of other occupations with the same name in the parish of St. Giles' Cripplegate and St. Saviour's Southwark. It is sometimes impossible to distinguish them.

The more important player, John Shank, sr., was a King's man throughout our period, but from 1610 to 1614 he had appeared as a member of the Prince Henry's–Palsgrave's company; the 1614 charge of receiving stolen goods at the playhouse implies that he had bought costumes for the Palsgrave's men, a practice which his will indicates he continued for the King's men. Shank himself said that in his youth he had been a Pembroke's and Queen Elizabeth's man, but we have no record of his connexion with these companies.

Shank came to the King's company some time between January 1612/13, when he was licensed as a Palsgrave's man, and March 1619, when he was in the King's men's patent. Mr. Baldwin thinks that he was the clown who succeeded to Armin's share after the latter's death in November 1615 (*Organization and Personnel*, p. 50). Mr. Baldwin Maxwell thinks that he came to the company not long after 1613 (*Phil. Quart.* v. 299–305). I do not see how the date can be fixed at present. Shank certainly succeeded Armin as clown, but he may have come to the company some time before Armin's death.

Shank's name does not appear in casts so often as those of other sharers because, as comedian, his roles often had few lines. Baldwin Maxwell (op. cit.) makes a good case for Shank as the hungry knave of the Beaumont and Fletcher plays—Corporal Judas in *Bonduca*, Geta in *The Prophetess*, Mallfort in *The Lover's Progress*, Lazarillo in *Love's Cure*, Onos in *The Queen of Corinth*, and Penurio in *Women Pleased*. His known roles of Sir Roger in *The Scornful Lady*, Hilario in *The Picture*, and Hodge in *The Soddered Citizen* are clown roles. In the last he provides low comedy, depending on a broad dialect, stupidity, and clownish capering. As Petella in *The Wild Goose Chase* he has no lines at all, and Mr. Baldwin suggests that Shank was simply assigned the part in order that he might be on hand to coach the two apprentices on whom he attends (*Organization and Personnel*, p. 176). It seems to me that such a supposition assumes a rather low standard for performances at Blackfriars, for each of the apprentices whom Shank attends had had at least six years' experience in the company. It is more probable that Shank was allowed to gag his lines, since the character has little real function in the play.

John Shank is associated with a larger number of apprentices than any other member of the King's company—Burt, Pollard, Thompson, Honyman, and Holcomb, and with three unnamed boys in 1635—a fact which suggests that he may have cared for extra boys as part of his service to the company. Shank himself implies this when he says that of his own purse he supplied the company for the service of His Majesty with boys. Possibly this apprentice boarding-house is the explanation of the large number of persons buried from Shank's house in Cripplegate.

Shank's fame as a jig maker and dancer is referred to in Heminges's line, 'Bass for a ballad, Iohn Shanke for a Iigg', in the line from Turner's *Dish of Lenten Stuff* (*Pepysian Garland*, p. 35), probably before 1616,

> Since Shanke did leaue to sing his rimes
> he is counted but a gull,

and probably in Sir Henry Herbert's licence of *Shanckes Ordinary* in March 1623/4. Since his talent is referred to by Heminges as late as 1632, the King's company must have made more use of the jig than is ordinarily supposed.

Probably 'Shankes Song', which J. P. Collier first noted, was associated by his contemporaries with his talent as a jig maker. Mr. W. J. Lawrence, who notes that the song exists in several versions as 'Shankes Song', 'The Irish Beggar', or 'The Irish Footman's Ochone', calls it a pathetic character song (*M.L.R.* xxv. 211). Versions were printed in *Wits Restored* (1658) and *Westminster Drollery*, Part II (1672).

These various references to his compositions suggest that Shank was more familiar to the Jacobean and Caroline audience than his assigned roles in plays would lead one to believe. That he was a well-known figure in the theatre is demonstrated by an interesting and flagrantly undramatic pun in Clavell's *Soddered Citizen*, acted about 1630. The MS. of this play contains a King's cast (see above, pp. 84–5) which shows that Shank played the role of the clown Hodge. At the end of the third scene of Act IV, Brainsicke orders, 'Goe & direct him *Shackle*, *Hodge*, about it, with all the speed thy nimble *shankes* can carry'. And Hodge replies, in the dialect which is his chief distinction in the play, 'Chill bee shanke all ore, to make the weeder strides'. Such a pun on his own name by the actor playing Hodge certainly depended on the familiarity of the audience with his identity. It indicates further that the audience was sufficiently interested in Shank to tolerate the reminder that the clown on the stage was not Hodge, the countryman of the play, but their old favourite, John Shank, comedian of the King's company.

The problem of disentangling the King's comedian from the other John Shanks at St. Giles' Cripplegate is a complex one. Since the actor calls himself a weaver in his will, the chandler, the cutler, and the grocer in St. Giles can be eliminated. I think that all the player entries must refer to the King's man, for my impression is that the Fortune actor of the same name, who does not certainly appear as a player until 1640, was too young to have been the father of Winifred in 1626. If this conjecture is true, none of the other player entries can refer to the Fortune player. Since the will of Sara Dambrooke, made three days before her burial, was witnessed by John and *Winifred* Shank, it was probably the player's house from which she was buried. And since the player was called gentleman in this instance, he is probably indicated in the other records of John Shank, gentleman. Of the other entries I am most uncertain. I have printed all the records in this period of men named John Shank at St. Giles in order to have all evidence for his identification at hand.

The John Shank who appears in the token books of St. Saviour's Southwark in 1605, 1617, 1620, and 1624, and in the registers as gardener and gentleman, was surely not the player, who seems always to have lived in St. Giles. The records of that parish show how common the name was.

1610, Dec. 31—'A sonne John Shanckes Player' bur. St. G.C.

1611/12, Feb. 10—'Elizabeth Daughter of John Shanck, Plaier' chris. St. G.C.

1614, Dec. 24—'Charles Mercy [Marcy] of St. Giles'-without-Cripplegate, gentleman, and Richard Moreton of London, ironmonger, for John Shanke of St. Giles' aforesaid, gentleman, to answer Henry Udall [Uvedall] of Drury Lane, linen-draper, for buying four network bands and a pair of cuffs at the Playhouse at an under-rate, being part of the goods which were stolen from the said Henry; and of William Flod [Flud] of St. Mary-le-Strand [Westminster], gentleman, and Edward Udall of Drury Lane, victualler, for the said Henry to give evidence against the said John; and of Henry Udall of the Strand, gentleman, and the said William and Edward for Richard Caulton of the same, yeoman, and for the said William and Edward; and of William Boulton of St. Mary-le-Strand, merchant-adventurer, and Robert Greene of the same, saddler, for the said Henry, all to appear.' (*Middx. Sessions*, ii. 188.)

1614/15, Mar. 22—'A dau. of John Shancke, Gentleman' bur. St. G.C.

1615/16, Mar. 16—'John Sonne of John Shanck yoman' chris. St. G.C.

1617, Oct. 7—'Robert sonne of Robert Petchey from John Shanck in Golding Lane' bur. St. G.C.

1617/18, Jan. 13—He witnessed Richard Cowley's will. (See Appendix, p. 642.)

1618, Oct. 16—'Susan Rodes, svant to John Shanckes player' bur. St. G.C.

1619,. Mar. 27—No. 12 in patent for King's. (*M.S.C.* i. 280–2.)

1619, May 19—No. 10 in livery allowance list for King's. (*Hist. MSS. Com.*, Report IV, p. 299.)

1619, Aug. 1—'James sonne of John Shancks, gentleman' chris. St. G.C.

1620/1, Feb. 2—'John Sonne of John Shanks, Chandler' chris. St. G.C.

1621, Apr. 7—No. 10 in livery allowance list for King's. (*Hist. MSS. Com.*, Report IV, p. 299.)

1621, Nov. 18—'Thomas sonne of John Shancks Gentleman' chris. St. G.C. Buried 1 Dec. 1621.

1622, May 14—No. 3 in King's cast for *The Prophetess*. (1679 folio B.M.)

1622, June 1—'Grace·wife of Blacknall of Oxford from the howse of John Shancks' bur. St. G.C.

1623—'Iohn Shancke' was twenty-fifth in the actor list of the Shakespeare folio. (First Folio B.M.)

1623, Aug. 3—'Wynefred d. of John Shancks, player' chris. St. G.C.

1623/4, Mar. 16—'For the king's company. *Shankes Ordinary*, written by Shankes himself, this 16 March, 1623,—1*l*. 0*s*. 0*d*.' (*Herbert*, p. 27.)

1624, Sept. 1—John[1] and Winifred Shank witnessed the will of Mrs. Sara Dambrooke. (See Appendix, p. 642.)

1624, Sept. 11—'Mrs. Sara Dambroake widow from the house of John Shanck, gentleman' bur. St. G.C.

1624, Nov. 12—'Maryan Porter, widow from yᵉ house of John Shanck gentleman' bur. St. G.C.

1624, Dec. 20—No. 8 in submission of King's for playing *The Spanish Viceroy*. (*Herbert*, p. 21; see above, pp. 14–15.)

1625, >May 5—'Iohn Shancke' was eighth in the list of 'The King Players' who received black cloth for James's funeral procession. (*M.S.C.* ii. 325.)

1625, June 24—No. 7 in King's patent. (Ibid. i. 282–3.)

1625, July 27—'Anne dau of John Shanke Cutler' bur. St. G.C.

1626, May 14—'Wynefred Da: of John Shankes, player' chris. St. G.C.

1628, May 11—'William sonn of John Shanks grocer' chris. St. G.C.

1628—'Iohn Shanck' was fourth in the King's cast for *The Lover's Melancholy* (the roles are not given), lic. 24 Nov. 1628. (1629 4° B.M.)

1629, May 6—'Iohn Shank' was fifth in the list of King's men named in a warrant for cloak allowances. (*M.S.C.* ii. 350.)

1629—'*Hilario*, seruant to *Sophia*. Iohn Shanucke' in King's cast for Massinger's *The Picture*, lic. 8 June. (1630 4° B.M.)

1629, June 16—'Wynefred Dau: of John Shanck Player' bur. St. G.C.

---

[1] This was pretty surely the player, as his will establishes the fact that his wife was named Winifred. Since we know, then, that the Shank called gentleman in the next entry was the player, the other entries concerning John Shank, Gentleman, may refer to him, too.

c. 1630—'*Hodge—A countrey fellowe*—John Shanke' in King's cast in the MS. of Clavell's (?) *Soddered Citizen*. '*A Mayde—Ser: to Miniona*—John: Shanks Boy.' (*Sod. Cit.*, p. 3.)

1630/1, Jan. 26—'John Shankes And Eliz Martin' mar. St. G.C.

1631, June 12—'Received of Mr. Shanke, in the name of the kings company, for the benefitt of their summer day, upon yͤ second daye of *Richard yͤ Seconde*, at the Globe, this 12 of June, 1631,— 5*l*. 6*s*. 6*d*.' (Herbert, p. 44.)

c. 1632—His fame as a jig maker is referred to in Heminges's *Elegy on Randolph's Finger*, one part of which has been frequently quoted under the title, *On the Time Poets*, 'Bass for a ballad, Iohn Shanke for a Iigg'. (Hemminges's *Elegy*, p. 14.)

1632—'PETELLA, their waiting-woman. Their Servant Mr *Shanck*' in the King's cast for the 1632 revival of *The Wild Goose Chase*, printed in 1652. (1652 ed. B.M.)

c. 1633—In his answer to the petition in 1635 of Benfield, Pollard, and Swanston, Shank said, 'That about allmost 2 yeeres since, your suppłt vpon offer to him made by William Hemings did buy of him one part hee had in the Blackfriers for about 6 yeeres then to come at the yeerly rent of 6ˡⁱ 5ˢ. & another part hee then had in yͤ Globe for about two yeeres to come & payd him for the same two partes in ready moneys 156ˡⁱ which sayd partes were offered to yʳ suppłt . . .' (*M.S.C.* ii. 367.)

c. 1634—In the same document Shank said, 'That about 11 months since the sayd Wᵐ Hemings offering to sell vnto yʳ suppͭ the remaining partes hee then had (viz) one in the Blackfriers, wherin hee had then about 5 yeeres to come & two in yͤ Globe wherin hee had then but one yeere to come, yoʳ suppłt likewise bought the same & payd for them in ready moneys more 350ˡⁱ . . .' (Ibid.)

1635, May 18–June 12—In the same petition, Shank said of himself that he 'hath still of his owne purse supplyed the company for the service of his Maᵗʸ wᵗʰ boyes as Thomas Pollard, Iohn Thompson deceased (for whome Hee payd 40ˡⁱ) yoʳ suppłt hauing payd his part of 200ˡⁱ for other boyes since his comîng to yͤ Company, Iohn Honiman, Thomas Holcome ·and diuerse others & at this time maintaines 3 more for the sayd service'. (Ibid., p. 369.)

1635, May 18—Benfield, Pollard, and Swanston in their petition to the Lord Chamberlain about shares in the Globe and Blackfriars say that several years before Shank had purchased three shares in the Globe from William Heminges (therefore not before Oct. 1630), and two shares in the Blackfriars from the same man. (Ibid. pp. 362–6.)

1635, June 6—It was probably John Shank, jr., and not John Shank, sr., who was at Norwich with Richard Weeks as the leader of a company. (Murray, ii. 357; see John Shank, jr.)

1635, Aug. 1—Shank said in a petition to the Lord Chamberlain that he had made a proposition to his fellows for the sale of his Globe and Blackfriars shares, but that they had refused it and restrained him from the stage. (*M.S.C.* ii. 372–3.)

1635, Dec. 31—'John Shanke one of his Maᵗˢ servants the Players, and Cittizen and weaver of London', made his will. He left legacies to his sons John and James, to his daughter Elizabeth Bowen, presumably a widow, and his 'little Grandchild' Winifrid

Bowen, and the bulk of his estate to his wife, Winifrid, who was made executrix. The estate, he said, 'doth consist for the most part in a Lease which I haue for a few yeares of Two Eight parts in the Blackfryers Playhouse, and of a Lease which I am to have of Three Eight parts in the moity of the Globe Playhouse for the Terme of Nyne yeares from Christmas last which I bought, and paid deere for.' (See Appendix, pp. 646–8.)

1635/6, Jan. 27—' Iohn Shanke, Player', bur. St. G.C.

>1639, Aug. 26—His wife seems to have married a man named Fitche. (See the will of Richard Benfield, Appendix, p. 634.)

>1642—Wright says, '*Burt* was a Boy first under *Shank* at the *Black-friers*' (*Hist. Hist.*, p. 3), and '*Pollard*, and *Robinson* were Come-dians, so was *Shank* who used to Act *Sir Roger*, in the *Scornful Lady*' (ibid., p. 4). Oliphant says of the *Scornful Lady*, ' It had, in fact, been acted by the King's men in 1624, when the part of the Curate had been played by Shanck' (Oliphant, pp. 207–8). I can find no evidence that there was a performance of this play by the King's company in 1624.

SHANK (SCHANCKES, SHANCKES, SHANKES, SHAUNKS), JOHN, jr. The John Shank who performed at the Fortune was probably a son of the King's comedian, who mentions his wild son John in his will. He may have been the John Shank christened at St. Giles in March 1615/16, but the name is too common and the designation yeoman too vague for certainty. He was probably the John Shankes who married Elizabeth Martin, for he did have a wife Elizabeth in 1638 or 1640. The son of the King's comedian, and presumably the Fortune actor, is identified in Benfield's will and the Fortune suit by the name of his mother, Winifred, who is conspicuous in the will of the elder John Shank.

The court's award of alimony to his wife in 1640 and the account of his conduct after the battle in October 1642 seem to confirm the opinion expressed in the will of John Shank, sr.

1615/16, Mar. 16—' John Sonne of John Shanck yoman' chris. St. G.C.

1630/1, Jan. 26—' John Shankes And Eliz Martin' mar. St. G.C.

1635, June 6—' This day Richard Weeks ånd John Shanke brought into this Court a Bill signed wth his Maties hand and privie signett dated the last day of Aprill in the nynth yeare of his Maties Reigne, and a lycence vnder the seale of his Maties Revells dated the second of March last & contynuinge till the second of September next, They have leaue to play here till the xviii^th of this moneth.' (Murray, ii. 357.)

1635, Dec. 31—John Shank, sr., in his will bequeathed ' vnto my Two sonnes John and James Shanke vnto, and for whom I have already disbursed diuers soṁes of money, amountinge togeither in the wholl to a farr greater somme then their parts in my estate would any way come vnto, the severall soṁes of Tenn pounds a peece of law-full english money, which I require them from rest satisfied with as my guift and bequeast vnto them, leaving them to their mother and my Executrix to deale better with them if they shalbe loving, and obedient vnto her. . . . And I doe hereby require charge, and

Commaund my said Two sonnes John and James Shanke, That they nor either of them doe goe about to molest, trouble or hinder my wife their mother in the receiving and taking of this my estate or in thexecucon of this my will. . . .' (See Appendix, pp. 646–8.)

c. 1638 or *c.* 1640—In a bill in Chancery *Dulwich College* v. *Tobias Lisle and Thomas Grymes* (three copies, two endorsed 1647 and one endorsed 1649), with answers, proofs, and notes, Lisle in his answer says that '"about 9 yeares synce" he became assignee of a half-share in trust for Elizabeth Shanckes, his interest in which, at the request of the same Elizabeth and her husband, he afterwards made over to Winifred Shanckes'. (*MSS. Dul.*, pp. 245–7.)

1639, Aug. 20—Richard Benfield in his will bequeathed 'to Mrs Winifred ffitche and her sonne Mr John Shancke vnto each of them the some of fforty shillings'. (See Appendix, p. 634.)

1639/40, Feb. 8—Acts of the Court of High Commission: 'John Shaunks, actor, of the "Fortune" playhouse. Appeared and was sworn.' (*C.S.P., Dom.*, 1640, p. 393.)

1639/40, Feb. 13—'John Shaunks, an actor at the "Fortune" playhouse. Referred to Sir Nathaniel Brent to ascertain his income from the playhouse and otherwise, and out of his means to allot alimony to his wife.' (Ibid., p. 396.)

1640, Dec. 17—'A warr^t to sweare Iohn Shanke a Groome of the Chamber in Ordinary w^thout ffee to attend the Prince his Highnes in ye Quality of a Player.' (*M.S.C.* ii. 396.)

1641, Oct. 12—'John sonne of John Shankes' bur. St. G.F.

1642, Oct. 25—The following account (quoted with inaccuracies by Collier, *H.E.D.P.* iii. 485–6) appears in *A Perfect Diurnall* under the date 'Tuesday 25. Octob:' [1642] (B.M. copy):

This day there came three of the Lord Generalls Officers post from the Army to London, signifying that there was a great fight on Sunday last, and being brought to the Parliament and examined, it appeared they were not sent from the Armie with any letters or otherwise, but in a cowardly manner run from their Captains at the beginning of the fight & had most basely possessed the people as they came away, and at their comming to towne with many false rumours, giving forth in speeches that there were 20000 men kill'd on both sides, and that there were not foure men in all their companies escaped with life besides themselves, and many other strange wonders though altogether false, it being rather conceived that their companyes like themselves upon the beginning of the fight, very valiantly took their heeles and ran away.

And after further enquiry was made after these Commanders, it was no wonder to heare their strange news, for they were Captaine *Wilson*, Lieutenant *Whitney*, and one *Shanks* a player; an Affadavit was offered to bee made that one of them said before he went out with the Earle of Essex, that he would take the Parliaments pay, but would never fight against any of the Kings party, and the other two were very rude and insolent persons, where-upon the House ordered they should all three be committed to the Gatehouse and brought to condigne punishment according to Martiall Law for their base cowardlinesse.

Confirmation of the facts of this episode is found in ' A Collection of Speciall Passages and Certaine Informations of all the most memorable Accidents and Remarkable Truths from . . . *Munday* Octob 17 till Tuseday Novemb. 1. 1642', under the date Tuesday, 25 October:

> There were three officers of the Lord Generalls Army namely one Captaine *Willson* Leiuetennant *Whitney* and Lieuetennant *Shankes* that came this day post to London, and being brought to the Parliament and examined, it appeared that they had run from their Companies at the beginning of the Skirmish, and had possessed the Country as they came along with false Rumors telling them that there were 20000. killed on both sides, and other false reports where upon they were sent to the Gatehouse by order of Parliament.

SHARPE, RICHARD. The large number of casts in which he is mentioned is good evidence that Richard Sharpe was one of the more important actors of the company, though his early death kept him from appearing so often in contemporary references as some of the others. After 1625 (his particular role is given in only one cast before this date) Sharpe played young romantic leads like Lysander in *The Deserving Favorite* and Wittworth in *The Soddered Citizen*, and he had not yet outgrown this type of part at the time of his death in January 1631/2.

Before 1625, however, he had acted for a number of years and is known to have had important parts in at least thirteen plays, though his particular role is mentioned only once. This one role was the Duchess in *The Duchess of Malfi*. From this fact and from an analysis of the plays in which Sharpe appeared and of the lines of certain characters, Mr. Baldwin concludes that for several years before 1623 Sharpe had been the leading lady of the company, playing queens and Amazonian types, beautiful, proud, and overbearing. The lines indicate that he was physically rather large. Mr. Baldwin assigns to him the roles, among others, of Enanthe in *The Humorous Lieutenant*, Hippolyta in *The Custom of the Country*, Cleopatra in *The False One*, Martia in *The Double Marriage*, and Quisara in *The Island Princess*. (*Organization and Personnel*, pp. 186, 220–1, 198.)

Mr. Baldwin's contention that Sharpe played Barnavelt's wife in *Barnavelt* and that the MS. stage direction ' nich ' is a misreading for ' rich ' is untenable, for an examination of the MS. (which Baldwin had not seen) makes it very clear that ' nich 'is the correct reading. Nevertheless, Mr. Baldwin's analysis of type and assignment of roles to Sharpe is one of the more effective applications of his method. He carries through his analysis of age references in the roles to conclude that Sharpe must have been born about 1602 and have come to the King's company about 1612 (op. cit., pp. 220–1). He had become a sharer by 1624, when he appeared in *The Spanish Viceroy* submission and in a certificate of

protection. Probably he had been admitted in the year 1623 or
1624; Mr. Baldwin thinks that he succeeded Robert Goffe (op.
cit., pp. 54 and 58).

Sharpe's bill for stockings, his debt which Heminges was to pay
by deductions from his earnings, and his illegitimate child suggest
that he was a rather dashing young actor of a type not yet wholly
extinct.

1616—No. 7 in King's cast for *The Mad Lover*. (1679 folio B.M.)

1616–18—No. 4 in King's cast for *The Knight of Malta*. (Ibid.)

1618, Nov. 16—No. 4 in King's cast for *The Loyal Subject*. (Ibid.)

1619?—No. 4 in King's cast for *The Laws of Candy*. (Ibid.)

1619?—No. 3 in King's cast for *The Humorous Lieutenant*. (Ibid.)

c. 1619–20—No. 7 in King's cast for *The Custom of the Country*.
(Ibid.)

1619–21—No. 4 in King's cast for *Women Pleased*. (Ibid.)

1619–21—No. 4 in King's cast for *The Island Princess*. (Ibid.)

1619–22—No. 7 in King's cast for *The Little French Lawyer*. (Ibid.)

1619–23—'The Dutchesse, R. Sharpe', in King's cast prefixed to the
1623 quarto of *The Duchess of Malfi*. Since only one name is given
for the part, he may have played the role in both the original production, >1614, and the revival of 1619–23. (1623 4° B.M.)

c. 1620—No. 4 in King's cast for *The False One*. (1679 folio
B.M.)

c. 1621—No. 8 in King's cast for *The Double Marriage*. (Ibid.)

1622, May 14—No. 4 in King's cast for *The Prophetess*. (Ibid.)

1622, Oct. 24—Fleay, followed by Professor Murray, says that Sharpe
is No. 6 in the King's cast for *The Spanish Curate*. This statement
is an error, for Benfield is No. 6 in the cast, and Sharpe is not listed
at all. (Ibid.)

1623, Dec. 6—No. 7 in King's cast for *The Lover's Progress*. (Ibid.)

1624, Dec. 20—No. 11 in submission of King's for playing *The Spanish
Viceroy*. (*Herbert*, p. 21; see above, pp. 14–15.)

1624, Dec. 29—'A certificate graunted to Richard Sharpe the 29° of
December 1624 not to bee arested or imprisoned dureinge the tyme
of the Revells.' (Halliwell-Phillipps, *Collection*, p. 17.)

1625, >May 5—'Richard Sharpe' was fifth in the list of King's men
named in a warrant to receive black cloth for James's funeral.
(*M.S.C.* ii. 325.)

1625, June 24—No. 12 in list of King's for a patent. (Ibid. i. 282–3.)

1626—'*Parthenius* a free-man of *Caesars*. Richard Sharpe', in King's
cast for Massinger's *Roman Actor*, lic. 11 October. (1629 4° B.M.)

1625–9—Probably he was the actor Sharpe, a friend of William
Condell, whom young Condell's master, the haberdasher Edward
Pate, says Condell allowed to run up a bill of 41s. 10d. for stockings.
(Barnard, *New Links*, p. 40.)

1628—No. 7 in King's cast for *The Lover's Melancholy*, lic. 24 Nov.
(1629 4° B.M.)

1628, Nov. 24—A Henry Jenkins petitioned the Lord Chamberlain
against Sharpe for a debt of 50s. The Lord Chamberlain told
Heminges to satisfy the petitioner out of money accruing to Sharpe
for his share or dividend. (*See* Heminges, p. 469.)

1629, May 6—No. 7 in list of King's for cloak allowance. (*M.S.C.* ii. 350.)

1629—'*Ferdinand* Generall of the army. *Richard Sharpe*', in King's cast for Massinger's *The Picture*, lic. 8 June. (1630 4° B.M.)

1629?—'M^r. *Sharpe, Lysander*', in King's cast for Carlell's *The Deserving Favorite*. (1629 4° B.M.)

c. 1630—'*Sr. Wittworth—A younge gent' of qualitie*—Richard Sharpe & Prologue & Epilogue', in the King's cast in the MS. of Clavell's (?) *The Soddered Citizen*. (*Sod. Cit.*, p. 3.)

1631, Sept. 6—' Richard sonne of the reputed father Richard Sharpe Player base born of the body of Margaret Smith singlewoman in the house of Wm Jones Taylor three herring Courte' chris. St. G.C. 'Richard sonne of Richard Sharpe, Player', bur. 17 September 1631.

1631—'The King of the Lombards—Sharpe', in the MS. of Arthur Wilson's *The Swisser* (B.M. Add. MS. 36759). (Feuillerat, *The Swisser*.)

1631/2, Jan. 25—' Richard Sharp, a Player' bur. St. Anne's Black-friars.

SHATTERELL (SHATTERALL, SCHOTTNEL), EDWARD. There were two actors named Shatterell, Edward and Robert. Both of them acted after the Restoration and both, probably, before the closing of the theatres. Since Wright does not give the Christian name of the Shatterell who he says was a boy under Beeston at the Cockpit and quartermaster in Sir Thomas Dallison's troop in Prince Rupert's regiment (see Appendix, pp. 692 and 694), it is difficult to tell which one he means. Robert seems a little more likely, because he was the better-known actor after the Restoration, but Wright himself may have confused the two.

Though there is no record of Edward Shatterell as an actor before 1642, his activity during the Commonwealth period implies that he must have been a player before the closing of the theatres. For his career after the Restoration, see Hotson.

1644, Nov.–1644/5, Feb.—' Edward Schottnel' was one of the English company at The Hague. (*See* Jeremiah Kite.)

1659, May 12 and 17—Edward Shatterall and Anthony Turner were bound over for appearance before the Sessions of the Peace for 'the unlawfull mainteining of Stage playes and enterludes att the Redd Bull in St. John's Street, which house he affirms that they hire of the parishioners of Clerkenwell at the rate of twenty shillings a day over and above what they have agreed to pay to-wardes releife of their poore and repairing their highwaies, and in the meane tyme to be of good behaviour and not to depart the Court without lycence'. (Sessions of the Peace Roll, *Middx. Co. Rec.* iii. 279–80.)

SHATTERELL, ROBERT. Though Robert Shatterell was a very well-known actor after the Restoration, we have just one record of his activity before the closing of the theatres. It was probably Robert, not Edward Shatterell (q.v.) of whom Wright spoke, for

Robert was the better-known actor in the time of Charles II. Robert died some time before 1684. For his Restoration career, see Hotson.

1639, Aug. 10—'Robert Shatterell' was ninth in a list of young players at the Cockpit for a ticket of privilege. (*M.S.C.* ii. 390–1.)

>1642—Wright says, '*Burt* was a Boy first under *Shank* at the *Black-friers*, then under *Beeston* at the *Cockpit*; and *Mohun*, and *Shatterel* were in the same Condition with him, at the last Place.' (*Hist. Hist.*, p. 3.)

>1645—Wright says, '*Hart* was a Lieutenant of Horse under Sir *Thomas Dallison*, in *Prince Rupert's*, Regiment, *Burt* was Cornet in the same Troop, and *Shatterel* Quartermaster.' (Ibid., p. 8. See Appendix, p. 694.)

SHERLOCK (SHEARLOCK, SHIRELOCK, SHIRLEY, SHURLOCK), WILLIAM. William Sherlock first appears as a member of Lady Elizabeth's company in 1622, though the late Chancery suit which Mr. Hotson discovered seems to indicate that Sherlock was the keeper of the theatre from the beginning. In 1625 he became a Queen Henrietta's man, and he remained with this company, so far as we know, until the theatres were closed at the beginning of the War. In 1637 Sherlock was transferred by Sir Henry Herbert, with three other leading members of the company, to the Salisbury Court theatre and joined to the best of the Revels company there. The new organization was henceforward known as Queen Henrietta's company.

The extant casts show that Sherlock played both comic and villainous roles, though more of the former than the latter. He was probably the William Sherlock of the 1638 entry in the registers of St. Giles in the Fields, for Mr. Hotson's suit shows that he lived in that parish for a number of years. One would surmise, however, that he had been succeeded as keeper of the Cockpit by Rhodes in 1636 or 1637, for he could hardly have retained this position after he went to the Salisbury Court. He may, however, have remained in the parish, or even have returned for the burial of his son. Montague Summers says (*The Playhouse of Pepys*, p. 88) that he was the William Shirley who acted in Killigrew's company after 1663.

c. 1617—He occupied the ' . . . tenement or house and a little Garden thereunto belonging next adjoining to the Cockpits . . .' as the agent of Christopher Beeston and keeper of the theatre, apparently from the opening of Beeston's theatre (between 9 Aug. 1616 and 1 Mar. 1616/17), until he was succeeded by John Rhodes some time before 1644. (Hotson, pp. 89–90.)

1622—'William Shurlock' is sixth in the list of 'the chiefe of them at the Phoenix' in Herbert's office-book. (*Herbert*, p. 63.)

1626—'*Lodam*, a fat Gentleman. *William Sherlocke*', in the Queen Henrietta's cast for Shirley's *Wedding*. (1629 4° HN.)

c. 1630—'M^r. Ruffman, *a swaggering Gentleman*; *by* William Shearlock' in the cast of Queen Henrietta's men prefixed to the 1631 quarto of Heywood's *The Fair Maid of the West*, Part I; since no actor is named for this role in the cast for Part II, he probably played it there as well. (1631 4° B.M.)

> 1634—'Brand, M. [Mr.] Shirelock, who performed excellently well', in the Queen Henrietta's cast for Davenport's *King John and Matilda*. (1655 4° B.M.)

1634, July 18—He was probably the 'Shirley' to whom Kendall referred as a leader of the Queen's company. (See above, pp. 231–2.)

1635—The Queen Henrietta's cast for Nabbes's *Hannibal and Scipio* shows that he played two parts, '*Maharball. By William Shurlock*', and '*Prusias. By William Shurlock*'. (1637 4° B.M.)

1637, *c*. Oct. 2—Herbert recorded in his office book, 'I disposed of Perkins, Sumner, Sherlock and Turner, to Salisbury Court, and joynd them with the best of that company'. (*Herbert*, p. 66.)

1638, Nov. 21—'William sonne of William Sherlock' bur. St. G.F.

SHIRLEY, JAMES. There is no evidence that the dramatist was an actor, but there is evidence that his connexion with Queen Henrietta's men at the Cockpit was closer than that of a dramatist occasionally writing for them. Some twenty of his plays were written for the company between 1625 and 1636, and on the title-page of one, *The Bird in a Cage* (1633), he is called 'Iames Shirley, Servant to Her Majesty'. This title might suggest an honour bestowed for his composition of *The Triumph of Peace*, but the play was entered in the Stationers' Register 19 March 1632/3, and the masque was not presented until 3 February 1633/4. Furthermore, when Crosfield recorded in his diary the names of the Queen's men at the Phoenix which Kendall had told him, he named 'Mr Beeston, Mr Boyer, Shirley Robinson, Clarke' (see above, pp. 231–2). Of course it is probable that Crosfield wrote Shirley in error for Sherlock, but it is also possible that he did not make a mistake.

The sum of this evidence does not prove that Shirley was attached to the Cockpit, but it does suggest the possibility that he was under contract to that theatre as Brome was to Salisbury Court, that he was associated with it in the minds of his contemporaries, and that he may have had some sort of protection as company poet. (See above, pp. 226–7.)

SILVESTER.

1625, Oct. 16—'Martyn Slatier, Robson, & Silvester late servants to the late queene Anne' were paid at Coventry. (Murray, ii. 250.)

SINCKLER, WILLIAM. While there is no assurance that William Sinckler was connected with the theatres, many of the musicians at St. Saviour's were.

1629, Sept. 6—'Elizabeth d of Willm Sinckler a Musitan' chris. St. S.S.

SLATER (SLATHIER, SLATOR, SLAUGHTER, SLAUTER), MARTIN.
Slater first appears as an Admiral's man in 1594, and he remained
with this company until 1597. Thereafter he is never found in
London except for a short period in 1608, when he was manager
of the Children of the King's Revels at Whitefriars; in a document
of this period he called himself citizen and ironmonger of London.
After he was ejected from his residence at the Whitefriars playhouse in 1608, he is not heard of again until Pembroke's order of
1616, which reveals that he had been touring as a Queen Anne's
man. He continued as the leader of a provincial troupe until 1625.
It is probable that he always travelled as a Queen's man, though
he was associated with the Children of Bristol in 1618 and though
he was twice called a servant of the late Queen Elizabeth—an
obvious mistake, perhaps of a clerk whose memories of the days
of Good Queen Bess were too strong for him—and once a servant
of the King. If Slater was a Queen's man in 1616, in the funeral
allowance list for that company in 1619, and still called a servant
'to the late queene Anne' in 1625, he is not likely to have been
a patented member of any other company in the intervening
years.

A Martin Slater is found in the token books at St. Saviour's:
from 1595 to 1601 at Bradshaw's Rents, though in the last year
the name is crossed out and replaced by that of Augustine
Phillips, and in 1602 at Norman's Rents.

1617, June 4—Pembroke sent an order of 16 July 1616 to Norwich
   condemning the use of duplicate patents and specifying amongst
   others two taken out by 'Thomas Swynnerton and Martin Slaughter
   beinge two of the Queens Ma^{ts} company of Playors hauinge sepated
   themselves from their said Company'. (Murray, ii. 343; see above,
   pp. 178–9, for full letter.)
1618, Apr.—John Edmonds, Nathaniel Clay, and Slater got a Privy
   Council Letter of Assistance for the 'Children of Her Majesty's
   Royal Chamber of Bristol'. (C.S.P., Dom., 1611–18, p. 549.)
1618, Oct. 28< >Dec. 6—'Marten Slaughter, the Queenes Players'
   received 5s. at Ludlow. (Murray, ii. 325.)
1619, >May 13—As a member of Queen Anne's company, 'Martin
   Slater' was listed eighth to receive black cloth for her funeral procession. (M.S.C. ii. 325.)
1620, Dec. 23—'Martyn Slathier one of the players of the late Queene
   Elizabeth' was paid 5s. at Coventry. (Murray, ii. 248–9.)
1621, Dec. 31—'A license vnder his Lo^{ps} hand and seale to Martyn
   Slatier, servaunt to the late Queene Ann^e and the rest of his
   fellowes and Associats to vse and exercise the acting of Tragedies
   Comedies Histories hr in London or any other towne demeaning
   themselves orderly and continuing not above 14 dayes in a yeare
   in any Cittie or other place where they travell, and not to exceed
   the nomber of eighteene persons.' (Ibid., p. 192.)
1623, Jan.< >Aug.—'Martin Slathier and other players of the late
   Queene Elizabeth' were paid 5s. at Coventry. (Ibid., p. 249.)

1625, Oct. 15—'Slator and his Companie beinge the Kings Playors' were paid £1 at Leicester. (Ibid., p. 316.) Since Slater had always been a Queen's man, Professor Murray thinks that this designation was a clerk's mistake, 'no doubt . . . because their licence was signed by the King'. (Ibid., i. 188.)

1625, Oct. 16—'Martyn Slatier, Robson, & Silvester late servants to the late queene Anne' were paid 5s. at Coventry. (Ibid. ii. 250.)

SMITH, ANTHONY. Smith was a member of Prince Charles's company from March 1615/16 to 1625 and a King's man by October 1626. Three Prince's men, Smith, Hobbes, and Penn, found their way to the King's company shortly after their patron came to his father's throne. Hobbes had become attached to the King's company by 23 May 1625, for by that date he was petitioning to be sworn; it seems probable that all three men came together. They were all members by 1629 when they appear in the livery allowance list. The four roles of Smith which are known suggest that he was not of first importance in the company; there is no indication of a 'line'. Mr. Baldwin recognizes this fact when he says that Smith and Penn were handy-men in the company. (*Organization and Personnel*, pp. 187–8.)

Smith's name is so common that it cannot be assumed that he was the gentleman whose son was christened in Cripplegate in 1627; the parish would not, however, have been an inconvenient residence for him when he was performing at the Red Bull. It seems to me improbable that he was the Anthony Smith who appears in the St. Saviour's token books in 1597, 1598, 1599, 1608, and 1609.

1615/16, Mar. 20—He was eighth to sign the debt-funding agreement of the players at the Hope, probably Prince's (Charles I), with Alleyn and Meade. (*Hens. Paps.*, pp. 90–1.)

1616–17—He was seventh to sign the Prince's letter to Alleyn for help in finding a theatre and a loan. (Ibid., p. 93; see above, p. 200, n. 3.)

1625, >May 5—'Anthonie Smith' was second in the list of Prince's men who received black cloth for James's funeral procession. (*M.S.C.* ii. 326.)

1626—'*Philargus* a rich Miser, Anthony Smith', in King's cast for Massinger's *The Roman Actor*, lic. 11 October. (1629 4° B.M.)

1626/7, Jan. 3< >9—'A peticõn of Richard Holden against Ioseph Taylor Anthony Smith and Thomas Hobbes Answered of course.' (*M.S.C.* ii. 400.)

1627, Apr. 29—'Anthony son of Anthony Smith gent' chris. St. G.C.

1628—His name was sixth in the King's cast for *The Lover's Melancholy*, lic. 24 November. (1629 4° B.M.)

1629, May 6—His name was tenth in a cloak allowance for the King's men. (*M.S.C.* ii. 350.)

1629 ?—'Mʳ. *Smith, Gerard*' in King's cast for Carlell's *The Deserving Favorite*. (1629 4° B.M.)

c. 1630—'*Clutch—his* [Brainsicke's] *Keeper*—Anthony Smith' and '*Querpo—A decayde gent—Clut: disguis'd*' in King's cast given in the MS. of Clavell's (?) *The Soddered Citizen*. (*Sod. Cit.*, p. 3.)

1631—According to the cast given in the MS. of Arthur Wilson's *The Swisser* (B.M. Add. MS. 36759), 'Smith' played 'Asprandus' in the Blackfriars' production. (Feuillerat, *The Swisser*.)

SMITH, JOHN. A John Smith, citizen and fishmonger of London, contracted with Christopher Beeston to furnish Queen Anne's company with all tinsel and loom stuffs. He made a number of deliveries from 1612 to 1616. In 1619 he sued Beeston, Cumber, Worth, and Perkins for payment (see Wallace, *Three Theatres*, pp. 30 ff.). It is possible that Smith had a business with other and later theatrical companies.

SMITH, LEONARD. If Smith and Allen were leaders of one of the regular provincial companies, it is curious that they are not found elsewhere. It is probable that they led a troupe of local players or even of medicine players like the companies of Francis Nicolini and John Puncteus, who were licensed by Sir Henry Herbert. (*Herbert*, p. 47.)

1640, Aug. 19—'Jeremy Allin & leonard Smith togeather wth the rest of theire company being stage-players' were paid 20s. at Coventry. (Murray, ii. 254.)

SMITH, MATHEW. Before he became a Prince Charles's man, Smith was evidently a King and Queen of Bohemia's man, as the petitions of John Atkins indicate. There is no way of telling how long he had belonged to this organization, but the fact that he is named in the petitions with leaders like Gunnell, Cartwright, and Fowler implies that he could not have been an inexperienced actor; the allusion to him in *Knavery in All Trades* suggests that he had some reputation.

It is not surprising to find Smith in St. Giles' Cripplegate, for this is the parish of the Fortune theatre, in which he performed for years. It would be hazardous to identify the player with either the brawler in St. Margaret's churchyard or the Mathew Smith about whom Sir John Kiddermister complained, though he might have been both.

1613, Oct. 1—'John Smith and Mathew Smith, both of Westminster; for makinge an affray and drawinge blood of one another in the Church yard of St. Margarettes in Westminster.' (*Middx. Co. Rec.* ii. 234.)

1627, Dec. 5—'A petition of Sr Iohn Kedermister against Mathew Smith answered (vizt) I desire Sr Robert Cocke to peruse this petition and either cause Mathew Smith to giue Sr Iohn Kedermister satisfaction or certifye mee what hee conceiueth fitt to bee done therin.' (*M.S.C.* ii. 401.) On 16 February 1627/8, the petition of 'Sr Iohn Kiddermister' was answered, 'If Mathew Smith doe not giue appearance vnto such Actions as Sr Iohn Keddermister shall commence agst him by the [*blank*] of Easter Terme next, Sr Iohn Keddermister may freely take the ordinary course of Law for his releife, provided that the priuiledge of Parliament bee not infringed therby.' (Ibid.) In 1630, 5< >7 June, the Lord Chamberlain replied to another petition, 'I desire Sr Robert Cock to peruse this petition, and take a Course that Sr Iohn Kedermister may receiue satisfaccōn and I bee noe more troubled wth theis Complaintes, or I will take a course to free myselfe of them.' (Ibid., p. 403.)

1631, Oct. 18—'A petition of Iohn Atkins against Richard Gunnell William Cartwright Richard Fowler & Mathew Smith Answered of course.' (Ibid., p. 406.)

1631, Nov. 28—John Atkins's second petition calls these men 'ye Queene of Bohemias Players'; Atkins was given permission to sue after one month if he did not receive satisfaction. (Ibid.)

1631, Dec.—'*Agurtes, an Imposter.* Mathew Smith', in the Prince Charles's cast of *Holland's Leaguer*, presented at Salisbury Court this month. (*Herbert*, p. 45; 1632 4° B.M.)

1631, Dec. 7—A warrant of this date was shown at Norwich 21 February 1637/8, 'authorizing Joseph Moore Ellias Worth Mathew Smyth & others to play Comedies &c. . . . They had as gratuity of iii^li and soe they willingly departed.' The sum is entered in the Chamberlains' Accounts for 1637–8 as 'soe much given to the Prynces Players'. (Murray, ii. 358, 372.)

1632, 10–15 May—'Mathew Smith' was named third in a warrant to swear eleven Prince Charles's (II) men as Grooms of the Chamber in ordinary without fee. (*M.S.C.* ii. 358.)

1634, July 18—Kendall told Crosfield that 'Mr Smith' was one of the Prince's players at the Red Bull.. (*Crosfield's Diary*, p. 72.)

1639, Sept. 28—'Joyce wife of Mathew Smith Player' bur. St. G.C.

1640, July 9—'John sonne of George Jolly Player in ye house of Mathew Smith Playe^r in Whitcrostrt' chris. St. G.C.

1641, July 6—'Judith, daugh^r: of Mathew Smith, Player' chris. St. G.C.

1664—In the third act of *Knavery in All Trades*, several gentlemen are in a coffee-house talking of the theatre before the wars. One says, 'But did you know *Mat. Smith, Elis Worth* and *Fowler* at the Fortune?' (1664 4° HN; see above, pp. 317–19.)

SNELL, Thomas (*see* SUELL, THOMAS).

SNELLER, James. It is not unlikely that James Sneller ought to be identified with James Kneller (q.v.) who was a Lady Elizabeth's boy in 1613 and one of the Company of the Revels to the late Queen Anne at Exeter in 1624. Sneller is certainly known, however, only as a Prince Charles's man. Though the identification of the actor and the householder buried in Clerkenwell seems an easy one, it is well to remember that there are no full lists of Prince Charles's men after 1632, and that the absence of records of Sneller after that date cannot be taken as evidence of his death.

1631, Dec.—'*Autolicus, his disciple.* Iames Sneller', in Prince Charles's (II) cast for *Holland's Leaguer*, acted at the Salisbury Court this month. (*Herbert*, p. 45; 1632 4° B.M.)

1632, 10< >15 May—'Iames Sneller' was sixth in a warrant to swear eleven Prince's men Grooms of the Chamber in ordinary without fee. (*M.S.C.* ii. 358.)

1632, Dec. 10—'A petition of William Crome against William Browne Henry Graddell, Iames Sneller, Thomas Bond William Cooke & William Hall yᵉ princes Players answered of course.' Permission to sue was granted 21 December. (M.S.C. ii. 408.)

1634, Dec. 1—'James Sneller, householder' bur. St. J.C.

SOMERSET, GEORGE. A George Somerset appeared in the Admiral's plot for *Alcazar*, and it has been conjectured that the same man is referred to as George in that company's plot of *Fortune's Tennis* and *Tamar Cam*. There is no direct evidence that the musician of St. Bartholomew the Less was connected with the stage, but the John Wilson (q.v.) at his house seems to have been.

When Collier printed this burial entry in his *Memoirs of the Actors* (p. xix), he indicated that it came from St. Giles' Cripplegate, but his notes in the Bodleian show that it was really from St. Bartholomew the Less. ,

1624, Sept. 3—'sonne to John Wilson gentleman from the house of George Somerset Musition' bur. St. Bartholomew the Less. (Bod.)

SOULAS, JOSIAS DE (*see* FLORIDOR, JOSIAS).

SOYLES, WILLIAM. A ghost name from Mrs. Stopes's misreading, followed by Nungezer, of William Styles.

SPARKES, THOMAS. The Fortune leaseholder may be the Thomas Sparkes at whose house in Ivy Lane Edward Alleyn agreed in 1610 to pay a bond. (*MSS. Dul.*, p. 239.)

1622, May 20—Alleyn granted 'Thomas Sparkes Cittizen and Merchantaylor of London' a lease of one share of the Fortune. (*Hens. Paps.*, pp. 29, 112.)

SPENCER, JOHN. John Spencer is one of the most conspicuous of the troupe leaders of English actors in Germany in the reign of James I. He is first found in the Netherlands in 1605 in the service of the Elector of Brandenburg and later in the service of various princes in Germany and the Netherlands until 1623. Various records show that he had the clown name of Hans Stockfish.

There are no records of Spencer in England, unless he is to be identified with the John Spencer, musician, whose twin daughters were christened at St. Saviour's Southwark in 1603. (See Cohn, *Sh. in Ger.*, pp. lxxxiii–lxxxviii, xci–cii; Herz, *Englische Schauspieler*, pp. 44–52; Meissner, *Englischen Comoedianten*, p. 58; Bentley, *T.L.S.*)

SPENCER, NICHOLAS. There are no records of an actor of this name before the closing of the theatres, but Professor Hyder Rollins has found that a dancer and entertainer of the name was active during the Commonwealth period and was restrained by Davenant after the Restoration (Rollins, 'Commonwealth Drama', pp. 306–7). He had probably had some training in the theatre before the war began.

STAFFIELD, GEORGE (*see* STUTVILLE, GEORGE).

STAGEKEEPER. There are two extant dramatic manuscripts in which it is shown that the stagekeeper performed on the stage. It is practically certain that two different stagekeepers at different theatres are referred to; we have no clue to the identity of either man.

1622–3 (?)—In the prompter's notes in the MS. of *The Two Noble Ladies* (B.M. MS. Egerton 1994), acted at the Red Bull by the Revels company, the stagekeeper appears twice, once as a guard—'guard Tay: Stage k:' (fol. 228[5]ᵇ)—and once as a soldier—'Tay. Gib: Stage k:' (fol. 233[10]ᵃ). (Greg, *Dram. Doc.*, pp. 276–7.)

1624, Sept. 3—The stagekeepers appear in the MS. stage directions of Heywood's *The Captives* (B.M. MS. Egerton 1994), licensed on this date for the company at the Cockpit, presumably Lady Elizabeth's men: iii. 2 (fol. 61ᵇ), 'Stage:' as country fellows; v. 2 (fol. 70ᵃ), 'stagekeepers as a guard'. (Ibid., pp. 286–7.)

STOCKFISH, HANS. A stage name used by John Spencer (q.v.) in Germany.

STR——, ROBERT. In the Duke of Portland's MS. of Middleton's *Hengist, King of Kent* there appears at II. i. 40–1, the following marginal note: 'Brigs / Robrt str / Blackson', evidently the names of three actors who took part in the dumb show (Bald, *Hengist, King of Kent*, p. xxviii). Though the play belonged to the King's men in 1641, Mr. Bald shows reason for believing that it was originally written 1616–20 for some other company, and that the actors' names belong to these earlier performances (ibid., pp. xvii–xxi). Robert Str—— cannot be identified. It is unlikely, as Bald points out, that he was the Robert Stratford who was apparently a boy in 1631.

STRATFORD, ROBERT. Robert Stratford is known only as a boy actor in 1631. He may have been a son of the actor William Stratford (q.v.). It does not seem likely that he was the Robert Str—— (q.v.) of Middleton's *Hengist, King of Kent*.

1631, Dec.—'*Triphœna, wife to Philautus*. Robert Stratford', in Prince Charles's (II) cast for *Holland's Leaguer*, acted at Salisbury Court this month. (*Herbert*, p. 45; 1632 4° B.M.)

STRATFORD, WILLIAM. William Stratford first appears in 1610 as a member of Prince Charles's company, and he is found in this organization, relicensed as the Palsgrave's men in January 1612/13, until his death. His presence in the bond made in 1624 to Richard Gunnell by certain Palsgrave's men to continue playing at the Fortune indicates that he was one of the leading members of the company.

Stratford's residence in the parish of the theatre in which he acted is quite characteristic of the players of the time. His death and that of Charles Massey in August 1625 probably contributed to the decline of the Palsgrave's men as an important London company.

1618, Oct. 31—His name was sixth in the list of Palsgrave's men who signed the lease of the Fortune from Edward Alleyn. (See above, pp. 138–9.)

1619/20, Mar. 22—'Mary daughter of William Stratford yeoman' chris. St. G.C. 'Mary, daughter of William Stratford playe^r' bur. 8 January 1622/3.

1622/3, Mar. 16—'Judith daughter of William Stratford Playe^r' chris. St. G.C.

1623, May 21—'William Stratford att the vpper end of white Crosse Streete aforesayd', 5s., in Markham's suit. (See Appendix, p. 682.)

1623/4, Jan. 29—Markham's suit says that he was an actor at the Fortune. (Ibid.)

1624, Apr. 30—With five others, he signed a bond to Gunnell to continue to play together at the Fortune. (Hotson, p. 52; see above, pp. 148–9.)

1625, Aug. 27—'William Stratford, Player' bur. St. G.C.

STRETCH, JOHN.

1634/5, Mar. 10—His name is in the very full list of players recorded at Norwich; some of them seem to be King's Revels men, though the records do not give the name of the company, which was probably an amalgamation. (Murray, ii. 356; see above, pp. 286 and 288–9.)

STUTVILLE (ESTOTEVILLE, ESTOUTEVILE, STAFFEILD, STUTFIELD, STUTVILE, STUTVILL), GEORGE. George Stutville is one of the most restless of the Caroline players of whom we have any record. He was a Red Bull Revels player, a Prince Charles's man, a King's Revels man, a Queen Henrietta's man, and a leader of the company of Beeston's Boys, all in a period of sixteen or eighteen years. The evidence for his association with the Red Bull Revels company is his appearance in the stage directions of *The Two Noble Ladies*. Dr. Greg has pointed out (*Dram. Doc.*, p. 216) that this stage direction is much more likely to belong to the presentation in 1622 or 1623 by the Revels company than to any later performance by another company, and the presence of Thomas Bond in the stage directions is a corroboration of his reasoning.

Stutville evidently became a member of Prince Charles's company later than the other members sworn in May 1632, for there is a separate warrant for him on the 1st of June, and Miss Boswell notes that Stutville's name is a later addition to the document of 10–15 May 1632. (*M.S.C.* ii. 358.)

As an actor in Queen Henrietta's company and a leader of Beeston's Boys, Stutville seems to have been of more importance than he was in his earlier companies. His only known acting roles (except for the minor ones in *Edmond Ironside* and *The Two Noble*

Ladies, which are quite small and might have been taken by almost any actor) are the two he took for Queen Henrietta's men in *Hannibal and Scipio*; both of them are comic.

Dr. Boas (*The Library* [1917], viii. 235), followed by Nungezer, has assigned Stutville a part in *Thomas of Woodstock*, but the evidence for this assignment is inadequate, being simply the use of the name 'George' in the stage directions.

It is interesting to find that Stutville must be added to the list of Caroline actors who found occasion to express themselves in verse. His tribute to Heywood does not lead one to wish for the discovery of other flights of his muse.

1622–3 ?—His name appears twice in the prompter's notes in the MS. of *The Two Noble Ladies* (B.M. MS. Egerton 1994), whose title-page says that it was acted 'At the Red Bull in St: Iohns Streete By the Company of ye Reuells'. He seems to have played a Spirit and a Triton: fol. 234(11)ᵇ, 'Ent Spirrit Geo Stut'; fol. 235(12)ᵇ, 'Tritons in: Bond Stutf.' (See the notes on Thomas Bond.) (Greg, *Dram. Doc.*, pp. 274, 277.)

1632, 10< >15 May—'George Stutvile' was a later addition to a list of ten Prince's players named in a warrant to swear them Grooms of the Chamber in ordinary without fee. (*M.S.C.* ii. 358.)

1632, June 1—'A Warraunt to sweare Mr George Stutvile A Groome of the Chamber in ordinary wᵗʰout ffee to attend the Prince his Highnes in yᵉ quality of a player.' (Ibid.)

1632, Nov. 16—'A warrᵗ for the apprᵉhension of Iohn Ierom gent. [*blank*] Roades a Stationer & [*blank*] Booker A serjeant at mace in London. vpon the complaint of George Stutvile.' (Ibid., p. 359.)

c. 1632—Probably he is the 'Stutf:' who appears (fol. 104ᵇ) in the prompter's notes of the MS. of *Edmond Ironside* (B.M. MS. Egerton 1994), apparently written 1590–1600, but revived *c.* 1632, probably by Prince Charles's men (see above, p. 323). It would appear that Stutville took the part of one of the two pledges noblemen's sons. (Greg, *Dram. Doc.*, p. 259.)

1634, July 18—Kendall told Crosfield that among the players at Salisbury Court were '7. Mr. Staffeild'. (*Crosfield's Diary*, p. 72; see Appendix, p. 688.)

1634/5, Mar. 10—'George Stutvile' was the leader of a very large company of players at Norwich. A number of the men, like Stutville, are Revels players, but the records do not give the name of the company, which was probably an amalgamation. (Murray, ii. 356; see above, pp. 286 and 288–9.)

1635—He played two parts ('Souldier. By George Stutfield', and 'Bostar. By George Stutfield') in Nabbes's *Hannibal and Scipio*, given by Queen Henrietta's company at Drury Lane. (1637 4° B.M.)

1638 ?—Professor W. J. Lawrence says that in Ashmolean MS. 38, item 114, are lines entitled 'The Genius of the stage Dep(l)oring the death of Ben Jonson' and signed 'Geo Stutvill'. (*M.L.R.* xxv [April, 1930], 211.)

1640, May 3—An order forbidding acting at the Cockpit until further notice because of the production of an unlicensed play was addressed 'To William Bieston. George Estoteville & the rest of the Company of the Players at the Cockpitt in Drury Lane'. (*M.S.C.* ii. 393–4.)

1640, May 3—'A warr^t of app^{r}hension & cõmittm^t to the Marshall-seas of William Bieston, George Estotevill & [*blank*] Moone vpon ye aboue specified Occasion.' (Ibid., p. 394.)

1640—The following verses are prefixed to Heywood's *The Exemplary Lives and Memorable Acts of Nine the Most Worthy Women of the World* (1640 4° B.M.):

To his worthy Friend Mr. *Thomas Heywood*,
on his Nine Female Worthies.

Will neither rugged time nor vast expence
Of thy unfathom'd fancy and cleare sence
Perswade thee to leave off, but thou wilt still
Make all 'twixt heaven & hell flow from thy Quill;
Nay Heav'n it selfe, and all those Angels there,
Those powr's and vertues will themselves declare
Thy Genuine searching soule: But these here
Thy female Angels, that doe grace this Spheare,
Thrice worthy, worthy women, whose great acts
Immortallize their mem'ries, and exacts
Not thee alone, but all the noblest wits
That in the courts of truth and judgment sits
To write their Legends: But thy learned Pen,
That writ (before) their Story hath agen
From thy owne workes subtracted Nine, to be
The great example to posteritie:
I doe not flatter but I may admire
To see fire turn'd t'Ashes returne to fire;
Thy age goes backward, and thy *Phaenix* braine,
From the old Ashes is growne younge Againe.

George Estoutevile.

STYLES, WILLIAM. We have only one record to indicate that William Styles was an actor, and then it is in an unimportant capacity. I think it fairly probable that all the parish register extracts refer to the William Styles of the ticket of privilege, for all but one occur in the parish in which Styles was employed in 1636/7, and the names and dates fit together so well that the same man must be concerned in all of them. It is unfortunate that the registers of St. Anne's almost never mention occupations.

1634, June 25—'William Stiles & Dorothy Rowe' mar. St. G.F. 'P. L.' in margin.

1635, Apr. 5—'William sonne to William and Dorothy Stiles' chris. St. Anne's Blackfriars. There was another christening of 'William Sonne to William and Dorothy Stiles' 23 December 1635, and on the 27th of December in that year 'William sonne to William and Dorothy Stiles' was buried.

1636/7, Jan. 12—The names of John Allington and 'Wm Styles' have been added in the marginal list but do not occur in the body of the order in which the Lord Chamberlain granted nine 'persons Dependantes on the [Blackfriars] Players' tickets of privilege. (*M.S.C.* ii. 380.)

1641, June 6—'Lanslet sonne to William and Dorothy Styles' chris. St. Anne's Blackfriars. 'Lancelet sonne to William and Dorothy Styles' bur. 27 March 1643.

1642, June 14—' John sonne to William and Dorothy Styles' chris. St. Anne's Blackfriars. 'John sonne to William and Dorothy Styles' bur. 16 June.

1643, Oct. 4—'Dorothy daughter to John [*sic*] and Dorothy Stiles' chris. St. Anne's Blackfriars.

SUELL, THOMAS.

1613, May 31—He is listed as a boy in a patent for Lady Elizabeth's of this date which was copied at Coventry 28 March 1615. (*R.E.S.* i. 183.)

SUMNER (SOMNER, SUMPNER), JOHN. John Sumner is found in every known list of Queen Henrietta's men except the short one which Kendall gave Crosfield at Oxford; his omission from Kendall's list is probably due to the fact that Kendall did not consider Sumner one of the leaders of the company, though Wright said, 'Those of principal Note at the *Cockpit*, were, *Perkins, Michael Bowyer, Sumner, William Allen,* and *Bird*, eminent Actors . . .' (See above, pp. 231–2.)

Sumner's roles in Queen Henrietta's plays are all fairly large ones, but he never has the lead. He plays rather dashing parts and parts demanding some authority, like the Basha of Aleppo.

Wright's statement that Sumner and Perkins were buried in Clerkenwell makes it somewhat more probable that the actor was the man buried in 1651 in that parish rather than the one buried in 1649 in St. Giles' Cripplegate though the proximity of the two parishes and the nearness of the dates make either record a fair possibility.

1625—'Mvstapha, *Basha of* Aleppo. Iohn Sumner', in Queen Henrietta's cast for Massinger's *The Renegado*. (1630 4° B.M.)

1626—' *Marwood,* friend to *Beauford, Iohn Sumpner*', in Queen Henrietta's cast for Shirley's *The Wedding*. (1629 4° HN.)

c. 1630—' *The D. of* Florence, *with followers. By* M^r. Ioh. Somner', in the Queen Henrietta's cast for Heywood's *The Fair Maid of the West*, Part II; he does not appear in the cast prefixed to Part I. (1631 4° B.M.)

>1634—' Young *Bruce,* M. [Mr.] *Sumner*', in Queen Henrietta's cast for Davenport's *King John and Matilda*. (1655 4° B.M.)

1635—'Himulco. By Iohn Sumner', in Queen Henrietta's cast for Nabbes's *Hannibal and Scipio*. (1637 4° B.M.)

1637, *c*. Oct. 2—'I disposed of Perkins, Sumner, Sherlock and Turner, to Salisbury Court, and joynd them with the best of that company.' (*Herbert,* p. 66.)

1646/7, Mar. 15—'Elizabeth d. of John Sumner, gent., & Mary vx' chris. St. J.C.

>1660—Wright says that after the wars '*Perkins* and *Sumner* of the

Cockpit, kept House together at *Clerkenwel*, and were there Buried
. . . some Years before the Restauration.' (*Hist. Hist.*, p. 10.)
1649, Aug. 10—'John Sumner gentleman' bur. St. G.C.
1651, Sept. 18—'Jnº Sumpner' bur St. J.C.

SWANSTON (SAWNSTON, SWAINSTONE, SWANSON, SWANSTEAD,
SWANSTED, SWANSTONE, SWANSTRID, SWANTTON, SWAUTTED),
EYLLAERDT. The scribes practised their ingenuity on the Chris-
tian name of Swanston more than on that of any other actor. We
have Eliard, Elliard, Ellyard, Ellyart, Elyard, Eylardt, Eyllaerdt,
Eylaerd, Eylaerdt, Eylyardt, Hilliard, Hillyar, Iliar, Illre, and
Ilra. The actor himself signed Eyllaerdt in his only known signa-
tures.

Though Swanston became one of the most prominent of the
members of the King's company, he had never been an apprentice
in the organization, for the Burbages said of Pollard, Swanston,
and Benfield in 1635, 'these new men that were neuer bred from
Children in the kings service . . .' (*M.S.C.* ii. 371). We hear of
Swanston first as one of the seven leading members of the Lady
Elizabeth's company listed in Herbert's office-book in 1622. It is
possible that he had previously been a member of Prince Charles's
company, for he was called a Prince's man at Stafford in December
1622, and the Prince's men had been the predecessors of Lady
Elizabeth's at the Cockpit. Possibly Swanston was travelling
with an old licence, as the provincial players so often did. I suppose, however, that it is equally possible that the Stafford clerk
meant Princess's.

Certainly Swanston had become a member of the King's company by 1624, for he appears in a formal list of the company in
that year, and Malone pointed out that he had joined in 1624;
Mr. Baldwin infers that he succeeded Underwood some time after
the latter's death in October 1624 (*Organization and Personnel*,
p. 57). He appears regularly in casts and other lists of the King's
men from 1624 until the closing of the theatres. After 1631
Swanston is frequently associated with Lowin and Taylor as the
recipient of grants and payments for the company. Considering
his prominence in the company as indicated by these grants, it is
not at all surprising to find Swanston, with Benfield and Pollard,
asking the Lord Chamberlain in 1635 to see that they obtain a
larger share of the company's profits.

Since Wright's statement about Swanston's politics and his
residence after the beginning of civil war is corroborated by other
records, we can probably accept his assertion about the ex-
player's occupation. It is interesting to find Swanston living for
more than twenty years in the parish best known as the residence
of Heminges and Condell.

Swanston seems to have performed various types of roles for
the company. In at least three plays he is known to have been

a villain; his line was not exclusively villainous, however, for he also played Othello and Bussy D'Ambois and Utrante. Mr. Baldwin thinks that he was a leading utility man for the company and that by 1633 he had begun to share the leads with the ageing Lowin and Taylor (*Organization and Personnel*, pp. 181–2). Gayton's statement that he played Bussy D'Ambois makes it probable that Swanston is the actor referred to in the prologue and epilogue to the 1641 quarto of that play. Professor Parrott has pointed out that this prologue and epilogue were probably written for the court performance of the play on 7 April 1634 (*Chapman Tragedies*, p. 547). Mr. Baldwin notes (op. cit., p. 182) that since *Richard III* was presented by the company at court about five months before, the line in the prologue to *Bussy*, '*As Richard he was lik'd*', probably refers to Swanston's performance as Richard III.

1619, Dec. 16—'Iliar. Swanston & Alice Ivieson L. F.' mar. St. Gregory by St. Paul. (Challen, *Marriages*.)

1620, Sept. 3—'a still borne childe of Elyard Swanson' bur. St. M.A.

1621, Nov. 15—'Alse d. of Ilyard Swanston' chris. St. M.A. 'Alice Swainstone Jllrre Swainstone' bur. 1625 (the month and day are not given for burials at St. M.A. during this plague year).

1622—Herbert listed 'Eliard Swanson' among 'The chiefe of them at the Phoenix'. (*Herbert*, p. 63.)

1622, Dec. 13—'Given Mr Saw[a]nston [Swanston] the princes player, Dec. 13 . . . 6s. 8d.' at Stafford. (Murray, ii. 401.)

1622, Dec. 28—'Eliard s. of Eliard Swanston' chris. St. M.A.

1624—Malone says, 'Eliard Swanston in 1624 joined the company at Blackfriars'. (*Herbert*, p. 63.)

1624, Dec. 20—His name was third in the submission of King's for playing *The Spanish Viceroy*. (Ibid., p. 21.)

1625, >May 5—'Ellyart Swanstone' was ninth in the list of King's men who received black cloth to wear in James's funeral procession. (*M.S.C.* ii. 326.)

1625, June 24—No. 10 in King's patent. (*M.S.C.* i. 282–3.)

1626—'*Aretinus Clemens, Caesars* spie—Eyllardt Swanstone' in King's cast for Massinger's *The Roman Actor*, lic. 11 October. (1629 4° B.M.)

1627/8, Jan. 16—'Elizabeth d. of Mr Swanstrid [?]' chris. St. M.A.

1628—'Eylyardt Swanston' was fifth in King's cast for *The Lover's Melancholy*, lic. 24 November. (1629 4° B.M.)

1629, May 6—'Elliard Swanson' was eighth in King's list for cloak allowance. (*M.S.C.* ii. 350.)

1629—'*Ricardo*, [one of] 2. wild courtiers. *Eylardt Swanstone*', in King's cast for Massinger's *The Picture*, lic. 8 June. (1630 4° B.M.)

1629?—'Mr. *Swanstone, the Count Vtrante*' in King's cast for Carlell's *The Deserving Favourite*. (1629 4° B.M.)

1630, May 25—'John s. of Jlrā Swanston' chris. St. M.A.

1631—According to the property list, 'Mr Swantton:' played Chrysalus in King's production of *Believe as You List*, lic. 6 May. (Sisson, *B.A.Y.L.*, pp. xxxi and 99.)

1631—In the MS. of Arthur Wilson's *The Swisser* (B.M. Add. MS. 36759) his name is given in the cast for the Blackfriars production: 'Alcidonus, Sonne to Antharis . . . Swanston'. (Feuillerat, *The Swisser*.)

1631/2, Feb. 22—A warrant for the payment of £120 for plays at court during Christmas was made payable to Lowin, Taylor, and 'Elliard Swanson'. (*M.S.C.* ii. 358.)

1632, Apr. 16—'Hanna d. of Mr Hilliard Swanston' chris. St. M.A.

1632—'LUGIER, the rough and confident Tutor to the Ladies . . . Acted by Mr. *Hilliard Swanston*' in the King's cast for the 1632 revival of *The Wild Goose Chase*. On p. 32 occurs the stage direction, '*Enter Leverduce, des Lugier, Mr. Illiard.*' (1652 ed. B.M.)

1632/3, Mar. 16—A warrant was issued to 'Iohn Lowen Ioseph Taylor & Ellyard Swanston his Mates Comaedians' for payment for twenty-three plays and one rehearsal by King's at court. (*M.S.C.* ii. 360.)

1633, Oct. 24—Lowin and Swanston apologized for their 'ill manners' in the matter of Fletcher's *The Tamer Tamed*. (*Herbert*, p. 21 ; see above, pp. 36–7.)

1633/4, Feb. 21—'Beniamin s. of Hilliard Swanston' chris. St. M.A.

1634, Apr. 27—A warrant was issued to Lowin, Taylor, and 'Elliard Swanston' for payment for twenty-two plays acted at court. (*M.S.C.* ii. 373.)

1635, May 18—Both the Burbages and John Shank assert in their petition to the Lord Chamberlain in 1635 that for the year Whitsun Monday 1634 to Whitsun Monday 1635 Swanston gained from the King's company, in addition to £34 for his one-third share in Blackfriars, 'as hee was a Player and noe Howskeeper 180li'. (Ibid., pp. 368, 372.)

1635, May 18 < > July 12—Benfield, Pollard, and Swanston petitioned the Lord Chamberlain that Shank, Cuthbert Burbage, and Mrs. Robinson be forced to sell them each one share in the Globe. They further petitioned that Shank be forced to sell one of his shares in the Blackfriars to be divided among the three of them. (Ibid., pp. 362–4.) Shank replied that Swanston had had one-third of one share in the Blackfriars for two or three years. (Ibid., p. 368.)

1635, July 12—The Lord Chamberlain complied with the request of Benfield, Pollard, and Swanston. (Ibid., p. 365.)

1635, Aug. 1—Since the actors were unable to agree on the price of the shares, Sir Henry Herbert, Sir John Finett, and Daniel Bedingfield were appointed to arbitrate. (Ibid., p. 373.) (Shank's will of 31 December 1635 indicates that he still claimed all his shares. See Appendix, pp. 646–8.)

1635, Aug. 18—'Hilliard Swanstons child' chris. St. M.A.

1636, Aug. 2—'Francis s. of Hilliard Swanston' chris. St. M.A.

1637, Apr. 22—A warrant for liveries was issued to 'Iohn Lowen, Ioseph Taylor & Eilardt Swanston for themselues & thirteene others his Mates comaedians'. (*M.S.C.* ii. 383.)

1637, July 6—On the back of the warrant for payment of £240 to the King's men for plays at court 1636–7 is a receipt for £200 of the sum signed 'Eyllaerdt Swanston'. (Law, *Forgeries*, App.)

1637/8, Mar. 15—'A Warrt. . . . for the payment of 150li vnto Iohn Lowen, Ioseph Taylor & Eillart Swanston or any of them for them-

selues & the rest of the Company of his Ma^{tes} Players for 14 Playes
Acted before his Ma^{ty}e . . .' (*M.S.C.* ii. 387.)

1638, June 5—At the foot of the warrant for payment of £240 to the
King's men for plays at court 1636–7 is a receipt for the full amount
signed 'Eyllaerdt Swanston'. (Law, *Forgeries*, App.)

1638/9, Jan. 21—'Stephen s. of Mr Swanstone' chris. St. M.A.
'Stephen Swanstone' bur. 22 January 1638/9.

1638/9, Mar. 12—A warrant was issued for payment 'vnto Iohn
Lowen, Ioseph Taylor & Eillardt Swanston or any one of them for
themselues & the rest of ye aforesayd Company of his Ma^{tes} Players'
of £300 for 24 plays in 1638–9. (*M.S.C.* ii. 388–9.)

1638/9, Mar. 14—'A warr^t for Liueryes for 16 of ye Kinges Players . . .
to bee d̄d̄ to Iohn Lowen, Ioseph Taylor & Eillardt Swanston.'
(Ibid., p. 389.)

1639, Aug. 26—Richard Benfield of Gray's Inn in his will bequeathed
'vnto my gossipp Eliardt Swanston and Thomas Pollard to each
of them the some of fforty shillings of like money'. (See Appendix,
p. 634.)

1640, Apr. 4—'A warr^t for payment of 230^{li} vnto Iohn Lowen, Ioseph
Taylor & Eillardt Swanston for himselfe & the rest of the Company
of ye Players for one & Twenty Playes Acted before their Ma^{ts} . . .'
in 1639–40. (*M.S.C.* ii. 392.)

1640/1, Mar. 20—'A warr^t for payment of 160^{li} vnto the Kinges Players
. . . to bee payd to Iohn Lowen. Ioseph Taylor & Eillardt Swanston
or any of them' for plays given at court in 1640–1. (Ibid., p. 397.)

1640/1, Mar. 20—A livery allowance was issued 'for Iohn Lowen,
Ioseph Taylor & Eillardt Swanston and fifteene others their
fellowes'. (Ibid., pp. 397–8.)

>1642—Wright says, '*Swanston* used to Play *Othello*:'. (*Hist. Hist.*,
p. 4; see Appendix, p. 693.)

< 1642—Wright says, 'I have not heard of one of these Players of any
Note that sided with the other Party, but only *Swanston*, and he
profest himself a Presbyterian, took up the Trade of a Jeweller,
and liv'd in *Aldermanbury*, within the Territory of Father *Calamy*.'
(Ibid., p. 8; see Appendix, p. 695.)

1647—His name—'Eylærd Swanston'—stands third in the list of ten
King's men who signed the dedication of the Beaumont and Fletcher
folio. (1647 folio B.M.)

1648—'From *A Key To the Cabinet of the Parliament, By Their Remembrancer* (1648), Professor Rollins has extracted a corroborative
passage which shows that Swanston was a Parliament's man:
"What need is there of any Playes? will not these serve well enough,
especially when they have gotten *Hillyar Swansted* the Player to
be one?"' (Hotson, p. 15.)

1651, June 24—He made his nuncupative will as 'Eylaeardt Swanston, of St. Mary Aldermanbury, London, gent.' (Hotson, p. 15.)
'He left all he possessed to be divided among his children, and he
desired his daughter Sarah, wife of Joseph Wilson, to see the same
carried out. Witnesses: Joseph Wilson, Elizabeth Vasely, Elizabeth Swanston, Sarah Wilson (*her mark*), Joseph Wilson Junior.'
Commission to administer the estate was made to Sarah Wilson
3 July 1651 and to Joseph Wilson, husband of Sarah deceased,
18 April 1666. (Ibid., p. 73, n. 48.)

1651, June 28—'Mr Elyard Swanston and his wife boeth in one grave in ye North Ile', bur. St. M.A.

1654—Gayton says in his *Pleasant Notes on Don Quixot*, '*Taylor*, acting *Arbaces*, or *Swanston D'Amboys*, were shadowes to him . . .' (1654 ed. B.M., p. 25.)

1664—In a coffee-house scene in the third act of Tatham's (?) *Knavery in All Trades*, a gentleman has mentioned a current play (1664 4° HN):

> *third*. . . . Bur [*sic*] sir, they say 'tis done rarely well.
> *fourth*. I cannot believe it, 'tis impossible they should do any thing so well as I have seen things done.
> *fifth*. When *Taylor Lowen*, and *Pollard* were alive.
> *fourth*. Did you not know *Benfield*, and Swautted?
> *fifth*. Did I not know 'em? yes, and hum'd them off a hundred times.

1676—Snarl, 'a great Admirer of the last Age', in Shadwell's *Virtuoso*, says (Act I), when it is suggested that he can see plays, '. . . I have seen 'em at *Black-Friers*; pox, they act like Poppets now in sadness. I, that have seen *Joseph Taylor*, and *Lowen*, and *Swanstead*: Oh a brave roaring Fellow! would make the house shake again. Besides, I can never endure to see Plays since Women came on the Stage; Boys are better by half.' (1676 4° B.M., pp. 15–16.)

SWAYNE, MARTIN. Richard Price (q.v.) was a prominent member of the Palsgrave's men at the Fortune, who are frequently found in the registers of St. Giles. It is possible that his servant Swayne's services were rendered in the theatre.

1625, Aug. 23—'Martin Swayne s^r to Richard Price, gent.' bur. St. G.C.

SWINARTON, ABELL. Like most of the puzzling Queen of Bohemia's company of 1628, Swinarton is not found in any other dramatic records.

1628, June 30—'Abell Swinarton' is eighth in the list of the 'Queene of Bohemias Players' sworn grooms of the chamber. (See above, pp. 188 ff.)

SWINNERTON (SWETHERTON, SWYNERTON), THOMAS. Swinnerton first appeared in March 1603/4 in the patent for Queen Anne's company; he is never found with any other organization. Professor Wallace found (*Three Theatres*, p. 18) that Aaron Holland in March 1604/5 had granted Swinnerton 'a seaventh parte of the said playhowse and gallaries with a gatherers place there[to] belonginge', and that he still held this share in 1620. In 1616 and after Swinnerton is found only in the provinces, where he seems to have led a Queen's company for twenty years. Some of the provincial records seem to indicate that Swinnerton was more successful in persuading local authorities to accede to his requests than most provincial managers.

There are records of Thomas Swinnertons in various London parishes—St. Leonard's Shoreditch, St. Mary's Aldermanbury,

St. James's Clerkenwell, St. Bartholomew the Less, and Allhallows London Wall—but the name is too common to allow
identification of the player.

1616, Mar. 30—Thomas Swinnerton and Robert Lee brought the
Queen's patent of 15 April 1609 to Norwich and finally received
permission to play, though the rest of the company was absent.
(Murray, ii. 340–1.)

1616, May 29—Swinnerton appeared again at Norwich as a leader
of Queen's, but without a patent. He was refused permission to
play because his company had been there so recently, said his
company would play in spite of the refusal, but when offered a
gratuity 'he was content to accept the same & pmised desitance
accòrdyngly'. (Ibid., p. 341.)

1616–17—' Tho: Swynerton and fellowes being her Mats players' were
given a pound at Southampton. (Ibid., p. 399.)

1617, June 4—Pembroke sent an order of 16 July 1616 to Norwich
condemning duplicate patents and specifying amongst others two
taken out by 'Thomas Swynnerton and Martin Slaughter beinge
two of the Queens Mats company of Playors hauinge sepated themselves from their said Company'. (Ibid., p. 343; see above,
pp. 178–9.)

1619, >May 13—'Thomas Swiñerton' was seventh in a list of Queen
Anne's men allowed black cloth for her funeral procession. (M.S.C.
ii. 325.)

1619—'Swynnerton and his Companye of Playos' received one pound
at Leicester. (Murray, ii. 313.)

1620, Mar. 29—See Daniel Swynnerton.

1624/5, Mar. 16—Ellis Guest, Thomas Swinnerton, and Arthuret
Grimes were leaders of a company with a licence of this date which
was shown at Norwich 28 May 1625 and at Leicester 6 March
1625/6. (Murray, ii. 352–3, 316.)

1628, July 19—'Mr Thomas Swynerton a player . . . by warrant
dated the xixth of July 1628' received 20s. as a gratuity at Norwich.
(Ibid., p. 371.)

1628—One pound was 'geuen to a Companie of Players, beinge Swinnerton and his Companie' at Leicester. (Ibid., p. 317.)

SWYNNERTON, DANIEL. Since Thomas Swinnertoñ was a
leader of Queen Anne's company in the provinces for years, and
since Daniel Swynnerton is unknown save for this one record, it
seems likely that Daniel is the Coventry clerk's mistake for
Thomas; one cannot, however, be certain.

1620, Mar. 29—'Daniel Swynnerton & the company of players
belonging to the late Queene Ann' received 10s. at Coventry.
(Murray, ii. 248.)

T., R. There are several actors whose initials were R. T., but
none is known to have been connected with the King's company.

1619, Aug.—The prompter's notes in the MS. of Sir John van Olden
Barnavelt show that some actor with these initials played an officer,
a huntsman, a servant, and a messenger in King's production of the
play. (Greg, Dram. Doc., p. 273.)

TATTERDELL, HUGHE.

1629, Nov. 10—He was named in a licence of this date granted to
William Perry and Richard Weeks, 'his Majestie's sworne servantes', which was shown at Reading 30 November 1629; the
players named were said to be 'all of the Red Bull company'.
(Murray, i. 272 and ii. 386.)

TAWYER (TAWIER, TOYER), WILLIAM. Sir Henry Herbert's
exemption from arrest indicates that Tawyer was more than a
personal servant of John Heminges who was occasionally employed about the Blackfriars and Globe. The stage direction
implies that he was a musician. Baldwin's statement that Tawyer
spent his life with the company (*Organization and Personnel*,
p. 147) is evidently based on the assumption that this stage
direction derives from the original production. This folio stage
direction, however, almost certainly belongs to a revival. (See
Wilson's discussion of the folio text in the Cambridge edition of
the play.)

>1623—The stage direction, 'Tawyer with a Trumpet before them',
occurs v. 1, in *Midsummer Night's Dream* in the First Folio; it is
not found in the quartos of 1600 and 1619. (1623 folio B.M.)
1624, Dec. 27—'William Toyer' was twentieth in a list of twenty-one
'Musitions and other necessary attendantes' of the King's company
who were exempted from arrest. (*Herbert*, p. 74.)
1625, June—'William Tawier, Mr Heminges man' bur. St. S.S. (Bod.)

TAYLOR. The Taylor in the play MSS. cannot be identified. If
either man is to be identified with any of the Taylors whose
Christian name is known, Thomas is the most likely candidate.

1622–3 ?—Probably an actor of this name is indicated in the prompter's notes in the MS. of *The Two Noble Ladies* (B.M. MS. Egerton
1994), whose title-page says that it was acted at the Red Bull by
the company of the Revels. He played a guard—fol. 228(5)^b,
'guard Tay: Stage k:'—and a soldier—fol. 233(10)^a, 'Tay: Gib:
Stage k:' and fol. 236(13)^b, 'Tay: Gibs:'. This evidence suggests
that he was a member of the Revels company, though his name
may belong to the prompter's notes for a later performance. (Greg,
Dram. Doc., pp. 276, 277.)
1624, c. Sept. 3—According to the stage directions in the MS. of *The
Captives* (B.M. MS. Egerton 1994), 'Taylor' appears as a country
fellow, iii. 2 (fol. 61^b). The play was licensed for the Cockpit and
probably belonged to the Lady Elizabeth's company. (Ibid.,
p. 286.)

TAYLOR (TAILOR), JOSEPH. In the reign of Charles I John
Lowin and Joseph Taylor were the most widely known members
of the King's company, the recognized leaders of the organization.
Unlike Lowin, Taylor was already a well-known actor when he
entered the company, some sixteen years after Lowin had joined.

The actor may be, as Collier suggested (*Mem. Act.*, p. 249), the
Joseph Taylor who was christened at St. Andrew's by the Ward-

robe 6 February 1585/6, for he is first found as an actor twenty-three years later when, with several other Duke of York's men, he bought costumes for the company from John Heminges. In 1611 he joined the new Lady Elizabeth's company, and he remained a member of that organization until it was reduced to a provincial status early in 1616 (see above, pp. 177–80), when with four other Lady Elizabeth's men he joined Prince Charles's company. Early in 1619 he again changed companies and became a King's man. It is easy to fix the approximate date of this change, since he performed with other Prince's men in *The Inner Temple Masque* in January or February 1618/19, but had become a King's man before the middle of May following. Since Taylor does not appear in the King's patent of 27 March 1619, he evidently became a member between the time of the first stages of the patent (probably early March) and the middle of May, when he appeared in the livery warrant. When one recalls that Taylor is known to have performed many of the roles created by Burbage and that Burbage was buried 16 March 1618/19, it becomes obvious that the company secured Taylor to fill the place of Richard Burbage immediately after the latter's death.

Taylor was as prominent in the roles written for him as he was in those written for Richard Burbage. In the assigned casts his part is nearly always first or second in number of lines; Mr. Baldwin has pointed out that he is usually the handsome, heroic young lover, though sometimes the handsome and dashing near-villain (*Organization and Personnel*, pp. 177–8, 200). After an analysis of the plays of the Beaumont and Fletcher folio, Mr. Baldwin suggests that Taylor played, among other roles, Demetrius in *The Humorous Lieutenant*, Arnoldo in *The Custom of the Country*, Dinant in *The Little French Lawyer*, Lisander in *The Lover's Progress*, and Perez in *Rule a Wife and Have a Wife* (ibid., p. 198). He must, eventually, have been succeeded in such roles by younger men like Richard Sharpe and Stephen Hammerton, but none of his later parts is known.

Taylor was not only a leading actor of the company but one of its business managers as well. As early as 1625 he had begun to perform functions for the company which had previously been undertaken by Heminges; after Heminges's death Lowin and Taylor handled the business affairs of the company until the closing of the theatres, though Swanston often acted with them. Lowin and Taylor acquired shares in the Blackfriars and Globe, apparently after the death of John Heminges, when they took charge as managers of the company. It is interesting to note that both managers obtained royal grants, Lowin as King's Porter and Taylor as Yeoman of the Revels. One would suppose that Taylor's post would offer more advantages to the company than Lowin's. He must have had the support of the Master of the

Revels in his candidacy, for in February 1635/6 Sir Henry Herbert recorded in his office book the King's promise that no Yeoman of the Revels would be appointed to succeed Hunt without consultation with Sir Henry (*Herbert*, p. 68).

Because of the commonness of his name, it is not always easy to establish Taylor's residence. Certainly he lived in St. Saviour's Southwark in 1610, 1612, 1614, 1616, 1617, and 1623, when he is called player in the parish registers. He is probably the Joseph Taylor in the token books of that parish in numerous years between 1606 and 1623. The Joseph Taylors in Allhallows London Wall and St. Botolph's Bishopsgate are more doubtful, though one would assume that the Joseph Taylor of Markham's suit in 1623 was an actor, and he lived in Bishopsgate. A Joseph Taylor was, however, buried in that parish 21 October 1623, and it may have been that man and not the King's player whom Markham sued.

Taylor's part in the 1633 revival of *The Faithful Shepherdess* seems to indicate that he had some acquaintance at court, since Sir Henry Herbert says that the Queen had given Taylor the costumes. Marmion's verses for the third quarto speak of Taylor as if he had revised the play, but the third quarto contains no noteworthy revisions or additions except the court prologue, which Taylor may have written ; Marmion's praise must, therefore, have been elicited by Taylor's acting, his second-hand costumes, and perhaps his production of the play.

1615/16, Jan. 11—'Jone Taylor d of Joseph a Player' chris. St. S.S.

1615/16, Mar. 20—He was third to sign the debt funding agreement of the players at the Hope, probably Prince Charles's (I) with Alleyn and Meade. (*Hens. Paps.*, pp. 90–1.)

1616–17—He was third to sign Prince Charles's (I) letter to Alleyn asking for his help in finding a theatre and a loan. (*Hens. Paps.*, p. 93; see above, p. 200, n. 3.)

1617, June 1—'Robert Taylor s of Joseph a player' chris. St. S.S.

1618, Apr. 12—'Hester daugh. of Joseph Taylor & Eliz. his Wife' chris. Allhallows.

1618, Oct. 4—Alleyn noted in his diary that 'Jo: Taylore dind w^t vs'. Warner identifies this name with the actor, since John Taylor, the water poet, 'did not reach London on his return from Scotland till 15th October'. (Young, ii. 109.)

1618/19, Jan. or Feb.—As one of Prince Charles's men, 'D. *Almanacke*. Ios. Taylor' appears in Middleton's *Inner Temple Masque or Masque of Heroes*. (1619 4° B.M.)

1619?—No. 5 in King's cast for *The Humorous Lieutenant*. (1679 folio B.M.)

1619?—No. 1 in King's cast for *The Laws of Candy*. (Ibid.)

1619, Aug. 8—'Ann da. of Joseph Taylor' chris. Allhallows.

1619, May 19—No. 12 in livery warrant for King's. (*Hist. MSS. Com.*, Report IV, p. 299.)

1619, Aug. 15—Probably the Taylor who dined with Alleyn; *see* Francis Grace. (Young, ii. 147.)

c. 1619–20—No. 1 in King's cast for *The Custom of the Country.* (1679 folio B.M.)

1619–21—No. 5 in King's cast for *The Island Princess.* (Ibid.)

1619–21—No. 1 in King's cast for *Women Pleased.* (Ibid.)

1619–23—'Ferdinand, 1 R. *Burbidge.* 2 I. *Taylor*', in the cast of King's men prefixed to the 1623 quarto of *The Duchess of Malfi.* Apparently he took the part in the revival after Burbage's death. (1623 4° B.M.)

c. 1620—No. 5 in King's cast for *The False One.* (Ibid.)

1620/1, Mar. 18—'Samuell the sonne of Joseph Taylor & Eliz. his Wife' chris. Allhallows.

1621—No. 1 in King's cast for *The Pilgrim.* (1679 folio B.M.)

1619–22—No. 1 in King's cast for *The Little French Lawyer.* (Ibid.)

1621, Apr. 7—No. 12 in livery warrant for King's. (*Hist. MSS. Com.,* Report IV, p. 299.)

1621, Sept. 7—'Joseph Taylor a child' bur. St. S.S.

1621/2, Mar. 19—'Wynifred, daughter of Joseph Tayler and Elizabeth' chris. St. B.B.

c. 1621—No. 1 in King's cast for *The Double Marriage.* (1679 folio B.M.)

1622, May 14—No. 5 in King's cast for *The Prophetess.* (Ibid.)

1622, June 22—No. 1 in King's cast for *The Sea Voyage.* (Ibid.)

1622, Oct. 24—No. 1 in King's cast for *The Spanish Curate.* (Ibid.)

1623, May 21—In Markham's suit, 'Joseph Taylor in Bishoppsgate neare the Spittle', 5s. (See Appendix, p. 682.)

1623, June 3—In his will, Tooley said, 'Item whereas I stand bound for Josephe Tayler as his surety for paiement of tenn pounds or thereabouts My will is That my executors shall out of my estate paie that debt for him and discharge him of that bond.' (See Appendix, p. 650.)

1623, Aug. 24—'Anne Taylor d of Joseph a Player' chris. St. S.S.

1623, Aug. 29—No. 1 in King's cast for *The Maid in the Mill.* (1679 folio B.M.)

1623, Dec. 6—No. 1 in King's cast for *The Lover's Progress.* (Ibid.)

1623—No. 21 in actor list in Shakespeare folio.

1624, May 27—No. 1 in King's cast for *A Wife for a Month.* (1679 folio B.M.)

1624, Dec. 20—No. 1 in submission of King's for playing *The Spanish Viceroy.* (Herbert, p. 21; see above, pp. 14–15.)

1624/5, Feb. 8—'For the king's company. An olde play called *The Honest Man's Fortune,* the originall being lost, was re-allowed by mee at Mr. Taylor's intreaty, and on condition to give mee a booke. . . .' (Ibid., p. 30.)

1625, >May 5—'Ioseph Taylor' was tenth in the list of King's men who received black cloth to wear in James's funeral procession. (*M.S.C.* ii. 326.)

1625, June 24—No. 4 in King's patent. (*M.S.C.* i. 282–3.)

1625, Dec.—At the King's order, Taylor was paid £66. 13. 8 to furnish the King's men with better apparel for the Christmas court performances. (See above, pp. 20–1.)

1626—'*Paris* the Tragaedian . . . Ioseph Taylor' in King's cast for

Massinger's *The Roman Actor*, lic. 11 October; he contributed prefatory verses to the 1629 quarto, 'to professe our loues Anti-quitie'. (1629 4° B.M.)

1626/7, Jan. 3< >9—'A peticõn of Richard Holden against Ioseph Taylor Anthony Smith and Thomas Hobbes Answered of course.' (*M.S.C.* ii. 400.)

1628—'Ioseph Taylor' was second in King's cast for *The Lover's Melancholy*, lic. 24 November. (1629 4° B.M.)

1628, Apr. 10—Warrant for payment to 'Iohn Hemings, Iohn Lowen, and Ioseph Taylor or to any one of them' of £100 for plays given by the King's company at court in 1627. (*M.S.C.* ii. 346.)

1629, May 6—'Ioseph Taylor' was named third in a cloak allowance for the King's men. (Ibid., p. 350.)

1629—'*Mathias* a knight of *Bohemia. Ioseph Taylor*', in King's cast for Massinger's *The Picture*, lic. 8 June. (1630 4° B.M.)

1629?—'Mr *Taylor, the Duke*', in King's cast for Carlell's *The Deserving Favourite*. (1629 4° B.M.)

1630/1, Feb. 18—'Received of Mr. Taylor and Lowins, in the name of their company, for the benefitt of my winter day, upon the second day of Ben Jonson's play of *Every Man in his Humour* ... 12*l.* 4*s.* 0*d.* (*Herbert*, p. 44.)

1631, Apr. 27—A warrant was issued for delivery 'vnto Ioseph Tailor for himselfe & thirteene others his ffellowes his Mates Players' of cloth for liveries. (*M.S.C.* ii. 355.)

1631—According to the stage directions, 'Mr Taylor' played Antiochus in King's production of *Believe as You List*, lic. 7 May. (Sisson, *B.A.Y.L.*, pp. xxxi ff.)

1631—The MS. of Arthur Wilson's *The Swisser* (B.M. Add. MS. 36759) gives his name in the cast for the Blackfriars production: 'Arioldus, A nobleman retir'd—Taylor.' (Feuillerat, *The Swisser*.)

c. 1631—Lowin and Taylor acquired housekeeper's shares in the Globe and Blackfriars. *See* Lowin.

1631/2, Feb. 22—'A Warraunt for payment of 120li vnto Iohn Lowing Ioseph Taylor & Elliard Swanson for themselues & the rest of their fellowes his Mates Comædians for 11 playes (one wherof at Hãpton Court) by them Acted before his Matye at Christmas 1631.' (*M.S.C.* ii. 358.)

1632—'MIRABELL, the *Wild-Goose*, a Travayl'd Monsieur, and great defyer of all Ladies in the way of Marriage, ... Incomparably Acted by Mr. *Joseph Taylor*' in the King's cast for the 1632 revival of *The Wild Goose Chase* which was printed in the 1652 edition. (B.M. copy.)

1632—Alexander Gill's slanderous verses on Jonson's *Magnetic Lady* (Wood's *Athenae*, ii. 598-9, from a Bodleian MS.) conclude:

> Lett playes alone, and yff thou needs wilte wright
> And thrust thy feeble muse into the light,
> Lett Lowine cease, and Taylore feare to touch
> The loathed stage, for thou hast made ytt such!

1632/3, Mar. 16—A warrant was issued for payment to 'Iohn Lowen Ioseph Taylor & Ellyard Swanston' of £270 for twenty-three plays and one rehearsal by the King's men at court. (*M.S.C.* ii. 360.)

1633, May 6—A warrant to 'take into yor Company any . . . Actor or Actors belonging to any of the lycensed Companyes wthin & about the Citty of London' was directed to 'Iohn Lowen and Ioseph Taylor two of the Company of his Ma^{tes} Players'. (Ibid., p. 361.)

1633, Oct. 24—Apologized to Herbert. See above, pp. 37–8.

1633/4, Jan. 6—'On Monday night, the sixth of January and the Twelfe Night, was presented at Denmark-house, before the King and Queene, Fletchers pastorall called *The Faithfull Shepheardesse*, in the clothes the Queene had given Taylor the year before of her owne pastorall.' (*Herbert*, p. 53.)

1634, Apr. 27—'A Warraunt for payment of 220^{li} vnto Iohn Lowen Ioseph Taylor & Elliard Swanston' for plays presented at court in the preceding year. (*M.S.C.* ii. 373.)

1634, July 18—Kendall told Crosfield. 'The Kings Company at ye private house of Blackfriars: The masters or cheife whereof are
{ Mr Talor
{ Mr Lowen.'
(*Crosfield's Diary*, p. 72; see Appendix, p. 688.)

1634—The third edition (1634) of Fletcher's *The Faithful Shepherdess*, whose title-page mentions the 1633/4 Twelfth Night court performance, contains a set of prefatory verses (the only addition to the front matter of the 1629 edition) signed 'Shack. Marmyon'. They read as follows:

Vnto his worthy friend M^r. *Ioseph Taylor* upon his presentment
of the *Faithfull Shepherdesse before the King and Queene, at Whitehall, on Twelfth night last. 1633.*

When this smooth Pastorall was first brought forth,
The Age twas borne in, did not know it's worth.
Since by thy cost, and industry reviv'd,
It hath a new fame, and new birth atchiv'd.
Happy in that shee found in her distresse,
A friend, as faithfull, as her Shepherdesse.
For having cur'd her from her courser rents,
And deckt her new with fresh habiliments,
Thou brought'st her to the Court, and made her be
A fitting spectacle for Majestie.
So have I seen a clowded beauty drest
In a rich vesture, shine above the rest.
Yet did it not receive more honour from
The glorious pompe, then thine owne action.
Expect no satisfaction for the same,
Poets can render no reward but Fame.
Yet this Ile prophesie, when thou shalt come
Into the confines of *Elysium*
Amidst the Quire of Muses, and the lists
Of famous Actors, and quicke Dramatists,
So much admir'd for gesture, and for wit,
That there on Seats of living Marble sit,
The blessed Consort of that numerous Traine,
Shall rise with an applause to entertaine
Thy happy welcome, causing thee sit downe,
And with a Lawrell-wreath thy temples crowne.

And meane time, while this Poeme shall be read,
Taylor, thy name shall be eternized.
For it is just, that thou, who first did'st give
Vnto this booke a life, by it shouldst live.

1636, Dec. 13—The warrant for a £20 weekly allowance to the King's players directed that payment should be made to ' John Lowen and Joseph Taylor, on behalf of their company'. (See above, p. 53.)

1636/7, Mar. 12—A warrant was issued directing payment to Lowin and Taylor for twenty-two plays given by King's at court, but Swanston signed the receipt 5 June 1638. (Law, *Forgeries*, App.)

1637, Apr. 22—A warrant for liveries for the King's men directed delivery to 'Iohn Lowen, Ioseph Taylor & Eilardt Swanston'. (*M.S.C.* ii. 383.)

1637, June 10—The Lord Chamberlain wrote the Stationers' Company that no plays should be published without the written consent of Taylor and Lowin for the King's company and Christopher Beeston for the King and Queen's young company, or their successors in management. (*M.S.C.* ii. 384–5.)

1637, Oct. 8—' Joseph Taylor Inf' bur. St. S.S.

1637—'Joseph Taylor, his Majesty's servant', petitioned for a waiter's place in the Custom House of London. (*C.S.P., Dom.*, 1637–8, p. 99.)

1637/8, Mar. 15—A warrant was issued for payment 'vnto Iohn Lowen, Ioseph Taylor & Eillart Swanston or any of them' for plays acted at court. (*M.S.C.* ii. 387.)

1638/9, Mar. 12—A warrant was issued for payment 'vnto Iohn Lowen, Ioseph Taylor & Eillardt Swanston or any one of them' for plays acted at court. (Ibid., pp. 388–9.)

1638/9, Mar. 14—A warrant for liveries for the King's men directed delivery to be made 'to Iohn Lowen, Ioseph Taylor & Eillardt Swanston'. (Ibid., p. 389.)

1639, Sept. 29—' A warrant to sweare Mr Ioseph Taylor yeoman of the Reuelles to his Matye in Ordinary in ye place of William Hunt deceased.' (Ibid., p. 391.)

1639, Oct. 21—A warrant was issued for the preparation of Taylor's patent as Yeoman of the Revels. (Ibid.)

1639, Nov. 11—The Letters Patent creating ' Ioseph Taylor' Yeoman of the Revels were copied into the L.C. Warrant Book. He was to receive sixpence a day, a yearly livery coat, 'one sufficient howse or mansion' for the safe-keeping of the vestures and trappings, 'together wth all manner of other comodities, and advantages to the sayd office to be due and accustomed'. The indenture was made 2 December 1639. (Ibid., pp. 343–6.)

1640, Apr. 4—A warrant was issued for the payment of £230 for plays given by King's at court 'vnto Iohn Lowen, Ioseph Taylor & Eillardt Swanston'. (Ibid., p. 392.)

1640/1, Mar. 20—A warrant was issued for the payment of £160 for plays given by King's at court 'to bee payd to Iohn Lowen. Ioseph Taylor & Eillardt Swanston or any of them'. (Ibid., p. 397.)

1640/1, Mar. 20—A warrant was issued for liveries 'for Iohn Lowen, Ioseph Taylor & Eillardt Swanston and fifteene others their fellowes'. (Ibid., pp. 397–8.)

1641—The following remark occurs in Act v, scene 1, of Killigrew's *Parson's Wedding*: '*Capt*. But who should I meet at the corner of the *Piazza*, but *Joseph Taylor*; he tells me, there's a new Play at the Fryers to day, and I have bespoke a Box for Master *Wild* and his Bride.' (1664 ed. B.M.)

1641—A list of the officers of the Revels in 1641 in the L.C. papers reads as follows (*M.S.C.* ii. 326) ·

Sᵣ Henry Herbert Mᵣ.
Alexander Stafford Clarke
Ioseph Taylor yeoman
Geo: Wilson Groome

>1642—In *Roscius Anglicanus* Downes tells of the Restoration performance of *Hamlet*, '. . . *Hamlet* being Perform'd by *Mr. Betterton*, Sir *William* (having seen *Mr. Taylor* of the *Black-Fryars* Company Act it, who being Instructed by the Author *Mr. Shaksepeur*) taught Mr. *Betterton* in every Particle of it'. Obviously Downes's genealogy is false, since Burbage preceded Taylor. Probably neither Burbage nor Shakespeare coached Taylor, since both were dead before he came to the company. (1708 ed. B.M.)

>1642—Wright says, '*Tayler* acted *Hamlet* incomparably well, *Jago*, *Truewit* in the *Silent Woman*, and *Face* in the *Alchymiʂt*', and that Lowin, Taylor, and Pollard were superannuated when the War began. (*Hist. Hist.*, pp. 4, 7; see Appendix, pp. 693 and 694.)

1645, Aug.—'For when the Stage at *Westminster*, where the two Houses now Act, is once more restored back againe to *Black-Fryers*, they have hope they shall returne to their old harmlesse profession of killing Men in Tragedies without Man-slaughter. Till then, they complaine very much that their profession is taken from them: and say 't was never a good World, since the Lord *Viscount Say and Seale* succeeded *Joseph Taylor*.' (Hotson, p. 19, from *Mercurius Anti-Britannicus*, B.M. E. 296. 9.)

1647—His name—'Joseph Taylor'—is sixth in the list of ten King's men who signed the dedication of the Beaumont and Fletcher folio. (1647 folio B.M.)

1647—In his verses to the Beaumont and Fletcher folio, Henry Harington says (1647 folio B.M.):

Judgement could ne're to this opinion leane
That Lowen, Tailor, ere could grace thy Scene:

1648—Taylor was playing Rollo in *Rollo or the Bloody Brother* when soldiers raided the Cockpit. (*Hist. Hist.*, p. 9; see Appendix, p. 695.)

1652—*The Wild Goose Chase* was published for the benefit of Lowin and Taylor; see John Lowin.

1652, Nov. 4—He was buried at Richmond. (Cunningham, *Revels*, p. l.)

1654—In his *Pleasant Notes on Don Quixot*, Gayton says, '*Taylor* acting *Arbaces* [in *A King and No King*] or *Swanston D'Amboys*, were shadowes to him. . . .' (1654 ed. B.M., p. 25.)

1656—In Gayton's 'Wit Revived or A New and Excellent way of divertisement, digested into most ingenious Qvestion and Answers' is the following (1656 ed. B.M., p. 45):

Q. *Which of our Tailors were the most famous?*
A. The Plaier and the Sculler.

1658—Flecknoe's character, '*Of one that imitates the good companion another way*', begins: 'He is on, who now the stage is down Acts the *Parasites* part at Table; and since *Tailors* death, none can play *Mosco's* part so well as he:' (*Enigmaticall Characters*, 1658 ed. B.M., p. 10.)

1664—In a coffee-house scene in the third act of Tatham's (?) *Knavery in All Trades*, a gentleman has mentioned a current play (1664 4° HN):

> *third.* . . . Bur [*sic*] sir, they say 'tis done rarely well.
> *fourth.* I cannot believe it, 'tis impossible they should do any thing so well as I have seen things done.
> *fifth.* When *Taylor Lowin*, and *Pollard* were alive.
> *fourth.* Did you not know *Benfield* and Swautted?
> *fifth.* Did I not know 'em? yes, and hum'd them off a hundred times.

1676—Snarl, 'a great Admirer of the last Age', in Shadwell's *Virtuoso*, says (Act I), when it is suggested that he can see plays, '. . . I have seen 'em at *Black-Friers*; pox, they act like Poppets now in sadness. I, that have seen *Joseph Taylor*, and *Lowen*, and *Swanstead*:'. (1676 4° B.M., pp. 15–16.)

TAYLOR, ROBERT. The Coventry clerk probably used the word 'players' simply in the sense of showmen; Robert Taylor is not known to have been connected with any company.

1638, July 12—'Paid given to Robert Tayler and Ann Mossock, players who came by warrant to shew the worlds creation' at Coventry. (Murray, ii. 253.)

TAYLOR, STAGE. A ghost name arising from Bullen and Murray's reading of the direction for two actors, 'Stage: Taylor' (Stagekeeper and Taylor), as the name of one actor in the MS. of *The Captives* (B.M. MS. Egerton 1994).

TAYLOR, THOMAS. Though we have only the assurance of the St. Giles registers that Thomas Taylor was an actor, the excerpts are quite sufficient to establish his occupation. His residence suggests that he may have been a hired man at the Fortune. The will of Thomas Taylor, pewterer, is doubtful, not because of his occupation, for Richard Errington (q.v.) the player styled himself pewterer, but because it was not proved for eleven years after the death of the St. Giles 'gent', who was probably the player.

1622–3?—*See* Taylor, ——.

1623, May 21—Markham's suit mentions 'Thomas Taylor of George Alley in Gouldinge Lane', 5s. (See Appendix, p. 683.)

1624, *c.* Sept. 3—*See* Taylor, ——.

1624/5, Jan. 10—'Sonne of Thomas Taylor, Player', bur. St. G.C.

1625, July 30—Thomas Taylor, citizen and pewterer of London, made his will; he left legacies to his sister-in-law, Margaret Taylor, and to his brothers Edward and Raphe. (See Appendix, pp. 648–9.)

1625, Aug. 4—'Thomas Taylor gent' bur. St. G.C.

1625, Aug. 21—'Roger sonne of Thomas Taylor Player' bur. St. G.C.
1636, May 13—The will which Thomas Taylor, pewterer, made in
   1625 was proved this date. (See Appendix, p. 649.)

TEODOR, JACOB. This man has sometimes been listed as an
English actor because he appeared in the company of Robert
Reynolds at Torgau in 1627 and at Cologne in 1628. At Torgau,
however, he was called 'der Hesse', and it seems unlikely that he
was English. (See Herz, *Englische Schauspieler*, pp. 31 and 54.)

THOMPSON (THOMSON, TOMPSON, TOMSON), JOHN. Young
Thompson was the leading boy actor in the King's company for
several years. He may have been the son of the 'Johne tomsone
player' to whom Henslowe made a loan in 1598, but nothing
certain is known of his antecedents or the date of his birth. We
know from Shank's reply to the players' petition in 1635 that he
had expended £40 for the company in connexion with Thompson,
but what this means we cannot be sure. Shank's statement may
mean that he had paid £40 to secure Thompson as his apprentice,
as Henslowe paid £8 for a boy in 1597 (*Hens. D.* i. 203). His
phrase, however, is not as definite as we could wish. The number
of boys Shank says he had paid for—more than four—and the
amount of money—£40 and his part of £200—seem rather exces-
sive if he is simply indicating the premiums he paid for apprentices. I have suggested (*see* John Shank) that Shank may have run
some sort of apprentices' boarding-house for the company (he
said he was maintaining three boys at the time) and that these
sums may represent the total fees which the company owed him
for the boys he boarded. In any case, Shank's statement indicates
that Thompson was closely associated with him.

From the casts of plays in which his name occurs, it is evident
that young Thompson played female roles for the company from
at least 1621 to 1631. In 1632, 1633, and 1634 he probably played
minor male roles, for, though he does not appear in any casts, he
was sworn a groom in 1633.

Mr. Baldwin (*Organization and Personnel*, p. 189) points out
that Thompson's roles are mostly those of the regal lady, haughty
queen, or proud villainess, and that the songs in several of his
parts indicate that he was something of a singer. Mr. Baldwin's
other comments on Thompson are sadly confused because he
assumes that the actor died in the plague of 1630 and was succeeded in all his roles by John Honyman, whereas we know now
that Thompson lived for four years after 1630. Far from succeed-
ing to Thompson's parts, Honyman had already begun to act
male roles when he played Sly in *The Soddered Citizen*, while
Thompson still had a female role, Miniona, in that play.

1619?—Fleay, followed by Professor Murray, says that Thompson is
   No. 6 in the cast of King's men for *The Laws of Candy* (1679 folio
   B.M.) This is an error, for Thompson is not mentioned in the cast.

1619–23—'The Cardinals Mⁱˢ. I. Tomson', in the cast of King's men
   prefixed to the 1623 quarto of *The Duchess of Malfi*. (1623 4° B.M.)
1621—No. 4 in King's cast for *The Pilgrim*. (1679 folio B.M.)
1623, Aug. 29—No. 5 in King's cast for *The Maid in the Mill*. (Ibid.)
1623, Dec. 6—No. 8 in King's cast for *The Lover's Progress*. (Ibid.)
1626—'*Domitia* the wife of *Aelius Lamia*—Iohn Tompson' in King's
   cast of Massinger's *The Roman Actor*, lic. 11 October. (1629 4°
   B.M.)
1628—No. 13 in King's cast for *The Lover's Melancholy*, lic. 24
   November. The roles are not given, but the position of his name
   indicates a woman's part. (1629 4° B.M.)
1629—'*Honoria* the Queene—*Iohn Tomson*' in King's cast for Massinger's *The Picture*, lic. 8 June. (1630 4° B.M.)
1629?—'*Iohn Tomson, Cleonarda*' in King's cast for Carlell's *The
   Deserving Favorite*. (1629 4° B.M.)
c. 1630—'*Miniona—his [Undermyne's] Daughter*—John Thompson'
   in King's cast given in the MS. of Clavell's (?) *The Soddered Citizen*.
   (*Sod. Cit.*, p. 3.)
1631—In the MS. of Arthur Wilson's *The Swisser* (B.M. Add. MS.
   36759) 'Panopia, The Kings sister—Tomson' appears in the cast
   for the Blackfriars production. (Feuillerat, *The Swisser*.)
1632, July 16—'Anne dau: of John Thomson, Player, in the house of
   Henry Hore, Carpenter in Wᵗcrss street' chris. St. G.C.
1632, Oct. 1—'Lettice dau: of John Thomson, player' bur. St. G.C.
1633, Apr. 15—In the L.C. Warrant books is 'A Warraunt to sweare
   Iohn Thompson A Groome of the Chamber in ordinary wᵗʰout ffee
   to attend in the quality of A Player.' (*M.S.C.* ii. 360.)
1634, Dec. 13—'John Thomson, Player' bur. St. G.C.
1635, May 18–July 12—John Shank said in his reply to the players'
   petition to the Lord Chamberlain that he had 'still of his owne
   purse supplyed the company for the service of his Maᵗy wᵗʰ boyes as
   Thomas Pollard, Iohn Thompson deceased (for whome Hee payd
   40ˡⁱ) . . . .' (*M.S.C.* ii. 369.)

THOMPSON, RICHARD. Richard Thompson was probably
simply a showman and no player.

1630—'Richard Tompson who had comission to play the Worlds
   wonder' was at Coventry. (Murray, ii. 251.)

THOMPSON (THOMSON, TOMSON), SAMUEL. Samuel Thompson
was apparently a fairly important member of the King's Revels
company; Kendall's account probably indicates that he was one
of the sharers of the company. He is the most likely candidate for
the player who 'died of the government' in 1652.

1634, July 18—Kendall told Crosfield that among the players at
   Salisbury Court was '6. Sam. Thompson'. (*Crosfield's Diary*, p. 72;
   see Appendix, p. 688.)
c. 1634 ?—'*Menester* an actor and Favorite compel'd by the Empresse
   —*Sam. Tomson*' in King's Revels cast for Richards's *Messalina*.
   (1640 ed. B.M.)
1652—In a satirical list of important events in Ralph Desmus's
   almanac, *Merlinus Anonymous*, for 18 November 1653 (B.M.

E. 1487[1]) is the following item: 'Thomson the player died of the govvt, 1652.' (Rollins, 'Commonwealth Drama', p. 304.)

TOBYE, EDWARD.

1624, Apr. 9—The Exeter records show that Edward Tobye was named in a confirmation of this date attached to a patent of 31 October 1617 and brought to Exeter and Norwich by William Perry in 1624. The Norwich record supplements the Exeter one, which is confused. The reference in the Exeter record to the company as 'Children of the Revells of the late Queene Anna' must have been copied from the confirmation, as the licence was issued more than a year before the death of Queen Anne. (*Hist. MSS. Com.*, Records of the City of Exeter, p. 171, and Murray, ii. 273, 347.)

?—He was perhaps the 'Toby:' in the prompter's notes of the MS. of *Thomas of Woodstock or Richard II* (B.M. MS. Egerton 1994, fol. 178b). 'Toby' apparently had the part of a servant. The date of the performance is uncertain; probably it was a revival. (Greg, *Dram. Doc.*, p. 255.)

TOOLEY (*alias* WILKINSON), NICHOLAS.

Nicholas Tooley, whose own will calls attention to his alias of Wilkinson, was a King's man from at least 1605 to 1623. Collier suggested (*H.E.D.P.* iii. 448) that he may have been the Nicholas, son of Charles Wilkinson, christened at St. Anne's Blackfriars, 3 February 1574/5. This is a good date for the player, but the names are not sufficiently unusual in London to make identification anything but hazardous.

Tooley was a member of the King's company before 4 May 1605, when Augustine Phillips left him a legacy as his 'fellowe'. Since Tooley had not been named in the patent of 19 May 1603, he must have succeeded to membership later in 1603 or in 1604. He must, however, have been connected with the company long before he succeeded to membership, for in his will he calls Richard Burbage 'my late Master', and the legacies and the burial record indicate that he was an intimate of the Burbage family. These facts make it pretty clear that Tooley had been Richard Burbage's apprentice, though the apprenticeship must have been completed—probably long completed—before Phillips called him 'fellowe'.

There are records of a number of plays in which Tooley acted, but his only known role is that of Forobosco in *The Duchess of Malfi*. Various writers have suggested that Tooley was one or another of the Nicks who appear in play MSS. and in the Henslowe papers. While Tooley may possibly be identified with one or more of the Nicks who appear before 1604, the Nicks in the play MSS. after 1616 are evidently hired men or boys and therefore possibly to be identified with Nicholas Burt or Nicholas Underhill, but certainly not with Nicholas Tooley.

Because the evidence as to his roles and his early connexions with the company is so inadequate, Mr. Baldwin's assignment of a 'line' and a career to him depends almost wholly upon conjecture and is not at all convincing.

It is obvious that Tooley's name was included in the cast of *A Wife for a Month* by mistake; he was buried nearly a year before the play was licensed.

1616-17—No. 7 in King's cast for *The Queen of Corinth*. (1679 folio B.M.)

1618, Nov. 16—No. 7 in King's cast for *The Loyal Subject*. (Ibid.)

1618/19, Mar. 12—He witnessed Richard Burbage's will. (See Appendix, p. 638.)

c. 1619-20—No. 3 in King's cast for *The Custom of the Country*. (1679 folio B.M.)

1619, Mar. 27—No. 5 in list of King's for patent. (*M.S.C.* i. 280-2.)

1619, May 19—No. 6 in King's livery allowance list. (*Hist. MSS. Com.*, Report IV, p. 299.)

1619?—No. 3 in King's cast for *The Laws of Candy*. (1679 folio B.M.)

1619, Sept. 6—'Confirmation to Nich. Tooley of a former grant of old debts due to the Crown, which grant was lately questioned.' (*C.S.P., Dom.*, 1619-23, p. 75.)

1619-21—No. 7 in King's cast for *Women Pleased*. (1679 folio B.M.)

1619-23—'Forobosco, *N. Towley*' and one of 'The seuerall mad men, *N. Towley, I. Vnderwood*, &c.' in the King's cast for *The Duchess of Malfi*. (1623 4° B.M.)

c. 1620—No. 6 in King's cast for *The False One*. (Ibid.)

1621—No. 2 in King's cast for *The Pilgrim*. (Ibid.)

1619-22—No. 5 in King's cast for *The Little French Lawyer*. (Ibid.)

1621, Apr. 7—No. 6 in King's livery allowance list. (*Hist. MSS. Com.*, Report IV, p. 299.)

c. 1621—No. 7 in King's cast for *The Double Marriage*. (1679 folio B.M.)

1622, May 14—No. 6 in King's cast for *The Prophetess*. (Ibid.)

1622, June 22—No. 3 in King's cast for *The Sea Voyage*. (Ibid.)

1622, Oct. 24—No. 3 in King's cast for *The Spanish Curate*. (Ibid.)

1623—No. 19 in the list of King's men in the Shakespeare folio.

1623, June 3—'Nicholas Tooley of London gentleman' made his will; there are numerous bequests to players, and Cuthbert Burbage and Henry Condell were made executors. In a codicil he affirmed that his name was 'Nicholas Wilkinson *als* Tooley'. (See Appendix, pp. 649-51.)

1623, June 5—'Nicholas Tooley, Gentleman, from the house of Cuthbert Burbidge, gentleman', bur. St. G.C.

1624, May 27—His name is third in King's cast for *A Wife for a Month*. (1679 folio B.M.)

TOSEDALL, ROGER.

1634/5, Mar. 10—His name is in the full list of players recorded at Norwich; some of them are King's Revels men, though the records do not give the name of the company, which seems to have been an amalgamation. (Murray, ii. 356; see above, pp. 286 and 288-9.)

TOWNSEND (TOWNESHEND), JOHN. John Townsend first appears in 1611 when he and Joseph Moore were named as the leaders of Lady Elizabeth's company in the patent of that year. For twenty years thereafter he appears as a leader of the company, almost always in the provinces. Of course Lady Elizabeth's men were only a provincial company during most of the years after 1616, but Townsend never appears with the company when it is found in London. Townsend and Moore generally appear together in the provincial records, but Moore, unlike Townsend, is often found in the London records of the company as well, and for at least one period he stopped acting entirely. There are several indications—notably in the Norwich records for 1624—that Townsend was thought by the local authorities to be a person of somewhat more consequence than the usual player.

Townsend's position in the 1634 patent for an unknown company—probably a provincial King's Revels organization—indicates quite a decline from his position as leader of the provincial Lady Elizabeth's men.

1616, June 5—Townsend brought the Lady Elizabeth's patent of 27 April 1611 to Norwich, but the company was forbidden to play and given a reward of 40s. (Murray, ii. 341–2.)

1617, July 11—Townsend and Joseph Moore were paid for three plays given during James's journey to Scotland. (Cunningham, *Revels*, xliv; see above, pp. 180–1.)

1617/18, Mar. 20—'Alexander ffoster John Townsend Joseph Moore & ffr Wamus servants to the Lady Elizabeth are lycensed to play in the Citty of London & by the space of xiiii^{en} dayes at any one tyme in the yeare in any other Citty. . . .' (Murray, ii. 344–5.)

1618, May 23—'This day John Towneshend brought' the above licence to Norwich. (Ibid.)

1619, Nov. 15—'Christopher Bodie servant servant [*sic*] to John Townesend a Player of Enterludes, . . . Stab'd with an All' bur. St. Bodolph's Aldgate. (Denkinger, p. 106.)

1620, Apr. 22—Waymus brought the patent of 20 March 1617/18 to Norwich; Moore was not with the company, but Townsend evidently was, for the Chamberlains' Accounts for the year 1620–1 contain records of two payments to him: 'Itm gyven to Townshend & others of the Lady Elizabeth her Company of players—xls' and 'Itm to Towneshend and other Players of the Lady Elizabeth's Company as by warrant appeareth—xls'. The Accounts are not dated by month and day, so that it is impossible to tell just when these two visits of the company occurred. (Murray, ii. 345, 370.)

1621, May 2—Townsend brought the Lady Elizabeth's licence of 20 March 1617/18 to Norwich, but 'none of the said Company but onely the said Towneshend are nowe in Towne'; permission to play was refused. (Ibid., p. 346.)

1621/2, Mar. 13—'A bill signed for John Townsend Alexander Foster & Joseph Moore the Lady Elizabeths graces her playe^{rs} and one Francis Wanibus name being added by the Clerke of ye Signett.' (Ibid., p. 193.)

1622, May 1—'This day Towneshend brought a Bill signed by his Matie authorisinge him & his Company as the Lady Elizabethes players to play. . . . They are denyed for many reasons alledged vnto them.' Norwich. (Ibid., p. 346.)

1623, May 10—He was named in the licence of 20 March 1621/2 which Waymus presented at Norwich. (Murray, ii. 346-7.)

1624, Apr. 24—Townsend was named in the Lady Elizabeth's patent of 20 March 1621/2 which Waymus showed at Norwich. When he was forbidden to play, Waymus defied the Mayor. (Ibid., p. 348.)

1624, Apr. 26—Townsend was summoned before the Mayor with others named in the Lady Elizabeth's patent for putting up a play-bill at Norwich; only Waymus was there, and he was committed to prison because he would offer no sureties for his good behaviour. (Ibid., pp. 348-9.)

1624, May 24—After nearly a month in prison, Francis Waymus desired 'tyme of deliberacion . . . till the comeinge of his fellowe Towneshend wᶜʰ should be this afternoone'. (Ibid., p. 349.)

1624, July 9—'Mʳ Townesend and his fellowes, being the Ladie Elizabeth her players', were paid 20s. at Leicester. (Ibid., p. 316.)

1624, Sept. 28 (morning)—The Norwich jailer was willing to discharge Francis Waymus and Bee, 'ffor he said Mʳ Towneshend had given his word to pay the chardges, And the said Wambus & Mʳ Towneshend beinge here in Court desired recompence for the imprisonment of Wambus'. (Ibid., p. 350.)

1624, Sept. 28 (afternoon)—'mʳ Wambus & mʳ Towneshend players' came to the special session of the Norwich court to ask recompence for the imprisonment of Waymus; they were given nothing. (Ibid.)

1628, July 17—A new licence was granted to 'Ioseph Moore, Robert Gilman, Alexander Foster and [blank] and the rest of their Company the Lady Elizabeths [Company] servantes', who were to have 'the same Priviledges as Iohn Townsend, Alexander Foster Ioseph Moore and Francis Wambus and their company haue heeretofore enjoyed in the time of oʳ Souueraigne Lord King Iames'. Probably Townsend's name belongs in the blank, since he is later mentioned as one of the new licensees. (M.S.C. ii. 347-8; see above, p. 189.)

1628, Dec. 9—'Joseph Tounsend' is named as one of four leaders in a docquet for a new licence for the Lady Elizabeth's company. (C.S.P., Dom., 1628-9, p. 406; see above, p. 189, n. 3.)

1629, June 27—Ellis Guest showed at Norwich a Master of the Revels licence of 8 June 1629 naming Moore, Foster, Guilman, and Townsend. He said that the rest of the company was at Thetford. (Murray, ii. 353.)

1629, Dec. 24—Moore, Foster, Guilman, and Townsend were at Reading with a licence of 15 December 1628. (Ibid., p. 386.)

1631, Mar. 30—With Joseph Moore, Townsend was payee for Lady Elizabeth's at Coventry. (Ibid., p. 251.)

1634, Nov. 28—In a licence of this date shown at Norwich 3 September 1635, the following players are named: William Daniel, William Hart, John Townsend, Samuel Minion, Hugh Houghton, and Thomas Doughton. The company is unnamed. Professor Murray thinks, with some evidence, that it was a new King's Revels company. (Ibid., pp. 8, 357.)

TOWYER, WILLIAM (see TAWYER, WILLIAM).

TRIGG, WILLIAM. Trigg was a boy in the King's company in the late twenties and early thirties, probably John Shank's apprentice, as the statement in Shank's will seems to imply. By 1636 Trigg was apparently a hired man of the company, since he appears in the players' pass of that year. He had joined Beeston's Boys before August 1639, the most likely time being the winter of 1636–7 when the company was formed.

Mr. Baldwin's reconstruction of Trigg's 'line' in the plays of the King's company is unsatisfactory because, as in so many other cases, he is forced to work from inadequate evidence. In only two of the plays which Professor Baldwin examined (*The Picture* and *The Wild Goose Chase*) does Trigg have a well-defined role, and one of these was written, certainly with another actor in mind, eleven years before the performance in which Trigg took part. Since Trigg's roles in these two plays were humorous and pert, Mr. Baldwin concluded that his 'line' was that of the 'pert, madcap waiting-maid, the female comedian', and assigned him this type of role in other plays (*Organization and Personnel*, pp. 191, 219, 368). Unfortunately Mr. Baldwin had not seen the casts of *The Swisser* and *The Soddered Citizen*. In both plays Trigg takes the part of a modest maiden in love, and in the latter he is Modestina, a very female prig, a smug lecturer on morality to her gay unconventional friend, Miniona. Trigg's roles illustrate the danger in assuming too easily that the actors of the Jacobean and Caroline dramatic companies always performed the same general types of roles.

The actor was probably the William Trigg found in St. Giles in the Fields from 1642 to 1652, for he was a member of the company performing in the theatre in that parish. It is possible that he was also the William Trigg of St. Botolph's Bishopsgate; if so, he must have been married, bereaved, and married again in a period of seven months. The William Trigg whom Collier found marrying Cicely Baker at St. Anne's Blackfriars in 1620 (Bod.) cannot have been the boy of the King's company, who was still acting female roles twelve years after this date.

Trigg's rank in 1642 is rather surprising, but not so puzzling as the reference to Trigg the turncoat. This epigram must have first appeared in the 1654 or 1663 edition of *Wit's Recreations*, which I have been unable to examine; it is not in the 1640 or 1641 editions. If it refers to the actor, Trigg must be coupled with Swanston as a second player who deserted the royal cause. It is unfortunate that the epigram does not identify Trigg more closely.

1626 —' *Iulia Titus* Daughter. William Trigge', in King's cast for Massinger's *The Roman Actor*, licensed·11 October. (1629 4° B.M.)

1628—'William Trigg' was No. 16 in King's cast for *The Lover's Melancholy*, lic. 24 November. The roles are not given, but the position of his name in the cast indicates that he took a woman's part. (1629 4° B.M.)

1629—'*Corsica, Sophias* woman. *William Trigge*', in King's cast for Massinger's *The Picture*, licensed 8 June. (1630 4° B.M.)

c. 1630—'*Modestina—his* [Undermyne's] *Orphant*—Will: Trigge', in King's cast in the MS. of Clavell's (?) *The Soddered Citizen.* (*Sod. Cit.*, p. 3.)

1631—In the MS. of Arthur Wilson's *The Swisser* (B.M. Add. MS. 36759), 'Selina, Daughter to Clephis—Trigg' appears in the cast for the Blackfriars production. (Feuillerat, *The Swisser.*)

1632—'*William Trigg*' took the part of 'ROSALURA', one of the 'Aërie Daughters of *Nantolet*', in the King's cast for the 1632 revival of *The Wild Goose Chase*, printed in 1652. (B.M. copy.)

1635, Dec. 31—Shank's will speaks of 'Two and Twenty shillings for Trigg' which the company owes him. (See Appendix, p. 647.)

1636, May 17—'Wm Trig' was third in a list of minor King's men named in a players' pass. (*M.S.C.* ii. 378–9.)

1639, Aug. 10—'William Trig:' was second in a list of 'ye young Company of [*sic*] at ye Cockpitt Players' named in a ticket of privilege. (Ibid., pp. 390–1.)

1641, June 6—'William Trig and Elizabeth Morton, b.' mar. St. B.B.

1641/2, Jan. 9—'William Trigge and Elisabeth Bird' mar. St. G.F.

1642, Dec.—'A satirical pamphlet addressed to Parliament in December, 1642, advocated religious stage plays with psalm-singing between the acts, and assured the august body that, if plays could be made to edify, "Captaine *Trig*, and the rest of the Players which are now in service, would doubtlessely returne to their callings, and much lessen the King's Army".' (Hotson, p. 13, from B.M. E. 179.28, reprinted *Antiquarian Repertory* [1808], iii.)

1641–63—The following couplet from *Wit's Recreations* is quoted in *Facetiae*, II, 139:

On Trigg

Trigg having turn'd his sute he struts in state,
And tells the world he's now regenerate.

1647/8, Feb. 4—'Thomas sonne of William and Elisabeth Trigge' chris. St. G.F. 'Thomas so: of William Trigg' was buried 8 November 1651.

1651, May 17—'Mathew sonne of William Trigg' bur. St. G.F.

1651, Nov. 16—'Elizabeth Da: of William Trigg' bur. St. G.F.

1652, May 28—'A stilborne childe of William Trigg' bur. St. G.F.

TRUNDLE, JOHN. There is only the fact that the majority of the defendants in Markham's suit were actors to suggest that Trundle was connected with the stage.

1623, May 21—'Iohn Trundle att the nobodye in Barbican', 5*s.*, is one of the defendants in Markham's suit. (See Appendix, p. 682.)

TUCKE, T. (*see* TUCKFIELD, THOMAS).

TUCKFIELD, THOMAS. Tuckfield was evidently a hired man of the King's company. The correspondence between the abbreviated name in the stage directions of *The Two Noble Kinsmen* and the name in Sir Henry Herbert's exemption and the dissimilarity between the abbreviation and all other names associated with the King's company make it easy to identify T. Tucke. The date of the revised MS. of *The Two Noble Kinsmen* is fixed, in part, by the appearance of 'Curtis' and 'T. Tucke' in the stage directions of the 1634 quarto. See Chambers, *Shakespeare*, i. 530.

1624, Dec. 27—'Thomas Tuckfeild' was twelfth in a list of twenty-one 'Musitions and other necessary attendantes' of the King's company whom Herbert exempted from arrest. (*Herbert*, pp. 74–5; see above, pp. 15–16.)

c. 1625–6—The stage directions for *The Two Noble Kinsmen*, v. 3, indicate that he had a minor part: 'some Attendants, T. Tucke: Curtis'. (1634 4° B.M.)

TURNER, ANTHONY. Turner first appears as a member of Lady Elizabeth's company at the Cockpit in 1622, and for fifteen years thereafter he was an actor at that theatre, appearing in all known casts of Queen Henrietta's men except that of *The Renegado*. He was evidently not an important member of the organization; Crosfield did not mention him among the five leaders of the company in 1634, though he was certainly a member at that time, and his roles in the five plays in which he is known to have had a part are not very conspicuous ones. In three of the plays he had the part of an old man.

As Herbert's office-book indicates, Turner formed part of the nucleus of old Queen Henrietta's men out of which the new Queen Henrietta's company was formed when Beeston installed his new company at the Phoenix in 1637 (see above, pp. 237–9). Turner seems to have remained with this company until the theatres were closed; the livery warrant of January 1641/2 indicates that he was of more importance in the new organization than he had been in the old.

Turner's arrest in 1659 for maintaining plays at the Red Bull suggests that he had acted for some time during the Commonwealth period, for the Red Bull was one of the more conspicuous theatres in this period (see Hotson, pp. 3–59).

There is no way of identifying the unfortunate Anthony Turner who was having trouble with his wife in 1624, but the Anthony Turner of St. Giles in the Fields may well have been the actor, who performed for at least fifteen years at the theatre in that parish. One would expect to find entries concerning his family 1622–36, but unfortunately the burial and christening registers for that period have been lost (see Bentley, *R.E.S.*, pp. 149–50).

1622—He was the last of seven named by Herbert as the 'chiefe of them at the Phoenix'. (*Herbert*, p. 63.)

1624, Oct. 23—'Recognizances, taken before Thomas Saunderson esq. J.P., of William Brooke of St. Michael's, Bashinshaw London smith and Stephen Hosier of St. James's Westminster, in the sum of forty pounds each; For the appearance of Dorothy Turner at the next Session of the Peace for Middlesex, to answer "for cruelly beatinge and abusinge her husband Anthony Turner".' (*Middx. Co. Rec.* ii. 185.)

1626—'Iustice *Landby*. *Anthony Turner*', in the Queen Henrietta's cast for Shirley's *The Wedding*. (1629 4° HN.)

c. 1630—'*A kitching Maid*; *by* M^r. Anthony Furner [*sic*]' in the cast of Queen Henrietta's men in the 1631 quarto of Heywood's *The Fair Maid of the West*, Part I; '*Bashaw* Alcade. *By* M^r. Anthonie Turner', in the cast prefixed to Part II, though Wilbraham had had this role in Part I. (1631 4° B.M.)

> 1634—'Old Lord *Bruce*, M. [Mr.] *Turner*', in Queen Henrietta's cast for Davenport's *King John and Matilda*. (1655 4° B.M.)

1635—'Piston. By Anthony Turner', in Queen Henrietta's cast for Nabbe's *Hannibal and Scipio*. (1637 4° B.M.)

1636, Nov. 26—'Mary Daughter of Anthony Turner' bur. St. G.F.

1637, *c.* Oct. 2—'I disposed of Perkins, Sumner, Sherlock and Turner, to Salisbury Court, and joynd them with the best of that company.' (*Herbert*, p. 66.)

1639/40, Feb. 8—'Jone wife of Anthony Turner' bur. St. G.F.

1639/40, Mar. 6—'A warr^t for payment of 80^li vnto Henry Turner &^c the Queenes Players for 7 playes by them Acted at Court Annis 1638 & 1639.' Since no Henry Turner is known elsewhere, the name here given is probably a mistake for Anthony Turner. (*M.S.C.* ii. 392.)

1640/1, Jan. 8—A warrant was issued providing liveries, to be delivered 'vnto Richard Perkins & Anthony Turner for them selues & twelue others their fellowes in all fowerteene & of the Queenes Ma^tes Company of Players'. (Ibid., p. 396.)

1641, Oct. 1—'Mary Daughter of Anthony Turner' bur. St. G.F.

1642, Apr. 4—'Jane Daughter of Anthony Turner' bur. St. G.F.

1650/1, Mar. 19—'A Crisom Child of Anthony Turner' bur. St. G.F.

1653—Heminges's *The Fatal Contract*, whose title-page says that it was 'Acted with great Applause by her *Majesties* Servants', has a dedication to James Compton, Earl of Northampton, signed 'A. T.' and 'A. P.' The initials may stand for Anthony Turner and Andrew Pennycuicke (for whom it was printed), since certainly Turner and possible Pennycuicke had been players in the company which performed the play. (1653 4° HN.)

1659, May 12 and 17—With Edward Shatterell, he was summoned before the Sessions of the Peace for 'the unlawfull mainteining of Stage plays and enterludes att the Redd Bull in St. John's Street'. *See* Edward Shatterell.

TURNER, DREW or TRUE. Turner was a member of the company of players which was arrested at Banbury because the local authorities said they were rogues with a forged licence. Turner's statement that he simply drove the horse and beat the drum is interesting evidence of important provincial functions, but it cannot be accepted as evidence that Turner did not act. He preempted a role which the Banbury Puritans would find less offensive than any other connected with a dramatic company, and since there were only six in the company, it is pretty certain that all of them had to appear on the stage.

1633, May 2—'Examination of Drewe Turner. Has been with this company of players these twelve months. Does nothing but drive the horse and beat the drum. Knows not where his master dwells, nor whether his master has a wife, nor does he know anything concerning the commission in question.' (*C.S.P., Dom.*, 1633-4, p. 48.)

1633, May 3—'Further examination of the same. Richard Bradshaw is his master, and Edward Whiting and Bradshaw were partners and went together.' (Ibid.)

1633, May 22—At the order of the Privy Council, he was fetched with others from the jail at Banbury where he had been imprisoned for playing with a forged licence. Since all the men were accused of giving false names, this one may be assumed. (Murray, ii. 163-7; *M.S.C.* i. 384-5.)

1633, June 3—He appeared before the Privy Council in London. (*M.S.C.* i. 385.)

1633, June 8—He was discharged upon bond; *see* Bartholomew Jones for other documents. (Ibid., p. 385.)

TURNER, HENRY. This name in the warrant of 6 March 1639/40 for payment for plays given at Court by Queen Henrietta's men is probably a mistake for Anthony Turner (q.v.).

UNDERHILL, NICHOLAS. Underhill was a hired man in the King's company whose roles, except for Shackle in *The Soddered Citizen*, are uncertain. I am inclined to think, however, that Underhill was both the 'nick' of *Barnavelt* and the 'Nick' of *Believe as You List*. His parts in the latter play are much the same as the role he is known to have had about the same time in *The Soddered Citizen*, and he is more likely than any other known candidate for the role of Barnavelt's wife in *Sir John van Olden Barnavelt*. (*See* Nick.)

A man named 'vnderell' was paid wages by Henslowe in October 1602; apparently he was a hired man of Worcester's company. It is possible that he was the man who later worked for the King's men, but if so he cannot have been the Nick of Barnavelt.

1619, Aug.—He was probably the 'nick' who played Barnavelt's wife in the King's production of *Sir John van Olden Barnavelt*. See Nick.

1624, Dec. 27—'Nicholas Vnderhill' is the eighth name is the list of twenty-one employees of the King's men exempted from arrest by Sir Henry Herbert. (*Herbert*, p. 74; see above, pp. 15-16.)

c. 1630—'*Shackle—his other Keeper*—Nich: Vnderhill' in King's cast in the MS. of Clavell's (?) *The Soddered Citizen*; also '*Brayde—A Haberd: of small ware—Shac: disguis'd*'. (*Sod. Cit.*, p. 3.)

1631—He was probably the Nick of *Believe as You List* who played a Carthaginian officer and two attendants. *See* Nick.

UNDERHILL (UNDERELL, UNDRILL), THOMAS. The musician and trumpeter at St. Saviour's is probably the same as the Thomas Underell who was a royal trumpeter, 1603-24 (*King's Musick*, *passim*). There is only a possibility that Underhill was connected with the stage as other St. Saviour's musicians were.

1602/3, Feb. 13—'Thomas Undrill s of Thomas musitian' chris. St. S.S

1608, July 19—'Alphonso Underhill s of Thomas the king's Trumperter' chris. St. S.S.

1631/2, Mar. 16—'daughter of Thomas Underhill, Musitian' bur. St. G.C. (Bod.)

UNDERWOOD, JOHN. Underwood first appears as a boy with the company of the Children of the Chapel, acting in *Cynthia's Revels* and *The Poetaster*. In 1608 he became a King's man with his fellow actor, William Ostler. Years later it was said that the King's men took over the Queen's Revels theatre, Blackfriars, partially out of a desire to possess Underwood and Ostler. Apparently both came in as members (see *Organization and Personnel*, p. 49). From this time until his death in 1624 Underwood appeared regularly in lists of the King's company.

Though Underwood's name is found in more than twenty casts, his only known role is that of Delio in *The Duchess of Malfi*. Mr. Baldwin thinks that he played 'princely libertines and rascals', 'gallant princes', and, for a time, juvenile leads for the King's men (op. cit., pp. 209–11, 253–4, 318). Though there is no doubt that these 'lines' are to be found in the company's plays during the time of Underwood's membership, Mr. Baldwin has assigned them to Underwood largely by a process of elimination—a method which is not very reliable. His assignments of roles are, therefore, too conjectural to be of much value.

Underwood's will shows that he owned shares in the Blackfriars, Globe, and Curtain theatres. It is not unlikely, as Mr. Baldwin suggests (op. cit., p. 102), that some time between 1612 and 1614 he had secured the shares which had been left to his heirs by Thomas Pope.

Since Underwood calls himself a resident of St. Bartholomew the Less in his will, it is not unlikely that he was the 'John Underwood, gent', whose son John was christened in that parish 27 December 1610. (Bod.)

1616–17—No. 3 in King's cast for *The Queen of Corinth*. (1679 folio B.M.)

1616–18—No. 3 in King's cast for *The Knight of Malta*. (Ibid.)

1618, Nov. 16—No. 6 in King's cast for *The Loyal Subject*. (Ibid.)

c. 1619–20—No. 4 in King's cast for *The Custom of the Country*. (Ibid.)

1619?—No. 6 in King's cast for *The Laws of Candy*. (Ibid.)

1619?—No. 7 in King's cast for *The Humorous Lieutenant*. (Ibid.)

1619, Mar. 27—No. 6 in patent for King's. (*M.S.C.* i. 280–2.)

1619, May 19—No. 5 in livery allowance list for King's. (*Hist. MSS. Com.*, Report IV, p. 299.)

1619–21—No. 2 in King's cast for *Women Pleased*. (1679 folio B.M.)

1619–21—No. 2 in King's cast for *The Island Princess*. (Ibid.)

1619-22—No. 3 in King's cast for *The Little French Lawyer*. (Ibid.)

1619-23—'Delio, *I. Vnderwood*', and 'The seuerall mad men, *N. Towley. I. Vnderwood*, &c', in the cast of King's men prefixed to the 1623 quarto of *The Duchess of Malfi*. Apparently he had the part in both the original production >1614 and the revival 1619-23. (1623 4° B.M.)

c. 1620—No. 2 in King's cast for *The False One*. (1679 folio B.M.)

1621—No. 6 in King's cast for *The Pilgrim*. (Ibid.)

1621, Apr. 7—No. 5 in livery allowance list for King's. (*Hist. MSS. Com.*, Report IV, p. 299.)

c. 1621—No. 3 in King's cast for *The Double Marriage*. (1679 folio B.M.)

1622, June 22—No. 5 in King's cast for *The Sea Voyage*. (Ibid.)

1623—No. 18 in the list of King's men in the Shakespeare folio.

1623, June 3—Nicholas Tooley in his will said, ' I doe release and forgiue vnto John Vnderwood and William Ecclestone all such sommes of monie as they doe severallie owe vnto mee.' (See Appendix, p. 650.)

1623, Aug. 29—No. 3 in King's cast for *The Maid in the Mill*. (1679 folio B.M.)

1623, Dec. 6—No. 6 in King's cast for *The Lover's Progress*. (Ibid.)

1624, May 27—No. 5 in King's cast for *A Wife for a Month*. (Ibid.)

1624, Oct. 4—' John Vnderwood, of the parish of St: Bartholomewes the lesse in London, gent.', made his will; he left theatre shares and mentioned several members of the King's company. (See Appendix, p. 651.)

VERNON, GEORGE. It is difficult to determine whether George Vernon was a member or a hired man in the King's company. He is included in the list of attendants of the company whom Sir Henry Herbert exempted from arrest 27 December 1624, and he is absent from all patent lists of the company and from the list of players who submitted to Herbert in the affair of *The Spanish Viceroy*, 20 December 1624. This evidence indicates that he was a hired man. Yet his presence in the company's livery lists of >5 May 1625 and 6 May 1629 would seem to indicate that he was a member. If he had become a member between *The Spanish Viceroy* list of December 1624 and the livery list of May 1625 he would have appeared in the patent of 24 June 1625, but he does not. After Charles came to the throne Vernon may, therefore, have belonged, as Mr. Baldwin suggests (*Organization and Personnel*, pp. 118-19), to some special class of hired men entitled to livery. His known roles are quite unimportant ones.

The registers of St. Saviour's Southwark establish both his residence in that parish and his connexion with the King's company. Collier (Bod.) says that in addition to the children mentioned below, George Vernon had a son Thomas baptized at St. Saviour's 21 September 1624. This is certainly a mistake, for I made a second search of the St. Saviour's registers, looking especially for a reference to Thomas Vernon in all burial and

christening entries of September 1623, 1624, and 1625; possibly
only the date is wrong.

1624, Dec. 27—He was tenth in a list of twenty-one attendants of
King's whom Herbert exempted from arrest. (*Herbert*, p. 74; see
above, pp. 15–16.)

1624/5, Feb. 8—He is probably the 'G: Ver:' who appears (fol. 5ᵃ)
with 'I: Rho:' (John Rhodes) as a creditor in the prompter's notes
of the MS. of *The Honest Man's Fortune* (Dyce MS. 9). Though
the play was first performed in 1613, it was probably in the revival
licensed by Herbert 8 February 1624/5 that Rhodes and Vernon
appeared. (Greg, *Dram. Doc.*, p. 291.)

1625, >May 5—He was seventh in the list of King's men who received black cloth for James's funeral procession. (*M.S.C.* ii. 325.)

1626—' 2. Lictors—George Vernon. Iames Horne', in King's cast for
Massinger's *The Roman Actor*, lic. 11 October. (1629 4° B.M.)

1626, July 23—'Elizabeth Vernon d of George ye ks player' chris.
St. S.S.

1628, July 7—'Anne Vernon d of George a player' chris. St. S.S.

1628—No. 11 in King's cast for *The Lover's Melancholy*, lic. 24
November. (1629 4° B.M.)

1629, May 6—He was thirteenth in a list of King's men named in a
livery allowance. (*M.S.C.* ii. 350.)

1630, Apr. 30—'George s of George Vernon a Player' chris. St. S.S.

VINCENT, THOMAS. Thomas Vincent is known only from Taylor's
anecdote. The story itself is simply an old one with new names
which offers no clue to the date of Vincent's connexion with the
company, but Taylor's association of Vincent with a player who
was dead before 1608 suggests that Vincent held the book in the
early days of the Globe. Mr. Baldwin (*Organization and Personnel*, pp. 124, 129, 134, 136, 141, n. 84, and 289, n. 14) builds
up quite a structure of conjectures about Vincent as book-holder
for the company in Shakespeare's time, but his only evidence is
Taylor's anecdote.

1638—In the seventeenth anecdote in *Taylors Feast*, Taylor says,
'I my selfe did know one *Thomas Vincent* that was a Book-keeper
or prompter at the Globe play-house neere the Banck-end in Maid-
lane: As also I did know *Iohn Singer*, who play'd the Clownes part
at the Fortune-play-house in *Golding-Lane* . . .' (1638 4° HN,
pp. 66–7.)

VINCENT, WILLIAM. William Vincent was the leader of a company of jugglers and tight-rope walkers which certainly offered
competition to the provincial companies. Vincent may well have
performed at the Fortune, for juggling and tight-rope walking
are known to have been presented at that theatre, and Vincent
lived in the parish.

1622, June 8< >Aug. 26—At Leicester ten shillings was 'given to
Vincent and his Company, by Mʳ Maiors Appointmᵗ, having
authoritye from the King to shew feats of Activitye'. (Murray,
ii. 314.)

1627, Dec. 13—'A license vnder the Signett vnto Wm Vincent wth the rest of his Company to exercise and practize the Arte of legerdemaine wth all his other feates of activitie, As vaulting, danceing on the ropes for his best Comodotie in any Convenient place w^thin any his Ma^ts Dominions, Any provinciall lawe or any other lawe or Restraint whatsoeuer to the contrary notw^thstanding . . .' (P.R.O., Signet Office Docquets, October 1627 to July 1630, C82./2024.)

1630, June 1—'Eliz: Thorpe sut to Willm Vincent Jugler' bur. St. G.C.

1630, Aug.—At Coventry five shillings was 'given to William Vincent who came wth comission from the Kings Maties to show feats of activitie & legerdemaine'. (Murray, ii. 251.)

1631, June 26—'Margaret dau. of Wm Vincent Tumbler' chris. St. G.C. 'Margaret dau: of Wm Vincent Jugler' bur. 12 May 1632.

1632, May 24—'James sonne of Wm Vincent Jugler' bur. St. G.C.

1635, Nov. 13—'Willm Vincent one of the patentees' showed a licence of 13 December 1627, confirmed by the Master of the Revels, at Norwich; 'hee hath tyme to exercise his feates till Wednesday night next'. (Murray, ii. 358.)

1636–7—He was at Gloucester twice between 29 September 1636 and 28 September 1637. On the first occasion £1. 6s. 8d. was 'payd vnto Vincente that caries sightes & shewes with dauncing on the Ropp wch was by order of the Justices'; on the second £0. 13s. 4d. was 'payd more vnto Vincent at his 2nd coming to towne in that the tyme of contagious sicknes might prove dangerous by order of the Justices'. (Ibid., 285.)

1642, Dec. >7—At Coventry ten shillings was 'given to William Vincent who had comission for him & his company to daunce vpon the ropes & shew other trickes of legerdemeane'. (Ibid., p. 254.)

WAIDE, JOHANN.

1650, Nov. 10—'Johann Waide' is one of the four members mentioned in a letter from the Emperor Ferdinand III asking safe conduct for a company of English comedians in Germany. (Cohn, *Sh. in Ger.*, p. c.)

WALPOLE, FRANCIS. Walpole must have left the company before the Baskervile suit was instituted in 1623. He is not found in the livery allowance of 1619.

1616, June—He was named in the Baskervile suit as a member of Queen Anne's at the time of the second settlement in favour of Francis Browne. (Fleay, *Stage*, p. 275.)

1617, June 3—He signed the new agreement of Queen Anne's with the Baskerviles, who said that he was a fellow and sharer of the company at the time. (Ibid., pp. 285–8.)

WAMBUS (WAMUS, WANIBUS, WAYMUS), FRANCIS. Francis Wambus first appears as a Lady Elizabeth's man in the company's bond to Henslowe in 1611. Thereafter he appears only with the provincial company, never in London. He was one of the leaders of the provincial organization, a man who demanded the players' rights whether local authorities wished them to play or not. The

affair in which Wambus figured at Norwich must be fairly characteristic of the adventures of the provincial companies, though
none of the other town clerks seems to have had the admirable
loquacity of the one at Norwich. Wambus probably died or gave
up playing between the time of the Norwich conflict and the
issuance of the new licence of 1628, for though he is named in the
new patent, it is as a former leader of the company and not as a
member of the new organization.

1617/18, Mar. 20—With Foster, Townsend, and Moore, 'ffr Wamus'
was licensed as 'servants to the Lady Elizabeth'. The licence was
shown at Norwich 23 May 1618, where the company was given
permission to play. (Murray, ii. 344–5.)

1620, Apr. 22—'ffrancis Wamus' brought the licence of 20 March
1617/18 to Norwich; Moore was absent. (Ibid., p. 345.)

1621, May 2—Townsend brought the 1617/18 patent to Norwich; he
was the only member of the company present and was refused permission to play. (Ibid., p. 346.)

1621/2, Mar. 13—A warrant for the Lady Elizabeth's new licence
names Townsend, Foster, and Moore, 'and one Francis Wanibus
name being added by the Clerke of ye Signett in drawing vp of the
bill allthough not menconed in his Lop warrant'. (Ibid., p. 193.)

1623, May 10—'ffrancis wambus' brought the Lady Elizabeth's
licence of 20 March 1621/2 to Norwich. (Ibid., pp. 346–7.)

1624, Apr. 24—When 'ffrancis wambus' presented the Lady Elizabeth's patent of 20 March 1621/2 at Norwich, he was shown the
Privy Council bill forbidding plays, 'wherevpon the said Wambus
pemtorily affirmed that he would play in this City & would lay in
prison here this Tweluemoneth but he would try whether the kings
comand or the Counsells be the greater. . . . And therevpon the
said wambus was . . . comanded to forbeare to play. . . . And he
neutheles answered that he would make tryall what he might doe
by the kings authority for he said he would play.' (Ibid., p. 348.)

1624, Apr. 26—After Wambus had fastened up a playbill announcing
that the company would perform *The Spanish Contract*, he was
called before the Mayor 'and saide confidently that he & his Company would play the Comedy aforesaid . . . he saide yt [the play-
bill] was his hand writinge & that he caused yt to be set vp this day
And . . . he said notwthstandinge that he would play & taxed Mr
Maior very falsely & scandalusly wth vntratges & beinge demanded
to find suerties for his good behavior he said he would finde none
wherevpon he was comitted. . . .' (Ibid., pp. 348–9.)

1624, May 24—'This day mr Maior & Justices of peace of this City
here assembled did offer to ffrancis Wambus who was comitted
vpon the 24th of Aprill last vntill he should finde suerties for his
good behavior that inasmuch as he beinge a stranger in this City
could not readily finde baill That therefore he might be dis-
chardged vpon his owne bond for his appearance at the next
Sessions of the peace to be holden after St. Michael next. And mr
Maior beinge further moved by mr Rosse in the behalfe of the said
Wambus that because he the said Wambus seemed very desirous
of inlargemt that therefore he might be enlarged wthout any bond

for further appearance, the said Wambus before any answer given therevnto by Mr Maior desired that he might have tyme of deliberacion therein till the comeinge of his fellowe Towneshend wch should be this afternoone.' (Ibid., p. 349.)

1624, May 26—'This day a warrant was deliv[er]ed to Richard Buller . . . for the dischardge of ffrancis Wambus and Willm Bee.' (Ibid., p. 350.)

1624, Sept. 28—'This day Mr Wambus shewed forth a Letter from Sr Henry Herbert dated in June last purporting that yt was my Lo: chambylns pleasure that he should be set at liberty And should giue his owne security for payment of his chardges in the beginnige of August followinge And the goaler beinge here in Court saith that vpon his receipt of the warrant for dischardginge of the said Wambus & of Bee he the said gaoler was contented to dischardge them ffor he said Mr Towneshend had given his word to pay the chardges, And the said Wambus & Mr Towneshend beinge here in Court desired recompence for the imprisonment of Wambus. . . . And because yt was remembred & conceiued that what was done concerninge them was by consent of the whole Court and that nothinge was done any way iniurious to them but that their imprisonment was occasioned by their owne miscariage, therefore yt was by gen[er]all consent agreed that nothinge should be gyven vnto them in that respect.' (Ibid., 350, two items.)

1628, July 17—'Francis Wambus' was the fourth of four men named as the leaders of the old Lady Elizabeth's company, but he was not one of the three leaders mentioned in the new warrant for the 'Queene of Bohemias Players'. (M.S.C. ii. 347–8.)

WANIBUS, FRANCIS (see WAMBUS, FRANCIS).

WAYMUS, FRANCIS (see WAMBUS, FRANCIS).

WEDWER, WILLIAM. A William Wedwer was named as a member of Robert Reynolds's company in Germany in 1640, but there is no assurance that he was English.

WEEKS (WEEKES, WICKS), RICHARD. Richard Weeks first appears as a proposed candidate for the new Queen of Bohemia's company of 1628; evidently it was learned that he would not be a member of the company before the players were finally sworn. One would guess that he had formerly belonged to the King and Queen of Bohemia's company and had been expected to be a member of the new organization, but found it more to his advantage to join William Perry as a leader of the Red Bull–King's company. For eight years Weeks is found in the provincial records as a leader of this company. It is not unlikely that he performed at the Red Bull in London as well, but we have no proof of his activity there. (See above, pp. 270 ff.)

Weeks is too common a name in seventeenth-century London to make identification of the player easy—there was a Richard Weeks in St. James's Clerkenwell after the Restoration and another in Allhallows London Wall, and a Richard Weeks, chandler,

lived in St. Peter's, Paul's Wharf, in 1616. The player may have
been the gentleman of St. James's Clerkenwell whose wife was a
recusant in 1635, for his theatre was in that parish; it is also
possible that he was the Richard Weeks of St. Giles in the Fields,
another theatrical parish.

1628, June 30—The name of 'Richard Wicks' has been deleted from
a warrant for swearing the Queen of Bohemia's players Grooms of
his Majesty's Chamber and that of 'Wm Rogers' substituted for it.
(*M.S.C.* ii. 347; see above, pp. 188–9.)

1629, Nov. 10—The licence which Herbert granted to 'William
Perrye and Richard Weekes, his Majestie's sworne servantes', and
six others, 'all of the Red Bull company', was shown at Reading
30 November 1629. (Murray, ii. 386.)

1630, Nov. 2—'William Perrey and Richard Wickes, the Kinge's
servantes, and their Company' were at Reading. (Ibid.)

1633, Apr. 30—'Richard Weeks and John Shanke' showed at Norwich a bill of this date authorizing them to play, and a Master of the
Revels' licence for six months dated 2 March 1634/5; they were
given permission on the 6th of June 1635 to 'play here till the
xviii^th of this moneth'. (Ibid., p. 357.)

1635, June 6—See above item.

1635, June 20—The following item probably refers to Weeks's company, though the marginal notation reads 'Game players': 'This
day Mr Maior sent for the Players who have exceeded their tyme,
And comanded them to forbeare playinge from this day forward.'
(Ibid.)

1635, Sept. 1 and Oct. 5—'Joan wife of Richard Weekes gentleman'
of St. James's Clerkenwell named for recusancy. (Gaol Delivery
Roll, *Middx. Co. Rec.* iii. 59.)

1635/6, Mar.—The Mayor of Canterbury wrote to the Archbishop
complaining of the disorders during Lent caused by 'the company
of the Fortune play house, and the principal of them were Weekes
and Perry'. See Perry for the full account. (*C.S.P., Dom.*, 1635–6,
pp. 354–5.)

1636, May 11—'This day Richard Wicks & other servants to his
Matie beinge his Maties players granted to Wm Perry & others did
bringe in a warrant dated' 30 April 1633, at Norwich. (Murray, ii.
358.)

1640, July 18—'Ann Daughter of Richard Weekes' bur. St. G.F.

WHEATON, ELIZABETH. Elizabeth Wheaton, a pensioner of the
Condell family, was a gatherer at the Globe and the Blackfriars
for several years. It is amusing to note that the masticating miss
who dispenses tickets from the glass cage at the movie palace had
a Caroline forerunner in the Widow Wheaton.

1627, Dec. 13—In the will of Henry Condell, Elizabeth Wheaton, an
old servant, was left forty shillings, a mourning gown, 'and that
place or priviledge which shee nowe exerciseth and enioyeth in the
howses of the blackfriers, London and the globe on the backside'
for life, 'if my estate shall so long continew in the premisses'. (See
Appendix, p. 642.)

1635, Sept. 1—Elizabeth Condell, widow of Henry, left to Elizabeth Wheaton, widow, various gifts, £20, and 'the gatheringe Place at the Globe during my Lease'. (See Appendix, p. 639.)

WHETSTONE, THOMAS. The easiest guess is that Whetstone was a hired man at the Fortune.

1630/1, Jan. 9—'Roger sonne of Thomas Whetstone, Player', chris. St. G.C.

WHITE, JOSIAS. Nothing is known of this company of Ellis Guest. It is unnamed in the Norwich records, and most of the thirteen players mentioned are otherwise unknown.

1628, July 2—Josias White was sixth in a list of thirteen players, of whom Ellis Guest was evidently the leader, named in a licence presented at Norwich on this date; the licence was from Herbert and was dated 7 June 1628. (Murray, ii. 353.)

1631, Oct. 23—'Mary d. of Josias White' chris. St. J.C.

WHITE, ROBERT. Professor Murray (Murray, i. 219) translates as Robert White the 'Robert Huyt' who appears in the cast of Prince Charles's men who performed Marmion's *Holland's Leaguer*. The man is otherwise unknown, but Hoyt seems to me a better guess than White. (*See* Robert Huyt.)

WHITEHEAD, CHRISTOPHER. Whitehead was a dancer and entertainer during the Commonwealth who may well have been an actor before the closing of the theatres, for it is difficult to imagine anyone who did not already have a stake in the entertainer's profession taking it up in the face of the hostility of Parliament. (See Rollins, 'Commonwealth Drama', pp. 306–7 and 315.)

WHITING, EDWARD. The members of the company of Richard Bradshaw who were imprisoned at Banbury in May 1633 gave varying testimony about Edward Whiting. Bartholomew Jones said that the commission under the privy seal belonged to Edward Whiting, Bradshaw's partner, and that both Bradshaw and Whiting were in London. When questioned further, Jones said that Bradshaw had bought the commission of Whiting at Nottingham some two years since. Richard Whiting testified that Edward was his father, and that he had led the company in Cornwall. Examined further, Richard Whiting said that his name was Johnson, that Bradshaw was his master, and that Bradshaw had bought the commission of Edward Whiting of Nottingham, surgeon. Edward Damport testified that Edward Whiting was his master, whom he was to serve for seven years, that Whiting lived in Coventry, and at the time was in London. Damport said on further examination that his master was Bradshaw and that Whiting had let the commission to some man who had pawned it. His further testimony is contradictory and confused, but seems to indicate that Whiting was a middleman in the transfer of the commission. Drewe Turner testified that Bradshaw and Whiting were partners and went together. Robert Houghton testified that Whiting had originally let the commission to Fluellen Morgan and William Cooke, puppeteers, who had pawned the commission for four shillings before Bradshaw got it. Robert Collewell testified that he was servant to Edward Whiting and had travelled with the company for two years, but when further examined Collewell said that Bradshaw was his master and had bought the commission from Whiting. (Murray, ii. 163–7.)

From this confusion of lies several facts are apparent. The three men who testified that they were servants of Whiting all admitted later that Bradshaw and not Whiting was their master. Several testify that Bradshaw got the commission one way or another from Whiting. Probably the commission was in Whiting's name, and the men lied to try to establish their right to it. I doubt if Whiting was ever Bradshaw's partner. Robert Houghton's version of the transactions is most circumstantial, most damning to the company, and therefore probably most accurate.

We are left with the information that Whiting had had some sort of a commission for provincial entertainment, that he had, apparently, rented his commission to two puppeteers, and that it had eventually come into the hands of Richard Bradshaw and his company of provincial players.

WHITING, RICHARD (*alias* RICHARD JOHNSON). It seems likely that this man's real name was Johnson and that he pretended to be Whiting's son in order to establish some legitimate connexion with the man in whose name the commission was apparently made. *See* Edward Whiting.

1633, May 2—'Examination of Richard Whiting of Cothelston, near Derby. Has been with this company of players about half a year. Met his father, Edward Whiting, in Cornwall. Thence they came to Bristol. Has acted a part with these players lately in divers places; at Leicester, Stratford, Meriden, Solihull, at Sir William Spencer's, and Sir Thomas Lucy's. On Saturday last they came to Keinton and there they played three days. They could answer where they had the commission under the privy seal well enough.'

1633, May 3—'Further examination of the preceding. His name is Richard Johnson, alias Bea . . ., and that Richard Bradshaw, his master, bought the commission and the motion of Edward Whiting, of Nottingham, a surgeon. Bradshaw is gone to London to renew the commission and to bring more company. He appointed to meet them at Marlow in Bucks. The commission from the Master of the Revels was out of date in January last, and it was rased and made June. Bradshaw bought the commission, with the privy seal, and the show, of Edward Whiting the last summer at Nottingham.' (*C.S.P., Dom.*, 1633–4, pp. 47–8.)

1633, May 22—The warrant in which the Privy Council directed Robert Cross to fetch the six players 'now in prison at Banbury' to London names 'Richard Whiting' second. (*M.S.C.* i. 384–5.)

1633, June 3—In the notice of the appearance of the players before the Privy Council, the name of 'Rich: Iohnson' appears in the place of Richard Whiting. (Ibid., p. 385.)

1633, June 8—'This day the Players form'ly sent for from Banbury were discharged . . . vpon Bond.' (Ibid.)

WIGPITT, THOMAS. Wigpitt had a financial interest in the Fortune and may have been a friend of Edward Alleyn.

1622, May 20—Alleyn granted 'Thomas Wigpitt Cittizen and Bricklayer of London' a lease of a half-share of the new Fortune. (*Hens. Paps.*, pp. 29, 112.)

1622, Aug. 18—He dined with Alleyn; see Thomas Downton.

WILBRAHAM, WILLIAM. Wilbraham was a Queen Henrietta's man for at least two or three years, probably longer. Professor Adams (Adams, p. 374) thinks that he had become a King's Revels man by 1629, when that company opened at the new Salisbury Court theatre. Though this conjecture is not unreasonable, if we allow for the uncertain date of the production of the first part of *The Fair Maid of the West*, there is no evidence that Wilbraham was connected with the King's Revels company before that organization appeared at Norwich in March 1634/5. There is no further record of Wilbraham as a player, but Mr. Hotson's suit indicates that his interest in theatres continued. St. Giles in the Fields is not an unlikely residence for a man who held a mortgage on the Phoenix.

1626—'*Isaac*, Sir *Iohns* man. *William Wilbraham*', in the Queen Henrietta's cast for Shirley's *The Wedding*. (1629 4° HN.)

c. 1630—'*Bashaw* Alcade; by M^r. Wilbraham', in the cast of Queen Henrietta's men prefixed to the 1631 4° of Heywood's *The Fair Maid of the West*, Part I; in Part II this role is assigned to Anthony Turner; and Wilbraham's name does not appear. (1631 4° B.M.)

1634/5, Mar. 10—His name is in the full list of players recorded at Norwich; some of them are King's Revels men, though the records do not give the name of the company, which seems to be an amalgamation. (Murray, ii. 356; see above, pp. 286 and 288-9.)

1640, July 7—Mr. Hotson says that on this date Christopher Beeston's widow, Elizabeth, was forced to borrow £150 from Wilbraham and mortgage the Cockpit property to him. (Hotson, p. 94.)

1644, May 4—'Avice wife of William Wilbraham' bur. St. G.F.

WILKINSON, NICHOLAS (*see* TOOLEY, NICHOLAS).

WILLANS, GEORGE (*see* WILLIAMS, GEORGE).

WILLIAMS (WILLANS), GEORGE. Though George Williams appears only in provincial and parish records, he may well have been a London player, for both the companies with which he is associated performed in London.

1629, Nov. 10—His name is last in a list of six men, 'all of the Red Bull company', whose leaders were Perry and Weeks, in a licence presented at Reading 30 November 1629. (Murray, ii. 386.)

1630, May 30—'Eliz. Dau: of George Williams, Player', chris. St. G.C.

1634/5, Mar. 10—'George Willans' is the twenty-fifth name in the full list of players recorded at Norwich; some of them seem to be King's Revels men, though the records do not give the name of the company, which was probably an amalgamation. (Murray, ii. 356; see above, pp. 286 and 288–9.)

WILLIAMS, JOHN. John Williams was a theatrical speculator whose ideas, if the clauses of the patent are any indication, were rather large. He sounds a bit like a seventeenth-century Tex Rickard. There is a reference to his second project in *Holland's Leaguer*, ii. 3.

1620, Sept. 29—The King wrote to the Privy Council to revoke a licence previously granted to John Cotton, John Williams, and Thomas Dixon to build an amphitheatre 'intended principally for martiall exercises, and extraordinary shewes and solemnyties', with the privilege to close other shows and sports one day a month on fourteen days' warning. (*H.E.D.P.* i. 405–8 and 444–5.)

>1626, Aug. 12—Cotton and Williams again applied for permission to build an amphitheatre in Lincoln's Inn Fields, and according to the Lord Keeper their intention was to present 'common plaies, or ordinary sports, now used or shewed at the Beare-garden or the common Playhouses about London, for all sorts of beholders, with a restraint to all other plaies and shewes, for one day in the weeke upon two daies warning'. On 28 September 1626 the Lord Keeper recommended that the grant should not be passed. (Ibid., pp. 444–5.)

WILLIAMS (WILLYAMS), WALTER. Williams was probably a boy in the King's Revels company, though neither of the lists in which he appears is known definitely to be made up wholly of Revels players.

1634/5, Mar. 10—'Walt^r Willyams' appears in the full list of players recorded at Norwich; some of them are King's Revels men, though the records do not give the name of the company, which was probably an amalgamation. (Murray, ii. 356; see above, pp. 286 and 288–9.)

c. 1635 ?—'Mr. Featherbrain—*Wal. Williams*' appears in the cast for *Money Is an Ass* printed in the 1668 quarto. (1668 4° B.M. *See* Thomas Jordan.)

WILLIS, RICHARD.

1628, June 7—His name appears in the new licence granted by Herbert to Ellis Guest's unnamed company on this date and shown at Norwich 2 July 1628. (Murray, ii. 353.)

WILSON, GEORGE. As Groom of the Revels, George Wilson had some dealings with the players, as is shown by Sir Henry Herbert's entry of 12 May 1636. No doubt he had others not noted in the office-book, or at least not copied by Malone and Chalmers.

1624/5, Feb. 4—He was sworn Groom of the Revels on this date. Chalmers says, 'He [Sir Henry Herbert], no doubt, received some useful assistance from George Wilson, who was sworn his Majesty's Servant, and a Groom of his Majesty's Revels, in ordinary, on the 4th of February, 1624–5. Whether this office of Groom of the Revels were distinct from the Yeoman of the Revels, I am unable to explain: Certain it is, that William Hunt, and after him, Joseph Taylor, were Yeomen of the Revels, while George Wilson was the Groom. With all those helps, Sir Henry Herbert's duty sometimes slept; owing to the multifarious nature of his office. (*S.A.*, 210–11.)' (*Herbert*, p. 68.)

1625, >May 5—Under the heading 'The Revills:' 'George Willson groome' was allowed black cloth for James's funeral procession. (*M.S.C.* ii. 326.)

1626, Aug. 28—'A Certificate signed and sealed to George Wilson a Groome of ye Revels in Ordinary declaring the Priviledges hee is to inioy by beeing his Maties serv^t.' (*P.R.O.*, L.C. 3/31, p. 358.)

1636, May 12—Sir Henry Herbert says that he gave his warrants for the closing of the theatres during the plague 'to George Wilson for the four companys of players, to be served upon them'. (*Herbert*, p. 65.)

1640 (?)—He was perhaps the George Wilson of Whitechapel whose wife was accused of infidelity. (*C.S.P.*, *Dom.*, 1640–1, p. 345.)

1641—'Geo: Wilson Groome' is in the list of officers of the Revels in the L.C. papers. (*See* Joseph Taylor.) (*M.S.C.* ii. 326.)

WILSON, HENRY. There were several musicians in Jacobean and Caroline times named Wilson, and it is sometimes impossible to disentangle them. There can be little doubt, however, that the King's attendant of 1624, the fiddler sued by Hemings in 1628, and the lute player of *Believe as You List* are the same man. Professor Sisson in his edition of *Believe as You List* suggests that Henry Wilson was a member of the family of Nicholas Wilson and Jack Wilson of the stage directions of *Much Ado* (*B.A.Y.L.*, p. xxxiv). It is possible that the King's players' musician was the singer Wilson who dined with Alleyn in 1620 and the cunning musician who was involved in the bishop's performance in 1631 (*see* John Wilson).

1624, Dec. 27—'Henry Wilson' was the fifth name in a list of twenty-one attendants of the King's men whom Herbert exempted from arrest. (*Herbert*, p. 74; see above, pp. 15–16.)

1628, Dec. 14—The Lord Chamberlain issued a warrant for the apprehension of 'Ambrose Beeland and Henry Wilson Fidlers at ye complaint of Mr Hemmings'. (*M.S.C.* ii. 348.)

1631—At line 1,968 of the MS. of *Believe as You List* is the stage direction, 'Harry: Willson: & Boy ready for the song at ye Arras:'. A later direction indicates that the singer was accompanied by the lute. (Sisson, *B.A.Y.L.*, pp. 65, 67.)

WILSON, JOHN. There were two musicians named John Wilson. One was the eminent lutanist, composer, and Professor of Music at Oxford (see *D.N.B.*), and the other was a musician with Shakespeare's company some time before 1623. The 'Iacke Wilson' of

Much Ado was probably the John, son of Nicholas Wilson, musician, who was christened at St. Bartholomew the Less in April 1585 (Bod.), and who was living in that parish in 1624. He must also have been the John Wilson recommended to the Lord Mayor and Aldermen. The *D.N.B.* says that Wilson was still a city wait in 1641, but I have been unable to find the reference. The Wilson who dined with Alleyn and the Wilson who planned the Bishop of Lincoln's dramatic evening might have been either Henry or John.

Rimbault's identification of the Jack Wilson of *Much Ado* and the Oxford Professor of Music is not generally accepted (Edward F. Rimbault, *Who Was 'Jack Wilson'?*, London, 1846).

1620, Oct. 22—'this daye wase our weding daye & ther dind w^t vs m^{rs} Knight m^r maund & His wife, m^r mylyon m^r Jeffe & 2 frends w^t them a precher & His frend m^r Willson ye singer w^t others.' (Alleyn's Diary, Young, ii. 192.)

1622, Oct. 21—'VIII. 48. Letter from H. Mandeville to the Lord Mayor and Court of Aldermen, soliciting for John Willson the place of one of the servants of the City for Music and Voice, vacant by the death of Richard Balls.' (*Remembrancia*, p. 303.)

1623—A stage direction in *Much Ado*, ii. 3, says, 'Enter . . . Iacke Wilson'. Evidently he played the part of Balthasar and sang the song. (1623 folio.)

1624, July 17—'Jone, wife of John Wilson musitian buryed from Little St Bartholomews'. (Bod.)

1624, Sept. 3—'sonne to John Wilson gentleman from the house of George Somerset Musitian' bur. St. Bartholomew the Less. (Bod.)

1631—'one Mr. Wilson a cunning Musition' was concerned in a Sunday performance of a play, possibly *Midsummer Night's Dream*, 27 September 1631, which offended the Puritans. (*See* Murray, ii. 148–50.)

WILSON, WILLIAM. William Wilson's connexion with the Palsgrave's men can only be inferred from his assumption that Alleyn could persuade the members of the company to make him a wedding gift. He may have been, as Professor Adams suggests, a gatherer at the Fortune, for Alleyn's friend John Russell (q.v.) was, and Robert Browne had written Alleyn in 1612 to try to get a gathering place for a friend (*Hens. Paps.*, p. 63). The dating of the letter depends upon the identification of the William Wilson married at St. Saviour's and the letter writer.

The bookseller's statement that Wilson was an actor of Shakespeare's company is, of course, absurd.

1617, >Nov. 2—The following letter was addressed 'To my most deare & especeall good frend m^r. Edward Alleyn at Dulwich dd thes'. 'Right worshipfull, my humble dutie rememberd—hoping in the Almightie of y^{re} health & prosperety, wch on my knees I beseeche him long to contyneue, ffor the many favor^s wch I haue from tyme to tyme received my poor abillety is not in the least degree able to give you satisfaction, vnless as I and myne haue byn bounden to yo^u for yor many kyndnes soe will wee duringe life pray for yor prosperety. I confess I haue found you my cheifest frend in midest of my extremeties, wch makes me loath to presse or request y^r favo^r any further, yet for that I am to be married on Sunday next, & yor kindnes may be a great help & furtherance vnto me towards the raisinge of my poore & deserted estate, I am enforced ·once agayne to entreat yor wopp^s furtherance in a charitable request, wch is that I may haue yor wopp^s Letter to m^r Dowton & m^r Edward Juby to be a meanes that the Company of players of the ffortune maie either offer at my wedding at St Saviors church, or of their owne good natures bestowe somthinge vppon me on that day. And as ever I and myne will not only rest bounden vnto y^r [woPP] but contyneually pray for y^r wopp^s health wth encreas of all happynes longe to contyneue. In hope of y^r wopp^s favo^r herin, I humbly take my leave. Resting / y^r worshipps during / life to be commanded / William Wilson'. (Joseph Quincy Adams, 'An "Hitherto Unknown" Actor of Shakespeare's Troupe?', *M.L.N.* xxxiv [1919], 46–7.)

1617, Nov. 2—'It appears from the registers of St. Saviour's Church, Southwark, that William Wilson was married there, to Dorethea Seare, on Sunday, Nov. 2, 1617.' (Ibid., p. 47, from Myers and Company, *Illustrated Catalogue of Rare Books*, 1918.)

WINTERSHALL (WINTERSALL, WINTERSCALE, WINTERSHULL), WILLIAM. William Wintershall's theatrical activities after the Restoration are fairly well known, but his career before the closing of the theatres is most obscure. We have only Wright's statement that he performed at the Salisbury Court, a statement which would presumably connect him with Queen Henrietta's men, the last company at that theatre before the wars. Wintershall's marriage to the daughter of Gunnell (manager of the Salisbury Court from 1629 to 1634) suggests that he may have been at the Salisbury Court before 1637, when Queen Henrietta's men came. If so, he may have been a King's Revels player, but this is pure conjecture.

Wintershall's appearance at court to assist Shatterell and Turner, the latter a former fellow member of the Queen's company, does not necessarily indicate that Wintershall himself was connected with the theatrical enterprise at the Red Bull, but it would not be surprising to find that he was. He might be the man at St. James's or the man at St. Anne's or neither or both.

1638/9, Feb. 6—'William Winterscale & Jane Hurd; lic. from the Facul.', mar. St. J.C.

1640, May 29—'William sonne to William and Jane Winterscal' chris. St. Anne's Blackfriars.

>1641—He married Margaret, daughter of Richard and Elizabeth Gunnell. (Hotson, p. 52, from a Chancery suit.)

>1642—Wright says, '*Cartwright*, and *Wintershal* belong'd to the private House in *Salisbury-Court*'. (*Hist. Hist.*, p. 3.)

1652, July 6—'W^m s. of Wm Wintersall' bur. St. J.C.

1654—Wintershall and his wife Margaret, daughter of Richard Gunnell, brought suit against Andrew·Cane on the old bond of the leading Palsgrave's men to Gunnell. The outcome of the suit is unknown. (Hotson, pp. 52–4.)

1659, May 12—'Recognizances, taken before Ra: Hall esq. J.P., of William Wintershall and Henry Eaton both of Clerkenwell gentlemen' for the appearance of Anthony Turner and Edward Shatterell, charged with maintaining stage plays at the Red Bull. (*Middx. Co. Rec.* iii. 279–80.)

1659, Oct. 2—'Margarett d. of Will'm Wintershull' bur. St. J.C.

WITTER, JOHN. Not an actor. He married Augustine Phillips's widow, apparently some time in 1605, and thus secured control of the housekeeper's share of the Globe which Phillips had held. He was a constant annoyance to the housekeepers until his last suit against them was finally dismissed, 29 November 1620. See the papers in the suit *Witter* v. *Heminges and Condell* (Wallace, *Sh. and Lond. Assoc.*).

WOOD, WILLIAM. It is unfortunate that so much more is known about Wood's family than about his professional activities. The Coventry record of 1623 seems to indicate that Wood was a member of the Red Bull Revels company active at that time, but it is odd that a payment was made to a man not otherwise known to have been connected with the company.

1595, June 10—'Anthony the s of William Wood' chris. St. Leonard's Shoreditch. 'Curtayn' is written after the entry. (Bod.)

1615, Sept. 27—'Abraham Wood, sonne to William wood, a Player of Interludes in Houndsditch', chris. St. Bodolph's, Aldgate. (Denkinger.)

1623, Aug. 28—'William Wood a player of the Revells' was paid 2s. 6d. at Coventry. (Murray, ii. 249.)

1623, Dec. 14—'Alice daughter of William Wood Player' bur. St. G.C.

1624, Sept. 18—'William sonne of William Wood yeomā' chris. St. G.C.

1625, Mar. 25—'John sonne of William Wood yeoman' chris. St. G.C.

WOODFORD, THOMAS. Woodford was not an actor but a well-to-do London merchant who was interested in theatrical investments. He was concerned with the Children of Paul's in 1600 and with the Whitefriars theatre, the Red Bull, and perhaps even the Globe. C. W. Wallace even went so far as to say that he was connected 'with nearly every theatre in London'. One cannot tell, however, whether this is simply a rash statement or another of Professor Wallace's references to unpublished suits. Woodford's activity is best known before 1616; after that date, so far as we know, he was simply trying to finish litigation which had grown out of earlier enterprises.

1619/20, Feb.—He made a deposition in the *Witter* v. *Heminges and Condell* suit over the Globe shares, but it is lost. (Wallace, *Sh. and Lond. Assoc.*, p. 74.)

1623–4—Professor Sisson writes that he has found a Chancery case in 1623–4 'which concludes the story of his [Aaron Holland's] relations with the Red Bull, and recapitulates the incidents of his long struggle with Thomas Woodford, which he finally won'. (Sisson, *Keep the Widow Waking*, p. 235.)

1630, Apr. 24—'Eliz. d. of Thomas Woodford & Eliz. vx.' chris. St. J.C.

1636, Oct. 3 and Dec. 1—Thomas Woodford of Hosierlane helped bury Samuel Underhill, a plague victim, with illegal splendour. (*See* George Bosgrave.)

1642—The decision in the old case of *Trevill* v. *Woodford* over the Whitefriars theatre was handed down. (Hillebrand, pp. 227 ff.)

WOODE, JOHN. Most of the defendants in Markham's suit were actors, and one is encouraged to think that John Woode was, too, by the appearance in 1604 of a John Woods as an English actor in Holland. (Cohn, *Sh. in Ger.*, p. lxxvii.)

1623, May 21—'Iohn Woode of Beech Lane London', 5s., appeared in Markham's suit. (See Appendix, p. 682.)

WORTH (WOORTH, WROTH), ELLIS. Worth seems to have been a member of Queen Anne's company as early as 1612, when Smith says that he was making deliveries to Beeston, Cumber, Perkins, and Worth as the responsible members of the company, and he is an important member in all the early agreements with the Baskerviles. Worth continued to be a Queen Anne's man until the death of the Queen, when, with a number of his fellows, he became one of the Players of the Revels at the Red Bull. Professor Sisson says (apparently on the basis of evidence in unpublished suits) that Worth was forced to leave the Red Bull to avoid the Baskerviles in 1623; certainly in January 1624/5 he professed complete ignorance of a recent Red Bull play.

Shortly after this time, Worth married the widow of Thomas Holcomb, the King's man, and moved to his wife's parish of St. Giles' Cripplegate. He may have been first associated with the Fortune theatre at this time—at any rate, he was at a later date. After a period of seven or eight years when there is no record of his theatrical activities, he appears as a Prince Charles's man in 1631, and he continued to be one of the two or three leading members of this company, certainly until 1638 and probably until 1642.

Worth evidently resided in St. James's Clerkenwell, so long as he performed at the Red Bull in that parish. He married Elizabeth Slead there 8 October 1612, and his daughter Jane was christened there 19 July 1613. After his second marriage in 1625/6 he moved to his wife's parish (*see* Thomas Holcomb).

Worth's one role, Ardelio in *Holland's Leaguer*, is that of a parasite, a fat man.

1616, June—He was named in the Baskervile suit as a member of

Queen Anne's at the time of the second settlement in favour of Francis Browne. (Fleay, *Stage*, p. 283.)

1616, Oct. 13—'Alexander Scrogge, serv^t to Ellis Worth', bur. St. J.C.

c. 1617—Possibly Worth is the 'Ellis' of the stage direction of the 1655 quarto of Daborne's *The Poor Man's Comfort*. If the stage direction dates 1617 (see Baldwin, *Organization and Personnel*, p. 424), he is the most likely candidate. Ellis Bedowe and Ellis Guest are possibilities if the direction dates, as W. J Lawrence says (*M.L.R.* xxv. 209), from a 1635 revival.

1617, June 3—As a fellow and sharer of Queen Anne's he signed the new agreement with the Baskerviles and signed two bonds as well. (Fleay, *Stage*, pp. 285–8.)

1617, Oct. 2—Beeston, Heywood, Perkins, Drew, Harrison, and Worth petitioned the Sessions of the Peace against highway repair presentments made against the Red Bull. (*Middx. Co. Rec.* ii. 170.)

1619—Worth, Perkins, and Cumber, when sued by John Smith, declared that Beeston had kept the company accounts fraudulently for the last seven or eight years. (Wallace, *Three Theatres*, pp. 35 ff.)

1619, >May 13—'Ellis Wroth' was ninth in the list of Queen Anne's men allowed black cloth to wear in her funeral procession. (*M.S.C.* ii. 325.)

1621/2, Mar. 2—'Ellisworth' was paid for a play presented by the 'late servaunts to Queene Anne and now the Companie of the Revells'. (Murray, ii. 192–3.)

1622, July 8—'Ellis woorth' was third in a list of seven 'late Commedians to Queene Ann^e. deceased' named in a warrant for the licensing of the Children of the Revels; the bill was signed 25 July. (Murray, ii. 193–4; see above, pp. 167–8.)

1622, Oct. 3—One of six Red Bull actors named in an order for repairing the highways. (See above, p. 169, n. 2.)

1622—'Ellis Woorth' was third in the list of 'the chiefe players at the Red Bull, called the players of the Revells', recorded in Herbert's office-book. (*Herbert*, p. 63.)

1623, May 23—Worth, Cumber, and Blaney, as 'late servants and players to the late Queens most excellent ma^{tie}', petitioned to be relieved from their payments to the Baskerviles since most of their company were 'dead, or departed' to some other company. (Fleay, *Stage*, pp. 270–9.)

1623—Professor Sisson says, 'He certainly had to leave the Red Bull in 1623, in order to strengthen his defence against Mrs. Baskerville's claim.' (Sisson, *Keep the Widow Waking*, p. 254, apparently from unpublished P.R.O. documents.)

1623, Sept. 27—'Elizabeth wife of Ellis Worth' bur. St. J.C.

1624/5, Jan. 31—When Worth was sued with others for contributing to the performance of *Keep the Widow Waking* at the Red Bull, he answered that he did not act in the play, nor did he ever see it. (Sisson, *Keep the Widow Waking*, pp. 237 and 243.)

1625/6, Jan. 13—'Ellis Worth, of St James, Clerkenwell, Middlesex, Gent., & Frances Holcombe, of St Giles, Cripplegate, London, widow of Thomas Holcombe; at All Hallows the Less, Thames Street, London.' (*Marriages, London.*)

1626, June 23—His case against the Baskerviles was finally dismissed. (Fleay, *Stage*, pp. 296–7.)

1628/9, Mar. 10—'Elizeus son of Ellis Worth Player' chris. St. G.C.

1629/30, Mar. 15—'Elizabeth Commens stᵉ to Ellis Worth gentle' bur. St. G.C.

c. 1630—He was possibly the 'Ellis' mentioned in the MS. of *The Wasp*; see Ellis Bedowe *and* Ellis Guest. (Greg, *Dram. Doc.*, p. 360.)

1631, Dec.—'*Ardelio, his parasite*. Ellis Worth', in Prince Charles's (II) cast for *Holland's Leaguer*. (1632 4° B.M.; *Herbert*, p. 45.)

1631, Dec. 7—A warrant of this date to Joseph Moore, Ellias Worth, and Mathew Smith was shown at Norwich 21 February 1637/8; probably Prince Charles's company. (Murray, ii. 358.)

1632, May 10< >15—'Ellis Worth' was first in a list of eleven players to be sworn Grooms of the Chamber 'to attend the Prince his Highnes in yᵉ quality of players'. (See above, p. 303.)

1634, July 18—Kendall told Crosfield that 'Mr Worth' was one of the Prince's men at the Red Bull. (*Crosfield's Diary*, p. 72; see Appendix, p. 688.)

1634, July 25—'Marie Worth, wid., mother to Mʳ Ellis Worth', bur. St. J.C.

1635, Nov. 3—Moore presented at Norwich a licence authorizing 'Andrew Kayne Elis Worth & others to play Comedies in Salisbury Court & otherwhere'. (Murray, ii. 358.)

1635, Dec. 10—A warrant for payment of £100 'to yᵉ Princes Com̃edians' was issued to Moore, Cane, and Worth. (*M.S.C.* ii. 377.)

1637/8, Feb. 21—The warrant of 7 December 1631 was shown at Norwich; see above.

1664—In the third act of *Knavery in All Trades*, several gentlemen are in a coffee house talking of the theatre before the wars. One says, 'But did you know *Mat. Smith, Elis Worth* and *Fowler* at the Fortune?' (1664 4° HN; see above, pp. 318–19.)

WRIGHT, JOHN. Before the closing of the theatres, John Wright had belonged first to Prince Charles's company and then to Beeston's Boys, but he seems to have been better known as a surreptitious player during the interregnum than he was as an actor in either of these companies. Professor Rollins says that he must have died about 1655 or 1656, for a ballad 'On the Death of Jo. Wright' first appears about 1656. (*Stud. Phil.* xviii. 314 n.)

1631, Dec.—'*Millescent, daughter to Agurtes*. Iohn Wright', in the Prince Charles's (II) cast for *Holland's Leaguer*. (*Herbert*, p. 45; 1632 4° B.M.)

1639, Aug. 10—'Iohn Wright' was eleventh named in a ticket of privilege for the young company of Cockpit players. (*M.S.C.* ii. 390–1.)

>1655—He is probably the John Wright who wrote and sang in the street a ballad on 'the Turk', the famous rope dancer. See Rollins, 'Commonwealth Drama', p. 314 n.

1655, Sept. 14—Professor Hotson (Hotson, p. 57, from *Sportive Wit*,

Bodleian Malone 391) quotes a verse which names him from a poem celebrating the rout of the players at the Red Bull on this date:

> Then *Jo: Wright* they met,
> Yet nothing could get,
>   And *Tom Jay* i' th' same condition:
> The fire [tire] men they
> Wou'd ha' made 'em a prey,
>   But they scorn'd to make a petition.

YOUNG, JOHN. As a Queen Henrietta's man, Young's roles are rather small ones, though Kendall's listing of the King's Revels men seems to indicate that Young was more important in that company than his known acting parts would imply. It is possible that Young was one of the original members of the King's Revels company in 1629, as Professor Adams says (Adams, p. 374), but I know of no definite evidence that he had joined the company before 1634.

1626—'*Hauer*, a yong Gentleman, louer of mistresse *Iane*. *Iohn Yong*', in Queen Henrietta's cast for Shirley's *The Wedding*. (1629 4º HN.)

>1634—'*Leister*, M. [Mr.] *Young*', in Queen Henrietta's cast for Davenport's *King John and Matilda*. (1655 4º B.M.)

1634, July 18—Kendail told Crosfield that among those at the Salisbury Court was '2. Mr. John Yongue'. (*Crosfield's Diary*, p. 72; see below, p. 688.)

1634/5, Mar. 10—He is named in the full list of players recorded at Norwich; some of them are King's Revels men, though the records do not give the name of the company which was probably an amalgamation. (Murray, ii. 356; see above, pp. 286 and 288–9.)

APPENDIX

WILLS OF THEATRICAL INTEREST

THOMAS BASSE

Consistory Court of London, Allen 202–3.[1]

T[estamentum] Thome Basse.

Memorandum that on or about the eleaventh daie of September . . . 1634 Thomas Basse of the parrish of St. James Clarkenwell in the county of Midd. gent. deceased . . . being sicke in bodye but of perfect mind & memory made . . . his last will and testament nuncupative in manner . . . following vizt he gaue and bequeathed to his sister Jane the some of fortie shillings To his sister Vrsula a Ring of ten shillings To his Godson Thomas Axon the sonne of Robert Axon the some of fortie shillings He further gaue . . . unto his loveing frends M^r. Xpofer Beeston and Elizabeth his wife M^r. William Robins & Cicely his wife Robert Axon and Mary his wife, Richard Perkins Michaell Bower and William Beeston gent. to each of them a Ring of the value of tenn shillings a peece to weare in remembrance of him The rest and residue of all his estate . . . his debts and legacies being payed he gaue and bequeathed vnto his wife Dorcas Basse whome he made the sole executrix wch words he the sayd Thomas [altered from 'John'] Basse spake . . . in the presence of vs . . . Robert Axon Anne Conisbey [or 'Comṣbey'] The mark of Elizabeth Miller

Probatum fuit testamentum huius modi tertio die Octobris Anno domini millesimo sexentesimo tricesimo quarto coram Magistro Thoma Wiborowe Clerico Surrugato etc. Juramento Testium supranominatorum et etiam Juramento Dorce Basse executricis etc. Cui commissa fuit administracio etc. . . . Jurat[e].

Commissary Court of London Probate Act Book 1627–38. Book 18, fo. 261. Administration of goods of Dorcas Basse, who died intestate of St. Giles in the Fields, Middx. Granted 18 November 1635 to William Atkinson, creditor. Inventory total [only]—£9. 18s. 2d.

CHRISTOPHER BEESTON alias HUTCHINSON[2]

Lee 172.

In the name of God Amen, the fowerth day of October, 1638 . . . I Christopher Hutchinson of the p[ar]ishe of Saint Gyles in the fieldes in the County of Midd[lesex] gentleman being sick, . . .

[1] All book and folio references are to the will registers of the Perogative Court of Canterbury, Somerset House, unless otherwise indicated.

[2] My transcript of this will was made before Mr. Hotson's appeared (Hotson, pp. 398–400); it is printed here for convenience of reference.

[direct my body] to be buried in Christian buriall in the parrishe Church of S^t. Gyles in the fields aforesaid . . . Imprimis I forthwith give will and bequeath vnto my loving Sonne William Hutchinson his heires and assignes forever All and Singuler my freehold land and the messuages or tenements thereupon erected and builte or vpon any parte or parcell thereof scituate lynge and beinge in the p[ar]ish of S^t. Leonard in Shorditch[1] in the County of Midd[lesex]. And all and singuler the deedes writings and Evidences concerninge the same And all leases thereof made to any p[er]son or p[er]sons whatsoever, more I give and bequeath unto him all my parte or parcell of ground nowe inclosed with a brick wall lyinge and beinge in Lyncolns Inn feilds in the p[ar]ishe of S^t. Gyles in the feilds aforesaid the deedes where of were by me delivered vnto Master Thomas Vaughan to keepe in trust for me, Item I give and bequeath vnto my eldest daughter Anne Bird wife of Theophilus Bird gent and to her sonne my godsonne Christopher Bird the some of three hundred poundes of lawfull mony of England if my twoe howses lately erected and built in Covent garden in the p[ar]ishe of S^t. Marten in the feilds in the said County of Midd[lesex] shalbe assured to amounte vnto the some of Six hundred poundes ster, and by reason I doe owe many greate debts and am engaged for greate somes of money wch noe one but my wife understands where or howe to receave pay or take in I therefore make her my beloved wife Elizabeth Hutchinson my full and sole executrix of this my p[rese]nte last will and testament, And I doe hereby give vnto my said executrix after my debts paied legacies performed and funerall charges defraied the residue of all and singuler my goods and Chattells whatsoever, And Overseers hereof I doe make nominate and appointe my Noble freind Captaine Lewis Kirk and my Worthy respected friend Thomas Sheppard esquier entereatinge them in the love of a true and dyinge freind that to theire vtmost as occasion shall serve they wilbe ayding and assisting to my executrix for the p[er]formance of this my last will and testament according to my true intent and honest meaninge, here specified and I do give vnto either of them a gold ring to weare in remembrance of me, And whereas I stand possessed of fower of the six shares in the Company for the King and Queenes service att the Cockpitt in Drury lane, I declare that twoe of my said fower shares be delivered vpp for the advancem^t of the said Company and the other twoe to Remaine vnto my said executrix as fully and amply as if I lived amongst them. And I will that my said executrix shall for the said twoe shares prouide and finde for the said Company a sufficient and good stock of app[ar]ell fittinge for their vse shee allowinge and payinge to my said sonne William Hutchinson for his care and industry in the said Company twentie

---

[1] From a Chancery suit of 1666 Mr. Hotson learned that part of this Shoreditch property was adjacent to the Curtain theatre (Hotson, p. 92).

poundes of lawfull mony of England p[er] ann[um], And I do hereby charge him by the love of a Childe to his ffather that he for my sake doe all good concerninge this or any other business to my said wife and her twoe daughters, And I doe hereby will and order that the legacies by me hereby given willed and bequeathed be paied by my said executrix within eighteene monethes nexte after my decease . . . Christopher Chutchinson [*sic*] Read signed, sealed, and as the last will and testament of the said Christopher Hutchinson published and deliuered in the presence of Bartho Bramfield Scr, The marke of Marie Haines, The marke of Marie Wilkes. Bar. Church.

7th die Octobris 1638,

Md that whereas the within named Christopher Hutchinson have willed ordered and devised by my last will and testament within written that my executrix within named, should pay vnto my within named Sonne .William Hutchinson, the yearely some of Twentie poundes of lawfull mony of England for his Care and industry to be taken in and about the Company w^thin menconed, Nowe my will and mynd is and I do hereby order and devise that my said Executrix in liewe of the said twentie poundes p[er] ann[um] shall allowe vnto him my said sonne William Hutchinson one halfe share of the twoe shares in the said Company within menconed for his care in the business shee findinge and providinge a stock of app[ar]ell for the said company as is within declared Witnes my hand .the day and yeare abovesaid Christopher Hutchinson Subscribed in the presence of Bar Church. The marke of Marie Haines, The marke of Mary Wilkes, Bartholomew Bromfield Scr.

Proved 30 December 1638.

RICHARD BENFIELD[1]

Harvey 180.

In the name of God Amen the sixe and twentieth Day of August anno D[omi]nj 1639 . . . I Richard Benefeild of Grays Inn in the County of Midd[lesex] gent . . . beinge desirous to limmitt

[1] Richard Benfield was not an actor; the will is included here because of the items concerning actors and the interesting material concerning an evident friend of the stage. Apparently he was the son of William Benfield, a well-to-do citizen of Southwark and the proprietor of Benfield's Rents, frequently mentioned in the Southwark token-books. William died in 1619 and left most of his property to his son Richard. He also left 40s. to a Robert Benfield of Aldgate, whom he made an overseer of the will and who may have been the actor. Probably his Southwark residence is the origin of Richard's friendship with the King's men. (Information from token-books and William Benfield's will, Parke 84.) Further theatrical associations are seen in Edward Alleyn's attendance at William Benfield's funeral 26 October 1619 (*MSS. Dul.*, p. 182).

a certaine course for the disposall of such estate and temporall blessings as it hath pleased God to bestowe vppon mee that peace may be setled amongst my freinds when I am departed this life doe make and declare this my present Testament conteyninge my last Will in forme following. . . . I coṁitt [my body] to the Earth to be decently interred within the parrishe of St Saviours in Southwarke in the County of Surrey at the discretion of my Executors hereinafter named. And my Will is that my Executors heerin after menċoned shall expend for and towards my funerall chardges the sume of one hundred pounds of lawefull money of England And that after my funerall solempnized they shall likewise expend in the makinge and erecting a Monument or Tombe with my ffigure to be represented there in the soṁe of forty pounds of like money. And my Will is that such Debts or soṁes of money as shalbee from mee payable at the time of my decease to any person or persons shallbee truely satisfied and paid within such convenient time as hereafter is lymitted. Item I give and bequeath vnto Thomas ffrench the sonne and vnto Anne and Sarah ffrench the daughters of my late Sister Rebecca ffrench deceased the suṁe of Thirty pounds of lawefull money of England to bee equally devided amongst them. Item I ['bequeath' in margin] vnto Anne the Daughter of my kinseman Robert Benefeild gent[1] the some of twenty and five pounds of like money Item I bequeath vnto Mrs Elizabeth Bowen Widdowe the some of Thirty pounds of like money to buy her a gowne and ringe. Item I bequeath vnto her Daughter Winifrid Bowen[2] the some of twenty pounds of like money to the intent aforesaid. Item I bequeath vnto my lovinge freind John Bugges Doctor in Phisicke the some of fifteene pounds of like money. Item I bequeath vnto my ffrend Robert Woodford the some of ffive pounds of like money. Item I bequeath vnto my gossipp Eliardt Swanston and Thomas Pollard to each of them the some of fforty shillings of like money Item I bequeath to Mrs Winifred ffitche and her sonne Mr John Shancke[3] vnto each of them the some of fforty shillings of like money. Item I bequeath to Edward Goodale and his nowe wife the some of fforty shillings of like money to be equally devided betwixt them. And my intent is that the somes of money soe bequeathed to my said ffreinds Robert Woodford Eliardt Swanston Thomas Pollard Winifred ffitch John Shancke, Edward Goodale and his said Wife shall buy them severall ringes to weare for my sake. Item I bequeath vnto Katherine Sadler nowe a Maide servant to my aforesaid kinesman Robert Benefeild the some of fforty shillings of like money Item I bequeath vnto every of the three severall liberties

---

[1] Apparently the King's player, who is known to have had a daughter Anne. See Hotson, p. 33.

[2] Elizabeth and Winifred Bowen were the daughter and granddaughter of the former comedian of the King's company, John Shank.

[3] The wife and son of the King's man.

herein after menčoned That is to saye the liberty of the Clinke within the parish of S^t: Saviours in Southwarke in the County of Surrey aforesaid the liberty of Whitecrostreete within the parish of S^t. Giles Cripplegate in the County of Midd[lesex] and the liberty of Grayes Inne Lane within the parish of St Andrews Holborne and County of Midd[lesex] aforesaid the some of tenn poundes of like money to bee paid and deliuered by my Executors vnto the Churchwardens of the said severall parishes to bee by them and their Successors kept and preserved as a perpetuall stocke for the same liberties and to be ymploid and Disposed to the best vse and advantage that maybee And my Will is that such money and advantage as may arrise thereby shalbee disbursed for bread and shalbe Distributed by the Churchwardens or Ouerseers of the parrishes aforesaid vnto such severall poore people within the same libertye as they shall thincke meete on the Sunday followeing the three and twentieth day of November every yeare yearely for ever.

[There is further mentioned in the will a cash estate of £303, 'Seueral' houses and tenements in Gray's Inn Lane als Perpoole Lane, at least four other houses, the Spread Eagle Inn, a horse, a war saddle, and armour.]

MICHAEL BOWYER

Rivers 137.

In the name of God Amen, ye six and twentith day of September Anno D[omini] 1645. et Reg: Caroli 21 I Michael Bowyer of Hounslow in the Countie of Midd[lesex] gent being sicke & weake in bodye but of good and p[er]fect memorie (thankes be giuen to god therfore) Doe make and ordayne this my last will and Testament in manner and forme following. ffirst I bequeath my soule into the hands of allmightie god . . . and my body to be decently buried at the discrecon of my execut[ors] hereafter named, Item I giue to my loveing frend Mr Richard Perkins of St Giles in the feilds London ffyftie pounds of currant English money to be payed vnto him by fyve shillings a weeke, yf he shall soe long lyve as to receave the sume as aforesaid: But if he shall decease before the said sume soe to be receaved Then the sayd payment alsoe to cease likewise. But yf ye said Richard Perkins shall overlive the full receipt of the said sume as aforesaid Then he shall haue foure shillings a weeke dureinge his naturall life to be paied out of my lands in Worcester sheire Item I̅ give to Henry Mildmay of Heston Esqr my Nagg wch he gave vnto me wth new Bridle Sadle & Cloth. Item to James Totnell in Shoe lane London in the parrish of St Brides my black lace suite and Cloake Item I giue to Nicholas Awnsham of Hownslowe gentl twentie shillings Item I give vnto my loveing wife Elizabeth Bowyer all my lands tenem[en]ts and herediturments whatsoever in Worcester-sheire in

Kiddermaster wth their app[er]ten[an]ces to her and her heires forever And alsoe I giue and bequeath all other my goods and Chattles whatsoever (not before bequeathed) vnto my said loueing wife Elizabeth Bowyer whome I make and ordaine full and whole executrix of this my last will and Testament In witnes whereot I the sayd Michaell Bowyer haue hereunto set my hand and seale the day and yeare aboue written Michaell Bowyer Signed sealed published and declared as the last will and testam[en]t of the said Michael Bowyer in the p^rsence of vs. Nicholas Awnsham ffrancis Harpar.

Proved 7 November 1645. In the margin, by the Latin Probate, is the following:

The Seaventh of May 1656 . . . a Lettē of Ado issued out to Thomas Morrison Husband & Ad^tor of Eliz: Morrison aîs Bowyer. Ex^rix of Michael Bowyer dec^d to Ad^er ye goods of ye sd dec^d according to ye tenor of ye Will of ye sd dec^d wch sd goods were-vuadst r. . . . [blurred] by the sd Elizabeth hee being first sworne truly to Ad^er/

WILLIAM BROWNE

Seager 105.

In the name of God Amen, The Three and twentieth daie of October One thousand six hundred thirtie fower . . . I William Browne of the parish of St James Clarkenwell in the Countie of Midd[lesex] gent being at this present sicke and weake . . . [direct my body] to be buried . . . in the Chancell of the parish Church of St James Clarkenwell aforesaid soe neere as maie be conveniently to my father Greene. . . . Imprimis I give and bequeath vnto my brother Robert Browne Haberdasher the somē of five poundes of lawfull money of England, and also my best suite of apparrell (vizt) hose, doublett and cloke, the same to be paid and delivered him within one moneth next after my decease Item I give and bequeath vnto the three Children of the said Robert Browne the somē of tenn pounds of lawfull money of England to be shared amongst them part and part alike And my will and mind is that if any of my said brothers Children shall depart this life before they shall accomplish theire full ages of one and twentie yeares, then his or theire part soe dying to remayne to the survivor of them, and if they shall all of them die before the accomplishment of theire said ages of one and twentie yeares then I will the same shall remayne vnto my said brother Item I give to my brother in lawe Thomas bond¹ my best blacke stuffe suite and cloke my wrought gold capp my best halfe shirt and my best band, and my white beaver hatt to be paid and delivered him imediately after my decease Item I give and bequeath vnto my sister Susan Bond wife of the said Thomas Bond the somē of fower pounds to be paid

¹ Probably the player of Prince Charles's company.

her wthin three moneths next after my decease And I doe also release acquite and discharge my said sister of the debt of twentie shillings wch she oweth me Item I give and bequeath unto my dearly beloved Mother Susan Greene als Baskervile All such some and somes of mony, debts, duties claymes chalenges and demaunds whatsoever as either is ought or shalbe due owing, or belonging vnto me forth, out of and from the redd Bull Playhouse scituate in St John streete in the Countie of Midd[lesex] whereof I am a member, and a fellow sharer, or of or by any of the shares or other person or persons players there or owners thereof, and of in or to any house or houses to the said playhouse adioyning And also all bonds, bills, debts and other things as I have formerly graunted or assigned vnto my said mother, or wherein by deede I have declared any trust to be reposed in me for the vse and benefitt of my said mother Item I further give and bequeath vnto my said mother my house clocke my pockett watch, my gold seale ring, my best beaver hatt, and all my wearing apparrell as well linnen as woollen not otherwise herein and hereby given, disposed willed or bequeathed Item I give to the said Company of players twentie shillings to buy them blacke ribbons to weare in remembrance of me Item I give and bequeath unto Phillipp Massam my sonne in lawe the some of ten pounds of lawfull money of England to be paid him at his age of one and twentie yeares if he shalbe then living And my will and minde is that if my said sonne shall depart this mortall life before he shall accomplish his age of one and twentie yeares aforesaid That then the said ten pounds which should have ben paid to him shalbe paid w^thin one moneth next after the said Phillipps decease vnto my foresaid brother Robert Browne his Executo^rs or assignes Item I give to the poore of the said parish of St James Clerkenwell the some of twentie shillings to be distributed amongst them at the discretion of my Executrix hereafter named And all other my goods chattells Cattell, plate ready moneys, debts and whatsoever else of myne, and not herein or by deed under my hand and seale otherwise disposed of my due debts being first payd and my funerall expences and legacies discharged I give vnto my wife Anne Browne And I doe make and ordayne my said Mother Susan Baskervile als Greene full and whole Executrix of this my Testament and last will And I doe hereby revoke and disanull all former wills and this onely to stand for and as my last will and testament Jn witnes whereof I the said William Browne have herevnto set my hand and seale yeoven the daie and yeares first above written p[er] me Willm Browne Signed, sealed published and delivered by the said testator for and as his last will and testam[en]t in the presence of us Robert Neale Johua Hill Richard Tuttells m[ar]ke Richard Merydale Scr.

Probated 10 November 1634.

638

APPENDIX

RICHARD BURBAGE[1]

Memorandum That on ffrydaye the Twelueth of Marche Anno
D[omi]ni. One thousande, sixe hundred, and eighteene, [' J '
crossed out] Richarde Burbadge of the p[ar]ishe of S[t]. Leonarde
in Shoreditch in the Countie of Midd[lesex] Gent. beinge sicke in
bodie but of good, & perfect remembrance, did make his last will,
and testament nuncupative in manner, and forme followinge:
vizt. He the said Richarde did nominate and appointe his welbeloved wife Winifride Burbage, to be his sole Executrix of all his
goodes and Chattels whatsoever, Jn the p[re]sence, & hearinge of
the p[er]sons vndernamed Cuthbert Burbadge, brother to the
Testator. The marke of Elizabeth his wife. Nicholas Tooley
Anne Lancaster. Richarde Robinson, The mark of Elizabeth
Graues. Henry Jacksonne.

Proved 22 April 1619.

ELIZABETH CONDELL[2]

Pile 13.

In the name of God Amen I, Elizabeth Cundall of ffulham in the
Countie of Midd[lesex] widdowe doe renounce all former wills
made by me and I doe make this my last will, and Testament, . . .
I doe desire M[r] Cuthbert Burbidge, and Thomas Seaman (whome
I doe nominate make and appoynt the Executors of this my last
will and Testament) to haue a Care vnto my grandchildren the
now Children of my daughter ffynch, and to performe this my last
will and Testament in such manner as I shall lymitt and appoynt
for certayne causes which I haue made knowne vnto my said
Executo[rs] touching as well my owne sonne William Cundall as
alsoe my sonne in lawe M[r]. Herbert ffynch the which I hold fitt
herein not to mencon. . . . And as touching my said sonne William
Cundall, I doe give vnto him twenty shillings to be payd vnto him
within One weeke next after my death, but if my said Executors
. . . shall think fitt to giue vnto my saide sonne William Cundall any
more then the some which they shall agree vpon or the survivor
thinke fitt for him to haue shalbee payd out of the interest lease
or Terme of yeares which I haue in the Globe, and ffryers at such
tyme and tymes and in such manner as they my said Executo[rs]
or the survivo[r]: of them shall likewise thinke fitt, and my reason
is for that I would haue noe parte of my estate neither prodigally
spent, nor lewdly wasted by him, and the residue out of the same
I doe giue vnto my said grandchildren, but if in case my said

---

[1] This will was published by Collier, *Mem. Act.*, pp. 45–6. It has been
corrected from the transcript at Somerset House, Parker 38.

[2] Mrs. Condell was not, of course, an actor. Her will is printed here
because of its references to actors and their families and to theatrical affairs.
The great length of the will has led me to summarize parts of it.

Executo^{rs} or the survivor of them shall find and see that my said sonne William Cundall shall not amend his Courses, but spend that estate and meanes which hee now hath, then my will is that he shall onely haue the said Twenty shillings vnlesse his extreame poverty and need shall cause my said Executors, or the survivor of them to afford him what in charity they shall think fitt. Item I doe giue and bequeath vnto Elizabeth Cundall the wife of my said sonne William Cundall, One siluer Porringer, and my will is that they the said William and Elizabeth hauing noe interest att all in those Twelve messuages scittuate in the Strond in the Countie of Midd[lesex] which I haue sold to John Hatt gent, shall leuy a ffyne of the same messuages, and assure the same as on their parts vnto the said John Hatt or some other person, or persons which he shall nominate, and appoint, or els they nor either of them to take any benefitt by my will, for that otherwise my said Executo^{rs}: and Estate wilbee troubled and encumbred by that deed which I gaue sealed to the said Hatt for more than One Thousands Pounds for the cleeringe of the Title, and freeing all Incumbrances vpon the said houses.

[A gift of £50 was left Elizabeth, daughter of William Condell, at the age of twenty-one or upon her marriage, and £10 apiece to the executors. Item I doe giue vnto M^{rs}: Burbidge a silver fork and a gold Purse.' A 'Case of strong waters with all that Doe belong vnto it' and a gold purse was left to Mrs. Seaman, 'and because the said Thomas Seaman hath done the office of a true freind vnto me, therefore and in performance of my promise I doe give vnto him all my bookes.'

Gifts were made to Mr. John Diodate, Isabella Underwood,[1] and Mrs. Norton, and twenty shillings left to Mary Norton. 'Item I doe give and bequeath vnto Elizabeth Wheaton Widdowe[2] the gatheringe Place at the Globe during my Lease'; also gifts and £20. Mrs. Condell left £10 to Mrs. Wheaton's daughter and some 'course' sheets, £20 to Jasper Smart, 40s. to Joane Smart, 40s. to the mother of the said Jasper, 40s. to the poor of Fulham, £20 to Mr. Norton 'of the money which he oweth vnto me', and cancelled a 40s. debt owed by 'one Jones'.]

And I doe nominate appoynte, and desire Mr Lowen,[3] and Mr John Diodate to be the Overseers of this my last will and Testament. [A piece of plate worth 50s. was given to each.] And I doe hereby declare, and make knowne vnto all men that I will have none of the Legatees aboue named hereafter to sue or trouble my said Executo^{rs} or either of them touchinge anythinge conteyned

---

[1] Probably the daughter of John Underwood, the actor, mentioned as a minor in his will in 1624. Henry Cóndell had been one of the executors of the will.

[2] She had received bequests and a confirmation of her gatherer's place in Henry Condell's will eight years before.

[3] Apparently the actor in the King's company.

in this my will in regards I doe knowe that they will honestly, and faithfully performe the same to the uttermost of their power. And I doe Charge them as they will answere the same att the day of Judgment that they, nor either of my said Executo^{rs} doe violate or breake anie the trust in them reposed, but that they and either of them p[er]forme the same to the best of Power, And if in Case that any of the Legatees shall sue or trouble my said Executo^{rs}: or either of them concerninge anie of the p^rmisses, Then my will is, That such person, and persons shall have noe benefitt by this my will. And whereas the said John Hatt hath bought of me the said Twelue Houses or Messuages in the Strond called the Helmett Courte for One Thousand ffower hundred, and ffiftie Pounds, and whereas hee the said Hatt hath already payd most parte of the same, and because the assurance in lawe is not as yet setled on him the said Hatt by reason of the vniust dealings of one Sir William Acton knight and Barronett with mee, for releese of which I haue now a Bill dependinge in the Chancery against him, therefore to the ende that all people may knowe that it is my will and meaninge that hee the said Hatt should enioy his bargaine made with me, and alsoe have the said houses I doe hereby give grante, and devise the said Twelue Messuages with their appurtenn[ances] vnto the said John Hatt his heires and assignes forever he or they paying vnto me or my Executo^{rs} the Remainder of the moneys in his hands for the said purchase, and I doe hereby order and appoynt William Danyell and Walter Acton Trustees for the said Sir William Acton to seale, and deliver, and acknowledge in Chauncery that deed and grant of bargaine and sale of the said Twelve messuages which I have already sealed vnto the said Hatt, and acknowledged before M^r: Page one of the Masters in Chauncery, In witnes whereof I haue herevnto put my hand and seale this ffirst daie of September. Anno Domini One Thousand six hundred thirty ffive, and I have published this to bee my last will, and Testament in the presence of vs, who are witnesses to the same, (vizt) (Elizabeth Condell) Robert Blumson, Thomas Blumson, The m[ar]ke of Mary Cole.

Probated 8 February 1635/6.

HENRY CONDELL[1]

'Henrie Cundall of London gentleman' directed his burial to be at night 'in such parish where it shall please god to call me'.

All 'ffrehould messuages, landes, tenements and hereditaments whatsoever with theire and everie of theire appurtenances scituate lying and being in Helmett court in the Strand and elsewhere in the Countie of Midd[lesex]' was bequeathed to his wife

---

[1] Because of the length of the will, parts of it are summarized. It was published by Collier, *Mem. Act.*, pp. 145–9. It has been checked from the transcript at Somerset House, Barrington 18.

Elizabeth for life; on her death to his son Henry; on his death without issue to his son William; on his without issue to his daughter Elizabeth Finch.

All 'freehold messuages', &c., in the parish of St. Bride, near Fleet Street, London, and 'elsewhere in the Cittie of London and the suburbes thereof' was bequeathed to his wife Elizabeth until William's term of apprenticehood was up, when it went to him; on his death without issue, to Henry or Elizabeth above.

'Jmprimis, whereas J am executor of the last will and testament of John Vnderwood deceased and by force of the same executorshipp become possessed of soe much of the personall estate of the said John Vnderwood which is expressed in an Jnventory made thereof and by me exhibited in due form of lawe into the Ecclesiasticall Court and whereas also in discharge of my said executorshipp J haue from time to time disbursed divers somes of money in the educacon and bringing vp of the Children of the said John Vnderwood deceased as by my Accomptes kepte in that behalfe Appeareth. nowe in discharge of my conscience and in full performance of the trust reposed in me by the said John Vnderwood, J doe charge my executrix faithfullie to pay to the surviuing Children of the said John Vnderwood All and whatsoever shalbe founde and appeare by my Accompts to belong vnto them, And to deliuer vnto them all such Rings as was theire late ffathers and which are by me kept by themselues aparte in a little Caskett.'

His wife, Elizabeth Condell, was made executrix. 'John Hemings gentleman Cuthbert Burbadge gentleman my sonne in lawe Harbert ffinch and Peeter Saunderson grocer' were made overseers and given £5 each for a piece of plate.

To his son William were bequeathed all rents and profits 'of and by my leases and tearmes of yeares of all my Messuages, howses and places scituate in the Blackfriars, London and at the banckside in the Countie of Surrey', until £300 was 'raised for a stocke'.

'Jtem for as much as J haue by this my will dealt very bountifully with my welbeloued wief Elizabeth Cundall Considering my estate', an annuity of £30 was bequeathed to Henry 'for his maintenance either at the Vniversitie or elsewhere' during Elizabeth's life.

To widow Martin and widow Gimber was given 20s. yearly apiece for life 'if my leases and tearmes of yeares of and in my howses in Aldermanburie in London, shall soe long continewe vnexpired'.

To the poor of the parish of Fulham, Middlesex, 'where J nowe dwell', was given £5 to be distributed by 'Master Doctor Clewett, and Master Edmond Powell of ffulham gentlemen'.

To his wife and daughter were given equal shares of the household stuff, his wife to have the preference.

His cousin, Frances Gurney alias Hulse, the daughter of his aunt, was bequeathed £5, and to her daughter the same, and a like sum to each of the daughters of his cousin Gilder, late of Norfolk.

Elizabeth Wheaton,[1] an old servant, was bequeathed a mourning gown and 40s. 'and that place or priviledge which shee nowe exerciseth and enioyeth in the howses of the blackfriers, London and the globe on the backside' for life, 'if my estate shall so long continew in the premisses'; £5 was left her daughter.

The rest of the estate was given to his wife. The will was witnessed by 'Robert Yonge, Hum. Dyson, N.P., and Ro. Dickins, servt. to N.P.' 13 December 1627, and proved 24 February 1627/8.

RICHARD COWLEY[2]

The xiii^th of January 1617.—Memorandu[m] that Richard Cowley in the p^rsence of vs herevnder written made and constituted his daughter Elizabeth Cowley sole Executrix of all his goods and Chattells; witnes John Heminges Cuthbert Burbaage, John Shancke, Tho. Ravenscroft.

Proved in St. Leonard's Shoreditch by Elizabeth Birch, *als* Cowley, daughter and executrix of the deceased, on the 6th April, 1619.

SARA DAMBROOKE[3]

The will was made 8 September 1624. The estate, which was not very large, went to her children and her uncle, Nathaniell Torpley, executor. It was signed by Sara Dambrooke in the presence of John and Winifred Shancke, who signed their marks, and proved 3 March 1624/5

THOMAS DOWNTON

Clarke 84.

In the name of God Amen I Thomas Downton of the p[ar]ish of St Gyles w^thout Cripplegate vinter . . . bequeath my body to [be] buried in the Churchyarde of the p[ar]ishe Church of St Giles where I yet live, as neare my firste wife Anne Downton as maybe founde place, wch I leaue to the discreçon of my Executrix hereafter named, Item I give to my sonne Thomas Downton all my Library of bookes both of devinitye & humanitye excepte fewe

---

[1] She was remembered and her place confirmed in the will of Mrs. Condell eight years later (see p. 639).

[2] Printed by H. R. Plomer, *N. & Q.* (Series X), vi. 368, from the Archdeaconry of London, vol. vi, folio 22. Checked from the transcript at Somerset House.

[3] The summary of this will (Clarke 29) is included because of the reference to the comedian John Shank, from whose house Sara Dambrooke was buried.

bookes of devinity and humanytie wch my wife shall Chuse, Item because my sonne hath bine a desperate sonne to me I giue a desperat Legacye ffifty pounds of one Hundred & Thirty pounds wch I haue sued to a Judgm[en]t in the Courte of pleas in the Exchequer office soe I giue him one Ringe of goulde wth a lyon Rampant & the two great l[ette]res of his name p[ro]vided that he shall not receiue those Legacies but vppon such occasin as my Executrix shall thinke fitt nor shall he Claime or seeke by anie senister meanes to Wreste the saide debte of ffifty pounds from my Executrix or else vntill he shall well approue the bonde, & money to be in the possession of my Executrix or her assignes, but yf he shall other wise doe, I doe vtterlye deprive him of any such legacye, Item I give and bequeath to my sonne Ed: my musquet wth the appurten[anc]es & the other ffiftye pounds of the saide bonde of one hundred & Thirty pounds vppon the like Condiĉons to be p[er]formed as before, Alsoe I giue & bequeath to my daughter Jane Downton the soñe of Thirty pounds wch is full soñe of one Hundred & thirty pounds due by that bonde, Also I give my saide daughter Jane one bonde of Sixty pounds & one Bill of Thirty pounds for the paym[en]t of ffifteene pounds, I give & bequeath to all my daughters some little remembrance of Edward shillings accordinge to my poore abillytie & I doe make & Constitute Jayne my welbeloved & Constant wife my sole Executrix of all my p[er]sonall estate or of whatsoever I did enioye before I married her or whatsoever I haue enioyed or possessed for her & to her vse since my marriage to her freeing my self of my p[ro]mise that I haue not altered anie estate of hirs since my marriage to her, soe to this will I make my Lovinge Cozen Andrew Wheatley & Richard Waight my overseers Sealed wth my seale and Subscribed wth my hande this ffifth of August one Thousand Sixe Hundred Twentie ffive . . . Tho: downton Signed Sealed & deliu[er]ed in the p[rese]nce of vs the m[ar]ke of Abraham Rissers Humphrey Marshall Robert Baxter.

Probated 19 August 1625.

JOHN HEMINGES[1]

' John Hemings Citizen and Grocer of [London]',[2] made his will 9 October 1630, directing his burial in St. Mary's Aldermanbury, near his wife Rebecca and under the same stone with her if possible, 'and that my funerall may be in decent and comely manner p[er]formed in the Evening without any vaine pompe or cost therein to be bestowed'.

[1] The will was printed in *Variorum*, iii. 191-6. It has been partly summarized here because of its length and corrected from the transcript at Somerset House.
[2] The word 'London' is not in the will; as no space was left for an insert, it was evidently omitted in the haste of copying.

He directed that all his debts be paid out of the sale of his goods, chattels, &c., and if that were not sufficient 'that the moiety or one half of the yeerely benefitt and proffitt of the severall partes which J have by lease in the severall Playhowses of the Globe and Blackffriers for and during such time and terme as J have therein be from time to time receaved and taken vp by my Executor herein after named and by him from time to time faithfully ymployed towards the payement of such of my said owne proper debts which shall remayne vnsatisfied and that proporconably to every person and persons to whome J shall then remaine indebted vntill by the said moiety or one half of the said yearly benefitt and profitt of the said partes they shalbe satisfied and paid without fraude or Coven'. If that should not be enough, the other half was to be used in like manner. After such debts were paid, the profit from the theatres was to be used in paying legacies and raising 'porcons for such of my said children as at the time of my decease shall have received from me no advancement'.

Bequests were made to his daughter Rebecca Smith, wife of Captain William Smith, to his daughter Margaret Sheppard, wife of Mr. Thomas Sheppard, to his daughter Elizabeth, and to his daughter Merefield. The children of his daughters Merefield and Sheppard were left 50s. each, and Richard Atkins, his grandchild, was given £5 to "buy him bookes'. His son-in-law, John Atkins, 'and his nowe wife' were left 40s. for two rings, if they were living with him at his decease.

'J giue and bequeath vnto every o1 my fellowes and sharers his Ma^ts servants which shalbe livinge at the time of my decease the some of tenn shillinges apeece to make them ringes for remembrances of me.'

'John Rice Clerke of St Saviours in Southwarke' was given 20s. for a remembrance (if living). The parish poor of St. Mary's Aldermanbury 'where J longe lived' were bequeathed 40s.

He directed 'that the severall legacies and somes of money by me herein before bequeathed to be paid in money be raised and taken out of the yeerley proffitt and benefitt which shall arrise or be made by my severall partes and shares in the severall Playhouses Called the Globe and Blackffriers after my said debts shalbe paid with as much speed as the same Conveniently may be'. His debts were to be paid first, then the legacies, from his estate, 'w^thout any lessening diminishing or vndervaluing thereof'. 'And for the better p[er]formance thereof my will minde and desire is that my said partes in the said Playhowses should be ymployed in playing the better to raise proffitt thereby as formerly the same have bine and haue yeilded good yearly proffitt as by my bookes will in that behalf appeare.'

After his debts and legacies were paid, the rest of his property was to be divided equally 'amongest such of my Children as at the time of my decease shalbe vnmarried or vnadvaunced and shall not have received from me any porcon in marriage or otherwise further then only for their educacon and breedinge p[ar]te and p[ar]te like'.

His son, William Heminges, was made executor, and 'my loving freinds Mr Burbage and Mr Rice' overseers.

The will was proved 11 October 1630.

JOHN HONYMAN

Pile 39.

In the name of God Amen, I John Honyman one of his Maties Servants the Players being weake, and infirme in bodie but of sound and perfect memory . . . bequeath my Body to bee Decently and Christianly buried in the Churchyard of S^t: Gyles without Criplegate, as neere as may bee to the place where my own ffather lyeth buried, And for that estate wherewithall it hath pleased God to bless mee in this world I dispose of it [in] manner and forme following, vizt (after my funerall Expences discharged and my debts paid which I desire may faithfully be done to all my Creditors) I give, and bequeath the one halfe, or moyety of all my goods, whether ready money debts apparrell bookes or what somme or somes shall growe due vnto mee from and amongst my ffellowes the Play[ers] or any other thing whatsoever equally to be devided to my deare and loving Mother Ellen Sweetman, and the other halfe I bequeath and comitt into the hands and custody of my said mother to be disposed of by her as shee in her discretion shall thinke fittest to the onely use Behalf and best benefitt of my onely Brother Richard Honyman, and to noe other use whatsoever, Item I give, and bequeath to my Loving ffather in lawe John Sweetman Twenty shillings to buy him a ring withall. Item I giue to euery one of my ffelowes the Players a Ringe of tenn shillings price. Item I give, and bequeath Twenty shillings to the Poore of the Parrish of S^t: Gyles without Criplegate aforesaid to be distributed amongst them according to the discretion of the Churchwardens of the said parrish, And I doe hereby will declare, and make my said mother the sole Executrix of this my last will, and testament not doubting but that out of her motherly Care and pietie shee will faithfully execute this my last will according to my true intent, and meaninge, In witnes whereof I haue herevnto sett my hand the seaventh day of Aprill, In the Twelft yeare of the reigne of our soveraigne Lord Charles . . . And in the yeare of our Redemption one thousand six hundred thirty sixe, John Honyman. Signed subscribed and published in the presence of Will Browne Robert Benefeild, Will Burbage.

Probated 26 April 1636.

John Shank

Pile 7.

In the name of God Amen the Last Day of December one Thousand and six hundred Thirty ffyve . . . I, John Shanke one of his Ma^ts: servants the Players, and Cittizen and weaver of London . . . will devise and appoint, That all such debts as I shall happen to owe at the tyme of my decease to any person or persons whatsoeuer be well and truely satisfied, and paid as soone after my decease as the same Conveniently may be raised out of my estate. Item, I will devise and appoint that my debts being paid and satisfied, and my funeralls discharged my lovinge wife Winifride Shanke have, and enioy to her owne use One whole Third part of my cleere estate (the same being personall, and consisting in goods Chattells, and Leases,) as being due and belonging vnto her my said wife, according to the laudable custome of the Citty of London whereof I am a ffreman, And I alsoe desire, will, deuise, and appoint that my said wife Winifride Shanke, whome I doe hereby make the sole Executrix of this my last will, and Testament doe take care that out of the other Two parts of my cleere estate theis Legacyes by me hereinafter given, and expressed be well and truely satisfied and paid according to my true meaninge herein declared (vizt) ffirst I give devise and bequeath vnto my Two sonnes John and James Shanke vnto, and for whom I have already disbursed diuers somes of money, amountinge togeither in the wholl to a farr greater somme then their parts in my estate would any way come vnto, the severall somes of Ten pounds a peece of lawfull english money, which I require them to rest satisfied with as my guift and bequeast vnto them, leaving them to their mother and my Executrix to deale better with them if they shalbe loving, and obedient vnto her. Item I give and bequeath vnto my daughter Elizabeth Bowen the some of One Hundred Pounds in lawfull english money. To be paid vnto her in manner, and forme following (vizt.) ffifty Pounds thereof att her next day of marriage, and the other ffifty pounds at the Birth of her next child that shee shall haue after such marriage. Item I give and bequeath vnto my grandchild Winifrid Bowen daughter of the said Elizabeth the some of Twenty Pounds of lawfull english money; To be deliuered into the hands of Mrs Morgan and shee to have the benefitt of the yearely Interest thereof during the minority of the said Childe towards her Cósts and charges in in the breeding and educacon of her, And the same Twenty Pounds to be paid vnto her my said Grandchild att her age of One, and twenty yeares, or day of marriage whichsoeuer shall first happen. And I further giue, devise, and bequeath vnto the said M^rs: Morgan the somme of Tenn Pounds in lawfull English money as a token of my gratitude, and thankefulnes vnto her for her loue and care in the educacon, and bringing vp of my said little

Grandchild: And which sayd some of Tenn Pounds I desire, and appoint to bee paid vnto her with asmuch Convenient speed as may be, Togeither wth the some of Three score and Tenn dounds [*sic*] Debt which I doe owe vnto her the said M^{rs}: Morgan and for which shee hath my bond. Item I give and bequeath vnto my loving Cozen Katherine Payne the some of fforty shillings in lawfull English money to make her a Ring for a remembrance, All the rest and residue of my goods chattells, and Credditts unbequeathed (my debts, funeralls and Legacies being paid, and discharged) I doe hereby wholly give, devise, and bequeath the same vnto my said loving wife Winifrid Shancke my Executrix desiring her, that she will take an especially Care that first and principally my debts and Legacyes be well and trully paid with asmuch Convenient speed as maybe out of my estate which doth consist for the most part in a Lease which I haue for a few yeares of Two Eight parts in the Blackfryers Playhouse, and of a Lease which I am to have of Three Eight parts in the moity of the Globe Playhouse for the Terme of Nyne yeares from Christmas last which I bought, and paid deere for: And by meanes thereof have benn put into debt. And I doe devise desire and appoint that the proffits yearelie comming and arising of and by the said parts may goe, and be ymployed for, and towards the payment of my debts, and legacys aforesaid, and that the same be not by my said Executrix apprized att an vnder value, and soe made part of my estate to the diminution thereof thereby to hinder the payment of my debts and Legacyes, And I doe desire my fellows his Ma^{ts}: Servants the players that they doe not abridge my said wife, and Executrix in the receiving of what is due vnto me, and my estate amongst them, as namely ffifty Pounds for my share in the stocke bookes apparrell, and other things according to the old Custome, and agreement amongst vs, fforty Pounds or more by them received of my share taken vp and remayning in the hands of John Lowen, or some other of them which they haue for a good space past receiued, and taken vpp of my share as I am a Player, and Sixteene Pounds and Twelve shillings which they owe mee for Two gownes, and Two and Twenty shillings for Trigg, and my share in the Courte moneyes behind, and that they will not goe about to hinder my wife in having her assurance amongst them for my parts in the Globe Playhouse according to a decree in the Court of Requests in that behalfe obteyned against S^r: Mathew Brend knight. And I doe hereby require charge, and Commaund my said Two sonnes John and James Shanke, That they nor either of them doe goe about to molest, trouble or hinder my wife their mother in the receiving and taking of this my estate or in thexecucon of this my will according to my true meaning herein declared, But that they, and either of them be loving and obedyent vnto her, which if they soe be, then I doubt not but shee will as I doe and haue required her be kind vnto and Carefull of them, and doe them the best good shee cann. And I doe hereby desire and appoint my loving freinds Phillipp Powell draper, and John Atkins Cittizen and Scrivener of London to be Overseers of this my last will and Testament desiring them to be ayding and assisting vnto my said wife, and Executrix with their best advice and Councell in thexecucon of this my will that the same may be p[er]formed according to my true meaning herein declared, And I doe hereby revoke all former wills by me heretofore made, and doe pronounce publish and declare this to be my last will and Testament, In witnes whereof I have herevnto putt my hand and seale the daye, and yeare first aboue written. John Shanke. Signed sealed pronounced published, and declared for and as the last will and Testament of the said John Shancke conteyned in seaven sheets of Paper in the p[re]sence of William Blagrave, Jonas Sage, John Atkins Scr.

Probated 28 January 1635/6.

EYLLAERDT SWANSTON[1]

'Eylaeardt Swanston late of the parish of S[t] Marie Alldermanburie London gentleman' made his nuncupative will 24 June 1651. He left all he possessed to be divided among his children, and he desired his daughter Sarah, wife of Joseph Wilson, to carry out his bequests. The witnesses were Joseph Wilson, Elizabeth Vasely (mark), Elizabeth Swanston, Sarah Wilson (mark), Joseph Wilson, Junior.

On 3 July 1651 a commission was granted to John Swanston and Sarah Wilson alias Swanston, to administer the goods, &c., and 18 April 1666 the like to Joseph Wilson, husband of Sarah Wilson alias Swanston, to administer the goods left unadministered by her, now deceased.

THOMAS TAYLOR

Hele 74.

In the name of God Amen: The thirtith daye of July anno d[omi]ni 1625 . . . J Thomas Taylor Cittizen and Pewterer of London beinge weake in body but of good and perfect mynde and memorie . . . will my body to be decentlie & Christianlyke buryed at the discreacon of myne executor hereafter named And as touchinge the disposicon of suche worldly estate as it hathe pleased the Lorde to lende in this lyfe J give will & bequeathe the same in manner and forme followinge (That is to saye) Jtem J give & bequeathe to my Sister in lawe Margerie Taylo[r] the some of

---

[1] This material is taken from Hotson, pp. 15 and 73, checked from the transcript at Somerset House, Grey 151.

ffourty shillings of lawfull monye of England To be payde vnto her oute of the Debt of Six poundes and three shillings oweinge vnto me by Bartholomewe Quoyten at suche tyme as myne Executor shall receive the same The residue of all & singuler my goods Chattells debts rights and Creditts not before bequeathed (my debts beinge payde, and ffunerall expenss Discharged) J give and bequeathe to my lovinge Brothers Edwarde Taylo[r] and Raphe Taylo[r] to be equallye devided betwne them p[ar]te & p[ar]te lyke And J ordaine and make my sayd brother Edward Taylo[r] sole executor of this my last Will and Testament Jn wittnes whereof hereunto J the sayd Thomas Taylo[r] haue sett myne hand & seale geven the daye and yeare firste above written. Thomas Taylor. Witnessed by John Pryce and Tho: Dutton, Scr.

Proved 13 May 1636.

Nicholas Tooley[1]

In the name of God Amen. I Nicholas Tooley of London gentleman . . . giue vnto my good freind M[r]. Thomas Adams preacher of gods word whome I doe entreate to preache my funerall sermon the summe of tenn pounds. Item I doe release and forgiue vnto my kinswoman Mary Cobb of London widowe the summe of fiue pounds which she oweth mee, and I doe giue vnto her the somme of fiue pounds more. Item I doe release and forgiue vnto her sonne Peter Cobb the summe of six pounds which hee oweth mee. Item I doe giue vnto her sonne John Cobb the somme of six pounds. Item I doe giue vnto her daughter Margaret Mosley the somme of fiue pounds. Item I doe giue vnto M[rs] Burbadge the wife of my good frend M[r]. Cuthberte Burbadge in whose howse I doe now lodge as a remembrance of my love in respect of her motherlie care over mee, the summe of tenn pounds over and besides, such sommes of monie as I shall owe vnto here, at my decease Item I doe giue vnto her daughter Elizabethe Burbadge als Maxey the summe of tenn pounds to be paied vnto her owne proper hands (therwithall to buy her such things as shee shall thincke most meete to weare in remembrance of mee. And my will is that an acquitance vnder her onlie hand and seale, shalbe a sufficient discharge in Lawe to my executo[rs] for paiement thereof to all intents purposes and construccons and as fullie as if her pretended husband should make and seale the same with her. Item I giue to Alice Walker the sister of my late Master, Richard Burbadge deceased the somme of tenn pounds to bee paied vnto her owne proper hands . . . Item I giue vnto Sara Burbadge the daughter of my said late M[r]. Richard Burbadge deceased that somme of twentie and nine pounds and thirteene shillings which is owing vnto mee

---

[1] Tooley's will was first printed *Variorum*, iii. 484–9. This transcript was taken from the copy at Somerset House, Byrd 83.

by Richard Robinson, to bee recovered deteyned and disposed of by my executo^{rs} herevnder named vntill her marriage, or age of twentie and one yeares which shall first and next happen without anie allowance to bee made of vse otherwise, then as they in theire discretions shall thinke, meete to allowe vnto her. Item I giue vnto Mrs Condell . . . the summes of tenn pounds. Item whereas I stand bound for Josephe Tayler as his surety for paiement of tenn pounds or thereabouts My will is That my executo^{rs} shall out of my estate paie that debt for him and discharge him of that bond. Item I doe release and forgiue vnto John Vnderwood and William Ecclestone all such sommes of monie as they doe severallie owe vnto mee. Item I doe giue and bequeathe for and towards perpetuall releife of the poore people of the parishe of Ste Leonard in Shorditche in the County of Midd[lese]x . . . the summe of fower score pounds to remaine as a stock . . . in such sorte as that on every sundaie after morning prayer, forever there may out of the encrease, which shall arise by the imployment thereof bee distributed amongst the poorer sorte of people of the same parishe, thirtie and two pennie wheaten loves, for theire reliefe. . . . Item I doe giue and bequeath for and towards the perpetuall reliefe of the poore people of the said parish of S^{te}: Gyles without Cripplegate London vnder the condition herevnder expressed the summe of twentie pounds to remaine as a stock [for the same use as above] . . . and my will and minde is that if my said guifte shalbe misimployed or neglected to bee performed in anie wise contrary to the true meaning of this my will Then and in such case I giue and bequeath the same legacie of twentie pounds for and towards the reliefe of the poore people of the said parishe of Ste Leonard in Shorditch to be imployed in that parishe in forme aforesaid. . . . All the rest and residue of all and singuler my goods Chattells Leases monie debts and personall estate What soever, and wheresoever (My debts Legacies and funerall Charges, discharged) I doe fullie and whollie giue and bequeath vnto my aforenamed Loving freinds Cutberte Burbadge, and Henry Condell to be equallie devided betwene them part and part alike, And I doe make name and constitute the said Cutberte Burbadge and Henry Condell the executo^{rs} of this my last will and testament. . . . In witnes Wherof to this my last will and testament, conteyning fowre sheetes of paper with my name subscribed to everie sheete, I haue set my seale the third daie of Iune one thowsand six hundred twentie three, and in the one and twentith yeare of the Raigne of our Soveraigne Lord Kinge James &c. Nicholas Tooley. Signed sealed pronounced and declared by the said Nicholas Tooley the Testator as his last will and testament on the daie and yeares aboue written in the presence of vs. The marke of Anne Asplin. The ma^{r}ke of Mary Dover, The marke of Joane Boothe. The marke of Agn[es] Dowson The marke of E B: Elizabeth Boulton

The marke of ffaith Kemsall The marke of Isabell Stanly Hum: Dyson Notary Publige and of me Ro: Dickens servant vnto the said Notary. Memorandum. That whereas I Nicholas Wilkinson als Tooley of London gentleman, haue on the daie of the date of theis presents by the name of Nicholas Tooley of London gentleman made my last will and testament ... Now for the explanation cleering avoyding and determination of all such ambiguities doubts scruples questions and variances aboute the validity of my said last will as may arise happen or bee moved after my decease by reason of omission of my name of Wilkinson therein I doe therefore by this my present Codicill by the name of Nicholas Wilkinson als Tooley ratifie confirme and approve my said last will and every guift Legacie and bequest therein expressed. ...

Proved 17 June 1624 by Cuthbert Burbage and Henry Condell.

John Underwood[1]

On 4 October 1624 ' John Vnderwood, of the parish of S^t: Bartholomewes the lesse in London, gent. ', made his will, leaving to his five children, John, Elizabeth, Burbage, Thomas, and Isabell, on reaching the age of twenty-one, equal shares of all his household goods, &c., 'and also all the right, title, or interest, part or share, that I haue and enioy at this present by lease or otherwise, or ought to have, possesse or enioye in any manner or kinde at this present, or hereafter within the blackefryars London or in the Company of his Maties: Servants my Loving and kinde fellowes in their house there or at the Globe on the Banckeside And also that my part and share or due in or out of the playhovse called the Curtaine scituate in or neere Holloway in the parishe of S^t: Leonard in Shoreditch London or any other place ... during their ... minorityes for and towards their education maintenance and placeing in the world. ... Provided allwaies ... that my said Executors shall not alienate change or alter by sale or otherwise directly or indirectly any my part ... in the said playhouses ... but that the increase and benefit ... shall come ... to my said Executors as now it is to me to the vse of my said Children'.

Henry Condell, Thomas Sanford, and Thomas Smith were named executors. John Heminges and John Lowen, 'my fellowes', were made overseers and each given 11s. for a ring.

A codicil, disposing of twelve rings, gilt and silver spoons and plate among his children, was made 10 October 1624 'or thereabouts' and added after his death.

Proved 1 February 1624/5.

---

[1] Underwood's will was first printed *Mem. Act.*, pp. 229–32. These extracts have been checked from the copy at Somerset House.

THE CLOSING OF THE THEATRES BECAUSE OF PLAGUE

IT has long been known that the London theatres were frequently closed as a precautionary measure against plague in the reigns of Elizabeth, James I, and Charles I. In the reign of Elizabeth, the precise number of plague deaths which was considered the signal for closing the theatres seems to have varied,[1] but during the first five or six years of the reign of James the number was thirty.[2]

There is evidence that before 1610 the danger mark was raised to forty, for in David, Lord Barry's *Ram Alley*, entered S.R. 9 November 1610 and probably acted in 1607 or 1608,[3] William Small-shanks says,

> For I dwindle at a serjeant in buff
> Almost as much as a new player does
> At a plague bill certified forty.[4]

So far as I can find, forty continued to be the danger mark until the final closing of the theatres in 1642. The 1619 licence for the King's men authorizes the company 'freely to use and exercise the Art and facultie of playing . . . when the infecčon of the Plague shall not weekely exceede the number of forty by the c'tificate of the lord Maior of london for the time being. . . .'[5] Precisely the same words appear in the company's licence of 1625, and a comparison of the closing dates of the theatres with the extant plague tables shows a rough correlation between dark theatres and mortality bills above forty.

It must not be thought, however, that the playhouses were closed promptly when forty plague deaths were reported and not before; nor must it be taken for granted that playing began again as soon as less than forty plague deaths appeared in the bills. After the plague of 1625 the players of the Phoenix were commanded to stop playing by an order of 6 December, though only fifteen were reported dead of the plague in the last bill. In 1630 Sir Henry Herbert sent the closing order to the theatres on the 17th of April, though the last two weekly reports had recorded two and eleven deaths. In 1636 the theatres were closed on 12 May and not opened for nine months, though the bills for 19 and 26 May recorded twenty-two and thirty-eight deaths respectively. In 1637

---

[1] See Murray, ii. 171–4, and Chambers, *E.S.* iv. 346–9, and i. 285–302.
[2] The 1603 patent for the Queen's men specified this number, and there are several other records whose precise statements indicate that thirty plague deaths was the number to be feared by the players. See Murray, ii. 174, and *Hens. Paps.*, pp. 61–2.
[3] Chambers, *E.S.* iii. 215.
[4] Act IV, scene i, Dodsley, v. 428; cited by Murray, ii. 175.
[5] *M.S.C.* i. 281.

Herbert did not allow the playhouses to open until 2 October, though for six preceding weeks the bills had indicated fewer than forty deaths. In 1640 the danger mark was passed on 23 July, and the death toll continued to mount for seven weeks before the theatres were closed on 11 September, when 105 plague deaths were listed. In 1641 the theatres were not closed, if my reading of Chalmers is correct,[1] until one hundred deaths had been recorded in the bills of mortality.

Such records as we have indicate that in Jacobean and Caroline times the usual procedure was for the Privy Council to notify the Master of the Revels that the theatres and other places of amusement were to be closed, and for Sir Henry Herbert to communicate directly with the companies.[2] The records of 1640 and 1641 suggest that the Privy Council had become somewhat remiss in its regulation of the players, no doubt because far more serious concerns were occupying the attention of their lordships in those years.

The weekly bills of mortality upon which the restraints of playing were based were issued every Thursday morning, in our period, from Parish Clerks' Hall.[3] Reports were submitted for the preceding seven days by the clerk of each parish, who drew his figures from the parish registers and from the reports of the searchers, two old women in each parish who were required to examine all corpses and report the cause of death. Comparatively few of these original bills are extant,[4] many of them having been burned in the fire at Parish Clerks' Hall in 1666. For the student of the seventeenth-century stage, the most valuable extant plague reports are those which John Bell printed from the records in Parish Clerks' Hall just before the fire of 1666. Bell's records for the period 1616–42, together with John Graunt's summaries of the yearly vital statistics for the same period, will be found on pp. 667–72.[5]

In the following pages I have set forth such evidence as I have been able to collect concerning the closing of the London theatres because of plague from the death of Shakespeare to the closing of the theatres. I have discussed only the years in which the theatres are known to have been closed, or in which I think the evidence shows that they were closed, though the closing has not been generally recognized. There is no discussion of the years in

[1] See below, pp. 666–7.
[2] See *M.S.C.* ii. 352; ibid. i. 391–2, and *Herbert*, p. 65; *M.S.C.* i. 395; and below, p. 666.
[3] According to Wilson, before 1626 and possibly for some time after these were printed only in plague time (Wilson, *Plague*, p. 197).
[4] See ibid., pp. 191–3.
[5] The most helpful modern discussion of the plague which I have found is F. P. Wilson's *The Plague in Shakespeare's London*, Oxford, 1927. Most of the facts of my discussion are derived from this book.

which there was no plague closing. There is one exception to this rule: the plague situation in 1635 has been considered because there are frequent assertions that the theatres were closed in that year. Though the evidence shows that the players were not restrained in 1635, I have thought it advisable, in the circumstances, to set forth the evidence in full.

1625

The plague of 1625 was, in the words of one historian, more deadly than any London had experienced since the days of the Black Death. The number of deaths increased gradually from the middle of March until the week ending 5 May, when they reached thirty, and the week ending 12 May, when they reached forty-five. Thereafter the death toll rose steeply to 4,463 in the week ending 18 August, and then decreased to forty-eight on 17 November, twenty-seven on 24 November, and fifteen on 1 December. Though there is no doubt that the theatres were closed in this time, we have no record of a closing or an opening order. It is possible, however, to ascertain the approximate period during which there were no public performances.

Almost certainly the theatres were closed at the death of King James, 27 March 1625,[1] and not expected to open until after his funeral on the seventh of May.[2] Such an action would have fol-

---

[1] Gardiner, v. 314.

[2] *M.S.C.* ii. 325. It is possible that the theatres were already closed when King James died, for Lent had begun nearly four weeks before on the 2nd of March, and it appears that usually there was some sort of limitation upon acting in this period. Unfortunately the records of Lent restrictions are confused and contradictory (see Chambers, *E.S.* i. 315–16). In 1615 representatives of all the London companies were summoned before the Privy Council for playing in Lent (*M.S.C.* i. 372), yet in 1617, 1619, 1622, 1624, 1625, and 1626 Sir Henry Herbert records fees paid him by the various companies for Lenten dispensations.

The Lenten restrictions are referred to by Francis Lenton in his *Young Gallants Whirligig*, 1629. When speaking of the frivolity of the young Inns of Court man, Lenton says (p. 7),

> Your Theaters hee daily doth frequent
> (Except the intermitted time of Lent).

Malone says specifically that the actors were not allowed to perform on Wednesdays and Fridays, sermon days, and that they could perform on other days in Lent only with special dispensations (*Herbert*, pp. 47–8). Malone's statement fits well enough with Sir Henry Herbert's remarks about the French players in February and March 1634/5, though Herbert seems to imply that all playing was ordinarily prohibited during Passion Week. He says (*Herbert*, pp. 60–1):

> 'This day being Friday, and the 20 of the same monthe [February], the kinge tould mee his pleasure, and commanded mee to give order that this Frenche company should playe the too sermon daies in the weeke, during their time of playinge in Lent, and in the house of Drury-lane, where the queenes players usually playe.

lowed the precedent of the procedure at the death of Prince Henry in 1612[1] and at the death of Queen Anne in 1619.[2] Even before the King's death, however, the Privy Council had been worried about the plague situation, for on 25 March they had written to the Lord Mayor and Aldermen rebuking them for neglecting to enforce the customary plague precautions,[3] and again on 29 March and on 5 April they wrote advising further precautions.[4] On 13 April a correspondent wrote to the Reverend Joseph Mead that King Charles was taking measures to protect the city against plague.[5] Since the Privy Council and the King were disturbed about plague conditions before and immediately after the death of James, and since plague reports grew steadily worse from his death until his burial, recording thirty plague deaths two days before the funeral, it is highly unlikely that the theatres were permitted to reopen after the funeral on the 7th of May.

'The kings pleasure I signifyed to Mr. Beeston, [the Manager of Drury-lane theatre,] the same day, who obeyd readily.

'The house-keepers are to give them by promise the benefit of their interest for the two days of the first weeke.

'They had the benefitt of playinge on the sermon daies, and gott two hundred pounds at least; besides many rich clothes were given them.

'They had freely to themselves the whole weeke before the weeke before Easter, which I obtaynd of the king for them.'

Customary, though not invariable, Lenten restrictions are also indicated in an account of a Privy Council meeting in March 1636/7 which Mr. Garrard wrote for the Lord Deputy in Ireland (*Strafforde's Letters*, ii. 56):

'Upon a little Abatement of the Plague, even in the first Week of *Lent*, the Players set up their Bills, and began to play in the *Black-Fryars* and other Houses. But my Lord of *Canterbury* quickly reduced them to a better Order; for, at the next Meeting at Council his Grace complained of it to the King, declared the Solemnity of *Lent*, the Unfitness of that Liberty to be given, both in respect of the Time and the Sickness, which was not extinguished in the City, concluding that if his Majesty did not command him to the contrary, he would lay them by the Heels, if they played again. My Lord Chamberlain stood up and said, that my Lord's Grace and he served one God and one King; that he hoped his Grace would not meddle in his Place no more than he did in his; that Players were under his Command. My Lord's Grace replied, that what he had spoken no ways touched upon his Place, &c. still concluding as he had done before, which he did with some Vehemency reiterate once or twice. So the King put an End to the Business by commanding my Lord Chamberlain that they should play no more.'

I think we can conclude from this evidence that there was always some sort of restriction on the players during Lent (probably plays were usually forbidden on Wednesdays and Fridays and on all days in Passion Week), but that it was generally possible to open the theatres part of the time providing the proper arrangements were made with Sir Henry Herbert. Unfortunately such a conclusion does not enable us to learn what any particular company did in a given year. In 1625 Sir Henry Herbert records two payments from Gunnell, manager of the Fortune, for the rope dancers, on 15 and 19 March (see above, p. 150). Evidently then, the Palsgrave's men had at least restricted their acting at the Fortune during Lent 1625.

[1] *M.S.C.* i. 88–9.   [2] See above, p. 6.   [3] Wilson, *Plague*, pp. 131–2.
[4] Ibid., pp. 132 n. and 133.   [5] Birch, *Charles I*, i. 11.

The probabilities are that there was no playing in London until about the end of November or the first week in December following. We have evidence that the company at the Cockpit or Phoenix in Drury Lane (and presumably the other companies as well) had begun to play again before the 6th of December, for on that date is recorded a court order by which the actors at the Cockpit were commanded to stop playing.

Forasmuch as it was conceyved by this Courte [Sessions of the Peace held at Hicks Hall] that the drawinge of people togeather to places was a great meanes of spreadinge and continewinge the infeccioun, Therefore according to the Letters of the right honourable the Lords and others of his Majesties most Honourable Privie Counsell, for the preventinge of such inconveniences, It is thought fitt, and this Courte doth prohibite the players of the howse at the Cockpitt, beinge next to his Majesties Courte at Whitehall, commaundinge them to surcease all such theire proceedinges untill his Majesties pleasure be further signified.[1]

It may be that this order was not enforced, for two weeks later the Lord Mayor and Council indicated to the Privy Council that playing was still going on in London. Their letter, superscribed 'From the L. Mayor about the players, xxj of Dcemb. To the righte honorable   Lordes and others of his Ma.ts most honorable privye councell', is as follows:

The remembraunce of the late grevious infeccon and contagion of the plague wherewth it pleased Almightie God so heavilye to afflicte vs this Citty and other p[ar]tes of this Kingedome, do make vs very circumspecte and warye so farr as lyeth in our powers to prevente all occasions that wee conceave may bee a meanes to renue or to spread the same, Soe accordingely wee haue benn very carefull to give order for the ayringe and clensinge of all houses and especially those that haue bene infected in this late visitacon as also for the cleane and sweete keepinge of our streetes and lanes, and for avoidinge of Jnmates and vndersitters that heretofore haue much pestered this Citty and especially the populous parrishes of the same, This haue wee carefully done, and yet ther is one thinge of late begonne wch in our opinions wilbe as greate a meanes as any of the rest both to renewe and increase the sicknes, namely comon stageplaies aboute the Citty out of our iurisdiccons wch lyeth not in our powers to redresse, And therefore wee haue prsumed to giue yor Lps notice thereof leavinge it to yo Lpps grave consideracons what is meete to bee done therein: But wee are of opinion that yf way bee given to contynue plaies, it wilbe a meanes to drawe together a greate concourse of people, and that of the meaner and lewder sorte, who there make matches and appointe theire meetinge places, and so consequently to indanger the renvinge & dispersinge of the sicknes, wch (blessed bee god) is nowe in a manner totally abated wthin this Citty. And so wee humbly take our leaves of yor Lpps This xxjth of December 1625
                    Yor Lpps most humble
                    [Signatures of the Mayor and nine others][2]

[1] Middx. Co. Records, iii. 6.   [2] B.M. Egerton MS. 2623, fol. 30.

Unfortunately the two documents here quoted fail to tell us just when playing began again after the plague of 1625. They do indicate, however, that at least one company, and presumably others, had resumed performances before the sixth of December, and that several were performing in the third week in December. These facts suggest that the reopening came in the last week in November after the weekly deaths had fallen below the stipulated total of forty, or in the first week in December after only fifteen had been reported on the first. I know of no evidence to show whether the Privy Council acted on the suggestion of the Lord Mayor. Presumably they did not.

Such evidence as we have, then, indicates that the theatres were probably closed from at least the 27th of March, when King James died, until the last week in November, after twenty-seven plague deaths had been reported on the twenty-fourth, or the first week in December after only fifteen deaths had been reported on the first.

1630

Though the plague of 1630 was mild as compared with that of 1625,[1] the theatres were closed for seven months, only one month less than in 1625. The extant records for the 1st, 8th, and 15th of April show only one, two, and eleven plague deaths respectively, but the Privy Council sent an order to the Lord Mayor on 14 April 1630 for the suppressing of 'Meetings & Stage playes. Bearebaytings, Tvmbling Dancing on ye Ropes, shewes, or scights',[2] and three days later, on the 17th of April, ordered Sir Henry Herbert to suppress all stage plays and other assemblies for sport and pastime.[3] The theatres remained quiet until November, as Malone discovered from the office-book of the Master of the Revels:

... the playhouses were shut up in April, and not permitted to be opened till the 12th of November, at which time the weekly bill of those who died in London of that distemper, was diminished to twenty-nine.[4]

[1] The total number of plague deaths for 1625 was 35,417; for 1630, 1,317. See pp. 668–9.   [2] M.S.C. i. 96.   [3] Ibid. ii. 352.
[4] Herbert, p. 64. This fact is roughly verified by a letter from the Reverend Joseph Mead at Cambridge to Sir Martin Stuteville, dated 27 November 1630: 'But to go on again with my first letter, which moreover relates: that the Dunkirkers have burned houses and taken away cattle in the Isle of Wight. That all the playhouses at London were now again open, since there had died that week of the plague but 18. . . .' (Birch, Charles I, ii. 80.) Evidently the news-writer in question was a little late with his observation. It was the plague bill of Thursday, 11 November, which recorded twenty-nine deaths, and Herbert opened the theatres on Friday. It was the bill of Thursday the 18th which recorded eighteen deaths (see p. 669). The news-writer did not get out his letter until after the players had been at work for a week. On 29 October 1630 Sir Thomas Rowe had written the Queen of Bohemia, 'No plays these six months, and that makes our statesmen see the good use of them' (C.S.P., Dom., 1629–31, p. 370).

Thus the theatres were closed for a little more than thirty weeks in 1630, from 17 April to 12 November. Apparently the plague of 1625 had made the authorities unusually cautious, for in fourteen of these thirty weeks less than forty deaths from plague had been reported; only twice were there more than seventy deaths. The theatres had been closed for twelve weeks before the first report of over forty plague deaths was entered, on the 8th of July.

1631

Although the theatres had been allowed to open in 1630 on 12 November, they must have been closed again because of plague some time between that date and 10 June 1631. There is no direct evidence of this closing order, and the weekly bills of mortality for 1631 are not extant, but the actors were evidently put under restraint again, for the following receipt was entered in Sir Henry Herbert's office-book:

Received of Mr. Benfielde, in the name of the kings company, for a gratuity for ther liberty gaind unto them of playinge, upon the cessation of the plague, this 10 of June, 1631,—3l. 10s. od.—This (Sir Henry Herbert adds) was taken upon *Pericles* at the Globe.[1]

It seems to me highly improbable that this notation should refer to the opening of seven months before; the evidence which we have shows that the King's men were not dilatory about gratuities. It must refer to a subsequent occasion. Such an occasion can scarcely have been in November or December of 1630, for we have the records of plague deaths for five weeks after the opening of 12 November: eighteen, seven, twenty, nineteen, five.[2] The theatres were open on 18 February 1630/1, for Sir Henry Herbert acknowledges his receipt on that day of £12. 4s. taken by the King's men at Blackfriars.[3] The closing referred to in the office-book must therefore have been between 18 February 1630/1 and 10 June 1631, when Sir Henry acknowledged the gratuity.

There is, moreover, evidence in the State papers that there was plague in and about London during this time. On 29 March 1631 the Justices of the Peace of Westminster wrote to the Privy Council giving a rather detailed account of the precautions they were taking 'on deaths of persons of the contagion of the sickness'.[4] And on 16 June 1631 the Lord Mayor of London the Privy Council as if the city were just recovering from a plague visitation: 'The sickness has been wholly withdrawn owing to the watchfulness of the officers.'[5] I realize that this evidence does not prove that the plague was serious enough for the theatres to be

---

[1] *Herbert*, p. 64. [2] See below, p. 669. [3] *Herbert*, p. 44.
[4] C.S.P., Dom., 1629–31, p. 557 (No. 50).
[5] Ibid., 1631–3, p. 78 (No. 10).

closed, but, taken with Herbert's acknowledgement, it constitutes more than a suggestion. John Graunt's iist of 274 plague deaths for the year 1631[1] as compared with 1,317 for 1630 shows that such plague as there was cannot have been very severe or, probably, very protracted. Though Graunt's figures cannot be said to prove or disprove a plague closing in 1631, they are not incompatible with the suggestion that there was a short period when playing was prohibited some time between 18 February 1630/1 and 10 June 1631.

1635

It has been asserted several times that there was a plague closing in 1635, though no order is extant, and the plague tables for that year—except for the last two weeks—have disappeared.[2] Hotson says, 'The London theatres had been going through hard times; plagues had closed their doors in 1635, and again, for eighteen months, in 1636–1637.'[3] Professor Hyder Rollins says, 'For one thing, plagues had caused a suppression of plays in 1635 and in 1636–1637.'[4] Professor J. Q. Adams implies that the theatres were closed in 1635: 'Towards the end of 1635 the plague was seriously interfering with their [the Red Bull company's] performance of plays',[5] and gives as his authority Young's *History of Dulwich College*, i. 114. Young, on this page, refers to MSS. I, 115, which is quoted at greater length in Warner, *MSS. Dul.*, p. 54. It is a 'Bill in Chancery preferred by Dulwich College against Margaret Gray, Edward Marrant, and John Roods for the non-payment of rent upon leases of the Fortune Theatre, with the answers of the defendants; Nov., 1637. . . .' The answer of the defendants concludes:

And they paid their rents vntill Christmas which was 12 monthe, which was Christmas 1635, and then the kinge to hinder the increase of the Plague did forbid Theaters in and about London, for to hinder concurse of people. And soe, acteing of playes being the way to rayse the rent (and forbiden), the defendants haue not euer since bene able, nor are chargeable as they conceiue, to pay rents, they being alsoe inhibited for imployeing the premises to any other vse then for playes.

Now the statement of the defendants is clearly that all was well

[1] See below, p. 672.
[2] The fact that John Graunt's annual table of deaths in London shows a total of 10,651 burials in 1635 but *no* plague deaths ought to be enough to disprove the assertion that there was a plague closing in 1635 (see below, p. 672). Graunt's reliability may, however, have been suspected, since he records 10,651 deaths exclusive of plague in 1635, but only 9,237 deaths, including 1,317 from the plague, in 1630. Probably the increase in 1635 was due to the growth of the city, but lest Graunt's evidence should be considered insufficient it may be well to set forth other evidence that the theatres were not closed in 1635.
[3] Hotson, p. 3.
[4] *Stud. Phil.* xviii (1921), 268.   [5] Adams, p. 287.

and the rent had been paid until Christmas 1635, *and then* the King closed the theatres, i.e. after Christmas 1635. The plague bills are extant for two years after Christmas 1635; they show that in the weeks ending 24 December 1635, 31 December 1635, and every week thereafter for three months there were no plague deaths at all. Evidently the theatres were not closed during the three months after Christmas 1635. The plague reappeared, however, in April 1636 and increased until forty-one deaths were recorded on 12 May, when Sir Henry Herbert ordered the theatres to be closed.

Clearly it is this plague closing *after* Christmas 1635 to which the defendants referred in November 1637. At the date of the defendants' answer, the playhouses had been closed for seventeen months, and it is no wonder that the assignees of the Fortune leases could not pay their rent.

I think we have disposed of the statement of the defendants as evidence for serious plague in 1635. There is more positive evidence that London was free from the scourge in that year. The *Calendar of State Papers, Domestic*, for 1635 records no references to the plague in London, though there are more than a dozen letters on the serious epidemic on the Continent, especially in the Low Countries. The calendar of extant references to theatrical activities in 1635 is unusually full. From these references alone we can rule out the possibility of any very long plague closing or of any closing at all in the months before the Fortune lessees paid their rent at Christmas, 1635. The title-pages of two plays, Nabbe's *Hannibal and Scipio* and Brome's *Sparagus Garden*, refer to their performance in the year 1635. The more precisely dated theatrical events of the year are as follows:

10 Jan. Herbert licensed Massinger's *Orator* (*Herbert*, p. 36).[1]
6 Feb. Herbert licensed Shirley's *Coronation* (ibid.).
19 Feb. Sir Humphrey Mildmay saw a play (see Appendix, p. 677).
20 Feb. Herbert allowed the visiting French players to act at the Phoenix 'the too sermon daies in the weeke, during their time of playinge in Lent' (*Herbert*, pp. 60–1).
25 Apr. Sir Humphrey Mildmay saw *The Elder Brother* at Blackfriars (see Appendix, p. 677).
28 Apr. Mildmay saw a play at the Blackfriars (ibid.).
6 May Mildmay saw *Othello* at Blackfriars (ibid.).
19 May George Garrard wrote Wentworth about a recent quarrel at Blackfriars (*Strafforde's Letters*, i. 426).
1 Aug. Herbert licensed Davenant's *News from Plymouth* (*Herbert*, p. 36).

[1] It may be objected that the extracts of Malone and Chalmers from Herbert's licences are not conclusive evidence that the theatres were open. Perhaps not, but the striking contrast between the twelve months of 1635, when eight plays were licensed, and the seventeen plague months, 12 May 1636 to 2 October 1637, when not a single one was allowed, speaks for itself.

16 Sep. Blagrave renewed the license for *Love's Pilgrimage* (ibid.).
15 Oct. Herbert licensed *The Lady of Pleasure* (ibid., p. 37).
6 Nov. John Greene saw *The Lady of Pleasure* (Symonds, 'Diary', p. 389).
16 Nov. Herbert licensed *The Platonic Lovers* (*Herbert*, p. 37).
25 Nov. Mildmay saw a play at Blackfriars (see Appendix, p. 677).
27 Nov. Mildmay saw a play (ibid.).
8 Dec. Mildmay saw *The Lady of Pleasure* (ibid.).
11 Dec. Mildmay's wife saw 'the Newe playe' (ibid.).
16 Dec. Mildmay saw a play at Blackfriars (ibid., p. 678).

1636–7

Of the several plague visitations between 1616 and 1642, that of 1636 and 1637 was second only to that of 1625 in severity. From the 1st of April 1636 to the 14th of December 1637, 13,482 plague deaths were recorded. For sixteen consecutive months more than thirty plague deaths were recorded each week, with only two exceptions. The first deaths were reported on 7 April, but the total did not reach forty until 12 May. when forty-one were announced.

Evidently the Privy Council heard that the death toll was mounting in the second week in May, though only four deaths had been reported on the 5th. On the 10th, two days before forty-one deaths were reported, they decided that the theatres should be closed.[1] Sir Henry Herbert sent his closing order to the theatres on the 12th.[2] Only once in the next fifteen months did the death toll drop below thirty a week. In spite of the alarming persistence

---

[1] *M.S.C.* i. 391–2. For some reason, the Privy Council issued two orders for the suppression of plays at the same sitting. The wording of the two orders is almost identical, except that one orders 'the Lo: Chamblaine of the Queens ma[ts]: Household . . . to cause the Players, that are her ma[ts]: Servants to forbeare all Stage Playes & other Enterludes whatsoeuer vntill further order', and the other orders that 'the Lo Chamblaine of his ma[ts]: Househould should be hereby prayed & required to cause all Stage Playes, Enterludes, Showes & Spectacles whatsoever, to be forthw[th] suppressed vntill further order'.
I know of no other record which indicates that it was thought necessary to make a distinction between the Queen's company and the other London troupes. Perhaps some matter of the prerogative of the Lord Chamberlain of the Queen's household was involved. There are several suggestions that the Queen's Chamberlain had some peculiar relationship to the players. (See 'Players'—Dorset, and the Baskerviles' statement [Fleay, *Stage*, p. 281], 'Shee the said Susan was informed, and accordinglie did peticion the Right Honorable the now Earle of Leicester, then Lord Chamberlaine of the Howshould of the said late deceased queene Anne, who hadd a kind of Gouernm[t] and suruey ouer the said Players.')
[2] 'This day the 12 May, 1636, I received a warrant from my lord Chamberlin for the suppressing of playes and shews, and at the same time delivered my severall warrants to George Wilson for the four companys of players, to be served upon them' (*Herbert*, p. 65). The four companies must have been King's, Queen's, King's Revels, and Prince Charles's.

of the high death-rate, the theatres were allowed to reopen on 24 February 1636/7, though they were shortly closed again.

Sir Henry Herbert's record of this opening·immediately follows his account of his closing the theatres on 12 May 1636. He says,

On thursday morning the 23 of February the bill of the plague made the number at forty foure, upon which decrease the king gave the players their liberty, and they began the 24 February 1636. [1636–7.]

The plague encreasinge, the players laye still untill the 2 of October, when they had leave to play.[1]

Though Sir Henry indicates that the theatres were closed again because of the increase of the plague, and though the plague tables show that the death-rate was high,[2] there was an additional reason for the closing of the theatres. On 23 March 1636/7 George Garrard wrote to the Lord Deputy in Ireland,

Upon a little Abatement of the Plague, even in the first Week of *Lent*, the Players set up their Bills, and began to play in the *Black-Fryars* and other Houses. But my Lord of *Canterbury* quickly reduced them to a better Order; for, at the next Meeting at Council his Grace complained of it to the King, declared the Solemnity of *Lent*, the Unfitness of that Liberty to be given, both in respect of the Time and the Sickness, which was not extinguished in the City, concluding that if his Majesty did not command him to the contrary, he would lay them by the Heels, if they played again. My Lord Chamberlain stood up and said, that my Lord's Grace and he served one God and one King; that he hoped his Grace would not meddle in his Place no more than he did in his; that Players were under his Command. My Lord's Grace replied, that what he had spoken no ways touched upon his Place, *&c.* still concluding as he had done before, which he did with some Vehemency reiterate once or twice. So the King put an End to the Business by commanding my Lord Chamberlain that they should play no more.[3]

Between the Archbishop and the plague, the players were put down after only a week of acting. The stormy meeting of the Privy Council to which Garrard refers must have been that of 1 March 1636/7, for in the records of that sitting we find:

Playes &cs.   An order to suppresse Playes, danceing on the Ropes &c:
suppressed   of the tenor of that entered the 10th of May last.[4]

After this short week of activity, the theatres remained closed until 2 October 1637.[5] One company at any rate found this long

[1] *Herbert*, p. 65.

[2] On 9 February there were ninety-two deaths; on 16 February, seventy-three; on 23 February, thirty-eight; on 2 March, fifty-seven; on 9 March, eighty-eight. See below, p. 670.

[3] *Strafforde's Letters*, ii. 56.

[4] *M.S.C.* i. 392.

[5] See below, p. 665. It is sometimes said that the theatres were allowed

period of the inhibition of acting too much for it. Beeston's young company at the Cockpit defied the restraint, as we learn from two contemporary documents. On the 12th of May 1637, just one year after Sir Henry Herbert's closing order, the following warrant is found in the Privy Council Registers:

A warrant to Iaspar Heyley Messenger to fetch before the Lords Christopher and W^m. Biston Theophil Bird Ezech: Fenn & Michaell Moone wth a Clause to Command the Keepers of the Playhouse called the Cockpit in Drury Lane who either live in it or have relaĉon to it not to permit Playes to bee Acted there till further Order. Dated ye 12th Signed Lo A Bp of Cant Lo Keeper Lo: Treãrer, Lo P: Seale Mr Sec Coke.[1]

It is probable that the second document should be dated shortly after the preceding one, though the petition is undated and has usually been arbitrarily dated 1636. It reads as follows:

Petition of Christopher Beeston to the Council. Petitioner being commanded to erect and prepare a company of young actors for their Majesties' service, and being desirous to know how they profited by his instructions, invited some noblemen and gentlemen to see them act at his house, the Cockpit. For which, since he perceives it is imputed as a fault, he is very sorry, and craves pardon.[2]

This petition seems nicely worded to mollify the Council. At any rate, the consequences of his rashness were not very serious for Beeston, for on 10 June 1637, less than a month after his summons from the Privy Council, the Lord Chamberlain interceded with the Stationers' Company to protect the plays claimed by Beeston's company.[3]

Before the theatres finally opened on the 2nd of October, the actors were making efforts to have the restrictions removed. At the meeting of 3 September 1637 the Council received a petition from the King's company that they be allowed to play at Michaelmas: 'Petition of the King's players; if there fall nothing

to open twice in this period, once on 23 February and once on 5 August. The notion of a second opening seems due to Chalmers. See below, pp. 666–7.

The long inhibition of the players is referred to in William Habington's 'Elegy upon the Death of Ben Jonson'. Jonson died 6 August 1637.

> . . . Heaven, before thy fate,
> That thou thyself might'st thy own dirges hear,
> Made the sad stage close mourner for a year;
> The stage, which (as by an instinct divine,
> Instructed) seeing its own fate in thine,
> And knowing how it ow'd its life to thee,
> Prepared itself thy sepulchre to be.
> (*Jonson Allusion Book*, p. 221, from *Jonsonus Virbius*, 1638.)

[1] *M.S.C.* i. 392, from P.C. Register, Charles I, xiii. 403.
[2] *C.S.P., Dom.*, 1636–7, p. 254.
[3] See above, pp. 53–5 and 328.

between this and Michaelmas, then at Michaelmas they may play, and all the schools.'[1]

' On the 17th of September Christopher Beeston made a similar petition that his new company be allowed to play:

Whereas Christopher Beeston their Ma[ties]: Servaunt did by his humble Peticon presented to the Boord shewe that having many young Actors lying at his Charge a long time vnpractised by reason of y[e] restraint occasioned by y[e] Infeccon of y[e] plague in and neare London, whereby they are much disabled to performe their desired Service, And therefore humbly besought that they might have leave to practise for y[e] better performance of their duties, when they shalbee commanded. It was therevpon Ordered his Ma[tie]: present in Councell that the said Beeston should bee at libertie to practise his said Actors, at Michaelmas next, if by that time there bee noe considerable encrease of the Sicknesse, or that there dye not of y[e] Infeccon in and about London more then there died this last weeke.[2]

At the same meeting the Council granted the King's men's petition on the same condition that plague deaths did not increase:

Order of the King in Council. His Majesty's servants, the players, having been for a long time restrained, and having spent what they got in many years before, and having prayed that they might now be at liberty to use their quality, it is ordered as in the article preceding [i.e. the answer to Beeston's petition].[3]

On 24 September, the reorganized Queen Henrietta's company petitioned the Council to the same effect:

Whereas her Ma[ts] Players did by their humble Peticon shew, that by reason of the Infeccon of the Plague in and neare about London they have for a long time, almost to their vtter vndoing (having noe other Imployment nor meanes to maintaine themselves and their families) been restrayned from vsing their quallity, And therefore humbly besought their Lo[pps] to bee restored to their former Liberty. It was therevpon Ordered (his Ma[tie-] present in Councell) that her Ma[ts]: said Players should bee at liberty to play at Michaelmas next, if by that time there bee noe considerable encrease nor that there dye not of the Infeccon in and about London, more then there died this last weeke.[4]

The references in these petitions to the players' suffering during

---

[1] C.S.P., Dom., 1637, p. 403. This petition, which was merely noted on the 3rd of September, was for some peculiar reason copied in full in the records for the Council meeting on the 24th, as follows: 'His Ma[ts] Servants y[e] Players having, by reason of the Infeccon of the Plague in and neare London, been for a long time restrained and having now spent what they got in many yeares before and soe not able any longer to subsist & mainteine their families did by their Peticon to his Ma[tie]: most humbly desire leave to bee now at libertie to vse their quallity.' (M.S.C. i. 394.)

[2] M.S.C. i. 393.

[3] C.S.P., Dom., 1637, pp. 420 and 421 (Nos. 86 and 87).

[4] M.S.C. i. 393–4.

plague closings only repeat what we know from many other sources.

At Michaelmas the players were again disappointed, for the report on the day before had shown an increase of five deaths. Nevertheless, three days later, on the 2nd of October, after nearly seventeen months of idleness, the theatres were allowed to open, for Herbert says, 'The plague encreasinge, the players laye still untill the 2 of October, when they had leave to play'.[1] On 9 October 1637 George Garrard wrote to the Lord Deputy in Ireland, 'The Players have obtained Leave to play again . . .',[2] and on 3 November 1637 Sir Humphrey Mildmay saw an unnamed play at Blackfriars.[3]

1640

In 1640 the plague again became alarming. Although the number of deaths from this scourge increased steadily from the 1st of July until the week of 10 September, when they reached 105 and began to decline,[4] it is not until September that we have any record that the theatres were closed. At the sitting of 11 September the Privy Council, considering that the plague 'doeth much increase in and about London', ordered that

all Players, both their Ma[ts] Servants and others as also the Keepers of Paris Garden bee hereby commanded and required forthw[th] to shut vp their Play houses, and not to exercise or play in any of them or in any other place w[th]in y[e] Citty or Suburbs of London till it shall please God to cease the Infec[c]on and that further Order shalbee given by the Boord. Hereof all the Masters and Actors of the said Play-houses are to take notice and to conforme themselves as they will answere it at their perills.[5]

We do not know just when the theatres were allowed to reopen, but the plague tables show only twenty-four deaths for the week ending 29 October and seventeen for the one ending 5 November. Sir Humphrey Mildmay saw plays on the 6th, 9th, and 16th of November;[6] Herbert licensed a play for the King's men on the 10th of November;[7] and on the same day the King's men began their Christmas season at court.[8] Evidently, then, the players

[1] *Herbert*, p. 65.   [2] *Strafforde's Letters*, ii. 118.
[3] See Appendix, p. 678.   [4] See p. 671.
[5] *M.S.C.* i. 395. Collier (*H.E.D.P.* ii. 34) printed a copy of this order which said that the playhouses were to close for six months, but was otherwise much the same. If the order ever contained a six months clause, it certainly was not enforced.
[6] See Appendix, p. 679.
[7] Shirley's *Imposture*. Herbert mentions no company, but the play was in the list of King's plays which Essex sent to the Stationers' Company (see above, p. 66), and it was printed in 1652 as 'Acted at the private House in Black Fryers' (*Herbert*, p. 39, and title-page of the 1652 edition).
[8] See above, p. 100.

were allowed to begin performing in October or early in November
—probably the first week in November, perhaps on the 6th, after
only seventeen plague deaths had been reported on the 5th.

1641

Plague raged in London in the summer and autumn of 1641.
The five weekly reports in July gave 33, 28, 42, 56, and 74 deaths;
the four in August, 100, 80, 131, and 139. Every week thereafter
more than one hundred deaths were reported, until the second
week in November, and not until the 9th of December did the
total drop below forty.[1]

Obviously the theatres must have been closed in this time,
though it is generally said that we have no record of the order.
I think, however, that Chalmers copied the account of this plague
closing from Sir Henry Herbert's office-book, though it has been
confused with the account of the plague of 1636–7. Chalmers's
transcript reads:

> On the 12th of May, 1636, warrants were sent to the *four* companies
> to stop the plays, on account of the pest. Owing to the same cause,
> Sir Henry, upon conference with the Earl of Essex, the Lord Cham-
> berlain, concerning the plague, which had increased to a hundred
> deaths a week, sent warrants, by Mr. Louens, on the 5th of August,
> to the several playhouses, for the purpose of preventing their repre-
> sentations: The plague, having decreased to eighty-six deaths a week,
> induced the Lord Chamberlain to open the theatres, for the profit of
> the players, and the amusement of the people.[2]

It has generally been taken for granted that this entire quota-
tion concerns the plague of 1636–7, but I believe that only the first
sentence has to do with that plague visitation, while the second
sentence refers to the plague of 1641. The facts which Chalmers
gives about the plague of 1636–7 are verified by Malone's extract
from the office-book.[3] The second sentence certainly does not
refer to the same visitation, because there was no plague report
on a 5 August in 1636 or 1637, there was no week when one hundred deaths were reported, and the Earl of Essex was not Lord
Chamberlain in 1636 or 1637. All these facts do, however, fit the
plague of 1641. On 5 August 1641, one hundred deaths were reported,[4] and on that date the Earl of Essex was Lord Chamberlain.[5] Furthermore, the unfamiliarity of the Earl of Essex with
his new duties, since he had come into his office only ten days
before on the 24th of July, may account for the fact that the
closing was delayed for three weeks after the number of plague

[1] See below, p. 671.
[2] *Herbert*, p. 65, from *Sup. Ap.*, pp. 211–12.
[3] Ibid., from *Variorum*, iii. 239.
[4] See below, p. 671.   [5] See *M.S.C.* ii. 322.

deaths reached the accepted danger mark. Unfortunately, I cannot account for the statement about the opening of the theatres when the plague decreased to eighty-six. It seems strange that the theatres would be allowed to reopen at such a time, and the figures do not fit any of the extant plague records (4 November, 106; 11 November, 79; 18 November, 61; 25 November, 44; 2 December, 41; 9 December, 15).[1] There is evidence, however, that some time in November the players were allowed to resume, for Sir Humphrey Mildmay saw a play on the 1st of December and another on the 10th.

I think we can conclude, therefore, that Chalmers confused two plague accounts in Sir Henry Herbert's office-book, that the theatres were ordered closed on 5 August 1641, and that they were allowed to reopen shortly before the first of December, probably on the 26th or 27th of November after the report of forty-four deaths on Thursday, the 25th.

PLAGUE TABLES

The following weekly tables with their explanations are taken from John Bell's *London's Remembrancer* (London, 1665), B$_2$v, B$_4$, C$_1$, C$_2$, and C$_2$v.

The table of annual totals which follows is taken from John Graunt's *Natural and Political Observations Mentioned in a following Index and made upon the Bills of Mortality* (5th ed.: London, 1676), pp. 115–16.

Instructions for the better understanding of the
following TABLES.

The 1 Column intimates to you the number of the Weeks, as the 1, 2, or 3. Week of the Year, beginning alwayes in December.
The 2. the several Dayes of the Moneth in which each Week expired.
The 3. the Totalls of the *Christnings* in each of the said Weeks.
The 4. the Totalls of the *Burials*.
The 5. the Totalls of the *Plague*.
And the 6. the Number of the Parishes infected.

I might also have added another Column to shew the *Weekly Increase* or *Decrease* of the *Burials*, but that is easily known by the number in the precedent Week, therefore I think it needless.

I shall here also Note unto you, that what Observations I shall make in this small Treatise shall follow the *Tables* for the 18 Years.

---

[1] See below, p. 671.

A TABLE of the *Christnings* and *Mortality,* for the Year 1624, and 1625.

Weeks	Days of Mon.		Christn.	Buried	Plague	Inf.
1	Decemb.	23	165	183	0	0
2		30	176	211	0	0
3	January	6	199	220	1	1
4		13	194	196	1	1
5		20	160	240	0	0
6		27	178	226	0	0
7	February	3	178	174	3	1
8		10	161	204	5	2
9		17	181	211	3	1
10		24	190	252	1	1
11	March—	3	185	207	0	0
12		10	196	210	0	0
13		17	175	262	4	3
14		24	187	226	8	2
15		31	133	243	11	4
16	April—	7	184	239	10	4
17		14	154	256	24	10
18		21	160	230	25	11
19		28	134	305	26	9
20	May—	5	158	292	30	10
21		12	140	332	45	13
22		19	182	379	71	17
23		26	145	401	78	16
24	June—	2	123	395	69	20
25		9	125	434	91	25
26		16	110	510	165	31
27		23	110	640	239	32
28		30	125	942	390	50
29	July—	7	114	1222	593	57
30		14	115	1741	1004	82
31		21	137	2850	1819	96
32		28	155	3583	2471	103
33	August—	4	128	4517	3659	114
34		11	125	4855	4115	112
35		18	134	5205	4463	114
36		25	135	4841	4218	114
37	Septemb.	1	117	3897	3344	117
38		8	112	3157	2550	116
39		15	100	2148	1672	107
40		22	75	1994	1551	111
41		29	78	1236	852	103
42	October	6	77	838	538	99
43		13	85	815	511	91
44		20	91	651	331	76
45		27	77	375	134	47
46	Novemb.	3	82	357	89	41
47		10	85	319	92	35
48		17	88	274	48	22
49		24	88	231	27	16
50	Decemb.	1	93	190	15	12
51		8	90	181	15	7
52		15	94	168	6	5
	The Totals—		6983	54265	35417	

A TABLE of the *Christnings* and *Mortality* for the Year 1629, and 1630.

Weeks	Days of Mom.	Christn.	Buried	Plague	Inf.
1	Decemb. 24	198	141	0	0
2	31	184	145	0	0
3	January 7	196	156	0	0
4	14	198	140	0	0
5	21	180	150	0	0
6	28	204	147	0	0
7	February 4	203	151	0	0
8	11	201	124	0	0
9	18	201	163	0	0
10	25	179	162	0	0
11	March— 4	219	170	0	0
12	11	220	161	2	2
13	18	187	153	4	1
14	25	205	172	0	0
15	April— 1	189	161	1	1
16	8	204	183	2	2
17	15	203	173	11	6
18	22	218	188	7	3
19	29	192	165	3	2
20	May— 6	177	196	15	6
21	13	175	194	13	9
22	20	158	187	20	10
23	27	158	209	24	8
24	June— 3	180	193	17	10
25	10	159	192	19	13
26	17	126	180	13	8
27	24	174	205	19	8
28	July— 1	149	209	25	12
29	8	141	217	43	16
30	15	148	250	50	20
31	22	163	229	40	16
32	29	172	279	77	26
33	August— 5	140	250	56	15
34	12	142	246	65	19
35	19	184	269	54	14
36	26	163	270	67	22
37	Septemb. 2	159	230	66	19
38	9	167	259	63	25
39	16	175	264	68	18
40	23	168	274	57	22
41	30	165	269	56	22
42	October 7	186	236	66	26
43	14	166	261	73	28
44	21	191	248	60	22
45	28	164	214	34	16
46	Novemb. 4	154	242	29	16
47	11	176	215	29	15
48	18	201	200	18	9
49	25	210	226	7	6
50	Decemb. 2	206	221	20	12
51	9	150	198	19	11
52	16	187	217	5	4
	The Totals—9315	10554	1317		

A TABLE of the *Christnings* and *Mortality* for the Year 1635, and 1636.

Weeks	Days of Mom.	Christn.	Buried	Plague	Inf.
1	Decemb. 24	231	170	0	0
2	31	195	174	0	0
3	January 7	217	189	0	0
4	14	242	174	0	0
5	21	220	190	0	0
6	28	214	171	0	0
7	February 4	227	183	0	0
8	11	234	160	0	0
9	18	207	203	0	0
10	25	198	238	0	0
11	March— 3	221	198	0	0
12	10	231	194	0	0
13	17	244	187	0	0
14	24	215	177	0	0
15	31	193	196	0	0
16	April— 7	202	199	2	1
17	14	221	205	4	2
18	21	204	205	7	3
19	28	271	210	4	3
20	May— 5	197	206	4	3
21	12	199	254	41	11
22	19	171	244	22	8
23	26	160	263	38	11
24	June— 2	189	276	51	13
25	9	153	275	64	15
26	16	145	325	86	16
27	23	149	257	65	12
28	30	141	273	82	15
29	July— 7	152	265	64	16
30	14	142	298	86	18
31	21	146	350	108	19
32	28	183	365	136	29
33	August— 4	152	394	181	35
34	11	166	465	244	35
35	18	167	546	284	43
36	25	161	690	380	45
37	Septemb. 1	163	835	536	51
38	8	153	921	567	55
39	15	166	1106	728	60
40	22	172	1018	645	64
41	29	168	1211	796	57
42	Octob.— 6	170	1195	790	62
43	13	164	1117	682	59
44	20	174	855	476	52
45	27	133	779	404	58
46	Novemb. 3	153	1156	755	67
47	10	164	966	635	64
48	17	143	827	512	59
49	24	162	747	408	46
50	Decemb. 1	168	550	291	48
51	8	175	385	143	34
52	15	134	324	79	23
	The Totals—9522	23359	10400		

A TABLE of the *Christnings* and *Mortality* for the Year 1636, and 1637.

Weeks	Days of Mom.	Christn.	Buried	Plague	Inf.
1	Decemb. 22	157	263	67	23
2	29	156	318	108	26
3	January 5	162	333	118	33
4	12	157	260	66	21
5	19	172	223	51	18
6	26	199	248	69	24
7	February 2	213	293	92	25
8	9	185	270	92	31
9	16	186	250	73	21
10	23	166	218	38	17
11	March— 2	186	214	57	25
12	9	204	274	88	29
13	16	193	255	67	29
14	23	177	222	57	25
15	30	194	299	101	30
16	April— 6	171	250	86	30
17	13	187	235	67	26
18	20	188	252	81	32
19	27	162	264	92	28
20	May— 4	168	251	72	31
21	11	163	242	85	29
22	18	157	250	66	27
23	25	172	255	67	23
24	June— 1	135	232	61	25
25	8	127	218	58	26
26	15	140	223	93	29
27	22	160	246	83	28
28	29	142	314	133	36
29	July— 6	147	303	141	34
30	13	145	254	109	32
31	20	148	263	125	36
32	27	143	256	86	27
33	August— 3	160	223	63	26
34	10	146	228	62	27
35	17	144	213	49	18
36	24	164	178	38	19
37	31	168	170	25	13
38	Septemb. 7	152	181	31	14
39	14	133	171	19	9
40	21	195	150	19	10
41	28	176	167	24	13
42	October 5	212	135	14	9
43	12	213	164	14	10
44	19	160	135	9	5
45	26	225	151	7	5
46	Novemb. 2	210	169	12	7
47	9	203	186	9	5
48	16	210	190	2	2
49	23	218	190	5	3
50	30	214	173	11	8
51	Decemb. 7	227	168	14	8
52	14	229	173	10	8
	The Totals—	9160	11763	3082	

A TABLE of the *Christnings* and *Mortality*, for the Year 1639, and 1640.

Weeks	Days of Mom.	Christn.	Buried	Plague	Inf.
1	Decemb. 19	219	197	3	2
2	26	180	143	4	2
3	January 2	210	172	8	5
4	9	217	184	2	2
5	16	186	178	2	2
6	23	189	181	1	1
7	30	201	220	0	0
8	February 6	213	213	1	1
9	13	215	217	3	3
10	20	229	257	1	1
11	27	224	222	1	1
12	March— 5	249	233	3	2
13	12	229	263	3	3
14	19	224	232	4	3
15	26	230	236	4	4
16	April— 2	239	247	3	2
17	9	188	231	1	1
18	16	209	208	4	4
19	23	225	219	2	2
20	30	213	239	3	3
21	May— 7	217	212	5	3
22	14	220	219	6	3
23	21	194	219	13	7
24	28	198	193	10	4
25	June— 4	209	224	19	8
26	11	165	238	34	10
27	18	180	236	15	6
28	25	175	207	25	9
29	July— 2	193	213	26	7
30	9	179	209	26	11
31	16	157	225	30	12
32	23	189	250	41	11
33	30	181	237	52	17
34	August— 6	210	266	68	19
35	13	215	298	81	21
36	20	195	320	98	24
37	27	209	336	89	25
38	Septemb. 3	219	343	98	27
39	10	219	331	105	24
40	17	193	331	98	25
41	24	210	332	94	23
42	October 1	197	314	69	22
43	8	201	314	63	27
44	15	217	294	55	19
45	22	158	260	42	18
46	29	181	246	24	13
47	Novemb. 5	192	210	17	12
48	12	200	240	33	17
49	19	201	228	23	12
50	26	234	224	13	8
51	Decemb. 3	208	220	9	6
52	10	200	219	6	4
53	17	245	271	10	5
	The Totals—	10850	12771	1450	

A TABLE of the *Christnings* and *Mortality* for the Year 1640, and 1641.

Weeks	Days of Mon.	Christn.	Buried	Plague	Inf.
1	Decemb. 24	235	374	4	4
2	31	202	322	3	2
3	January 7	210	220	3	2
4	14	184	194	4	1
5	21	206	222	5	4
6	28	210	218	3	3
7	February 4	222	214	2	2
8	11	230	235	6	6
9	18	230	219	5	3
10	25	221	259	3	2
11	March— 4	222	232	2	1
12	11	209	242	2	2
13	18	205	233	3	2
14	25	221	234	3	3
15	April— 1	228	226	8	4
16	8	218	272	5	3
17	15	216	229	4	3
18	22	234	267	7	7
19	29	193	225	7	6
20	May— 6	208	241	12	8
21	13	204	254	13	10
22	20	191	234	11	10
23	27	192	245	16	10
24	June— 3	168	289	27	13
25	10	191	300	20	13
26	17	138	268	19	11
27	24	174	256	15	10
28	July— 1	171	305	33	15
29	8	161	304	28	17
30	15	163	311	42	17
31	22	190	376	56	16
32	29	183	458	74	28
33	August— 5	212	467	100	25
34	12	179	507	80	28
35	19	192	558	131	30
36	26	203	610	139	35
37	Septemb. 2	201	703	183	36
38	9	202	659	185	38
39	16	206	652	197	38
40	23	210	660	239	50
41	30	176	630	204	50
42	Octob.— 7	202	654	239	49
43	14	196	604	234	54
44	21	198	518	184	48
45	28	174	464	144	36
46	Novemb. 4	177	408	106	31
47	11	183	337	79	25
48	18	209	316	61	20
49	25	223	296	44	16
50	Decemb. 2	198	279	41	17
51	9	209	245	15	10
52	16	190	246	17	10
	The Totals—10370	18291		3067	

A TABLE of the *Christnings* and *Mortality* for the Year 1641, and 1642.

Weeks	Days of Mon.	Christn.	Buried	Plague	Inf.
1	Decemb. 23	213	208	15	9
2	30	196	267	51	23
3	January 6	213	253	26	14
4	13	193	202	11	9
5	20	180	208	14	8
6	27	235	234	31	16
7	February 3	213	214	29	15
8	10	259	250	23	14
9	17	215	187	14	7
10	24	210	231	26	9
11	March— 3	237	239	17	10
12	10	232	232	18	11
13	17	206	214	5	5
14	24	203	219	13	5
15	31	221	204	17	11
16	April— 7	211	213	23	13
17	14	191	190	20	11
18	21	211	205	22	10
19	28	211	239	20	11
20	May— 5	193	241	21	15
21	12	198	230	29	11
22	19	201	245	25	15
23	26	174	217	27	15
24	June— 2	174	241	37	16
25	9	165	208	25	14
26	16	157	202	23	15
27	23	177	178	14	10
28	30	167	164	15	7
29	July— 7	170	163	18	12
30	14	165	165	24	12
31	21	192	170	24	12
32	28	200	187	29	18
33	August— 4	213	185	30	13
34	11	235	224	48	14
35	18	235	224	48	18
36	25	219	236	58	13
37	Septemb. 1	237	227	60	20
38	8	188	274	70	21
39	15	218	279	66	23
40	22	228	351	103	23
41	29	206	362	126	33
42	Octob.— 6	205	331	83	24
43	13	235	281	81	29
44	20	227	315	98	29
45	27	190	275	51	23
46	Novemb. 3	198	275	51	22
47	10	186	232	37	15
48	17	217	303	46	21
49	24	219	256	13	10
50	Decemb. 1	223	250	19	13
51	8	228	250	18	9
52	15	181	247	12	10
	The Totals—10670	12167		1824	

The Table of Burials, and Christnings, in London.

Anno Dom.	97 Parishes	16 Parishes	Out-Parishes	Buried in all	Besides of the Plague	Christned
1615	2446	3791	1613	7850	37	7682
1616	2490	3876	1697	8063	9	7985
1617	2397	4109	1774	8280	6	7747
1618	2815	4715	2066	9596	18	7735
1619	2339	3857	1804	7999	9	8127
1620	2726	4819	2146	9691	21	7845
1621	2438	3759	1915	8112	11	8039
1622	2811	4217	2392	8943	16	7894
1623	3591	4721	2783	11095	17	7945
1624	3385	5919	2895	12199	11	8299
1625	5143	9819	3886	18848	35417	6983
1626	2150	3285	1965	7401	134	6701
1627	2325	3400	1988	7711	4	8408
1628	2412	3311	2017	7740	3	8564
1629	2536	3992	2243	8771	0	9901
1630	2506	4201	2521	9237	1317	9315
1631	2459	3697	2132	8288	274	8524
1632	2704	4412	2411	9527	8	9584
1633	2378	3936	2078	8393	0	9997
1634	2937	4980	2982	10399	1	9855
1635	2742	4966	2943	10651	0	10034
1636	2825	6924	3210	12959	10400	9522
1637	2288	4265	2128	8681	3082	9160
1638	3584	5926	3751	13261	363	10311
1639	2592	4344	2612	9548	314	10150
1640	2919	5156	3246	11321	1450	10850
1641	3248	5092	3427	11767	1375	10670
1642	3176	5245	3578	11999	1274	10370

THE RECORDS OF SIR HUMPHREY MILDMAY[1]

THE diary and account-book of Sir Humphrey Mildmay, from which the following extracts are taken, give us a valuable record of the London theatre in the reign of Charles I. So far as I know, it is the most complete account of any individual's theatre attendance which exists for any Englishman before Pepys.

The manuscript, which is preserved in the British Museum (Harl. MS. 454), is a large book, $11\frac{1}{2} \times 7\frac{1}{8}$ inches. The diary occupies the front portion and consists of 104 leaves covering the period 3 July 1633 to 9 July 1652; the accounts, which are entered in the back of the same manuscript book reversed, consist of 75 leaves covering the period from 21 January 1631/2 to 22 July 1652. Both diary and accounts are so closely written that they are sometimes difficult to decipher, though the hand is not a bad one. In his history of the family (*A Brief Memoir of the Mildmay Family* [London: John Lane, The Bodley Head, 1913]) Lieutenant-Colonel Herbert A. St. John Mildmay says that a copy of this diary was sold at Sotheby's on 10 July 1857, and is probably the one which is now the property of Mr. Humphrey St. John-Mildmay, of Shoreham, Kent. The second part of Sir Humphrey Mildmay's diary, from 11 July 1652 to 2 June 1666, is now among the papers of the Marquis of Ormond at Kilkenny Castle.

Sir Humphrey Mildmay (1592–?1666) was the oldest surviving son of Sir Anthony Mildmay, of Danbury, Essex, and the grandson of Sir Walter Mildmay, of Apethorpe, Northamptonshire, Chancellor of the Exchequer to Queen Elizabeth. His younger brother, Sir Henry Mildmay, was the Master of the Jewel House under Charles I who deserted the royalists in 1641 and was imprisoned as a regicide in 1660. Another brother, Anthony, who is frequently mentioned in the diary and who seems to have been Sir Humphrey's boon companion, was a sewer at the Court of Charles I, later one of the four gentlemen in attendance on the king in the last months of his life, and, after the execution, custodian of the royal children at Carisbrook (see the *D.N.B.* accounts of Sir Walter and Sir Henry Mildmay, Lieutenant-Colonel Mildmay's *Memoir*, and the *Visitations of Essex*).

Sir Humphrey was less active in public affairs than his two brothers. He seems to have concerned himself chiefly with the management of his estates and the social pleasures of London, dividing his time between London and Danbury, in Essex, with occasional visits to his estate at Queen Camel, Somerset.

The diary, which gives a short account of from one to five lines

---

[1] This material is printed here by the kind permission of *Modern Philology* and the University of Chicago Press.

of nearly every day Sir Humphrey spent in London and of many of those he spent in the country, is generally little more than a bare relation of activities. It gives ample evidence, however, that the author was a regular patron of the theatres, since he recorded about six visits a year in the ten years between the opening of the account-book in January 1631/2, and the closing of the theatres at the beginning of the Civil War. Whenever there is a lapse of two months or more in the records of dramatic entertainment, it is almost invariably accounted for by Sir Humphrey's absence from London or by some temporary prohibition of acting. It is unfortunate that his theatrical items are not more explicit.

So far as I know, most of these extracts from Sir Humphrey's diary have never been published before. Collier noticed about one-third of them (*H.E.D.P.*, vols. i and ii, *passim*), but since Collier is most suspect in his handling of just this sort of material not much use has been made of his extracts. There is, however, no evidence that Collier tampered with the manuscript except, perhaps, in one place. On 30 May 1633 Sir Humphrey recorded (fol. 180) a payment for spurs to 'Mr Shakespere his man'. A modern hand, slightly disguised, has written in the margin opposite, 'No Player now'. Since Collier inserted a short speculation as to the meaning of 'these remarkable words' in the first edition of his *History of English Dramatic Poetry* (i. 469, and ii. 42 n.), one suspects that he wrote the marginal note himself; Sir Edmund Chambers speaks of it as 'a clear forgery' (Chambers, *Shakespeare*, ii. 386–7). Though his other extracts are not altogether accurate and a few are complete misreadings (such as 'Dorcrutch' for 'Bor Anth' in the accounts for 8 June 1633, and 'Com. Panheard' for 'Company eod' in those for 27 January 1633/4; see *H.E.D.P.*, i. 482 n. and 489 n.), they are not fabrications.

I have taken all references to plays, masques, or theatres from the beginning of the diary and accounts through the year 1643. Other references to purchases of books, political and social events, or merely amusing activities I have ignored unless they seemed to have some bearing on the play records, though in one or two instances the temptation to quote has proved too much for me.

The entries are given in chronological order; the record from the account-book is listed first and marked 'A', followed by the entry from the diary, marked 'D'. Occasionally there is the record of a play in the diary with no corresponding record in the accounts, or vice versa. Since the diary does not begin until some eighteen months after the beginning of the account-book, the first dozen or so entries from the accounts stand alone.

1631/2, Jan. 26 or 27. A, 183v. 'To a play wth Sr ffra: Wortely . . . . 00–02–06'
1632, June 25. A, 182v. 'To Marke Waxe, ets & a playe eod . . . . 00–03–00'

1632, Nov. 17. A, 181ᵛ. 'To a play = 17 . . . . 00–01–06'
1632, Nov. 30. A, 181ᵛ. 'To a playe ets [?] the laste A . 00–04–00'
1632, Dec. 19–22. A, 181. 'Expences att a playe wᵗʰ my
wyfe . . . . 00–07–06'
1632/3, Jan. 16. A, 181. 'To a play eod. . . . . . 00–01–00'
1632/3, Jan. 22. A, 181. 'To a play att the bla: ffryers = 22 00–01–00'
1633, May 14. A, 180. 'To a playe eod . . . . . 00–02–00'
1633, May 16. A, 180. 'To a play that day beinge Thursday att the globe . . . . 00–02–00'
1633, May 23. A, 180. 'To a play Called Rolloe, & the
globe: 23 . . . . 00–01–06'
(Fletcher's *Rollo, Duke of Normandy or the Bloody
Brother*.)
1633, June 6. A, 179ᵛ. 'To a pretty & Merry Conedy att
the Cocke . . . . 00–01–00'
(The Phoenix, or Cockpit, in Drury Lane.)
1633, June 8–10. A, 179ᵛ. 'To a playe att the globe, wᵗʰ
Bor [?] Anᵗʰ . . . . 00–01–06'
1633, July 18. A, 179. 'To a playe att the globe this 18ᵗʰ 00–01–10'
1633/4, Jan. 14. A, 178ᵛ. 'To Mʳ and my selfe att a play:
14 . . . . 00–03–00'
1633/4, Jan. 21. A, 178. 'To a playe att Bla: fryers eod 00–01–06'
D, 5ᵛ. '21: Ja: warde was hanged att grayes Inn lane,
eande, & one att longe lane eande for a foule rape|'
(Apparently the criminal news drove the play from Sir
Humphrey's mind.)
1633/4, Jan. 22. A, 178. 'To a playe att the fryers, the
Witts . . . . 00–01–00'
D, 5ᵛ. '22: att a playe att the bl = fryers.' (The play
is Davenant's; Sir Henry Herbert had licensed it only
three days before. The entry in the accounts is undated,
but its position between entries for 21 January and
23 January, together with the diary entry, makes the
date clear.)
1633/4, Jan. 27. A, 178. 'To a playe wᵗʰ Company eod. . 00–03–00'
D, 5ᵛ. '. . . this day I was att the Newe play et'
1633/4, Feb. 3. A, 178. 'To a Coachman that day . . . 00–01–00'
D, 5ᵛ. 'att nighte in the strande, att the lodgeinge of
Monsʳ: Bobarre where wee supped, & sawe the stately
Masque . . .' (The masque performed this night was
Shirley's *Triumph of Peace*.)
1633/4, Feb. 6. A, 178. 'for a boate, to Whitehall: eod. 00–00–06'
'To a barbir for my bearde ets· . . . . . . 00–01–06'
'For a booke & the play of pastorell [?] . . . . 00–02–00'
D, 5ᵛ. '. . . this nighte I was att Whitehall att the
daunceinge & playe, & laye all nighte wᵗʰ Bor Anth:'
(The dates are uncertain here, but both accounts and
diary entries seem to belong to 6 February. The play
at court this night was Shirley's *Gamester*.)
1633/4, Feb. 7. A, 178. (Nothing of plays in this day's
accounts.)
D, 5ᵛ. 'I came home to dynner, wente to th bl = fryers wᵗʰ Mʳ Prince. . . .'

1633/4, Feb. 13. A, 178. 'To a Middwife & a Nurse to Ben: Wallinger his Chilαe this: 13th of feb . . . . 00–12–00'
D, 5^v. '. . . this nighte was againe the famous Masque before there Ma^{ts}: att Marchant Taylers hall in London . . .' (This was the second performance of Shirley's *Triumph of Peace*.)

1633/4, Feb. 18. A, 178. 'for the Masque of his Ma eod . 00–00–06'
D, 5^v. '. . . att nighte was pformed his Ma^{ts}: Masque of Lordes et att Whitehall.' (The masque was Carew's *Coelum Britannicum*.)

1633/4, Mar. 20. A, 177^v. 'To a base play att the Cocke pitt eod. . . . . 00–01–06'
D, 6. '. . . this after noone J wente to the Cocke pitt to a playe wth Bor Anth: a fooleishe one . . .'

1634, May 1. A, 176^v. 'To a Newe play Called the spartan Lady: 1 . . . . 00–01–03'
D, 6^v. '. . . after dynner att a play alone . . .' (This play, by Lodowick Carlell, is not extant. It was entered in the Stationers' Register, 4 September 1646. Sir Humphrey's record gives us the date of the play, since he calls it new.)

1634, May 8. A, 176^v. 'To a play wth Bor Ch: Abdy: 8 . 00–01–00'
D, 6^v. '. . . this day dined My Brother Abdy wth mee, & then wee wente to the playe together|'

1634, May 21. A, 176^v. 'To a playe wth Company: 21 . 00–06–00'
D, 7. '. . . after dynner wth Sr Henry Skipwith My wife, Ned: Boteler, Nann: Mildmay att the play Called Lasander & Callista, beinge a poem|' (This play was probably *The Lover's Progress*, in which Lisander and Calista are the leading characters. Several scholars think it was a revision of *The Wandering Lovers*, licensed to the King's men, 6 December 1623. Mildmay's title may indicate the one used on the playbills for this performance, or it may indicate his familiarity with the French romance of the same name on which the play was based.)

1634, Nov. 9. A. (There is no entry in the accounts for the ninth.)
D, 8. '. . . att nighte to the Cou^rte wth a freinde to see' Catteline Acted|' (This performance of Jonson's play is first recorded here. Perhaps the court performance led to the second edition of 1635.)

1634, Nov. 29. A, 175^v. 'To a play after dynner wth Dr Doriela: 29 . . . . 00–04–00'
D, 8^v. '. . . att dynner An^{thie}: Croftes Ser: Ma: Wentworth from thence to a playe a fine one|'

1634, Dec. 12. A, 175. 'To a play wth the :2: South^{lan}des: 12 . . . . 00–04–06'
D, 8^v. 'To a play of Loue & honnor wth the :2: Southlandes . . .' (Davenant's tragi-comedy, which had been licensed to the King's men three weeks before, on the 20th of November. Mildmay evidently saw the play at the Blackfriars.)

1634, Dec. 29. A. (No entry.)

D, 9. '. . . This nighte Dame Sisly Croftes Supped heere wth her sweete harte Mr Tho: Killigraue| . . .'

1634/5, Feb. 14. A. (No entry.)

D, 9^v. 'beinge St Vallentine was a wett day, . . . att nighte wee both of vs wayted onn My Lady Cooke to a pretty Masque of Ladyes, . . .' (In the margin is written, 'The Masque'. This masque was probably Davenant's *The Temple of Love,* which was first presented by the Queen and her ladies on Shrove Tuesday, but the Venetian ambassador wrote that it was repeated three times.)

1634/5, Feb. 19. A, 174^v. 'To Expences Jn wine ets: 19   00–03–00'

D, 9^v. 'att home vntill dynn^r To a play, & to Supper came good Company Jn plenty.'

1635, Apr. 25. A, 173^v. 'To a playe eod: Called the Elder Brother . . . . 00–01–00'

D, 10^v. '. . . after dynner to the Elder Brother att the bla: ffryers & was idle|' (Fletcher's play, which had probably been revised by Massinger [E. H. C. Oliphant, *The Plays of Beaumont and Fletcher,* pp. 230–4]. It was presented at court in the following Christmas season.)

1635, Apr. 28. A, 173^v. 'Expended att the bla: fryers— 28 . . . . 00–03–00'

D, 10^v. '. . . this after Noone, J spente att a playe wth good Company.'

1635, May 6. A, 173^v. 'To other Expenses: 5: 6: 7: 8: et: 9   00–07–02'

D, 10^v. 'not farre from home all day att the bla: ffryers & a play this day Called the More of Venice|' (Shakespeare's *Othello.* It was presented at court 6 December 1636.)

1635, Nov. 25. A. (No entry in the accounts for the twenty-fifth.)

D, 12^v. '. . . after dynner to a fooleishe play att the fryers,| . . .'

1635, Nov. 27. A, 172^v. 'To a playe wth Dr Doriila: 27   00–03–00'

D, 12^v. '. . . the after Noone J spente wth the D^r att a playe & came home Jn peace|'

1635, Dec. 8. A, 172. 'To the playe Called the La: of pleasure . . . . 00–01–00'

D, 13. '. . . dined wth Rob: Dowgill wente to the La: of pleasure & sawe that rare playe came home late Supped . . .' (Shirley's comedy. It had been licensed two months before. Since it was printed two years later as a Queen's men's play, Mildmay must have seen it at the Cockpit. The account-book entry is not dated, but it occurs between the items for the 6th and the 10th, and the diary shows that it belongs to the 8th.)

1635, Dec. 11. A. (No entry in the accounts for the eleventh.)

D, 13. 'To dynner came Sr Chr: Abdy & wente to the Newe playe wth my wife J wente abroade by myselfe to worse places alone|'

1635, Dec. 16. A, 172. 'To a playe att bla: fryers wth good Company . . . . 00–03–06'
D. (No diary entries from 14 December to 20 December.)

1637, Nov. 3. A, 169. 'To my Exp: att the play ets: 3 . 00–02–06'
D, 18^v. '. . . dined att home & wento the fryers blacke to a play & home to Supper & bed in Peace|'

1637/8, Feb. 3. A, 168^v. 'Espenses att White hall ets . 00–05–00'
D, 20. 'a Sad durty wett & windy Morneinge| I wente to Westmi. by water & dined wth m^r Layton & Came home by Ned: Herris et wth Ben: Wallinger J have beine all soe & Scene a sawsie Accoumpte| To White hall I wente Supped wth Mr Secretary Cooke & Came home durty & weary| the playe beinge full.'

1637/8, Feb. 5. A, 168^v. 'Expences in botehire & the play: 5 . . . . 00–02–06'
D, 20. 'dined wth Dr Doriela, Wente & sawe the fooleishe Newe play . . .'

1638, Oct. 27. A, 167^v. 'To see the foxe playe wth fra: Wortley . . . . 00–04–06'
D, 21^v. 'fayre & Cleere all this day I wente to Westmi: dined att Whitehall & after dynner to the fox playe = att bl: fryers wth my Cozen fra. Wortley & my Brother Anth,: & Came Jn Peace to Supper & bedd, I bles god.' (Jonson's *Volpone*, generally called by its subtitle in this time. It was acted at court two weeks later. The account-book entry is undated. It stands between entries for 26 October and 3 November. The diary shows that it should be dated 27 October.)

1638/9, Feb. 12. A, 167. 'To a playe & after supper eod . . . . 00–05–00'
D, 22^v. '. . . To a play wth m^{rs} James, & to supper wth Dr Doriela & Tho: Chichley & home.'

1638/9, Feb. 13. A. (Nothing about plays in the accounts.)
D, 22^v. '. . . then I wente to a playe wth Dr Doriela & home late.'

1638/9, Feb. 14. A. (Nothing about plays in the accounts.)
D, 22^v. '. . . after Noone I wente to a playe & was soe Jmployed that day.'

1638/9, Feb. 18. A, 166^v. 'To him att the playe Jn full 00–06–00'
D, 23. '. . . dined wth Mrs James & wente to a playe wth her . . . ' (The accounts entry is one of several undated items between February 17 and February 19. The diary indicates the proper date.)

1639, May 18. A, 166^v. 'To the Alchemist eod . . . 00–05–00'
D, 23^v. '. . . home to dynner| after to a playe wth Mrs James & her goodman, a wett day . . .' (The King's men owned Jonson's play. Since this is just about the time that the company usually moved from the Blackfriars to the Globe, it is difficult to tell which theatre Mildmay visited.)

1639, May 21. A, 166^v. 'To the Mad louer: 21 . . . 00–06–00'
D, 23^v. '. . . after Noone To the playe wth' (Fletcher's

play belonged to the King's men. Mildmay probably
saw it at the Globe, though the company may still have
been at Blackfriars.)

1639, Nov. 8. A, 164. 'To a playe: 8 . . . . 00–02–00'
D, 27ᵛ. '. . . to dynner from thence wᵗʰ my Lawer Mʳ
Banfeilde to see a playe . . .'

1639, Nov. 14. A, 164. 'To Jone & a playe . . . . 00–02–00'
D, 27ᵛ. '. . . To dynner & then to a playe . . .' (The
account entry is undated, between entries for 8 November and 17 November. The diary entry indicates
that the probable date is 14 November.)

1640, May 8. A, 162ᵛ. 'Expended att a play 8 . . . 00–03–00'
D, 31ᵛ. '. . . to a playe & loitred all the day . . .'

1640, May 15. A, 162ᵛ. 'To the playe house wᵗʰ my wife &
Company . . . . 00–11–00'
D, 31ᵛ. '. . . to dynner & then to the Newe play att
Bl: fryers wᵗʰ my Company where I loste the whole
day . . .'

1640, Nov. 6. A, 158. 'To Pigge & the Play: 6 . . . 00–02–06'
D, 36ᵛ. '. . . after Noone to a playe all the day ets: . . .'
(The Privy Council had ordered all theatres closed
because of plague on 11 September in this year. It
has not been known heretofore when they were
allowed to reopen, but Mildmay's records show that
they were functioning at least as early as the 6th of
November.)

1640, Nov. 9. A, 158. 'To a play: 9: wᵗʰ my Wife & Com-
pany that . . . . 00–09–00'
D, 36ᵛ. '. . . Came home to dynner & founde good
Company there after Noone to a playe . . .'

1640, Nov. 16. A, 158. 'To a Playe wᵗʰ good Company:
16 . . . . 00–08–00'
D, 36ᵛ. '. . . after Noone wᵗʰ my wife & Pretty Cozen
to a playe & home late . . .'

1640/1, Feb. 15. A, 157ᵛ. 'To a Playe eod : 15 . . . 00–08–06'
D, 38ᵛ. '. . . to dynner & soe to the playe & supper
wᵗʰ Dʳ Doriela & late home to bed . . .'

1641, May 18. A. (No record of a play in accounts.)
D, 40ᵛ. '. . . to the Hall J wente by boate, to dynner
& after I loitered att a playe . . .'

1641, May 19 [?]. A, 156ᵛ. 'To the play att Blacke fryers 00–01–06'
D. (No diary record of a play. This accounts entry is
undated and comes between entries dated 19 May and
20 May. In spite of this fact one is tempted to think
that it refers to the diary account of the 18th, for there
is only one play record in the accounts and one play
record in the diary between the theatre entries of 15 February 1640/1 and 24 May 1641.)

1641, May 24. A, 156. 'To a playe ets . . . . . 00–01–08'
D, 40ᵛ. '. . . after Noone I Loitered att a playe et . . .'

1641, Dec. 1. A, 154ᵛ. 'To a playe: 1: Decembris . . 00–02–00'
D, 46. '. . . after Noone to a Playe & home to Supper

& bed, . . .' (This account affords our best evidence
of the date of the opening of the theatres after the
plague of the summer and autumn of 1641.)

1641, Dec. 10. A. (No play expenses in the accounts about
this date.)

D, 46. '. . . to dynner & after to a play . . .

1643, July 18 (?). A, 148. 'To My Expences att the
Danceinge of the Ropes w^th: all oure famely.   .   .   .   00–03–06'
D, 60. '. . . to the Danceinge of the Ropes w^th: all oure
famely this after Noone . . .' (The entry in the accounts is undated and comes between entries for 19
July and 20 July. It must, however, refer to the same
occasion as the diary of the 18th; the dates in the
diary seem more trustworthy, since each separate entry
is dated there.)

1643, Aug. 21. A, 147^v. 'To a Playe & other foleryes .   00–02–01'
D, 60^v. '. . . I was att a Playe & home Late to Sup . . .'

1643, Nov. 16. A, 146. 'To a Playe of Warre   .   .   .   00–00–06'
D, 62^v. '. . . then w^th: Company to a Playe where was
a Disaster home to Sup.' (The accounts entry is undated but comes between entries dated 15 November
and 21 November. The diary makes it evident that the
date should be the 16th.)

In addition to its value for the individual facts recorded, Sir
Humphrey's diary as a whole suggests several interesting generali-
zations. It is noticeable that though he does not, as a rule, give
the name of the theatre he visited, Blackfriars is clearly his
favourite. He mentions it fourteen times, the Globe four times,
and the Cockpit, or Phoenix in Drury Lane, three times. The
plays which he refers to by title indicate that he visited the Blackfriars four times and the Cockpit once when no theatre is named.
The Fortune, the Red Bull, and Salisbury Court are not mentioned
at all. Mildmay's preference for the Blackfriars and his neglect
of the Fortune and Red Bull agree with other evidence of the
popularity of the Blackfriars with the upper classes (though
proximity probably was an influence on Mildmay; see the entry
for 6 May 1635) and the low reputation of the other two. One
would have expected him to attend the Salisbury Court occasionally, and it may be that he simply neglects to mention it.

The accounts are also interesting as confirmation of Malone's
statement that 'the king's company usually began to play at the
Globe in the month of May' (*Variorum*, iii. 70–1). Apparently the
precise day in May for the transfer depended on the season, for
Mildmay was at the Globe on the 16th and 23rd in 1633 and at the
Blackfriars on the 6th in 1635, the 15th in 1640, and 19th in 1641.
He was usually out of town at the probable time of transfer back
to Blackfriars in the winter. His earliest autumnal attendance at
a play was 27 October 1638, when he saw Jonson's *Volpone* at
Blackfriars.

In the ten years following January 1631/2—he mentions no dramatic entertainment in 1642—Sir Humphrey records his attendance at fifty-seven plays and four court masques. Though in most instances he gives no titles, all the masques can be identified, and on twelve occasions he mentions the name of the play he saw. If we can assume that Sir Humphrey specifically mentioned the name of a play because he thought it somewhat above the ordinary run, then his taste, as demonstrated by the relative popularity of the different authors on his list, is much the same as that indicated in the miscellaneous allusions to dramatists in the reign of Charles I. Four of the plays were by Fletcher (*Rollo, Duke of Normandy, The Lover's Progress, The Elder Brother,* and *The Mad Lover*), three were by Jonson (*Catiline, Volpone,* and *The Alchemist*), two by Davenant (*The Wits* and *Love and Honour*), and one each by Shakespeare (*Othello*), Shirley (*The Lady of Pleasure*), and Carlell (*The Spartan Ladies*). All but two of these plays appear in the extant lists of performances at the courts of James I and Charles I—a further suggestion that Sir Humphrey was a typical Cavalier in his dramatic taste.

Sir Humphrey's comments on the plays he saw tell us very little about him or about the audience of which he was a part, because in only one instance is his comment coupled with the name of a play, when he calls Shirley's *Lady of Pleasure* 'that rare playe'. On five occasions he says that the play was new—further testimony to the well-known appeal of novelty in the theatre of the time. Three times he calls the plays he saw 'foolish'. One is tempted to think that Sir Humphrey was anticipating some modern readers in their attitude towards many of the love and honour tragi-comedies, but a close reading of the diary suggests that he was more probably expressing annoyance at time wasted in the theatre, since he so frequently chides himself for his theatre attendance in phrases like '& was idle'. '& loitred all the day', 'I loste the whole day', 'I loitered att a playe'. Such phrases remind one of the half-hearted struggles of a more famous diarist to resist the lure of the theatre.

THE MARKHAM SUIT

C. W. Wallace in his article on 'Gervase Markham, Dramatist' (*Shakespeare Jahrbuch*, xlvi [1910], 345–50), says, 'The following records are from the Court of Requests, 21 James I (1623), Public Record Office, London. The Bill is preserved among the un-calendered documents, the affidavit in one of the miscellaneous books of that court.' The Bill and affidavit come from Markham's suit to collect the given sums from the persons named. The money had been subscribed 'vppon Bills of Adventure' when Markham proposed to go on foot from London to Berwick, using only 'an ordinarye Leape staffe or staffe to leape wthall' for crossing all bodies of water. When he returned after accomplishing the feat, his backers refused to pay, hence the suit in the Court of Requests. I quote the parts of the Bill and affidavit which certainly or possibly refer to theatrical people; the bracketed sums are those which the various individuals 'did seu*er*allye Assume . . . to paye'. The Bill, which is headed 'Gervase Markham *vs* Thirty-nine Defendants, chiefly Actors', was filed 'xvvj^{to} die Maij Anno Regni Jacobi Regis Angl francie et Hibrnie xxj° et Scotie lvj^{to}'.

'. . . to ffrancis Acton att the white harte in the ould Balye London [10s.] to Edmond Barbor on Charkenwell hill [22s.], to Ambrose Broughton of the Crowne office in the Midle Temple London [5s.], to Raphe Keyes att the Crosse Keyes in Knighte Ryder streete London [5s.], to Iohn Woode of Beech Lane London [5s.], to Iohn Trundle att the nobodye in Barbican [5s.], to Henry Gosson over the gate att London bridge [5s.], to Henrye Sheppey a Turner in Chauncerye Lane [5s.], to Richard Robinson att the vpper end of Shoreditch [10s.] to Joseph Taylor in Bishoppsgate neare the Spittle [5s.], to Roberte Gough on the Banckesyde [5s.], to George Burgh att the vpper end of Shoreditch [5s.], to William Pattricke on the Banckesyde neare the Bargehouse [5s.], to Roberte Leigh in Clarkenwell Close [5s.] to Richard Perkins att the vpper end of St Iohns Streete [5s.], to Iohn Blanye neare the Red Bull in St Iohns Streete [5s.], to Iohn Cumber in Aldermanburye [5s.], to Thomas Haywarde neare Clarkenwell Hill [5s.], to Edwarde Shakerley in Clarkenwell Close [5s.], to Joseph More att the Harowe in Barbican [5s.], to William Carpenter porter at the Marshallsey [5s.], to Edwarde Knighte att the George Alley in Gouldinge Lane [5s.] to William Penn at the George Alley in Gouldinge lane aforesayd [5s.], to ffrancke Grace att the George Alley in Gouldinge lane aforesayd [10s.] to William Cartwrighte att the vpper end of white Crosse Streete [6s.] to William Stratford att the vpper end of white Crosse Streete aforesayd [5s.], to Richard ffowler in Redcrosse Streete [5s.], to Richard Claytone in Goulding Lane [5s.], to Abraham Pedle of George

Alley in Gouldinge lane aforesayd [5s.], to Thomas Taylor of George Alley in Gouldinge Lane aforesayd [5s.] to Richard Grace in Gouldinge Lane aforesayd [5s.], to Edward Bridge att the vpper end of Shoreditch [5s.], to Richard Browne of Toothill Streete [11s.], to Iohn Lowen of Lambeth [10s.], to Iohn Rice of the Bancksyde [5s.], to William Robins on Clarkenwell hill [5s.], to Thomas Hobbes att the vpper end of Shoreditch [6s. 8d.] to Richard Price in White Crosse Streete [5s.] to Robert Keyes of S^t: Brydes Lane [5s.] . . . .'

The affidavit, which is from Affidavit Book, 21 & 22 James I, Miscellaneous Books, 132, is dated 'xxix° die Januarij A° &c 21° et 57°'.

'Paull Tey (messenger of this Court) sent to warne diuerse persons at the sute of Gervis Markham gent: sayeth that on or about the xxiijth day of May last he warned Richard Clayton, Richard Grace, William Stratford and Abraham Pedle gent (all Acto^{rs} at the fortune neere Golding lane) & one Robt Gough gent on the banksyde in theire seuerall persons, and left seuerall notes in wryting for Raphe Keyes wth his wief neere Docto^{rs} Commons, and for John Trundle at his howse in Barbican, That all & euery of them should vpon the xxvth day of the same moneth make theire personall apparances in this court to answere A bill of complaint at the sute of Gervase Markham gent plaintiff.'

HETON'S PAPERS

Peter Cunningham published the following documents in *Shakespeare Society Papers*, iv. 95–100, without discussion or any hint as to source.

The following 'Instructions' are endorsed 'Mr. Heten's Paper'.

That the Pattent for electing her M^{ts} Company of Comedians be graunted only to my selfe, that I may alwaies haue a Company in readines at Salisberry Co^{r}t for her M^{ts} service, and that if all or any of the Company goe away from Salisberry Co^{r}t, to play at any other Playhouse already built or hereafter to be built, they from thenceforth to cease to be her M^{ts} servants, and only the Company remayning there to have that hono^r and tytle. My selfe to be sole governo^r of the Company. The Company to enter into Articles wth me to continew there for 7 yeares, upon the same condicons they haue had for a yeare and halfe last past, and such as refuse to be removed, and others placed in their roomes; for if they should continew at libertie as they now are, and haue power to take her M^{ts} service alonge wth them, they wold make use of o^r house but untill they could p'vyde another upon better termes, and then leave us as in one yeare and halfe of their being here they haue many tymes threatned, when they might not exact any new imposicons upon the housekeepers at their pleasure. And some of them have treated upon Condicons for the Cockpit playhouse, some gone about to begge o^r house from the King, and one nowe of the cheife fellowes, an Agent for one that hath gott a grant[1] from the King, for the building of a new playhouse wch was intended to be in Fleet Street, wch noe man can judge that a fellow of o^r Company, and a wellwisher to those that owe the house, would ev'r be an actor in.

When her M^{ts} servants were at the Cockpitt, beinge all at liberty, they disperst themselves to severall Companies, soe that had not my lo: of Dorsett taken care to make up a new Company for the Queene, she had not had any at all.

How much I haue done for the uphoulding of this Company, I gave you some p'ticulers of in a peticon to my lo: of Dorsett.

And wheras my lo: of Dorsett had gotten for a former Company at Salisberry Co't the Princes service, they being left at liberty, took their opportunity of another house, and left the house in Salisberry Co^{r}t destitute both of a service and Company.

This setling of the service and Company upon condicons certane, and of a knowne governo^r, would be the occasion to avoyd

---

[1] Cunningham says (op. cit., p. 96) that this passage refers to the patent Davenant got in March 1639 for a large new theatre at 3 King's Ordinary in Fleet Street.

many differences and disturbances that hapen both betwene the Company and housekeepers, amongst the Company themselves, and many generall discontents—to the great credit of the house, and p'fitt of the Company.

Richard Heton
One of the Sewers of her M^ts Chamber Extraord:

The following document is endorsed, '*Heton's draught of his pattent*'.

Charles, by the grace of God, King of England, Scotland, Fraunce, and Ireland, Defender of the Faith, &c., To all mayors, sheriffs, justices of the peace, bayliffs, constables, headborrowes, and all other his M^ts officers, ministers, and loving subjects, to whom these p^rsents shall come, greetinge. Whereas o^r servant, Richard Heton, one of the Sewers of the Chamber to o^r deare Consort, the Queene, hath disbursed great somes of money in provyding a convenient Playhouse in Dorset house yard for her M^ts Comedians to practise and act Playes in, that they may be there resident and in readines for the said service when they shalbe comanded, and hath lykewise disbursed good somes of money for the maintayning and supporting the said Actors in the sicknes tyme, and other wayes to keepe the said Company together, w^thout wch a great part of them had not bene able to subsist, but the Company had bene utterly ruyned and dispersed. And whereas, upon every smale occasion, for their owne benefite companies of Actors have removed from their residence, and dispersed themselves into severall places, soe that noe certaine place of abode is knowne where they may be found when We are pleased to comand their attendance for o^r owne or o^r deare Consort's solace, pleasure, and disport. Now, know yee that We, of o^r especiall grace, certaine knowlege, and meere mocon, haue lycensed and aucthorized, and by these o^r l'res patent doe lycence and aucthorize o^r said servant Richard Heton, or his assignes, from tyme to tyme, and at all tymes hereafter to select, order, direct, sett up, and governe a company of Comedians in the said private house in Dorset house yard, for ye seruice of o^r deare Consort the quene, and there to exercise their quality of playinge Comedies, Tragedies, Histories, Pastoralls, Maskes, Enterludes, Moralls, Stageplayes, and such lyke, what they have already studyed, or hereafter shall study or cause to be studyed, as well for the solace and pleasure of o^r deare Consort, the Queene, and of o^r selfe, when We shall think fit to see them, as the recreacon of o^r louing subiects. And the said Comedies, Tragedies, Histories, Pastoralls, Maskes, Enterludes, Morralls, Stageplayes, and such like, to shew, act, and exercise, to their best p^rfitt and comodity, as well w^thin their foresaid playhouse in Dorset house yard, as in any city, university, towne, or borough of o^r said realmes and dominions, there to soiourne and abide, if at any tyme they wth their Company and Associats (whom o^r said servant Richard Heton shall thinke fitting to select) shall have occasion (by reason of sicknes in London or otherwise) to travell, to exercise publikely, to their best p^rfitt, comodity, and advantage, their aforesaid Comodies, Tragedies, &c., at all tyme or tymes, (the tyme of Divine service only excepted) before or after supper, w^thin any townehalls, guildhalls, moothalls, schoolehouses, or any other convenient places whatsoever. And the same Comedyes, Tragedyes, &c., wth the tymes they are to be acted, to proclayme in such places as afores'd wth drums, trumpetts, and by publike bills, if they thinke fitt, Notwithstanding any statute, act, proclamacon, pr'vision, restraint, or matter whatsoever to the contrary.

My Intencon for the rest.

That such of the company as will not be ordered and governed by me as of their governor, or shall not by the M^r of his M^ts Revells and my selfe bee thought fitt Comedians for her M^ts service, I may have power to discharge from the Company, and, wth the advice of the M^r of the Revells, to putt new ones in their places; and those who shalbe soe descharged not to have the honor to be her M^ts servants, but only those who shall continew at the aforesaid playhouse. And the said Company not to play at any tyme in any other place but the forsaid playhouse without my consent under my hand in wryting, (lest his M^ts service might be neglected) except by speciall comand from one of the Lo. Chamberlaines, or the M^r of his M^ts Revells, &c.'

Cunningham says, 'The short memorandum subjoined was found with the preceding documents'. It was indorsed, 'INSTRUCTIONS TOUCHING SALESBERY CO^RT PLAYHOUSE, 14 SEPTEM., 1639.'

The diffrence betwixt the first Articles and the last.

The housekeep^s enioy not any one Benefit in the last wch they had not in the first.

And they paid only by the first.
1, All Repaires of the house.
2, Halfe the gathering plačs.
    Halfe to the Sweepers of the house, the stagekeep^s, to the Poor, and for carying away the soyle.

By the last Articles.

We first allow them a Roome or 2 more then they form'ly had.
All that was allowed by the former Articles, and
Halfe the Poets wages wch is 10^s a week.[1]

---

[1] Evidently the theatre paid the poet 20s. a week. This is the wage Brome was to receive from the Salisbury Court according to his contract of August 1638 (see Andrews, *Brome*, pp. 13–15).

Halfe the lycencing of every new play wch halfe is also xx^s.

And one dayes p'ffitt wholly to themselves every yeare in consideration of their want of stooles on the stage, wch were taken away by his M^ts comand.

We allow them also that was in noe Articles.

Halfe for lights, both waxe and Tallow, wch halfe all winter is near 5^s a day.

Halfe for coles to all the Roomes.

Halfe for rushes, flowers, and strowings on the stage.

Halfe for all the boyes' new gloves at every new play, and every revived play not lately plaid.

All the rest of the Articles are some indifferent Rules fitt to be observed for the generall creditt of the house and benfitt of both Housekeep^s and Players.

THEATRICAL NOTES FROM CROSFIELD'S DIARY

The following extract is from *The Diary of Thomas Crosfield* (London: Oxford University Press, 1935), edited by Frederick S. Boas.[1] Crosfield was a Fellow of Queen's College, Oxford, whose diary, 1626–40 and 1653–4, contains an interview with Richard Kendall, wardrobe keeper of the Salisbury Court players. The significant entries, pp. 71–3, dated 18 July 1634, follow:

One Richard Kendall about yᵉ age of 50 or upwards, belonging to yᵉ Company of players of Salsbury Court that came to Oxford this yeare came to see me & related unto me diverse particular stories vizᵗ.

1. of his particular state & education in his youth at Kirkby Lonsdall where he served his Apprenticeship to a Talor, & afterward went to Cambridge where he stayd but litle, & then went to London where he became servant to Sir Wᵐ Slingsby—and nowe he is one of yᵉ 2. Keepers of the Wardrobe of the said Company.

['Stories' 2, 3, and 4 are not of theatrical interest.]

5. of the severall Companies of Players in London wᶜh are in number 5.

1. The Kings Company at yᵉ private house of Blackfriars: The masters or cheife whereof are { Mr Talor { Mr Lowen
2. The Queen's servants at yᵉ Phoenix in Drury Lane. Their master Mr Beeston, Mr Boyer, Shirley Robinson, Clarke—
3. The Princes Servants at yᵉ Red-bull in St Johns street, yᵉ cheife Mr Cane a goldsmith, Mr Worth Mr Smith 2000ˡⁱ.[2]
4. The Fortune in Golden Lane, yᵉ cheife Mr Wᵐ Cartwright, Edward Armestead, John Buckle, John Kirke.
5. The Company of Salisbury Court at yᵉ further

end of fleet street against yᵉ Conduit: The cheife whereof are 1. Mr. Gunnell a Papist. 2. Mr. John Yongue. 3. Edward Gibbs a fencer. 4. Timothy Reed. 5. Christofer Goad. 6. Sam. Thompson. 7. Mr. Staffeild. 8. John Robinson. 9. Courteous Grevill. These are yᵉ cheife whereof 7 are called sharers i.e. such as pay wages to yᵉ servants & equally share in the overplus: other servants there are as 2 Close keepers { Richard Kendall { Anthony &c { Dover

Of all these Companies yᵉ first if they please may come to Oxõn, but none without speciall lettres from the Chancellor obtained by meanes of yᵉ Secretary to the ViceChancelour./ Mr Gunnell

---

[1] The extract is printed here with the kind permission of Professor Boas.
[2] Professor Boas says (p. 136), 'I cannot explain "2000ˡⁱ" here.'

akin to ye Nappers.[1] A Crosse mischance happened to this company bec*ause* of a boy y^t quarrelled with a Scholar in ye Taverne./ They came furnished with 14 playes. And lodged at ye Kings Armes, where Franklin hath about 3^li a day while they stay, i.e. for every play 4 nobles besides ye benefit of seats.—

[1] A well-known Oxford family to whom Crosfield often refers.

MISCELLANEOUS

An Order of the Lords and Commons concerning Stage-playes[1]

Whereas the distressed Estate of Ireland, steeped in her own Blood, and the distracted Estate of England, threatned with a Cloud of Blood, by a Civill Warre, call for all possible meanes to appease and avert the Wrath of God appearing in these Judgements; amongst which, Fasting and Prayer having bin often tryed to be very effectuall, have bin lately, and are still ejoyned; and whereas publike Sports doe not well agree with publike Calamities, nor publike Stage-playes with the Seasons of Humiliation, this being an Exercise of sad and pious solemnity, and the other being Spectacles of pleasure, too commonly expressing laciuious Mirth and Levitie: It is therefore thought fit, and Ordeined by the Lords and Commons in this Parliament Assembled, that while these sad Causes and set times of Humiliation doe continue, publike Stage-Playes shall cease, and bee forborne. Instead of which, are recommended to the people of this Land, the profitable and seasonable Considerations of Repentance, Reconciliation, and peace with God, which probably may produce outward peace and prosperity, and bring againe Times of Joy and Gladnesse to these Nations.

Die Veneris, Septemb. 2. 1642.

Ordered by the Lords and Commons in Parliament, that this Order be forthwith Printed and published.

John Browne Cler. Parl.

Contemporary Theatrical Comment

The following quotations are taken from Edmund Gayton's *Pleasant Notes upon Don Quixote*, 1654.

I have heard, that the Poets of the Fortune and red Bull, had alwayes a mouth-measure for their Actors (who were terrible tearethroats) and made their lines proportionable to their compasse, which were *sesquipedales*, a foot and a halfe. [Page 24.]

. . . yet men come not to study at a Play-house, but love such expressions and passages, which with ease insinuate themselves into their capacities . . . to them bring *Jack Drumm's* entertainment, *Greens tu quoque*, the *Devill of Edmunton*, and the like; or if it be on Holy dayes, when Saylers, Water-men, Shoomakers, Butchers and Apprentices are at leisure, then it is good policy to amaze those violent spirits, with some tearing Tragaedy full of fights and skirmishes: as the *Guilphs* and *Guiblins*, *Greeks* and *Trojans*, or the three *London Apprentises*, which commonly ends in six acts, the spectators

[1] Downes, Appendix.

frequently mounting the stage, and making a more bloody Catastrophe amongst themselves, then the Players did. I have known upon one of these *Festivals*, but especially at *Shrove-tide*, where the Players have been appointed, notwithstanding their bils to the contrary, to act what the major part of the company had a mind to; sometimes *Tamerlane*, sometimes *Jugurth*, sometimes the Jew of *Malta*, and sometimes parts of all these, and at last, none of the three taking, they were forc'd to undresse and put off their Tragick habits, and conclude the day with the merry milk-maides. And unlesse this were done, and the popular humour satisfied, as sometimes it so fortun'd, that the Players were refractory; the Benches, the tiles, the laths, the stones, Oranges, Apples, Nuts, flew about most liberally, and as there were Mechanicks of all professions, who fell every one to his owne trade, and dissolved a house in an instant, and made a ruine of a stately Fabrick. It was not then the most mimicall nor fighting man, *Fowler*, nor *Andrew Cane* could pacifie; Prologues nor Epilogues would prevaile; the Devill and the fool were quite out of favour. Nothing but noise and tumult fils the house, untill a cogg take 'um, and then to the Bawdy houses, and reforme them; and instantly to the Banks side, where the poor Beares must conclude the riot, and fight twenty dogs at a time beside the Butchers, which sometimes fell into the service; this perform'd, and the Horse and Jack-an-Apes for a jigge, they had sport enough that day for nothing. [Pages 271–2.]

HISTORIA HISTRIONICA

HISTORIA HISTRIONICA: An Historical Account of the English-Stage, Shewing The ancient Use, Improvement, and Perfection, of Dramatick Representations, in this Nation. In a Dialogue, of Plays and Players . . . London . . . 1699. (B.M. 641.e.15.)

A DIALOGUE OF PLAYS AND PLAYERS

Lovewit, Truman.

Lovew. Honest Old Cavalier! well met, 'faith I'm glad to see thee.

Trum. Have a care what you call me. Old, is a Word of Disgrace among the Ladies; to be Honest is to be Poor and Foolish, (as some think) and Cavalier is a Word as much out of Fashion as any of 'em.

Lovew. The more's the pity: But what said the Fortune-Teller in *Ben. Johnson's* Mask of *Gypsies*, to the then *Lord Privy Seal*,

Honest and Old!
In those the Good *Part of a Fortune is told.*

Trum. Ben. *Johnson*? How dare you name *Ben. Johnson* in these times? When we have such a crowd of Poets of a quite different Genius; the least of which thinks himself as well able to correct *Ben. Johnson*, as he could a Country School Mistress that taught to Spell.

Lovew. We have indeed, Poets of a different Genius; so are the

Plays: But in my Opinion, they are all of 'em (some few excepted) as much inferior to those of former Times, as the Actors now in being (generally speaking) are, compared to *Hart, Mohun, Burt, Lacy, Clun,* and *Shatterel*; for I can reach no farther backward.

Trum. I can; and dare assure you, if my Fancy and Memory are not partial (for Men of my Age are apt to be over indulgent to the thoughts of their youthful Days) I say the Actors that I have seen before the Wars, *Lowin, Tayler, Pollard,* and some others, were almost as far beyond *Hart* and his Company, as those were beyond these now in being.

Lovew. I am willing to believe it, but cannot readily; because I have been told, That those whom I mention'd, were Bred up under the others of your Acquaintance, and follow'd their manner of Action, which is now lost. So far, that when the Question has been askt, Why these Players do not revive the *Silent Woman,* and some other of *Johnson's* Plays, (once of highest esteem) they have answer'd, truly, Because there are none now Living who can rightly Humour those Parts, for all who related to the *Black-friers* (where they were Acted in perfection) are now Dead, and almost forgotten.

Trum. 'Tis very true, *Hart* and *Clun,* were bred up Boys at the *Blackfriers*; and Acted Womens Parts, *Hart* was *Robinson's* Boy or Apprentice: He Acted the Dutchess in the Tragedy of *the Cardinal,* which was the first Part that gave him Reputation. *Cartwright,* and *Wintershal* belong'd to the private House in *Salisbury-Court, Burt* was a Boy first under *Shank* at the *Black-friers,* then under *Beeston* at the *Cockpit*; and *Mohun,* and *Shatterel* were in the same Condition with him, at the last Place. There *Burt* used to Play the principal Women's Parts, in particular *Clariana* in *Love's Cruelty*; and at the same time *Mohun* Acted *Bellamente,* which Part he retain'd after the Restauration.

Lovew. That I have seen, and can well remember. I wish they had Printed in the last Age (so I call the times before the Rebellion) the Actors Names over against the Parts they Acted, as they have done since the Restauration. And thus one might have guest at the Action of the Men, by the Parts which we now Read in the Old Plays.

Trum. It was not the Custome and Usage of those Days, as it hath been since. Yet some few Old Plays there are that have the Names set against the Parts, as, *The Dutchess of Malfy*; *the Picture*; *the Roman Actor*; *the deserving Favourite, the Wild Goose Chace,* (at the Black-friers) *the Wedding*; *the Renegado*; *the fair Maid of the West*; *Hannibal and Scipio*; *King John and Matilda*; (at the Cockpit) and *Holland's Leaguer,* (at Salisbury Court.)

Lovew. These are but few indeed: But pray Sir, what Master Parts can you remember the Old *Black-friers* Men to Act, in *Johnson, Shakespear,* and *Fletcher's* Plays.

Trum. What I can at present recollect I'll tell you; *Shakespear,* (who as I have heard, was a much better Poet, than Player) *Burbadge, Hemmings,* and others of the Older sort, were Dead before I knew the Town; but in my time, before the Wars, *Lowin* used to Act, with mighty Applause, *Falstaffe, Morose, Vulpone,* and *Mammon* in the *Alchymist; Melancius* in the *Maid's* Tragedy, and at the same time *Amyntor* was Play'd by *Stephen Hammerton,* (who was at first a most noted and beautiful Woman Actor, but afterwards he acted with equal Grace and Applause, a Young Lover's Part) *Tayler* acted *Hamlet* incomparably well, *Jago, Truewit* in the *Silent Woman,* and *Face* in the *Alchymist; Swanston* used to Play *Othello: Pollard,* and *Robinson* were Comedians, so was *Shank* who used to Act Sir *Roger,* in the *Scornful Lady.* These were of the *Blackfriers.* Those of principal Note at the *Cockpit,* were, *Perkins, Michael Bowyer, Sumner, William Allen,* and *Bird,* eminent Actors. and *Robins* a Comedian. Of the other Companies I took little notice.

Lovew. Were there so many Companies?

Trum. Before the Wars, there were in being all these Playhouses at the same time. The *Black-friers,* and *Globe* on the *Bankside,* a Winter and Summer House, belonging to the same Company called the King's Servants; the *Cockpit* or *Phaenix,* in *Drury-lane,* called the Queen's Servants; the private House in *Salisburycourt,* called the Prince's Servants; the *Fortune* near *White-crossstreet,* and the *Red Bull* at the upper end of St. *John's-street:* The two last were mostly frequented by Citizens, and the meaner sort of People. All these Companies got Money, and Liv'd in Reputation, especially those of the *Blackfriers,* who were Men of grave and sober Behaviour.

Lovew. Which I admire at; That the Town much less than at present, could then maintain Five Companies, and yet now Two can hardly Subsist.

Trum. Do not wonder, but consider, That tho' the Town was then, perhaps, not much more than half so Populous as now, yet then the Prices were small (there being no Scenes) and better order kept among the Company that came; which made very good People think a Play an Innocent Diversion for an idle Hour or two, the Plays themselves being then, for the most part, more Instructive and Moral. Whereas of late, the Play-houses are so extreamly pestered with Vizard-masks and their Trade, (occasioning continual Quarrels and Abuses) that many of the more Civilized Part of the Town are uneasy in the Company, and shun the Theater as they would a House of Scandal. It is an Argument of the worth of the Plays and Actors, of the last Age, and easily inferr'd, that they were much beyond ours in this, to consider that they cou'd support themselves meerly from their own Merit; the weight of the Matter, and goodness of the Action, without Scenes and Machines: Whereas the present Plays with all that shew, can hardly draw an Audience, unless there be the additional Invitation of a *Signior Fideli*, a *Monsier L'abbe*, or some such Foreign Regale exprest in the bottom of the Bill.

Lovew. To wave this Digression, I have Read of one *Edward Allin*, a Man so famed for excellent Action, that among *Ben. Johnson's* Epigrams, I find one directed to him, full of Encomium, and concluding thus

> *Wear this Renown, 'tis just that who did give*
> *So may Poets Life, by one should Live.*

Was he one of the *Black-friers*?

Trum. Never, as I have heard; (for he was Dead before my time.) He was Master of a Company of his own, for whom he Built the *Fortune* Play-house from the Ground, a large, round Brick Building. This is he that grew so Rich that he purchased a great Estate in *Surrey* and elsewhere; and having no Issue, he Built and largely endow'd *Dulwich* College, in the Year 1619, for a Master, a Warden, Four Fellows, Twelve aged poor People, and Twelve poor Boys, &c. A noble Charity.

Lovew. What kind of Playhouses had they before the Wars?

Trum. The *Black-friers*, *Cockpit*, and *Salisbury-court*, were called Private Houses, and were very small to what we see now. The *Cockpit* was standing since the Restauration, and *Rhode's* Company Acted there for some time.

Lovew. I have seen that.

Trum. Then you have seen the other two, in effect; for they were all three Built almost exactly alike, for Form and Bigness. Here they had Pits for the Gentry, and Acted by Candle-light. The *Globe, Fortune* and *Bull*, were large Houses, and lay partly open to the Weather, and there they alwaies Acted by Daylight.

Lovew. But prithee, *Truman*, what became of these Players when the Stage was put down, and the Rebellion raised?

Trum. Most of 'em, except *Lowin, Tayler* and *Pollard*, (who were superannuated) went into the King's Army, and like good Men and true, Serv'd their Old Master, tho' in a different, yet more honourable, Capacity. *Robinson* was Kill'd at the Taking of a Place (I think *Basing House*) by *Harrison*, he that was after Hang'd at *Charing-cross*, who refused him Quarter, and Shot him in the Head when he had laid down his Arms; abusing Scripture at the same time, in saying, *Cursed is he that doth the Work of the Lord negligently.* *Mohun* was a Captain, (and after the Wars were ended here, served in *Flanders*, where he received Pay as a Major) *Hart* was a Lieutenant of Horse under Sir *Thomas Dallison*, in *Prince Rupert's*, Regiment, *Burt* was Cornet in the same Troop, and *Shatterel* Quartermaster. *Allen* of the *Cockpit*, was a Major, and Quarter Master General at *Oxford*. I have not heard of one of these Players of any Note that sided with the other Party, but only *Swanston*, and he profest himself a Presbyterian, took up the Trade of a Jeweller, and liv'd in *Aldermanbury*, within the Territory of Father *Calamy*. The rest either Lost, or expos'd their Lives for their King. When the Wars were over, and the Royalists totally Subdued; most of 'em who were left alive gather'd to *London*, and for a Subsistence endeavour'd to revive their Old Trade, privately. They made up one Company out of all the Scatter'd Members of Several; and in the Winter before the King's Murder, 1648, They ventured to Act some Plays with as much caution and privacy as cou'd be, at the *Cockpit*. They continu'd undisturbed for three or four Days; but at last as they were presenting the Tragedy of the *Bloudy Brother*, (in which *Lowin* Acted Aubrey, *Tayler* Rollo, *Pollard* the Cook, *Burt* Latorch, and I think *Hart* Otto) a Party of Foot Souldiers beset the House, surprized 'em about the midle of the Play, and carried 'em away in their habits, not admitting them to Shift, to *Hatton-house* then a Prison, where having detain'd them sometime, they Plunder'd them of their Cloths and let 'em loose again. Afterwards in *Oliver's* time, they used to Act privately, three or four Miles, or more, out of Town, now here, now there, sometimes in Noblemens Houses, in particular *Holland-house* at *Kensington*, where the Nobility and Gentry who met (but in no great Numbers) used to make a Sum for them, each giving a broad Peice, or the like. And *Alexander Goffe*, the Woman Actor at *Blackfriers*, (who had made himself known to Persons of Quality) used to be the Jackal and give notice of Time and Place. At Christmass, and Bartlemew-fair, they used to Bribe the Officer who Commanded the Guard at *Whitehall*, and were thereupon connived at to Act for a few Days, at the *Red Bull*; but were sometimes notwithstanding Disturb'd by Soldiers. Some pickt up a little Money by publishing the Copies of Plays never before Printed, but kept up in Manuscript. For instance, in the Year 1652, *Beaumont* and *Fletcher's Wild Goose Chace* was Printed in Folio, *for the Publick use of all the Ingenious*, (as the Title-page says) *and private Benefit of* John Lowin *and* Joseph Tayler, *Servants to his late Majesty*; and by them Dedicated *To the Honour'd few Lovers of Dramatick Poesy*: Wherein they modestly intimate their Wants. And that with sufficient Cause; for whatever they were before the Wars, they were, after, reduced to a necessitous Condition. *Lowin* in his latter Days, kept an Inn (the three Pidgions) at *Brentford*, where he Dyed very Old, (for he was an Actor of eminent Note in the Reign of K. *James* the first) and his Poverty was as great as his Age. *Tayler* Dyed at *Richmond* and was there Buried. *Pollard* who Lived Single, and had a Competent Estate; Retired to some Relations he had in the Country, and there ended his Life. *Perkins* and *Sumner* of the *Cockpit*, kept House together at Clerkenwel, and were there

Buried. These all Dyed some Years before the Restauration. What follow'd after, I need not tell you: You can easily Remember.[1]

.   .   .   .

Some of these Chappel Boys, when they grew Men, became Actors at the Black-friers; such were *Nathan Feild*, and *John Underwood*.

[1] The above material occupies pp. 1–10; the following sentence is from p. 16.

INDEX

Abdy, Sir Chr., 677.
Abell, William, 314.
Acton, Francis, **343**, 682.
Acton, Walter, 640.
Acton, Sir William, 640.
Actor-dramatists, *see* Players.
Actors, *see* Players.
Adams, J. Q., 27 n. 2.
'An "Hitherto Unknown Actor"
of Shakespeare's Troupe', 623.
Adams, Thomas, 649.
Adkinson, Will, **343**.
Admiral's company, 1, 135, 322, 486,
490, 507.
Adson, F., *see* Adson, J.
Adson, John, **343**.
Courtly Masquing Ayres, 343.
Adye, Mr., 510.
Aglaura, *see* Suckling.
Albany, Duke of, 198.
Albertus Wallenstein, see Glapthorne.
Alchemist, The, see Jonson.
Alcimedon, see Duryer.
Alderman, 314.
Aldermanbury, *see* London, streets
of.
Alderson, Thomas, 265, 432.
Aldgate, *see* London, streets of.
Alexius, see Massinger.
Alfonso, see Anon., *Alphonsus, Em-
peror of Germany.*
Alice and Alexis, see Anon.
Allen, Alice, **345**.
Allen, Ann, **345**.
Allen, Edward, *see* Alleyn, Edward.
Allen, Elizabeth, **346**.
Allen, Hester, **345**.
Allen, Jeremy, **344**.
Allen, John, **345**.
Allen, Mary, **345**.
Allen, Michael, **345**.
Allen, Richard, **344**.
Allen, Robert, **345**.
Allen, Samuel, **345**.
Allen, Thomas, 137.
Allen, William, 56, 57, 64, 69 n. 2,
73–89, 220, 221, 226, 231, 239,
246, 247, **344–6**.
Alleyn, Edward, 6, 135, 136, 137,
138, 142, 143, 144, 146 and n. 1,
152, 153, 177, 198, 199 and n. 2,
200, 201 n. 2, 202, 209, **346–9**, 507,
528, 633, 694.
Alleyn, Mathias, 144.

All Hallows, London Wall, 589, 592,
593, 615.
All Hallows the Less, 626.
Allington, John, 49 n. 2 cont'd., 73–
89, **349**.
All's Lost by Lust, see W. Rowley.
Almanacs, 243 n. 2.
Alnwick Castle, 363.
Alphonsus, Emperor of Germany, see
Anon.
Altar upon the stage, 277–8.
Amends for Ladies, see Field.
Amphitheatre, 423, 620.
Amsterdam, 267.
Amyntas, see Randolph.
Andrewes, William, 483.
Angel King, The, see Anon.
Angell, Thomas, 510.
Angels Inn, 348.
Anne, Queen, death of, 6, 139 n. 7,
164.
Funeral of, 6, 7.
Company of, 137 n. 3, **158–75**,
177, 178, 183 n. 2, 185 n. 9,
200, 202 and n. 6, 208, 222,
308. Queen Anne–Red Bull
Revels, 165–75, 308, 309;
Livery allowance, 164–5, 171.
Wardrobe, 204.
Warrant for patent, 167–9.
Anonymous, *Alice and Alexis*, 123.
Alphonsus, Emperor of Germany,
27, 48 n. 5, 51, 66, 96, 98, 132–3.
Angel King, The, 150, 157.
Battle of Alcazar, The, see Peele.
Beggars, The, 66, 133.
Black Lady, The, 185, 196–7, 205
n. 5.
Bloody Banquet, The, 331, 341,
427.
Bridegroom and the Madman, The,
66, 95 n. c, 133.
*Brief Description of the Notorious
Life of John Lambe, A*, 267.
Buck Is a Thief, The, 95, 133.
Cardinal's Conspiracy, The, 278,
282.
City Shuffler, The, 293 n. 2.
Conceited Duke, The, 331, 342.
Costly Whore, The, 175, 301.
Doctor Lambe and the Witches, 41,
294 and n. 1, 301.
*Dutch Painter and the French
Brawle, The*, 205, 216.

Anonymous (*contd.*):
Edmond Ironside, 323, 388–9, 443, 450, 509, 510, 580, 581.
Fair Star of Antwerp, The, 150, 157.
False Friend, The, 111.
Famous Victories of Henry the Fifth, The, 133.
Father's Own Son, The, see Beaumont and Fletcher, *Monsieur Thomas.*
Fool and Her Maidenhead Soon Parted, A, 331, 342.
Fortune's Tennis, 578.
Four Sons of Amon, The, 206 n. 3, 216.
Frederick and Basilea, 481.
George a Greene, 331, 342.
Gramercy Wit, 166, 173, 175.
Great Duke, The, see Massinger, *The Great Duke of Florence.*
Greeks and Trojans, The, 690.
Guelphs and Ghibellines, The, 690.
Honest Lawyer, The, 174.
Honour in the End, 150, 157.
Honour of Women, The, 134.
Induction for the House, 28 and n. 1, 96, 97 n. 1 †.
Irish Rebellion, The, 493.
Italian Night Masque, The, 551, 552.
Italian Night-piece or the Unfortunate Piety, The, 126.
Jugurth, King of Numidia, 150 and n. 4, 151, 157, 691.
Key to the Cabinet of Parliament, A, 549.
Knave in Grain New Vampt, The, 13 n. 2, 282.
Lasander and Callista, 676.
Late (and the Last) Will and Testament of the Doctors Commons, The, 319.
Love's Aftergame, see The Proxy.
Love Tricks with Compliments, see Shirley, *The School of Compliment.*
Lysander and Calista, see Beaumont and Fletcher, *The Lover's Progress.*
Mad Couple Well Met, A, 331, 342.
Man in the Moon Drinks Claret, The, 205, 213, 216.
Masque, The, see Gunnell.
Merry Devil of Edmonton, The, 28, 94, 96, 99, 133, 690.
Musarum Deliciæ, 472.
Nice Valour, The, 133.

Anonymous (*contd.*):
'On the Time Poets', *see* William Heminges, *Elegy on Randolph's Finger.*
Parricide, The, 216.
Pastoral, The, 97, 133, 675.
Peaceable King or the Lord Mendall, The, 206, 216.
Plantation of Virginia, The, 206.
Proxy or Love's Aftergame, The, 294 and n. 2, 296, 299 and n. d, 301.
Queen or the Excellency of Her Sex, The, 447.
Runaways' Answer to a Book Called, A Rod for Runaways, The, 19, 20, 410, 412.
Second Maiden's Tragedy, The, 448, 550
Seven Deadly Sins, 363, 410, 447.
Sir Giles Goosecap, 301.
Spanish Contract, The, 197, 614.
Spanish Viceroy, The, 14, 15 n. 1, 80–1, 101 n. a, 102, 104 and n. 1, 133–4, 375, 377, 448, 501, 532, 533, 547, 552, 557, 565, 569, 570, 593, 611.
Sportive Wit, 627.
Stage Players' Complaint, The, 65 n. 2, 317 and n. 1, 398, 399, 400, 540, 541.
Swetnam the Woman Hater, 174.
Tamar Cam, 485, 578.
Thomas of Woodstock or Richard II, 441, 445, 450, 581.
Three London Apprentices, The, 690.
Two Merry Milkmaids, The, 166, 173, 175, 417–18, 691.
Two Noble Ladies, The, 166, 175, 382, 388, 389, 441, 579, 580, 581, 590.
Tyrant, The, see Massinger.
Valiant Scholar, The, 185, 197, 205 n. 5.
Valiant Scot, The, 13 n. 2, 278, 282.
Vow and a Good One, A, 205, 213, 216.
Wasp, The, 362, 363, 453, 627.
Welsh Ambassador, The, 175.
Welsh Traveller, The, 167, 175, 205 n. 5.
Westminster Drollery, 563.
Whore in Grain, The, 150, 157.
Whore New Vamped, The, 13 n. 2, 157, 314, 323, 400.
Witch of Edmonton, The, see Dekker.

Anonymous (*contd.*):
Wits Restored, 563.
Woman Is Too Hard for Him, The, 94, 134.
World, The, 331, 342.
Younger Brother, The, 202, 216–17, 346.
Antipodes, The, see Brome.
Antiquarian Repertory, The, 606.
Antiquary, The, see Marmion.
Antwerp, 512.
Anything for a Quiet Life, see Middleton.
Apethorpe, Northamptonshire, 310, 673.
Apperley, Elizabeth, 350.
Apperley, John, **349–50**.
Apperley, Margaret, 350.
Appius and Virginia, see Webster.
Apple-wives, 268, 315.
Apprentices, 3, 137 n. 6, 161, 163, 166–7, 167, 207, 207 n. 4, 267, 268, 318 n. 1, 335, 443, 463, 475, 484, 491, 496, 499, 517, 532, 544, 550, 553, 559, 563, 572, 584, 599, 601, 604, 688, 690.
  Acting, 35 n. 2, 692.
  Boarding-house, 599.
  Cost of, 45.
  Riot of, 161 n. 2.
Apsley, Sir Allen, 354.
Arcadia, The, see Shirley.
Archer, Robert, **350**.
Argalus and Parthenia, see Glapthorne.
Argyll, Earl of, 436.
Argyll, Lady, 436.
Aristotle, 538.
Armiger, Edward, 272, 275, 281, **350**.
Armstead, Edward, *see* Armiger, Edward.
Armyn, Robert, 2, 5 n. 6.
Army plot, 335, 421.
Arnold, William, 357.
Arrest, players' exemption from, 15–16.
Arszch, Robert, *see* Archer, Robert.
Arundel, Earl of, 349.
Arviragus and Felicia, I and II, *see* Carlell.
Ashborne, Edward, 15, 73–89, **350–1**.
Ashley, Sir Anthony, 415.
Ashley, Sir Francis, 416.
Ashmolean Museum, 500.
Ashton, Edward (*see also* Ashboïne, Edward), 351.
Asken, Aaron, **351**.
Askewgh, William, 355.

Asplin, Anne, 650.
Assize Sermon, An, 418.
Astley, Sir John, 471.
As You Like It, see Shakespeare.
Atkins, John, 261 and n. 3, **351**, 577, 644, 648.
Atkins, Richard, 644.
Atkinson, William, 631.
Attendants (*see also under* individual companies), 332.
Atterley, John, *see* Apperley, John.
Attwell, Hugh, 199 and n. 2, 200 and n. 3, 203, 211, **351–3**.
Attwell's Jig, 352.
Audience, behaviour of, 279–80, 690–1.
  Courtly character of, 47 n. 3.
Austen's Rents, Southwark, *see* London, streets of.
Authors, *see* Playwrights.
Awnsham, Nicholas, 461, 635, 636.
Axall or Axell, Robert, *see* Axen, Robert.
Axen, Everelda, 353.
Axen, Robert, 142, 220, 223 n. 6, 239, 246, 324, 326 n. 6, 332, 336, **353**.
Axen, Symon, 353.
Axen, William, 353.
Axon, Robert, *see* Axen, Robert.
Ayloffe, John, 404.

Baber, Francis, 355.
Babham, Christopher, 35, **353–4**.
Babthorpe, Dame Grace, 471.
Babthorpe, Sir Ralph, 471.
Babties, Mr., 486.
Backer, Dr., 142, 353.
Backstead, William, *see* Barkstead, William.
Bacon, Francis, 347.
Bacon, Lady Jane, 42 n. 3.
Bacon, John, 49 n. 2 cont'd., 73–89, **354**.
Baggont, Anne, 488.
Bagnall, William, 413.
Bagshot, 50.
Bagshot Park, 561.
Bagstare, Richard, *see* Baxter, Richard.
Bailiff, 348, 438.
Baker, 486.
Baker, Cicely, 605.
Baldron, Mathew, 412.
Baldwin, Henry, 162, 366.
Baldwin, Katherine, 428.
Ball, The, see Shirley.
Ballets, 30 n. 6 cont'd.
Balls, Francis, 73–89, **354–5**.

Balls, Richard, 202, **355**, 622.
Balsams, 517.
Banbury, 292 n. 4, 409.
Band, Thomas, *see* Bond, Thomas.
Bankes, Ralph, 356.
Bankes, Thomas, 356.
Bankes, William, 311, 321, **355–6**.
Bankside, *see* London, streets of.
Barber chirurgion (*see also* Doctor, Physician, and Surgeon), 143, 437, 484.
Barbican, *see* London, streets of.
Barbor, Edmond, **356**, 682.
Barclay, Will, 58.
Barefield, Roger, *see* Barfield, Roger.
Barfield, Anthony, 357.
Barfield, Isabell, 357.
Barfield, Roger, **356–7**.
Barfield, Susan, 357.
Barfoote, Roger, *see* Barfield, Roger.
Bargehouse on the Bankside, *see* London, streets of.
Barkham, Edward, 416.
Barking, Essex, 497.
Barksted, William, 176, 177 and n. 2, 199 and n. 2, 200, 211, **357–8**.
  Hiren, 357.
  Myrrha, 357.
Barnavelt, *see* Beaumont and Fletcher, *Sir John van Olden Barnavelt*.
Barnes, —, *The Madcap*, 206 n. 3, 214.
Barnes, Thomas, 190, 192, **358–9**.
Barnstaple, 172, 193, 212.
Barratt, Gustavous, 359.
Barrett, John, 285, 286, 287, 288, 289 n. 4 cont'd., 290, 297, **359**.
Barrett, Walter, 168 n. 1, **359**.
Barrett, William, 359.
Barry, David (Lord), *Ram Alley*, 652.
Bartholomew Fair, *see* Jonson.
Bashful Lover, The, *see* Massinger.
Basing House, 548, 549, 694.
Baskervile, Francis, *see* Browne, Francis.
Baskervile, James, 158, 159.
Baskervile papers, 207.
Baskervile suit, 158–60.
Baskervile, Susan, 158, 159, 171, 310, 368, 545, 548, 637.
Baskerviles, new agreement with, 171.
Basket-maker, 431, 486.
Basse, Jane, 631.
Basse, Thomas, 167, 168 n. 2, 171, 176, 177 and n. 6, **360**.
  Will of, 631.

Basse, Ursula, 631.
Battle of Alcazar, The, *see* Peele.
Batty, 318, **360**.
Baxted, William, *see* Barksted, William.
Baxter, Constance, 361.
Baxter, Elizabeth, 362.
Baxter, Jane, 361.
Baxter, Joane, 361.
Baxter, John, 361.
Baxter, Michael, 361.
Baxter, Richard, 49 and n. 2 cont'd., 73–89, 166, 167, 168 n. 1, 171, **360–2**.
Baxter, Robert, 361, 643.
Baxter, Susan, 361.
Baylie, Ann, 392.
Bayly, Edward, **362**.
Bearbaiting, 201, 510, 657, 691.
Bear-garden, 225, 265, 315, 423, 510, 620.
Beaulieu, 20.
Beaumont and Fletcher, 2, 6, 22 n. 2, 66, 68, 225, 436, 557, 692.
  Popularity of, at court, 29.
  Folios, 69 n. 2, 88–9, 177 nn. 3 and 6, 345.
  Beggar's Bush, The, 28, 51, 94, 96, 98, 100, 109.
  Bloody Brother, The, 28, 30, 51, 69 n. 2, 88–9, 96, 98, 99 n. v, 109, 397, 505, 534, 556, 597, 675, 681, 695.
  Bonduca, 66, 109, 429, 465, 500, 550, 562.
  Captain, The, 66, **95** n. c, 109–10.
  Chances, The, 28, 66, 96, 100, 110, 426, 430.
  Coronation, The, *see* Shirley.
  Coxcomb, The, 51, 66, 94, 98, 110, 344, 425, 539.
  Cupid's Revenge, 186 n. 7, 194, 325, 330–1, 336, 337.
  Custom of the Country, The, 24, 27, 66, 74–5, 96, 100, 110, 374, 407, 430, 475, 501, 569, 570, 591, 593, 602, 610.
  Demetrius and Enanthe, *see* The Humorous Lieutenant.
  Devil of Dowgate, The, 103, 110, 127.
  Double Marriage, The, 66, 78–9, 110, 126, 375, 377, 501, 552, 569, 570, 593, 602, 611.
  Elder Brother, The, 48, 51, 98, 110, 660, 677, 681.
  Fair Maid of the Inn, The, 104, 110, 447, 476, 500, 556.

Beaumont and Fletcher (*contd.*):
Faithful Shepherdess, The, 39 and
n. 1, 58 n. 3, 97, 110–11, 133,
592, 595.
False One, The, 74–5, 111, 375,
377, 430, 501, 547, 569, 570,
593, 602, 611.
*Father's Own Son, see Monsieur
Thomas.*
Four Plays in One, 435.
Henry VIII, 2, 22, 318, 506.
Honest Man's Fortune, The, 66,
104, 111, 435, 539, 544, 547, 593,
612.
Humorous Lieutenant, The, 66,
74–5, 111, 374, 411, 416, 430,
475, 500, 501, 532, 533, 534,
569, 570, 591, 592, 610.
Island, Princess, The, 66, 74–5,
94, 111, 374, 377, 430, 500, 501,
533, 569, 570, 593, 610.
Jeweller of Amsterdam, The, see
Field.
King and No King, A, 28, 51, 96,
98, 111, 343, 541, 597.
Knight of Malta, The, 66, 72–3,
95 n. c, 111, 374, 396, 411, 435,
475, 501, 570, 610.
Knight of the Burning Pestle, The,
236, 248 n. i, 249, 250, 330, 337,
441.
Laws of Candy, The, 74–5, 111,
377, 430, 501, 533, 570, 592,
599, 602, 610.
Little French Lawyer, The, 65,
76–7, 111, 374, 430, 475, 501,
570, 591, 593, 602, 611.
Lover's Progress, The, 66, 80–1, 95,
103, 111–12, 112, 124 n. 1, 375,
377, 476, 501, 533, 562, 570,
591, 593, 600, 611, 676, 681.
Love's Cure, 65, 112, 562.
Love's Pilgrimage, 51, 66, 98, 107,
112, 351, 354, 381, 425, 475, 661.
Loyal Subject, The, 51, 65, 72–3,
97, 98, 106, 112, 396, 411, 430,
435, 475, 501, 570, 602, 610.
Mad Lover, The, 28 and n. 1, 62,
66, 72–3, 84–5, 94, 96, 112, 177,
361, 362, 374, 396, 411, 430,
435, 479, 480, 501, 570, 678–9,
681.
Maid in the Mill, The, 66, 78–9,
95, 103, 112, 375, 476, 500, 501,
533, 556, 557, 593, 600, 611.
Maid's Tragedy, The, 28, 51, 95
n. c, 96, 98, 113, 505, 693.
*Martial Maid, The, see Love's
Cure.*

Beaumont and Fletcher (*contd.*):
Monsieur Thomas, 62, 113, 330,
331, 337.
*Nice Valour or the Passionate
Madman, The, see* Anon., *The
Bridegroom and the Madman.*
Night Walker, The, 226 n. 7 cont'd.,
230, 249, 250, 330, 337.
Noble Gentleman, The, 66, 104,
113.
Philaster, 28, 52, 95 n. c, 96, 98,
113.
Pilgrim, The, 66, 76–7, 94, 113,
375, 377, 479, 501, 593, 600,
602, 611.
Prophetess, The, 24, 66, 78–9, 103,
113, 377, 375, 475, 501, 562,
565, 570, 593, 602.
Queen of Corinth, The, 66, 72–3,
113, 177, 396, 411, 435, 475,
501, 533, 562, 602, 610.
*Rollo, Duke of Normandy, see The
Bloody Brother.*
Rule a Wife and Have a Wife, 13,
95, 104, 114, 447, 556, 591.
Scornful Lady, The, 28, 37, 67, 96,
100, 114, 562, 567, 693.
Sea Voyage, The, 78–9, 103, 114,
430, 475, 501, 593, 602, 611.
Sir John van Olden Barnavelt, 7,
74–5, 114, 377, 415, 448, 475,
499 and n. 1, 511, 516, 533, 546,
550, 552, 589, 609.
Spanish Curate, The, 65, 78–9, 94,
100, 103, 114, 375, 429, 430,
501, 533, 570, 593, 602.
*Tamer Tamed, The, see The
Woman's Prize.*
Thierry and Theodoret, 114, 435.
Two Noble Kinsmen, The, 82–3,
95 n. c, 114, 418, 452, 606–7.
Valentinian, 66, 115, 465, 500.
*Wandering Lovers, The, see The
Lover's Progress.*
Widow, The, see Middleton.
Wife for a Month, A, 52, 66, 80–1,
98, 103, 115, 375, 377, 476, 552,
556, 593, 602, 611.
Wild Goose Chase, The, 24, 36, 65,
86–7, 94, 115, 376, 430–1, 446,
447, 460, 477, 503, 505, 524,
532, 534, 553, 562–3, 566, 586,
594, 597, 605, 606, 692, 695.
Wit without Money, 250, 325, 330,
336, 337, 509, 510.
Woman Hater, The, 115.
Woman's Prize, The, 37 and n. 2,
38, 66, 86–7, 97, 114, 115, 487,
495, 503, 586.

Beaumont and Fletcher (*contd.*) :
Women Pleased, 76-7, 115, 374, 430, 475, 501, 562, 570, 593, 602, 610.
Beauty in a Trance, see Ford.
Becher, Sir William, 54 n. 2.
Beckland, Ambrose, *see* Beeland, Ambrose.
Bedford, Lord, 47.
Bedingfield, Daniel, 46, 376, 534, 586.
Bedingfield, Nicholas, 350.
Bedowe, Ellis, 286, 297, **362.**
Bee, William, **362.**
Beech Lane, *see* London, streets of.
Beedome, Thomas, *Poems, Divine and Humane*, 509 n. 1.
Beeland, Ambrose, 15, 72-88, **362-3.**
Beeston, Andrea, 370.
Beeston, Augustine, 364.
Beeston, Christopher, 1, 54, 55, 57, 137 n. 3, 141 n. 6, 158, 159, 160, 162-3, 163, 165, 169 n. 2, 171, 183 and n. 2, 184, 187, 188, 192, 202 and n. 6, 203, 204 and n. 4, 205 n. 3, 211 and n. b, 218, 219 and n. 3, 222, 223 and n. 6, 224, 225 n. 1, 228, 229, 230 n. 2, 231, 234, 236, 237, 241, 246, 247, 248 n. i, 249 n. e, 324, 325 and n. 4, 326 and nn. 2, 6, and 7, 327, 328, 329 and n. 6, 336 and n. b, 338, **363-70,** 527.
Will of, 631-3.
Beeston, Elizabeth, 330, 335, **370.**
Beeston, George, 373.
Beeston, Jane, 345, 364, 365, 366, 373.
Beeston, John, 369.
Beeston, Mary, 372.
Beeston, Robert, 158, 364, **370.**
Beeston, William, 35, 36, 62, 242, 291, 324, 326 nn. 6 and 7, 327, 330 and n. 3, 331 and n. 4, 332, 333, 334 n. 1, 335, 336, 338, **370-4,** 371.
Beeston's Boys, 54, 55, 57, 187, 204 n. 4, 219 n. 3, 283, **324-42.**
Beggars, The, see Anon. and Beaumont and Fletcher, *The Beggar's Bush*.
Beggar's Bush, The, see Beaumont and Fletcher.
Behel, Jacob, *see* Pedel, Jacob.
Beland, Ambrose, *see* Beeland, Ambrose.
Believe as You List, see Massinger.
Bell, John, *London's Remembrancer*, 667.
Bellermyne, 538.

Bellman of Paris, The, see Dekker.
Belvoir, 310.
Benches in theatre, *see* Theatre.
Benefit performances, 230, 295 n. 4.
Benfield, Anne, 376, 634.
Benfield, Bartholomew, 375.
Benfield, Elizabeth, 375.
Benfield, James, 375.
Benfield, Richard, **374,** 376, 534, 568, 587, 679.
Will of, 633-5.
Benfield, Robert, 4 n. 2, 5 and n. 6 cont'd., 14, 17, 35 n. 1, 37, 43, 46, 47, 69 n. 2, 72-88, 129, 177 and n. 5, 318, **374-6,** 633, 634, 645.
Benfield, William, 633.
Benfield's Rents, *see* London, streets of.
Bennyfield, Mary, 375.
Beoley, Worcester, 411.
Bequests to the poor, 635, 637, 639, 641, 644, 645, 650.
Berkeley, William, *The Lost Lady*, 99, 115.
Berwick, 147, 682.
Best, John, 160, 365.
Best, John, widow of, 368.
Betterton, Thomas, 165 n. 8, 506, 546, 597.
Biel, Jacob, *see* Pedel, Jacob.
Biland, Ambrose, *see* Beeland, Ambrose.
Bilboe's the Best Blade, see S. Rowley, *Hardshift for Husbands*.
Bills of Adventure, 682.
Birch, Elizabeth, 642.
Birch, Ewin, 404.
Birch, George, 14, 16, 17, 24, 72-88, **377,** 682.
Birche, Bridget, 377.
Birchen Lane, *see* London, streets of.
Bird, Anne, 378.
Bird, Christopher, 632.
Bird, Elizabeth, 379, 606.
Bird, Theophilus, 56, 57 and n. 2, 64, 69 n. 2, 73-89, 220, 221, 238, 246, 251, 324, 326 nn. 6 and 7, 327, 332, 336, **377-9.**
Bird, William, 135, 136, 138, 139, 140, 143, 147, 155, **379-80.**
Bird in a Cage, The, see Shirley.
Birredge, Bridget, 452.
Birredge, Elizabeth, 452.
Birredge, Robert, 452.
Bishops, 65 n. 2.
Bishopsgate, *see* London, streets of.
Bishops War, 244.
Blackboy alley, *see* London, streets of.

Blackfriars Gate, *see* London, streets of.

Blackfriars theatre, 2, 3 and n. 7, 4, 5 and n. 5, 16 n. 6, 17, 21, 25, 30 and n. 2, 31, 35, 37, 43, 47 and n. 3, 58, 59, 60, 61, 63, 101, 103, 104, 105, 149 n. 4, 184, 208, 225 n. 1, 264, 268, 273 n. 1, 319, 638, 692, 693, 694, 696.
Average takings, 30 n. 6.
Box at, 48.
Coaches ordered not to park near, 33; order rescinded, 33–4.
Cost of share in, 45.
Courtly audience at, 47 n. 3.
Favourite theatre of Sir Humphrey Mildmay, 48.
Gentlewomen at, 33.
Music at, 40.
Musicians at, 363.
Patrons of, 38–40.
Playing at, stopped by local petition, 5.
Popularity of, 30 n. 6.
Prestige of, 16 n. 6, 30 n. 6, 42, 225 n. 2, 307 and n. 1.
Proposal for removal of, 32.
Quarrels in, 42, 47, 48.
Queen's visit to, 39, 48 n. 5.
Receipts at, 68.
Rent of, 44.
Shareholder in, 466.
Shares in, 43–7.
Superiority of music at, 40.
Time of performance, 5.
Total takings, 23–4.
Transfer from, to the Globe, 3 n. 7.
Value of, 32 and n. 3.
Yearly rent, 45.
Black Lady, The, see Anon.
Blacknall, Grace, 565.
Blacksmith, 314.
Blackson, **380.**
Blackwall, Stepney, 265, 266.
Blagrave, Thomas, 380.
Blagrave, William, 35, 36, 40, 41, 42, 107, 112, 239 n. 3, 283 n. 7, 284, 291 and n. 6, 292, 299 n. b, 300, **380–1,** 648.
Blake, John, **381.**
Blaney, John, 167, 168 n. 2, 169, 171, 183 n. 2, 220, 221, 222, 246, **381–2,** 682.
Blind Beggar of Bethnal Green, The, see Day.
Bloody Banquet, The, see Anon.
Bloody Brother, The, see Beaumont and Fletcher.
Blumson, Robert, 640.
4595.2

Blumson, Thomas, 640.
Boarne, Thomas, *see* Bourne, Thomas.
Boar's Head, 158.
Bobarre, Monsieur, 675.
Bodie, Christopher, 603.
Bodleian Library, 104, 123, 127, 132.
Bodymaker, 455.
Boger, Jo., 474.
Bohemia, King and Queen of, company of, 153, 188, 219, **260–9,** 291 and n. 1, 308, 309.
Bohemia, King of, company of, *see* Palsgrave's company.
Bohemia, Queen of, company of, *see* Lady Elizabeth's company.
Bolland, James, 449.
Bond, Susan, 636.
Bond, Thomas, 168 n. 1, 303, 307, 308, 312, 321, **382–3.**
Bondman, The, see Massinger.
Bonduca, see Beaumont and Fletcher.
Bonen, William, *The Cra . . . Merchant, or Come to My Country House,* 185, 194, 206.
Two Kings in a Cottage, 150, 156.
Bonus, John, 390.
Booker, —, 545, 581.
Book-keeper, 118, 492, 494, 612.
Bookseller, 405, 473, 544, 545.
Boorne, Thomas, *see* Bourne, Thomas.
Booseley, Edward, 384.
Boothe, Joane, 650.
Borne, Mr., 139.
Borne, Theophilus, *see* Bird, Theophilus.
Borne, William, *see* Bird, William.
Borrose, —, **383.**
Bosgrave, George, 168 n. 1, **383–4,** 384.
Boteler, Ned, 676.
Boulton, Elizabeth, 650.
Boulton, William, 564.
Bourne, Constance, 385.
Bourne, Edmond, 385.
Bourne, Elizabeth, 384.
Bourne, Francis, 385.
Bourne, Mary, 385.
Bourne, Richard, 385.
Bourne, Susan, 384.
Bourne, Temperance, 385.
Bourne, Theophilus, *see* Bird, Theophilus.
Bourne, Thomas, 286, 297, **384–5.**
Bourne, William, *see* Bird, William.
Bowen, Alice, 371, 373.
Bowen, Elizabeth, 634, 646.
Bowen, Thomas, 371.

Bowen, Winifrid, 634, 646.
Bowers, Jeremiah, 385.
Bowers, John, 385.
Bowers, Mary, 385.
Bowers, Richard, 49 n. 2 cont'd., 73–89, **385.**
Bow Lane, *see* London, streets of.
Bowman, Francis, 301.
Bowrne, Thomas, *see* Bourne, Thomas.
Bowyer, Elizabeth, 635, 636.
Bowyer, Isabell, 386.
Bowyer, Michael, 56, 57, 64, 69, 73–89, 220, 221, 231, 232, 239, 246, **385-7.**
Will of, 635–6.
Bowyer, William, 386.
Box for money, *see* Theatre.
Box in theatre, *see* Theatre.
Boxer tumblers, 485.
Boy actors, *see* Players.
Bradford, 50.
Bradshaw, —, 318.
Bradshaw, Alexander, 356.
Bradshaw, John, 350.
Bradshaw, Richard, **387-8.**
Bradshaw's Rents, *see* London, streets of.
Bradstreet, John, **388.**
Bramfield, Bartholomew, *see* Bromefield, Bartholomew.
Brande, Thomas, 25.
Brandenburg, Elector of, 350, 578.
Brathwaite, Richard, *Wit's Recreations*, 605, 606.
Bray, Anthony, 286, 297, **388.**
Braybrooke, Richard Griffin, *The Private Correspondence of Lady Jane Cornwallis, 1613–44*, 42 n. 3.
Brend, Sir Mathew, 30, 647.
Brennoralt, *see* Suckling.
Brent, Nathaniel, 568.
Brentford, 500, 695.
Brew, Anthony, **388-9.**
Brewer, 482.
Brewer, Anthony, *The Lovesick King*, 388.
Brewer's servant, 431.
Bricklayer, 143, 619.
Bride, The, *see* Nabbes.
Bridegroom and the Madman, The, *see* Anon.
Bridge, Edward, **389**, 683.
Bridgewater, John, Earl of, 416.
Bridport, 213.
Briggs, Robert, **389.**
Brigham, Marke, 138, 143.
Bristol, 92, 151 n. 5, 156, 179, 193, 212, 282, 530, 574.

Bristol, Youths of Her Majesty's Royal Chamber of, 419.
Bristow Merchant, The, *see* Ford.
Broken Heart, The, *see* Ford.
Brome, Alexander, *The Cunning Lovers*, 331, 337.
Brome, George, 139.
Brome, Henry, 116.
Brome, Josias, 357.
Brome, Lucia, 390.
Brome, Richard, 63, 188 and n. 4, 192, 227, 241, 292 n. 1, 295 and n. 5, 330 n. 3, 334 n. 1, **389-90**, 488, 696 n. 1.
  Jealous of *Aglaura*, 58–60.
  Poet for the Cockpit, 330.
  Antipodes, The, 58–9, 242, 243 n. 2, 250, 283, 338, 372, 390.
  Court Beggar, The, 59–60, 63, 115, 243 n. 2, 324, 334, 337–8, 372–3.
  English Moor, The, 56 n. 1, 241, 250.
  Fault in Friendship, A (with Jonson), 206, 214.
  Five New Plays, 319.
  Honour of Young Ladies, The, *see The Lovesick Maid*.
  Jovial Crew, A, 324 n. 1 cont'd., 335, 338.
  Late Lancashire Witches, The, *see* Heywood.
  Lovesick Maid, The, 66, 96, 105, 115, 469.
  Mad Couple Well Matched, A, 338, 342.
  Northern Lass, The, 12, 13, 100, 105, 115–16.
  Novella, The, 66, 116.
  Queen and Concubine, The, 295, 300 and n. 1.
  Queen's Exchange, The, 116.
  Sparagus Garden, The, 285, 295, 300 and n. 1, 337, 444, 660.
Brome, Robert, 357.
Brome, Sara, 390.
Bromefield, Bartholomew, 633.
Bromefield, Richard, 137, **390.**
Brooke, William, 607.
Brothers, The, *see* Shirley.
Broughton, Ambrose, **390**, 682.
Browne, Anne, 637.
Browne, Cisley, 548.
Browne (*alias* Baskervile), Francis, 159, **391.**
Browne, John, 690.
Browne, Joseph, **391.**
Brown (*alias* Robins), Judith, 406.
Browne, Lucretia, 391.
Browne, Richard, **391**, 683.

Browne, Robert, **391**, 637.
Browne, Robert (haberdasher), 636.
Brown, William, 159, 169, 303, 307, 308, 310, 312, 321, 391, **391–2**, 645.
Will of, 636–7.
Bruce, Mrs., 16 n. 6.
Brunswick, Duke of, 16 n. 6.
Bryan, Mary, 392–3.
Buc, Sir George, 103, 106, 110, 112, 127, 130, 195, 206, 216, 422.
A Commentary upon the New Roll of Winchester, 422.
Buck Is a Thief, The, see Anon.
Buckingham, 535.
Buckingham, Duke of (First), 10 n. 6 cont'd., 22, 23 and n. 1, 128, 223 and n. 8, 224, 253, 266, 347.
Masque of, 518.
Buckingham, Duke of (Second), *Rehearsal, The*, 481.
Buckle, Elizabeth, 393.
Buckle, John, 275, 281, **393**.
Buckle, Mary, 393.
Bucksted, William, see Barksted, William.
Budsdell, Alse, 350.
Bugge, Andrew, 393.
Bugge, John, 190, 192, **393–4**, 634.
Bugge, Mary, 394.
Builder, 348.
Building forbidden, 365–7.
Buklank, Alexander, 16 n. 1, **394**.
Bullard, Alexander, 15, 16 n. 1, 73–89, **394**.
Bull-baiting, 510.
Bullen, George, in *The Athenaeum*, 23 n. 1.
Buller, Richard, 615.
Bullocke, Richard, 459.
Burbage, Alice (Walker), 9, 649.
Burbage, Cuthbert, 1, 2, 3, 4 nn. 1 and 2, 9, 30, 32 n. 3, 43, 44, 45, 46, **394–5**, 638, 641, 642, 649, 651.
Burbage, Mrs. Cuthbert, 9, 649.
Burbage, Elizabeth (Maxey), 9, 649.
Burbage, James, 135, 394, 395.
Burbage, Richard, 1, 2, 3, 4 n. 2, 5, 6, 7, 30, 43, 72–88, 137 n. 3, **395–7**, 436, 649.
Will of, 638.
Burbage, Sara, 9, 396, 552, 649.
Burbage, William, 32 n. 3, 43, 46, 396, 553, 645.
Burbage, Winifred (Robinson), 4 nn. 1 and 2, 46, 396, 638, 639.
Burfeild, Roger, see Barfield, Roger.
Burght, see Birch, George.

Burroughs, —, *The Fatal Friendship*, 116, 117, 123.
Burt, Nicholas (*see also* Nick), 69 n. 2, 73–89, 327 n. 3, 336, **397**.
Burton, Antony, **397**.
Burton, Samuel, 411.
Bussy D'Ambois, see Chapman.
Butcher, 690, 691.
Butler, Jos., 279, 545.
Byfield, Pentronill, 350.
Byland, Ambrose, see Beeland, Ambrose.

Cain, Andrew, see Cane, Andrew.
Calcot, Allin, 345.
Cambridge, 491, 537, 538, 539, 657 n. 4, 688.
Camby, —, **398**.
Campion, Thomas, 554.
Candlelight, see Theatres.
Cane, Andrew, 65 n. 2, 147 and n. 1, 148 and n. 5, 149, 152, 153, 155, 183, 184, 187, 192, 219, 263, 269, 275, 295, 302, 303 n. 1, 307, 308, 309, 311, 312 and n. 7 cont'd., 314 and n. 4, 315, 317 and n. 2, 321, 323, **398–401**, 691.
Cane, Mary, 399.
Cane, Thomas, 399.
Canterbury, 92, 213, 275, 276, 420.
Canterbury, Archbishop of, 16 n. 6, 38, 122, 327, 545, 654 n. 2 cont'd.
Capon, John, **401**.
Captain, The, see Beaumont and Fletcher.
Captives, or the Lost Recovered, The, see Heywood.
Capuchins, 329.
Cardinal, The, see Shirley.
Cardinal's Conspiracy, The, see Anon.
Careless Shepherdess, The, see Goffe.
Carew, Thomas, 224, 225, 228.
Coelum Britannicum, 676.
Carisbrook, 673.
Carlell, Lodowick, 676.
Arviragus and Felicia, I and II, 48, 51, 98, 99 n. s, 116.
Deserving Favourite, The, 84–5, 116, 117 n. 1, 375, 477, 479, 480, 502, 552, 569, 571, 575, 585, 594, 600, 692.
Fool Would Be a Favourite, The, 116, 117, 250.
Osmond, the Great Turk, 103, 116–17, 250.
Passionate Lovers, The, I and II, 66, 99, 100, 117, 446, 447.
Spartan Ladies, The, 39, 117 and n. 1, 123, 676, 681.

Carleton, Sir Dudley, 6, 10 nn. 2 and 3, 16 n. 6, 140, 141, 349, 396.
Carlisle, Earl of, 349.
Carpenter, 143, 358, 482, 499.
Carpenter, Anne, 402.
Carpenter, Elizabeth, 402.
Carpenter, Francesse, 402.
Carpenter, Robert, 401.
Carpenter, William, 176, 203 and n. 3, 208, 209, 210, 211, **401–2**, 682.
Carr, John, 298, 384, **402**.
Carrier, 486.
Carter Lane, see London, streets of.
Cartwright, Ann, 404.
Cartwright, Jane, 403.
Cartwright, Katherine, 404.
Cartwright, William (dramatist), The Royal Slave, 51, 52, 53 and n. 1, 58 n. 3, 98, 99 n. u, 117.
Cartwright, William, Senior, 136, 137, 138, 140, 142, 147, 148, 152, 153, 155, 261 and n. 3, 262 and n. 4, 263 and n. 1, 269, 275, 277, 281, 285, 286, 287, 288, 289 n. 4 cont'd., 290, 297, **402–4**, 682.
Cartwright, William, Junior, 286, 297, **404–5**.
Actor's Vindication, The, 405.
Carver, James, 265, 432.
Carver, William, 15, 73–89, **405**.
Cashe, Katherine, alias Nurse, alias Hutchenson, 365.
Casse, Robert, **406**.
Castle Ashby, 310.
Castle, Hester, 405.
Castle, Nicholas, 405.
Castle, Thomas, **405**.
Castleton, John, 522.
Catholicism, 329, 454.
Catiline, see Jonson.
Caue, Andrew, see Cane, Andrew.
Caulton, Richard, 564.
Cavalier taste, 681.
Cavendish, William, Duke of Newcastle, 512.
Country Captain, The, 66, 118, 343, 344.
Variety, The, 118.
Censorship, 7, 60, 277–8, 332–4.
Evasion of, 14.
Overruled, 103, 106–7.
Certificate of privilege, see Tickets of privilege.
Chabot, Admiral of France, see Chapman.
Challenge for Beauty, A, see Heywood.
Chamberlain, John, 3, 6, 10 n. 3, 16 n. 6, 136, 141, 149, 161, 162, 163, 349, 396.

Chamberlain, Lord, see Lord Chamberlain.
Chambers, William, 15, 72–88, **406**.
Chancellor, Ellen, 476.
Chancery records, 158.
Chancery suit, 56, 205 n. 3.
Chances, The, see Beaumont and Fletcher.
Chandler, 479, 564, 565, 615.
Changeling, The, see Middleton.
Changes, or Love in a Maze, see Shirley.
Chapman, George, 557.
Alphonsus, Emperor of Germany, see Anon.
Ball, The, see Shirley.
Bussy D'Ambois, 95 n. c, 97, 99, 118, 383, 436, 489, 585, 597.
Chabot, Admiral of France, 226 n. 7, 235, 251, 331, 338.
Conspiracy and Tragedy of Charles Duke of Byron, The, 118.
Revenge for Honour, see Glapthorne.
Wars of Pompey and Caesar, The, 118.
Widow's Tears, The, 117, 118.
Chapman, Henry, 317 n. 2.
City of Bath Described, The, 401.
Charing Cross, see London, streets of.
Charles I, 18, 34, 48, 52, 53, 218, 311 n. 1.
As censor, 61, 106–7.
Company of, see King's company.
Complaint about play, 333.
Gift to King's company from, 20, 26–7.
Journey to North, play on, 333.
Personal interest in the King's company, 35.
Prohibits stools on stage, 687.
Charles, Prince of Wales (later Charles I), 9, 10 n. 6 cont'd.
Company of, see Prince Charles's (I) company.
Charles, Prince of Wales (later Charles II), 424.
Company of, see Prince Charles's (II) company.
Charles Lewis, Prince of the Palatinate, 48, 51 and n. 2, 99 n. r, 133.
Charley, Alexander, 530.
Charterhouse, 142, 353.
Charterhouse, Master of, see George Garrard.
Chaste Gallant, The, see Massinger, Alexius.

Chaste Lover, The, see Massinger, *Alexius.*
Chatterton, —, 318, **406.**
Cherrington, Will, **406.**
Chettle and Dekker, *Troilus and Cressida,* 481.
Chichester, 513.
Chickley, Thomas, 678.
Children, company of, 167, 171, 283, 324–5.
Children of Her Majesty's Revels, 122.
Children of Paul's, 115.
Children of the Chapel, 118, 121 n. 1, 434.
Children of the King's Revels, 178.
Children of the Revels, 2, 114, 168, 194, 205 n. 5.
Chimney-boys, 315.
Christ Church, Oxford, 52, 117, 470.
Christenings, tables of, 667–72.
Church, Bar., 633.
Churchwarden, 466.
Church robes used in a play, 294.
Cid, The, see Rutter, Joseph.
Citizens' theatres, 693.
City Madam, The, see Massinger.
City Match, The, see Mayne.
City Night Cap, The, see Davenport.
City Shuffler, The, see Anon.
Claracilla, see Killigrew.
Clark, Hugh, 56, 57, 64, 69 n. 2, 73–89, 220, 221, 231, 232, 239, 246, **406–7.**
Clark, Sill, **407.**
Clarke, Elizabeth, 407.
Clarke, Ezekiell, 407.
Clarke, Mary, 431.
Clarke, Robert, 15, 72–88, **407.**
Clavell, John, *The Soddered Citizen,* 70, 84–5, 118, 194, 375, 446, 447, 452, 476, 477, 502, 516, 532, 534, 562, 563, 566, 569, 571, 575, 599, 600, 605, 606, 609.
Clay, Henry, 15, 72–88, **407–8.**
Clay, John, 407.
Clay, Nathaniel, 298, **408.**
Clay, Susanna, 408.
Clayton, Richard, 145, 147, 155, **408,** 682, 683.
Cleander, see Massinger.
Clement, Elizabeth, 499.
Cleodora, Queen of Aragon, see Habington, *The Queen of Aragon.*
Clerk, 350, 504, 644.
Clerk of the Bills, 438.
Clerkenwell, *see* London, streets of.
Clerkenwell Close, *see* London, streets of.

Clerkenwell Hill, *see* London, streets of.
Clewett, Master Doctor, 641.
Clearke, Hugh, *see* Clark, Hugh.
Clerke, Hugh, *see* Clark Hugh.
Cley, Henry, *see* Clay, Henry.
Clifford, Lady Anne, 112.
Clifford, Lord, 414.
Clifford family, 254.
Clifton, Sir Gervase, 42, 126, 552.
Clink, liberty of the, *see* London, streets of.
Clothmaker, 443.
Clown, 30 n. 6 cont'd.
Clun, Walter, 73–89, **408.**
Coaches, 4, 5 n. 1, 32, 42.
Ground for turning in, 32 n. 3.
Hackney, 4.
Cobb, John, 649.
Cobb, Mary, 649.
Cobb, Peter, 649.
Coborne, Edward, *see* Colborne, Edward.
Cock, Sir Robert, 576, 577.
Cockpit, *see* Phoenix.
Cockpit in Court, 28 n. 1, 67, 108, 118, 223 n. 8, 234.
Coffee House, 318.
Cokayne, Sir Aston, 319, 476.
Small Poems of Divers Sorts, 478.
Coke, Sir Edward, 396, 474.
Coke, Sir John (Mr. Secretary), 327, 354, 502, 678.
Coke, Lady, 396, 677.
Colborne, Alice, 409.
Colborne, Bartholomew, 409.
Colborne, Edward, 136, 139, 155, **408–9.**
Colborne, Elizabeth, 408, 409.
Colborne, John, 409.
Colborne, Margaret, 408.
Colborne, Martha, 409.
Cole, Mary, 640.
Cole, Thomas, 403.
Coley, Alice, 555.
College of God's Gift at Dulwich, 346, 395, 434, 506, 527, 659, 694.
College of Physicians, 190.
College plays, 52.
Collewell, Richard, **409.**
Collier, 508.
Collins, Edward, 49 n. 2 cont'd., 73–89, **409,** 508.
Collins, Ellen, 404.
Collins, Jeffrey, 15, 72–88, **409.**
Collison, William, 265, 266.
Colman, Elinor, 507.
Cologne, 451.

Comedians, 215, 287, 401, 415, 466, 499, 516, 532, 540, 541, 543, 548, 549, 550, 556, 562–7, 572, 580–1, 605, 612, 693.
Comedy, French, 25.
Come See a Wonder, see Day.
Commens, Elizabeth, 627.
Commission fraudulently obtained, 618–19.
Companies, breaking of, 69 and n. 2, 151–3, 165, 169–70, 177–8, 186–8, 209–10, 236–9, 268–9, 296, 684, 685.
  Capital stock of, 647.
  Competition between, 225 n. 2.
  In London, reduced in number, 1.
  Shares in, 632–3, 637, 651.
Company contract with theatre owners, 684.
Company financing, 474.
Company governors, 325, 330, 331, 334–5, 684, 685.
  Powers of, 686.
Company leaders, 176, 309.
Company managers, 3, 26 n. 5, 36, 54, 135, 137, 148–9, 159, 190, 198, 218, 229, 231, 241, 242, 324 n. 1, 364–5, 369, 390, 454, 465–7, 471–2, 492, 500, 512–13, 529, 537, 544, 560, 574, 590–8, 602–4, 613–15, 615–16, 665, 694.
Company relations with theatre owners, 684.
Company repertories, 108–34, 156–7, 174–5, 194–7, 214–17, 250–9, 282, 300–1, 322–3, 337–42.
Company treasurer, 503–4.
Composer, 432.
Compter, 267.
Compton, Sir Henry, 283 n. 7.
Compton, James, Earl of Northampton, 525, 608.
Comsbey, Ann, *see* Conisbey, Ann.
Conceited Duke, The, see Anon.
Condell, Elizabeth (Mrs. Henry Condell), 4 nn. 1 and 2, 44, 409–10, 413, 650.
  Will of, 638–40.
Condell, Henry, 1, 2, 4 n. 2, 5, 9, 17, 18, 19, 24, 30, 34 n. 3, 46, 72–88, 184, 410–12, 651.
  Will of, 640–2.
Condell, Judith, 413.
Condell, William, 413, 570, 638.
Conisbey, Anne, 631.
Conjurer, 266.
Conspiracy, The, see Killigrew, Henry.

Conspiracy and Tragedy of Charles Duke of Byron, The, see Chapman.
Constable, 266.
Constant Maid, The, see Shirley.
Contractor, 143.
Conway, Sir Edward, 11, 12, 47 n. 3, 277.
Cooke, Alexander, 429.
Cooke, Elizabeth, 405.
Cooke, John, *Greene's Tu Quoque*, 185 n. 9, 186 n. 8, 194, 690.
Cooke, Thomas, 5 n. 6, 7, 95 n. b.
Cooke, William, 308, 311, 321, 413.
Cooling, John, 413.
Cooper, 579.
Copyright, 54, 65.
Corden, Georg, 414.
Cordwainer, 265.
Cornet, 508.
Cornwall, 617.
Coronation, The, see Shirley.
Corporal, The, see Wilson.
Corporation of London, 5 n. 5.
Costine, John, 414.
Costly Whore, The, see Anon.
Costumes, 20, 21, 44, 58–60, 120, 136, 141, 144, 162, 199 n. 2, 202 n. 1, 204, 228, 234, 242–3 and notes, 312, 330, 367, 413, 417, 436, 453, 491, 512, 534, 555, 562, 564, 576, 591, 592, 595, 632, 633, 654 n. 2 cont'd.
  Gift of, 39 and n. 1, 58 and n. 3.
  Letter about, 211.
  Loan of, 52.
  Repair of, 558.
Cothelston, near Derby, 618.
Cotterell, Sir Charles, 512.
Cotton, John, 414.
Counterfeiting, 536.
Country Captain, The, see Cavendish.
Courage of Love, The, see Davenant, *Love and Honour*.
Coursing of a Hare, or the Madcap, see Heminges.
Court Beggar, The, see Brome.
Court of Common Council, 400.
Court of High Commission, 38, 440, 442, 561, 568.
Court of Probate, 314.
Court of Requests, 46, 475.
Court performances, 1, 3, 4, 7, 20, 21, 23, 27–9, 51–2, 57, 60, 62, 64, 94–100, 176, 186, 194, 213, 224, 229, 233, 249, 299, 322, 336.
  Cost of, 53 n. 1.
Court Secret, The, see Shirley.
Covent Garden, see Nabbes.
Covent Garden, *see* London, streets of.

Coventry, 92, 93, 156, 172, 173, 179, 193, 212, 213, 248, 274, 280 n. 2, 282, 298, 299, 322, 344, 419, 420, 421, 452, 458, 484, 514, 530, 600, 613, 617.
Cow Cross, see London, streets of.
Cowley, Abraham, Love's Riddle, 553.
Cowley, Elizabeth, 377, 414, 642.
Cowley, Richard, 2, 3, 5 n. 6 cont'd., 414.
Will of, 642.
Cox, Andrew, 415.
Cox, Beatrice, 415.
Cox, Katherine, 415.
Cox, Robert, 327 n. 4, 332, 336, 414-15.
Coxcomb, The, see Beaumont and Fletcher.
Craddell, see Gradwell.
Cra . . . Merchant, or Come to My Country House, The, see Bonen.
Crane, Ralph, 127, 415-16.
Pilgrim's New Year's Gift, The, 416.
Works of Mercy, The, 415, 416.
Crate, Christopher, 416.
Crate, Kathe, 416.
Craven District, 92, 173, 212, 248.
Craven, Elisabeth, 370.
Crawford, James, 416-17.
Creswell, Thomas, 384.
Crew, 26.
Cripplegate, see London, streets of.
Criticism, see Plays, criticism of.
Croftes, Anthony, 676.
Croftes, Cecily, 677.
Croftes, Mr., 20.
Crofts, Edward, 355.
Crofts, Jack, 47.
Crofts, Will, 47.
Crome, William, 417, 578.
Cromes, —, 294, 417.
Cromwell, Oliver, 487.
Crosfield, Thomas, 26 n. 5 cont'd., 30 n. 6, 231, 246, 274, 285, 293, 297 and n. b, 309, 310.
Diary of, 688-9.
Cross, Robert, 618.
Cross Keys, 1, 491, 682.
Crosse, Katherine, 370.
Cruel Brother, The, see Davenant.
Cuffle, Major, 549.
Cumber, John, 165, 167, 168 n. 2, 169, 171, 183 n. 2, 204, 417-18, 682.
Cunning Lovers, The, see Brome, Alexander.
Cupid's Festival, see Anon.

Cupid's Revenge, see Beaumont and Fletcher.
Cupid's Vagaries, see Rowley, Samuel, Hymen's Holidays.
Curt, 418.
Curtain, The, 1, 158, 201 n. 2, 205 and n. 3, 206, 207, 208, 370, 531, 555, 558, 651.
Custom House of London, 596.
Custom of the Country, The, see Beaumont and Fletcher.
Cutler, 564.
Cymbeline, see Shakespeare.
Cynthia's Revels, see Jonson.

D., J., The Knave in Grain New Vampt, see Anon.
D., T., The Bloody Banquet, see Anon.
Daborne, Robert, 176, 177 n. 5, 199 n. 2, 418.
Poor Men's Comfort, The, 174, 362, 453, 509, 510, 559, 560, 626.
Dallison, Sir Thomas, 397, 463, 571, 694.
Dambrooke, Sara, 562, 564, 565.
Will of, 642.
Damport, Edward, 418-19.
Danbury, Essex, 673.
Dance, Ann, 421.
Dancer, John, Nicomede, 473.
Dancers, 53 n. 1, 496, 515, 517-18, 522, 541, 563, 578, 617.
Dancers on the ropes, 150, 456, 517, 521, 522, 613, 657, 662, 680.
Dancing in theatres, see Theatres.
Dancing master, 517.
Daniel, John, 419-20.
Daniel, Samuel, 419.
Daniel, William, 298, 299, 420-1, 640.
Danner, John, 190 n. 2, 421.
Danzig, 486.
D'Aunay, Josias, see Floridor, Josias.
Daunce, John, 190, 192, 421.
Dausse, Robert, see Dawes, Robert.
Davenant, William, 225, 240 n. 2, 303 n. 1, 324, 334, 335, 421-2.
Courage of Love, The, see Love and Honour.
Cruel Brother, The, 104, 118.
Distresses, The, 66, 119.
Fair Favorite, The, 66, 99, 100, 108, 119.
Just Italian, The, 26, 105, 119, 224, 228.
Love and Honour, 40, 51, 66, 98, 107, 119, 676, 681.
News from Plymouth, 66, 107, 119, 660.

Davenant, William (*contd.*):
Nonpareilles or the Matchless Maids, The, see Love and Honour.
Platonic Lovers, The, 107, 119, 503, 661.
Playhouse to Be Let, The, 13.
Temple of Love, The, 677.
Unfortunate Lovers, The, 48 n. 5, 66, 99, 107, 119.
Wits, The, 39, 61, 97, 106–7, 119, 675, 681.
Davenport, Edward, 327 n. 4, 332, 336, **422.**
Davenport, Rebecca, 422.
Davenport, Robert, *City Night Cap, The,* 186, 194, 219 n. 4, 251, 331, 338.
Crown for a Conqueror, A, 387, 553.
History of Henry the First, The, 103, 119–20.
King John and Matilda, 221 n. 1, 246, 249, 251, 331, 338, 345, 353, 387, 407, 445, 482, 525, 528, 573, 583, 608, 628, 692.
New Trick to Cheat the Devil, A, 331, 338.
Davenport, Thomas, 514.
Davies, Sir John, 557.
Davige, Lawrence, 266.
Dawbridgecourt, George, 561.
Dawes, Robert, 198, 211, **422.**
Cupid's Festival, 422.
Day, Hugh, 479.
Day, John, 426.
Bellman of Paris, The, see Dekker.
Blind Beggar of Bethnal Green, The, 322, 407.
Come See a Wonder, 206.
Day, Thomas, **422–3.**
De Caine, Andrew, *see* Cane, Andrew.
Dekker, Thomas, 20, 170 n. 1, 184, 208.
Bellman of Paris, The, 206, 209, 214.
Bristow Merchant, The, see Ford.
Fairy Knight, The, see Ford.
Fatal Dowry, The, see Massinger.
Guy of Warwick (with Rowley), 228.
Honest Whore, The (with Middleton), 251.
Late Murder in Whitechapel, or Keep the Widow Waking (with Ford, Rowley, and Webster), 170 n. 1, 208, 209, 214, 380.
Match Me in London, 185 and n. 5, 195.

Dekker, Thomas (*contd.*):
Owl's Almanack, 161 n. 2.
Roaring Girl, The (with Middleton), 136 n. 3.
Rod for Run-aways, A, 19.
Shoemaker's Holiday, The, 535.
Sun's Darling, The (with Ford), 185, 195, 331, 336, 338–9, 379, 525.
Virgin Martyr, The (with Massinger), 166, 174.
Witch of Edmonton, The (with Ford and Rowley), 202 n. 6, 204 n. 1, 205, 209, 213, 214, 215, 251–2, 378, 425, 433, 459–60, 506, 554.
de Lau, Hurfries, *see* Lau, Hurfries de.
Demetrius and Enanthe, see Beaumont and Fletcher.
Denham, John, *The Sophy,* 120.
Denmark House, 201 n. 1 cont'd., 232.
Denshfield, Katherine, 449.
Denygten, *see* Downton, Thomas.
Derby House, 401.
Dermiere, Barbara, 456.
Dermiere, John, 456.
Deserving Favourite, The, see Carlell.
Desmus, Ralph, *Merlinus Anonymous,* 600.
de Soulas, Josias, *see* Floridor, Josias.
Devil in plays, 30 n. 6 cont'd.
Devil Is an Ass, The, see Jonson.
Devil of Dowgate, or Usury Put to Use, The, see Beaumont and Fletcher.
Devil's Law Case, The, see Webster.
D'Ewes, Sir Simonds, 64.
Diaries, 94, 112, 114, 123, 128, 132, 673–81.
Diaries and Despatches of the Venetian Embassy at the Court of King James I in the Years 1617–18, translated by Rawdon Brown, 136 n. 4.
Diary or an Exact Journal, A, see Newspapers.
Dicconson, Frances, 41.
Dickens, Ro., 642, 651.
Digby, Sir Kenelm, 42, 47, 416, 493.
Digby, Lady Venetia, 248 n. h.
Dillon, —, 413.
Diodate, John, 639.
Discontented Colonel, The, see Suckling, *Brennoralt.*
Dishley, *see* Distle.
Distle, —, **423.**
Distresses, The, see Davenant.

Dixon, Thomas, 201 n. 1, 422, **423**.
Dobson, John, 220, 246, **423.**
Doctor (*see also* Barber-Chirurgion, Physician, and Surgeon), 641.
Doctor in physic, 634.
Doctor Faustus, see Marlowe.
Doctor Lambe and the Witches, see Anon.
Doctors' Commons, *see* London, streets of.
Doge, letter to, 204.
Doncaster, 92, 93, 193, 248, 282, 423, 496
Doncaster, Viscount, 6.
Donne, Constance, 349.
Donne, John, 349, 468, 557.
Don Quixote, 541.
Donstone, James, 135.
Dorchester, Viscount, 302.
Doriela, Dr., 676, 677, 678.
Dorney, Margaret, 363.
Dorney, Richard, 363.
Dorset, Edward Sackville, Earl of, 223, 238, 239 and n. 3, 283 n. 7, 303, 304 and n. 2, 309, 380, 423–4, 684.
Dorset, Mary, Countess of, 424.
Double Marriage, The, see Beaumont and Fletcher.
Doubtful Heir, The, see Shirley.
Doughten or Doughton, Thomas, *see* Downton, Thomas.
Dounton, Thomas, *see* Downton, Thomas.
Doutone, Thomas, *see* Downton, Thomas.
Dover, 92, 156, 172, 173, 180, 193, 212, 213, 218, 313, 322.
Dover, Anthony, 286, 288, 290, 297, **425.**
Dover, Mary, 650.
Dowdeswell, Roger, 403.
Dowghton, Thomas, *see* Downton, Thomas.
Dowgill, Robert, 677.
Dowland, Robert, *see* Dulandt, Robert.
Dowle, Rowland, 49 n. 2 cont'd., 73–89, **425–6.**
Downes, John, *Roscius Anglicanus*, 545.
Downton, Anne, 426, 642.
Downton, Ed., 643.
Downton, Jane, 426, 643.
Downton, Thomas, Senior, 135, 136, 137, 139, 142, 155, **426**, 623.
Will of, 642–3.
Downton, Thomas, Junior, 299, **426–7.**

Dowson, Agnes, 650.
Dowten or Dowton, Thomas, *see* Downton, Thomas.
Dramatic coach, 371.
Dramatists, *see* Playwrights.
Draper, 544, 545, 648.
Drapers' company, 545.
Drayton, Michael, 557.
    Oldcastle (with Hathway, Munday, and Wilson), 28, 96, 99, 120.
Draytwiche, Worcester, 469.
Dresden, 451.
Drewe, Bartholomew, **427.**
Drewe, Elizabeth, 428.
Drewe, Francis, 428.
Drewe, George, 427.
Drewe, Robert, 428.
Drewe, Thomas, 163, 169 n. 2, 171, 202, **427–8.**
Drewe, Thomas, *Daniel Ben Alexander, the Converted Jew*, 428.
Dreydon, Sir John, 442.
Drington, Richard, *see* Errington, Richard.
Drinking Academy, The, see Randolph.
Drue, Thomas, *Life of the Duchess of Suffolk, The*, 150, 156, 427, 428.
    Woman's Mistake, The, 427, 428.
Drum, to advertise provincial performances, 608–9, 686.
Drummer, 473.
Drummond, William, 436.
Drury Lane, 675.
Dublin, 131.
    First theatre in, 518.
Duchess of Malfi, The, see Webster.
Dudley, Lord, 423.
Dudlowe, Joane, 536.
Duke, John, 1, 158, **428–9.**
Duke, The, see Shirley.
Duke of Lerma, The, see Henry Shirley, *The Spanish Duke of Lerma*.
Duke of Milan, The, see Massinger.
Duke's Mistress, The, see Shirley.
Dulandt, Robert, **429.**
Dulwich, 138, 143, 403, 405, 483, 486, 510.
    Mayor of, 346.
Dulwich College, *see* College of God's Gift at Dulwich.
Dulwich College *v.* Tobias Lisle and Thomas Grymes, 568.
Dumb Bawd of Venice, The, see Henry Shirley.
Dumb show, 579.
Dunkirk, 657 n. 4.
Dunwich, 93, 172, 212.

Durham, Henry, 558.
Du Rocher, R. M., *La Melise*, 234.
Duryer, *Alcimedon*, 235 n. 1.
Dutch Courtesan, The, see Marston.
Dutch Painter and the French Brawle, The, see Anon.
Dutton, Henry, 400.
Dutton, Thomas, 649.
Dylke, Joane, 390.
Dyot, Richard, 471.
Dysart, Earl of, 61.
Dyson, Hum., 642, 651.

Earle, John, 316, 321, **429.**
East Anglia, 509 n. 1.
Easton, 310.
Easton, Jane, 426.
Easton, Oliver, 426.
East Smithfield, see London, streets of.
Eaton, Henry, 624.
Eaton, William, **429.**
Ecclesiastical Court, 641.
Eccleston, William, 5 and n. 6, 9, 16, 72–88, 176, **429–31,** 650.
Edinburgh, 180 and n. 12.
Edisbury, Kenrick, 473.
Edmans, John, see Edmonds, John.
Edmonds, John, 137, 141 and n. 1, 171 and n. b, **431.**
Edmondes, Sir Thomas, 349.
Edmund Ironside, see Anon.
Edward II, see Marlowe.
Eglestone, William, see Eccleston, William.
Elder Brother, The, see Beaumont and Fletcher.
Elector Palatine, see Palsgrave, The.
Eliot, Tom, 47.
Elitt, Joane, 361.
Elizabeth, Lady, Princess of England, Electress Palatine, Queen of Bohemia, 48, 267, 657 n. 4.
   Company of, 121 n. 1, 137 n. 3, 153, **176–97,** 183, 200, 202 n. 6, 203 n. 1, 205, 206, 208, 219, 220, 221, 261, 262 and n. 3, 263, 268, 308.
   Marriage of, 136, 185 n. 7.
Elizabeth, Queen of England, 1, 2.
   Company of, 562.
   Servant of, 466.
Ellis, see Guest, Ellis, and Bedowe, Ellis.
Ellis, William, 471.
Elton, Richard, 393.
Emmerson, Margaret, 433.
Emperor of the East, The, see Massinger.

Emperor Valentinian, The, see Beaumont and Fletcher, *Valentinian.*
Endfield, Middlesex, 428.
English Moor or the Mock Marriage, The, see Brome.
English Profit, The, see Rowley, Samuel, *Richard the Third.*
English Traveller, The, see Heywood.
Entertainer, 578, 617.
Entertainment, The, see Randolph, *The Muses' Looking Glass.*
Epicoene, see Jonson.
Epilogues, 440, 691.
   Contract to write, 390.
Errington, Richard, 271, 281, 299, **431–2.**
Ertzer, Robert, see Archer, Robert.
Esdaile, Arundel, 487–8.
Essex, Earl of, 65, 106, 132, 504, 568, 666.
Essex House, 283 n. 7 cont'd.
Estoteville, George, see Stutville, George.
Estoutevile, George, see Stutville, George.
Evans, Gouldwais, **432.**
Evans, Thomas, 2, 4 n. 2.
Every Man in His Humour, see Jonson.
Ewer, Richard, 502.
Example, The, see Shirley.
Exeter, 168 n. 1, 180, 193, 212, 485.
Extras in plays, 318.
Eydwartt, Johann, **432.**

Fair Anchoress of Pausilippo, The, see Massinger.
Fair Favourite, The, see Davenant.
Fair Foul One or the Baiting of the Jealous Knight, The, see Smith.
Fair Maid of the Inn, The, see Beaumont and Fletcher.
Fair Maid of the West, The, see Heywood.
Fair Quarrel, A, see Middleton.
Fair Star of Antwerp, The, see Anon.
Fairy Knight, The, see Ford.
Faithful Servant, The, see Shirley, *The Grateful Servant.*
Faithful Shepherdess, The, see Beaumont and Fletcher.
False One, The, see Beaumont and Fletcher.
Falstaff, see Shakespeare, *Henry IV, Parts I and II.*
Famous Victories of Henry the Fifth, The, see Anon.
Fancies Chaste and Noble, The, see Ford.

Fancies' Theatre, see Tatham.
Fane, Sir Henry, 64.
Farnaby, Giles, 432.
Farnaby, Richard, **432.**
Farnborough, Warwick, 371.
Fatal Contract, The, see William Heminges.
Fatal Dowry, The, see Massinger.
Fatal Friendship, The, see Burroughes.
Father's Own Son, see Beaumont and Fletcher, *Monsieur Thomas.*
Faulkland, Lord, 123.
Faulkner, Thomas, 264, 265, **432–3.**
Fault in Friendship, A, see Brome.
Fawne, Catherine, 452.
Fearne, Sir John, 349.
Febure, M. le, riding-school of, 235.
Feltmaker's Apprentice, 167.
Fencer, 318, 360, 406, 442, 688.
Fenn, Ezekiel, 238, **2**46, 251, 326 nn. 6 and 7, 327, 332, 336, **433–4.**
Fenn, Lucie, 433.
Fenn, Mauritii, 433.
Ferdinand III, Emperor, 406.
Ferret, James, 286, 297, **434.**
Ferris, Deavid (?), 272, 281, **434.**
Fiddlers, 363, 469, 621.
Fideli, Signior, 694.
Field, Henry, 286, 297, **434.**
Field, John, 434.
Field, Nathan, 5 and n 6 cont'd., 8, 72–88, 124 n. 2, 176, 177 and n. 3, 203 n. 1, **434–6,** 696.
Amends for Ladies, 176, 198, 201 n. 2, **435,** 436.
Fatal Dowry, The, see Massinger.
Jeweller of Amsterdam, The (with Fletcher and Massinger), 435.
Woman Is a Weathercock, A, 435.
Field, Nathaniel, 434, 436.
Field, Theophilus, Bishop of Llandaff, 434.
Finch, Elizabeth, 641.
Finch, Harbert, 641.
Finch, Mary, 506.
Fine Companion, A, see Marmion.
Finett, Sir John, 46, 376, 534, 586.
Finsbury Fields, *see* London, streets of.
Fintrye, Robert, **437.**
Fisher, John, 143, 144, **437,** 545.
Fishmonger, 576.
Fitche, —, 567.
Fitche, Winifred, 568, 634.
Fitzmorris, Robert, 413.
Five New Plays, see Brome.
Flanders, 512, 694.

Flecknoe, Richard, *Epigrams of All Sorts,* 436.
Love's Dominion, 324, 373–4.
Love's Kingdom, 436.
Fleet Conduit, *see* London, streets of.
Fleet street, *see* London, streets of.
Fletcher, John, *see* Beaumont and Fletcher.
Fletcher, Jone, 442.
Fletcher, Lawrence, 2.
Flod, William, 564.
Floridor, Josias, 235 n. 1, **437.**
Flower, Edmund, 363.
Folger Shakespeare Library, 443.
Publications, 27 n. 2.
Fool and Her Maidenhead Soon Parted, A, see Anon.
Fool Would Be a Favorite, The, see Carlell.
Forced Lady, The, see Massinger.
Ford, John, of Gray's Inn, 477.
Ford, John, 184, **488.**
Beauty in a Trance, 28, 65, 96, 120.
Bristow Merchant, The, 150, 151, 156.
Broken Heart, The, 120.
Fairy Knight, The, 206 n. 3, 214.
Fancies Chaste and Noble, The, 252.
Lady's Trial, The, 329, 338, 378.
Late Murder in Whitechapel, The, see Dekker.
Lover's Melancholy, The, 82–3, 104, 120, 361, 375, 447, 452, 474, 477, 479, 502, 524, 533, 546, 565, 570, 575, 585, 594, 600, 605, 612.
Love's Sacrifice, 252, 331, 338.
Perkin Warbeck, 252.
Queen, The, see Anon.
Sun's Darling, The, see Dekker.
'Tis Pity She's a Whore, 252, 331, 338.
Witch of Edmonton, The, see Dekker.
Formido, Cornelius, *The Governor,* 52, 98, 120.
Forster collection, 132.
Fortune by Land and Sea, see Heywood.
Fortune's Tennis, see Anon.
Fortune (ship), 473.
Fortune Inn, 137 n. 6.
Fortune theatre, 4 n. 3, 25, 135, 136, 137 and n. 6, 138, 138–9, 140, 141, 145, 153, 163, 184, 207, 208, 263, 264, 264–9, 273 n. 1, 274, 275, 276, 280, 289 n. 4 cont'd., 292, 306 n. 3, 307, 309,

Fortune theatre (*contd.*):
312 and n. 7 cont'd., 315 and n. 2, 317 and n. 2, 319, 320, 346, 347, 348, 558, 612, 680, 683, 690, 693, 694.
Conduct of audiences at, 318.
Contractors for, 143.
Early distinction of, 136–7, 140.
Fire at, 141 and n. 4.
First, 146.
Leases, 138–9, 143–4.
Manager of, 279.
New, 144.
Opening of new, 144–6 and 144 n. 4.
Playwrights for, 690.
Raided, 278.
Rebuilding of, 142–6.
Rent of, 138.
Reputation of, 268, 280, 315, 319.
Riot at, 264–6.
Stock in, 144.
Taphouse at, 138, 143.
Typical audience at, 268.
Foster, —, 510.
Foster, Alexander, 176, 181, 182, 188, 189 and n. 3, 192, **437–8**.
Foster, Francis, 264, 265.
Foster, Thomas, 199 n. 2.
Foster, William, 265.
Fouch, Richard, 307, 308, 321, **439**.
Four companies, 194, 206, 236, 621, 666 and n. 1.
Four Plays in One, see Beaumont and Fletcher.
Four Sons of Amon, The, see Anon.
Fowler, Adam, 439.
Fowler, Elizabeth, 439.
Fowler, Jane, 439.
Fowler, Richard, 138, 139, 147, 148, 152, 153, 155, 261 and n. 3, 262 and n. 4, 263 and n. 1, 269, 303, 307, 308, 318, 319, 321, **439–40**, 682, 691.
Fowler, Thomas, 439.
Fox, The, see Jonson, *Volpone.*
Foxley, 401.
France, 421.
Franke, Robert, 265, 266.
Frankfort, 451.
Franklin, —, 293, 689.
Fraud in players' activities, 190.
Fraud in swearing players, 358–9.
Frederick and Basilea, see Anon.
Frederick V, *see* Palsgrave, The.
Freeman, Elizabeth, 439.
French ambassador, 6, 283 n. 7 cont'd.
French, Anne, 634.

French players, 25, 207, 233–5, 272–3 and 273 n. 1, 437, 496, 654 n. 2.
French, Rebecca, 634.
French, Sarah, 634.
French, Thomas, 634.
Friar Bacon and Friar Bungay, see Greene.
Fulham, 19, 412, 638, 639, 641.
Fynch, Herbert, 638.

Galleries, 136, 199 n. 2, 202, 318.
Receipts from, 44.
Game at Chess, A, see Middleton.
Game players, 616.
Gamester, The, see Shirley.
Gaoler, 354.
Gardener, 352, 564.
Garfield, Benjamin, 380.
Garland, John, 198, 211.
Garman, —, 142.
Garrard, George, 33, 39 n. 1, 47, 48, 56 n. 3, 58, 131, 244, 329, 654 n. 2 cont'd., 660, 662, 665.
Garrell, —, 558.
Garrett, John, 164 n. 4 cont'd., 171 and n. b, 440.
Garrett, William, 497.
Garst, *see* Guest, Ellis.
Garter King of Arms, 469.
Gary, Giles, 176.
Gascoigne, Alice, 441.
Gascoigne, Jane, 441.
Gascoigne, William, 15, 73–89, **440–1**.
Gate House, 568.
Gatherer, 346, 558, 588, 616, 622, 684.
Gathering places, 686.
Gawthorpe Hall, Lancs., 172, 423.
Gayton, Edmond, *Pleasant Notes upon Don Quixote*, 690–1.
Gee, John, *New Shreds of the Old Snare*, 207–8, 396–7.
Gell, Robert, 129, 253.
Gellius, Gedeon, 441.
Gentleman of Venice, The, see Shirley.
George, **441**.
George a Greene, see Anon.
George Alley in Golding Lane, *see* London, streets of.
Gerard, Lord, 496.
Gerdler, Adam, **441**.
Germany, 6.
English actors in, 165, 350, 351, 388, 391, 406, 429, 432, 441, 451, 473, 484, 486, 495, 521, 522, 537, 543, 553, 559, 561, 578, 579, 599, 613, 615.

Gerrard, Edward, 358, 359.
Gersley, Sir George, 239 n. 3, 283 n. 7 cont'd., 284.
Gest, Ellis, *see* Guest, Ellis.
Geyst, Ellis, *see* Guest, Ellis.
Ghost writing, 60.
Gibbens, Margaret, 465.
Gibbes, George, **441**.
Gibbon's Tennis Court, 373.
Gibborne, Thomas, *see* Gilbourne, Thomas.
Gibbs, Alice, 442.
Gibbs, Anthony, **441–2**.
Gibbs, Edward, 285, 287, 288, 290, 297, 318, 324, 327 n. 1, 332, 336, **442**.
Gibbs, Jone, 442.
Gibbs, Mary, 442.
Gibbs, Susan, 442.
Gibes, Anthony, *see* Gibbs, Anthony.
Gibson, —, **442–3**.
Gibson, H., 323, **443**.
Gilbourne, Thomas, **443**.
Gilburne, Samuel, **443**.
Gilbye, John, 266.
Gilder, —, 642.
Giles, George, 189, 192, **443–4**.
Giles, Gideon, *see* Gellius, Gedeon.
Giles, Launcelot, 384.
Gill, Alexander, 42, 122, 268, 503, 594.
Gill, John, 166 and n. 5, 361.
Gilman, Robert, 188, 189 and n. 3, 192, **444**.
Gimber, Widow, 641.
Glapthorne, Henry, 509 n. 1.
  Albertus Wallenstein, 120.
  Argalus and Parthenia, 336 and n. d, 339.
  Hollander, The, 236 and n. 6, 252, 336 and n. f, 339.
  Ladies' Privilege, The, 336 and n. e, 339.
  Lady Mother, The, 300, 381, 482.
  Love's Trial, see The Hollander.
  Parricide, The, 206 n. 3.
  Poems, 433.
  Revenge for Honour, 213 n. b, 216.
  Wit in a Constable, 339.
Globe Alley, *see* London, streets of.
Globe theatre, 1, 2, 3 and n. 7, 4 and n. 1, 5, 10 and n. 6 cont'd., 17, 30 and n. 6, 40, 43, 44, 101, 103, 129, 141 n. 4; 146, 149 n. 4, 207, 208, 225 n. 1, 264, 307, 319, 612, 638, 651, 658, 675, 694.
  And Blackfriars, relative importance of, 30 n. 6.

Globe theatre (*contd.*) :
  Character of audience at, 10 n. 6.
  Cost of share in, 45.
  First, 146.
  Garden of, 44.
  Intended riot at, 21.
  Large stage of, 30 n. 6 cont'd.
  Lease of, 30, 31, 45.
  Performance at, 22.
  Proportion of plays seen at, 30 n. 2.
  Rent of, 44.
  Second, 146.
    Cost of building, 45.
    Income from shares in, 45.
    Shareholder in, 466.
  Shares in, 43–7.
  Taphouse, 44.
  Tenement, 44.
  Total takings, 23–4.
  Type of plays at, 30 n. 6 cont'd.
  Yearly rent, 45.
Gloucester, 299, 411, 421, 613.
Gloves for boy actors in new plays, 687.
Goad, Christopher, 220, 223 n. 6, 246, 249 n. f cont'd., 285, 286, 288, 289 n. 4, 290, 291 n. 2, 297, **444–5**.
Goad, Constance, 445.
Goad, Elizabeth, 445.
Goad, John, 445.
Goad, Mary, 445.
Goad, Michael, 445.
Goad, Roger, 444.
Goad, Ruth, 445.
Goad, Symon, 445.
Goad, Timothy, 445.
Goblins, The, see Suckling.
Godwin, Richard, 307, 308, 321, **445**.
Goffe, Alexander, *see* Gough, Alexander.
Goffe, Robert, *see* Gough, Robert.
Goffe, Thomas, *The Careless Shepherdess*, 540, 541.
Golding, —, **445–6**.
Golding Lane, *see* London, streets of.
Goldsmith, 275, 398, 401, 499.
Gollancz, Sir Israel, 412.
Gomond, Edward, 421. [*at Chess*.
Gondomar, see Middleton, *A Game*
Gondomar, Count of, 12, 140 n. 9.
Good, Christopher, *see* Goad, Christopher.
Goodale, Edward, 634.
Goodman, Jo., 490.
Gord, Francis, 533.
Gore, John, 366.
Gore, William, 366.

Goring, Lord, 414.
Gosson, Henry, **446**, 682.
Gost, Ellis, *see* Guest, Ellis.
Gouge, William, 5.
Gough, Alexander, 49, 70, 73–89, **446–7**.
Gough, Robert, 5, 16, 72–88, **447–8** 682, 683.
Govell, R., *A Mask*, *see* Gunnell, Richard.
Governor, The, see Formido.
Governor of the company, *see* Company governors.
Gowdy, Framlingham, 312.
Grace, Charles, 449.
Grace, Elizabeth, 449.
Grace, Francis, 136, 138, 140 and n. 1, 147, 149, 155, **448–9**, 682.
Grace, Increase, 449
Grace, John, 449.
Grace, Margaret, 449.
Grace, Richard, 145, 147, 155, **449– 50**, 683.
Grace, Sara, 449.
Gradell, Henry, *see* Gradwell, Henry.
Gradwell, Alice, 450.
Gradwell, Anne, 451.
Gradwell, Elizabeth, 451.
Gradwell, Francys, 450.
Gradwell, Henry, 303, 307, 308, 321, 323, **450**.
Gradwell, Jane, 450.
Gradwell, Richard, **450–1**.
Gramercy Wit, see Anon.
Grateful Servant, The, see Shirley, *The Faithful Servant*.
Graunt, John, *Natural and Political Observations Mentioned in a Following Index and Made upon the Bills of Mortality*, 667.
Graves, Elizabeth, 638.
Gravesend, 145.
Gray, Margaret, *see* Grey, Margaret.
Gray, Patrick, 265.
Gray's Inn, 477, 488, 633.
Gray's Inn Lane, *see* London, streets of.
Great Duke, The, see Massinger, *The Great Duke of Florence*.
Great Duke of Florence, The, see Massinger.
Greeks and Trojans, The, see Anon.
Greene, John, 110, 114, 123, 128, 132, 235, 250, 255, 258, **451**.
Greene, Robert, saddler, 564.
Greene, Robert, *Friar Bacon and Friar Bungay*, 156.
George a Greene, the Pinner of Wakefield, see Anon.

Greene Robert (*contd.*):
Looking Glass for London and England, A (with Lodge), 542, 543.
Greene, Susan Baskervile, 637.
Greene, Thomas, 158, 364, **451**, 531, 636.
Greene's Tu Quoque, see Cook.
Greville, Curtis, 73–89, 147 and n. 1, 149, 155, 183, 187, 192, 285, 287, 288, 290, 297, **451–2**.
Greville, Fulke, *Alaham*, 213 n. b.
Grey, Margaret, **452**, 545, 659.
Griffin, Henry, 384.
Grigg, Michael, 457.
Grimes, Arthuret, *see* Grymes, Anthony.
Grimes, Thomas, 545.
Grimsthorpe, 310.
Grivell, *see* Greville, Curtis.
Grocer, 564, 641, 643.
Grooms of the Chamber, 2, 7, 56, 64, 88–9, 188–9, 189, 190, 191, 271, 303, 309, 311, 315 n. 2, 321, 324 n. 1.
Grooms of the Revels, 620.
Grub street, *see* London, streets of.
Grymes, Anthony, **452**.
Grymes, John, 162, 366.
Grymes, Thomas, **453**.
Guardian, The, see Massinger.
Guelphs and Ghibellines, The. see Anon.
Guest, Ellis, **453–4**.
Guilman, Robert, *see* Gilman, Robert.
Gunnell, Anne, 455.
Gunnell, Edward, 455, 456.
Gunnell, Elizabeth, 549.
Gunnell, Ellenor, 456.
Gunnell, Hellen, 456.
Gunnell, John, 457.
Gunnell, Margaret, 455, 623.
Gunnell, Martyne, 454.
Gunnell, Penelope, 456.
Gunnell, Richard, 136, **137**, **138**, 140 and n. 1, 142, 143, 144, 147, 148, 151, 152, 153, 184, 261 and n. 3, 262 and n. 4, 263 and n. 1, 264, 269 and n. 3, 283 and n. 7, 285, 286–7, 288, 290, 291 n. 6, 295, 297, 308, **454–8**.
Hungarian Lion, The, 150, 156, 456.
Masque, The, 150 n. 7, 157, 456.
Way to Content All Women, or How a Man May Please His Wife, The, 150, 156, 456.
Gurney, Frances, 642.
Gwalter, William, 142, 143, 144, **458**.

Gylman, Robert, *see* Gilman, Robert.
Gypsies Metamorphosed, The, see
Jonson, *The Masque of Gypsies.*

Haberdasher, 412, 636.
Habington, William, 63, 662 n. 5
cont'd.
Queen of Aragon, The, 62 and
nn. 5 and 6, 120.
Hague, The, 6, 335.
English actors in, 413, 493–4, 523,
571.
Haines, Marie, 633.
Haley, Richard, *see* Hawley,
Richard.
Hall, Afrika, 459.
Hall, Ann, 459.
Hall, Frances, 459.
Hall, George, **458.**
Hall, Joan, 499.
Hall, Ra., 624.
Hall, Sarah, 459.
Hall, William, 285, 287, 290, 291
n. 1, 297, 303, 308, 321, **458–9.**
Halley, Richard, *see* Hawley,
Richard.
Halliwell-Phillipps, J. O., 23 n. 1.
Halsey, Bernard, **459.**
Hamerton, Henry, 311, 312, 321,
459.
Hamerton, Nicholas, 312.
Hamlen, Robert, 176, 177 and n. 2,
199 and n. 2, 200 and n. 3, 209,
210, 211, **459.**
Hamlet, see Shakespeare.
Hamlett, Robert, *see* Hamlen,
Robert.
Hamluc, W., 252, **459–60.**
Hammersley, Affryca, 459.
Hammersley, Henry, *see* Hamerton,
Henry.
Hammerton, Mary, 460.
Hammerton, Nicholas, **460.**
Hammerton, Richard, 460.
Hammerton, Stephen, 35, 36, 64,
69 n. 2, 73–89, 123, 312, **460–61.**
Hammond, William, 416.
Hammonds, Captain, 559.
Hamond, John, 361.
Hamond, Dorothy, 479.
Hampton Court, 27, 28 n. 1, 50, 52,
53, 97 n. 1†, 117, 133, 249 n. b,
311.
Hanley, Richard, *see* Hawley,
Richard.
Hannibal and Scipio, see Nabbes.
Hanson, Nicholas, 298, **461.**
*Hardshift for Husbands, or Bilboe's
the Best Blade, see* Samuel Rowley.

Harfield, George, **464.**
Hargreaves, Mrs., 41.
Harington, Henry, 461, 597.
Harison, Toby, 558.
Harpar, Francis, 636.
Harredye, Jone, 459.
Harris, John, 286, 288, 297, **462**
Harrison, Major, 549.
Harrison, Richard, 163, 169 n. 2,
171, **462.**
Harrow in Barbican, 514, 682.
Harsenett, Isaak, 404.
Hart, The, 142, 348.
Hart, Anne, 463.
Hart, Charles, 462–3.
Hart, Mary, 464.
Hart, William, 49 and n. 2 cont'd.,
69 n. 2, 73–89, 299, **463–4.**
Harte, Winifred, 464.
Harvey, William, **464.**
Hathway, *Oldcastle, see* Drayton.
Hatt, John, 639, 640.
Hatton House, 695.
Haughton, Hugh, 299, **464.**
Haughton, Robert, *see* Houghton,
Robert.
Hawle, Richard, *see* Hawley,
Richard.
Hawley, Francis, 465.
Hawley, Joanna, 465.
Hawley, Jone, 465.
Hawley, Joyce, 465.
Hawley, Richard, 49 and n. 2 cont'd.,
73–89, **465.**
Hawley, Roger, 465.
Hawley, Sara, 465.
Hawley, Thomazine, 465.
Hay, Lord, 436.
Haynes, —, 474.
Hayward, Haywood, Thomas, *see*
Heywood, Thomas.
Hayward, Mabel, 546.
Hayward, Peter, 438.
Hearne, John, *see* Herne, John.
Heath, Attorney General, 471.
Heath, Ezechiel, 400.
Heath, Francis, 393.
Heather, Edward, 264, 266.
Heaton, Elizabeth, 472.
Heaton, Hellen, 472.
Hebrew, Professor of, 470.
Hector of Germany, The, see W.
Smith.
Heir, The, see May.
Hellifield, York, 460.
Helmet Court in the Strand, *see*
London, streets of.
Heminges, Alice, 351.
Heminges, Edward, 470.

Heminges, Elizabeth, 644.
Heminges, George, 469.
Heminges, John, 1, 2, 3, 4 nn. 1 and
    2, 5, 17, 18, 20 n. 6 cont'd., 21,
    22, 23, 26 and n. 5, 30, 34 n. 3,
    35 n. 1, 45, 46, 72–88, 90, 95
    nn. a, d, e, f, g, i, k, 103, 117,
    130, 137 n. 3, 142 n. 4, 184, 270,
    279, 283, **465–9**, 590, 642, 651.
    Will of, 643–5.
Heminges, Rebecca, 468, 470, 643.
Heminges, Ruth, 470.
Heminges, William, 12, 44, **470**.
    Coursing of a Hare, or the Madcap,
        The, 293, 470.
    Elegy on Randolph's Finger, 13,
        470, 537, 566, 570.
    Fatal Contract, The, 252, 470, 525,
        608.
    Jew's Tragedy, The, 470.
    'On the Time Poets', *see Elegy on*
        Randolph's Finger.
Hengist, King of Kent, see Middleton.
Henrietta Maria, Queen, 38, 99 n. r.
    At Oxford, 52.
    Company of, 24, 52 n. 2, 55, 56,
        64, 121 n. 1, 185 n. 9, 187, 188,
        204 n. 4, **218–59**, 264, 289 n. 4
        cont'd., 290, 291, 296, 305 n. 3,
        326 and n. 4, 327, 331 n. 4, 684–7.
    Lord Chamberlain of, 223, 236
        n. 8 cont'd., 239, 304 n. 2, 424,
        661 n. 1.
    Marriage of, 218.
    Personal interest of, in her com-
        pany, 223.
    Visit to Blackfriars, 39, 99 nn. t
        and y.
Henry IV, Part 1, see Shakespeare.
Henry IV, Part 2, see Shakespeare.
Henry VI, see Shakespeare.
Henry VIII, see Shakespeare.
Henry, Prince, company of, 135.
    Death of, 136, 655.
    Household Book of, 136.
Henslowe, Mrs., 558.
Henslowe, Philip, 1, 135, 136, 158,
    176, 177 nn. 2 and 3, 198, 199 and
    n. 2, 200 n. 3, 322, 435, 490, 519,
    525, 599, 609.
Herbert, Sir Henry, 10 and n. 6
    cont'd., 11, 12, 14, 15, 21, 22
    n. 2, 25, 30 n. 6, 35, 38, 40, 46,
    49, 54, 61, 67, 101–8, 147, 151,
    165 n. 8, 167, 168 n. 1, 178, 182,
    183, 184, 199, 201 n. 2, 207, 222,
    228, 229, 233, 234, 236, 240,
    285 n. 1, 288, 291, 292, 304, 323
    n. 1, 324, 325, 326, 332, 463, **471**.

Herbert, Sir Henry (*contd.*):
    His censorship, 36, 39.
    His fee, 23, 24, 36.
    His interest in Salisbury Court,
        239 n. 3.
    His office-book, 2, 3 n. 7, 29, 183,
        218, 270, 279, 293, 305, 329.
Herne, Benjamin, 471.
Herne, John, **471**.
Herne, Susanna, 471.
Herod and Antipater, see Markham.
Herringe, Robert, 265.
Herris, Ned, 678.
Hester, a foundling, 399.
Heston, 635.
Heton, Richard, 237, 238, 239, 240,
    241, 295, 296 n. 1, 299 n. c, 303,
    304, 309, **471–2**.
Heton's Papers, 684–7.
Hewitt, Mr., 347.
Heydon, Drue, 358.
Heyley, Jaspar, 327, 663.
Heywood, Thomas, 158, 163, 169 n. 2,
    171, 183 n. 2, 184, 364, **472–3**,
    488, 557, 682.
    Apology for Actors, 264, 519.
    Captives, or the Lost Recovered,
        The, 185, 187 n. 5, 195, 442,
        482, 579, 590, 598.
    Challenge for Beauty, A, 120–1.
    English Traveller, The, 252.
    Exemplary Lives and Memorable
        Acts of Nine the Most Worthy
        Women of the World, 582.
    Fair Maid of the West, The, 220,
        221 n. 1, 246, 249 n. b, 252, 345,
        353, 378, 386, 398, 406, 444,
        445, 528, 547, 548, 572–3, 583,
        608, 619, 692.
    Fortune by Land and Sea (with
        Rowley), 253.
    Hierarchie of the Blessed Angels,
        The, 364, 369, 372.
    If You Know Not Me You Know
        Nobody, 252–3.
    Late Lancashire Witches, The (with
        Brome), 40, 41, 121, 343, 381.
    Love's Mistress, 232–3, 249, 253,
        331, 339, 472.
    Maidenhead Well Lost, A, 253.
    Pleasant Dialogues and Dramas,
        28 n. 1, 249 nn. b and d, 252,
        400, 540.
    Rape of Lucrece, The, 22, 174, 223
        and n. 8, 253, 331, 339.
    Royal King and the Loyal Subject,
        The, 253.
    Woman Killed with Kindness, A,
        174.

Hichinbrook, 310.
High Commission Court, 65 n. 2,
122, 278, 317 n. 1.
Highway repairs, see Red Bull, peti-
tion about highway repairs.
Hill, Alyce, 473.
Hill, John, 281, **473.**
Hill, Johua, 637.
Hill's list of plays, 216, 217.
Hint, Robert, 272, 281, **473.**
Hired men, 3, 16, 35 n. 2, 44, 80–1,
187 n. 5, 316, 332, 558, 598, 605,
609, 611.
Wages of, 44.
*History of the Duchess of Suffolk,
The,* see Drue, *The Life of the
Duchess of Suffolk.*
History of Henry I, The, see Daven-
port.
Hitchens, Francis, **473.**
Hitchens, Katherine, 473.
Hobbes, Alice, 474.
Hobbes, Anne, 474.
Hobbes, Thomas, 18, 24, 49, 73–89,
, 198, 199 and n. 2, 200, 209, 211
and n. a, **473–4,** 683.
Hodgeson, Edward 383, 384.
Hodgson, James, 384.
Hodgson, Jane, 405.
Hog Hath Lost His Pearl, The, see
Tailor.
Hog Lane, see London, streets of.
Holborn, see London, streets of.
Holcomb, Frances, 626.
Holcomb, George, 475.
Holcomb, Thomas, 45, 72–88, **475,**
626.
Holden, Richard, 474, 575, 594.
Holdenby, 310.
Holland, see Netherlands.
Holland, Aaron, **475,** 560, 588.
Holland, Earl of, 23, 37, 48, 128.
Hollander, The, see Glapthorne.
Holland House, 695.
Holland's Leaguer, see Marmion.
Holloway, 651.
Holman, Thomas, 298, **475.**
Holmes, Thomas, 416.
Holt, James, 158, 171, **475–6.**
Honest Lawyer, The, see Anon.
Honest Man's Fortune, The, see
Beaumont and Fletcher.
Honest Whore, The, see Dekker.
Honeyman *or* Honiman, John, *see*
Honyman, John.
Honeyman *or* Honiman, Richard,
see Honyman, Richard.
Honour in the End, see Anon.
Honour of Women, The, see Massinger,

Honour of Young Ladies, The, see
Brome, *The Lovesick Maid.*
Honyman, Alice, 476.
Honyman, Anthony, 476.
Honyman, Hellin, 478.
Honyman, John, 45, 70, 73–89, 316,
476–8.
Will of, 645.
Honyman, Rachael, 479.
Honyman, Richard, 316, 321, **478–9,**
645.
Hope theatre, 176, 199 and n. 2, 200
n. 3, 346, 510.
Hore, Henry, 600.
Horne, James, 16, 35 n. 1, 72–88,
479.
Horton, Edward, 73–89, **479–80.**
Hosier, 413.
Hosier Lane, see London, streets of.
Hosier, Stephen, 607.
Hotspur, The, see Shakespeare,
Henry IV, Part 1.
Houghton, Edward, 404.
Houghton, Robert, **480.**
Hoult, James, see Holt, James.
Houndsditch, see London, streets of.
Hounslow, see London, streets of.
Housekeepers, 2, 4, 23, 46, 234, 351,
466, 500, 654 n. 2 cont'd., 685.
Benefits of, 686–7.
Expenses of, 44.
Receipts of, 44.
House of Commons, 64.
Hovell, William, 510.
How a Man May Please His Wife,
see Gunnell, *The Way to Content
All Women.*
Howard, Lord, company of, 135.
Howell, James, letter of, 184.
Epistolae Ho-Elianae, 184 n. 4.
Howes, Oliver, **480.**
Howson, Margaret, 371, 372.
Hoyt, Robert, see Huyt, Robert.
Hubert, 73–89, **480.**
Hudsone, widow, 490.
Hull, John, 473.
Hulse, Frances, 642.
Humorous Courtier, The, see Shirley.
Humorous Lieutenant, The, see Beau-
mont and Fletcher.
Humours Reconciled, see Jonson, *The
Magnetic Lady.*
Hungarian Lion, The, see Gunnell.
Hunnieman, John, see Honyman,
John.
Hunnyman, John, see Honyman,
John.
Hunnyman, Richard, see Honyman,
Richard.

Hunsdon, Lord, his players, 1.
Hunt, —, 140 and n. 6, 155.
Hunt, John, **481.**
Hunt, Robert, **481.**
Hunt, Thomas, 176, **481.**
Hunt, William, 596, 621.
Hunter, Susan, 383.
Hurd, Edward, 355.
Hurd, Jane, 623.
Hutchinson, Alice, 373.
Hutchinson, Christopher, *see* Beeston, Christopher.
Hutchinson, Elizabeth, *see* Beeston, Elizabeth.
Hutchinson, Jane, 373.
Hutchinson, William, *see* Beeston, William.
Huyt, Richard, 321.
Huyt, Robert, 307, 308, **481.**
Hyde Park, see Shirley.
Hymen's Holiday, or Cupid's Vagaries, see Rowley.

If You Know Not Me You Know Nobody, see Heywood.
Imposter, The, see Shirley, *The Imposture.*
Imposture, The, see Shirley.
Inconstant Lady, The, see Wilson.
Induction to the House, An, see Anon.
Ingleby, C. M., &c., *The Shakespeare Allusion-Book* (Oxford, 1932), 121.
Ingram, Sir Arthur, 10 n. 1.
Inner Temple, 164.
Inner Temple Library, 166,' 167, 182.
Inner Temple Masque, The, see Middleton.
Innholder, 458.
Innkeeper, 500, 513.
Inns and taverns:
  Angels, 348.
  Cross Keys, 1, 491, 682.
  Fortune, 137 n. 6.
  Harrow in Barbican, 514, 682.
  Hart, 142, 348.
  King's Arms, 293, 689.
  King's Head, 558.
  Leopard's Head, 486.
  Lord of Arundle tavern, 142.
  Mermaid in Bread street, 137, 347.
  Nobody in Barbican, 606, 682.
  Paul's Head, 140.
  Prince's Arms, 201 n. 2.
  Spread Eagle Inn, 635.
  Three Kings Ordinary, 421, 684 n. 1.
  Three Pigeons at Brentford, 505, 695.

Inns and taverns (*contd.*):
  White Hart in the Old Bailey, 343, 682.
  Windmill Tavern in Lothbury, 266.
Inns, plays at, 293.
  Plays written in, 473.
Inns of Court man, 654 n. 2.
Insatiate Countess, The, see Marston.
Interludes, 685.
Ipswich, 92, 172, 193, 212.
Ireland, 165, 539.
  Lord Deputy in, 47, 56 n. 3, 329.
Ireland, Peter, 444.
Irish Rebellion, The, see Anon.
Ironmonger, 574.
Isham, Sir Charles, 128.
Isham, Thomas, 129.
Island Princess, The, see Beaumont and Fletcher.
Isle of Dogs, The, see Nashe.
Islipp, Adam, 143, 144, **481.**
Italian actor, 517.
Italian motion, 507.
Italian Night Masque, The, see Anon.
Italian Night Piece, The, see Anon.
Ives, Mr., 40.
Ivieson, Alice, 585.
Ivory, Abraham, **481.**
Ivy Lane, *see* London, streets of.

Jack, **482.**
Jack Drum's Entertainment, see Marston.
Jack of Oxford, 462.
Jackson, —, **482.**
Jackson, Edward, 143, 144, **482.**
Jacksonne, Henry, 638.
Jacob, Thomas, 314.
James I, company of, *see* King's company.
  His death, 19, 151, 186.
  Disapproves of play, 204.
  His funeral, 16, 19, 200, 209.
  Mitigates players' punishment, 12.
  Progress to Scotland, 180–1, 181 nn. 1, 3, and 4.
James, Mrs., 678.
Jarman, Anthony, 143, 144, **482.**
Jarvice, **482.**
Jay, Tom, **482.**
Jeffes, Anthony, 135, 136, **482-3.**
Jeffes, Humphrey, 135, 136, 137, 139, 155, 178, **483.**
Jeffes, Richard, 482.
Jeffes, Sara, 483.
Jeffes, William, 482.
Jenkins, Henry, 22, 469, 570.
Jermyn, Henry, 335, 422.

Jerom, John, 545, 581.
Jesuits, 396, 538, 543.
Jeube, Edward, *see* Juby, Edward.
Jewbe or Jewbey, *see* Juby, Edward.
Jewell, John, 189, 192, **483**.
Jeweller, 554, 587, 695.
Jeweller of Amsterdam, The, see Field.
Jew of Malta, The, see Marlowe.
Jew's Tragedy, The, see W. Heminges.
Jig, 103 n. 2, 401, 691.
Jig maker, 563.
Johnson, James, 363.
Johnson, George, 527.
Johnson, Richard, 285, 287, 290, 297, **483**.
Johnson, Thomas, 400.
Johnson, William, 384, **483**.
Jolly, George, **484**, 577.
Jolly, John, 484, 577.
Jolly, Mary, 484.
Jones, Ann, 485, 486.
Jones, Bartholomew, 292 n. 4, **484**-5.
Jones, Edward, **485**.
Jones, Elizabeth, 485, 486.
Jones, Inigo, 53, 117, 229, 233, 349, 456.
Jones, James, 168 n. 1, **485**.
Jones, John, **485**-6.
Jones, Oliver, 189, 192, **486**.
Jones, Richard, 135, **486**-7.
Jones, William, 571.
Jonson, Ben, 2, 7, 26, 59, 66, 68, 95 n. b, 115, 150 and n. 7, 225, 435, 436, 444, 456, 468, 496, 550, 557, 662 n. 5 cont'd., 692, 694.
    1616 folio, 1.
    Alchemist, The, 24, 62, 94, 121, 429, 465, 505, 597, 678, 681, 693.
    Bartholomew Fair, 117, 121 n. 1.
    Catiline, 39, 98, 121, 429, 465, 676, 681.
    Cynthia's Revels, 117, 121 n. 1, 422.
    Devil Is an Ass, The, 121, 551.
    Epicoene, 51, 95 n. c, 98, 99 n. s, 122, 344, 505, 523, 597, 692, 693.
    Every Man in His Humour, 1, 24, 28, 96, 121, 363, 502, 594.
    Fox, The, see Volpone.
    Gypsies Metamorphosed, The, see The Masque of Gypsies.
    Magnetic Lady, The, 30, 38 and n. 2, 42, 105, 121-2, 268, 495, 503, 594.
    Masque of Christmas, The, 396, 467.
    Masque of Gypsies, The, 691.
    New Inn, The, 104, 105, 122.

Jonson, Ben (*contd.*):
    Poetaster, The, 422, 610.
    Sejanus, 499.
    Silent Women, The, see Epicoene.
    Staple of News, The, 12, 13, 97 n. h, 122, 557.
    Tale of a Tub, A, 117, 121 n. 1, 229, 230, 249, 253, 496.
    Volpone, 28, 61, 95 and n. c, 96, 99, 122-3, 505, 598, 678, 680, 681, 693.
    Widow, The, see Middleton.
Jonson, 'Young', *A Fault in Friendship, see* Brome.
Jonsonus Virbius, 662 n. 5 cont'd.
Joones, Haris, 486.
Jordan, Anne, 488.
Jordan, Elisabeth, 489.
Jordan, Richard, 489.
Jordan, Thomas, 285, 286, 287, 288, 290, 297, **487**-90.
    Money Is an Ass, 406, 487, 488, 498, 508, 560, 620.
    Nursery of Novelties, A, 487, 488, 489, 493.
    Piety and Poesy, 493.
    Poetical Varieties or Variety of Fancies, 457, 477, 488, 509, 510.
    Rules to Know a Loyal King from a Disloyal Subject, 489.
    Tricks of Youth, 487-8, 489.
    Walks of Islington and Hogsdon, 13 n. 2, 489.
    Wit in the Wilderness of Promiscuous Poetry, 489.
Jordan, William, 5 n. 1.
Jovial Crew, The, see Brome.
Juby, Edward, 135, 136, 138, 147, 155, **490**, 623.
Juby, Frances, 143, 144, **490**.
Juby, Richard, 490.
Juby, Tabitha, 490.
Juby, William, 490.
Judge, The, see Massinger.
Jugglers, 612.
Jugurth, King of Numidia, see Anon.
Julius Caesar, see Shakespeare.
Jupe, Edward, 384.
Just Italian, The, see Davenant.

Kane, Andrew, *see* Cane, Andrew.
Kayne, Andrew, *see* Cane, Andrew.
Keep the Widow Waking, see Dekker, *The Late Murder in Whitechapel*.
Keepers of the Wardrobe, 688.
Kein, Andrew, *see* Cane, Andrew.
Keinton, 480, 484, 618.
Kellock, John, **491**.
Kellock, Philadelphia, 491.

Kelly, Philadelphia, 527.
Kemble, John Philip, 382, 383.
Kempe, William, 1, 4 n. 1.
Kempston, Robert, 298, **491**.
Kemsall, Faith, 651.
Kendall, Joan, 491.
Kendall, Richard, 26 n. 5 cont'd.,
    30 n. 6, 231–2, 274, 285–8, 289
    n. 4, 290, 293, 297 and n. b, 309,
    310, **491**.
Kendall, Tomazine, 404.
Kent, 421.
Kerbye, John, 266.
Kerke, John, see Kirke, John.
Keyes, Ralph, **491**, 682, 683.
Keyes, Robert, **492**, 683.
Keyne or Keynes, Andrew, see Cane,
    Andrew.
Keyne, Mary, 400.
Kiddermaster, Worcs., 636.
Kiddermister, Sir John, 576–7.
Kilkenny Castle, 673.
Killigraue, Thomas, see Killigrew,
    Thomas.
Killigrew, Henry, The Conspiracy,
    123.
Killigrew, Thomas, 117 and n. 1, 677.
    Claracilla, 253.
    Parson's Wedding, The, 123, 461,
    597.
    Princess, The, 117, 123.
    Prisoners, The, 253.
Kimpton, Robert, see Kempston,
    Robert.
Kinde, Dorothy, 525.
King and No King, A, see Beaumont
    and Fletcher.
King and Queen of Bohemia, see
    Bohemia, King and Queen of.
King and Queen's Young Company,
    see Beeston's Boys.
King and the Subject, The, see Mas-
    singer.
King, John, 160, 367, **492**.
King of Kent, see Middleton, Hen-
    gist, King of Kent.
King John and Matilda, see Daven-
    port.
Kingdom's Weekly Intelligencer, The,
    see Newspapers.
King's Arms, 293, 689.
King's Bench, 42.
King's Bill, 273.
King's company, 1–**134**, 141 n. 6,
    149, 200, 209, 226, 242, 264, 270
    n. 4, 278, 290, 327, 337, **494–5**.
King's Head, 558.
King's Head Yard, see London,
    streets of.

King's Lynn, 273.
Kingsmill, Lady Bridget, 442.
King's Porter, 500, 591.
King's Revels company, 36, 41, 152,
    231, 268, **283–301**, 304, 305, 306
    n. 3, 307, 309, 327, 332.
Kirby Lonsdale, 491, 688.
Kirke, Elizabeth, 493.
Kirke, John, 272, 275, 281, 308, 311,
    312, 321, **492–3**.
    Seven Champions of Christendom,
    The, 312, 493.
Kirke, Marie, 493.
Kirke, Parry, 493.
Kirk, Lewis, 632.
Kirkman, Francis, 473.
    Loves and Adventures of Clerico
    and Logis, The, 373.
    Wits, or Sport upon Sport, The,
    415.
Kite, Francis, 494.
Kite, Jeremy, **493–4**.
Kite, William, 494.
Knave in Grain New Vampt, The,
    see Anon.
Knavery in All Trades, see Tatham.
Knell, Rebecca, 466.
Knell, William, 466.
Kneller, James, 168 n. 1, **494**.
Knight, —, 37, 121, **494–5**.
Knight, Anthony, 15, 73–89, **495**.
Knight, Edward, 15, 72–88, 199 n. 2,
    495, 682.
Knight, Mrs., 622.
Knight of Malta, The, see Beaumont
    and Fletcher.
Knight of the Burning Pestle, The,
    see Beaumont and Fletcher.
Knight, Philip, 384, 495.
Knight Rider, see London, streets of.
Knipton, Robert, see Kempston,
    Robert.
Knowsley Hall, 464.
Kostressen, Johan, **495**.
Kyd, Thomas, The Spanish Tragedy,
    440.
Kynaston, Edward, 545, 546.

L'abbe, Mònsieur, 694.
Labourer, 431, 486.
Lacrymae Cantabrigiensis, 444.
Lacy, John, 327 n. 4, 332, 336,
    495–6.
    Ladies' Privilege, The, see Glap-
    thorne.
Lady Mother, The, see Glapthorne.
Lady of Pleasure, The, see Shirley.
Lady's Trial, The, see Ford.
Laighton, Ned, 142, 349.

Lake, Sir Thomas, 10 n. 6.
Lambard Volume, The, 132.
Lambe, Dr., 266–8.
Lambeth, see London, streets of.
Lamport Hall, 23 n. 1.
Lancaster, Anne, 637.
Lancaster, Silvester, 316, 321, **496**.
Landgrave of Hesse-Darmstadt, 432.
Langley, Francis, 384.
Langlies Rents, see London, streets of.
Lanier, Henry, 343.
Lanier, William, 343.
Lasander and Callista, see Beaumont and Fletcher, *The Wandering Lovers.*
Late Lancashire Witches, The, see Heywood.
Late Murder in Whitechapel, The, see Dekker.
Lau, Hurfries de, **496**.
Laud, Archbishop, 276.
Laws of Candy, The, see Beaumont and Fletcher.
Lawyer, 3 n. 7, 266.
Lawyers as theatre patrons, 3 n. 7.
Layton, Mr., 678.
Leadenhall, see London, streets of.
Leake, Robert, 42.
Leakes, Madame, 161 n. 2.
Leap staff, tour with, 682.
Lecherpiere, S., 428.
Lee, Robert, 137 n. 3, 158, 165 n. 8, 167, 168 nn. 1, 2, and 3, 171 and n. b, 172 n. 1, 179 n. 2, **496–7**, 561, 682.
Le Febure's riding academy, 437.
Leicester, 92, 156, 172, 173, 180, 193, 212, 213, 282, 298, 299, 322, 423, 452, 484, 494, 530, 612, 618.
Leicester, Earl of, 414, 661 n. 1.
Leigh, Robert, see Lee, Robert.
Lenox, Duke of, 6, 48, 198.
Lent, 5, 22, 186, 275, 276, 654 n. 2.
Lenton, Francis, *Young Gallant's Whirligig*, 654 n. 2.
Leopard's Head, 486.
Lesley, Robert, 356.
Leslie, Shane, 443.
Letters patent, theft of, 420.
Lewes, Christopher, 162, 366.
Lewin, John, *see* Lowin, John.
Licences, 5, 19, 49, 50, 181, 188, 189, 271, 272, 273 and n. 5, 274, 275, 302, 321.
 Forged, 484–5, 486.
Lichfield, Leonard, 301.
Lieutenants of the county of Middlesex, 163.

Life of the Duchess of Suffolk, The, see Drue.
Lights of theatre, cost of, 44.
Lillie, George, 189, 192, **497**.
Lillie, John, 188, 192, 438, **497–8**.
Lilly, William, 398.
Lilypot Lane, see London, streets of.
Lincoln, Bishop of, 622.
Lincoln Cathedral, 381.
Lincoln's Inn, 160.
Lincoln's Inn Field, see London, streets of.
Lisle, Tobias, 393, 545.
Little Britain, see London, streets of.
Little French Lawyer, The, see Beaumont and Fletcher.
Liverpool, 64.
Livery allowances, 1, 3 n. 1, 7, 8, 16, 24, 53, 61, 72–3, 76–7, 80–1, 82–3, 90–1, 164–5, 171, 211, 223 and n. 6, 229, 247–8.
Lodge, Thomas, 415.
 Looking Glass for London and England, A (with Greene), 542, 543.
 Scillaes Metamorphosis, 415.
Loffday, Thomas, see Loveday, Thomas.
London and the Country Carbonadoed, see Lupton.
London, Bishop of, censors play, 7.
 Complaints to, 32.
London Common Council, 5.
London companies, representative of, 466.
London mortality tables, 667–72.
London, streets and districts of:
 Aldermanbury, 587, 641, 682, 695.
 Aldgate, 633.
 Austen's Rents, Southwark, 448.
 Bankside, 200 n. 3, 201, 682, 683.
 Barbican, 384, 606, 682, 683.
 Bargehouse on the Bankside, 520, 682.
 Beech Lane, 625, 682.
 Benfield's Rents, Southwark, 633.
 Birchen Lane, 504.
 Bishopsgate, 140, 593, 682.
 Bishopsgate street, 374.
 Bishopsgate street without, 374.
 Blackboy Alley, 467.
 Blackfriars, citizens of, 34.
 Blackfriars Gate, 33.
 Blackfriars, precinct of, 5.
  Inhabitants of, 4.
  Residents of, petition against players, 4–5, 31–2, 64.
  Rosseter's plan to erect a theatre in, 176.

London streets and districts (*contd.*) :
Bow Lane, 455.
Bradshaw's Rents, Southwark, 574.
Carter Lane, 33.
Chancery Lane, 682.
Charing Cross, 546, 694.
Clerkenwell, 526, 528, 571, 584, 624, 695.
Clerkenwell Close, 561, 682.
Clerkenwell Hill, 473, 682, 683.
Clink, Liberty of the, 635.
Conduit, 688.
Covent Garden, 228, 632.
Cow Cross, 384.
Cripplegate, 7, 384.
Crown office in the Middle Temple, 682.
Doctors' Commons, 683.
East Smithfield, 551.
Finsbury Fields, 161.
Fleet Conduit, 33.
Fleet street, 33, 240, 455, 688.
Proposed new playhouse in, 684.
George Alley in Golding Lane, 495, 521, 523, 598, 682, 683.
Globe Alley, 467.
Golding Lane, 138, 143, 384, 408, 448, 449, 452, 536, 564, 612, 682.
Gray's Inn Lane, 496, 635, 675.
Liberty of, 635.
Grub street, 384.
Helmet Court in the Strand, 640.
Hog Lane, 370.
Holborn, 314.
Hosier Lane, 384, 625.
Houndsditch, 523.
Hounslow, 461, 635.
Ivy Lane, 578.
Kensington, 695.
King's Head Yard, 370.
Knight Rider street, 491, 682.
Lambeth, 38, 683.
Langlies' Rents, Southwark, 519
Leadenhall, 453.
Leadenhall street, 201 n. 2.
Lilypot Lane, 365.
Lincoln's Inn Fields, 161, 201 n. 1, 228 n. 1, 369, 620, 632.
Little Britain, 545.
London Bridge, 682.
Long Lane, 228, 294.
Ludgate, 4, 33, 64.
Maiden Lane, 500, 612.
Marshalsea, 294, 324, 333, 401, 582, 682.
Moorgate, 266, 267.
Moor Lane, 484.

London streets and districts (*contd.*) :
Newgate, 33.
Norman's Rents, Southwark, 574.
Oare's Rents, Southwark, 490.
Old Bailey, 682.
Palmer's Rents, Southwark, 448.
Perpoole Lane, 635.
Poultry, 267.
Queen's street, 228 n. 1.
Red Cross street, 456, 682.
Red Lion Alley, 561.
St. Bride's Lane, 492, 683.
St. John's street, 309, 310, 384, 401, 527, 571, 637, 682, 693.
St. Paul's Churchyard, 33.
Shoe Lane, 635.
Shoreditch, 161 n. 2, 164, 552, 682, 683.
Smithfield, 142.
Southwark, 1, 633.
Soare's Rents, Southwark, 519.
Spittle, 593, 682.
Spittlegate, 558.
Strand, 564, 639, 640.
Thames street, 626.
Three Herring Court, 571.
Toothill street, 683.
Tower Hill, 276.
Turnstile Alley, 405.
Tuttle street, Westminster, 546.
Westminster, 27, 244, 546, 550, 658.
Whitecross street, 138, 143, 384, 452, 484, 536, 577, 580, 600, 635, 682, 683, 693.
Liberty of, 635.
Whitehall, 28 n. 1, 34, 39 n. 1, 49, 104, 133, 178, 222, 223, 230, 234, 244, 284, 311, 333, 695.
Wood street, 467.
Long, George, 265–6.
Long Lane, *see* London, streets of.
Longe, Alice, 392.
Longe, Christopher, 162, 366.
Longe, Nicholas, 165 n. 8, 176, 498.
Looking Glass for London and England, A, see Lodge.
Lord Admiral's company, 135–6.
Lord Chamberlain, 6, 8, 22, 28 n. 1, 34 and n. 3, 35, 36, 41, 42, 43, 45, 46, 48, 53, 54, 55, 63, 65, 160, 166, 167, 178, 194, 195, 209, 236, 260, 283 n. 2, 324 n. 1, 328, 333, 334, 467, 542, 657 n. 2 contin'd., 661 n. 1.
Company of, 1, 121.
Lord Chamberlain's Warrant Books, 188, 190, 271, 273, 278, 310.
Unpublished entries from, 260 n. 2, 302, 384, 399, 421, 422, 463, 469.

Lord Chamberlain to the Queen, 223, 236 n. 8 cont'd., 239, 304 n. 2, 424, 661 n. 1.
Lord Keeper, 16 n. 6, 201 n. 1, 327.
Lord Mayor, 161, 162 n. 3.
Lord of Arundel tavern, 142.
Lord Privy Seal, 46, 327.
Lord Treasurer, 327.
Lorkin, Thomas, 436.
Lost Lady, The, see Berkeley.
Lost Recovered, The, see Heywood, *The Captives.*
Lott, Francis, 389.
Love and Honour, see Davenant.
Loveday, Thomas, 286, 297, **398.**
Lovelace, Richard, *The Scholars,* 253–4.
Love Lies a Bleeding, see Beaumont and Fletcher, *Philaster.*
Lovell, Thomas, 286, 297, **498.**
Lover's Melancholy, The, see Ford.
Lover's Pilgrimage, The, see Beaumont and Fletcher.
Lover's Progress, The, see Beaumont and Fletcher.
Love's Aftergame, see Anon, *The Proxy.*
Love's Cruelty, see Shirley.
Love's Cure, or the Martial Maid, see Beaumont and Fletcher.
Love's Dominion, see Flecknoe.
Lovesick King, The, see Brewer.
Lovesick Maid, The, see Brome.
Love's Labour's Lost, see Shakespeare.
Love's Mistress, see Heywood.
Love's Pilgrimage, see Beaumont and Fletcher.
Love's Riddle, see Cowley.
Love's Sacrifice, see Ford.
Love's Trial, see Glapthorne, *The Hollander.*
Love Tricks with Compliments, see Shirley, *The School of Compliment.*
Lowe, George, 10 n. 1.
Lowe, Nicholas, **498–9.**
Lowen, G., 72–88, **499.**
Lowen or Lowens, John, *see* Lowin, John.
Lowen, John, clerk, 504.
Lowin, Elizabeth, 499.
Lowin, Joane, 499, 504.
Lowin, John, 4 nn. 1 and 2, 5, 14, 17, 26 n. 5, 34, 35 n. 1, 37, 44, 53, 54, 55, 57, 60, 61, 69 n. 2, 72–88, 90, 97 nn. i, n, and p, 99 nn. u, x, z, and aa, 100 n. bb, 121, 125, 318, 328, **499–506,** 647, 651, 666, 683.
Lowin, Katherine, 501.

Lowin, Richard, 499.
Lowine or Lowing, John, *see* Lowin, John.
Lowther, Richard, 455.
Lowyn, John, *see* Lowin, John.
Loyal Subject, The, see Beaumont and Fletcher.
Lucasta, see Lovelace, *The Scholars.*
Lucy, Sir Thomas, 484, 618.
Ludgate, *see* London, streets of.
Ludgate Prison, 470.
Ludlow, 172, 271, 282, 432.
Lupton, D., *London and the Country Carbonadoed,* 146 n. 6 cont'd.
Lupton, Francis, *The Young Gallant's Whirligig,* 225 n. 2.
Lutanist, 554, 621.
Lute, bass, 554.
Luther, Martin, 538.
Lydall, Mrs., 121.
Lyly, George, *see* Lillie, George.
Lyly, John, *see* Lillie, John.
Lyme Regis, 193.
Lysander and Calista, see Beaumont and Fletcher, *The Lover's Progress.*

Madcap, The, see Barnes.
Mad Couple Well Matched, A, see Brome.
Mad Couple Well Met, A, see Anon.
Maddox, Ronald, 455.
Mad Lover, The, see Beaumont and Fletcher.
Mad World My Masters, A, see Middleton.
Magnetic Lady, The, see Jonson.
Mago, William, 15, 73–89, 251, **506.**
Maid, 349, 353, 634.
Maidenhead Well Lost, A, see Heywood.
Maiden Lane, *see* London, streets of.
Maid in the Mill, The, see Beaumont and Fletcher.
Maid of Honour, The, see Massinger.
Maid's Revenge, The, see Shirley.
Maid's Tragedy, The, see Beaumont and Fletcher.
Maivrin, 286, 297, **506.**
Malcontent, The, see Marston.
Mallory, Thomas, 552.
Malvolio, see Shakespeare, *Twelfth Night.*
Manager, *see* Company manager.
Manchester, 414, 507.
Mandeville, Viscount, 355.
Mandeville, H., 622.
Man in the Moon, The, see Newspapers.

Man in the Moon Drinks Claret, The,
see Anon.
Manneroy, Samuel, *see* Mannery,
Samuel.
Mannery, Ann, 506.
Mannery, Mary, 506.
Mannery, Samuel, 308, 321, 327 n.
2, 332, 336, **506.**
Man servant, 349, 353.
Manuray, Samuel, *see* Mannery,
Samuel.
Mapes, Richard, 530.
Marcy, Charles, *see* Massey, Charles.
Margrave, Richard, 265.
Market Bosworth, 484.
Markham, Gervase, 145, 147, 682.
Herod and Antipater, 166, 174.
His suit, 682–3.
Marlborough, 92, 173, 180, 193, 211.
Marlow, Bucks., 618.
Marlowe, Christopher, *Doctor Faus-*
tus, 157, 318, 319.
Edward II, 174.
Jew of Malta, The, 28 n. 1, 249,
254, 472, 528, 691.
Tamburlaine, 691.
Marmion, Shakerley, 110, 595.
Antiquary, The, 254.
Fine Companion, A, 322, 323.
Holland's Leaguer, 13 n. 2, 152 n.
3, 226, 239 n. 3, 292, 303, 304,
305, 306–7, 307, 308, 311, 321,
323 and n. 1, 383, 392, 398,
399, 423, 439, 445, 450, 458,
481, 506, 509, 560, 577, 579,
617, 620, 625, 627, 692.
Soddered Citizen, The, see Clavell.
Marovin, —, *see* Maivrin.
Marrant, Edward, **506,** 545, 659.
Marshalsea, *see* London, streets of.
Marshall, Charles, 137, 178, **507.**
Marshall, Humphrey, 643.
Marston, John, *The Dutch Courte-*
san, 195.
Insatiate Countess, The, 357, 358.
Jack Drum's Entertainment, 690.
Malcontent, The, 123, 395.
Marston Moor, 398.
Martial Maid, The, see Beaumont
and Fletcher, *Love's Cure.*
Martin, Elizabeth, 566, 567.
Martin, Widow, 641.
Martyn, Charles, **507.**
Martyred Soldier, The, see Henry
Shirley.
Mason, Bridget, 392.
Maskell, Thomas, **507.**
Masque, The, see Anon.
Masque of Christmas, The, see Jonson.

Masques, 185, 681, 685.
Massam, Phillip, 637.
Massam, Thomas, 412.
Massey, Charles, 136, 137 n. 4, 138,
140, 141 and n. 2, 142, 143, 144,
147, 148, 152, 153, 155, 263,
507–8, 564.
Malcolm, King of Scots, 507.
Siege of Dunkirk with Alleyn the
Pirate, The, 507.
Massey, Elinor, 507, 508.
Massey, George, 144, **508.**
Massey, John, 508.
Massey, Margaret, 508.
Massie, Charles, *see* Massey, Charles.
Massinger, Philip, 63, 184, 218,
557.
Alexius the Chaste Gallant, 65, 108,
123.
Bashful, Lover, The, 66, 107, 108,
123–4.
Believe as You List, 84–5, 101 n. b,
105, 124, 354, 355, 375, 397,
418, 425, 441, 452, 474, 477,
480, 502, 506, 516, 521, 524,
534, 585, 594, 609, 621.
Bondman, The, 185, 186 and n. 5,
194, 195, 331, 339.
City Madam, The, 30, 66, 105,
124.
Cleander, 39 and n. 2, 97, 107, 124
and n. 1.
Duke of Milan, The, 124.
Emperor of the East, The, 97 n. m,
105, 124.
Fair Anchoress of Pausilippo,
The, 108, 124.
Fatal Dowry, The, 28, 96, 124,
435, 436.
Forced Lady, The, 65, 125.
Great Duke of Florence, The, 218,
223 and n. 4, 254, 331, 339.
Guardian, The, 66, 97, 106, 125.
Honour of Women, The, see Anon.,
The Spanish Viceroy.
Jeweller of Amsterdam, The, see
Field.
Judge, The, 66, 104, 125.
King and the Subject, The, 60–1,
60 n. 4, 107, 108, 125, 504.
London's Lamentable Estate, 416.
Maid of Honour, The, 254, 331,
339.
Minerva's Sacrifice, 66, 105, 125.
New Way to Pay Old Debts, A,
248 n. 2, 254, 331, 339–40.
Noble Bondman, The, see The Bond-
man.
Noble Choice, The, 125.

Massinger, Philip (*contd.*):
Orator, The, 107, 125, 660.
Parliament of Love, The, 186, 195–6.
Picture, The, 82–3, 105, 125, 375, 447, 477, 502, 524, 533, 562, 565, 571, 585, 594, 600, 605, 692.
Renegado, The, 185, 187, 196, 218 n. 3, 219 n. 4, 220–2, 246, 254, 331, 340, 344, 345, 378, 382, 386, 526, 543, 548, 553, 561, 583, 607, 692.
Roman Actor, The, 82–3, 104, 125–6, 375, 447, 452, 476, 479, 502, 521, 533, 546, 552, 570, 575, 585, 593–4, 600, 605, 612, 692.
Sir John van Olden Barnavelt, see Beaumont and Fletcher.
Tyrant, The, see The King and the Subject.
Unfortunate Combat, The, 126.
Unfortunate Piety, The, 105, 126, 552.
Very Woman, A, 107, 126.
Virgin Martyr, The, see Dekker.
Woman's Plot, The, 66, 94, 126.
Massy, Charles, see Massey, Charles.
Master of the Jewel House, 673.
Matchit, Amb., 508.
Match Me in London, see Dekker.
Match or No Match, A, see Samuel Rowley.
Mathew, Jo., 379.
Matthew, Sir Tobie, 10 n. 6 cont'd.
Maund, Mr., 622.
Maxey, Elizabeth Burbage, 649.
May, Clare, 510.
May, Edward, 286, 290, 297, 307, 308, 321, 323, 488, 509–10.
May, Edward, Epigrams Divine and Moral, 509 n. 1.
May, Edward, physician, 509 n. 1.
May, Francis, 510.
May, Mary, 510.
May, Nathan, 510.
May, Thomas, The Heir, 166, 175.
Mayne, Jasper, The City Match, 126.
Maynwaring, Mary, 510.
Mayor of Quinborough, The, see Middleton, Hengist, King of Kent.
Mead, Jacob, waterman, 510.
Mead, Joseph, 20, 266, 349, 655, 657 n. 4.
Meade, Jacob, 176, 177 n. 3, 198, 199 and n. 2, 200, 201, 209, 510.
Measure, William, 463.
Medicine show, 517, 537.
Medus, Dr., 349.
Megus, Katherine, 511.

Megus, William, 511.
Melise, ou les Princes Reconnus, La, see Du Rocher.
Mell, Davies, 363.
Melton, John, Astrologaster, 157.
Members of company, new, money, advanced by, 57 and n. 2.
Membership, 'Mr.' as indication of, 287.
Merchant, 486, 493.
Merchant adventurer, 564.
Merchant tailor, 143, 508, 555, 578.
Merchant Tailors' company, 546.
Merchant Tailors' School, 414.
Mercurius Democritus, see Newspapers.
Mercurius Fumigosus, see Newspapers.
Mercurius Impartialis, see Newspapers.
Mercurius Militaris, see Newspapers.
Mercurius Pragmaticus, see Newspapers.
Mercy, Charles, see Massey, Charles.
Merefield, Mrs., 644.
Meriden, 419, 484, 618.
Mermaid in Bread street, 137, 347.
Merrell, Anne, 511.
Merrell, Joane, 511.
Merrell, John, 511.
Merricke, Ann, 121.
Merry Devil of Edmonton, The, see Anon.
Merry Wives of Windsor, The, see Shakespeare.
Merydale, Richard, 637.
Messalina, see Richards.
Messenger, 448, 683.
Michael, 72–88, 511.
Microcosmus, see Nabbes.
Middlesex, 428, 458,
Middlesex Special Session, 162.
Middleton, Edward, 12.
Middleton, Thomas, 6 and n. 7 cont'd., 11, 184, 557.
Anything for a Quiet Life, 126.
Changeling, The (with Rowley), 183, 185, 186 n. 6, 187, 194, 196, 219 n. 4, 254–5, 331, 340, 540.
City Madam, The, 524, 525.
Fair Quarrel, A (with Rowley), 213, 215, 331, 340.
Game at Chess, A, 9–15, 104, 126–7, 295 n. 6, 416, 556, 557.
Hengist, King of Kent, 66, 95 n. c, 127, 380, 389, 579.
Inner Temple Masque, The, 164, 203, 211, 352, 401–2, 464, 516, 556, 557, 591, 592.

Middleton, Thomas (contd.):
 Mad World, My Masters, A, 254.
 Mayor of Quinborough, The, see
  Hengist, King of Kent.
 More Dissemblers besides Women,
  66, 95, 103, 110, 127.
 Roaring Girl, The, see Dekker.
 'Song in several parts, A', 416.
 Spanish Gypsy, The (with Row-
  ley), 185, 186 n. 4, 187, 194,
  196, 219 n. 4, 255, 331, 340.
 Widow, The (with Fletcher and
  Jonson), 66, 127, 447.
 Witch, The, 127, 416.
 Witch of Edmonton, The, see
  Dekker.
 World Tossed at Tennis, The (with
  Rowley), 201 n. 2, 205, 214,
  342.
Middlewich, Chester, 511.
Midsummer Night's Dream, see
 Shakespeare.
Mildmay, Sir Anthony, 673.
Mildmay, Sir Henry, 635, 673.
Mildmay, Herbert A. St. John, A
 Brief Memoir of the Mildmay
 Family, 673.
Mildmay, Sir Humphrey, 3 n. 7, 30
 and nn. 2 and 6, 39, 47, 48,
 56 n. 3, 61, 62, 231 and n. 1,
 235, 245, 258.
 Records of, 673–81.
Mildmay, Humphrey St. John, 673.
Mildmay, Nann, 676.
Mildmay, Sir Walter, 673.
Miller, Elizabeth, 631.
Miller, Richard, 527.
Minerva's Sacrifice, see Massinger.
Mingay, Anthony, 312.
Minion, Samuel, 299, 511.
Minshall, Edward, see Minshaw,
 Edward.
Minshaw, Edward, 511.
Minshaw, Huon, 511.
Minshaw, Jane, 511.
Minshaw, John, 511.
Minshaw, Joyce, 511.
Minshaw, Julyan, 511.
Minshaw, Mary, 511.
Minshaw, Willi, 511.
Mistale or Misdale, 286, 297, 511.
Mohun, Lady Catherine, 447.
Mohun, Michael, 327, and n. 4, 332,
 336, 511–12.
Money is an Ass, see Jordan.
Monk, General, 545.
Monke, Samuel, 512.
Monke, William, 512.
Monopolers, 65 n. 2, 317 n. 1.

Monsieur Thomas, see Beaumont
 and Fletcher.
Montgomery, Earl of, 349.
Moone, Michael, see Mohun, Michael.
Moor Lane, see London, streets of.
Moor of Venice, The, see Shake-
 speare, Othello.
Moore, Captain Alexander, 438.
Moore, John, 64.
Moore, Joseph, 176, 178, 179, 180
 and n. 13, 181, 182, 183, 187, 188,
 189 and nn. 3 and 4, 190, 192, 219,
 302, 303, 307, 308, 311, 315, 321,
 512–15, 682.
Moore, Robert, 438.
Moorgate, see London, streets of.
Morals, 685.
More Dissemblers besides Women,
 see Middleton.
More, Roger, see Nore, Roger.
Moreton, Richard, 564.
Morgan, Fluellen, 515.
Morgan, General, 521.
Morgan, Mrs., 646, 647.
Morgan, William, 385.
Morris, John, 470.
Morris, Matthias, 285, 287, 290, 297,
 515.
Morrison. Elizabeth Bowyer, 635,
 636.
Morrison, Thomas, 69 n. 2, 88, 89,
 376, 387, 636.
Mortality tables, 667–72.
Mortimer, Mr., 350.
Morton, Sir Albert, 10. n. 6.
Morton, Elizabeth, 606.
Moseley, Humphrey, 116, 117, 123,
 276.
Mosley, Margaret, 649.
Mossock, Ann, 515, 598.
Mountsett, John, 515.
Moxie, James, 394.
Much Ado about Nothing, see Shake-
 speare.
Munck, Lewin, 416.
Munday, Anthony, Oldcastle, see
 Drayton.
Muntford, John, see Mountsett, John.
Murray, John, 385.
Murray, William, 60, 61.
Musarum Deliciae, see Anon.
Muses' Looking Glass, The, see
 Randolph.
Music in theatres, 136–7.
 Cost of, 44.
Musicians, 3, 15, 20, 40, 142, 343,
 347, 349, 354, 355, 363, 400, 422,
 426, 427, 429, 432, 441, 443, 479,
 482, 487, 495, 508, 511, 512, 543,

Musicians (*contd.*) :
544, 554, 560, 561, 573, 578, 590, 609, 610, 621, 622.
Myers and Company, *Illustrated Catalogue of Rare Books*, 623.
Mylyon, Mr., 622.

Nabbes, Thomas, 488, 509 n. 1.
Bride, The, 340.
Covent Garden, 227, 255.
Hannibal and Scipio, 221 n. 1, 231, 235, 246, 251, 255, 344, 345, 353, 377, 378, 387, 407, 433, 518, 528, 573, 581, 583, 608, 660, 692.
Microcosmus, 255.
Tottenham Court, 255–6.
Unfortunate Mother, The, 444.
Nabes, Joane, 491.
Nappers, —, 457, 689.
Nashe, Thomas, *The Isle of Dogs*, 1.
Navarro, John, **515**.
Naworth, Castle, 212.
Neale, Robert, 637.
Netherlands, 578.
    Ambassador from, 20.
    English actors in, 6, 335, 413, 493, 494, 523, 571, 625.
    Vaulter from, 502.
Nethersole, Sir Francis, 10 nn. 2 and 5, 267.
Newcastle, Duke of, *see* Cavendish, William.
Newcastle, King's visit to, 388–9.
New College, Winchester, 514.
Newgate, *see* London, streets of.
Newington Butts theatre, 1.
New Inn, The, see Jonson.
Newmarket, 61.
Newport, Lady, 329.
New Prison, 266.
News from Plymouth, see Davenant.
Newsletter, 223 n. 8.
Newspapers:
    Diary or an Exact Journal, A, 549.
    Kingdom's Weekly Intelligencer, The, 481.
    Man in the Moon, The, 462, 531.
    Mercurius Democritus, 415.
    Mercurius Fumigosus, 515, 523.
    Mercurius Impartialis, 462.
    Mercurius Militaris, 462.
    Mercurius Pragmaticus, 531, 555.
    Perfect Occurrences, 548.
    Royal Diurnal, 462.
    Second Discovery by the Northern Scout, A, 13 n. 2.
    True Diurnal Occurrences, 67.
    Vox Borealis, or the Northern Discovery, 277, 282.

Newton, Francis, 384.
Newton, John, 137 n. 3, 176, 198, 199 and n. 2, 200 and n. 3, 203 and n. 1, 209, 210, 211, **515–16**.
Newton, William, 516.
New Trick to Cheat the Devil, A, see Davenport.
New Way to Pay Old Debts, A, see Massinger.
New Wonder, a Woman Never Vexed, A, see Rowley.
Nice Valour, or the Passionate Madman, The, see Beaumont and Fletcher.
Nicholas, Sir Edward, 473, 512.
Nicholson, James, 276.
Nick, **516–17**.
Nicolini, Francis, **517**.
Nicols, John, 502, 552.
Night playing, *see* Plays at night.
Night Walker, The, see Beaumont and Fletcher.
Nill, John, **517**.
Noar or Noer, Roger, *see* Nore, Roger.
Noble Choice, The, see Massinger, *The Orator*.
Noble Gentleman, The, see Beaumont and Fletcher.
Nobleman, The, see Tourneur.
Noble Stranger, The, see Sharpe.
Nobody in Barbican, 606, 682.
Nonpareilles, or the Matchless Maids, The, see Davenant, *Love and Honour*.
Nore, Amellicoe, 517.
Nore, Elizabeth, 517.
Nore, John, 517.
Nore, Roger, 316 and n. 2, 321, **517**.
Norfolk, 642.
Norman's Rents, *see* London, streets of.
Northern Lass, The, see Brome.
Norton, Mary, 639.
Norton, Mrs., 639.
Norwich, 144 n. 4, 156, 172, 173, 178, 179, 181, 182, 193, 197, 212, 213, 248, 273, 274, 275, 276, 282, 286, 288, 289 and n. 4, 294, 297, 298, 299, 302, 303 and n. 1, 312 and n. 7 cont'd., 322, 420, 427, 452, 454, 458, 485, 530, 613.
    Bishop of, 274.
    Mayor of, 179.
Notary Public, 651.
Nott, Dr., 347.
Nottingham, 92, 172, 173, 180, 193, 212, 213, 310, 419, 617.

Novella, The, see Brome.
Nuremberg, 451, 561.

Oare's Rents, *see* London, streets of.
Oaths, *see* Profanity.
Oatlands, 50.
Occupations:
Apple-wives, 268, 315.
Bailiff, 348.
Baker, 486.
Barber-chirurgion (*see also* Doctor, Physician, and Surgeon), 143, 437, 484.
Basket-maker, 431, 486.
Blacksmith, 314.
Body-keeper, 118, 492, 494, 612.
Body-maker, 455.
Bookseller, 405, 473, 544, 545.
Boxer tumbler, 485.
Brewer, 482.
Brewer's servant, 431.
Bricklayer, 143, 619.
Builders, 348.
Butchers, 690, 691.
Carpenter, 143, 358, 482, 499.
Carrier, 486.
Chandler, 479, 564, 565, 615.
Churchwarden, 466.
Clerk, 350, 504, 644.
Clothmaker, 443.
Collier, 508.
Composer, 432.
Conjurer, 266.
Constable, 266.
Contractor, 143.
Cooper, 579.
Cordwainer, 265.
Cutler, 564.
Dancers, 53 n. 1, 496, 515, 517–18, 522, 541, 563, 578, 617.
Dancers on the ropes, 150, 456, 517, 521, 522, 613, 657, 662, 680.
Dancing master, 517.
Doctor (*see also* Barber-chirurgion, Physician, and Surgeon), 641.
Doctor in Physic, 634.
Draper, 544, 545, 648.
Drummer, 473.
Entertainer, 578, 617.
Felt-maker, 167.
Fencer, 318, 360, 406, 442, 688.
Fiddler, 363, 469, 621.
Fishmonger, 576.
Game player, 616.
Gaoler, 354.
Gardener, 352, 564.
Gatherer, 346, 558, 588, 616, 622, 684.
Goldsmith, 398, 401, 499.

Occupations (*contd.*):
Grocer, 564, 641, 643.
Haberdasher, 412, 636.
Hosier, 413.
Innholder, 458.
Innkeeper, 500.
Ironmonger, 574.
Jeweller, 554, 587, 695.
Jig maker, 563.
Juggler, 612.
Labourer, 431, 486.
Lawyer, 3 n. 7, 266.
Lutanist, 554, 621.
Maid servant, 349, 353, 634.
Man servant, 349, 353.
Merchant, 486, 493.
Merchant adventurer, 564.
Merchant tailor, 143, 508, 555, 578.
Messenger, 448, 683.
Musicians, 3, 15, 20, 40, 142, 343, 347, 349, 354, 355, 363, 400, 422, 426, 427, 432, 441, 443, 479, 482, 487, 495, 508, 511, 512, 543, 544, 554, 560, 561, 573, 578, 590, 609, 610, 621, 622.
Organist, 422.
Packthread-maker, 357.
Painters, 48, 395.
Pewterer, 431, 598.
Physician (*see also* Barber-chirurgion, Doctor, and Surgeon), 509 n. 1.
Porter, 682.
Preacher, 435, 649.
Printer, 434, 436.
Property-maker, 53 n. 1.
Puppeteer, 413, 618.
Saddler, 564.
Sailor, 21, 265–6, 267, 431, 690.
Scene painters, 53 n. 1.
Scrivener, 351, 415–16, 511, 551, 648, 649.
Sergeant at mace, 545, 581.
Serving man, 449.
Shoemaker, 690.
Showman, 507.
Sidesman, 466.
Smith, 607.
Stage keeper, 686.
Stationer, 143, 481, 545.
Surgeon (*see also* Barber-chirurgion, Doctor, and Physician), 139, 265, 453, 617.
Taverner, 497.
Tailor, 413, 446, 455, 486, 491, 688.
Theatre caretakers, 432, 462, 544, 572.

Occupations (*contd.*):
. Tight-rope walker (*see also* Dancers on the ropes), 612.
Trumpeter, 357, 483, 609.
Tumbler, 459, 486, 522.
Turner, 682.
Undercook, 546.
Vaulter, 486, 502, 522, 613.
Victualler, 564.
Vintner, 314, 426, 642.
Wardrobe-keeper, 26 n. 5 cont'd., 491, 546.
Waterman, 486, 510, 690.
Weaver, 464, 564, 566, 646.
Workman, 348.
Ogilby, John, 517–18.
Oldcastle, see Drayton.
Oley, Henry, 518.
Oliphant, E. H. C., *The Plays of Beaumont and Fletcher*, 677.
Opportunity, The, see Shirley.
Orator, The, see Massinger.
Orchestra at Blackfriars, 40.
Organist, 422.
Ormond, Marquis of, 673.
Orton, Mary, 518.
Orton, Thomas, 518.
Osborne, Dorothy, 415, 416.
Osborne, Thomas, 383.
Osmond, the Great Turk, see Carlell.
Ossulston, the Hundred of, Middx., 458.
Ostler, William, 5 n. 6 cont'd., 374.
Othello, see Shakespeare.
Ottewell or Ottwell, Hugh, *see* Attwell, Hugh.
Outer doors of theatre, receipts from, 44 and n. 3.
Oxford, 2, 19, 50, 52, 92, 172, 212, 293, 309, 565, 688.
Vice-chancellor of, 688.
Oxford, Lady Ann, Countess of, 525.

Packthread-maker, 357.
Page, John, 220, 239, 246, 324, 326 n. 6, 332, 336, 518.
Page, Mr., 640.
Page of the Bedchamber, 438.
Page, William, 518.
Painter, 48, 395.
Palatinate, the, 10 n. 6 cont'd.
Prince of the, *see* Charles Lewis.
Palatine, Elector, *see* Palsgrave.
Pallant, Robert, senior, 158, 171, 177 and n. 2, 199 and n. 2, 200 and n. 3, 203 n. 1, 211, 518–19.
Pallant, Robert, junior, 15, 72–88, 519–20.

Pallantus and Eudora, see Killigrew, *The Conspiracy.*
Palmer's Rents, *see* London, streets of.
Palsgrave, the, Frederick V, Elector Palatine, 136, 140 n. 2, 185 n. 7.
Company of, 4 n. 3, 135–57, 178, 183, 188, 261, 262 and n. 3, 263, 264.
Papist, 549, 688.
Paris, 218, 235.
Paris Garden, 63, 501.
Parish Clerk's Hall, 653.
Parkins, Richard, *see* Perkins, Richard.
Parliament of Love, The, see Massinger.
Parr, Richard, 520.
Parr, William, 136, 137, 138, 140, 147, 155, 178, 520.
Parricide, The, see Glapthorne.
Parrott, Henry, *Cures for the Itch*, 413.
Parson, John, 143.
Parson's Wedding, The, see Killigrew.
Partridge, John, 352.
Partridge, Mary, 352.
Pascal, Thomasin, 559.
Passionate Lovers, The, see Carlell.
Passionate Madman, The, see Beaumont and Fletcher, *The Nice Valour.*
Pastoral, The, see Anon.
Pastorals, 685.
Pate, Edward, 412, 413, 570.
Patent to build a theatre, 198.
Patents, 3 n. 1, 5, 17, 72–3, 80–1, 137, 155, 167–9, 182, 211, 274.
Duplicate, condemned, 178.
Exemplifications of, 178–9.
Proposed, for Queen's company, 685–6.
Patrick, Margaret, 520.
Patrick, William, 15, 49 and n. 2 cont'd., 72–88, 520–1, 682.
Paul's Head, 140.
Payne, Katherine, 647.
Payne, Richard, 486.
Peaceable King, or the Lord Mendall, The, see Anon.
Peadle, Abraham, 145, 147, 155, 521, 682, 683.
Peadle, Anne, 522.
Peadle, Cornelius, 522.
Peadle, Jacob, 521.
Peadle, Thomas, 522.
Peadle, William, senior, 522.
Peadle, William, junior, 522–3.

Peagott, Richard, 455.
Pedel *or* Pedle, *see* Peadle.
Peele, George, *The Battle of Alcazar*, 481, 578.
    Alphonsus, Emperor of Germany, *see* Anon.
Peet, Nathan, **523.**
Pembroke, Earl of, 6, 7, 12, 34 n. 3, 53, 179, 349.
Pembroke and Montgomery, Earl of, 34 n. 3, 62.
Pembroke's company, 562.
Pendle Forest, 41, 294 n. 1.
Penn, Anne, 524.
Penn, John, 524.
Penn, Marie, 523.
Penn, Sibilla, 523.
Penn, William, 18, 24, 49, 73–89, 199 and n. 2, 200, 209, 211, **523–4,** 682.
Penneycuick, Andrew, *see* Pennycuicke, Andrew.
Pennicooke *or* Pennycooke, Andrew, *see* Pennycuicke, Andrew.
Pennington, Alderman, 64.
Pennycuicke, Andrew, 246, **524–5.**
Pennycuicke, Dorothy, 525.
Pennycuicke, Jacobi, 525.
Pennycuicke, Margaret, 525.
Perckens, Richard, *see* Perkins, Richard.
Perfect Occurrences, see Newspapers.
Pericles, see Shakespeare.
Perkin Warbeck, see Ford
Perkins, Elizabeth, 527.
Perkins, John, 526.
Perkins, Richard, 16, 24, 73–89, 90 n. a, 158, 163, 165, 167, 168 nn. 2 and 3, 169 and n. 2, 171, 204, 220, 221, 222, 231, 237, 238, 244, 245, 246, 247, **525–8,** 682.
Perkins, William, 484.
Perpoole Lane, *see* London, streets of.
Perrie, William, *see* Perry, William.
Perry, Jone, 529.
Perry, William, 24, 25, 158 n. 1, 178, 271, 272, 273 nn. 3 and 5, 274, 275, 276, 280 n. 2, 281, 282 n. 1, 288, 510, **529–31.**
Perryn, Richard, 535.
Perspectives, 52.
Petchey, Robert, 564.
Peters, Hugh, 401, **531,** 548, 549.
Petre, Sir George, 10 n. 6 cont'd.
Pett, John, 384.
Pettingham, Henry, 49 n. 2 cont'd., 73–89, **531.**
Pettington, Henry, **531.**

Pewterer, 431, 598, 648.
Philaster, see Beaumont and Fletcher.
Phillips, Augustine, 1, 2, 4 n. 1, 46, 363, 411, 443, 447, 468, 624.
Phillips, John, *The Impartial Doom*, 58.
Phoenix or Cockpit theatre, 3 n. 7, 26, 28 and n. 1, 137 n. 6, 161–3, 164, 165, 174, 178, 182, 183, 184, 185 and n. 9, 187, 188, 194, 195, 196, 201 n. 2, 202 and nn. 1 and 6, 204 and n. 1, 205, 207, 208, 218, 219, 220, 223, 224, 225 and n. 1, 226, 227, 228, 231, 234 and n. 3, 236, 242, 264, 268, 305 n. 3, 307, 319, 325, 327, 329 n. 6, 331, 334, 675, 676, 692, 693, 694, 695.
    Chief actors at, 182, 183.
    Early reputation of, 164.
    Environs of, 228 n. 1.
    Objections to, 160.
    Prestige of, 184, 226, 234, 307 and n. 1.
    Royal visit to, 232.
Physician (*see also* Barber-chirurgion, Doctor, and Surgeon), 509 n. 1.
Pickleherring, *see* Reynolds, Robert.
Picture, The, see Massinger.
Pierry, William, *see* Perry, William.
Pilgrim, The, see Beaumont and Fletcher.
Pinder, widow, 474.
Pinnocke, Thomas, 313.
Pirkyns, Richard, *see* Perkins, Richard.
Pit, *see* Theatre, pit in.
Plague, 2, 17, 20 and n. 6 cont'd., 63, 65, 129, 260 n. 3, 262, 270, 271, 296, 313, 316, **652–72.**
    Closing regulations violated, 56 n. 1.
    Gratuities on raising of restrictions after, 658.
    King's assistance during, 53.
    Players petition to open after, 55–6, 240, 328.
    Precautions against, 656, 658.
    Reason for provincial tours, 686.
    Table of deaths from, 667–72.
    Theatre closed because of, 19, 26–7, 29, 49, 186, 222, 652–72.
Plantation of Virginia, The, see Anon.
Platonic Lovers, The, see Davenant.
Playbill, 197, 541, 604, 614, 686.
Playbooks, 162, 534.

Players:
Accidents to, 689.
Attendance of, on King's progress, 309 n. 3, 310–11.
Benefit performance for, 507.
Benefit publication for, 505.
Bonds of, 148–9, 176, 198, 211, 263.
Boys, 285, 308, 487, 599.
  Care of, 563.
  Comparisons of, with women, 588.
  Gloves for, 687.
  Impersonations by, 551.
  Wages of, 44.
Dramatists as, 357, 388–9, 389, 417, 427, 434–6, 454–8, 472, 476–8, 487–90, 492–3, 507, 555, 555–6, 581.
Estates of, 396, 412, 502, 535, 551, 587, 631–51.
Expenses of, 44.
Fined, 277.
Fraudulent activities of, 190.
Fraudulent swearing of, 190, 358–9.
Hired men, see Hired men.
Imprisonment of, 332–3, 336, 480, 484–5, 604, 609, 614.
In Civil War, 694–5.
Incomes of, 43, 45.
Mutes, 318.
Pass for, 86–7.
Petitions against, 4–5, 22, 31–3, 35, 43–7, 64, 190, 351, 355, 356, 358, 359, 383, 392, 393, 403, 404, 413, 417, 438, 439, 440, 456, 457, 459, 463, 469, 497, 497–8, 514, 531, 570, 576–7, 577, 578.
Petitions of, 55–6, 56 n. 1, 122, 201 n. 1, 240, 260, 327–8, 328–9, 663, 664.
Popularity of, 460.
Portraits of, 382, 395, 403, 405, 434, 500, 527.
Punishment of, 11–12.
Recruiting of, 34.
Share of profits, division of, 44.
Stayed too long at Norwich, 274.
Summoned for playing during plague, 327, 336.
Support of in plague time, 685.
Suppressed, 1, 12, 241 and n. 3, 327, 332–3.
Suspension from stage as punishment, 46.
Theatre duties, 474.
Training of, 692.

Players (contd.):
Warrant to recruit, 34, 35 and n. 2.
Women, 25.
Playgoers, 673–81.
Playhouse, see Theatre.
Playhouse to Be Let, The, see Davenant.
Playhouse scrivener, 415–16.
Playing, actor's pleasure in, 505.
  At court, see Court performances.
  At night, 180 n. 10, 276, 312.
  Prohibition of, 6, 222.
  Surreptitious, 362, 695.
Plays, anti-Anglican, 277–8.
  Anti-Catholic, 9–15.
  Anti-Spanish, 9.
  At court, see Court performances.
  Attempt to suppress, 67.
  Authors' contract to write, 241–2.
  Average number of performances of, 135.
  Caroline vs. Restoration, 691–2, 693.
  Censored, 7, 36–9, 103, 105, 106, 106–7, 107–8, 115, 121–2, 124, 125, 150, 314.
  Composition of, 473.
  Conduct at, 276.
  Corrupt printing of, 54.
  Criticism of, 31, 58–60, 107, 122, 126, 224, 230, 681.
  Cutting of, 242.
  Expurgated, 495.
  Illegally sold, 279.
  Illegal use of by King's, 278–9.
  In company repertory, protected, 53–4, 65–7, 328, 330–1.
    Destruction of, 141.
  In folio, 243 n. 2.
  In manuscript, 103, 111, 114, 118, 120, 123, 124, 126–7, 127, 132, 173–4, 175, 195, 195–6, 216, 216–17, 300, 323.
  Licensing fees for, 687.
  New, annual production of, 149 n. 4.
  Number of, per year, 135.
  Offensive, 493.
  Offensive at court, 204.
  Personal satire in, 228–9, 229, 314.
  Political allusions in, 333.
  Political satire in, 9–15, 60–1.
  Popular, 10, 13 n. 2, 105.
    Income from, 295 and n. 6.
  Printing of, prohibited without company's consent, 54.
  Private performances of, 6, 39, 48 and n. 5, 327–8.

Plays, anti-Anglican (*contd.*):
Publication of, 295.
Relicensed, 103, 104, 106, 107, 115, 150, 174–5, 185, 206, 229–30, 250, 277, 293–4.
Request performances of, 23 n. 1.
Revisions of, 41, 149, 174–5, 230, 277, 293–4.
Revivals of, 23, 62, 124, 687.
Rights in, 330–1.
Runs of, 13 n. 2, 278, 282, 303.
Selling of, 545.
Subsidized, 59.
Suppressed, 10–15, 36–9, 277–8.
Surreptitious, 489, 608, 624, 680.
Taste in, 681.
Titles changed, 107, 107–8, 108, 113, 125, 256–7, 258, 291 and n. 8.
Topical, 7, 9–15, 40–1, 60–1, 204, 208–9, 228–9, 277–8, 314, 333.
Unlicensed, 14, 332–3.
Penalty for acting, 332–3, 336.
Witches in, 40.
Playwrights, 44.
Benefit performances for, 295 n. 4, 390.
Contracts of, 63, 227, 241, 242, 292 n. 1, 295 and nn. 4 and 5, 390, 538, 555.
Play of, rejected, 242 n. 1.
Wages of, 242, 295, 686.
Plumfield, Thomas, 303, 308, 321, 531.
Plymouth, 180, 193, 212.
Pocklington, York, 473.
Poetaster, The, see Jonson.
Poets, *see* Playwrights.
Politicians, The, see Shirley.
Politics in plays, *see* Plays.
Politique Father, The, see Shirley, *The Brothers.*
Pollard, Thomas, 4 n. 2, 14, 16, 17, 35 n. 1, 43, 45, 46, 69 and n. 2, 72–88, 318, 532–5.
Poor Man's Comfort, The, see Daborne.
Pope, Thomas, 1, 4 n. 1, 447.
Porter at the Marshalsea, 682.
Porter, Endymion, 39, 61, 106.
Porter, Maryan, 565.
Portland, Duke of, 579.
Portsmouth, 23 n. 1.
Portugal, Sebastian, King of, 105.
Poultry, *see* London, streets of.
Powders, 517.
Powell, Edmond, 641.
Powell, Edward, 535.
Powell, George, 535.
Powell, Margery, 543.

Powell, Martin, 535.
Powell, Philip, 648.
Prague, 451.
Praise of Hemp-seed, The, see John Taylor.
Prat, Samuel, 535.
Preacher, 435, 649.
Pregion, John, 381.
Presbyterian, 587, 695.
Price, Henry, 536.
Price, Mary, 536, 537.
Price, Morgan, 536.
Price, Richard, 136, 138, 140, 143, 144, 147, 148, 152, 153, 155, 261, 262 and n. 4, 263 and n. 1, 269, 535–7, 683.
Price, Richard, junior, 536, 537.
Prince Charles's (I) company, 7, 18, and n. 8, 22 and n. 2, 24, 36, 137 n. 3, 152 n. 3, 164, 165, 176, 177, 178, 183, 193 n. 2, **198–217**, 270 and n. 3.
Prince Charles's (II) company, 184, 269, 274, 279–80, 282, 290, 291 n. 1, 292, 293 n. 2, **302–23**, 327.
Prince, Mr., 675.
Prince's Arms, 201 n. 2.
Princes Reconnus, Les, see Du Rocher.
Princess, The, see Killigrew.
Printer, 434, 436.
Printers and stationers, company of, 53.
Prisoner, The, see Massinger, *The Fair Anchoress of Pausilippo.*
Prisoners, The, see Killigrew.
Private performances, 10 n. 6 cont'd., 327.
Privilege, certificates of, *see* Tickets of privilege.
Privy Council, 1, 10, 11, 21, 63, 137, 161, 162 n. 3, 163, 176, 198, 228 n. 1, 236 n. 7, 296, 324 n. 1, 327.
President of, 12.
Privy Seal Office, 415.
Profanity, 37, 106–7.
Progress, royal, 311 n. 1.
Itinerary of, 310.
Players' attendance during, 309 n. 3, 310–11.
Projectors, 65 n. 2, 314, 317 n. 1.
Projects, 314.
Prologues, 228, 440, 691.
Contract to write, 390.
Properties, value of, 57.
Property makers, 53 n. 1.
Prophetess, The, see Beaumont and Fletcher.

Proude, Searles, 464.
Provincial audiences, 312–13.
Provincial companies suppressed, 178–9.
Provincial performances, conduct at, 276.
Provincial tours, players dislike of, 146 n. 6.
Provincial visits, 92–3, 156, 172–3, 193, 212–13, 248, 282, 298–9, 322.
    Length of, 274, 275, 276.
Proxy, or Love's Aftergame, The, see Anon.
Pryce, John, 649.
Prynne, William, 25 n. 5, 329, 454, 457.
Pryore, Richard, *see* Price, Richard.
Puckering, Sir Thomas, 52, 239 n. 3, 283 n. 7 cont'd., 284, 436.
Puddle Wharf theatre, *see* Rosseter's Puddle Wharf or Blackfriars theatre.
Pudsey, Edward, **537.**
Puncteus, John, **537.**
Puppeteer, 413, 618.
Puppet play, 480.
Puritan feeling against the players, 67.
Puritan minister, 5.
Puritan residents in Blackfriars, 31.
Puritans, 537, 538.
Pyne, Arthur, *Musarum Deliciae*, 472.
Pyrkyns, Richard, *see* Perkins, Richard.

Queen and the Concubine, The, see Brome.
Queen Camel, Somerset, 673.
Queen of Aragon, The, see Habington.
Queen of Corinth, The, see Beaumont and Fletcher.
Queen, or the Excellency of Her Sex, The, see Anon.
Queen's College, Oxford, 26 n. 5 cont'd., 688.
Queen's company, *see* Anne and Henrietta Maria.
Queen's Exchange, The, see Brome.
Queen's Lord Chamberlain, *see* Lord Chamberlain to the Queen.
Queen's Revels, 198, 200.
Queen's street, *see* London, streets of.
Quoyten, Bartholomew, 649.

Rainescrofte, Thomas, *see* Ravenscroft, Thomas.

Raison, Gilbert, *see* Reason, Gilbert.
Raleigh, Sir Edward, 371.
Ram Alley, see David, Lord Barry.
Randolph, Ambrose, 42 n. 3.
Randolph, Thomas, 291 n. 8, 292 n. 1, 416, **537–9.**
    Amyntas, 292, 299 n. a, 300, 538.
    Drinking Academy, The, 538.
    'Eclogue to Master Jonson', 538.
    Entertainment, The, see *The Muses' Looking Glass.*
    Muses' Looking Glass, The, 291, 292, 301, 537, 538.
Ranting in theatres, 280.
Rape, execution for, 675.
Rape of Lucrece, The, see Heywood.
Ravenscroft, Thomas, **539,** 642.
Rawlins, Thomas, *The Rebellion*, 13 n. 2, 301, 319 n. 1, 440, 444, 446, 489.
Rayer, Alice, 403.
Rayne, Andrew, *see* Cane, Andrew.
Reade, Edward, 541.
Reade, Emanuel, 171, 177 and n. 6, **539.**
Reade, Pennella, 541.
Reade, Timothy, 65 n. 2, 165, 220, 246, 285, 286, 287, 288, 290, 291 and n. 2, 297, **540–1.**
Reading, 92, 172, 189 n. 3, 193, 212, 272, 273, 282, 298, 350, 453, 475, 604.
Reason, Gilbert, 178, 198, 209 and n. 2, 210, 211, **541–3.**
Rebellion, The, see Rawlins.
Receipts from popular plays, 10.
Recusants, 364, 365, 366, 370, 385, 457, 460, 471, 543, 616.
Red Bull theatre, 22 n. 2, 25, 26, 137 n. 6, 158, 160, 161, 163, 164, 165, 166, 170 n. 1, 174, 188 n. 4, 190, 194, 201, 202 and n. 1, 203, 206, 207, 208, 220, 224, 225 and n. 1, 228, 270, 272, 273 and n. 1, 274, 275, 279, 280, 309, 310, 312 n. 7, 314, 315, 317 and n. 2, 319, 320, 346, 560, 571, 637, 680, 690, 693, 694, 695.
    Chief players at, 167, 171.
    Conduct of audiences at, 316.
    Dancing at, 523.
    Disturbance at, 313–14.
    Footways about, 169.
    Mishap on the stage of, 166.
    Petition about highway repairs near, 171.
    Playwrights for, 690.
    Reputation of, 280, 319.

Red Bull–King's company, 22 and n. 2, 25 n. 3, 171, **270–82**, 290, 308, 311, 312, 315.
Red Bull Revels company, 203, 208.
Red Cross street, *see* London, streets of.
Red Lion Alley, *see* London, streets of.
Redman, —, 347.
Reed, Timothy, *see* Reade, Timothy.
Rehearsal, The, see Buckingham.
Rehearsals, 503, 552.
Reignolds, William, 220, 221, 222, 246, **543.**
Renegado, or the Gentleman of Venice, The, see Massinger.
Repertories, *see* Company repertories.
Revels, Master of the, 159, 239, 272. Bonus for, 105.
Revels, Players of the, *see* Queen Anne's Company—Players of the Revels, 158–75.
Revenge for Honour, see Glapthorne *The Parricide.*
Reynolds, Jane, 543.
Reynolds, Margery, 543.
Reynolds, Robert, 165, 171, 543.
Reynolds, William, *see* Reignolds, William.
Rheade, Timothy, *see* Reade, Timothy.
Rhodes, Ann, 545.
Rhodes, John, 15, 73–89, 279, **544–6,** 659.
Rhodes, John (Restoration manager), 694.
Rice, John, 8, 14, 17, 24, 72–88, 117, 176, **546–7,** 683.
Rice, John, clerk of St. S.S., 644.
Richard II, see Shakespeare.
Richard III, see Shakespeare.
Richard the Third, or the English Profit, see Samuel Rowley.
Richards, Nathaniel, *Messalina, the Roman Empress,* 285, 286, 287, 288, 289 n. 4, 290, 291 n. 1, 297, 301, 359, 402, 404, 444, 445, 459, 483, 487, 488, 489, 515, 549, 550, 600.
Richmond, 315, 597, 695.
Richmond, Duchess of, 420.
Richmond and Lennox, Mary, Duchess of, 447.
Richmond, Duke of, 349.
Rick, G., *see* Rickner, George.
Rickner, George, 15, 16 n. 1, 72–88, **547.**
Rimbault, Edward F., 302.
'Who was " Jack Wilson " ?', 622.

Rissers, Abraham, 643.
Ritual, satire of, 277–8.
Roades *or* Roads, *see* Rhodes, John.
Roades, —, 581.
Road troupe, 51.
Roaring Girl, The, see Dekker.
,Robbins, Alice, 548.
Robbins, William, 56, 57, 64, 73–89, 167, 168 n. 2, 171, 183 n. 2, 220, 221, 231, 232, 239, 246, **547–9,** 693.
Robins, Andria, 405.
Robins, William, *see* Robbins, William.
Robinson, Elizabeth, 549.
Robinson, Humphrey, 116, 117, 123.
Robinson, James, 434, 550.
Robinson, John, 285, 286, 288, 290, 297, 457, **549–50.**
Robinson, Margaret, 41.
Robinson, Richard, 3, 5 and n. 6, 14, 17, 35 n. 1, 45 and n. 1, 69 n. 2, 72–88, 126, **550–3,** 637, 650, 682.
Robinson, Mrs. Richard, 44, 45 n. 1.
Robinson, Thomas, **533.**
Robinson, William, *see* Robbins, William.
Robinson, Winifred, 43, 553.
Robson, William, *see* Robbins, William.
Rod for Run-aways, A, see Dekker.
Rodd, Thomas, 302.
Rodes, John, *see* Rhodes, John.
Rodes, Susan, 565.
Roe, William, **553.**
Rogers, Abraham, 384.
Rogers, Edward, 220, 221, 246, **553.**
Rogers, Hester, 554.
Rogers, William, 189, 192, 272, 438, **553–4.**
Roles, characteristic, 318.
Rollo, Duke of Normandy, see Beaumont and Fletcher, *The Bloody Brother.*
Roman Actor, The, see Massinger.
Roods, John, *see* Rhodes, John.
Rope dancers, *see* Dancers on the ropes.
Rosania, see Shirley, *The Doubtful Heir.*
Roscio, I. L., *Conclusions upon Dances,* 499.
Roscius Anglicanus, see John Downes.
Rose, Adam, 384.
Rose theatre, 135, 158, 176.
Rosee, Mr., 614.
Rosenbach, A. S. W., 443.

Rositer, Sara, 421.
Rosseter, Dudley, 554.
Rosseter, Hugh, 554.
Rosseter, Philip, 168 n. 1, 198, **554**.
Rosseter's Puddle Wharf or Black-friars theatre, 201 n. 2, 346, 554.
Rosseter's Queen's Revels, 176.
Rossingham, Edward, 52, 277.
Rossiter, Philip, *see* Rosseter, Philip.
Rotterdam, 531.
Rowe, Dorothy, 582.
Rowe, Sir Thomas, 657 n. 4.
Rowl, *see* Dowle, Rowland.
Rowland, 252, **554–5**.
Rowley, Grace, 558.
Rowley, Samuel, 136, 139, 151, 155, 507, **555**.
 Bilboe's the Best Blade, see *Hard-shift for Husbands*.
 English Profit, The, see *Richard the Third*.
 Hardshift for Husbands, or Bilboe's the Best Blade, 150, 157, 555.
 Hymen's Holiday, or Cupid's Vagaries, see William Rowley.
 Match or No Match, A, 150, 157, 555.
 Richard the Third, or the English Profit, 149, 555.
Rowley, William, 14, 17, 18 and n. 8, 72–88, 137 n. 3, 176, 184, 198, 199 and n. 2, 200 and n. 3, 203 and n. 1, 208, 209 and n. 3, 211, **555–8**.
 All's Lost by Lust, 187, 196, 215 and n. 1, 219 n. 4, 256, 331, 340, 556, 557.
 Changeling, The, see Middleton.
 Fair Quarrel, A, see Middleton.
 Fortune by Land and Sea, see Heywood.
 Guy of Warwick, see Dekker.
 Hymen's Holiday, or Cupid's Vagaries, 230, 249, 256, 331, 340, 368.
 Late Murder in Whitechapel, or Keep the Widow Waking, The (with Dekker, Webster, and Ford), 208, 209, 214, 402, 556, 557, 560, 626.
 New Wonder, a Woman Never Vext, A, 558.
 Search for Money, The, 473.
 Spanish Gypsy, The, see Middleton.
 Witch of Edmonton, The, see Dekker.
 World Tossed at Tennis, The, see Middleton.

Rowly, Mr., 486.
Royal Diurnal, see Newspapers.
Royal King and the Loyal Subject, The, see Heywood.
Royal Slave, The, see Cartwright.
Royston, 50.
Rudyard, Sir Benjamin, 10 n. 6.
Rudyard, Nicholas, 499.
Rule a Wife and Have a Wife, see Beaumont and Fletcher.
Runaways' Answer to a Book Called A Rod for Runaways, The, see Anon.
Rupert, Prince, 463, 571, 694.
Russell, Elizabeth, 345.
Russell, John, 138, 143, **558–9**.
Rutter, Joseph, *The Cid*, 325 n. 2, 336 and n. c, 340.
 Shepherd's Holiday, The, 249, 256.

Sackville, Edward, *see* Dorset, Earl of.
Sackville, Sir John, 283 n. 7.
Sackville, Thomas, **559**.
Saddler, 564.
Sadler, Katherine, 376, 634.
Saffron Walden, 92, 172, 173, 212, 213.
Sage, Jonas, 648.
Sailors, 21, 264, 265–6, 267, 431, 690.
St. Aldermary, *see* St. Mary Alder-mary.
St. Andrew's Holborn, 266, 511, 635.
St. Andrew's by the Wardrobe, 452, 488, 515, 590–1.
St. Anne's, Blackfriars, 5 and n. 1, 31, 383, 385, 406, 407, 436, 485, 489, 520, 535, 551, 553, 559, 571, 582, 583, 601, 605, 623.
St. Bartholomew the Great, 426, 428.
St. Bartholomew the Less, 457, 578, 589, 610, 611, 622, 651.
St. Bodolph's, Aldgate, 386, 485, 496, 523, 561, 603, 624.
St. Botolph's, Bishopsgate, 439, 476, 478, 479, 499, 517, 533, 592, 593, 606.
St. Bride's, 64, 421, 635, 641.
St. Bride's Lane, *see* London, streets of.
St. Catherine's, 161.
St. Clement Dane's, 471, 500, 501, 505, 511.
St. Clement's, Eastcheap, 536.
St. Dionis Backchurch, 442.
St. Dunstan's in the West, 421, 511.

St. Giles without Cripplegate, 138, 143, 149, 262, 312, 316, 357, 359, 384, 385, 391, 393, 399, 401, 402, 403, 404, 405, 407, 408, 409, 415, 426, 439, 440, 445, 449, 450, 451, 452, 454, 455, 456, 459, 463, 464, 465, 471, 473, 475, 482, 483, 484, 494, 498, 499, 508, 510, 516, 517, 518, 522, 523, 524, 536, 537, 541, 543, 544, 545, 550, 555, 556, 562, 564, 565, 567, 571, 575, 576, 577, 578, 580, 584, 588, 598, 599, 600, 602, 610, 613, 617, 624, 626, 627, 635, 642, 645, 650.
St. Giles in the Fields, 184, 329, 344, 346, 364, 369–70, 371, 372, 378, 379, 403, 405, 421, 436, 441, 445, 465, 472, 485, 489, 496, 506, 509, 511, 522, 525, 526, 559, 568, 572, 573, 582, 606, 608, 616, 631, 632, 635.
St. Gregory by St. Paul, 390, 421, 449, 507, 585.
St. Helen within Bishopsgate, 521.
St. James's, Clerkenwell, 308, 310, 312, 353, 361, 364, 383, 390, 392, 400, 405, 407, 428, 429, 432, 445, 450, 473, 474, 486, 492, 493, 496, 497, 518, 523, 524, 526, 527, 528, 529, 531, 543, 548, 557, 583, 584, 589, 615, 616, 617, 623, 625, 626, 627, 631, 636, 637.
St. James's palace, 230, 236, 324, 325.
St. James's, Westminster, 607.
St. Leonard's, Shoreditch, 147, 364, 369, 380, 394, 395, 396, 399, 414, 495, 523, 553, 588, 624, 632, 638, 642, 650, 651.
St. Margaret's, Westminster, 265, 460, 576.
St. Martin's, 64.
St. Martin's, Aldersgate, 484.
St. Martin's in the Fields, 433, 496, 525, 545, 632.
St. Martin Orgar, 491.
St. Mary's, Aldermanbury, 26 n. 5, 343, 410, 411, 412, 413, 418, 466, 467, 468, 469, 470, 501, 585, 587, 588, 643, 644, 648.
St. Mary Aldermary, 455.
St. Mary-le-Strand (Westminster), 564.
St. Michael's, Bassishaw, 389, 607.
St. Michael's, Crooked Lane, 555.
St. Michael's in Bedwardine, 486.
St. Michael le Querne, 495.
St. Paul's Cathedral, 140.
St. Paul's Churchyard, see London, streets of.

St. Peter's Cornhill, 453.
St. Peter's, Paul's Wharf, 616.
St. Saviour's, Southwark, 24, 199 n. 2, 391, 418, 426, 427, 431, 432, 447, 448, 467, 472, 473, 490, 491, 500, 501, 504, 510, 511, 512, 519, 520, 522, 547, 560, 562, 564, 573, 574, 575, 578, 590, 592, 593, 596, 610, 611, 612, 623, 634, 635, 644.
St. Swithin's, 479.
Sale, Charles, 522.
Salisbury Court theatre, 26 n. 5 cont'd., 36, 41, 56, 152 and n. 3, 188 n. 4, 196, 226, 227, 231, 237, 238, 239, 240, 242, 269, 283 and n. 7, 291, 292, 293, 302, 303, 304, 305, 306 n. 3, 307, 308, 309 and n. 3, 319, 330, 379, 538, 623, 680, 684–7, 692, 694.
Dramatist for, 295.
Manager of, 241.
Masque at, 255.
Receipts from, 239 n. 3.
Salisbury family, 412.
Salusbury, Thomas, Masque at Knowsley, 464.
Sampson, William, Herod and Antipater, see Markham.
    Widow's Prize, The, 206 n. 3, 215–16.
Sanders, Elizabeth, 559.
Sanders, Thomasin, 559.
Sanders, William, 15, 72–88, 559.
Sanderson, Georg, 559.
Sanderson, Gregory, 171, 174, 384, 559.
Sands, James, 559–60.
Sands, Thomas, 286, 297, 560.
Sanford, Thomas, 651.
Satire, political, see Plays.
Saul, Thomas, 262, 403, 537.
Saunderson, Peter, 641.
Saunderson, Thomas, 607.
Savage, John, 411.
Savage, Raphe, 560.
Savill, Arthur, 307–8, 308, 321, 560.
Savoian ambassador, 23, 128.
Sawnston, see Swanston, Eyllaerdt.
Scene painters, 53 n. 1.
Scenery, see Theatre, scenery in.
Schadleutner, Sebastian, 561.
Schankes, or Schanks, see Shank.
Scholars, The, see Lovelace.
School of Compliment, The, see Shirley.
Schottnel, Edward, see Shatterell, Edward.
Scornful Lady, The, see Beaumont and Fletcher.

Scotland, 180, 181, 293 n. 2, 311 n. 1.
Scott, Mr., 139, 347.
Scrivener, 351, 415–16, 511, 551, 648, 649.
Scrogge, Alexander, 626.
Scudéry, Georges de, *Le Trompeur Puni*, 235 n. 1.
Seabrooke, Thomas, 190, 192, **561**.
Seaman, Mrs., 639.
Seaman, Thomas, 638, 639.
Search for Money, The, see Rowley.
Seare, Dorothea, 623.
Sea Voyage, The, see Beaumont and Fletcher.
Sebeck, Henry, **561**.
Second Discovery by the Northern Scout, A, see Newspapers.
Second Maiden's Tragedy, The, see Anon.
Sejanus, see Jonson.
Sergeant at mace, 545, 581.
Serving man, 449.
Seven Champions of Christendom, The, see Kirke.
Seven Deadly Sins, see Anon.
Sewers of Her Majesty's Chamber, 685.
Shadwell in Stepney, 265.
Shadwell, Thomas, *The Virtuoso*, 598.
Shagbutts, 348, 508.
Shakerley, Edward, 220, 221, 222, 246, **561**, 682.
Shakespeare, William, 1, 2, 4 nn. 1 and 2, 5 n. 6 cont'd., 22, 46, 66, 68, 120, 146 n. 6, 177, 270 and nn. 3 and 4, 410, 435, 436, 462, 463, 467, 469, 478, 506, 537, 597, 674, 692, 693.
First folio, 8, 22 n. 2, 34 n. 3, 184, 270 n. 4 cont'd., 467.
As You Like It, 137 and n. 7, 157, 347.
Cymbeline, 97, 127.
Hamlet, 51, 95 n. c, 98, 99 n. v, 127–8, 597, 693.
Henry IV, Part 1, 95, 128, 447, 489, 505, 693.
Henry IV, Part 2, 95 n. c, 128–9.
Henry VIII, 2, 22, 318, 506.
Julius Caesar, 51, 98, 99, 129.
Love's Labour's Lost, 447.
Merry Wives of Windsor, The, 99, 129.
Midsummer Night's Dream, A, 27, 96, 129, 590, 622.
Much Ado About Nothing, 621, 622.
Othello, 24, 48, 51, 98, 129, 587, 597, 660, 677, 681, 693.

Shakespeare, William, *(contd.)*:
Pericles, 94, 129, 375, 658.
Richard II, 1, 24, 129, 566.
Richard III, 97, 128, 129, 395, 585.
Romeo and Juliet, 347.
Taming of the Shrew, The, 97, 129–30.
Twelfth Night, 94, 130.
Two Noble Kinsmen, The, see Beaumont and Fletcher.
Winter's Tale, The, 94, 95 and n. c, 97, 103, 130, 468.
Shanbrooke, Elizabeth, 562.
Shanbrooke, John, **561–2**.
Shanbrooke, Rachel, 562.
Shanbrooke, William, 562.
Shanck, Shancke, Shanckes, *or* Shancks, *see* Shank.
Shank, Anne, 565.
Shank, Elizabeth, 564, 566, 567, 568.
Shank, James, 565, 566, 567, 646, 647.
Shank, John, senior, 4 nn. 1 and 2, 5 and n. 6, 14, 17, 31, 35 n. 1, 43, 44, 45, 46, 47, 57 n. 2, 72–88, 129, 136, 139, 155, 281, 321, **562–7**, 642.
Will of, 646–8.
Shank's Ordinary, 103 and n. 2, 130, 565.
Shank, John, junior, 275, 315 n. 2, **567–9**.
Shank, Thomas, 565.
Shank, Winifred, 46, 564, 565, 566–7, 568, 646, 647.
Shank's Ordinary, see Shank, John.
Shanks, William, 565.
Shanucke, John, *see* Shank, John, senior.
Sharer Papers, 43–7, 86–7.
Sharers, 310, 688.
Sharpe, Lewis, *The Noble Stranger*, 256.
Sharpe, Richard, 14, 16, 17, 22, 35 n. 1, 70, 72–88, **569–71**.
Shatterell, Edward, **571**.
Shatterell, Robert, 327 n. 4, 332, 336, **571–2**.
Shaunks, John, *see* Shank, John, junior.
Shaw, Robert, 135.
Shearlock, William, *see* Sherlock, William.
Sheldon, Edward, 411.
Shepherd's Holiday, The, see Rutter.
Sheppard, Margaret, 644.
Sheppard, Thomas, 632, 644.
Shepperd, John, 365.

Sheppey, Henry, 682.
Sherlock, William, 163, 183, 187, 192, 219, 220, 221, 222, 231, 232, 237, 238, 246, **572-3**.
Shirelock, William, *see* Sherlock, William.
Shirley, Henry, *The Dumb Bawd of Venice*, 96, 130, 469.
    Martyred Soldier, The, 256, 493.
    Spanish Duke of Lerma, The, 66, 130.
Shirley, James, 63, 184, 229, 230 n. 2, 231, 305 n. 3, 306 n. 2, **573**.
    Herbert's commendation of, 230.
    Plays of, for Queen Henrietta's men, 226.
    Possible contract of, with Phoenix, 227.
    Relation of, with Salisbury Court, 306 and n. 2.
    Arcadia, The, 104, 111, 226 n. 7, 227, 256.
    Ball, The, 226 n. 7, 228-9, 230 n. 2, 250-1.
    Bewties, The, see *The Bird in a Cage*.
    Bird in a Cage, The, 226 n. 7, 227 n. 2, 256, 573.
    Brothers, The, 63, 66, 108, 130-1, 258.
    Cardinal, The, 63, 108, 131, 462-3, 534, 692.
    Chabot, Admiral of France, see Chapman.
    Changes, or Love in a Maze, 227, 285 and n. 1, 301, 304, 305-6, 311, 323.
    Constant Maid, The, 227, 256-7, 378.
    Coronation, The, 226 n. 7, 257, 331, 337, 340, 660.
    Court Secret, The, 63, 131.
    Doubtful Heir, The, 30 n. 6, 63, 66, 108, 131, 461.
    Duke, The, see *The Humorous Courtier*.
    Duke's Mistress, The, 226 n. 7, 236, 248 n. i, 249, 257.
    Example, The, 226 n. 7, 257, 331, 340.
    Faithful Servant, The, see *The Grateful Servant*.
    Gamester, The, 226 n. 7, 230, 231, 249, 257, 675.
    Gentleman of Venice, The, 244, 257.
    Grateful Servant, The, 226 n. 7, 257, 331, 340-1.
    Humorous Courtier, The, 226 n. 7, 257.

Shirley, James (*contd.*):
    Hyde Park, 226 n. 7, 257-8, 331, 341.
    Impostor, The, see *The Imposture*.
    Imposture, The, 63, 66, 108, 131, 665 n. 7.
    Lady of Pleasure, The, 226 n. 7, 231 n. 1, 235, 258, 331, 341, 661, 677, 681.
    Love's Cruelty, 226 n. 7, 258, 331, 336, 341, 397, 512, 692.
    Love Tricks with Compliments, see *The School of Compliment*.
    Love Will Find out the Way, see *The Constant Maid*.
    Maid's Revenge, The, 218 n. 3, 222, 223 n. 1, 226 n. 7, 258, 331, 341.
    Night Walker, The, see Beaumont and Fletcher.
    Opportunity, The, 226 n. 7, 258, 331, 341.
    Politician, The, 258.
    Politique Father, The, see *The Brothers*.
    Rosania, see *The Doubtful Heir*.
    School of Compliment, The, 186 and n. 3, 187, 196, 219 n. 4, 226 n. 7, 258, 331, 341.
    Sisters, The, 63, 67-8, 108, 131.
    Traitor, The, 226 n. 7, 258, 331, 341.
    Triumph of Peace, The, 573, 675, 676.
    Wedding, The, 218, 220, 221 and n. 1, 222, 223 and n. 6, 226 n. 7, 231, 246, 259, 331, 341, 345, 386, 406, 423, 518, 528, 540, 548, 553, 572, 583, 608, 619, 628, 692.
    Witty, Fair One, The, 223, 226 n. 7, 259, 331, 341.
    Young Admiral, The, 226 n. 7, 230, 249, 259, 331, 341.
Shoe Lane, *see* London, streets of.
Shoemaker, 690.
Shoemaker's Holiday, The, *see* Dekker.
Shoreditch, *see* London, streets of.
Shoreham, Kent, 673.
Showman, 690.
Shrewsbury, 212.
Shrove Tuesday riot, 161-4, 691.
Shurlock, William, *see* Sherlock, William.
Sidesman, 466.
Signet Office Docquet Book, 168, 302.
Silent Woman, The, *see* Jonson, *Epicoene*.
Silvester, **573**.

Simpson, Elizabeth, 554.
Simpson, William, 554.
Sinckler, Elizabeth, 573.
Sinckler, William, **573.**
Singer, John, 135, 612.
Sir Gyles Goosecap, see Anon.
Sir John van Olden Barnavelt, see
Beaumont and Fletcher.
Sisters, The, see Shirley.
Skooleing, Mary, 421.
Skragg, Mr., 379.
Slater, Martin, 135, 160, 165, 171
and n. b, 172 n. 1, 178, **574–5.**
Slathier, Martin, *see* Slater, Martin.
Slaughter *or* Slauter, *see* Slater,
Martin.
Slead, Elizabeth, 625.
Slight of hand, 486.
Slingsby, Sir William, 491, 688.
Sly, William, 1, 2, 4 n. 2.
Smart, Jasper, 639.
Smart, Joane, 639.
Smith, 607.
Smith, Amye, 543.
Smith, Anthony, 18, 24, 35 n. 1,
73–89, 199 and n. 2, 200 and n. 3,
209, 210, 211 and n. a, **575–6,**
607.
Smith, Henry, 142 n. 6, 143.
Smith, John, 160, 161, 202 n. 6,
204 n. 3, 211 n. b, 527, **576.**
Smith, John, *vs.* Christopher Bees-
ton, 527.
Smith, Captain John, *A Descrip-
tion of New England*, 455.
Smith, Joyce, 577.
Smith, Judith, 577.
Smith, Lady, 10 n. 6.
Smith, Leonard, **576.**
Smith, Margaret, 571.
Smith, Mathew, 261 and n. 3, 262,
263 n. 1, 269, 275, 303, 307, 308,
309, 318, 319, 321, **576–7.**
Smith, Rebecca, 644.
Smith, Richard, 365.
Smith, Thomas, 651.
Smith, Wentworth, *The Hector of
Germany*, 207 n. 4.
Smith, William, *The Fair Foul One,
or the Baiting of the Jealous Knight*,
206.
Smith, William, 503.
Smith, Captain William, 644.
Smithfield, *see* London, streets of.
Smyth, William, 265.
Sneller, James, 303, 307, 308, 312,
321, **577–8.**
Soare's Rents, *see* London, streets
of.

Soddered Citizen, The, see Clavell.
Soham, Cambridgeshire, 438.
Soldiers, 438.
Solihull, 419, 484, 618.
Somerset, George, **578.**
Somerset House, 39, 46, 110, 117,
329, 401.
Somner, John, *see* Sumner, John.
Songs, contract to write, 390.
Sophia, Princess, 432.
Sophy, The, see Denham.
Sotheby's, 673.
Southampton, 20, 50, 92, 172, 212,
322, 349.
Southampton, Earl of, *see* Wriothes-
ley, Thomas.
Southlande, —, 676.
Southwark, *see* London, streets of.
Soyles, William, 578.
Spain, 9.
Ambassador from, 2, 9, 10, 140.
Play against, 15.
Spanish Contract, The, see Anon.
Spanish Curate, The, see Beaumont
and Fletcher.
Spanish Duke of Lerma, The, see
Henry Shirley.
Spanish Gypsy, The, see Middleton.
Spanish marriage, 9.
Spanish players, 515.
Spanish Tragedy, The, see Kyd.
Spanish Viceroy, The, see Anon.
Sparagus Garden, The, see Brome.
Sparkes, Thomas, 143, 144, **578.**
Spartan Ladies, The, see Carlell.
Speckart, Mr., 184.
Spectators on the stage, 166–7.
Spencer, Gabriel, 135.
Spencer, John, **578.**
Spencer, Mary, 41.
Spencer, Nicholas, **578–9.**
Spencer, Sir William, 480, 618.
Spittle, *see* London, streets of.
Spittlegate, *see* London, streets of.
Spread Eagle Inn, 635.
Sprigg, Joshua, *Anglia Rediviva*,
549.
Squibs, 30 n. 6 cont'd.
Squier, John, 553.
Staffeild *or* Staffield, George, *see*
Stutville, George.
Stafford, 213, 585.
Stafford, Alexander, 597.
Stage, accident on, 166–7.
Bason on, 277–8.
Candlesticks on, 277–8.
Rushes on, 687.
Sitting on, 225 n. 2.
Stools on, 687.

Stage keeper, **579**, 686.
Stage Players' Complaint, The, see Anon.
Stanley, Thomas, 335.
Stanly, Isabell, 651.
Stanton, 484.
Staple of News, The, see Jonson.
Star Chamber, 47, 65 n. 2, 208, 317 n. 1.
Stationer, 143, 481, 545.
Stationers' Company, 65, 328, 504.
Staughton, E., 520.
Stephens, Mr., 479.
Stevens, —, 520.
Stevens, William, 438.
Steward, Robert, 453.
Stockfish, Hans, **579**.
Stoddard, Sir Nicholas, 140.
Stoner, William, 404.
Str——, Robert, **579**.
Strafford, Earl of, 58.
Strand, *see* London, streets of.
Strange, Lord, company of, 1, 135, 466, 496, 518.
Strangwick, Sir John, 47.
Stratford, Judith, 580.
Stratford, Mary, 580.
Stratford, Robert, 307, 308, 321, **579**.
Stratford, William, 136, 138, 145, 147, 148, 152, 153, 155, 263, **579–80**, 682, 683.
Stratford-on-Avon, 92, 463, 464, 484, 618.
Street, Andrew, 400.
Streets, paving of, 228 n. 1.
Stretch, John, 286, 297, **580**.
Strowd, Thomas, 322.
Styles, Dorothy, 582, 583.
Styles, John, 583.
Styles, Lanslet, 583.
Styles, William, 49 n. 2 cont'd., 73–89, **582–3**.
Styles, William, junior, 582.
Stutfield, George, *see* Stutville, George.
Stutville, George, 246, 285, 286 and n. 1, 287, 288, 289 and n. 1, 290, 291 n. 1, 297, 303, 308, 321, 323, 324, 326 n. 6, 327 nn. 1, 2, and 4, 332, 333 and n. 1, 336, **580–1**.
Stutville, Sir Martin, 20, 129, 253, 266, 657 n. 4.
Suckling, Sir John, 42 and n. 3, 58, 243, 335.
  Aglaura, 57–8, 58–60, 63, 99 and n. x, 131, 243 nn. 1 and 2.
  Brennoralt, or the Discontented Colonel, 66, 131.
  Goblins, The, 66, 131–2, 461.

Suell, Thomas, **583**.
Summer and winter theatres, 3 n. 7.
Summer performances, income from, 24.
Sumner, Elizabeth, 583.
Sumner, John, 220, 221, 231, 237, 238, 246, **583–4**.
Sumner, Mary, 583.
Sumpner, John, *see* Sumner, John.
Sun's Darling, The, see Dekker.
Suppression of the theatre, petition for, 31, 64.
Surgeon (*see also* Barber-chirurgion, Doctor, and Physican), 139, 265, 453, 617.
Surrey, 21.
Sutton, —, 435.
Swainstone, —, *see* Swanston, Eyllaerdt.
Swallow, Richard, 400.
Swan theatre, 176.
Swanstead *or* Swansted *or* Swanstrid, *see* Swanston, Eyllaerdt.
Swanston, Alice, 585.
Swanston, Benjamin, 586.
Swanston, Elizabeth, 585, 587, 648.
Swanston, Eyllaerdt, 4 n. 2, 14, 16, 17, 26 n. 5, 35 n. 1, 37, 43, 46, 57, 60, 61, 69 n. 2, 73–89, 90, 97 nn. n and o, 99 nn. u, x, z, and aa, 100 n. bb, 183, 187, 192, 219, 318, **584–8**.
Will of, 648.
Swanston, Francis, 586.
Swanston, Hanna, 586.
Swanston, John, 585.
Swanston, Stephen, 587.
Swantton *or* Swautted, *see* Swanston, Eyllaerdt.
Swayne, Martin, 536, **588**.
Sweetman, Ellen, 477, 645.
Sweetman, John, 476, 477, 645.
Swetherton, Thomas, *see* Swinnerton, Thomas.
Swetnam the Woman Hater, see Anon.
Swinarton, Abell, 189, 192, **588**.
Swinnerton, Thomas, 158, 160, 165, 171 and n. b, 172 n. 1, 178, **588–9**.
Swisser, The, see Wilson.
Swynerton, Thomas, *see* Swinnerton, Thomas.
Swynnerton, Daniel, **589**.
Symes, —, 504.

T., R., 72–88, **589**.
Tailor, 413, 446, 455, 486, 491, 688.
Tailor, Joseph, *see* Taylor, Joseph.

Tailor, Robert, (*see also* Taylor), *The Hog Hath Lost His Pearl*, 207 n. 4.

Tale of a Tub, A, see Jonson.

Tamburlaine, see Marlowe.

Tamer Cam, see Anon.

Tamer Tamed, The, see Beaumont and Fletcher, *The Woman's Prize*.

Taming of the Shrew, The, see Shakespeare.

Target fighting, 30 n. 6 cont'd.

Taste, popular, 541.

Tatham, John, *The Fancies' Theatre*, 279, 315–16, 444.

Knavery in All Trades, 317–19, 360, 376, 388, 406, 439, 440, 442, 505, 535, 576, 577, 588, 598, 627.

Tatterdell, Hughe, 272, 281, 590.

Taverner, 497.

Taverns, *see* Inns and taverns.

Tawier, William, *see* Tawyer, William.

Tawyer, William, 15, 73–89, 590.

Taylor, —, 590.

Taylor, Ann, 592, 593.

Taylor, Edward, 598, 649.

Taylor, Elizabeth, 592, 593.

Taylor, Hester, 592.

Taylor, John, *Praise of Hempseed, The*, 557.

Taylor's Feast, 612.

Wit and Mirth, 358, 436.

Taylor, Jone, 592.

Taylor, Joseph, 4 nn. 1 and 2, 7, 9, 14, 17, 20, 26 n. 5, 34, 35 n. 1, 37, 44, 53, 54, 55, 57, 60, 61, 69 n. 2, 72–88, 90, 97 nn. i, n, p, 99 nn. u, x, z, aa, 100 n. bb, 104, 121, 123, 140, 164, 176, 177, and n. 2, 198, 199 and n. 2, 200 and n. 3, 203 and n. 1, 211, 318, 328, 590–8, 621, 650, 682.

Taylor, Joseph, junior, 593, 596.

Taylor, Margaret, 598.

Taylor, Margerie, 648.

Taylor, Mary, 474.

Taylor, Raphe, 598, 649.

Taylor, Robert (*see also* Tailor), 592, 598.

Taylor, Roger, 599.

Taylor, Samuel, 593.

Taylor, Stage, 598.

Taylor, Thomas, 598–9, 683. Will of, 648–9.

Taylor, Winifred, 593.

Taylor, *vs.* Heminges, 198.

Temple of Love, The, see Davenant.

Tennant, Thomas, 356.

4595.2

Tent for players' use on progress, 310.

Teodor, Jacob, 599.

Terry, William, *see* Perry, William.

Tey, Paull, 683.

Thame, Oxford, 484.

Thames, *see* London, streets of.

Theatre, The, 1, 135.

Theatre, *see also* Blackfriars, Cockpit in Court, Curtain, Fortune, Globe, Hope, Newington Butts, Phoenix, Red Bull, Rose, Rosseter's Puddlewharf, Salisbury Court, Swan, Theatre, Whitefriars.

Theatre, accident in, 166–7.

Annual fee for, 370.

Appearance of, 694.

Benches in, 26, 30 n. 6 cont'd., 225, 691.

Box for money at, 541, 558.

Boxes in, 44, 48, 283 n. 7 cont'd., 597.

Burned, 2, 141.

Candle-light in, 694.

Caretakers of, 432, 462, 485, 506, 544, 572.

Closed, 21, 68.

By plague, 652–72.

In Lent, 654 n. 2.

Competition between, 225.

Conduct at, 693.

Construction of, 283 n. 7.

Contractors for, 143.

Cost of, 283 n. 7 cont'd.

Cost of lights in, 44, 687.

Dancing in, 136–7, 523.

Demonstrations in, 25.

Expenses of, 44.

Favourite, 680.

Fires in rooms of, 687.

Flowers in, 687.

Galleries, 44, 136, 199 n. 2, 202, 318.

Gatherers at, 558, 588, 616, 622, 684.

Holiday audiences at, 690–1.

Leases of, 30, 138–9, 143–4.

Length of time for building, 146.

Lights, cost of, 44.

Managers of, 147, 263–4, 279, 286, 295, 518.

Music, cost of, 44.

New, for French players, 235.

Order closing, 690.

Patent for new, 421.

Patron of, 674.

Petitions for suppression of, 31–3.

Pit in 30 n. 6 cont'd., 694.

Theatre (*contd.*):
  Profits from, 43, 330.
  Raided, 278, 695.
  Ranting in, 690.
  Rent of, 138.
  Repairs of, 686.
  Reputations of, 693.
  Rooms in, 686, 687.
  Scenery in, 52, 53, 58, 59, 117, 120, 233, 243 n. 2, 693–4.
  Shares in, 1, 2, 3–4, 303, 329–30, 638, 644, 647, 651.
  Stage hangings in, 534.
  Suppression of, 68–9.
  Sweepers of, 686.
  Tiles in, 691.
  Time of performance at, 5.
  Tiring-house, 44 and n. 3, 318, 440.
  Viewing rooms, 283 n. 7 cont'd.
  Wardrobe-keeper in, *see* Occupations.
Theatrical anecdotes, 318, 440.
Theatrical dinner, 140.
Thelwall, Simon, 165 n. 8.
Theobalds, 50, 178.
Thetford, 453, 604.
Thicknis, Mr., 142.
Thierry and Theodoret, see Beaumont and Fletcher.
Thomas of Woodstock, or Richard II, see Anon.
Thomas, John, 476.
Thomas, William, senior, 411.
Thomas, William, junior, 411.
Thompson, Anne, 600.
Thompson, John, 45, 72–88, 455, **599–600**.
Thompson, Lettice, 600.
Thompson, Richard, **600**.
Thompson, Samuel, 285, 288, 290, 297, **600–1**.
Thorpe, Elizabeth, 613.
Three Herring Court, *see* London, streets of.
Three Kings Ordinary, 421, 684 n. 1.
Three London Apprentices, The, see Anon.
Three Pigeons at Brentford, 505, 695.
Tickets of privilege, 15, 49 n. 2, 80–1, 86–7, 260, 262 n. 6, 316, 321, 332, 336, 379, 561, 570.
Tight-rope walkers (*see also* Dancers on the ropes), 612.
'Tis Pity She's a Whore, see Ford.
Titus Andronicus, see Shakespeare.
Tobacco pipe, 318.

Tobye, Edward, 168 n. 1, **601**.
Todd, Mary, 428.
Token books, 448, 467, 486, 490, 500, 510, 519, 546, 560, 564, 574, 575, 592, 633.
Tooley, Isabell, 556.
Tooley, Nicholas, 5, 9, 16, 72–88, 556, **601–2**, 638.
  Will of, 649–51.
Torgau, 451.
Torpley, Nathaniel, 642.
Tosedall, Roger, 286, 297, **602**.
Totnell, James, 635.
Tottenham Court, see Nabbes.
Touring companies, 146 n. 6, 178, 228.
  Fees of, paid, 293, 689.
  Precautions about audiences of, 312.
  Quarrelling between, 294.
  Repertory of, 293, 689.
  Size of, 288–9, 298.
Tourneur, Cyril, *The Great Man*, 132.
  Nobleman, The, 66, 132.
Tower Hill, *see* London, streets of.
Towne, Thomas, 135, 136.
Townsend, John, 176, 180 and n. 13, 181, 182, 189 and n. 3, 192, 299, **602–4**.
Towyer *or* Toyer, William, *see* Tawyer, William.
Traffic problems, 4–5, 33.
'Tragedy of Doctor Lamb, The', 267–8.
Traitor, The, see Shirley.
Transome, Nicholas, 357.
Travis, Edward, 346.
Trevill *vs.* Woodford, 625.
Trick to Cheat the Devil, A, see Davenport, *A New Trick to Cheat the Devil*.
Tricks of Youth, see Jordan, *Walks of Islington and Hogsdon*.
Trigg, Elizabeth, 606.
Trigg, Mathew, 606.
Trigg, Thomas, 606.
Trigg, William, 49, 73–89, 327 n. 3, 332, 336, **604–6**, 647.
Triumph of Peace, The, see Shirley.
Troilus and Cressida, see Chettle.
Trompeur Puni, Le, see Scudéry.
True Diurnal Occurrences, see Newspapers.
Trumbull, Sir William, 436.
Trumpeter, 357, 483, 609.
Trumpets, to advertise provincial performances, 686.
Trundle, John, **606**, 682, 683.

Tuchborne, —, 347.
Tucke, T., *see* Tuckfield, Thomas.
Tuckfield, Thomas, 15, 72–88, **606–7.**
Tumbler, 459, 486, 522, 657.
Turner, 682.
Turner, Anthony, 183, 187, 192, 219, 220, 221, 222, 231, 237, 238, 244 and n. 2, 245, 246, 247, 248 n. j, **607–8.**
Turner, Dorothy,· 607.
Turner, Drew or True, **608–9.**
Turner, Henry, 244 n. 2, 248 n. j, 608, **609.**
Turner, Jane, 608.
Turner, Jone, 608.
Turner, Mary, 608.
Turner, W., *A Dish of Lenten Stuff*, 563.
Turney, Edmund, 444.
Turnstile Alley, *see* London, streets of.
Tutbury, 310.
Tuttells, Richard, 637.
Tuttle, Westminster, *see* London, streets of.
Twelfth Night, see Shakespeare.
Two Kings in a Cottage, see Bonen.
Two Merry Milkmaids, or the Best Words Wear Garlands, The, see Anon.
Two Noble Kinsmen, The, see Beaumont and Fletcher.
Two Noble Ladies, The, see Anon.
Tychebourne, Leonell, 139.
Tyldesley, Thomas, 471.
Tyrant, The, see Massinger, *The King and the Subject.*

Udall, Edward, 564.
Udall, Henry, 564.
Undercook, 546.
Underell, Thomas, *see* Underhill, Thomas.
Underhill, Alphonso, 610.
Underhill, Nicholas, 15, 72–88, **609.**
Underhill, Samuel, 384, 625.
Underhill, Thomas, **609–10.**
Underwood, Burbage, 651.
Underwood, Elizabeth, 651.
Underwood, Henry, 144.
Underwood, Isabella, 639, 651.
Underwood, John, 5, 9, 16, 44 and n. 6, 72–88, 584, **610–11,** 641, 650, 696.
Will of, 651.
Underwood, John, junior, 651.
Underwood, Thomas, 651.
Undrill, Thomas, *see* Underhill, Thomas.

Unfortunate Lovers, The, see Davenant.
Unfortunate Mother, The, see Nabbes.
Unfortunate Piety, The, see Massinger.
Unnatural Combat, The, see Massinger.
Upper stage, 283 n. 7 cont'd.
Upton on Severn, 486.

Valentinian, see Beaumont and Fletcher.
Valiant Scholar, The, see Anon.
Valiant Scot, The, see Anon.
Van Dyke, 48.
Vanham, William, 356.
Variety, The, see Cavendish.
Vasely, Elizabeth, 587, 648.
Vaughan, Thomas, 632.
Vaulter, 486, 502, 522, 613.
Venetian ambassador, 20, 204.
Vernon, Anne, 612.
Vernon, Elizabeth, 612.
Vernon, George, 15, 16, 35 n. 1, 72–88, 611–12.
Very Woman, A, see Massinger.
Vestments used in a play, 294.
Victoria and Albert Museum, 132.
Victualler, 564.
Villiers, George, *see* Buckingham, Duke of.
Vincent, James, 613.
Vincent, Margaret, 613.
Vincent, Thomas, 612.
Vincent, William, **612–13.**
Vintner, 314, 426, 642.
Virgin Martyr, The, see Dekker.
Virtuoso, The, see Shadwell.
Visitations of Essex, The, 673.
Volpone, see Jonson.
Vow and a Good One, A, see Anon.
Vox Borealis, see Newspapers.
Vox Graculi, or Jack Daw's Prognostication, 145.

W., J., *Valiant Scot, The, see* Anon.
Wabes, —, 413.
Wadd, Thomas, 384.
Waide, Johann, **613.**
Waight, Richard, 643.
Wales, National Library of, 412.
Walker, Alice Burbage, 9, 649.
Walks of Islington and Hogsdon, The, see Jordan.
Wallace, C. W., 'Gervase Markham, Dramatist', *Shakespeare Jahrbuch,* xlvi (1910), 682–3.
Wallinger, Ben, 676, 678.
Walpole, Francis, 165, 171, **613.**

Wambus, Francis, 176, 181, 182, 189, 192, 197, **613–15.**
Wamus, Francis, *sbe* Wambus, Francis.
Wandering Lovers, The, see Beaumont and Fletcher, *The Lover's Progress.*
Wanibus, Francis, *see* Wambus, Francis.
Wapping, 161, 265.
Warburton, —, 376.
Warburton, Ann Benfield, 376.
Warburton's Play List, 60 n. 4, 108, 120, 123, 125, 132, 134.
Warde, Ja:, 675.
Wardrobe, great, 505.
Wardrobe, theatrical, *see* Costumes.
Wardrobe keeper, 26 n. 5 cont'd., 491, 546.
Wars of Pompey and Caesar, The, see Chapman.
Warwick, 484.
Warwick Castle, 60.
Washbourne, William, 411.
Wasp, The, see Anon.
Waterman, 486, 510, 690.
Waymus, Francis, *see* Wambus, Francis.
Way to Content All Women, The, see Gunnell.
Weaver, 464, 564, 566, 646.
Webster, John, 526.
　Appius and Virginia, 331, 341.
　Devil's Law Case, The, 174.
　Duchess of Malfi, The, 28, 76–7, 96, 132, 374, 375, 395, 410, 465, 501, 519, 520, 533, 547, 552, 569, 570, 593, 600, 601, 602, 610, 611, 692.
　Late Murder in Whitechapel, or Keep the Widow Waking, The, see Rowley.
　White Devil, The, 259, 526.
Webster, John, *The Displaying of Supposed Witchcraft*, 1677, 41 n. 3.
Wedding, The, see Shirley.
Wedwer, William, **615.**
Weeding of Covent Garden, The, see Brome.
Weeks, Ann, 616.
Weeks, Joan, 616.
Weeks, Richard, 189, 192, 272, 273, 275, 276, 281, 282 n. 1, **615–16.**
Welbeck, 310.
Weldon, 181.
Welsh Ambassaor, The, see Anon., *The Welsh Traveller.*
Welsh Traveller, The, see Anon.
Wentworth, Sir John, 47 n. 3, 368, 371, 660, 676.

West, Sibilla, 523.
West Harling, Norfolk, 312.
Westminster, *see* London, streets of.
Westminster Abbey, organist of, 422.
Westminster Hall, 145.
Westminster school, 470.
Weston, Thomas, 551.
Wharton, Rachel, 478.
Wheatley, Andrew, 643.
Wheaton, Elizabeth, **616–17**, 639.
Whetstone, Roger, 617.
Whetstone, Thomas, **617.**
Whitbee, William, 457.
White, Josias, **617.**
White, Mary, 617.
White, Robert, **617.**
Whitechapel, 621.
Whitecross street, *see* London, streets of.
Whitecross street, liberty of, *see* London, streets of.
White Devil, The, see Webster.
Whitefriars theatre, 176, 540, 554, 574.
Whitehall, *see* London, streets of.
White Hart, 343, 682.
Whitehead, Christopher, **617.**
Whitelocke, Bulstrode, *Whitelocke's Coranto*, 40.
Whiting, Edward, **617–18.**
Whiting, Edward, surgeon, 617.
Whiting, Richard, **618–19.**
Whitney, Lieutenant, 568.
Whore in Grain, The, see Anon.
Whore New Vamped, The, see Anon.
Wicks, Richard, *see* Weeks, Richard.
Widow, The, see Middleton.
Widow's Prize, The, see Sampson.
Widow's Tears, The, see Chapman.
Wife for a Month, A, see Beaumont and Fletcher.
Wiggett, Thomas, *see* Wigpitt, Thomas.
Wight, Isle of, 657 n. 4.
Wigpitt, Thomas, 142, 143, 144, 545, **619.**
Wilborowe, Thomas, 631.
Wilbraham, Avice, 619.
Wilbraham, William, 220, 246, 286, 290, 297, **619.**
Wild Goose Chase, The, see Beaumont and Fletcher.
Wilkes, Marie, 633.
Wilkinson, Charles, 601.
Wilkinson, John, 384.
Wilkinson, Nicholas, *see* Tooley, Nicholas.
Willans, George, *see* Williams, George.

Williams, Edmond, 357.
Williams, Elizabeth, 620.
Williams, George, 272, 281, 286, 290, 297, **619–20.**
Williams, John, 201 n. 1, **620.**
Williams, Walter, 286, 297, **620.**
Willington, Thomas, 442.
Willis, Richard, **620.**
Willoughby, Sir Henry, 42.
Wilson, Arthur:
  Corporal, The, 66, 101 n. a, 105–6, 132.
  Inconstant Lady, The, 27 and n. 2, 66, 96, 132.
  Observations of God's Providence in the Tract of My Life, 106.
  Swisser, The, 66, 70, 84–5, 132, 375, 446, 447, 451, 452, 502, 524, 532, 534, 571, 576, 586, 594, 600, 605, 606.
Wilson, Captain, 568.
Wilson, Dover, 11 n. 6 cont'd.
Wilson, George, 236, 597, **620–1,** 661 n. 1.
Wilson, Henry, 15, 72–88, **621.**
Wilson, John, 355, 578, **621–2.**
Wilson, Jone, 622.
Wilson, Joseph, 587, 648.
Wilson, Joseph, junior, 587.
Wilson, Robert, *Oldcastle, see* Drayton.
Wilson, Sarah, 587, 648.
Wilson, William, **622–3.**
Wiltshire, 382.
Winchester, 92, 156, 180, 193, 212, 213, 349.
Winden, Elizabeth, 534.
Windmill Tavern, 266.
Windsor, 93.
Wines, new duty on, 314.
Winter and summer theatres, 3 n. 7.
Winter performances, income from, 24.
Wintersall, *or* Winterscale, William, *see* Wintershall, William.
Wintershall, Jane, 623.
Wintershall, Margaret, 400.
Wintershall, William, 400, 623–4.
Wintershall, William, junior, 623.
Winter's Tale, The, see Shakespeare.
Witch, The, see Middleton.
Witch of Edmonton, The, see Dekker.
Witches in plays, 40–1.
Wither, George, 557.
Wit in a Constable, see Glapthorne.
Wits, The, see Davenant.
Witter, John, 411, 468, **624.**
Witter, *vs.* Heminges and Condell, 468, 624.

Witty Fair One, The, see Shirley.
Wit without Money, see Beaumont and Fletcher.
Woking, 20.
Wolgast, Duke of, 429.
Woman Hater, The, see Beaumont and Fletcher.
Woman is a Weathercock, A, see Field.
Woman is Too Hard for Him, The, see Anon.
Woman Killed with Kindness, A, see Heywood.
Woman's Mistake, The, see Drue.
Woman's Plot, The, see Massinger.
Woman's Prize, The, see Beaumont and Fletcher.
Wombwell, William, 355.
Women actors, 25.
Women Pleased, see Beaumont and Fletcher.
Wood, Abraham, 624.
Wood, Alice, 624.
Wood, Anthony, 624.
Woode, John, 624, **625,** 682.
Wood, Randall, 347.
Wood, William, **624.**
Wood street, *see* London, streets of.
Wooden, Katherine, 501.
Woodford, Elizabeth, 625.
Woodford, Robert, 634.
Woodford, Thomas, 384, **624–5.**
Woodruff, Joan, 533.
Woodstock, 20.
Worcester, 92, 282.
Worcester, Earl of:
  Company of, 158, 363, 469, 486, 499, 518, 525, 609.
Worcestershire, 635.
Workmen, 348.
World, The, see Anon.
'World's wonder', 600.
World Tossed at Tennis, The, see Middleton.
Worsley, Thomas, 471.
Worth, Elizabeth, 626.
Worth, Elizeus, 627.
Worth, Ellis, 163, 165, 166, 167, 168 n. 2, 169 and n. 2, 170 n. 1, 171, 174, 183 n. 2, 204, 208, 275, 302, 303, 307, 308, 309, 311, 318, 319, 321, **625–7.**
Worth, Marie, 627.
Wortham, John, 356.
Wortley, Sir Francis, 674, 678.
Wotton, Sir Henry, 10 n. 6, 126, 551, 552.
Wriothesley, Thomas, Earl of Southampton, 379, 525.

Wright, John, 307, 308, 321, 327 n. 2, 332, 336, **627-8.**

Wright, James, *Historia Histrionica*, 691-6.

Wright, Louis B., 11 n. 6 cont'd.

Wroth, Ellis, *see* Worth, Ellis.

Yeoman of the Revels, 591, 596, 621.

Remuneration of, 596.

Yonge, Robert, 642.

York, 67. 271, 273 and n. 3, 471, 473, 529.

His Majesty's servants for the city of, 24.

York, Duke of, 129, 191, 198, 424.

Yorkshire, 496.

Young, John, 220, 246, 249 n. f cont'd., 285, 286, 287, 288, 290, 291 n. 2, 297, **628.**

Young, Dr., 531.

Young Admiral, The, see Shirley.

Younger Brother, The, see Anon.

PRINTED IN GREAT BRITAIN
AT THE UNIVERSITY PRESS, OXFORD
BY VIVIAN RIDLER
PRINTER TO THE UNIVERSITY